THE CRITICAL TURN IN TOURISM STUDIES

INNOVATIVE RESEARCH METHODOLOGIES

ADVANCES IN TOURISM RESEARCH

Series Editor: **Professor Stephen J. Page**
University of Stirling, UK
s.j.page@stir.ac.uk

Advances in Tourism Research series publishes monographs and edited volumes that comprise state-of-the-art research findings, written and edited by leading researchers working in the wider field of tourism studies. The series has been designed to provide a cutting edge focus for researchers interested in tourism, particularly the management issues now facing decision-makers, policy analysts and the public sector. The audience is much wider than just academics and each book seeks to make a significant contribution to the literature in the field of study by not only reviewing the state of knowledge relating to each topic but also questioning some of the prevailing assumptions and research paradigms which currently exist in tourism research. The series also aims to provide a platform for further studies in each area by highlighting key research agendas, which will stimulate further debate and interest in the expanding area of tourism research. The series is always willing to consider new ideas for innovative and scholarly books, inquiries should be made directly to the Series Editor.

Published:

Benchmarking National Tourism Organisations and Agencies
LENNON, SMITH, COCKEREL & TREW

Extreme Tourism: Lessons from the World's Cold Water Islands
BALDACCHINO

Tourism Local Systems and Networking
LAZZERETTI & PETRILLO

Progress in Tourism Marketing
KOZAK & ANDREU

Destination Marketing Organisations
PIKE

Indigenous Tourism
RYAN AND AICKEN

An International Handbook of Tourism Education
AIREY & TRIBE

Tourism in Turbulent Times
WILKS, PENDERGAST & LEGGAT

Taking Tourism to the Limits
RYAN, PAGE & AICKEN

Tourism and Social Identities
BURNS & NOVELLI

Micro-clusters & Networks – The Growth of Tourism
MICHAEL

Tourism and Politics
BURNS & NOVELLI

Tourism and Small Businesses in the New Europe
THOMAS & AUGUSTIJN

Hospitality: A Social Lens
LASHLEY, LYNCH & MORRISON

Forthcoming:

Tourism Research
AIREY & TRIBE

Travel Medicine: Tales Behind the Science
WILDER-SMITH, SCHWARTZ & SHAW

For other titles in the series visit: www.elsevier.com/locate/series/aitr

Related Elsevier Journals — sample copies available on request
Annals of Tourism Research
International Journal of Hospitality Management
Tourism Management

THE CRITICAL TURN IN TOURISM STUDIES

INNOVATIVE RESEARCH METHODS

EDITED BY

IRENA ATELJEVIC

Wageningen University, The Netherlands

ANNETTE PRITCHARD

University of Wales Institute, Cardiff, UK

NIGEL MORGAN

University of Wales Institute, Cardiff, UK

ELSEVIER

Amsterdam • Boston • Heidelberg • London • New York • Oxford
Paris • San Diego • San Francisco • Singapore • Sydney • Tokyo

Elsevier
Linacre House, Jordan Hill, Oxford, OX2 8DP, UK
Radarweg 29, PO Box 211, 1000 AE Amsterdam, The Netherlands

First edition 2007
Reprinted 2007

Notice
No responsibility is assumed by the publisher for any injury and/or damage to persons
or property as a matter of products liability, negligence or otherwise, or from any use
or operation of any methods, products, instructions or ideas contained in the material
herein. Because of rapid advances in the medical sciences, in particular, independent
verification of diagnoses and drug dosages should be made

British Library Cataloguing in Publication Data
A catalogue record for this book is available from the British Library

Library of Congress Cataloging-in-Publication Data
A catalog record for this book is available from the Library of Congress

ISBN: 978-0-08-045098-8

For information on all Elsevier publications
visit our website at books.elsevier.com

Printed and bound in *Hungary*

07 08 09 10 10 9 8 7 6 5 4 3 2

Working together to grow
libraries in developing countries

www.elsevier.com | www.bookaid.org | www.sabre.org

ELSEVIER   BOOK AID International   Sabre Foundation

Contents

**Part 2: Methodologies, Innovative Techniques, Methods of
         Interpretation and Writing Strategies**

List of Figures and Exhibits

List of Tables

Contributors

Cara Carmichael Aitchison is a Professor in human geography at the University of the West of England, Bristol, where she is Director of the Centre for Leisure, Tourism and Society (CELTS). Cara's teaching and research focus on the integration of social, cultural and spatial theories and policies of leisure, sport and tourism as sites and processes of inequality, identity, inclusion and social justice.

Martine Abramovici is a PhD candidate in tourism in the Faculty of Business at Auckland University of Technology. Martine's PhD focuses on Italian women and tanning, revealing the body to be a focal point in understanding Italian contemporary society. Her research interests include postmodern consumer society and identity, socio-cultural issues, gender issues, the body and embodiment, and critical approaches to research.

Irena Ateljevic received her doctoral degree in human geography in 1998 at the University of Auckland, New Zealand. She is currently positioned within the Socio-Spatial Analysis Group at Wageningen University, The Netherlands. Interested in the post-structural analysis of economy and culture, she explores the cultural complexities of gender, class, age and ethnicity in the production and consumption of tourist spaces and experiences and how their intersection reproduce power relations of injustice and inequality. She has engaged with those issues in the context of various subjects, reflective in her published work on tourism imagi(in)ing, backpacker phenomenon, peripheral regional development and small tourism firms. Her most recent research interest lies in analysing the political implications and powers surrounding the production of academic knowledge, which shape and condition our academic lives and of those we 'research' and interact with.

Maureen Ayikoru is a PhD candidate at University of Surrey in United Kingdom. Her PhD thesis looks at the way discourses construct social reality by specifically focusing on tourism higher education in England. The on-going research entails an analysis of various texts (documents) that seem to have direct and indirect implications for tourism in higher education. Thus the field of study is tourism, and main research interests include tourism in higher education, theoretical and philosophical issues in social (tourism) inquiry, sustainability in tourism and tourism in developing countries.

David Botterill is a Professor and Director of research in the Cardiff School of Management at the University of Wales Institute, Cardiff. His current interest is in the interface between the philosophies of the social sciences and the practices of tourism researchers.

Graham Brown is a Professor of Tourism Management at the University of South Australia. He gained his PhD from Texas A&M University, has taught tourism at universities in England, Canada, Mauritius and Australia and serves on a number of academic and editorial boards.

Kath Browne works in the area of geographies of sexualities and genders. Her research interests include: non-heterosexual women/lesbians, queer theories, feminist geographies, Pride festivals, 'gay' Brighton and Hove, civil partnerships.

Donna Chambers studied International Relations at both undergraduate and masters level in Jamaica and Trinidad respectively prior to spending 5 years in the tourism public sector in Jamaica. She subsequently did a masters degree in Tourism Management and completed a PhD in tourism with Brunel University in 2003. Donna's research interests include tourism and politics, heritage representation, discourse theory and postcolonial perspectives. She has presented in these areas at national and international tourism conferences and published journal articles and book chapters also in these areas. She is currently a lecturer in Tourism and Programme Leader for postgraduate tourism programmes at Napier University, Edinburgh.

Susanna Curtin is a senior lecturer in Tourism Management at Bournemouth University. Her research is focused on wildlife tourism, particularly that related to marine mammals. She is currently in the writing-up stages of her PhD and has published several journal articles from her preliminary findings as well as other related research projects.

Stephen Doorne has a background in human geography and development studies. His research interests focus on tourism in developing countries, community development, tourism and periphery. He currently shares his time between academia and consultancy and has been contracted to the University of the South Pacific since 2002.

Ria Ann Dunkley is a research student and part-time lecturer at the Welsh Centre for Tourism Research in the Cardiff School of Management, University of Wales Institute, Cardiff. Her research focuses on the thanatourism experience and she is passionate about alternative methodologies such as autoethnography.

Jeff Everett is an Assistant Professor in the Haskayne School of Business, The University of Calgary, Calgary, Canada. His main focus is on social and environmental accounting and organisational accountability, as well as the application of sociological and cultural theories to the study of protected areas.

Adrian Franklin is a Professor of sociology at the University of Tasmania, Australia and has held professorial positions at the University of Bristol and the University of Oslo. Recent books include *Tourism* (London: Sage), *Nature and Social Theory* (London: Sage), *Animals Nation* (Sydney: University of New South Wales Press) and Animals and Modern

Cultures (London: Sage) and he is co-editor (with Mike Crang) of the journal *Tourist Studies*. New tourism papers include the problems of wilderness as a concept, the theoretical implications for consumptive wildlife tourism, tourism theory and ordering, and an interview with Zygmunt Bauman on the sociological significance of tourism.

Derek Hall has degrees in geography and social anthropology from the University of London and a postgraduate qualification in linguistics. He has latterly been Head of the Leisure and Tourism Management Department at the Scottish Agricultural College where he has also had a personal chair in Regional Development. He is currently visiting professor at HAMK University of Applied Sciences, Mustiala, Finland. With around 300 publications, his interests have included tourism, transport and regional development.

Candice Harris is a senior lecturer in Management and Employment Relations in the Faculty of Business at Auckland University of Technology. Candice's PhD (Victoria University) focused on New Zealand women as business travellers. Her research interests include gender and diversity issues in tourism and management, human resource management, and qualitative and critical approaches to research.

Bente Heimtun is a PhD student at the Faculty of the Built Environment, University of West of England and a research fellow at Lillehammer University College, Norway. Her research coheres around the sociology of tourism, gender and identities. The current PhD research project focuses on the importance of social capital in the holiday, based on the experiences of midlife single women.

Keith Hollinshead is an Anglo-Australian researcher of the interface that tourism and travel have today with the cultural inheritances and the received understandings of the world's populations. Having first been trained light-years-ago in Romano-British history, he worked in various public and private sector marketing and development positions in recreation management in Wales and Australia (mainly in outback locales in Western Australia and the Northern Territory), before undertaking a Foucauldian study of the politics of heritage at Texas A&M University in the USA. Principally a transdiciplinary cum adisciplinary thinker, Keith's main critiques concern the way peoples, places, and pasts are 'represented' today and supposed/presupposed cosmologically. His current investigations focus upon those critical but slippery questions of traditonality/transitionality that arise in the projection of both *indigeneity* (especially in Australasia and The Pacific) and *otherness*. His work is much in debt to the insights of his father (Charles James) and his mother (Joyce), and to the outsights of Homi Bhabha, Edward Sampson, Nicholas Thomas, Stuart Hall, and Carwyn James.

Stephanie Hom Cary is in the Italian Studies PhD programme at the University of California, Berkeley, and is a co-founder of the UC Berkeley Tourism Studies Working Group. Her current research focuses on tourism, colonialism, and the modern Italian nation-state.

Tazim B. Jamal is an Associate Professor in the Department of Recreation, Park and Tourism Sciences at Texas A&M University. Her main research areas are community-based tourism planning, sustainable tourism (theory and pedagogy), heritage tourism.

Gayle Jennings is an Associate Professor in Tourism Management in the Department of Tourism, Leisure, Hotel and Sport Management, Griffith Business School, and Director, Tourism Management Cluster, Service Industry Research Centre, Griffith University. Gayle, along with Erica Wilson, Southern Cross University is co-founder of the *Qualitative Research in Tourism and Hospitality Network*. Her research interests include theoretical paradigms informing research processes, research methodologies, qualitative research, tourism education at the tertiary level, impacts of tourism, tourism and development studies, policy and planning, special interest tourism, marine and national park tourism rural tourism, adventure tourism, and sport tourism.

Olga Junek is a lecturer in Tourism and Event Management in the School of Hospitality, Tourism and Marketing at Victoria University. Her professional experience in the education sector has fostered her interest in tertiary international students and their leisure and travel experiences, an area in which she is currently undertaking her PhD research. Her other research interests include event visitation, sustainable tourism, Chinese inbound tourism and risk and crisis management in tourism.

Jo-Anne Lester is a senior lecturer at the Centre for Tourism Policy Studies, University of Brighton. Key interests in teaching and research include tourism and visual culture. Jo-Anne is currently registered for a PhD programme at University of Wales Institute Cardiff (UWIC) investigating discourses of cruise tourism with a focus on popular film.

Scott McCabe has main research interests in the field of tourist experience and touristic consumption, particularly the mundane, practical and rhetorical uses of language that makes up human social life and tourist interaction. He has written a number of journal articles and book chapters on subject including the construction of place identity in tourists talk, and the rhetorical function of the term *tourist* in everyday discourse. Centre for Tourism and Cultural Change, Faculty of Organisation and Management, Sheffield Hallam University, Howard Street, Sheffield. S1 1WB.

Nigel Morgan is a Professor of Tourism Studies at the Welsh Centre for Tourism Research in the Cardiff School of Management at the University of Wales Institute, Cardiff. His research interests embrace the socio-cultural dimensions of tourism and destination marketing and critical tourism studies and he is currently working on *Tourism, Identities and Embodiments*, to be published by Channel View.

Chaim Noy (PhD) is an independent scholar, presently teaching in the Departments of Communication and Anthropology at the Hebrew University in Jerusalem, Israel. His research interests combine performance and semiotic perspectives with language-oriented research, in the contexts of travel, tourism and transportation. His recent publications include "*A Narrative Community: Voices of Israeli Backpackers*" (Wayne State University Press, 2006), and "*Israeli Backpackers: From Tourism to a Rite of Passage*" (SUNY Press, 2005), co-authored with Erik Cohen.

Tomas Pernecky is a PhD Candidate at the Wageningen University, The Netherlands. In his PhD thesis, Tomas draws on the recent debates in tourism studies with respect to new ways of tourism theorising also addressed under the term 'Critical Turn'. In his work, he explores the New Age *becoming* and the role tourism and travel play in the process. Tomas is interested in New Age tourism, tourism theory, constructivism, qualitative methods, Hermeneutic phenomenology and Out-of-Body experiences.

Annette Pritchard is a Reader in tourism studies and Director of the Welsh Centre for Tourism Research in the Cardiff School of Management at the University of Wales Institute, Cardiff. Her research interests focus on the relationships between tourism, representation and social structures, experiences and identities and her next book will be *Tourism, Gender and Embodiment* (CABI, 2007).

Diane Sedgley is a senior lecturer in tourism and leisure studies at the Cardiff School of Management at the University of Wales Institute Cardiff. Her research interests include minority groups in tourism and leisure. She has published work on lesbian and gay tourism and leisure and, more recently, has been involved in research looking at the role of leisure in the lives of older women. Her current research interest is focussed on examining the role of biographical research in understanding leisure and tourism behaviour. She also plays an active role in the Welsh Centre for Tourism Research.

Dr Jennie Small is a senior lecturer in the School of Leisure, Sport and Tourism at the University of Technology, Sydney. Her specific research interest is tourist behaviour in terms of gender, age, disability, and the life-course. More generally, she is interested in a Critical Tourism approach to tourist behaviour.

Margaret Byrne Swain teaches at University of California Davis Women and Gender Studies. Her research applies feminist analysis to tourism and other issues of globalization, with a particular focus on Yunnan China and the Sani of Stone Forest. She directs the Gender and Global Issues Program, and co-directs the Women's Resources and Research Center.

Julia Trapp-Fallon is head of centre for tourism, leisure and events and MSc Award Director in the Cardiff School of Management at the University of Wales Institute, Cardiff. Her work in the Welsh Centre of Tourism Research concentrates upon oral history methodology and its application in tourism and leisure.

John Tribe is a Professor of Tourism at the University of Surrey, UK. He has authored books on strategy, economics, education and environmental management in tourism and his research concentrates on sustainability, epistemology and education in tourism. He is Chair of the ATHE (Association for Tourism in Higher Education) and edits the Journal of Hospitality, Leisure Sport and Tourism Education for the Higher Education Academy Subject Network.

René van der Duim since 1991 is an Assistant Professor at the Socio-spatial Analysis Group (Department of Environmental Sciences) of Wageningen University. His research focuses on the relation between tourism and sustainable development and he executed research project in Costa Rica, Kenya and The Netherlands. He has published his results in professional and scientific journals (e.g. *Journal of Sustainable Tourism, Annals of Tourism Research, Current Issues in Tourism* and *Vrijetijdstudies*) and has presented intermediate results at several conferences and workshops. In 2005 he completed his dissertation, titled *Tourismscapes, an actor-network perspective on sustainable tourism development.*

Soile Veijola is a sociologist and works at the University of Lapland, in Rovaniemi, Finland, as Professor of cultural studies of tourism. Her earlier publications include feminist critique of theorising on tourism (mostly co-authored with Eeva Jokinen) and analyses of mixed social orders in sport and society. She is currently leading an interdisciplinary research project entitled *Tourism as Work.*

Sheena Westwood is a senior lecturer in Marketing and Research Methods at Cardiff School of Management, University of Wales Institute, Cardiff. Her research interests include tourist consumption behaviour, marketing and progressive qualitative research inquiry. She has published work on gender issues in airline marketing, tourism branding and tourism experiences for the Welsh Centre for Tourism Research. Forthcoming work includes papers on the age–time–leisure paradox, and tourism shopping experiences.

Erica Wilson is a lecturer in the School of Tourism and Hospitality Management at Southern Cross University in Lismore, Northern NSW. Her doctoral thesis (Griffith University) focussed on the solo travel experiences of Australian women, particularly the constraints they face and how these are negotiated. Her research interests are with gender and tourism, the tourist experience, leisure constraints/negotiation and critical/qualitative research methodologies.

Acknowledgements

No book is ever the result of three people's efforts and this book is certainly no exception. We thank all our contributors for agreeing to be part of this project and then for speedily and cheerfully meeting our deadlines and for allowing us to edit their hard work. We express our gratitude to our editors at Elsevier for their assistance and guidance throughout the project, particularly the book series editor, Stephen Page for giving us the opportunity to publish the book in the first place. We owe a special debt of gratitude to Renee Pryce for all her painstaking editorial work on the manuscript — you know we could not have done it without you! Finally, the three of us owe so much to so many wonderful and beautiful people — our families, our friends and our colleagues — that to attempt to name you here would be an invidious task. Please forgive us and accept our simple thank you for inspiring and supporting us in this and all our efforts.

Irena Ateljevic
Murter, Croatia

Annette Pritchard
Cardiff, Wales

Nigel Morgan
Cardiff, Wales

26th July 2006

Foreword

As in any field of research, the cornerstone of tourism studies consists of *people talking* — and, preferably, being encouraged to publish their talks for a wider audience to read, and to talk about some more. The volume at hand distinguishes itself from many previous academic conversations, launched for the field of tourism and hospitality studies, by its spirit — and stamina — of a self-reflexive and engaged freedom fighter.

From what should the field of research be liberated, then? According to the editors of the volume, tourism studies are handicapped by an internal dichotomy of interests — between, on the one hand, critical social and cultural studies of tourism and, on the other, business-oriented tourism management. Writing in an academic context, the construction of the reader causes additional distress: should one accept the notion of an 'objectivist' discourse of 'events reporting themselves' or explore the possibilities opened through the use of personal experience in an academic enterprise? A third source of constraint is that work at universities is increasingly affected by new managerialism and the promotion of applied studies at the expense of independent research. This makes it difficult to enhance and maintain a sustained, focussed conversation between academic and applied research — no matter how much the travelling world would benefit from such a connection.

The numerous writers in this volume have turned the tables in order to articulate their theoretically and empirically based critique of the mainstream discourse of tourism research as a relatively isolated field, quantitative in nature and biased in favour of business applications rather than critical and reflexive research. The mainstream discourse is, furthermore, claimed to be masculinist in nature, which means that it excludes the perspectives and contributions of women and others who were not born with a white male body.

Do we need outspoken books like this in tourism research? In my view, they are pivotal. They articulate the often by-passed *constitutive rules* of both knowledge production and tourism scholarship. Moreover, they challenge readers from first-year students to the gate-keepers of academic journals, not to mention people wishing to learn and benefit from the research, to approach issues in tourism and travelling as a power-charged field of interdisciplinary expertise, firmly rooted in the lived realities of tourism, travelling or other mobilities and immobilities. Tourism in itself is as scientific as a glass of Piña Colada is. It needs to be theorised into a research field trough multiple research and knowledge strategies.

This is mainly what the individual chapters of this book are doing. They outline a future ethics for research on tourism, whereby traversing other schools of thought may be done with respect and curiosity. They also provide an impressing cavalcade of methodological insights for qualitative and theoretical research.

After alerting the academic community to its own unsustainable and biased practices, the same community needs to proceed with an even harder task: freeing knowledge from exclusive academic forums. How to *make sense* to all the hosts and guests of the mobile world in real life terms — without trivialising knowledge or wrapping it into promises of easy money?

Soile Veijola

Editors' Introduction: Promoting an Academy of Hope in Tourism Enquiry

Irena Ateljevic, Nigel Morgan and Annette Pritchard

'To travel is to discover that human beings in other lands and cultures are also people with whom we can share our laughter and our tears, and that what we have in common is a great deal more than the sum of all our differences'. (Margaret Silf, 2006, p. 178)

The Story of the Book, or about Poetry and the Political

Every book has a story to tell and we'd like to welcome you, our reader, into the story of this book. So, to begin at the beginning, over the last two decades a quiet revolution has been taking place in tourism enquiry as the field has begun to engage with the new work on identity, difference, the body, gender and post-structural theories of language and subjectivity which has forced such a rethinking in the social sciences. In many ways, this collection of essays is part of this turn to 'the critical' in tourism research although we do not want to review this new knowledge here since it is more than effectively discussed in the essays themselves. In fact, we do not see this as a conventional editors' introduction such as you would find at the beginning of most collections of tourism essays. We rather hope to take you on a poetic journey, to tell you this book's story and to unravel what we understand by the phrase 'critical tourism studies' before we sketch out the themes which the individual contributions capture. The book you have now in your hands is a physical object which appears to tell a neat, orderly and linear set of narratives, yet we prefer to think of it more as a series of on-going dialogues, conversations and entanglements, which we hope we can all take beyond these pages — into our classrooms, offices, conference rooms and even our homes. They are a series of dialogues which help us all to talk openly and honestly 'about the ways we work for change and are changed . . . to illuminate the space of the possible where we can work to sustain our *hope* and create community with justice as the core foundation' (hooks, 2003, p. xvi, italics in original).

In a very real sense this book has been inspired by every relationship and interaction which we have experienced over many years and across many countries. Whilst our three individual names might be on the book's cover and many other contributors' names appear within it, this collection owes its origins to a much wider community of people, and

The Critical Turn in Tourism Studies: Innovative Research Methodologies
Copyright © 2007 by Elsevier Ltd.
ISBN: 0-08-045098-9

particularly to those colleagues who inspired us to organize the first Critical Tourism Studies Conference in Dubrovnik in 2005. We planned it as the first conference where 'second generation tourism scholars' (Jamal & Kim, 2005) could take centre stage instead of acting on the margins and peripheries of the academy. Whilst we knew that there were many who shared our desire to challenge the field's dominant discourses, we were overwhelmed by the reaction to the event. Perhaps more significant than the numbers of people who came, however, was the strength and energy which this collective quickly created, soon transforming a series of personal relationships and loose groupings into a genuine community. This collection of essays is in no way a set of conference proceedings but it is a child of that conference and quite a few of its contributors were there in Croatia when hitherto isolated scholars and marginalized research clusters became a coalition of like-minded people. Revolution was in that warm summer air in 2005 and 'since there can be no revolution without poetry' (Steinem, 1993, p. 359) we would like to share with you Marge Piercy's inspirational poem which seems to so encapsulate our collective project:

> Alone, you can fight,
> you can refuse, you can
> take what revenge you can
> but they roll over you.
>
> But two people fighting
> back to back can cut through
> a mob, a snake-dancing file
> can break a cordon, an army
> can meet an army.
>
> Two people can keep each other
> sane, can give support, conviction,
> love, massage, hope, sex.
> Three people are a delegation,
> a committee, a wedge. With four
> you can play bridge and start
> an organisation. With six
> you can rent a whole house,
> eat pie for dinner with no
> seconds, and hold a fund raising party.
> A dozen make a demonstration.
> A hundred fill a hall.
> A thousand have solidarity and your own newsletter;
> ten thousand, power and your own paper;
> a hundred thousand, your own media;
> ten million, your own country.
>
> It goes on one at a time,
> It starts when you care
> to act, it starts when you do

it again after they said no,
it starts when you say *We*
and know who you mean, and each
day you mean one more.

In retrospect Dubrovnik (2005) seems to have been a key moment in the evolution of what we have now begun to describe as an emerging 'academy of hope' in tourism studies, a movement which comes at a time when more than ever we are all being challenged to 'shift to a new level of consciousness, to reach a higher moral ground. . . . to shed our fear and give hope to each other' (Wangari Maathai, 2004, Nobel Peace Prize lecture). In the aftermath of the conference and in the planning of this book, we found ourselves struggling with the notion of a 'critical' or a 'new' school in tourism enquiry and how this could be (mis)construed since labels create boundaries and academic schisms (Tribe, 2006). To be labelled as a critical scholar also tends to exclusively associate one with the Frankfurt School that relied heavily on Marxist theory in its explanations of social processes. Yet, our understanding of critical tourism scholarship is that it is more than simply a *way of knowing,* an ontology, it is a *way of being,* a commitment to tourism enquiry which is pro-social justice and equality and anti-oppression: it is an academy of hope. It transcends ontological shift and paradigmatic transformations. Advocacy of critical scholarship, however, is not about replacing one dominant school with another, merely substituting one rigid 'ism' with another — in other words it is not about 'either/or' thinking. Such polarities simply replicate and further legitimise the underlying masculinist academic structures, which so constrain us. Moreover, in critical studies there has been too much emphasis on marking a difference and too little focus on making a difference (Aitchison, this volume) — too much attention on identifying problems without suggesting solutions. Instead, our community of hope/resistance is a holistic and broad-based movement of tourism scholars that encompasses a range of interpretative, critical and emancipatory (amongst other) paradigms without being confined by them. Indeed, we would contest the de-humanising academic ideologies and practises that force us into 'either/or' thinking and challenge our academy to embrace more 'both/and' thought.

In this sense, our commitment to tourism research which challenges oppression also requires the emancipation of ourselves — clearly you cannot advocate the emancipation of others if you yourself are not free. Most universities today are straight-jacketed by institutional and governmental research assessment exercises and most academic appointments, tenures and promotions are determined by publications and/or citation indices. As institutions embrace neo-liberal economic discourses they commercialise and consumerise tertiary education, promote institutional and individual competition at the expense of collaboration and often stunt the ability of scholars to be captains of society's critical consciousness. The imposition of such masculinist metric-based structures also stifles creativity in research (see Page, 2005 for its impact on tourism enquiry), promotes a collective fear of radical change and entrenches a culture of domination — ensuring a de-humanising obedience — separating what we study from how we live (Steinem, 1993). As teachers and researchers therefore, we have a responsibility to be self-actualised individuals, for as bell hooks reflects (1994, p. 15) 'the practice of a healer, therapist, teacher should be directed toward his or herself first, because if the helper is unhappy, he or she cannot help many people.'

In a way, this book is one moment in our response to this acclaimed cultural critic and feminist theorist's call for academics to embrace honest and supportive communication in their efforts to produce social change. From our locations in privileged and powerful positions (as permanently employed senior academics in Western universities), we conceived this book as a means for 'new' and 'established' voices in the tourism academy to: speak about the power relations underpinning the production of academic knowledge; present a range of qualitative data collection methods which confront the field's dominant (post)positivist approaches; foreground the emotional dynamics of research relations and explore the personal, the political and the situated nature of research journeys. Such journeys are not without risk, however, as:

> . . . [I]t is not only the hostility of others that may prevent us from questioning the status quo. Our will to doubt can be just as powerfully sapped by an internal sense that societal conventions must have a sound basis, even if we are not sure exactly what this may be, because they have been adhered to by a great many people for a long time. . . . We stifle our doubts and follow the flock because we cannot conceive of ourselves as pioneers of hitherto unknown, difficult truths'. (de Botton, 2000, p. 13)

Although it is a characteristic conceit of the modern era to assert that each generation is transformatory, we are living through sharply transitional times, which are calling into question many conventions and orthodoxies that, until recently, felt relatively fixed. New perspectives are emerging across disciplines and research fields as western consciousness seeks to evolve beyond the limitations of Newtonian and Cartesian thought — from relativity theory in physics, from the findings of depth psychologists, to new approaches in anthropological and ecological studies. As a result of these and other related developments, the post-imperial, de-industrialising world is witnessing the increasing deconstruction of the largely masculine tradition of western thought — developments which are combining to stimulate a new awareness of 'reality' as a construction of human imagination. Place, space, time and identity — none are now conceived as fixed but as mutable, represented, relative and constructed. If relativity and imagination have replaced fixity and objectivity, then reality becomes contested and, as a result — together with an increasing awareness that the intellectual tradition of the west is no longer the dominant wisdom tradition — there is a greater interest now than at any other time in what has previously been marginalised, oppressed and unrecognised.

Central to such global awareness is an increased recognition of the need to live consciously and to promote self-acceptance, self-responsibility, self-assertiveness and personal integrity. All of this also connects with the broader movement of so-called 'spiritual activism', which reaffirms individual growth and spirituality and counters contemporary global discourses of fear, alienation and disempowerment (e.g. Diamant, 2005; Fonda, 2004; Fox, 2004; Maathai, 2005; Tacey, 2004). As tourism teachers and researchers, we have emotional and spiritual responsibilities to those with whom we co-create tourism knowledge, to our students and also to ourselves and we must try to reconnect what we study with how we live. This is not some self-centred self-indulgence, but rather a reintegration of mind/body/spirit; rational/emotional; feminine/masculine; subject/object; internal/external; winner/loser; dominant/passive; man/nature; and agency/structure/resistance. Challenging such destructive dichotomies, polarizations, linearities and hierarchies (incidentally all key dimensions of tourism enquiry's prevailing positivistic paradigm) Gloria Steinem (1993, 2004) suggests that the next step towards recognizing that our lives and our fate are intimately connected to those of everyone else on the planet is the new paradigm of *circularity*. Only when we balance our inner lives with our passion to contribute to the world will we be able to tune into our own powerful voices as the source for envisioning and actualizing a power paradigm shift. Describing this as a 'new circular paradigm', Gloria Steinem (1993, pp. 189-190) deserves to be quoted at length:

> As each person completes herself or himself and contributes what is authentic, a new paradigm emerges: circularity. At rest, it is a circle, and in motion, a spiral. If we think of ourselves as circles, our goal is completion — not defeating others. Progress lies in the direction we haven't been. . . . Progress is appreciation. If we think of work structures as circles, excellence and cooperation are the goal — not competition. Progress becomes mutual support and connectedness. If we think of nature as a circle, then we are part of its reciprocity. Progress means interdependence. If we respect nature and each living thing as a microcosm of nature — then we respect the unique miracle of ourselves. And so we have come full circle.

This is our vision of tourism scholarship's engagement with the critical and its potential to create an academy of hope which nurtures open minds and open hearts and is founded on principles of interdependence, respect, equity and humanity. At the dawn of what may be an era of engagement with 'sacred' social science epistemologies (Denzin & Lincoln, 2005), our field cannot claim to lead this movement, but it is important that we add our tourism voices to the collective. In our seriously fractured world where the evolving struggles between liberal and neo-conservative/neo-liberal views have become progressively sharper and more distinct, one might question such an endeavour as ambitious and naïve. Maybe so, but we must try to examine critically the purpose of our research and ask whether our knowledge has served to enhance social justice or whether it has simply served to reify historical power and social relations. It is our responsibility to take into our institutions, classrooms, offices, conferences, consultancy projects, writings, and lives the values of ethical scholarship. In the face of global conflicts and chaos, we need to (re) discover the power of our own agency and our own processes of becoming.

About the Book, or Moments in an On-Going Conversation

The collection of essays has been divided into two parts, with the first eleven essays establishing a fresh, context-specific framework for engaging philosophical and theoretical debates in contemporary tourism enquiry. The second set of twelve essays which constitute part two of the book then present, discuss and critique specific methodologies, research techniques, methods of interpretation and writing strategies, all of which are in some sense illustrative of 'critical' tourism research. With such a neatly woven structure, one could imagine that this was our intention from the outset, but that would be to deny the fact that every book has its own hidden history — from proposal to publication. At every stage of its revision the book has evolved, especially as its contributors began to create their own pieces and whilst their essays are presented here 'stuck' in their final published state, each individual contribution (and the book as a whole) is less an end point and more a pause in a series of on-going dialogues about tourism enquiry. It would be remiss of us if we did not acknowledge our own editorial power here and by deciding to structure the book in this way, we have consciously (and unconsciously) created particular linkages and divisions between ideas and contributors. Of course, the whole collection could have been differently shaped, arranged and presented, with a different list of contributors. In this last, it is important to point out that we intended to capture here a *sample,* not a definitive list of critical tourism scholars (clearly this is an impossible and also an inappropriate task).

What is profoundly attractive about these contributors is that they are all 'critical'. Although they might not all echo your particular view of critical scholarship or share your own epistemological or methodological leanings, our hope is that some of the work in this book at least resonates with your experiences of the research process. The contributors range from postgraduate students to established professors with two to over twenty years of experience as teachers, researchers and academic writers. Their various relationships with the English-speaking academy thus range from relative 'outsider' to well-positioned 'insider' and, drawn from both the geopolitical margins (e.g. Croatia, Jamaica, Israel and India) and the 'powerbases' of the tourism academy (North America, UK, Australia, Canada and New Zealand), they occupy a range of locations within the complexly spun web of academic power relations and social divisions (determined also by sex, age, gender, class background, expressions of sexuality, race, ability and ethnicity).

The collection begins with four essays which explore: the discursive formations which underpin and structure tourism's architecture of knowledge (Annette Pritchard and Nigel Morgan); tourism's 'rules' and the potential for resistance (John Tribe); researchers' entanglements, 'coping' strategies and voices (Candice Harris, Erica Wilson and Irena Ateljevic); experiences of researchers struggling in the liminal zones between traditional modernist and critical postmodernist research (Tazim Jamal and Jeff Everett). The focus then shifts to three compelling personal accounts of how as tourism researchers we can *make a difference* through inclusive ways of knowing and ways of being (Cara Aitchison, Margaret Swain and Derek Hall) in spite of the broader structural processes which affect research(er) emancipation and transformation. These are followed by two essays which explore the strengths and weaknesses of critical theory and the roles of engaged and situated researchers (Donna Chambers and David Botterill), followed in turn by essays by Adrian Franklin and Rene van der Duim which argue that what tourism studies actually requires is less a further theorization and more an engagement with new ontologies — such as tourism as ordering. As a counter balance to these ideas, this part of the book is closed with an essay by Keith Hollinshead, who calls for a greater theorization of the field and addresses the conceptualization of tourism as 'worldmaking'.

The second half of the book focuses on issues of research praxis in a series of essays which convincingly translate some of these conceptual formations into specific methodologies, research techniques, methods of interpretation and writing strategies. The first three chapters explore the potential of grounded theory (Gayle Jennings and Olga Junek), constructivism (Tomas Pernecky) and ethnmethodology (Scott McCabe). Next, four contributors

(Bente Heimtun, Jennie Small and her collective authors, Maureen Ayikoru and John Tribe) directly challenge the often unarticulated role of epistemology in determining methodological choices in tourism research, before three contributors explore how we can give more voice to those with whom we co-create that knowledge. In these essays Sheena Westwood discusses the potential of using projective techniques, Julia Fallon examines oral history and Diane Sedgley explores life-course analysis. The collection then closes with several powerful examples of the personal, situated but above all emotional nature of tourism research. Chaim Noy and Ria Dunkley expose the challenging and sometimes painful nature of the research process and put a compelling case for passionate scholarship, before the last chapter presents a series of short autobiographical reflections on their individual academic journeys by Stephen Doorne, Stephanie Hom Cary, Graham Brown, Jo-Anne Lester, Kathe Browne, Tomas Pernecky, Susana Curtin, Martine Abramovici and Nigel Morgan.

Using the Book, or Taking on Critical Research

Approaching your research from a critical perspective has an impact on every aspect of the research process — from your choice of topic, through to your research framework, to choosing particular methods for collecting and analyzing information. As we have seen from our brief overview of the essays here, the maturity of the methodological arguments developed by so many 'critical' tourism scholars over recent years makes tourism studies a rich field from which to draw out specific research practices. Being a critical scholar matters when taking on research in tourism in that your position (whether it is based on anti-oppression, social justice, pro-woman, advocacy of emancipation or self-determination, or any other similar worldview) influences every aspect of the research process. Thinking about your research and those with whom you co-create that research (including your participants, co-researchers and your audiences) from a critical point of view sharpens an approach to a project in that your appreciation of the complexly spun web of academic power relations brings into focus the varied contexts in which our research takes place. Above all, taking on research as a critical scholar means that we all should consider the wider impacts of our research — whether you are an undergraduate or postgraduate student or a more established researcher and teacher. We hope that this book will be of use to anyone who is thinking about or practicing critical tourism research. Of course there are gaps and omissions — some foreseen, most unanticipated. That after all is the nature of any project — it is never and nor should it be complete. Read, learn, get entangled, get engaged, get critical, but above all, enjoy.

References

De Botton, A. (2000). *The consolations of philosophy.* London: Hamish Hamilton.

Denzin, N. K., & Lincoln, Y. S. (2005). Introduction: The discipline and practice of qualitative research. In: N. K. Denzin, & Y. S. Lincoln (Eds), *The Sage handbook of qualitative research* (3rd ed., pp. 1–33). London: Sage.

Diamant, A. (2005). Keynote speech. *Proceedings of the Women and Power Omega Institute 4th Annual Conference*, New York, September 9–11.

Fonda, J. (2004). The new feminism. Keynote speech. *Proceedings of the Women and Power Omega Institute 4th and V-Day Annual Conference*, New York, September 9–11.

Fox, M. (2000). *One river, many wells.* Dublin: Gateway.

Hooks, B. (1994). *Teaching to transgress: Education as the practice of freedom.* New York: Routledge.

Jamal, T., & Kim, H. (2005). Bridging the interdisciplinary divide: Towards an integrated framework for heritage tourism research. *Tourist Studies*, 5(1), 55–83.

Maathai, W. (2005). Keynote speech. *Proceedings of the Women and Power Omega Institute and V-Day 4th Annual Conference*, New York, September 10–13.

Page, S. (2005). Academic ranking exercises: Do they achieve anything meaningful? - A personal view. *Tourism Management*, 26(5), 633–666.

Piercy, M. (1980). *The moon is always female.* New York: Alfred Knopf.

Silf, M. (2006). *The way of wisdom.* Oxford: Lion Hudson plc.

Steinem, G. (1993). *Revolution from within.* USA: Gloria Steinem.

Steinem, G. (2004). New leaps of consciousness. Keynote speech. *Proceedings of theWomen and Power Omega Institute 4th and V-Day Annual Conference*, New York, September 9–11.

Tacey, D. (2004) *The spirituality revolution.* New York: Brunner-Routledge.

Tribe, J. (2004). The truth about tourism. Paper presented at the Creating Tourism Knowledge, 14 th international research conference of the Council for Australian University Tourism and Hospitality Education, The University of Queensland, Brisbane, February 10–13.

PART 1:

THE CRITICAL SCHOOL OF TOURISM STUDIES: CRAFTING THE EPISTEMOLOGICAL GROUNDS

Chapter 1

De-centring Tourism's Intellectual Universe, or Traversing the Dialogue Between Change and Tradition

Annette Pritchard and Nigel Morgan

Introduction

The phenomenal growth of the travel and tourism industries in the past five decades has dramatically changed global lifestyles. But, as tourism has grown as an industry, so has it matured as a field of enquiry, especially in the last two decades when the totality of tourism research has developed beyond the narrow confines of an applied business field to reach out to new learnings, particularly in post-colonialism, production–consumption and power, practice, and agency. Yet the putative coalitions and alliances which have emerged to fore-ground these critical and interpretative modes of tourism inquiry still have much to do if they are to truly decentre the tourism academy and secure a paradigmatic shift in tourism scholarship and theory. There remains a crucial challenge to develop conceptualizations of tourisms that encompass multiple worldviews and cultural differences and research praxis that recognizes and reflects the plurality of all positions, practices, and insights. In this chapter, therefore, we confront the scale of the task facing those of us who would promote progressive transformation and academic renewal in tourism enquiry. We begin the chapter by challenging and deconstructing the tourism academy, before moving to critique its production of academic knowledge and its dominant discourses. We end our contribution with a call for more resistance from within the academy to those sites of power, which shore up existing points of privilege and stand in the way of more inclusive scholarship.

This current volume which focuses on the recent shift towards the 'critical' in tourism studies provides us with a rare opportunity (untrammeled by the expected norms of journal articles) to critique tourism study, its dominant epistemologies, its academy and perhaps most crucially, to speculate on its future. The establishment of tourism as a legitimate field of study owes much to the groundbreaking work of those who have been termed its first-generation scholars (Jamal & Kim, 2005) — the academics from a range of disciplines (but dominated by economics, sociology, and geography), who did much in the 1970s and 1980s to establish a number of the field's key journals and write a range of its seminal texts. Since those early days, there has been a tremendous growth in students interested in studying tourism at undergraduate and postgraduate levels and a subsequent explosion in the numbers of university departments offering courses in a range of tourism-related and cognate areas around the world. Indeed, such has been the rise of the field over the past 20 years that there are now over 40 professors of tourism management and tourism studies in the UK alone (Tribe, 2003); most of the world's leading academic publishers carry tourism book series and there has been a dramatic growth in the number and variety of tourism journals. These now number in excess of 75 (Pechlaner, Zehrer, & Abfalter, 2002), of which 40 are recognized internationally (McKercher, 2002) and which publish a wide variety of research papers from academics worldwide (Dowling, 2000; Jogaratnam, Chon, McCleary, Mena, & Yoo, 2005). Arguably, it is a sign of just how much tourism's academic reputation has grown that in 2008 (as a result of considerable lobbying by subject associations such as the Association for Tourism in Higher Education) tourism will for the first time, be a recognized sub-field of study in the UK Research Assessment Exercise.

And yet, while this growth has been identified by some as evidence of a healthy, democratic, global tourism research culture (McKercher, 2005), we would argue that such expansion has not always brought increased innovation and diversity; it could be said to have resulted in simply a greater volume of research which is mainly confirmatory and reproductive rather than scholarship which has sought to break new epistemological, conceptual or ethical ground. Indeed, writers such as Stephen Page (2005) have suggested that research creativity in tourism is being undermined by research assessment processes, which promote formulaic responses from academics anxious to guard against rejection. In the UK for instance, the impact of such funding mechanisms on the 'shape' of tourism enquiry is particularly acute since tourism scholarship is largely submitted to units of research assessment in sports-related or business and management studies — both of which are heavily dominated by positivist approaches. Indeed, despite some isolated dissenting voices there are a number of forces at work which are actively cementing the already dominant tradition of (post)positivist approaches in the field, including: location of tourism, leisure and hospitality studies in business and management schools, often in vocationally oriented higher education institutions; hostile environments created for inter- and multi-disciplinary work by funding mechanisms; pressures to produce technically useful, policy-oriented research; reluctance of funding bodies to consider tourism a 'serious' area of study. This last point continues to frustrate many tourism academics, who despite studying the world's largest and fastest growing industry are constantly challenged to demonstrate their academic credibility. Politicians and media and social commentators frequently characterize subjects such as tourism, leisure, hospitality and sports studies as intellectually insubstantial and unable to provide a sustained contribution to liberal education and independent critical thinking. Typical of such discourses are the comments of Gloria Ladson-Billings and Jamel Donnor (2005, p. 295) who suggest that:

> Courses and programs of study in hotel and restaurant management, criminal justice, and sports management, while representing legitimate job and career choices, are less likely to promote overall university goals of educating people

to engage with knowledge and critical thinking across a wide variety of disciplines and traditions.

At the same time, while academics in other disciplines and fields of enquiry frequently use tourism sites and experiences as the context for their study, they often regard tourism management/studies itself as intellectual lightweight, epistemologically and methodologically stunted by positivist industry prerogatives. Whether this is a fair characterization of our field can be debated, but what is clear is that analyses of social injustice, disenfranchisement and human and spatial marginalization have been all too rare in tourism enquiry, while its academy has seemed to be largely resistant to or oblivious of epistemological shifts occurring elsewhere. This is particularly depressing because, as Margaret Swain (2004, p. 103) reminds us:

> within tourism studies we have ample opportunities to act from an ethical position, to engage the oppressed, identifying possibilities for agency and resistance.

Not only this, but despite 40 years of tourism scholarship we still know too little about tourism identities, relationships, mobilities and consumptions and much of the new work on identity, difference, the body, gender and post-structural theories of language and subjectivity which has forced a rethinking of the social science intellectual universe remains on the margins of our subject. This is why, important though it was for us to begin our chapter by highlighting the constraining influence of governmental and institutional straightjacketing on tourism studies, at the heart of our discussion is the suggestion that there are greater and potentially more explosive intellectual rumblings beneath the apparent quiet surfaces of tourism scholarship. As marginalized and underrepresented voices clamour to be heard in tourism's essentially inward-looking and conservative academy, there are coalitions forming which could ignite and explode the power-bases of the field's knowledge gatekeepers. It is just possible that the academic culture of tourism and its modes of thinking about tourism may be on the verge of a seismic shift as these alternative voices (many of them women and Indigenous peoples whose scholarship is guided by self-determination and by democratic and social justice-oriented inquiry) begin to critique the academy's composition and the dominance of an overly narrow agenda for tourism research.

Deconstructing the Academy

It is expected of engaged, reflexive researchers that they should be aware of the nature of their own academic collectives so that they are conscious of the power structures and ideological underpinnings, which shape knowledge production in their particular fields. Yet, until relatively recently, researchers have been rather reluctant to address such issues critically in our area. This is beginning to change and contributions reflecting this new introspection include David Botterill's (2000) discussion of social scientific ways of knowing hospitality, Cara Aitchison's (2001) exploration of engendered leisure research, John Tribe's (2005) consideration of tourism's 'truths' and the thought-provoking contributions in Jenny Phillimore and Lisa Goodson's (2004a) collection on qualitative tourism research.

In this part of our chapter we want to expand this debate by exploring those academic hierarchies which exert power in and control over the tourism field so that we may build a picture of 'who controls what, how hierarchies are built, maintained and changed and how equity occurs' (Swain, 2004, p. 102). In this foray into the murky foucauldian world of power and discourse, we are responding to Michael Hall's (2004) criticism that the tourism academy has failed to critique the roles of its academic gatekeepers or to explore their interrelationships and influence on the nature and direction of tourism knowledge.

The importance of certain key gatekeepers to the networks of power which shape and determine knowledge production and academic discourse is well established in the sociology of knowledge (Spender, 1981). Collectively, these gatekeepers are responsible for setting the 'parameters in which individuals are encouraged to work if they wish to be at the centre of issues in their discipline' (Spender, 1981, p. 186) and at the heart of these networks of knowledge production and knowledge codification in a field such as tourism are the international refereed journals and the editorial hierarchies which support them. Of some considerable concern for our field, however, is the gendered nature of these academic elites. Cara Aitchison's 2001 study of the composition of leisure and tourism journal editorial boards revealed that tourism journals are very highly male-dominated, do not address gender issues in their editorial policy statements, and do not publish any equal opportunities information. Almost a decade later (the data for her study actually relates to 1997), we thought it would be instructive to examine the editorial board composition of a selection of tourism journals, especially as several new journals have been launched since the turn of the century. As Table 1.1 shows, women appear to have made only marginal progress in penetrating these largely masculine clubs and even in the newer journals such as *Tourist Studies, Tourism and Cultural Change*, and *Journal of Heritage Tourism* women constitute less than a third of editorial board members.

Table 1.1: The gender balance of a selection of international tourism journals.

Journal title	Date established	Editorial board size (number)	Male members (%)	Female members (%)
Annals of Tourism Research	1973	108	89	11
Tourism Management	1979	19	84	16
Journal of Sustainable Tourism	1992	29	69	31
Journal of Vacation Marketing	1994	37	81	19
Tourism Analysis	1996	73	88	12
Current Issues in Tourism	1997	13	85	15
Tourism & Hospitality Research	1999	23	82	18
Tourist Studies	2000	11	73	28
Journal of Ecotourism	2001	21	81	19
Tourism & Cultural Change	2003	33	70	30
Journal of Heritage Tourism	2006	20	70	30
Journal of Sport & Tourism	2006	9	78	22

Despite these journals' commitment to what could be broadly termed critical social science, gender equality initiatives and equal opportunities policies remain stubbornly absent from their editorial policies and when we contacted them, most publishers and/or editors were unaware of the gender breakdown of their own journals. In contrast, *Leisure Studies* (established in 1981) has become a model of good practice since Cara Aitchison's study in its commitment to (and subsequent achievement of) a gender-balanced, time-limited editorial board with transparent editorial policies and practices. By comparison tourism journal editorial boards have ignored and/or resisted such calls for gender equality and as can be seen from the table, any progress has been marginal. They continue to resemble some kind of priesthood, ignoring the intelligence and talents of more than half of humanity and this continuing male domination of these key agents of academic communication and the consequent cementing of masculinist research traditions and approaches has had real consequences for tourism scholarship. Two of the most obvious are the marginalization of female academics and a close correlation between those journals with the most heavily male-dominated editorial boards and those with the highest percentage of male article authors (Aitchison, 2001). Such a situation does not make for inclusive scholarship — especially at a time when many countries are witnessing a feminization of higher education. The numbers of female students now outnumber men in many countries (where there are equality of opportunities) and the proportion of female academics is rising worldwide — thus in the UK now there is almost a 50:50 mix (Fazackerley & Hughes, 2006).

The ongoing failure of the tourism academy to take gender inequality seriously and to recognize its role in perpetuating particular hegemonic worldviews, value systems, and ideologies is both worrying and indefensible. Indeed, the silencing of female voices is typical of tourism's discursive formation. A recent article by Weibing Zhao and Brent Ritchie (2006) which attempts to 'rank' tourism's leading academics over the past 20 years identifies only three women in the top 54 most prolific scholars under their criteria. While these authors comment that they were expecting men to outnumber women, they remark that the overwhelming dominance of male academics did take them by surprise. Interestingly, this article is one of a number of similar recent attempts to map the topology of the tourism academy (e.g. Jogaratnam et al., 2005; Ryan, 2005; Xiao & Smith, 2006), which have revealed its gendered segregation and provoked considerable debate among second-generation tourism scholars. In many ways, the appearance of these articles could not have been more timely for our chapter as they discuss (and at times reify) the attributes which tourism's gatekeepers consider constituting 'good' scholarship and which many of the contributors to this current volume are actively challenging. Weibing Zhao and Brent Ritchie's (2005) article is an empiricist quantitative analysis ranking the most prolific scholars during 1988–2004 and while subjective judgements are embedded in the paper, quantity of output (10 published articles in the study period in selected journals) is taken to provide the 'gold standard' of academic leadership: a productivity-based metric which directly equates authorship with leadership. As with the other recent articles which describe the patterns of tourism scholarship, Weibing Zhao and Brent Ritchie do not problematize the gender imbalance and thus there is no discussion of the consequences of the patriarchal structures that they uncover. Indeed, in their suggestion that their ranking system could be used by universities to recruit and reward staff and by the International Academy for the Study of Tourism (IAST) to identify potential new members, the authors are actually reinforcing the masculinist dominance of the tourism academy.

Interestingly, the IAST (established in 1986) still employs the traditional personal nomination process to consider and induct new members, of which there are currently 74 — including only 9 women. The 'clubby' nature of this group has been the subject of some critique elsewhere (see Swain, 2004), and one of its members, Erik Cohen (2005, p. 3) recently said of it that 'rather than an association of the best people in the field, it is unwittingly becoming an association of the best of friends . . . some of the best people in major disciplines have not yet been induced into the Academy'. This reveals a further feature of this gatekeeper community — its exclusivity. Many of the same academics appear on most of the main journal editorial boards and more than half of the editorial board members of *Tourism Management* and the *Annals of Tourism Research* have been inducted into the IAST, most of whose annual conference delegates are 'almost all male' (Tribe, 2005, p. 364). The particular dynamics of self-selecting clubs — such as associations and academic journals which rely on invitation — also means that their membership continues to be largely drawn from first-generation (male) tourism scholars (many IAST members are emeritus or approaching retirement age) while second-generation (and female) scholars remain largely overlooked.

The consequences of this male domination and how it 'makes for a very masculinist research community' (Swain, 2004, p. 105) continues to remain unproblematized, and yet its impact is far-reaching. Take for instance the fact that most professorial appointments processes around the world are based on recommendation and referees' reports — usually restricted to those already holding the title. It comes as little surprise then, in view of all of the above that there is not one female full professor of tourism in New Zealand, while only 6% of professors of tourism in the UK are women (Pritchard, 2005), a figure well below the (itself unacceptably low) national average of 14% across all academic disciplines (Fazackerley & Hughes, 2006). At the beginning of the twenty-first century, the tourism academy remains highly patriarchal and continues to privilege the knowledge systems of its first-generation scholars, many of whom have largely failed to problematize their middle class white identities; they have 'no class, no race, no gender [they are] the generic person' (Kimmel, 1996, p. 4). Such 'elders' or 'power brokers' are firmly entrenched in the key power bases of the academy, from where they are able to police the commissioning and dissemination of its knowledge (Tribe, 2005, p. 372).

Not only are our academy's gatekeepers typically male, first-generation scholars, it also emerges that they are more likely than not to be grounded in Western Anglocentric epistemic research traditions. Two recent studies (Pechlander et al., 2004; Jogaratnam et al., 2005) have demonstrated that journal output is dominated by institutions in the USA, UK, Canada and more recently Australia — a situation which has shown little change in over a decade (Sheldon, 1990). Similarly, Weibing Zhao and Brent Ritchie (2005) also reveal the power of these four English-speaking nations in producing tourism academics. Thus, according to their ranking of the top 54 tourism scholars only 3 non-English-speaking nations have educated one leading scholar. Leading scholars are more likely to be well-established academics (receiving their doctoral degrees earlier); they are most likely to have been educated in the USA (21) or UK (13), followed by Canada and Australia (8 each). These same English-speaking nations dominate current affiliations and publications opportunities and their leading tourism academics are most likely to be in business and management collectives (20), compared to tourism (9). Given this situation, it is unsurprising that over three-quarters of tourism journal editors are based in the USA, UK, Australia, Canada, and New Zealand.

Interestingly, however, in contrast to the gender imbalance of journal authors and editorial board members, this 'highly uneven geographical distribution of editorships and therefore the locations of the gatekeepers to journal publishing' are seen to be an issue of concern (Hall, Williams, & Lew, 2004, p. 9). However, what no one seems to have asked is just what does the fact that its academic elite is so unrepresentative mean for tourism scholarship? Indeed, how will the academy's currently marginalized and underrepresented groups ever join the knowledge power broker networks when 'those in powerful and privileged positions rarely give up power and privilege voluntarily' (Aitchison, 2001, p. 17)? Very few tourism journals attempt to destabilize points of privilege by specifically time-limiting editorial board tenure (Westwood, Pritchard, & Morgan, 2006) and while some journals such as *Tourist Studies* and *Leisure Studies* (which publishes tourism scholarship) actively welcome submissions from non-English-speaking authors to counter such anglo-centrism, such initiatives are as yet isolated examples. It seems to us that, despite the key role they play in shaping tourism knowledge (and of course the two of us are implicated here as journal editorial board members, book editors, manuscript reviewers, and doctoral student supervisors and examiners), the personal identities of the gatekeepers and the role of the personal remains 'almost completely ignored in discussions of tourism research' (Hall, 2004, p. 148). Such silence is a major omission in any discussion of knowledge production since 'all of what I am affects the problems I see and the power dynamics I experience as a researcher' (Swain, 2004, p. 102). The time has come to scrutinize just how this masculine, Anglo-Saxon, business-focused domination of the field has shaped its architecture of knowledge.

Discourses of Knowledge Production

If academic renewal means anything it must be accompanied by a commitment to critique how we produce tourism knowledge at particular times and places. This production is a process which:

> rules in certain ways of talking about a topic, defining an acceptable and intelligible way to talk, write or conduct oneself, so also by definition, it 'rules out', limits and restricts other ways of talking, of conducting ourselves in relation to the topic or constructing knowledge about it. (Hall, 1997, p. 44)

To scrutinize the codification of knowledge is in no sense an act of self-indulgent academic introspection but a fundamental engagement with how as knowledge creators and producers we define the ways in which our knowledge, our 'truth' is 'represented, thought about, practiced and studied' (Hall, 1997, p. 6). We are all complicit to some degree in this process of production. As researchers, authors, editorial board members, journal manuscript reviewers, teachers/supervisors, and examiners, we regularly engage with mechanisms which mediate and exercise power that then influences and regulates appropriate and acceptable behaviours. Indeed, we ourselves are also products of these regimes of truth.

Norman Denzin and Yvonna Lincoln (2005, p. 6) argue that: 'the narratives, or stories, scientists tell are accounts couched and framed within specific storytelling traditions, often defined as paradigms'. Here, we ask just how equipped are we as an academy to deal with diverse story-telling traditions? Thus, in this section of the chapter, we want to briefly map the topography of tourism enquiry and reflect on the development and constitution of the field before moving on to consider the doctoral work being undertaken in tourism study. This latter is crucial since doctoral students, as the creators of 'new' knowledge are a barometer of the paradigmatic health and diversity of the field — although their influence has yet to be felt in an academy where tourism PhD graduates remain a minority group (Zhao & Ritchie, 2006).

It is very clear that despite the work of a number of leading scholars (whose work is referenced throughout this volume and whose scholarship has inspired our own work), positivist discourses and a commitment to empiricism, quantification, neutrality, objectivity, distance, validity, and reliability continue to be the appropriate markers of the authoritative voice in much tourism research. Various dissenting voices have challenged this dominance, both from within and outside of the tourism academy, highlighting that 'much tourism scholarship . . . reflects this bias in favour of rigorous, quantitative and scientific methods' (Walle, 1997, p. 524). Others, such as the social historian John Walton (2000, p. 18) have described the field as 'unduly present minded and dominated by economics', while the leisure scholar Cara Aitchison (2000) has noted a growing dissatisfaction with the theoretical bases of tourism and leisure scholarship over-reliant on business prerogatives. Indeed, many of us would agree with Keith Hollinshead's (2004, pp. 65–66) assertion that:

> tourism studies is not yet in rude "qualitative" health and pays little cross-disciplinary attention to the subjective, the discourse of the interpretative, in short to those elements which are the essence of qualitative research.

But to what extent have members of the wider academy reflexively engaged with such critiques? The most recent historiography of tourism research (published in the *Annals of Tourism Research*) reveals that there is little evidence of any paradigmatic shift in tourism. Indeed, Honggen Xiao and Stephen Smith (2006, p. 503) conclude that 'this research confirms previous findings that the field is still dominated by the scientific-positivistic paradigm'. While these scholars recognize that alternative ways of knowing such as interpretive and critical paradigms are beginning to make some contribution to tourism ontology, they describe this as an emerging trend (see Phillimore & Goodson, 2004b for a more detailed review of this development). Tourism continues to demonstrate a poorly developed disciplinary base prompted by a failure to engage with paradigmatic shift and theoretical challenge. Moreover, its ontological framework remains dominated by four major foci: definitional and typological concerns; economic industry and socio-cultural/environmental studies; an increasing emphasis on marketing and management topics which is mirrored by a decline in recreation and hospitality studies; a geographical focus overwhelming dominated by North America, although this is gradually being balanced by European, Asian, Australian and New Zealand studies — although citations of Central and South Americas, Africa and Pacific Island States remain low (Xiao & Smith, 2006).

Thus, not only is our field's publication output shaped by positivist paradigms, many of the journal conventions, manuscript guidelines and submission criteria also continue to reflect the power that objective scientific measures exert over the codification of knowledge.

But if we as tourism scholars feel disempowered by these restrictive practices, their influence on the doctoral candidate community can be even more corrosive. As academics we all actively engage in the socialization of students into dominant academic structures, for example, through our entry requirements (such as research training courses which might privilege 'scientific' approaches), our ideological parameters and our expectations of writing styles. But how open is the worldwide tourism academic community to alternative paradigms? How many supervisors would encourage their students to embrace qualitative approaches defined by Norman Denzin and Yvonna Lincoln (2005) as fifth, yet alone eighth moment research? And perhaps even more pertinent, just how receptive are institutional research degree committees and doctoral thesis examiners to these ways of knowing and writing about tourism?

There have been several studies mapping the topography of tourism's doctoral landscape, particularly in the UK and North America and such work reveals that tourism PhD research is overwhelmingly defined in terms of its ability to provide 'useful' contributions to society — be they in the form of industry-specific questions (e.g. to establish best practice or problem resolution) or policy-oriented approaches. Arguably, the tendency to locate tourism scholarship in generic business/management schools has reinforced this trend towards industry-focused, (post)positivistic research and in turn further hampered the development of alternative epistemological and methodological prescriptions in tourism's postgraduate research community. Indeed, David Botterill's (1999, pp. 6–7) review of PhDs undertaken at universities in the UK during the previous decade fell into the categories of: development and impact studies (26); tourism management and policy planning (23) and industry-specific studies (12); tourism behaviour and motivation (11) and imagery (4). Of even more concern were the findings of a follow-up study by David Botterill, Tim Gale and Claire Haven-Tang (2003) of doctoral theses in UK and Ireland which found little evidence of 'critical thinking' at this level.

Instead, it seems that PhD candidates who wish to challenge and confront tourism's pre-eminent paradigm regularly face hostile learning environments and academic scrutiny which is often resistant to qualitative approaches (Wilson, 2004). In the USA, the post-graduate framework and culture promotes doctoral candidates who are 'bound to a positivistic empiricism that tends to quantitative-based research that often draws upon a restricted literature' (Ryan, 2005, p. 659). Similarly, when reviewing the experiences of memory work researchers in Australia, Jennie Small (2004) has underlined how feminist scholars can feel isolated and disempowered in an academic climate saturated by positivist discourses and framed by patriarchal structures. The depths of isolation and marginalization felt by qualitative researchers working on tourism studies in academic collectives steeped in functionalist and post-positivistic approaches and departments oriented towards management and industry-driven applied research should not be underestimated, as Erica Wilson's (2005) reflective account testifies:

> I often felt alone as a qualitative, gender-based researcher in a discipline where objectivity, generalization and distance were the norm . . . I understood and was told . . . that the gates to academia were held by the quantitative researchers and that a qualitative PhD was held in a less serious regard. (Ateljevic, Harris, Wilson, & Collins, 2005)

In a similarly reflective account, Tazim Jamal and Hyounggon Kim discuss how qualitative dissertation proposals are victimized by the scientific tradition which dominates tourism research. They argue that:

> Newtonian style reductionism was engrained in our academic training. The scientific method appropriated into the philosophy of social research that conditioned us left little room for "risky" critical or big-picture explorations, or reflexive writing.

As a result, they faced 'intradisciplinary methodological prejudices [and] interdisciplinary theoretical challenges' (Jamal & Kim, 2005, p. 56). Such prejudicial discourses not only limit those approaches deemed to be 'appropriate' but they also constrain a student's choice of research topic and in this it appears that 'exploring issues of gender in research often seems too contentious and is therefore avoided in favour of "easier", more academically accepted topics' (Ateljevic et al., 2005). Almost unbelievably, a recent survey of 377 North American tourism doctoral dissertations was able to classify only one as women's studies (Meyer-Arendt & Justice, 2002). Add to these prejudicial academic discourses arrayed against gender studies in tourism the reluctance of funding bodies at governmental and institutional level to support unusual or less economically useful research and projects 'will often be kept within relatively safe boundaries' (Hall, 2004, p. 144). Speaking from our personal experiences, government-funded overseas doctoral students have frequently been channelled towards technically useful, (post)-positivist-oriented studies by their sponsoring bodies and by their home academic institutions and mentors. In such circumstances, students can be actively discouraged from studying 'difficult' or 'challenging' issues such as gender, which is often also dismissed as a topic not serious enough to warrant a funded PhD project (Pritchard, 2005).

In spite of these forces, a number of doctoral students have and are responding to scholars such as Kevin Meethan's (2003) call for tourism researchers to adopt a more critical lens and to advance issues of political representation, cultural commodification, hegemony, and globalization in the study of tourism. Such studies require the adoption of inter/trans-disciplinary frameworks and diverse research methodological strategies and conferences such as the one held in Dubrovnik in 2005, which confirm that students do want to challenge epistemological and methodological conventions, despite the difficulties posed by their institutional and disciplinary frameworks. While the challenge of resisting such dominant discourses needs recognition and these students need greater support and encouragement, the winds of change may have begun to blow through tourism studies, as our next section outlines.

A New Approach?

Our analysis of the micro-politics of the tourism academy in terms of power, policies, discourses, pedagogy, and interpersonal relationships has clearly exposed the need for change and academic renewal. Yes, there are and have always been challenges to its dominant knowledge production and dissemination structures, new journals and book series have emerged in recent years and some existing gatekeepers have been prepared to embrace the recent paradigmatic shifts and progressive methodologies and to create spaces for second-generation scholars. Special issues of certain journals (such as the 2005 and 2006 issues of *Tourism Recreation Research*) have begun to foreground the new debates and approaches, while new journals such as *Tourism and Cultural Change* and *Tourist Studies* have been established to create more space for critical scholars. For instance, *Tourist Studies* (established in 2000) 'provides a critical social science approach to the study of the tourist', while *Tourism and Cultural Change* was launched in 2003 to examine 'the relationships, tensions, representations, conflicts and possibilities that exist between tourism/travel and culture/cultures'. However, despite such advances, as we have seen, this has not fundamentally altered tourism's scholarship basis which remains dominated by Anglocentric, masculinist ways of knowing, philosophies, and methodologies. Clearly, within this research climate, there is a crucial challenge for tourism management/studies to embrace academic renewal and to develop conceptualizations of tourisms that work across historical eras, traditional practices, worldviews, and cultural differences, and is inclusive of multiple research and knowledge strategies.

Our work as social science researchers advocating critical tourism scholarship must be not merely to replicate the work of previous scholars 'in a cookie-cutter fashion but rather to break new epistemological, methodological, social activist, and moral ground' (Ladson-Billings & Donnor, 2005, p. 291). At the same time, we are not advocating the replacement of one particular perspective with another. Instead, the complex nature of social reality demands plural epistemological bases and multi-dimensional approaches (Layder, 1997). Critical tourism scholarship depends on moving away from 'one dimensional epistemological prescriptions and competitive and antagonistic research environments', instead, cooperation will enable researchers to 'find what is of value in each approach' (Seale, 1998, p. 2). As Rosengren (2000, p. 10) observes of theoretical cross-fertilization 'the really interesting problems are to be found when we combine . . . [these] . . . seemingly contrary alternatives'. At the same time, particular theoretical perspectives (which once guided method selection) should not be allowed to dictate the choice of research methods; instead, reflexive researchers should use and shape methods as appropriate (Filmer, Jenks, Seale, & Walsh, 1998) enabling the production of creative work within and across theories and disciplines (Outhwaite, 1998).

Many second-generation tourism scholars are actively embracing and engaging with these challenges as they seek to piece together this 'new tourism picture' (Jamal & Kim, 2005, p. 56). Such second-generation scholarship is not defined by geography or age but by a way of thinking about enquiry. For many of these researchers, their work is guided by the search for intellectual enrichment, social justice, and social equity. As reflexive tourism researchers we must 'play a more active and progressive role in the fight for equity and social justice. [Our] work must transcend narrow disciplinary boundaries if it is to have any impact on people who reside in subaltern sites or even on policymakers' (Ladson-Billings & Donnor, 2005, p. 294). In transcending these boundaries, as researchers, we must begin to articulate and confront the ethnocentricity, which has shaped much of tourism research. Clearly, tourism is a base which is closely entwined with the imperial project and colonialism. Most tourism research is Eurocentric study that privileges and is interconnected with capitalism and linear thinking, while most of the research has been conducted or grounded in English and from limited scholarly perspectives. As such, the conceptualization and scholarship related to extant tourism literature has been created largely by white, Anglo-centric, masculine voices. Other voices (particularly those of women, ethnic minorities and aboriginal peoples) have struggled to be heard. We must use this knowledge then with critical reflections, decolonizing processes, and caution (Fox, 2006). Certainly, future tourism scholarship needs to comprehend, resist, and transform the crises related to the effects of colonization on indigenous peoples and the ongoing erosion of indigenous languages, knowledge and culture as a result of colonization. As Karen Fox has said of leisure research, so this is true for tourism enquiry:

> Although there has been some move towards collaborative research, the majority of leisure research connected with indigenous peoples is framed in Eurocentric perspectives, focuses only on positive outcomes as defined within Eurocentric categories, and isolates leisure and related concepts from holistic indigenous language perspectives, cultures and political strategies for self governance and self-determination. (Fox, 2006)

Indigenous scholarship with its emphasis on self-determination, critical analysis, collectivism, and dialogue challenges Western cultural practices, as Russell Bishop (2004, p. 131) says of indigenous scholars 'We know about a way that is born of time, connectedness, commitment and participation'. Such complex understandings also directly challenge Eurocentric tourism imaginaries as they require the development of polythetic comparisons in our conceptualizations of tourisms and in our research praxis. And yet, ours is a tourism scholarship where indigenous voices are rarely heard. As reflexive researchers we must act to decentre the tourism academy and respond to the challenges and critiques being articulated by indigenous scholars so that we may begin to create knowledge centred on indigenous epistemologies and ontologies. Academic decolonization is a necessity and a responsibility. It must be based on dialogues characterized by respect, reciprocity, equality, collectivity, and empathy between indigenous minorities, indigenous researchers, and their non-indigenous counterparts. Such decolonization is both a political and disruptive act:

> Because anything that requires a major change of worldview, that forces a society to confront its past and address it at a structural and institutional level that challenges the systems of power is, indeed, political. (Tuwai Smith, 2005, p. 9)

It is not enough to merely articulate a demand for a new, ethical scholarship. We must all shoulder some of the responsibility to create spaces for alternative voices to be heard — especially by encouraging emerging researchers to publish and present their work. Indeed, a recent study has warned that across academia 'Younger and less experienced academics are finding it harder to make a name for themselves in a peer-review system weighted in favour of established research stars' as time-pressured academic referees are increasingly 'opting for senior academics with proven records in research at the expense of those in the early stages of their careers' (Baty, 2006, p. 2). This current volume (which includes contributions from well established and emerging scholars) is itself an agent for change and academic renewal and stems from the first conference dedicated to critical studies in tourism enquiry where many of the presenters were recent and current doctoral students. This first international Critical Tourism Studies (CTS) conference, held in Dubrovnik in 2005 was organized to specifically foreground issues of researcher positionality, embodiment, and critical and interpretative modes of tourism inquiry, and a second conference will be held in Split in 2007 to continue these explorations of tourism in the context of material, discursive, and social practices. Inspired by bell hooks' calls for academics to embrace honest and supportive communication in their efforts to produce social change, we intend this event to provide an inclusive environment for new and alternative voices in the tourism academy. Moreover, to reflect the project which we have outlined here (and in our introduction with Irena Ateljevic), this conference will specifically address: the potential of tourism theory and practice as a progressive force for engagement in and analysis of global social justice; the de-centring and decolonizing of tourism studies; the emotional dynamics of research relations and the personal, the political, and the situated nature of research journeys.

Such conferences and the networks which underpin them bring together established and emerging researchers — and we need greater dialogues between first and second (and in the future third) generation scholars if we are to seek a more holistic understanding of tourism as a social, cultural and political phenomenon. Such conversations and reflections are already evident, especially in some of the recent 'thought pieces' on journals and journal outputs (e.g. Hall, 2005; Page, 2005; Ryan, 2005). Our criticism here of the academic elites does not mean that we advocate adopting a position of scepticism in which all of the assumptions and ideologies upon which their knowledge is based are seen as nothing more than sets of beliefs which justified a status quo that is historically irrelevant. That is far from our position. What we are challenging the academic gatekeepers to do is to listen more closely to the voices of the second-generation scholars and to those of currently marginalized and underrepresented groups (including female, black and ethnic minority, and indigenous scholars) in the tourism management/studies community. We would urge journal editors to consider *how* they could address equal opportunities rather than ask *why* they should. The need for such bodies to be more representative of the diversity that is the human race goes far beyond notions that they should in some way be representative of the composition of the tourism academy. How can we create holistic understanding of tourism (or any phenomenon) if we rely on knowledge traditions dominated by certain positionings at the expense of others? We need more dialogues, entanglements, and conversations — characterized by reciprocity, fairness, and understanding — if we are to develop conceptualizations of tourisms that encompass multiple worldviews and cultural differences and research praxis that recognizes and reflects the plurality of *all* our positions, practices, and insights.

Conclusion, or a Pause in the Conversation

It would be a fair characterization of the present intellectual climate to describe it as very confused since there are multiple voices speaking about cultures and societies undergoing rapid and complex change, so much so that any student of the social sciences is confronted by a bewildering array of interdisciplinary ideas that do not seem to have any great connection or coherence. Plurality is endemic to the post-modern condition and despite some claims to the contrary, disciplinary borders in the humanities and social sciences are being crossed all the time and the cross-fertilization of theories and ideas cannot be ignored. Our intellectual horizon is no longer one of apparent calm and certain consensus and yet, as we have seen, the tourism management communities remain rather too certain of themselves and do not have a history of embracing other knowledge traditions. Yet, we have also argued that there are those who would challenge the cosy orthodoxies of the first generation of tourism scholars and welcome more de-centred and critical perspectives.

Such dialectic between change and tradition has become very powerful in the humanities and social sciences, especially since the political and cultural upheaval of the 1960s made shifts in thinking and theorizing a constant in Western academia and the information revolution of the 1990s hugely accelerated the spread of new ideas. This can be an extremely confrontational dialectic, however, as that which is new has a particular appeal to a younger generation, and that which carries the patina of age can often seem a form of wisdom to those who lived in a particular tradition. While some of us who would locate ourselves in the new tourism research have yet to win battles which have already been fought elsewhere — such as gaining legitimacy for using the first person or writing ourselves into our research (see Morgan & Pritchard, 2005) — there are those in other disciplines launching an insurgency that many tourism academics do not even know exists or could not imagine existing. It is little wonder that the rapid transformations which left many disciplines in turmoil and forced a rethinking of the intellectual universe in the 1980s — a decade characterized by the rise of post-modernism, post-colonialism, feminism, and post-feminism, cultural studies, cybernetics and cyberpunk, de-constructionism, and post-structuralism — left the tourism academy remarkably unscathed.

But, as we have said, our criticism of the existing power bases does not mean that we see all of the assumptions and ideologies upon which they are based as irrelevant. Albert Einstein once said that you cannot solve problems with the same way of thinking that led to their creation; so we cannot replace one dominant ideology and academy with another. Indeed, as we said with Irena Ateljevic in the introduction to this volume, new tourism enquiry is more than just a *way of knowing*, an ontology, it is a *way of being*, a commitment to embracing moral discourse. It transcends ontological shift and paradigmatic transformations. It is not about replacing one dominant school with another, rather it is about replacing 'either/or' thinking with 'both/and' approaches and breaking the mould of 'clubbism' so that tourism management/studies ceases to be a dichotomy and begins to become a whole. The methodological strengths of tourism management/studies encompass in-depth, qualitative explorations and positivist, longitudinal studies of tourism among diverse social groups. Together, both approaches offer the potential to achieve complex understandings and combining the knowledge of researchers schooled in the traditions of both approaches enables us to gain what is strong and redress what is weak in either approach (Henderson, 2006; Pritchard, 2006). We argue that to simply replace one rigid 'ism' with another is to be boxed in by the polarized linear thinking so typical of the masculinist discourses which have for too long constrained tourism scholarship and the tourism academy. Institutions, academies and fields draw lines, we must aim to read between them; membership organizations create definitions, boundaries and battlelines; we must aim to be inclusive and holistic, crossing frontiers and making connections. The new tourism research should strive to be characterized by sensitivity, depth, openness, flow, feeling, paradox, being and becoming. Instead of shoring up existing privilege, we must become good listeners to silent voices and sharp observers of invisible objects. We may never achieve such goals, but we must at least aim for them, since in the words of Carl Schurz, 'Ideals are like the stars; we never reach them, but like the mariners of the sea, we chart our course by them' (quoted in Silf, 2006, p. 152).

The study of tourism in all its aspects has the potential to fully embrace some of the new learnings, which are reshaping approaches to academic teaching, learning, research and writing. The opportunity is there for tourism scholars to answer Norman Denzin and Yvonna Lincoln's call (2005, p. 3) for researchers to be:

> concerned with moral discourse, with the development of sacred textuali-
> ties. The eighth moment asks that the social sciences and the humanities
> become sites for critical conversations about democracy, race, gender, class,
> nation-states, globalization, freedom and community.

This can only be truly possible, however, if we embrace more reflexivity and promote a de-centred, decolonized, more gender-balanced academy, especially among our gate-keepers. These changes will nurture a transformation of how we know tourism and open up new lines of enquiry since 'Complex understanding occurs when we begin to see a phe-nomenon from various perspectives, as well as relationship among these perspectives' (Newhouse, 2004, p. 143).

In recent centuries Western culture has spread across the globe, pushing everything before it like a tidal wave, carried high on a hubris of a belief that our way must always be the best way, and must therefore be imposed upon the world. Only recently have we begun to hear the voices from what we once termed the 'Third World' (which, of course, is actu-ally the First World, in the sense that it is where all humankind has its origins) saying that we may have more to learn from traditional societies than we have to teach them (Silf, 2006). If we are to create an inclusive tourism academy and to create new tourism knowl-edge, we must be willing to learn from every knowledge tradition, from Africa, Asia and from indigenous peoples around the world. Such peoples have been suppressed and almost eliminated by the imperial project, and our world will remain forever psychologically unbal-anced until it has done justice to them. As social science researchers we have a responsi-bility to produce scholarship which is socially meaningful and morally responsible and which creates 'ethical' and 'sacred' epistemology which 'recognizes and interrogates the ways in which race, class and gender operate as important systems of oppression in the world today' (Denzin & Lincoln, 2005, p. 37). Yet, we cannot begin to advocate emanci-pation or self-determination for marginalized or subaltern peoples if our own community shores up points of privilege and exclusion.

Despite the at times negative tone of our discussion in this chapter, we do feel that in spite of a great deal of evidence to the contrary, our world is moving towards a process of change and growth. Half a century ago few people would question the legitimacy of war as a means of resolving international disputes, now millions protest against the use of mil-itary force. Fifty years ago few people were ecologically aware, now it is unacceptable not to be concerned about the environment. Fifty years ago social, gender and economic inequality were 'just the way of the world'. Today, many people and organizations fight for justice, especially on behalf of the oppressed and the marginalized and the world's poorest countries. We may feel that we are floundering in a collective chaos, in which old certainties have been lost and the new way ahead remains uncharted but such a chaos can also be a space for new growth and an opportunity for transformation. The challenge for us in the tourism academy is to become an agency for positive transformation and to find more spaces for dialogue, reflexivity, equality, empowerment and co-created knowledge in our scholarship. As Gandhi once said, 'we must be the change we wish to see in the world'.

References

Aitchison, C. (2000). Poststructuralist feminist theories of representing others: A response to the "crisis" in leisure studies discourse. *Leisure Studies*, *19*, 127–144.

Aitchison, C. (2001). Gender and leisure research: The codification of knowledge. *Leisure Sciences*, *23*, 1–19.

Ateljevic, I., Harris, C., Wilson, E., & Collins, F. (2005). Getting "entangled": Reflexivity and the "critical turn" in tourism studies. *Tourism Recreation Research*, *30*(2), 9–21.

Batty, P. (2006). Young blood loses out to the old guard. *The Times Higher Education Supplement*, *May 19*, 2.

Bishop, R. (2005). Freeing ourselves from neocolonial domination in research: A Kaupapa Maori approach to creating knowledge. In: N. K. Denzin, & Y. S. Lincoln (Eds), *The Sage handbook of qualitative research* (3rd ed., pp. 109–139). London: Sage.

Botterill, T. D. (1999). An epistemology of tourism research or tourism research epistemology. Paper presented at UWIC First Tourism Research Colloquium, Gregynog, January.

Botterill, T. D. (2000). Social scientific ways of knowing hospitality. In: C. Lashley, & A. Morrison (Eds), *In search of hospitality: Theoretical perspectives and debates* (pp. 177–197). Oxford: Butterworth Heinemann.

Botterill, D., Gale, T., & Haven, C. (2003). A survey of doctoral theses accepted by universities in the UK and Ireland for studies related to tourism 1990–1999. *Tourist Studies*, *2*, 283–311.

Cohen, E. (2005). Letter to the president. *International Academy for the Study of Tourism Newsletter*, *15*(3) November, 3.

Denzin, N. K., & Lincoln, Y. S. (2005). Introduction: The discipline and practice of qualitative research. In: N. K. Denzin, & Y. S. Lincoln (Eds), *The Sage handbook of qualitative research* (3rd ed., pp. 1–33). London: Sage.

Dowling, R. (2000). Tourism management: Towards the new millennium. *Annals of Tourism Research*, *28*(4), 1074–1076.

Fazackerley, A., & Hughes, L. (2006). Lecturing now women's work as men seek cash. *The Times Higher Education Supplement*, July 14, 2006, 4.

Filmer, P., Jenks, C., Seale, C., & Walsh, D. (1998). Developments in social theory. In: C. Seale (Ed), *Researching society and culture* (pp. 23–36). London: Sage.

Fox, K. (2006). Thinking about a connection between "leisure" and indigenous peoples. *Leisure Studies*, *25*(4), 403–410.

Foucault, M. (1980). *Power/Knowledge*. Harvester: Brighton.

Hall, C. M. (2004). Reflexivity and tourism research: Situating myself and/with others. In: J. Phillimore, & L. Goodson (Eds), *Qualitative research in tourism: Ontologies, epistemologies and methodologies* (pp. 137–155). London: Routledge.

Hall, C. M. (2005). Systems of surveillance and control: Commentary on "An analysis of institutional contributors to three major academic tourism journals: 1992–2001". *Tourism Management, 26,* 653–656.

Hall, S. (1997). The work of representation. In: S. Hall (Ed), *Representation: Cultural representations and signifying practices* (pp. 13–74). London: Sage and the Open University.

Henderson, K. (2006). False dichotomies and leisure research. *Leisure Studies, 25*(4), 391–396.

Hollinshead, K. (2004). A primer in ontological craft: The creative capture of people and places through qualitative research. In: J. Phillimore, & L. Goodson (Eds), *Qualitative research in tourism: Ontologies, epistemologies and methodologies* (pp. 63–82). London: Routledge.

Jamal, T., & Kim, H. (2005). Bridging the interdisciplinary divide: Towards an integrated framework for heritage tourism research. *Tourist Studies, 5*(1), 55–85.

Jogaratnam, G., Chon, K., McCleary, K., Mena, M., & Yoo, J. (2005). An analysis of institutional contributors to three major academic tourism journals: 1992–2001. *Tourism Management, 26*(5), 641–648.

Kimmel, M. (1996). *Manhood in America: A cultural history.* New York: Free Press.

Ladson-Billings, G., & Donnor, J. (2005). The moral activist role of critical race theory scholarship. In: N. K. Denzin, & Y. S. Lincoln (Eds), *The Sage handbook of qualitative research* (3rd ed., pp. 279–302). London: Sage.

Layder, D. (1997). The reality of social domains: Implications for theory and method. In: T. May, & M. Williams (Eds), *Knowing the social world* (pp. 86–102). Buckingham: Open University.

McKercher, B. (2002). The privileges and responsibilities of being a referee. *Annals of Tourism Research, 29,* 856–859.

McKercher, B. (2005). A case for ranking tourism journals. *Tourism Management, 26*(5), 649–651.

Meethan, K. (2003). Mobile cultures? Hybridity, tourism and cultural change. *Journal of Tourism and Cultural Change, 1*(1), 11–28.

Meyer-Arendt, K., & Justice, C. (2002). Tourism as the subject of North American doctoral dissertations 1987–2000. *Annals of Tourism Research, 29*(4), 1171–1174.

Morgan, N., & Pritchard, A. (2006). On souvenirs and metonymy: Narratives of memory, metaphor and materiality. *Tourist Studies, 5*(1), 29–53.

Newhouse, D. (2004). Indigenous knowledge in a multicultural world. *Native Studies Review, 15*(2), 139–154.

Outhwaite, W. (1998). Naturalisms and anti-naturalisms. In: T. May, & M. Williams (Eds), *Knowing the social world* (pp. 22–36). Buckingham: Open University Press.

Page, S. (2005). Academic ranking exercises: Do they achieve anything meaningful? — A personal view. *Tourism Management, 26*(5), 633–666.

Pechlander, H., Zehrer, A., & Abfalter, D. (2002). How can scientific journal quality be assessed? An exploratory study of tourism and hospitality journals. *Tourism, 50*(4), 395–399.

Pechlander, H., Zehrer, A., Matzler, K., & Abfalter, D. (2004). A ranking of international tourism and hospitality journals. *Journal of Travel research, 42*(4), 328–332.

Phillimore, J., & Goodson, L. (2004a). *Qualitative research in tourism: Ontologies, epistemologies and methodologies.* London: Routledge.

Phillimore, J., & Goodson, L. (2004b). Progress in qualitative research in tourism: epistemology, ontology and methodology. In: J. Phillimore, & L. Goodson (Eds), *Qualitative research in tourism: Ontologies, epistemologies and methodologies* (pp. 3–30). London: Routledge.

Pritchard, A. (2005). *Keynote address: Gender, globalisation and cultures of tourism.* Inaugural Special Meeting of Women Ministers of Culture, Reykjavik.

Pritchard, A. (2006). Guest editorial: Listening to leisure voices: Getting engaged in dialogues, conversations and entanglements. *Leisure Studies, 25*(4), 373–378.

Rosengren, K. E. (2000). *Communication: An introduction.* London: Sage.

Ryan, C. (2005). The ranking and rating of academics and journals in tourism research. *Tourism Management, 26*, 657–662.

Seale, C. (Ed.) (1998). *Researching Society and Culture.* London: Sage.

Silf, M. (2006). *The way of wisdom.* Oxford: Lion Hudson.

Sheldon, P. J. (1990). Journals in tourism and hospitality: The perceptions of the publishing faculty. *Journal of Tourism Studies, 1*(1), 42–48.

Spender, D. (Ed.) (1981). *Men's studies modified: The impact of feminism on the academic disciplines.* Oxford: Pergamon press.

Swain, M. (2004). (Dis)embodied experience and power dynamics in tourism research. In: J. Phillimore, & L. Goodson (Eds), *Qualitative research in tourism: Ontologies, epistemologies and methodologies* (pp. 102–118). London: Routledge.

Tribe, J. (2003). The RAE-ification of tourism research in the UK. *International Journal of Tourism Research, 5*, 225–234.

Tribe, J. (2005). The truth about tourism. *Annals of Tourism Research, 33*(2), 360–381.

Tuhiwai Smith, L. (1999). *Decolonizing methodologies: Research and indigenous peoples.* Dunedin: Zed Books: University of Otago Press.

Tuhiwai Smith, L. (2005). On tricky ground: Researching the native in an age of certainty. In: N. K. Denzin, & Y. S. Lincoln (Eds), *The Sage handbook of qualitative research,* (3rd ed., pp. 85–109). London: Sage.

Wilson, E. C. (2004). *A 'Journey of Her Own?' The impact of constraints on women's solo travel.* Unpublished Ph.D., Griffith University.

Walle, A. H. (1997). Quantitative versus qualitative tourism research. *Annals of Tourism Research, 24*(3), 524–536.

Walton, J. K. (2000). *The British seaside. Holidays and resorts in the twentieth century.* Manchester: Manchester University Press.

Westwood, S., Morgan, N., & Pritchard, A. (2006). Situation, participation and reflexivity in tourism research: Furthering interpretative approaches to tourism enquiry. *Tourism Recreation Research, 31*(2), 33–44.

Xiao, H., & Smith, S. (2006). The making of tourism research: Insights from a social sciences journal. *Annals of Tourism Research, 33*(2), 490–507.

Zhao, W., & Ritchie, B. (2006). A supplementary investigation of academic leadership in tourism research: 1985–2004. *Tourism Management,* article in press.

Chapter 2

Critical Tourism: Rules and Resistance

John Tribe

What it is to be Critical

In this chapter I will rehearse some of the key features that distinguish critical from other approaches to tourism studies and offer some examples of critical research. I will then examine the intellectual environment within which tourism studies operates in order to determine those factors which may inhibit the development of greater criticality (rules). I will also discuss how some researchers have made a move to critical theory and the circumstances that can encourage critical research to develop (resistance). I conclude the chapter by considering the prospects for greater criticality in tourism studies as well as the ways in which the realisation of greater criticality might be achieved.

Typically studies into research methodology classify research approaches into between three and five paradigms. These include approaches characterised by positivism and post-positivism, interpretivism, constructionism and critical theory. Critical theory is the research paradigm developed by the Frankfurt School (Horkheimer, Adorno, Marcuse and Habermas). Critical theorists trace their intellectual roots to Marx, Hegel and beyond and it is perhaps best to understand its meaning by reference to its difference from other research paradigms.

One key feature that distinguishes critical theory from other paradigms is its focus on ends rather than means and on emancipatory outcomes. It is described by Best and Kellner (1997, p. 223) as follows:

> Rejecting the positivist dichotomy between fact and value, theory and politics, critical theory interrogates the "is" in terms of the "ought," seeking to grasp the emancipatory possibilities of the current society as something that can and should be realized in the future.

Critical theory is thus very different from positivism. For the very basis of positivism is to exclude questions of a moral or ethical nature which cannot be settled by an appeal to facts. Hence the constraint of positivism to deal with empirically verifiable "facts". Positivism

The Critical Turn in Tourism Studies: Innovative Research Methodologies
Copyright © 2007 by Elsevier Ltd.
All rights of reproduction in any form reserved.
ISBN: 0-08-045098-9

separates out means and ends, facts and values and theory and practice, so that only means, facts and theory remain. In contrast, critical theory seeks to challenge the limitations of positivism by actively engaging with questions of values and desirable ends. Critical theory admits values, moral issues and repercussions into the frame of critical thinking. Gibson (1986, p. 37) summarises critical theory where:

> knowledge and interest in emancipation coincide and thus make for those unities which positivism severs – theory and practice, means and ends, thought and action, fact and value, reason and emotion.

Critical theory also distinguishes itself from interpretivism in one important way. It does not necessarily trust the accounts of the researched to give a true reading of the world. It is wary of the possibility of their false (or at the very least, not fully engaged) consciousness. Barnett (2003, p. 56) describes this as the situation where:

> That which is contingent is seen as inevitable. That which is iniquitous is seen as just. That which is imposed is seen as natural.

In other words whilst interpretivism might offer a voice to the researched and attempt thereby to reduce the power of the researcher this move does not necessarily relinquish the grip of other forms of power on the researched. So what are the other essential features of critical theory? First, critical theory is interested in power relations. Indeed its key point of departure from positivism is its wish to expose the interests that are associated with different research paradigms. For critical theory the current ordering of things is deliberately foregrounded. Power is a key issue to be researched and a critical approach to tourism would seek to expose whose interests are served and the exercise of power and the influence of ideology in the researched situation and research itself. Now an important aspect of ideology is that it provides a system of beliefs that directs the policies and activities of its adherents. The job of critical theory is initially to sniff out ideological influences. This is done as a prelude to ideology critique that then seeks to identify whose interests are being served by a particular ideology. A common feature of ideology is its overwhelming nature, i.e. the fact that ideologies are so all-encompassing and saturate our everyday lives and thoughts that it is difficult to think and act outside of their rules. A result of this can be a controlling aspect of culture that occurs without recourse to physical threat or violence or indeed explicit policing. Here Kincheloe and McLaren (2003, p. 436) point up the ways in which mass contemporary culture can contribute to the situation where:

> . . . individuals . . . have been acculturated to feel comfortable in relations of domination and subordination rather than equality and independence.

In other words some basic inequalities in the world (including the tourism world) are so entrenched, so taken for granted that they are infrequently questioned and when they are questioned they are pursued with so little effort or effect that they no longer appear significant to us. Where they do we are able to bracket them out of our everyday existence and actions. For example we pick up issues on the television news or in the papers but somehow this becomes a ritualised way of seeing but not fully realising the gravity of things. Each item is quickly displaced by the next item and all wrapped up within a designated time slot. The theme tune of the television news designates our return to our privileged world and our regularised routines. More specifically for tourism we sleep in hotels, cruise the oceans and consume food the production of which often entails some of the starkest issues of inequality and subordination. But our roles in this have again become so ritualised, we are supported by so many accomplices, and our actions are so well designed in terms of deserved pampering that we barely recognise any critical implications of our actions or our complicity in perpetuating the status quo. In terms of ideological blindness we may be able to recognise and abhor apartheid in distant lands whilst being unable to recognise less formalised social stratification that may result in similar outcomes close to home. Additionally the direct act of tourism often deposits those from the wealth generating regions into the less developed host regions. Here we can mingle with poverty, catch its smell and observe the interestingly different lives that it supports. We may offer sweets or pens to the child-poor or engage in other ad-hoc gestures, but somehow feelings of solidarity are soon lost as the return plane throttles down the runway and we are re-engaged with the signs that signal a return to the way things are: pre-dinner drinks, a copy of the inflight magazine "High Life", duty-free sales. In doing so perhaps we miss an ironic poetic message — that High Life suggests a corresponding Low Life and that duty free might suggest freedom from duty.

A final feature of critical theory which might be seen as its goal is its interest in emancipation, described by Grundy as leading to a "transformation in the way in which one perceives and acts in 'the world'" (1987, p. 99).

The emancipation that is sought here is action that results in a move to a better production and consumption of tourism. In other words critical theory entertains ideas about utopia and the good life for tourism.

It is also instructive to consider how the critical school differs from the Marxist school. A neo-Marxist critique of tourism research would be that the superstructure of society that includes universities along with institutions such as the law and the government is determined by the base of economic and material factors. Under this "base determines superstructure" theory, tourism faculties and researchers would be charged with training a workforce for the base with the necessary personalities and attitudes and providing research that offered a more efficient exploitation of the tourism resource. However Kincheloe and McLaren (2003, p. 437), explain that critical theory rejects crude forms of economic determinism and rather posits that there are "multiple forms of power". Indeed the simple Marxist deterministic model cannot account for the considerable autonomy enjoyed by educational institutions in the superstructure and also their ability to turn their critical sights against the interests of the economic and material base. The concepts of ideology and discourse are more relevant to tourism research than that of crude economic determinism.

On the whole, as pointed out by Riley and Love (2000, p. 180), tourism studies is dominated by positivist research with some contribution by interpretivist researchers. Critical theory is not well represented but does have a small number of advocates and I will use the work of Aitchison and Hollinshead to illustrate examples of critical approaches to tourism studies. Aitchison has particularly investigated the below the surface, taken for granted existence of patriarchal power in tourism research and demonstrated some of its consequences and in particular some of its hegemonic tendencies. In an early study, Aitchison (1996) found that key mechanisms by which patriarchal power and control are exerted in leisure and tourism include research and consultancy, publications, professional associations, educational management and teaching. She showed these mechanisms to be crucial to the construction of knowledge and its communication, legitimation and reproduction. In a follow-up study she found that male authors outnumbered female authors by four to one after a gender analysis of authors in international refereed journals in leisure and tourism studies (Aitchison, 2001a). In the same year (Aitchison, 2001b) she reviewed the interface between structural and cultural power in the construction of gender relations and gendered others in tourism arguing that tourism knowledge creation has a significant gender dimension.

Much of the work of Hollinshead has also demonstrated a strong critical influence. Like Aitchison, Hollinshead has probed the deeply entrenched and systematised privileging of knowledge that can benefit some groups at the expense of others. One of the targets of Hollinshead's critique is the power and exclusivity of the western liberal tradition that can often seem to be beyond self-critique. It is a tradition that has privileged and even fetishised universities and intellectuals. These knowledge brokers have their powers confirmed by and within socially sanctioned sites of knowledge production (universities). By this process other forms of knowledge are marginalised. Following the lead offered by critical theory Hollinshead asks how it might be possible to escape the discourse of ethnocentric Western portrayals of indigenous North Americans (Hollinshead, 1992). His technique for doing this is to understand and promote the acceptance, validity and logic of native North Americans' own visions of the world. This represents a clear example of the deployment of critical theory since a key aspect of his study is to recognise the power and position that researchers can bring to such an analysis (critical enlightenment) and an attempt to relinquish it (critical emancipation).

Criticality Contained

This part of the chapter considers the factors governing the development of critical tourism studies. Interestingly many of the insights offered by critical theory enable us to see more clearly the factors that inhibit its growth. In this section a number of areas will be explored which govern the emergence of criticality within the field of tourism studies. These are:

- Paradigms and permeability
- Ideology and independence
- Discourse and resistance
- Disciplines and unruliness
- Traditions and mavericks

We turn our attention first to paradigms and permeability. In a broad sense critical theory is about uncovering implicit and sometimes hidden rules in research and therefore one measure of critical tourism is its ability to escape the bounds of such rules. In an extreme form rules can build into paradigms (Dann, 1997). For Kuhn (1970) a paradigm represents "accepted examples of actual scientific practice . . . from which spring particular coherent traditions of scientific research" (p. 10).

Kuhn's analysis of paradigms demonstrated that the progress of scientific discovery was characterised by a series of all-encompassing systems such as the Newtonian and Einsteinian physics. Each would characterise a period of "normal science" with its governing paradigm. The point about a paradigm was that it set out the rules and defined the boundaries of the acceptable in research and knowledge creation. During any period the adherents of a particular paradigm often fought hard to protect its coherence and validity against emerging subversive theory. Because paradigms can represent a significant power dimension disciplining a research agenda it is necessary to ask whether there is such an influence operating in tourism studies defining "normal tourism studies". And in particular we might ask whether a "business of tourism paradigm" prevails.

It is not possible to present tourism studies as operating in the grip of a paradigm. Kuhn's analysis though highly plausible, describes a situation where the monopolisation of knowledge was possible, where patronage had a strong influence and where the communication of ideas was tightly controlled. It was therefore easier to suppress new truths or alternative perspectives. The postmodern (Lyotard, 1984) truth free-for-all has disabled the power of paradigm and an example demonstrates why this is also the situation in tourism. Like many others, Franklin and Crang wished to promote a particular aspect of tourism research that they saw as underresearched and underpublished. To rectify this they launched a new journal (*Tourist Studies*) "which provides a platform for the development of critical perspectives on the nature of tourism as a social phenomenon" (Franklin & Crang 2001, p. 6).

A truly established business of tourism paradigm would have been able to resist such a step through its patronage over employment and control over communications. Hence the notion of the existence of an all-encompassing paradigm that polices tourism studies is rejected. Rather the core of the subject is seen to be permeable.

What then of ideology and its potential threat to research independence? Is it possible to discern ideological influence that act to constrain the development of criticality in tourism studies? It is instructive to examine two different aspects of ideology (Althusser, 1969, 1984). On the one hand the term is used to describe specific, coherent subsets of beliefs (generally "-isms"). On the other hand ideology is a broader belief system that permeates a group (e.g. society, tourism scholars) and which guides thought and action.

Taking ideology's meaning as coherent belief sub-systems we might ask to what extent tourism researchers find themselves under the influence of particular ideologies. There is of course a plethora of "-isms" that researchers may subscribe to wittingly or unwittingly but a few examples will suffice to make the point. For example consumerism refers to a system of beliefs where consumer satisfaction is the end of theory and practice. Managerialism refers to a system of beliefs that privileges business management and in particular elevates profitability to the key end for appropriate action. At the other end of the ideology spectrum we have Marxism.

In a fascinating auto-ethnographic account of his personal research journey, David Botterill explains how the ideologies that permeated different Universities influenced his own research:

> At [Texas A&M] I had encountered the epitome of what Delanty (1997) describes as the 'technical useful knowledge' that emanates under institutionalised positivism. (Botterill, 2003, p. 100)

Botterill's experience demonstrates how ideologies discipline thinking. He explains that the taken for granted approach at Texas A&M was "so visible, so normal" that against it his comments often appeared as "heretic" (2003, p. 100). Subsequently Botterill explains how a move to a "social science subject group at a small college . . . brought [him] up sharply against the influence of Marxian thought" (2003, p. 103).

He then explains how later employment at a "'vocational' university . . . [made] it difficult to retain a high profile in a critical network" (2003, p. 103). Barnett also sounds the alarm about the influences of ideologies on universities noting that:

> Ideologies have entered the university from several directions, within and beyond the university. Ideology has gained such a grip in universities that it is no longer clear that the idea of the university — as pointing to a site of reason — can be realised. (2003, pp. 1–2)

In particular Barnett argues that universities as sites of freedom and reason are undermined not only by external ideologies but also internal ones such as entrepreneurialism, competition, quality and managerialism.

Taking ideology a single dominant belief system Marx argued that the dominant ideology is that which serves the dominant class. This idea was developed by Gramsci (1971) as hegemony that describes a subtle concept of power not as physical force but as empowerment of the cultural beliefs, values and practices of a dominant group and the suppression and partial exclusion of those of others. A key question here is for example whether tourism research falls under the hegemonic influences of the ideology of Western capitalism and consumerism. But again the post-modern facts of life argue strongly against a simple Marxist version of ideology and for this reason Bell (2000, p. 40) is able to argue for the end of ideology as evidenced by the collapse of Marxist politics and the fact that large political ideas have lost their "power to persuade". So it appears that ideologies can exert a strong power to influence the direction of tourism research. However they too are permeable as illustrated by tourism researchers such as Botterill who have exerted their independence and made successful bids for intellectual freedom.

The Foulcauldian notion of discourse (and the possible sites of resistance that discourse can engender) (Foucault, 1971, 1974, 1980) provides an even more subtle reading of the rules that can govern tourism researchers. Here the rules of admissibility and legitimation are much less overtly policed than in a paradigm. Hall (1997, p. 44) explains discourse as "a group of statements which provide a language for talking about . . . a particular topic at a particular historical moment".

Hence we have a discourse that explains madness, sickness and even success and Cheong and Miller (2000) bring a Foucauldian analysis to demonstrate the productive effects of power in the formation of knowledge in the field of tourism. Hall further explains that Foucault was interested in unearthing the rules and practices that gave statements meaning and regulated what could and could not be said. Sets of social relations and discursive formations legitimise what counts as knowledge and what does not and whose ideas are given authority and whose not. In this way discourse can help to construct subjects such as madness and tourism and determine what we enable ourselves to know (Shotter, 1993).

Hollinshead (1999) takes the Foucauldian idea of the gaze — the eye-of-power — and explains how it acts in tourism research to direct:

> . . . the way its members learn to see and project preferred versions of reality, and historically the way that such seeing and projecting privileges certain persons and their inheritances, and subjugates certain others and their inheritances. (Hollinshead, 1999, p. 9)

Hollinshead skilfully demonstrates how discourse can lead to:

> Entrenched a priori understandings in or of cultural, environmental matters and preformulated understandings about . . . a distant interpreted population. (Hollinshead, 1999, p. 17)

He thereby implores tourism researchers to consider:

> what . . . we repeatedly and systematically privilege in tourism representations . . . [and] what we . . . systematically deny and frustrate. (Hollinshead, 1999, p. 15)

But we should avoid the temptation to see discourse as a totalitarianising force in tourism research, for as Foucault observed "where there is power there is resistance" (1980, p. 95). Indeed all of these rules — paradigms, ideology and discourse — invite rule breakers, in this latter case notably Hollinshead, and this makes it difficult to argue the case for a discourse of tourism research. Similarly, Franklin and Crang clearly offer a site for resistance in tourism when they ask contributors to *Tourism Studies* to (among other things):

> . . . provide an alternative to the existing positivist, managerially oriented material which predominates in the current literature on tourism. These approaches may include qualitative, humanistic and ethnographic methodologies, and feminist and ethnic perspectives on tourism. (Franklin & Crang, 2001, p. 15)

But it does seem possible to identify dominant discursive formations. Here we are drawn back to managerialism as a powerful discourse disciplining tourism research. After Foucault, Ball (1990, p. 156) suggests that "management is a professional, professionalizing discourse". It is a discourse that tends to promote the legitimacy of issues such as efficiency, consumer satisfaction, marketing, competition and profitability and markets and sideline issues such as equity, power-politics, gender and exploitation.

Disciplines provide yet another focus for setting the rules of tourism research. Of course disciplines provide protocols to ensure the reliability and validity of research. But beyond this it is possible to see what Aronowitz and Giroux (1991) refer to as the tyranny of the disciplines. More recently Sayer (1999, p. 2) provides additional insight into this tendency by pointing up the parochialism of disciplines where:

> They tend to be incapable of seeing beyond the questions posed by their own discipline, which provide an all-purpose filter for everything.

Additionally Kincheloe and McLaren (2003, p. 435) view disciplines as "manifestations of the discourses and power relations of the social and historical contexts that produced them".

For these authors then, disciplines can over-discipline knowledge creation leading to "a recipe for misunderstanding the social world" (Sayer, 1999, p. 1). A number of studies (Jafari & Aaser, 1988; Meyer-Arendt & Justice, 2002; Botterill et al., 2003; and Tribe, 2006) underline the importance of the disciplines of economics, geography, sociology, business studies and anthropology in the study of tourism. Each of these disciplines offers a partial reading of the world. For example economics, as Robinson (1942) pointed out, persistently takes the world order as given avoiding questions of what should be in favour of a factual explanation of its mechanisms. The economics of tourism similarly offers a factual account of wage differentials without any interest in their justness or the power dynamics that bring them about. We are alerted to how the market mechanism works without any consideration of its justice.

Rojek and Urry advert to another blindness of economics which:

> Deliberately . . . abstract[s] most of the important issues of social and cultural practice and only consider[s] tourism as a set of economic activities. Questions of taste, fashion and identity would thus be viewed as exogenous to the system. (1997, p. 2)

So disciplines often mean that critical aspects of tourism are overlooked. Economics for example prides itself on its concentration on positivism and its unwillingness to deal in normative issues. However it should not be overlooked that some disciplines provide the platforms for sustained critique — particularly those of sociology, cultural studies and philosophy. Such disciplines can foster unruliness amongst their followers.

Finally in this section the rules provided by traditions, camps and networks are considered. A tradition (MacIntyre, 1985) provides a looser disciplining of thought than a paradigm and its idea points to a steady build-up rules and protocols about the way things are done. Traditions develop and become entrenched as researchers build on the emerging core values and routines attracting new supporters and dropping dissidents. They are less rigid than paradigms since different traditions often co-exist within a field of study and unlike paradigms they are more flexible and adaptable. However they are prone to create infrastructures based around people, publications, research agendas and departments. Camps and networks represent perhaps the loosest coalitions and groupings. Camps as the name implies are readily set up and disbanded and they are more informal. They are likely to be built around specific research issues rather than representing a large conglomeration of ideas, attitudes and rules. Networks are perhaps the most adaptable and unstable of groupings. There are of course multiple networks each with individual researchers at their centre as well as networks (often based around an e-list) around themes.

Perhaps it is also necessary to consider somewhat outside of these corralling forces the individualist, the maverick, the lone researcher, the discipline crosser, the post-disciplinary researcher. In the case of tourism studies it is probable that the development of criticality originated in the maverick researchers who found their sustenance in traditions and disciplines outside of the field of tourism. It is then possible to point to a bottom-up building of critical tourism studies starting from informal networks and establishing itself into a camp.

Conclusion

This chapter initially identified the meanings of "critical" as applied to tourism studies. Taking a lead from the Frankfurt School of critical theorists it identified what it is to be critical in this sense. The second line of enquiry entailed investigating the factors that militate against the development of critical tourism studies. Here a number of factors were seen to be important. These included paradigms, ideology, discourse, disciplines and traditions. However none of these was found to offer a totalitarianising grip on tourism studies and indeed a dialectic was established where each factor began an oppositional idea. Thus permeability, independence, resistance, unruliness and mavericks all seem to offer points for the crystallisation, nurturing and growth of critical approaches.

Tribe (1997, p. 654) had offered a pessimistic reading of the development of what he termed the indiscipline of tourism where "the business world of tourism is pushing out at the expense of other parts . . .."

This pointed to a strong tradition growing around the business of tourism — a tradition that could be quite hostile to other approaches whose proponents exercised alien rituals. But an increasing presence of criticality in tourism studies may be seen from the emergence of various coalitions and camps. All of which led Tribe (2005, p. 1) to revisit his prognosis and report on a new turn:

> This new turn is showing signs of organisation and dissemination through articles, journals, texts networks and conferences. Articles reflecting this new turn include Veijola and Jokinen's (1994) *The Body in Tourism*, Aitchison's (2001) *Theorizing Other Discourses of Tourism, Gender and Culture: can the subaltern speak (in tourism)?*, Botterill's (2003) *Autoethnographic Narrative on Tourism Research Epistemologies*, Fullagar's (2002) *Narrative of Travel: desire and the movement of feminine, subjectivity* and Hollinshead's (1999) *Surveillance of the Worlds of Tourism: Foucault and the eye-of-power*. Journals which actively promote this new turn include *Tourist Studies* and the *Journal of Tourism and Cultural Change*. Phillimore and Goodson's (2004) *Qualitative Research in Tourism: ontologies, epistemologies and methodologies* represents a text that signals a mainstream publisher's interest of new approaches to tourism research (and thus by implication an emerging market) whilst conferences which such as *Embodying Tourism Research: Advancing Critical Approaches* (Dubrovnik, 2005) and its follow up in Split 2007, explicitly invite contributions "that demonstrate innovative theoretical and methodological approaches.

So there are promising signs of and for criticality in tourism studies. But its ability to take hold depends upon its regular nourishment and the growth of a supporting infrastructure. For it is inevitably pitched against deeply embedded projects such as vocationalism, managerialism, consumersism, the Washington consensus, the Bushification of the terms "democracy and freedom" and the RAE-ification of research (Tribe, 2003). As Kincheloe and McLaren (2003, p. 436) put it:

> A reconceptualised critical theory questions the assumption that societies such as the United States, Canada, Australia, New Zealand and the nations in the European Union, for example are unproblematically democratic and free . . . individuals in these societies have been acculturated to feel comfortable in relations of domination and subordination rather than equality and independence.

More importantly whilst for criticality the first stage is critical thought and expression the ultimate aim must be critical action and practice. The ultimate test of success of critical tourism studies is logically that the position of those without power should be improved. This traditionally includes people of colour, woman, the disabled, the geographically peripheral and the poor. Success here would be measured by a greater voice and equitable positioning of these groups in the Academy and beyond this a better outcome for them in the wider production and consumption of tourism.

References

Aitchison, C. (1996). Patriarchal paradigms and the politics of pedagogy: A framework for a feminist analysis of leisure and tourism studies. *World Leisure & Recreation, 38*(4), 38–40.

Aitchison, C. (2001a). Gender and leisure research: The "codification of knowledge". *Leisure Sciences, 23*(1), 1–19.

Aitchison, C. (2001b). Theorizing other discourses of tourism, gender and culture: Can the subaltern speak (in tourism)? *Tourist Studies, 1*(2), 133–147.

Althusser, L. (1969). Ideology and ideological state apparatuses. In B. Cosin (Ed.), *School and society* (pp. 79–88). London: Routledge and Kegan Paul.

Althusser, L. (1984). *Essays on ideology.* London: Verso.

Aronowitz, S., & Giroux, H. (1991). *Postmodern education: Politics, culture, and social criticism.* Minneapolis: University of Minnesota Press.

Ball, S. (1990). Management as moral technology: A Luddite analysis. In S. Ball (Ed.), *Foucault and education: Disciplines and knowledge* (pp. 20–32). London: Routledge.

Barnett, R. (2003). *Beyond all reason: Living with ideology in the university.* Buckingham: SRHE and Open University Press.

Bell, D. (2000). *The end of ideology.* Cambridge, MA: Harvard University.

Best, S., & Kellner, D. (1997). *The postmodern turn.* New York: Guildford Publishing.

Botterill, D. (2003). An autoethnographic narrative on tourism research epistemologies. *Loisir et Société, 26*(1), 97–110.

Botterill, D., Gale, T., & Haven, C. (2003). A survey of doctoral theses accepted by universities in the UK and Ireland for studies related to tourism 1990–1999. *Tourist Studies, 2*(3), 283–311.

Cheong, S., & Miller, M. (2000). Power and tourism. A Foucauldian observation. *Annals of Tourism Research, 27*(2), 371–390.

Dann, G. (1997). Paradigms in tourism research. *Annals of Tourism Research, 24,* 472–474.

Delanty, G. (1997). *Social science: Beyond constructivism and realism.* Buckingham: Open University press.

Foucault, M. (1971). *L'ordre du Discours*. Paris: Gallimard.

Foucault, M. (1974). *The Archaeology of Knowledge*. London: Tavistock.

Foucault, M. (1980). *Power/Knowledge: Selected interviews and other writings, 1972–77*. Brighton: Harvester Press.

Franklin, A., & Crang, M. (2001). The trouble with tourism and travel theory. *Tourist Studies, 1*(1), 5–22.

Fullagar, S. (2002). Narratives of travel: Desire and the movement of feminine, subjectivity. *Leisure Studies, 21*(1), 57–74.

Gibson, R. (1986). *Critical theory and education*. Kent: Hodder and Stoughton.

Gramsci, A. (1971). *Selections from the Prison Notebooks* (Q. Hoare, & G. Smith, Trans.). New York: International Publishers.

Grundy, S. (1987). *Curriculum: Product or praxis*. Sussex: Falmer Press.

Hall, S. (1997). The work of representation. In S. Hall (Ed.), *Representation: Cultural representations and signifying practices* (pp. 13–74). London: Sage.

Hollinshead, K. (1992). 'White' gaze, 'red' people — shadow visions: The disidentification of 'Indians' in cultural tourism. *Leisure Studies, 11*(1), 43–64.

Hollinshead, K. (1999). Surveillance of the worlds of tourism: Foucault and the eye of power. *Tourism Management, 20*(1), 7–23.

Jafari, J., & Aaser, D. (1988). Tourism as the subject of doctoral dissertations. *Annals of Tourism Research, 15*(3), 407–429.

Kincheloe, J., & McLaren, P. (2003). "Rethinking critical theory and qualitative Research". In: N. Denzin, & S. Lincoln (Eds), *The handbook of qualitative research*. (pp. 279–313). Thousand Oaks, CA: Sage.

Kuhn, T. (1970). *The structure of scientific revolutions*. Chicago: University of Chicago Press.

Lyotard, J. (1984). *The postmodern condition: A report on knowledge* (G. Bennington, & B. Massumi, Trans.). Manchester: Manchester University Press.

MacIntyre, A. (1985). *After virtue: Study in moral theory*. London: Duckworth.

Meyer-Arendt, K., & Justice, C. (2002). Tourism as the subject of North American doctoral dissertations, 1987–2000. *Annals of Tourism Research, 29*, 1171–1174.

Phillimore, J., & Goodson, L. (2004). Progress in qualitative research in tourism. In: J. Phillimore, & L. Goodson (Eds), *Qualitative research in tourism* (pp. 4–29). London: Routledge.

Riley, R., & Love, L. (2000). The state of qualitative tourism research. *Annals of Tourism Research, 27*, 164–187.

Robinson, J. (orig. 1942) (1960). *An essay on Marxian economics*. London: MacMillan and Co.

Rojek, C., & Urry, J. (Eds) (1997). *Touring cultures*. London: Routledge.

Sayer, A. (1999). *Long live postdisciplinary studies! Sociology and the curse of disciplinary parochialism/imperialism*. Retrieved April 1, 2005, from Lancaster University Website: <http://www.lancs.ac.uk/fss/sociology/papers/sayer-long-live-postdisciplinary-studies.pdf>.

Shotter, J. (1993). *Conversational realities*. London: Sage.

Tribe, J. (1997). The indiscipline of tourism. *Annals of Tourism Research, 24*, 638–657.

Tribe, J. (2003). The RAE-ification of tourism research in the UK. *International Journal of Tourism Research, 5*, 225–234.

Tribe, J. (2005). New tourism research. *Tourism Recreation Research, 30*(2), 5–8.

Tribe, J. (2006). The truth about tourism. *Annals of Tourism Research, 33*(2), 360–381.

Veijola, S., & Jokinen, E. (1994). The body in tourism. *Theory, Culture and Society, 11*, 125–151.

Chapter 3

Structural Entanglements and the Strategy of Audiencing as a Reflexive Technique

Candice Harris, Erica Wilson and Irena Ateljevic

Introduction

Tourism studies has been moving steadily towards a 'critical turn' (Ateljevic, Harris, Wilson, & Collins, 2005), demonstrating a post-modern/post-structural effort to deconstruct the cultural politics of tourism research and the dominant processes involved in the so-called 'making of knowledge'. Questions and debates in tourism studies surrounding ontology, epistemology, methodology and reflexivity have been central within this critical turn, reflecting elements of Norman Denzin and Yvonna Lincoln's (2000, 2005) Seventh, Eighth and Ninth moments of qualitative research. The Seventh moment heralded a:

> new age where messy, uncertain, multivoiced texts, cultural criticism, and new experimental works will become more common, as will more reflexive forms of fieldwork, analysis, and intertextual representation. (Denzin & Lincoln, 2000, p. 24)

Indeed, the body of work presented in this book, and at conferences such as the *Embodying Tourism Research: Advancing Critical Approaches* event held in Dubrovnik, 2005 (at which we presented some of the ideas that make up this chapter), demonstrates our immersion in the Seventh moment, as we embrace critical approaches and question the assumptions which underpin tourism research. Norman Denzin and Yvonna Lincoln (2005) describe the future — that is, 2005 onwards — as the 'fractured future', which will consist of the emergence of the Eighth and Ninth moments. The Eighth moment, in particular, will confront the methodological backlash associated with the evidence-based social movement, and will ask:

> that the social sciences and the humanities become sites for critical conversations about democracy, race, gender, class, nation-states, globalisation, freedom, and community. (Denzin & Lincoln, 2005, p. 3)

The Critical Turn in Tourism Studies: Innovative Research Methodologies
Copyright © 2007 by Elsevier Ltd.
All rights of reproduction in any form reserved.
ISBN: 0-08-045098-9

But how does the critical turn influence us in our everyday and research lives? Broadly speaking, what we call the critical turn can be placed under the larger umbrella of what John Tribe (2005) terms 'new' tourism research — a phase marked by a move beyond the traditional strait-jacketed obsession with applied, empirical and industry-driven business research. In the new/critical tourism phase, academics strive to embrace reflexive and critical forms of academic inquiry, keen to seek the stories behind the data and search for more in-depth and complex understandings surrounding the tourism phenomenon. The critical turn asks that we, as students, academic researchers, teachers and communicators, think about the impacts of our research on those that we study, the communities in which we work and live, and the various audiences with whom we engage. While reflexive practices emphasise the agency of researchers and the researched, and the dynamics of their intersubjective relationships, it is the act of interpretation and representation of knowledge, which is the most *public* testament to reflexive practice. Researchers charged with this act can then be viewed as interlocutors (McLafferty, 1995), making choices about interpretation and forms of representation as a process of discovery of the subject, problem, and of the self (Guba & Lincoln, 2005; Hollinshead, 2004).

Building on our previous work (Ateljevic et al., 2005) on the joys, entanglements and difficulties inherent in the reflexive research process, this chapter explores a specific strategy for negotiation, which we call 'audiencing'. Essentially, we frame audiencing as a concept which encapsulates the complexities and issues involved in speaking about our research in different voices, and to different audiences. By 'audiences', we mean research participants, research gatekeepers, readers of books such as the one you are reading now, powerholders within universities, wider academic and research communities, journal boards and editors, external research users — even our families, partners and colleagues, among others that we interact with on a day-to-day level and with whom we share our research joys, questions and frustrations. To demonstrate how we audience to different groups and individuals, towards the end of the paper we adopt a collective narrative approach (Davies et al., 2004; Ellis & Bochner, 2000) and include our own personal, reflexive stories as examples. This style of writing has been popular within both feminist (e.g. Reinharz, 1992) and indigenist research (Tuhiwai Smith, 2005, p. 85), as academics struggled through "tricky ground" to portray their research experiences and relationships within the confines of positivist, depersonalised convention.

Indeed, the very act of writing this current chapter, falling back on the accepted and privileged tenets of academic language but wanting at the same time to be a little playful, is an example of how we 'audience'. In writing this chapter, we are playing with particular styles of communication (academic discourse combined with personal narrative) to send a particular message (embrace reflexivity; be aware of our audience/s) to a particular audience (academic/postgraduate readers who are most likely familiar with the critical school of thought). In these ways, we are being reflective on the process of reflexivity. Bronwyn Davies et al. (2004, p. 360) refer to this process as the "double reflexive arc", in which authors come together to "tell and write stories about reflexivity . . . [and] examine themselves at work" in the reflexive project.

Getting 'Entangled' in the Project of Reflexivity

In being reflexive, we understand that the researcher should fashion him or herself as the *bricoleur*, who:

> understands that research is an interactive process shaped by his or her per-
> sonal history, biography, gender, social class, race, and ethnicity, and those of
> the people in the setting. The *bricoleur* knows that science is power, for all
> research findings have political implications. (Denzin & Lincoln, 2000, p. 3)

We know also that reflexivity is an important way of "seeing what frames our seeing" (Lather, 1993, p. 675), and that there is no fixed reality or power hierarchy in the work that we do. These sound like fairly straightforward if not idealistic goals, yet we found that we share Bronwyn Davies et al.'s (2004) 'ambivalences' and Patti Lather's (1993) 'deep tensions' about how one actually *practices* reflexivity. As Patti Lather (1993, p. 685) posits:

> there are few guidelines for how one goes about the *doing* of it [reflexiv-
> ity], especially in a way that is both reflexive and, yet, notes the limits of
> self-reflexivity.

Further questions about the project of reflexivity are voiced by Bronwyn Davies et al. (2004, p. 362):

> . . . reflexivity turns out to be much more complex and demanding than we
> had at first thought. Not only must we engage in such an apparently fraught
> practice as reflexivity but also, in our engagement with research, invent our
> own methods of meaning making as we go *and* catch ourselves in the act
> of engaging in old practices and modes of meaning making that we are in
> the process of deconstructing and moving beyond.

Perhaps it can be said then that it is the *process* of reflexivity that is important, not the *outcome*. In reflecting on our own struggles with meaning making and reflexivity, then, it becomes important to explain how this chapter came into being. Our story starts with an article we wrote, with Francis Leo Collins, for a special issue of Tourism Recreation Research entitled *Getting 'Entangled': Reflexivity and the 'Critical Turn' in Tourism Studies* (Ateljevic et al., 2005). The impetus for the article came in 2004 when we were attending an annual international tourism conference, and collectively noticed and reflected upon a dominance towards mainstream, industry-driven themes. Critical, alternative research or methodological approaches seemed largely ignored (or at least unconsciously not addressed) within paper streams ordered by topic rather than paradigm or perspective. Over the several days of the conference, at which we ourselves were presenters, we spoke of our shared concerns about the replicated tourism conference product, which, through mainstreamed programming and themeing designed for broad appeal, did not allow critical voices to be heard. Following the conference, Irena, Candice and Erica began a three-way process of emailing and phoning one another, reflecting on the conference and a number of other concerns and constraints we faced trying to yet again locate our interpretive/gender/critical research within the dominant tourism research structure. From this discussion, combined with our awareness of the growing legitimisation of new tourism research, we felt inspired to collaborate to produce a paper exposing the (often left unexposed) personal and political side of tourism research, taking a particular focus on reflexivity. Following months of reading and communication by distance, the three of us decided to meet in person for a mini writing workshop in Auckland, New Zealand (where Irena and Candice then lived) to tell each other and write down our stories face-to-face. During the four days we worked together, we struggled to bring together all of our varying definitions and interpretations of being reflexive and of embracing critical approaches and methodologies as tourism academics. We defined these joys, frustrations and differing interpretations as the 'entanglements' of reflexivity (Ateljevic et al., 2005).

By entanglements, we mean those forces that influence, constrain and shape the act of producing and reproducing knowledge within academic structures. We found that our entanglements tended to focus around four main themes (which do not constitute an exhaustive list, by any means): the dominant *ideologies and legitimacies* which govern and guide our tourism research outputs; the *research accountability* environment which decides what is 'acceptable' as tourism research; our *positionality* as embodied researchers whose lives, experiences and worldviews impact on our studies, and our *intersectionality with the 'researched'* (for want of a better term) as we carry out our research relationships with the people that we profess to study. We acknowledge that to enter a reflexive, critical dialogue, we must go through a process of 'getting entangled' in these forces and constraints. While getting entangled is often a messy and frustrating process, at the same time it opens up an empowering and rich dialogue, as we search for new ways to improve and diversify the relevance of our research to varied audiences. To demonstrate the entanglements of reflexivity, we chose the visual metaphor of an atom to symbolise that reflexivity can be viewed as an energetic process where many interwoven elements fuse to create a knowledge–practice nexus (see Figure 3.1).

The entanglement of intersectionality with the researched is perhaps the most entwining force involved in being reflexive. It forces us to ask: how do we relate to, and voice the experiences of, those that we study? Furthermore, how do the 'researched' view us, in our supposed goal to be emancipatory and critical in our research. And how do our engagements with the so-called 'researched' help us as academics to re-think our assumptions brought to the research? Being reflexive helps us to question how we see ourselves and others, and to avoid coming to our research projects with essentialised, value-laden perspectives. We recognise that the goal of reflexivity is to not just position ourselves within texts or write in the 'first person':

> but to engage in a critical reflection on one's relationship with others, as circumscribed by institutional practices and by history, both within and outside of the academy. (Young & Meneley, 2005, p. 7)

Being reflexive and searching out collaborative knowledge production means critically engaging with the different systems and structures that constitute our institutions; the relationships

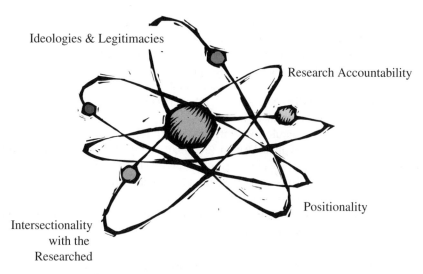

Ideologies & Legitimacies

Research Accountability

Positionality

Intersectionality
with the
Researched

Figure 3.1: The Entanglements of Reflexivity.
(*Source*: Ateljevic et al., 2005)

among fellow academics both within and across disciplines and research areas; the relation-ships between the knowledge produced in journals, conferences and elsewhere and those who read, listen and engage with that knowledge, and certainly the manner in which knowl-edge is produced and communicated between academics and students. Stacy Holman Jones (2005) describes the drama of representation, legitimation and praxis as being part of an ongoing dialogue between self and world, which hinges on questions of ontology, episte-mology, method and praxis. Such questions include: what is the nature of knowing, what is the relationship between knower and known, how do we share what we know and with what effect? One such strategy we identified as a means of dealing with the tensions, ambivalences and structural entanglements of reflexivity is 'audiencing'. It is this strategy, which we discussed at the *Embodying Tourism Research* conference in Croatia in 2005 and which has now led to this current chapter.

Coping with the Entanglements of Reflexive Research: Proposing the Strategy of Audiencing

The interpretive practice of making sense of one's research process is both an artistic and a political endeavour (Denzin & Lincoln, 2005). As discussed above, we offer 'audiencing' as a strategy in which to cope with the entanglements and politics of reflexive practice. Audiencing essentially refers to a method for how we write and position our voices, but it is also much broader than that. Audiencing depicts how we speak and translate research into various forms to engage with various groups and individuals; and how decisions are made about the ways in which we represent ourselves and those with whom we work. We should note that the idea of audiencing is not entirely a new concept, and has been discussed in varying ways by qualitative academics working at the reflexive, post-structuralist front. The term has also been used directly in the context of tourism studies. Keith Hollinshead (2004) refers to the four pillars which make up the messy, creative art of qualitative tourism research, these being matters of text, matters of reflexivity, matters of voice and matters of audiencing. By audiencing, Keith Hollinshead (2004, p. 2) refers to the 'poetics and politics of interpreting to specific audiences . . . the increasingly contested nature of all such projective public endeavours these days'.

Several scholars offer examples of strategies, which relate to our concept of audiencing. Norman Lincoln and Yvonna Denzin (2005) draw attention to what they call 'the decolonisation of the academy', which they argue has occurred because of the contribution of women, postgraduate students, non-native born faculty members and "faculty of colour". Such shifts are important, posit Norman Lincoln and Yvonna Denzin (2005, p. 1121), because these new members of the faculty feel far less tied to traditional forms of academic reporting than do their predecessors:

> As a consequence, the very shapes and forms of texts — whether books journal articles, or conference presentations — are likely to be less traditional. Experimental, "messy", layered poetic and performance texts are beginning to appear in journals and on conference podiums.

Dietmar Mieth (1997, p. 93) alludes to audiencing by highlighting our 'interpersonal responsibility' and moral obligation as qualitative researchers — to participants, to respondents, to consumers of research, and to themselves as qualitative fieldworkers. This includes the quality of "being with and for the other, not looking at" the other (de Laine, 2000, p. 16). Norman Denzin (2005), in arguing for a dialogue between critical and indigenous theories, recognises that he must acknowledge his position as an outsider to the indigenous colonised experience, and that he writes as a privileged Westerner. At the same time, he seeks to be an:

> 'allied other' . . . a fellow traveller of sorts, an antipositivist, an insider who wishes to deconstruct the Western academy and its positivist epistemologies from within. I endorse a critical epistemology that context notions of objectivity and neutrality. I believe that all inquiry is moral and political. (p. 736)

Consequently, he values collaborative, autoethnographic and performative methodologies, which are reflexive, ethical, critical, respectful and humble, and which allow him to audience in different ways to different groups.

Laurel Richardson (2000) uses the term creative analytic practice (CAP) to describe the varying ways in which people can write reflexively and communicate to their varying audiences. Such methods include performance autoethnography, short stories, conversations, fiction, personal narratives, creative non-fiction, poetic representation, photographic essays, personal essays, personal narratives of the self, personal histories and performance writings that blur the edges between text, representation and criticism. Autoethnography in particular has gained much popularity in recent years, as a writing style and methodology, which is involved with '. . . making a text present. Demand attention and participation. Implicating all involved. Refusing closure or categorisation' (Holman Jones, 2005, p. 765).

Carolyn Ellis and Arthur Bochner (2000) adopted a most playful form of audiencing in their contribution to the 2000 edition of the *Handbook of Qualitative Research*. They used an autoethnographic, personal narrative approach to discuss their own experiences of working as qualitative academics, supervisors and teachers within the social sciences. Most of their chapter is written as a conversation between Carolyn and Art (who are husband and wife), and begins with the challenges they faced in writing the chapter for the *Handbook*. This initial conversation contains the frustrations Art faced in terms of content, approach and time management, but in particular the constraints imposed by the genre of the handbook chapter as a form of writing. The two-way conversation between Art and Carolyn introduces readers to their lives, taking us through the discussion they (and many of us have had) around the power of conventions expected in academic writing and, as Carolyn states, 'how so many of our texts argue in post-modern abstract jargon for greater accessibility and experimental forms' (p. 735).

They decided to find a way to transgress the conventions by creating a story that would work within the handbook genre but also outside of it. Their chapter incorporates a story of Carolyn's interaction with Sylvia, a PhD student who wanted to write an autoethnographic dissertation on breast cancer, but struggled to justify a personal style of writing to her thesis committee and fellow academics. Cleverly, the chapter weaves a story of the interactions of Art, Carolyn and Sylvia, using personal experiences and narratives to not only address the topic of reflexivity but to also illustrate how three academics grappled with such issues in their normal academic lives.

Ellis and Bochner strike an interesting balance between conventional academic writing and personal narrative, producing a very readable and approachable account. Fine, Weis, Weseen, and Wong's (2000) essay, also in the second edition of the *Handbook of Qualitative Research* (Denzin & Lincoln, 2000), plays with a similar form of writing to communicate to and with their audience. Fine et al., incorporate narratives and stories regarding the politics of representation, to bring to life issues of informed consent, whose voice to use, what it is safe to say aloud and our responsibilities as researchers and interpreters.

In summary, a review of the literature on reflexivity and the academic writing project would suggest that audiencing requires us to make decisions about the following:

- Who do we want to talk to? Do we know our 'audiences' and do they know us?
- What is our relationship with our audiences now, and how do we want the relationship to be developed and/or maintained?
- What do we want to say to our audiences and for what reasons?
- How we will design our messages to be best received by our audiences, to appeal to their interests and conventions, but at the same time to achieve our own goals?
- What media (for example, texts, performance, reports, oral presentations) will we use that will allow us access to reach to our audiences?
- What are the power relationships and political implications for us and them that we need to consider prior to, during, and after we have delivered our texts, presentations, etc.?
- How will we retain our values and positions as academics, while embracing the flexibility that audiencing can offer us to talk with a variety of stakeholders about our research?

How Do We 'Audience'? Stories of Audiencing in Action

As indicated in the introduction, one of our goals in this chapter was to demonstrate the strategy of audiencing by drawing on our own personal narratives of the research experience. In doing this, we want to highlight the importance of acknowledging the researcher's voice and position in the research process, and honestly explain our own entanglements and struggles — which we should note are not fixed and which change over time depending on our work, lives and current research projects. Returning then to Patti Lather's (1993) reflexive tensions, how *do* we, as academic researchers and teachers, effectively 'audience'? That is, how do we use audiencing to speak about our research in different voices, to different audiences and for different purposes?

For instance, if talking or writing to a critical academic audience engaged with reflexivity and issues of epistemology (as we assume we are now), we may decide to write more of ourselves into texts and presentations. In these cases, we may feel safer in presenting more personal reflexive accounts and stories of ourselves and our research participants. At the *Embodying Tourism Research* conference in Dubrovnik, 2005, for example, we (Candice, Erica and Irena) considered ourselves to be in a safe academic environment in which to experiment and be more playful with our presentation as Candice explains:

> We decided to begin our presentation at the Dubrovnik conference with a role play based on a series of international phone and email conversations that had taken place in the preceding months between the three of us. In fact, we simply read directly from our emails, using these as embodied discursive texts upon which to reflect. Much of this conversation centred on an email that had appeared on TRINET, about how well-received qualitative and critical approaches were within the tourism academy — but we wanted to tell an alternative story of how we still felt marginalised as reflexive, qualitative researchers. The audience at our conference presentation seemed to enjoy this playful, conversational approach, which we used to begin our presentation. It was interesting that some of the delegates asked us at the end of our paper why we reverted to a more formal presentation after our initial role play, and that in fact they would have preferred more of the personal narrative approach. Such feedback has encouraged us to feel confident to go further in future to include more personal, reflexive accounts and stories. It is hoped that by doing so we engage our audiences more than just 'talking at them' with PowerPoint slides.

In our recognition of being entangled in the masculine world, underpinned by the traditional and well-acknowledged dichotomies of work/life, mind/body, rationality/emotions, etc. this reflective quote on our Dubrovnik experience illustrates how the legitimisation of the collective support is crucial to liberate and re-assure us to trust our inner voices, to write ourselves in and to speak out. In other words, the 'safety net' of our audience gives us the necessary credibility in the outside world as well as the internal comfort of belonging and acceptance.

Indeed, the Dubrovnik event triggered much more than the intended objective of legitimising more interpretative and critical modes of tourism enquiry. In its efforts to de-centre and decolonise tourism studies by providing a forum for alternative voices, texts and approaches, we believe the conference has created a special sense of community, providing an 'academy of hope' which bell hooks (2003) describes as a crucial transgression practice to freedom from systems of hierarchy and domination. Responding to hooks' call to 'highlight all the positive, life-transforming rewards that have been the outcome of collective efforts to change our society, especially education, so that it is not a site for the enactment of domination in any form' (hooks, 2003, p. xiii), Irena describes her own journey of 'being liberated' once finding the power of a collective audience in embracing a more human approach to our academic practises:

> The Dubrovnik event represents for me an important turning point in my own academic, personal and spiritual growth. For the first time ever I could speak openly without a feeling of being 'Othered', of a feeling that I have finally arrived 'at home'. As an immigrant to New Zealand (from a war-thorn country of Yugoslavia) who received a scholarship to do my doctoral study I was always (and remain to be) grateful to get a chance, hence never questioning the authority and practises of the established academic system. So, I did what all other young academics did around me, I played the game (albeit unconsciously) and bought into the 'publish or perish' pressure, never questioning why. Driven by strong personal reasons to survive economically and emotionally, I was simply doing my job. However enthusiastically I approached it, I learned fast that good teaching does not necessarily get you far, while research was my ticket into the bright future of career promotion. Not being able to negotiate huge teaching loads and also lacking the self-confidence (based on perceiving myself as a 'lucky immigrant'), I accepted that working in the weekends and evenings was perfectly normal. I guess that was what Michel Foucault calls the notion of self-governance or what bell hooks describes as a lack of self love. Or what Gloria Steinem claims to be a low self-esteem in disguise, often characteristic even to the most politically active and successful people. Yet, slowly but surely I began to recognise my own agency and power. Feeling no sense of community in a dispersed field of tourism studies dominated by business approaches and networks of male gatekeepers, I began creating my own small collaborative connections with whom I shared feelings of alienation and isolation from the broader tourism community. The small space occupied by those who were feeling marginalised has grown to the point that now we are organising the second critical tourism studies conference that aims to promote an academy of hope. So here you go my dear bell hooks, you have a positive example of life rewarding experience, of a respond to your outcry, of a vision that comes from a heart which you inspired in many ways . . . and just wait — you might get an invitation to be a keynote at our third conference!

Audiencing might also be about devising ways to use our own epistemological voices, while at the same time working within the structures of the academic system. For example, we could be strategic when choosing appropriate journals in which to publish, by selecting those that allow and encourage reflexive work and the use of our own voices. Or alternatively, in order to be 'publishing smart', we can twist our main argument and engage with different disciplines, theories or issues that fit into the positioning, rationale and objectives of a particular journal. Irena's example of her publication background which combined human geography and tourism studies demonstrates this point:

> Doing my PhD in human geography I've learned that many empirical socio-economic and cultural phenomena serve as contexts in which to investigate and raise broader questions of politics, economy and society. So, for my doctorate I looked at how tourism played an important political and economic role in the processes of colonising Aotearoa/New Zealand. When I entered the interdisciplinary arena of tourism studies I continued to use the same approach. Applying broader social science theories (e.g. power, cultural capital, space, place, etc.) in the context of tourism as a powerful economic and socio-cultural agent, I stepped into the exciting territory of blurring disciplinary boundaries. I will give you an example of my research and published work (together with my great collaborative colleague Stephen Doorne) in the area of backpacker travel and tourism entrepreneurship. While these subjects became recognised as being our 'expertise' *per se* (ironically enough), we were rather 'playing' and adopting the same research interest to different theories, depending on our decision of positioning and excitement with particular theories. So, sometimes we would stress the issues of sustainability (e.g. for *Journal of Sustainable Tourism*); or the blurring of economy and culture (e.g. for *Tourism Geographies*); or social and cultural capital and inequality of global political economy (e.g. *Tourist Studies*); or market segmentation (for a book on a consumer psychology in tourism); the power of agency and criticism of structuralist reductionism of tourism commodification (e.g. *Tourism and Cultural Change*). The fact that we were taking the same research focus to different economic–cultural contexts (e.g. New Zealand, Fiji, China, Croatia) only helped us to contextualise it and be even more 'playful' with our different audiences.

We may also adjust our methodological preferences from time to time to work within the boundaries of the academic research funding system. For example, if applying for government funding from a provider interested in industry implications, then we may opt to use certain methods, which do not necessarily 'fit' into our preferred paradigm (for example, a quantitative survey of tourists), but are essential for so-called 'generalisability of results'. Another methodological example of audiencing might be that we are conducting a tourism planning consultancy for a local government that often seeks this type of research and wants easy-to-understand, numerical results which will be easily translatable to their own audiences, while ultimately serving particular political objectives. Irena's involvement with collaborative research at Victoria University in New Zealand provided her with an important learning experience about how one can simultaneously satisfy the demand for policy and industry-oriented research and engage with theoretical endeavours:

> I have to go back to the early origins of my backpackers and small tourism firms research which also reminds me how one can take a particular research direction by triggers of one's contextual elements, albeit often unconsciously. Namely, our Victoria tourism team obtained funding to conduct research in four central regions of New Zealand in order to help local authorities in their regional (tourism) development strategies. Combining the complementary skills of our group (with both qualitative and quantitative methods), we developed a common methodology that could be replicated in all four regions. All being geographers, we looked at the various issues of local economy, history and culture, while at the same time conducting 'pure' market research of tourism supply and demand. Accordingly, we produced various reports for regional tourism organisations and developed particular policy, marketing and industry recommendations. In the process, however, we collected many empirical data that could be 'translated' into various publishing outlets. And that is how Stephen Doorne and myself (both of us being mostly responsible for qualitative research in the field) ended up writing up about backpackers and tourism entrepreneurship.

We may also adopt more accessible writing and communication strategies, which appeal to our research participants, students or the wider community. For example, Candice has been involved in small–medium enterprise research teams that produce reports for participants at the end of each project:

> The report is written specifically for the participants, outlining how the research was carried out, what the research revealed and conclusions. It is specifically written in plain English, without theory. It presents succinctly to the participants what we did and what we found. After receiving the report, several of the participants have contacted us to thank us for the report, saying they enjoyed reading it, and that it gave them a feeling of community; that there are others out there who have experienced similar issues in their own businesses. For the research team, such reports are about giving back to the participants, a product that thanks them for their time and shows them how what they shared with us was used to build the greater study.

Erica finds that her job as a tourism lecturer, which involves a combination of research, teaching and community interaction, requires getting to know all of these audiences well:

> I think one of the best examples of audiencing is to reflect on how I communicate in different ways when speaking to students, fellow academics or people in the wider community. It is important for me to write and speak to each of these groups in plain, clear English, no matter how 'theoretical' the

topic matter may be. I try to translate complex theories, ideas or language into words that my undergraduate students can understand. If students cannot understand, then they are being done a disservice. I also present from time to time to local women's business groups, and attempt to make my research findings relevant and palatable to them. I don't believe in making language convoluted as it runs the risk of isolating different audiences. At the same time, I don't want to feel the pressure of 'dumbing down' my research so that it appeals to the masses. Ideas can be expressed in different ways depending on the situation and the audience. It is indeed a tricky ground, but one which must always be negotiated and reflected upon in my effort to be a better teacher, researcher and community member. Writing for books like this allows me a chance to 'indulge' a little in a personal style of writing, but also frame it within a wider, more complex academic context. Often the two are seen as incongruous, particular in business faculties, but balancing the two is an important challenge — and one that keeps me interested in my job.

We must also consider how we translate our academic thinking and writing into words and terms, which resonate with, and even have the potential to empower, our research participants or other audiences. For example, in her PhD thesis, which focussed on solo women travellers, Erica held a two-hour post-analysis focus group with a number of the women:

> While this focus group had the primary aim of 'checking' the accuracy of themes developed from interview data, I realised the empowering aspect of the workshop in that the women found it beneficial to share their travel stories with others. Such a workshop did not only verify data and make people feel like they were somehow included in the study; it showed to me how research participants can be affected by research, that it can have an impact on their lives, and that their input creates new and interesting ways of looking at data.

Another audiencing question centres on how we allow for reciprocity in our research projects: that we consciously think and plan what we can 'take from' our participants, *and* what and how they would like us to give back to them. We may need to engage potential audiences and end-users earlier in the research process, such as in the stages of research design and analysis, so that we can decide how best to capture and produce knowledge. Greater and earlier collaboration would facilitate better understanding the demands of our various audiences. Ongoing collaboration with our participants will enable theorisations to be revisited and new insights to be gained. As Adrian Franklin and Mike Crang (2001) stress, much of the very thinking about tourism, most of its meaning and significance, resides far outside of a week or fortnight away. Candice can provide an example in relation to her PhD, when she tested her survey with participants who had also come to her focus groups:

> The women in my focus groups provided a wealth of information on their business travel experiences. I was surprised with each focus group, conversations on new themes occurred, issues that I had even not considered prior to conducting these groups. This led me to involve the women in the design of my survey. While this is generally known as 'pre-testing' I sent it out for them asking them to comment on a range of things such as the design, the

content, usability and as well as what else they felt could be added. Fifteen women were involved in this process of collaboration, and almost all came back with valuable comments on the design, as well as ideas to improve it. Their involvement improved the survey, made them feel involved and increased my pride in how the project was developing. Their enthusiasm helped sustain mine during the long PhD process.

Irena invokes a memory of numerous research conversations in the field with female travellers and entrepreneurs, and the sense of connectedness she felt based on their shared structural experience of being *a woman*.

Because fieldwork involves an embodied researcher who tries to build trust with people she 'researches', you inevitably engage with people, you connect, you understand, you become emotional, you begin to share. That is so human! For example, my research with more mature female backpacker travellers taught me how complex is their need to escape into travel spaces, the need that I often feel myself. My 'respondents' would regularly acknowledge those emotions of being understood and connected, or just curious and excited for being involved, re-affirmed, heard and listened to. It is that kind of reciprocity that may appear to be small, but it can go a long way.

Conclusion

While demonstrating a critical shift in thinking, social science and tourism literature offers limited guidance on how one actually undergoes the practice of being reflexive (for examples of tourism studies which have addressed reflexivity, see Hall, 2004; Hollinshead, 2004; Jamal & Everett, 2004; Veijola & Jokinen, 1994). Indeed, David Botterill (2001, p. 199) argues that the 'assumptions that underlie social science research in tourism are seldom made explicit'. Addressing such reflexive gaps, and framed within the 'new tourism' discourse, this chapter provided a critical analysis of the use of reflexivity in tourism research, drawing on our own research experiences and methodological confrontations while working at the 'critical turn' in tourism studies.

We have argued in this paper that consideration of audiencing is central in determining how best to engage our various research stakeholders; to understand: who are 'they'? What are their worldviews and social realities? What are their dominant ideologies? How are they themselves held accountable? What is their positionality in our research? What will our audiences understand of our findings, and how will those findings be useful for them? As researchers, contemplating these questions can assist us in devising ways to 'audience' to these groups — to speak with them in their language with content that meets their needs and is meaningful to them. Knowing our audience/s also enables us to make decisions regarding the content and style of the knowledge we package for them, to ideally bring us closer to them.

Audiencing, as a strategy of recognising the politics of reflexive research and the impacts of such research on ourselves and those we involve, allows us to find legitimate spaces for our voices, while at the same time allowing us to work within — and challenge — the boundaries of the academic system. Another advantage of audiencing is that it shows the multiple meanings and plurality of research and avoids an assumption of our research findings as objective 'truth'. It further implores us to recognise the broader relevance and impact of our research for our study participants and others in non-academic circles (Dupuis, 1999; Reinharz, 1979).

As there are entanglements in the reflexive research process, there are also tensions and challenges in our audiencing. For example, the widely touted notion of 'giving back to' research participants is often sacrificed in the interests of time to invest in the more rewarded priorities in our academic systems, such as formal publications. Other challenges include whether we choose to take our research to many groups and how we package it to appeal to their interests. It is essential that we make reflexive practice active, not only considering ourselves as the researchers and those that we study, but also the dynamics and relationships in engaging with multiple audiences (Ellis & Bochner, 2000). We must then enact strategies to appropriately engage with those audiences.

Further, while we advocate the importance of engaging with many audiences through our work, audiencing is not merely about massaging our results so that they are palatable to everyone. Audiencing should not be concerned with doing research about which we feel morally or ideologically uncomfortable, just to secure research grants and publication points. Nor is it about 'dumbing down' our academic results merely to appeal to industry, the public or media and commercial interests. All groups and institutions have their own cultures, norms and requirements, thus it must be acknowledged that they do have influence in shaping the parameters and rules within which we work. The reality is that we work and publish within these 'rules'. Rather than simply being servant to more interest groups and publication outputs, we do have power and agency within these systems, and need to be confident to put forward the relevance of our research and its findings.

In conclusion, we feel that there is much excitement at the critical turn in tourism studies. There is now a small, but growing, audience of peers and students for which to write and with whom to collaborate on projects which deconstruct assumptions regarding tourism and the tourist experience. Through such engagement and collaboration, we are further establishing our own acceptance as legitimate researchers, authors and academics. Strengthening these networks also acts to subtly remove us from disputing with the original power holders about ontological, epistemological and methodological issues. Instead, we are advancing our own platforms rather than banging our heads against their doors. Ultimately, how we each 'audience' will be influenced by the tensions and entanglements we face in being reflexive, which by its very nature is a messy and difficult process. Yet, it also opens up an empowering and rich dialogue, as we search for new ways to improve and diversify the relevance of our research to ourselves, and to the varied audiences and stakeholders with whom we must communicate.

References

Ateljevic, I., Harris, C., Wilson, E., & Collins, F. L. (2005). Getting 'entangled': Reflexivity and the 'critical turn' in tourism studies. *Tourism Recreation Research, 30*(2), 9–21.

Botterill, D. (2001). The epistemology of a set of tourism studies. *Leisure Sciences, 20*, 199–214.

Davies, B., Browne, J., Gannon, S., Honan, E., Laws, C., Mueller-Rockstroh, B., & Bendix Petersen, E. (2004). The ambivalent practices of reflexivity. *Qualitative Inquiry, 10*(3), 360–389.

de Laine, M. (2000). *Fieldwork, participation and practice: Ethics and dilemmas in qualitative research.* London: Sage Publications.

Denzin, N. K. (2005). Emancipatory discourses and the ethics and politics of interpretation. In: N. K. Denzin, & Y. S. Lincoln (Eds), *The Sage handbook of qualitative research.* Thousand Oaks, CA: Sage Publications.

Denzin, N. K., & Lincoln, Y. S. (2000). Introduction: The discipline and practice of qualitative research. In: N. K. Denzin, & Y .S. Lincoln (Eds), *Handbook of qualitative research* (pp. 1–28). Thousand Oaks, CA: Sage Publications.

Denzin, N. K., & Lincoln, Y. S. (2005). *The Sage handbook of qualitative research.* Thousand Oaks, CA: Sage Publications.

Dupuis, S. L. (1999). Naked truths: Towards a reflexive methodology in leisure research. *Leisure Sciences, 21*, 43–64.

Ellis, C., & Bochner, A. P. (2000). Autoethnography, personal narrative, reflexivity: Researcher as subject. In: N. K. Denzin, & Y. S. Lincoln (Eds), *Handbook of qualitative research* (2nd ed., pp. 733–768). Thousand Oaks, CA: Sage publications.

Fine, M., Weis, L., Weseen, S., & Wong, L. (2000). For whom? Qualitative research, representations, and social responsibilities. In: N. K. Denzin, & Y. S. Lincoln (Eds), *Handbook of qualitative research* (2nd ed., pp. 107–132). Thousand Oaks, CA: Sage Publications.

Franklin, A., & Crang, M. (2001). The trouble with tourism and travel theory? *Tourist Studies, 1*(1), 5–22.

Guba, E. G., & Lincoln, Y. S. (2005). Paradigmatic controversies, contradictions and emerging confluences. In: N. K. Denzin, & Y. S. Lincoln (Eds), *The Sage handbook of qualitative research* (3rd ed., pp. 191–215). London: Sage Publications.

Hall, M. (2004). Reflexivity and tourism research: Situating myself and/with others. In: J. Phillimore, & L. Goodson (Eds), *Qualitative research in tourism: Ontologies, epistemologies and methodologies.* London: Routledge.

Hollinshead, K. (2004). *Tourism and the dynamics of knowing: The consolidating craft of qualitative research.* Paper presented at 'Creating Tourism Knowledge', 14th International Research Conference of the Council for Australian University Tourism and Hospitality Education (CAUTHE), The University of Queensland, Brisbane, 10–13 February.

Holman Jones, S. (2005). Autoethnography: Making the personal political. In: N. K. Denzin, & Y. S. Lincoln (Eds), *The Sage handbook of qualitative research* (3rd ed., pp. 763–792). Thousand Oaks, CA: Sage Publications.

hooks, b. (2003). *Teaching community: A pedagogy of hope.* New York: Routledge.

Jamal, T. B., & Everett, J. (2004). Resisting rationalisation in the natural and academic life-world: Critical tourism research or hermeneutic charity? *Current Issues in Tourism, 7*(1), 1–19.

Lather, P. (1993). Fertile obsession: Validity after poststructuralism. *The Sociological Quarterly, 34*(4), 673–694.

Lincoln, Y., & Denzin, N. (2005). Epilogue: The eighth and ninth moments — qualitative research in/and the fractured future. In: N. K. Denzin, & Y. S. Lincoln (Eds), *The Sage handbook of qualitative research.* Thousand Oaks, CA: Sage Publications.

McLafferty, S. (1995). Counting for women. *Professional Geographer, 47*, 436–442.

Mieth, D. (1997). The basic norm of truthfulness: Its ethical justification and universality. In: C. G. Christians, & M. Traber (Eds), *Communication ethics and universal values* (pp. 87–104). Thousand Oaks, CA: Sage Publications.

Reinharz, S. (1979). *On becoming a social scientist.* San Francisco: Jossey-Bass.

Reinharz, S. (1992). *Feminist methods in social research*. New York: Oxford University.

Richardson, L. (2000). Writing: A method of inquiry. In: N. K. Denzin, & Y. S. Lincoln (Eds), *Handbook of qualitative research* (2nd ed., pp. 923–948). Thousand Oaks, CA: Sage Publications.

Tribe, J. (2005). New tourism research. *Tourism Recreation Research: Theme — Tourism and Research*, *30*(2), 5–8.

Tuhiwai Smith, L. (2005). On tricky ground: Researching the native in the age of uncertainty. In: N. K. Denzin, & Y. S. Lincoln (Eds), *The Sage handbook of qualitative research* (3rd ed., pp. 85–107). Thousand Oaks, CA: Sage Publications.

Veijola, S., & Jokinen, E. (1994). The body in tourism. *Theory, Culture and Society*, *11*(3), 125–151.

Young, D. J., & Meneley, A. (2005). Introduction: Auto-ethnographies of academic practices. In: A. Meneley, & D. J. Young (Eds), *Auto-ethnographies: The anthropology of academic practices*. Plymouth: Broadview Press.

Chapter 4

Resisting Rationalisation in the Natural and Academic Life-World: Critical Tourism Research or Hermeneutic Charity?

Tazim B. Jamal and Jeff Everett

Introduction

From within the interpretive turn of the 20th century and the post-modern challenge to Enlightenment visions of certainty and foundational truths arise a set of scholars and researchers seeking new ways to describe and understand the natural and social world. They are faced with the challenge of being interdisciplinary 'bricoleurs' (Denzin & Lincoln, 1994), cobbling together multiple methods and perspectives, synthesising social theory, epistemology and methodology in ways that leave them open to critiques of superficiality and lack of rigour in their research approaches (Kincheloe, 2001). This struggle is particularly well illustrated in tourism studies, situated as it is as a fledging intruder in the liminal zones between traditionally established or academically legitimised disciplines such as economics, commerce (including marketing), sociology, geography, anthropology and psychology, to name a few. As discussed below, understanding how these struggles play out in natural area destinations offers insights for conducting 'critical' research, and is important for academic and social praxis. How we relate to the natural world ourselves makes us complicit in the battle for environmental and cultural sustainability, embedded as it is within a complex web of globalisation and technological structures. Social research, said Macbeth (2001, p. 37), needs to encompass and go beyond positional and textual reflexivity, as:

> an inquiry into the very possibilities of our unreflective knowledge and practices, and in this way, the reflexive move is an aggressive one for bringing more of an unsettled field into view.

Using the example of a national park destination, this paper's investigations in the unsettled field of tourism studies represents such an attempt to bring more of tourism research into a culturally critical and reflexive scholarship.

Making knowledge claims is not a neutral activity, conducted by a disinterested researcher, for all such claims require justification, a task that falls under epistemology. Epistemology is a philosophic discipline having to do with the nature and conditions of knowledge. Ontology is concerned with the nature of existence. For analytical philosophers studying ontology, the focus is typically on the task of formulating an inventory of the things that exist in the universe. Existentialists, by contrast, have tended to focus on the nature of personal existence. Research methods are embedded in assumptions about ontology and epistemology, though researchers may hold these tacitly and not be aware of their commitments to particular versions of the world and ways of knowing, and how these implicit rules influence their research programmes and results (Moring, 2001; Usher, 1996). Neither may some be aware of the extent to which socio-political influences privilege certain research paradigms or theoretical views and ways of doing research within a particular discipline or field of study. Foucault (1980) points out that societies and institutions have regimes of truth supported by political as well as economic apparatuses and discourses infused with social struggle. In tourism studies, the split between the economics-externalities camp (the industry-oriented aspect) and the impacts-internalities camp (the social and cultural aspect) is well recognised, as is the 'indiscipline' of tourism studies (Tribe, 1997). Tourism marketing, economics, 'management' and control of visitor impacts and experiences, i.e. the functionalist and applied approaches, have dominated the literature until recently, and the rich varieties of qualitative research methodologies have been slow to catch on (Jamal & Hollinshead, 2000). Within the field of leisure studies, Weissinger, Henderson, and Bowling (1997, p. 436) also noted that 'the use of qualitative data as a building block for the body of knowledge appears to be slow in forthcoming'.

These authors conducted a mail survey of active leisure researchers (including graduate students and scholars from within and outside the US, but biased towards North American researchers). Their results indicated that many of their respondents conducted qualitative research, valued the contributions made by qualitative research, and mentored students to be equally positive about qualitative research. But, as these authors noted, most leisure researchers in their study had little formal training in qualitative methods and the philosophical tenets that underlie them. This is a sobering insight which raises questions about the assumptions that frame the gathering and interpretation of qualitative data, and how 'the Other' is being represented in the process.

Considering the relative newness of tourism studies as a field of inquiry, surprisingly little debate has occurred on issues pertaining to the methodologies and philosophy of social (and in this case, tourism-related) research. For instance, what is the purpose of social (tourism) research? Is it to contribute to prediction and control (amenable to quantitatively oriented empirical–analytical methods) of resources, places and populations, or to enhance understanding and meaning-making (via interpretive methods) of phenomena in the social world? Or, as a student argued in a Philosophy of Social Science class in Fall, 2001, is it to change the world (praxis)? Or perhaps all of the above? Additionally, postmodern and cultural critiques are challenging taken-for-granted views and assumptions about 'Nature', culture and society. No longer can Nature be studied as a neutral, objective concept. Rather, it is as much an ideological marker as it is something real, for understandings about nature are deeply embedded in geopolitical and cultural influences, symbolic meanings, social constructions and historical influences (Wang, 2000). Yet, while the urgency for economic equity and environmental sustainability has been forwarded in reports such as Our Common Future (World Commission on Environment and Development (WCED) 1987), mainstream tourism research has generally avoided casting a critical glance at the notion of sustainability or at the adequacy of traditionally employed methodologies for studying natural and cultural destinations. What are the impacts of this lack of critical research, and how can such inquiry be conducted effectively in the complex arena of tourism studies? This paper aims to address these questions under the following objectives:

(1) Address the importance of critically examining nature-based destinations as producers of cultural meanings that influence tourist motivations, use and development of these areas.
(2) Illustrate how critical-cultural perspectives like critical theory can be applied to understanding issues such as rationalisation and representation of national parks, as well as rationalisation and colonisation of the hermeneutic domain of the academic researcher.
(3) Offer philosophical and methodological insights for researchers conducting social and cultural inquiry, particularly with respect to the ethical responsibility of the critical researcher when it comes to 'gazing' upon the natural world and those who inhabit it.

Serendipitously, the critical research approach laid out in this paper became useful for illustrating yet another relationship, that of the academic to her research. The basic argument we commenced crystallised into a much stronger thesis as a new and sobering realisation emerged, that (1) alongside the colonisation of the natural world, and (2) the rationalisation of the everyday world of human interests, was (3) the colonisation of the social research world of tourism studies. Furthermore, these three domains are interrelated with respect to social research and tourism, for we ourselves are interwoven into the life-world we study, as researchers, residents, societal members and tourists. Hence we, too, are complicit in contributing to the impacts being experienced by natural-human spaces and places, by the ways in which we study and engage with them personally and professionally. It raised a spectre of something many tourism researchers avoid questioning or engaging in debate about: what is the purpose of social research? Jafari's (2001) set of evolutionary platforms in tourism studies raises the issue of building 'scientific knowledge' for the knowledge-based platform, but asking 'to what end does tourism research aspire' reveals a host of academic and practical implications.

Critical theorists might respond with the answer: praxis, which is related to participatory and emancipatory action in the natural-cultural space being investigated. It requires the researcher to be fully engaged in understanding the issues in the problem domain and acting to change them. And so this paper metamorphosed to a richer purpose, not merely to illustrate the global, local and social myths by which Nature is constructed for human use and consumption but, more importantly, to argue for the imperative of a critical yet charitable scholarship. To not do so means that we, too, risk being complicit in the global decline of biodiversity as well as cultural and ethnic diversity, as local and indigenous people are displaced from their natural homelands (Stone & D'Andrea, 2001). In order to achieve the objectives mentioned above, the next section of the paper commences with a short theoretical discussion on the relevance of the critical paradigm to the study of natural areas and tourism studies. We draw particularly from critical theory and the work of Jurgen Habermas (1978). This is followed by a section that uses the example of Yellowstone

National Park to describe the cultural construction and representation of 'Nature', and thus how such natural areas act as sites of meaning-making and identity formation. A historical and cultural analysis provides narratives that illustrate the importance of a critical theoretical approach to the study of natural area destinations. Issues related to academic rationalisation, ontological and epistemological assumptions and research praxis are discussed in the final section.

It should be noted that 'tourism in natural areas', 'nature tourism' and 'nature-based tourism' are used in this paper as broad, umbrella terms that include ecotourism, a type of nature-based tourism characterised by ecologically ethical or responsible activities. 'Nature' and 'nature' are used interchangeably to denote the physical, natural world not including the built environment, though we recognise that this separation may itself be based on a false dualism (Merchant, 1982).

Rationalisations in the Everyday Research(ed) World

The area of tourism studies has evolved in various (sub)disciplinary areas over the last three to four decades, finding homes in domains such as anthropology, sociology, social psychology, geography, economics, marketing and management, to name a few. However, the sociology of knowledge in tourism studies has been little studied, though debates within the sub-disciplinary areas are slowly contributing to this area (Echtner & Jamal, 1997). For example, following Grano's (1981) model of external influences and internal change in geography, Hall and Page (1999) examine the geography of tourism and recreation under the three interrelated areas of Grano's model: knowledge (substantive content of the study area); action (research within the context of research praxis); and culture (academics and students within the research community and wider society). The area of action has seen debates over radical approaches and over the focus of the discipline, whether an 'applied focus' is appropriate and how geographers should contribute their skills to the solution of societal problems. As Hall and Page (1999) discuss, conservatism and critiques over lack of methodological rigour in applied geography, as well as lack of recognition of the significance of tourism and recreation research by some geography departments, professional organisations and countries, have resulted in the creation of alternative multidisciplinary settings to which a significant number of geographers of tourism and recreation have migrated. Here, they are able to take up problem-solving needs and non-traditional research approaches to address challenges such as global economic restructuring and environmental conservation.

One of the challenges that face the developing field of tourism and recreation studies is the prevalence of quantitatively oriented, empirical–analytical methods to study natural and cultural areas, impact and resource management tools and techniques, and visitor experiences, behaviours and activities (Riley & Love, 2000). Such studies are appealing because their methodologies attempt to provide epistemological justification for generalisation, prediction and control ('management') of the destination domain. While useful for such purposes, a number of such studies rely on the legitimacy of the scientific method to avoid examining what the numbers mean, in terms of those who live in the built and natural environments, as well as those who recreate there. Sustainability principles related to access, equity, and social justice (WCED, 1987) suggest that there are tough questions to address, for example, on a proposed development project: Why is this project being proposed, for what purpose, and to what end, i.e. who benefits? What interests are involved, which individuals and groups stand to be impacted and whose needs are being left out, not heard or not included in the decision-making?

Such political questions increase the burden of the (sustainable) tourism researcher, who may then require non-traditional theoretical and methodological approaches such as post-structuralism, to examine unfamiliar discourses of power, representations of 'the Other', and production or consumption of cultural experiences and practices (Britton, 1991). Such disquieting research strategies compete against the uncertainty-reducing comfort and historical privilege of the (social) scientific method in traditional tourism research curricula. But in the face of growing concern about the sustainability of natural destinations worldwide (UNEPICLEI, 2003), it has become increasingly incumbent upon the tourism researcher to reconceptualise ways of researching and dealing with new local–global challenges, as well as face up to often implicit methodological and theoretical 'biases' in the process — a new ethical moment in research (Lincoln, 1995).

In the Autumn of 2001, a new Philosophy of Social Science course was offered to 14 Masters and PhD level graduate students in a recreation, park and tourism department at a large American university (one was a student from the Education department). Also described as a course on methodological issues, since it raised questions about the assumptions underlying quantitative and qualitative approaches, the syllabus provided a historical and philosophical overview of the natural and social sciences, and included insights into empiricism, logical positivism, post-positivism, critical theory and post-modernism. Most of the class participants saw the world through functionalist paradigms and modernist worldviews and had not yet been exposed to the variety of research paradigms that enrich leisure and tourism studies. None had experienced the challenge of developing critical interpretive scholarship amidst a culture of predominantly quantitative applied research, where the latter has historically been perceived to be more legitimate since it allows for 'objective' research versus the 'subjective' claims mistakenly attributed to the epistemology of the former (see Table 4.1).

At one point the instructor was asked by the students why they needed to understand critical theory – the Frankfurt School's concern with instrumental reason (see below) and post-modernism. Various tacks could be taken to answer such a question, one being to say 'wait and see how the world looks at the end of the course'. Or offer a safe pragmatic response suitable to mainstream tourism research, such as:

> Recognising the global and cultural discourses that shape natural area destinations helps one to identify and better manage areas where tourism-related activities generate unintended consequences.

Alternatively, take a deep breath and plunge into an intellectual debate (hopefully) using a polemic statement such as:

> I/we truly believe that the scholar's subjugation (or reluctant flight to safety)
> in disciplinary settings where applied research and quantitative methods are

Table 4.1: Basic beliefs (metaphysics) of alternative inquiry paradigms.

Item	Positivism	Post-positivism	Critical Theory et al.	Constructivism
Ontology	Naïve realism — 'real' reality but apprehendable	Critical realism — 'real' reality but only imperfectly and probabilistically apprehendable	Historical realism — virtual reality shaped by social, political, cultural, economic, ethnic, and gender values; crystallised over time	Relativism — local and specific constructed realities
Epistemology	Dualist/objectivist; findings true	Modified dualist/objectivist; critical tradition/community; findings probably true	Transactional/subjectivist; value-mediated findings	Transactional/subjectivist; created findings
Methodology	Experimental/manipulative; verification of hypotheses; chiefly quantitative methods	Modified experimental/manipulative; critical multiplism; falsification of hypotheses; may include qualitative methods	Dialogic/dialectical	Hermeneutic/dialectical

Source: Guba and Lincoln, 1998.

favoured over other approaches reflects a struggle for legitimation of the study area and of the social sciences overall. (Rosenau, 1992)

It is a struggle that unfortunately affects both graduate students concerned about future jobs and faculty members climbing tenure-track or other promotional ladders. Since this might not make much sense without theoretical and historical contextualisation, a smarter alternative might be to describe the concerns of critical theorists like those of the Frankfurt School, and to provide illustrative examples, as done below.

The Frankfurt School

Understanding and choosing appropriate research perspectives and paradigms take on even greater significance for nature-based tourism research when juxtaposed against the concerns of the Frankfurt School in the early to mid 20th century. The critical school's roots go back to 1923 and Frankfurt, Germany, where a group at the Institute of Social Research began the development of a body of work that effectively critiqued modern society by linking Marxian, Weberian and other sociological theories. Behind this body of work were the members of what came to be known as the 'Frankfurt School', a group that included Max Horkheimer, Theodor Adorno, Erich Fromm, Herbert Marcuse and, later, Jurgen Habermas. Why this body of work endures is because it does not attribute the problems of the modern world simply to capitalism (as some Orthodox Marxist readings do), but more generally to the growing dominance of instrumental rationalism (Weber's contribution). As Ritzer (1996a) notes, this group saw the future as an 'iron cage' of increasingly rational structures with little hope of escape. Focusing on one particular aspect of Weber's notion of formal rationality, Marcuse (1964) warned that instead of making technology subservient to the needs and well-being of society, modern capitalist society used technology to suppress individuality, critical thinking and inner freedoms, thus creating, in Marcuse's terms a 'one-dimensional society' (Marcuse, 1964).

Horkheimer and Adorno (1979) were particularly concerned about the entrenchment of the scientific view of the world, which they believed had resulted in a domination of nature and culture through the privileging of instrumental reason. Instrumental reason refers to a means–end rationality where objects and events are treated as means to a predetermined end, usually associated with the scientific objective of discovering natural and physical laws, and the modernist project of human progress and economic growth through the applications of scientific knowledge (technology). Aided by the Enlightenment's emphasis on reason and the autonomous, thinking subject (the Cartesian cogito), the subsequent explosion of scientific discoveries and technological advances resulted in increasing discourses of prediction, control and use of the natural world for human ends (Merchant, 1982) and for human recreation (Ritzer, 1996b). Drawing from this, it can be similarly argued that a historically scientific and modernist approach to tourism studies has the double effect of impacting not only the kinds of knowledge being generated in tourism studies, but also the ways in which the natural world is characterised, studied, taught and 'managed' by those who pass through tourism and recreation programmes.

An interesting approach to the study of natural areas lies in the work of a later critical theorist, Jurgen Habermas, who further took up the themes of technological domination and rationalisation. In contrast to the earlier critical theorists, Habermas believes that the Enlightenment project can be fulfilled by ensuring that the public sphere operates freely on the basis of consensus through communicative rationality and communicative action. His fears relate more to the increasing complexity of the modern world, its specialisations, and those forms of governance and knowledge constitution that rely on instrumental reason. Built upon many of the same concerns that occupied the early critical theorists, his theories of the public sphere and of knowledge constitutive interests (Habermas, 1978, 1989) help to identify some of the mechanisms by which public spaces (natural and social) come under the rationalising influences of academic research and scientific management interests.

Elaborating on the relationship between knowledge and human activity, Habermas sets knowledge constitution within the historical material conditions of human society. These have produced a form of knowledge (technical knowledge) and a realm where such knowledge is valourised, i.e. in the system-world. Against this form of knowledge exists practical knowledge and a realm called the life-world (*Lebenswelt*), which is the everyday world of lived experience. Each of these two forms of knowledge is supported by a 'knowledge constitutive interest' and a form of scientific inquiry: 'empirical–analytical science' in the realm of the system-world and 'historical-hermeneutic science' in the realm of the life-world. Problems can and do arise when technical interests are used to influence practical interests so as to create technological control over society. As a consequence, a third form of knowledge, supported by an 'emancipatory interest', is needed. This form, 'critical knowledge', valourises the human capacity for self-reflection, critical apprehension and rational action. The emancipatory interest stands as a necessary corrective element of modernity; it helps identify the contradictions and dialectic tensions that exist between the system-world and life-world. It is in this way that critical inquiry becomes fundamentally necessary inquiry (Table 4.2).

Habermas's 'knowledge constitutive interests' framework provides a useful research strategy for identifying the conflict that occurs between economic, technical, scientific and practical interests in protected areas such as national parks. Potential problems arise when scientific rationalisation (where measurement, monitoring and prediction are dominant discourses) and economic rationalisation (through increasing commodification, control, efficiency and productivity-generating activity) intersect the life-world of people in and around the protected areas. Without participatory opportunities in decision-making and governance of the park's economic and ecological well-being, practical knowledge (e.g. local and indigenous knowledge in this instance) risks becoming marginalised in park management. Life-world rationalisation results when the interests and well-being of the local residents living in and around the park are excluded or delegitimised by technical interests. The rationalisation of park spaces extends, moreover, to control over visitor movement, experience and understandings, which are mediated by a range of interests such as those of park interpreters, park planners and other local–global intermediaries (see next section).

Habermas's works suggest that to the extent that critical research and practical interests are excluded from activities such as interpretation and cultural appreciation, alternative meanings and narratives may remain suppressed, thereby inhibiting the emancipatory potential of national parks as protected places of nature, enabling meaningful interactions between visitors, locals and 'the Others' of the natural world (Berman, 1981). By examining the concerns, focal points and desired outcomes of the respective interests, and reading these against the parks and protected areas literature (e.g. Lowry, 1994; McNeely, 1995; Mott,

Table 4.2: Academic research interests and Habermas's knowledge constitutive interests.

Interest: Research	Technical	Practical	Emancipatory
Research paradigm	(Post) Positivistic	Interpretive	Critical research
Domain	Empirical–analytical sciences	Hermeneutic sciences	Critical, post-structural, post-colonial, feminist, cultural and Marxist studies
Concern	Measuring, modelling and predicting	Experience, meaning and understanding	Marginalised voices and the role of the researcher
Focal point	Systems, variables indicators, causality, certainty	Perceptions, values and beliefs, interpretations	Justice, disciplinary practices, domination, language, identity, resistance, contingency
Desired outcomes	Control, management, reduction of uncertainty	Inclusion of local voices, practical knowledge, experience and insights	Praxis, intervention, change, self-direction, emancipation

Note: This table adapts Habermas (1978) to show how his theory of knowledge constitutive interests relates to academic research interests.

1989; Nelson, Needham, Nelson, & Scace, 1978; Phillips, 1994, 1998), it could be argued that protected areas research is dominated by instrumental–technical reason and the system-world (for exceptions see Brandon, 1997; Ghimire & Pimbert, 1997; Kemp, 1993; Sanderson & Bird, 1998). The following section, therefore, attempts to exhibit the value of bringing a resistant reading or 'emancipatory' interest to research in this area. Yellowstone National Park is used as an example to demonstrate the importance of focusing on textuality, discourse and interests in this study setting. It is not intended to only show that this protected area is a politically and ideologically contested terrain. Rather, such discourses are intended to generate action and change (praxis). For instance, more radical critique might develop in the sociology of knowledge of tourism and recreation through scholarly activity in this area, and praxis-oriented researchers may facilitate the ability of locals and visitors to take a much more active role in managing experiences and activities of living or recreating in these natural spaces.

The Myth of Yellowstone National Park

The inception and development of Yellowstone National Park (USA) can be traced to a number of complex political and cultural factors in the 19th century, such as:

- the need to demonstrate America's political independence from its European roots. This was expressed in part by extolling the grandeur, stability and apparent timelessness of monumental landscapes like Yellowstone, thus providing the new country an opportunity to 'acquire a semblance of antiquity' (Runte, 1987, p. 41);

* cultural insecurity and political anxiety about the accomplishments of the newly established country, and living up to Europe's achievements. As Runte (1987, p. 32) notes, it was not until the discovery of 'landmarks of unquestionable uniqueness' that nationalists felt confident in urging Europeans to heed Thomas Jefferson's advice and visit the New World. Monumentalism thus facilitated cultural independence, cultural nationalism and national pride;
* the emergence of a favourable aesthetic regard of wild places in European intellectual thought (the European Romantic Movement) that emerged subsequent to takeover some of North America's 'howling wilderness' by early European settlers (Hall & Page, 1999);
* economic and railroad interests (like the Northern Pacific Railroad) that used the park's wonders to promote visitation, free enterprise and pioneer settlement in the region; the closing of the American frontier in the late 19th century, which made it imperative that the symbols of free rugged individualism in America be preserved and propagated, such as through protected wilderness environments like the national parks (Nash, 1973); and the scientific authorisation of the US Geological and Geographical Survey of the Territories.

Consider, for instance, the early accounts of one of the respected and well-known heads of the above organisation, Dr Ferdinand V. Hayden. These described Yellowstone in terms of sublime nature tamed by romantic descriptions of a 'Wonderland' whose landscapes were identified and valued by reference to treasures of middle and upper class American life. Yellowstone was 'worthless' for the material well-being of the public in terms of resource exploitation, argued Hayden, but it was vital to society's cultural needs for exotic, romantic nature (Magoc, 1999). The same 'worthlessness' argument had already been instrumental in granting Yosemite and four miles of the Redwoods to California. Additionally, vivid religious metaphors that blanketed its alien wilderness as divine sublimity and invoked responsibility for protecting a supernatural gift helped the passage of the Yellowstone bill into law on 1 March 1872, when President Ulysses S. Grant approved setting Yellowstone 'apart as a public park or pleasureing ground for the benefit and enjoyment of the people' (The Organic Act; cited in Magoc, 1999, p. 19). This protection was clearly necessary in a society where a utilitarian use ethic countered the land's aesthetic value, and necessitated a 'worthless' argument to enable preservation of certain areas (Runte, 1987). In this regard, distinct parallels with the US model could be seen in national park development elsewhere. As Hall and Page (1999, p. 220) point out, these familiar US:

> themes of aesthetic romanticism, recreation and the development of "worthless" or "waste" lands through tourism characterised the creation of the first national parks in Australia, Canada, and New Zealand.

Transatlantic travel and the expansion of the railroads were integrally linked to the development of national parks in the United States and the growth of tourism to these natural landscapes. In the decades following the inception of the park, myths of Yellowstone circulated through various symbolic media that ordered the tourist experience within a set of facts, beliefs and expectations. Certain natural features were identified and established by park officials as sights that merited viewing. Maps, guidebooks and brochures, other guided trips, travel writings and other related texts codified, organised and certified an 'authentic' tourist experience. The strange and picturesque wonders of the park were thus reduced to a subtle domination over nature, for it was particularly important that the stories that attracted visitors contained just the right mix of wildness and familiarity — too much strangeness might dissuade visitation (too dangerous), too little might send them elsewhere (not excit-ing enough). Nineteenth century European travellers, for instance, spent substantial time and money in transatlantic and continental crossings to experience the alluring wildness of the 'Wild West'. They were often courted by imagery that linked the New World to familiar Old World images and nature attractions such as England's Dover Cliffs, in order to make the strange familiar and not so threatening (Figure 4.1). The birth of the tourist guidebook in the 19th century played an important role in this romanticising of Yellowstone to local and European visitors. Like various other promotional materials, it prepared visitors to gaze upon a nature anthropomorphised to represent an American Europe (Figure 4.1). Banished to borderland reservations around the park and relegated to the tourist gaze were the native people who hunted and travelled through this area, for they didn't fit the mod-ern world's emerging needs and notions. Representations of these 'others' included the wild and exotic Noble Savage, a distinct contrast to the righteous and sacred space that constituted Yellowstone in the 19th century public imagination.

By the early 20th century, a new image began to shape this mythical space. It was one of physical and spiritual renewal intertwined with national values of democracy, family life and freedom (Nash, 1973). Yellowstone National Park was now being promoted as a site of estab-lished history and American pride. American identity and social order were reinforced and maintained through controlling the leisure activities and leisure time of the American work-force (Rast, 1998). Such formulations of tourist and civic identification were important in an identity and stability-seeking modern society. The public culture mirage of national life (so that a modern nation-state can exist) is that 'true citizens share common values and a com-mon life' (Horne, 1992, p. 168). Hence, the social constructions of nature in Yellowstone's 'Wonderland' helped to affirm the dynamically constitutive public values and political her-itage of a growing nation. This was carried out historically through the public space of the national park as a destination for local and global visitors, assisted by a range of travel inter-mediaries and symbolic tools. Such constructions and contestations over the park's meaning and use are not easily detected by the tourist, whose movements and learning are closely con-trolled by interpretive and trail management techniques, among other strategies (see, e.g. Peterson, 1988; Wilson, 1992). Neither are they easily visible without critical reflexive schol-arship to identify the discourses that influence use and preservation in these natural areas.

Adopting a cultural-critical approach, such as that of the critical theorists of the Frankfurt School, requires the researcher to view natural area destinations as politically, economi-cally and culturally contested spaces. It facilitates an analysis of how various interests play out in the nature-based domain, and how nature is socially 'constructed' to suit these inter-ests. It permits more sophisticated investigations of issues such as environmental justice and indigenous cultural relationships with the land. A framework of knowledge constitu-tive interests (Table 4.2) is particularly helpful in examining aspects like the role of scien-tific and traditional knowledge in interpreting and managing 'nature' in protected areas, the destination discourses that shape perceptions of Nature and visitor experiences, and how

Figure 4.1: Alice's adventures in the new wonderland. Northern Pacific Railroad. The Yellowstone National Park, Chicago (1884), available at: http://www.library.ubc.ca/spcoll/alice/. *Note*: Like the Northern Pacific Railroad's promotion of 'Wonderland', many other early guidebooks and tourist brochures used this term. As Schullery (2001) notes, the origin of this name has been attributed by some to imitations of Lewis Carroll's book *Alice's Adventures in Wonderland*' (1866). The little girl that Carroll wrote his story for visited Yellowstone National Park as a grownup.

the practical interests of those living and recreating in the life-world of the park may be colonised by economic, political and other interests in the system-world.

The socio-political factors described above also mean that the critical reflexive researcher has to pay close attention to the interrelationships between the global and the local. While any commodity can be understood as a production of signs interpretable in relation to its cultural and socio-political context, tourism is particularly unique as a commodity for it is differentiated in time and space (Lash & Urry, 1994; Mowforth & Munt, 1998). As such, touristic places like the national parks can be appropriated as local–global vehicles for shaping cultural and socio-political meanings. Neuman (1991, p. 30), in his study of Grand Canyon National Park, observed how:

> [a]t a time when moral, social and scientific consensus is shattered by the divergent values and practices of various interests groups, tourist sites stand out as cultural beacons where knowledge, history, and aesthetics seem to be in harmony.

The tourist only sees a few selected elements of the public culture of a nation in a compressed tour itinerary, enough to form some favourable impression of the culture, nationhood or identity of the society or area being visited. Similarly, the tourist on an interpretive tour in Yellowstone experiences a slice of nature, structured for the visitor through social constructions and symbolic translations — but again, which slice? Whose interpretations of nature? As discussed in the final section below, these meanings are partly dependent on the praxis-oriented role of the tourism researcher in the destination domain.

The Critical Reflexive Researcher

The narrative in the previous section indicates that natural sites and protected areas such as Yellowstone National Park are located within a globally institutionalised tourism system where nature is commodified for visual and aesthetic consumption. This paper therefore emphasises the need for a critical cultural approach to studying nature-based destinations. It requires the researcher to resist the rationalisation of the tourism academic's life-world and to engage in research praxis. Adopting a critical research paradigm and approach (such as that of the critical theorists of the Frankfurt School) enables the researcher to oppose 'one-dimensional' packaging of nature and seek a careful interrogation of the phenomenon of tourism itself, and of the philosophical and methodological complexities involved. It necessitates being critically reflexive and action oriented towards (re-)conceptualising what it means to be positioned in this area of study, and how one's research actions and assumptions affect the natural and social world. Some implications of this approach are discussed briefly here.

The Researcher's Own Assumptions

The social construction and post-modern turn in the social sciences raises challenging questions about what constitutes a visitor experience in the natural parks and how that experience is structured by a global tourism industry. It shows that 'Nature' and 'wilderness' in the national parks are contested concepts with multiple meanings and interpretations. This then turns the 'critical' gaze back on to the social and academic domain of the tourism researcher. What are the researcher's own assumptions in relation to Nature and the purpose of the national parks? More specifically, what are the researcher's ontological and epistemological assumptions, and methodological leanings? As Luke (1997, p. 196) points out, every ecocritique (including his):

> becomes an expression of another competing, alternative environmentality with its own new codes of ecoknowledge and systems of geopower, articulating fresh theoretical and practical answers to [one's] respective appraisals of the ecological crisis.

Every researcher makes certain presuppositions and assumptions about nature and human society that influences how the research is conducted and presented, even if they are not voiced or recorded. Scholars trained in the modernist tradition (which includes a large number of leisure and tourism researchers) tend to be metaphysical realists with varied assumptions about the 'nature' of nature, and generally hold foundational assumptions about truth and knowledge.[1] Ontologically, it can be argued that most researchers and practitioners trained in the modernist tradition tend to hold a commonsense, or 'naive', realism about the world of appearance. In this view, Nature is simply there and can be known by 'discovering' the laws of nature. Those holding such a view do not differentiate physical and social realities in a highly sophisticated manner unlike, for instance, Searle (1995), who separates brute facts (e.g. dinosaur extinction) from institutional facts (e.g. socially constructed facts like money, the economy and the stock market). In the case of Yellowstone National Park, understanding the social facts and political context provides insights into park formation, as does understanding the role of the tourism industry in the social construction of nature and the park as a destination area. Unfortunately, the philosophical assumptions of social constructionism and post-modernism also tend to put Nature 'under erasure' (to borrow a term from Derrida). While we debate endlessly about the multiple socially constructed views about Nature, how many species are going extinct every hour? Understanding one's own assumptions and beliefs about Nature is an important aspect of methodological inquiry, for this influences how one studies and interprets natural spaces such as national parks and other protected areas.

Our approach in this paper is situated as a critical-interpretive narrative within Guba and Lincoln's (1998) critical paradigm (Table 4.1). Tables 4.1 and 4.2 indicate that assumptions about human nature and about the external world play an important role in the research paradigm adopted, the preference accorded to 'objective' technical knowledge, and in considering the practical knowledge of local residents in the study area. For instance, in order to be able to take a stance that points out how rationalisation and domination is occurring, critical theorists have to be realists of some ilk, for example, be moral

---

[1]Not surprisingly, a realist view is generally compatible with a foundationalist epistemology of basic, knowable truths. A pure foundationalism such as espoused by Descartes claims that there are fundamental basic beliefs that can be known with certainty and don't require justification, or are self-justified (a priori knowledge). However, for empiricists such as John Locke, basic knowledge is empirical knowledge, known through perceptions only (see Jamal et al., 2002, for a discussion of metaphysical realism in the context of environmental groups and nature in the national parks).

universalists able to say '*x*' is universally wrong. Focused on the task of critique, it may be easy to omit addressing how to make things 'right' (even though praxis is a key component of the critical theory paradigm), or ensure that the researcher's own assumptions and action do not adversely impact those being 'emancipated'. Forms of 'ecological imperialism' occur when nature-based forms of tourism development and promotion 'fail to appreciate the role of social values within sustainable tourism development and the maintenance of biodiversity' (Hall, 1994, p. 141).

Praxis, Resistance and Hermeneutic Charity

A common criticism launched at critical researchers and theorists is that they willingly point out problems and reveal domination and exploitation in a particular domain, but their 'praxis' stops at actions that shake up worldviews and reveal structural (often) and cultural contradictions. In this sense, the critical theorist's worldview may be perceived as being inherently suspicious and disruptive, more inclined to criticise than offer suggestions to mend the problem(s), structures and relationships that may have been disrupted through the critical inquiry. An important question thus emerges from this criticism of domination and rationalisation theses. How can instrumentally oriented local and global discourses that structure natural-cultural destinations like Yellowstone National Park be resisted or altered? Since many critical theorists believe that ideology 'interpellates' the subject (Althusser, 1984), they may be inclined to treat human beings as having little ability to resist rationalisation and domination. Yet, local action and new social movements worldwide indicate that agency and change in these areas are possible and do occur, as Harvey (1998) points out.

Drawing from the concerns of the critical theorists discussed earlier and the above discussion suggests that careful attention must be paid to ensure that economically and sociopolitically driven interests in the system-world do not dominate practical interests in the natural world, in the everyday life-world of modern human societies, and in the academic world. One avenue by which life-world colonisation may be interrupted is through a critical interpretive praxis where change occurs through active intervention and disruption of dominant discourses, both in the academic world and the social world of practice. However, in light of the criticism of critical research noted above, two actions may be particularly helpful to ensure that hermeneutic charity is exercised in the task of critical interpretation and praxis: (1) Interdisciplinary scholarship and being open to the rich variety of theoretical and methodological approaches by which the complex ecopolitics of natural destinations may be addressed, and (2) Engaging participants in the academic life-world (e.g. students) and in the natural-cultural life-world (e.g. those who live in and around Yellowstone, if that was the study area) in dialogue and meaning-making about social research and the outcomes of the research. Such participatory action may also play a useful role in reconceptualising new localised ethics of place and space, such as bioregional narratives (Cheney, 1986). Hermeneutic interpretive approaches are sometimes dismissed by critical theorists like Habermas as being too trusting, lacking in appreciation of the power-related issues by which language can be used to control human behaviours and practices. Somewhere between these two poles, however, lies the role of the ethical researcher who attempts to bring hermeneutic charity to the critical gaze. It is a critical gaze, but a sensitive one, which disrupts the domination of instrumental rationality and retrieves these diminishing public spaces for meaningful human interactions with the natural world.

Epilogue

The first offering of a Philosophy of Science course for graduate students in a department of recreation, park and tourism 'sciences' in North America took place in the Autumn of 2001. It challenged the students to take a long hard look at their own philosophical and methodological assumptions. It was a theory-heavy course, but the intensive dialogue and reflection that occurred suggest that theory and critique did not colonise the life-world of course participants. Several wondered aloud why they had never learned previously about the historical and philosophical issues surrounding the statistic methods they had been taught to use in the past. One with firm post-positivistic views subsequently took a course in social theory elsewhere on campus and chose a challenging cultural study for his dissertation. The semester ended with another challenge to the 14 Masters and PhD level students: to bake a meaningful social research cake with the kaleidoscope of ingredients presented in the course (Figure 4.2). The required final report offered an opportunity to struggle with the social researcher's self. What is the purpose of social research (understanding, explanation, intervention and praxis)? How does one engage in it in a way that does justice to the topic and the life-world of research? What is the role of 'theory', since its meaning in science includes the laws governing physical phenomena, hence tending towards generalisation, prediction and control of the natural world?

The post-modern critique of grand theories and universal truths also raises new issues with respect to research practices. One issue is how to engage in post-modern critique without eschewing the ethical, both with respect to the researcher and the social world — ethical

Figure 4.2: The social research 'cake' in a philosophy of social science class in the Autumn of 2001.

action, conduct and interventions for a sustainable society and sustainable world. Another is how to manage the tensions between the universal and the particular in developing theoretical and practical understandings of the globalised economy and ecology of the nature tourism production system. Since 9/11, a number of social researchers are soul-searching about the possible failures of social science research, and:

> about ways in which a radically reformulated social science directed toward communitarian ethics and social justice might address our understanding of this horror. . . . (Denzin & Lincoln, 2002, p. 133)

Perhaps part of the answer lies in those places where educators, researchers, students and the general public fail to engage in critical reflection and participatory praxis. A good start may lie in the local and the particular, with questioning our intellectual traditions, our research methodologies and relationships to the natural and social communities that constitute the 'subject' of tourism studies. There is an omnipresent need to challenge taken-for-granted assumptions, whether these concern 'development' and 'progress', or, in the case of natural area destinations, 'nature as commodity' and 'nature as object to be controlled'.

So where do we go from here? Each one of us must pick our own pathways, and every research activity imposes an ethical responsibility on us as researchers and practitioners in the tourism domain. If the question is, how does one proceed with hermeneutic charity to being a critical scholar, the discussion above would suggest that we reflexively (1) examine how we view 'Nature' and conduct tourism research, (2) understand the historical antecedents to methods and methodologies of social sciences, and the recent intrusions of alternative research approaches and (3) engage in critical but charitable praxis. In this paper we have argued for incorporating such a critical and charitable perspective to bring practical wisdom into the theoretical and methodological lore of scholarship pertaining to natural area destinations.

> We shall not cease from exploration
> And the end of all our exploring
> Will be to arrive where we started
> And know the place for the first time.
>   (T.S. Elliot, *Four Quartets*)

Acknowledgements

We thank those who supported the publishing of this non-traditional research narrative. It offers hope for alternative discourses and ways to conceptualise social research in the context of tourism studies. We also thank Multilingual Matters for permission to reprint this article, which originally appeared in *Current Issues in Tourism*, 7(1), pp. 1–19, 2004.

References

Althusser, L. (1984). *Essays on ideology*. London: Verso.
Berman, M. (1981). *The reenchantment of the world*. Ithaca, NY and London: Cornell University Press.

Brandon, K. (1997). Policy and practical considerations in land-use strategies for biodiversity con-servation. In: R. Kramer, C. V. Schaik, & J. Johnson (Eds), *Last stand: Protected areas and the defence of tropical biodiversity* (pp. 90–114). New York: Oxford University Press.

Britton, S. (1991). Tourism, capital and place: Towards a critical geography of tourism. Environment and Planning D. *Society and Space, 9,* 451–478.

Cheney, J. (1986). Postmodern environmental ethics: Ethics as bioregional narrative. *Environmental Ethics, 11,* 117–134.

Denzin, N. K., & Lincoln, Y. S. (1994). Introduction: Entering the field of qualitative research. In: N. K. Denzin, & Y .S. Lincoln (Eds), *Handbook of qualitative research.* Thousand Oaks, CA: Sage.

Denzin, N. K., & Lincoln, Y. S. (2002). Editors' introduction: Special partial issue — Qualitative inquiry and the events following September 11, 2001. *Qualitative Inquiry, 8*(2), 133–134.

Echtner, C., & Jamal, T. (1997). The disciplinary dilemma of tourism studies. *Annals of Tourism Research, 24,* 868–883.

Foucault, M. (1980). *Power/knowledge: Selected interviews and other writings.* New York: Pantheon.

Ghimire, K. B., & Pimbert, M. P. (Eds) (1997). *Social change and conservation: Environmental pol-itics and the impacts of national parks and protected area.* London: Earthscan.

Grano, O. (1981). External influence and internal change in the development of geography. In: D. R. Stoddart (Ed.), *Geography, ideology and social concern* (pp. 17–36). Oxford: Blackwell.

Guba, E. G., & Lincoln, Y. S. (1998). Competing paradigms in qualitative research. In: N. K. Denzin, & Y. S. Lincoln (Eds), *The landscape of qualitative research* (pp. 195–220). Thousand Oaks, CA: Sage.

Habermas, J. (1978). *Knowledge and human interests* (2nd ed.). Boston: Beacon.

Habermas, J. (1989). *The structural transformation of the public sphere: An inquiry into a category of bourgeois society* (6th ed.). Cambridge, MA: MIT.

Hall, C. M. (1994). Ecotourism in Australia, New Zealand and the South Pacific: Appropriate tourism or a new form of ecological imperialism? In: E. Cater, & G. Lowman (Eds), *Ecotourism: A sus-tainable option?* (pp. 137–158). Chichester, UK: Wiley.

Hall, C. M., & Page, S. J. (1999). *The geography of tourism and recreation: Environment, space and place.* London and New York: Routledge.

Harvey, D. (1998). What's green and makes the environment go round? In: F. Jameson, & M. Miyoshi (Eds), *The cultures of globalization.* Durham and London: Duke University Press.

Horkheimer, M., & Adorno, T. W. (1979). *Dialectic of enlightenment.* New York: Continuum.

Horne, D. (1992). *The intelligent tourist.* Smithfield, NSW: Margaret Gee.

Jafari, J. (2001). The scientification of tourism. In: V. L. Smith, & M. Brent (Eds), *Hosts and guests revisited: Tourism issues of the 21st century* (pp. 28–41). New York: Cognizant communication.

Jamal, T., & Hollinshead, K. (2000). Tourism and the forbidden zone: The underserved power of qualitative research. *Tourism Management, 22,* 63–82.

Kemp, E. (1993). *The law of the mother: Protecting indigenous peoples in protected areas.* San Francisco, CA: Sierra Club.

Kincheloe, J. L. (2001). Describing the bricolage: Conceptualizing a new rigor in qualitative research. *Qualitative Inquiry, 7,* 679–692.

Lash, S., & Urry, J. (1994). *Economies of science and space.* London: Sage.

Lincoln, Y. S. (1995). The sixth moment: Emerging problems in qualitative research. *Studies in Symbolic Interaction, 19,* 37–55.

Lowry, W. R. (1994). *The capacity for wonder: Preserving national parks.* Washington, DC: Brookings Institution.

Luke, T. W. (1997). *Ecocritique: Contesting the politics of nature, economy, and culture.* Minneapolis, MN: University of Minnesota Press.

Macbeth, D. (2001). On 'reflexivity' in qualitative research: Two readings, and a third. *Qualitative Inquiry, 7,* 35–68.

Magoc, C. J. (1999). *Yellowstone: The creation and selling of an American landscape*. Albuquerque: University of New Mexico Press.

Marcuse, H. (1964). *One-dimensional man*. Boston: Beacon.

McNeely, J. (1995). Partnerships for conservation: How to expand public support for protected areas. In: J. McNeely (Ed.), *Expanding partnerships in conservation* (pp. 1–12). Washington, DC: Island Press.

Merchant, C. (1982). *The death of nature: Women, ecology, and the scientific revolution*. San Francisco, CA: Harper and Row.

Moring, I. (2001). Detecting the fictional problem solvers in time and space: Metaphors guiding qualitative inquiry analysis and interpretation. *Qualitative Inquiry*, 7, 346–369.

Mott, W. P. (1989). National parks: Year 2000. *National Parks*, 18–19.

Mowforth, M., & Munt, I. (1998). *Tourism and sustainability in the third world*. London: Routledge.

Nash, R. (1973). *Wilderness and the American mind* (1st ed.). New Haven: Yale University Press.

Nelson, J. G., Needham, R. D., Nelson, S. H., & Scace, R. C. (1978). Proceedings of the Canadian National Parks: Today and Tomorrow II Conference. In: J. G. Nelson, R. D. Needham, S. H. Nelson, & R. C. Scace (Eds), *Conference proceedings*. Waterloo: University of Waterloo.

Neuman, M. (1991). *Tourism and American culture: A study of the meanings of leisure travel at grand canyon National park*. Unpublished PhD Thesis, University of Utah, Salt Lake City.

Peterson, T. (1988). The meek shall inherit the mountains: Dramatistic criticism of grand Teton National Park's interpretive program. *Central State Speech Journal*, 39(2), 121–133.

Phillips, A. (1994). *Protected areas*. UNESCO Environmental Education Dossiers.

Phillips, A. (1998). Working landscapes and protected areas for the 21st century. In: N. W. P. Munro, & J. H. M. Wilson (Eds), *Proceedings of third international conference on science and management of protected areas: Linking protected areas with working landscapes/conserving biodiversity*. Wolfville, Canada, pp. 3–17.

Rast, R. W. (1998). Vistas, visions, and visitors: Creating the myth of Yellowstone National Park, 1872–1915. *JOW*, 37, 80–89.

Riley, R. W., & Love, L. L. (2000). The state of qualitative tourism research. *Annals of Tourism Research*, 27, 164–187.

Ritzer, G. (1996a). *Modern sociological theory* (4th ed.). McGraw Hill: New York.

Ritzer, G. (1996b). *The McDonaldization of society: An investigation into the changing character of contemporary life* (revised ed.). Thousand Oaks, CA: Pine Forge.

Rosenau, P. M. (1992). *Postmodernism and the social sciences: insights, inroads and intrusions*. Princeton, NJ: Princeton University.

Runte, A. (1987). *National parks: The American experience* (2nd ed.). Lincoln and London: University of Nebraska Press.

Sanderson, S. E., & Bird, S. (1998). The new politics of protected areas. In: K. Brandon, K. H. Redford, & S. E. Sanderson (Eds), *Parks in peril* (pp. 441–454). Washington, DC: Island.

Schullery, P. (2001). Privations and inconveniences: Early tourism in Yellowstone National Park. In: D. M. W. Wrobel, & P. T. Long (Eds), *Seeing and being seen: Tourism in the American west* (pp. 227–247). Lawrence: University Press of Kansas.

Searle, J. (1995). *The construction of social reality*. New York: Free Press.

Stone, R. D., & D'Andrea, C. (2001). *Tropical forests and the human spirit*. Berkeley and Los Angeles: University of California Press.

Tribe, J. (1997). The indiscipline of tourism. *Annals of Tourism Research*, 24, 637–657.

United Nations Environment Programme (UNEP) and International Council for Local Environmental Initiatives (ICLEI) (2003). Tourism and Local Agenda 21: The Role of Local Authorities in Sustainable Tourism. Paris: United Nations.

Usher, R. (1996). *Understanding educational research*. London: Routledge.

Wang, N. (2000). *Tourism and modernity: A sociological analysis*. Amsterdam: Pergamon.

Weissinger, E., Henderson, K. A., & Bowling, C. P. (1997). Towards and expanding methodological base in leisure studies: Researchers' knowledge, attitudes and practices concerning qualitative research. *Society and Leisure, 20*, 435–451.

Wilson, A. (1992). *The culture of nature: North American landscape from Disney to the exxon valdez*. Cambridge, MA: Blackwell.

World Commission on Environment and Development (WCED). (1987). *Our common future*. New York: Oxford University Press.

Chapter 5

Marking Difference or Making a Difference: Constructing Places, Policies and Knowledge of Inclusion, Exclusion and Social Justice in Leisure, Sport and Tourism*

Cara Carmichael Aitchison

Introduction

I thought it would be useful, first, to try and explain where the rather long title for this talk came from. In many ways it is a reflection of me and my multiple disciplinary and subject field backgrounds and interests: geographers speak of places, sociologists speak of social policies, educationalists speak of knowledge construction and I have spent over 20 years in higher education as a student, teacher and researcher working across these disciplinary boundaries and relating these disciplinary perspectives to the developing subject fields of leisure studies, sport studies and tourism studies. But perhaps the words that are most asso-ciated with my work are those of inclusion, exclusion and social justice reflecting the nature of my research which acknowledges leisure, sport and tourism as a series of two-faced coins.

On one side we are able to see the exclusionary nature of these contemporary cultural forms and on the other we can view the ways in which these cultural sites and processes can be harnessed as mechanisms through which the policy objectives of inclusion and social justice can be pursued. Thus my research has focussed on how we move beyond *marking difference* through exclusionary identities, places, policies and practices to *making*

* This text is the unedited version of my Inaugural Professorial Lecture presented at the University of the West of England, Bristol on 10th July 2006. The lecture marked the launch of the Bristol UWE Research Centre for Leisure, Tourism and Society (CeLTS) and took place on the eve of the 31st Annual Leisure Studies Association Conference, *Making Space: Leisure, Tourism and Renewal* hosted by Bristol UWE. I am deeply grateful to everyone who attended the lecture, the research cen-tre launch and the conference, to those who have supported my journeys towards these destinations and to those who have 'made a difference' in leisure, sport and tourism theory, policy and practice.

a difference through inclusive ways of knowing and ways of being. In a world where difference is increasingly marked by patterns of consumption rather than modes of production, leisure, sport and tourism have become key markers of economic, social and cultural capital formation shaping identities of class, nation, ethnicity, religion, race, gender, disability, age and all of the myriad intersections between these identities.

Following this introduction I seek to provide a brief contextualisation of policy developments and theoretical perspectives informing my research. I then want to offer a more personal contextualisation that situates me within the research process by acknowledging my own subjectivity, history and research journey. The talk then focuses on three specific research case studies selected to provide illustrative examples of the efficacy of 'the social–cultural nexus' as a conceptual framework for understanding inclusion, exclusion and social justice in leisure, sport and tourism. The first case study explores leisure and disability, the second gender and sport in the UK and Iran and the third gender and tourism studies including the intersections between gender, race and ethnicity.

Policy Context

Within the UK, economic poverty, relative deprivation and lack of social and cultural capital inform leisure, sport and tourism participation and non-participation. Two-thirds of adults in England do not take sufficient exercise to maintain health, there has been little increase in women's participation in sport and physical activity over the last ten years and, at intensive levels, the gap between women and men's participation is greater in the UK than in any other European county (Sport England and UK Sport, 1999). For children, obesity has not only become, as one of my students rather unfortunately put it in a recent exam paper, 'a growing problem' but also, more seriously, is a reflection of low levels of physical activity and poor diet. Turning from sport to tourism, almost 40% of the UK population does not take at least one holiday each year and half of this group never takes a holiday, reflecting levels of inequality that have changed little during my lifetime (Corlyon & La Placa, 2006).

At an international scale, tourism is of critical importance to developing countries that already account for almost half of all global international tourist arrivals (Pro-Poor Tourism Partnership, 2004). Twelve of the world's countries are home to 80% of the world's poor and international tourism is growing in all these countries (Department for International Development, 1999). Virtually all of these countries now have national tourism development strategies focusing on promoting economic growth and increasing foreign exchange earnings, but often without specifically considering the social, cultural or environmental impacts of tourism or taking the needs of the poor into account — a strategic approach that has become known as 'pro-poor tourism' (Ashley, Boyd, & Goodwin, 2000).

Recognition of the role of leisure, sport and tourism in addressing social exclusion has been slow to be realised within UK domestic public policy and in overseas development policy (Botterill & Klemm, 2005). While many other Western European countries have a long tradition of ministries of culture, the UK Department for Culture, Media and Sport (which includes tourism) is still less than 10 years old and does not enjoy the levels of budget, research funding, prime ministerial support or media attention that other cabinet portfolios benefit from. The Social Exclusion Unit, formed shortly after New Labour first came to power in 1997, included sport and the arts as one of the 18 Policy Action Teams established in an attempt to tackle social exclusion (Collins, 2003; Department for Culture, Media and Sport, 1999; Social Exclusion Unit, 1998). However, the approach adopted tended to equate exclusion with economic poverty, losing sight of exclusion as a relational rather than a distributive concept and failing to recognise sufficiently that social exclusion can be experienced materially as economic poverty *and* culturally as prejudice, discrimination, fear and/or hatred of the other (Commins, 1993; Knight & Brent, 1998; Room, 1995).

My work has been concerned with the interplay between these different forms of exclusion, the ways in which the material and cultural intersect and interact to form exclusionary practices and discourses, and how we might move from the identification of the negative ways in which difference is marked to positive ways in which difference can be made. I am interested in how we develop links between theory and practice to create theoretically informed practice, what feminists have previously referred to as 'praxis' and how, as Fred Coalter has recently suggested, we move from developing 'cultural services in communities' to 'developing communities through cultural services' (Coalter, 2004; Stanley, 1990).

Theoretical Context

My research has drawn on structuralist and post-structuralist accounts of gender, leisure, sport and tourism in recognition of the interconnections between social and cultural relations and their respective material and symbolic representations of power. I have articulated this accommodation of the social and the cultural through the conceptualisation of 'the social–cultural nexus' (Aitchison, 2000a, 2003a, 2005a, 2005b). The social–cultural nexus is explained as both a site and a process of construction, legitimation, reproduction and reworking of power relations where power is inherently related to identity. This linking of the social and the cultural within sociology has, as Mary Evans (2003, p. 69) pointed out, 'persuaded many people that social life is now organised and regulated through culture' thus serving to disrupt the rather dualistic late 20th century discourse between the social sciences, with their primary concern with economic production, and the humanities with their greater focus on cultural consumption.

Within tourism studies the turn to culture can, in part, be attributed to the influence of recent social and cultural geographies with their commensurate underpinning of post-structural theory. In geography, this shifting emphasis from the material to the cultural followed Peter Jackson's (1989) proclamation that a 'new' cultural geography was required. Cultural geography had, since the 1920s, been strongly associated with the work of Carl Sauer and the Berkeley School who were interested in the ways in which culture shaped landscape to create 'cultural landscapes'. By the 1960s, however, the Chicago School of urban geographers were turning their attention to urban culture, everyday culture and sub-cultures in attempts to make sense of the spatially constructed but socially regulated dimensions and impacts of culture with their work informed by the increasingly dominant Marxist and neo Marxist sociological perspectives developed by the Frankfurt School and others.

We can look to these developments of cultural and critical theory from the 1920s to the 1980s as encompassing a series of perspectives that sought to examine the relationships *between* cultural or symbolic *and* economic or material forms of power. Such theory has formed the basis of the structural Marxism of Althusser, the Marxian humanism of Adorno and Marcuse of the Frankfurt School, the critical theory of Habermas and Anthony Giddens' theory of structuration, all pointing to the inter-relationships between material power, ideology and cultural conditions (Aitchison, 2003b).

By the late 1980s the UK was experiencing a period of increasing cultural consumption in relation to both the materiality and symbolism of new forms of leisure, sport and tourism. The new social and cultural geographies of the 1990s began to rework earlier geographical perspectives with the sociological analyses of Bourdieu (1984), de Certeau (1984), Foucault (1977) and others offering insights into the role of cultural capital, productive consumption and the power of surveillance, respectively. Similarly, in sociology, and reflecting the increasing proximity of sociology and geography since the 1990s, Michelle Barrett's (1992) assertion that the 'turn to culture' signalled the 'decimation of the claims of materialism', whilst rather polemic, nonetheless offered new scope for the development of cultural theory where previously critical theory held sway. This turn to culture signalled a discursive shift from tourism management to tourism studies and, by the late 1990s, could be seen in a series of publications addressing leisure and tourism as predominantly cultural phenomena.

However, by the turn of the 21st century a number of writers were urging caution in the wholesale adoption of the cultural over the social or the post-structural over the material. Mary Evans, in 2003, for example, pleaded that 'If the "cultural turn" means anything, it must, I would argue, mean that as much as studying culture as an object, we also integrate the understandings offered to us by culture in our accounts of the social world'. In social geography a similar plea had been made by Liz Bondi, in 1992, when she urged against prioritising the cultural over the social or the 'unharnessing of the symbolic and the sociological' and this was reiterated almost a decade later by Gill Valentine, in 2001, who asked 'Whatever happened to the social?' in a paper exploring the impact of 'The "cultural turn" in British human geography'.

In addition to stressing the dangers of neglecting the social such discussions have emphasised the importance of maintaining the dual influences of the social and the cultural, the material and the symbolic, and the social sciences and the humanities in analyses of leisure, sport and tourism; sites, forms and processes which are themselves both social *and* cultural phenomena.

Auto-Ethnography

It has become customary within the right of passage, that is the inaugural lecture, to reveal something of the self. As someone who is known to be fairly private, both professionally and personally, this represents something of a challenge. Nonetheless, the writing of this talk has provided an opportunity to reflect on where it all began. I reckon it was somewhere around the age of eight when I was challenged by schoolmates and teachers as to why I played football with my neighbours — three boys, Philip, Paul and David. You might think this challenge to my sporting practice came because I was displaying inappropriate gender behaviour or, indeed, because playing with boys would mark me as a tom boy or 'even worse'. Neither of these markers of identity as gender or sexuality were what provoked this challenge. Instead, my behaviour was challenged on the grounds of religion — all the more curious as I was not actually aware that I had a religion as none of my extended family appeared to practise any religious belief. The religious or sectarian conflict was assumed as our football team was mixed catholic and protestant, and in 1970s central Scotland there was little mixing of the two religions.

Whilst religion was marked locally by educational segregation, social class was marked by spatial segregation. The natural geographical divide of a small river, or what we called a 'burn', marked those who lived on 'this side of the burn' as 'middle class' and those who lived on the other side 'across the burn', as working class with limited mixing between the two communities even though we all attended the same school.

The following year, 1974 and aged nine to be precise, I became a feminist. Having established my credentials as a footballer the boys at my own school wanted me to play centre forward in the school team; a position which I, rather immodestly, thought I rightly deserved. Interestingly, it was the women staff that quickly put a stop to my footballing ambitions and the male janitor who offered the substitution of a girls' team which he would manage and I would captain. This proposal, again, was quickly stopped by the women teachers and my footballing days drew to a close as my feminist awakening dawned.

Having encountered the uneven playing field of identity politics of religion, social class and gender at a young age, my own experience of disability then fell upon me suddenly and dramatically when at the age of 21 and entering my fourth and final year at Edinburgh University I went from being university basketball captain, keen cyclist, canoeist, hill walker, swimmer, full-time top class student, part-time paid worker and weekend party-goer to someone with Myalgic Encephalomyelitis or ME and all its crippling manifestations. After four months the illness resulted in my having to move back to my parents' house as I could no longer climb the stairs to my apartment nor had the strength or energy to shop, cook or clean let alone study. It was a rude awakening, was to by part of my every-day life (although often felt like a living death) for the next twelve years, by which time it had officially been defined as a disability, and demonstrated all too clearly how we con-struct identities around how we appear and what we do rather than who we are and how we are. Having gained a sponsored place on a post-graduate course in recreation and leisure practice at the time of the onset of the illness my own ambition (or perhaps fantasy) of establishing Scotland's first outdoor pursuits centre for women was clearly in tatters and I turned my attention instead to the 'desk job' of leisure theory.

I now want to move on a decade from 1988 and introduce the first of the three case stud-ies that serve to illustrate aspects of my research.

Case Study One: Leisure (Young People, Disability and Social Exclusion in Leisure)

Between 1999 and 2003, and undoubtedly influenced by my own personal experience, I developed a series of publications exploring the nature of the relationship between disabil-ity and leisure, and disability studies and leisure studies (Aitchison, 2000b, 2001a, 2003b) This research examined the nature of exclusion within a wider framework of social justice and, echoing the work of other disability researchers adopting a social model of disability, demonstrated that in addition to material forms of exclusion relating to physical access and economic resources disabled people also encountered forms of cultural exclusion relating to attitude, fear, prejudice and discrimination (Davis, 2000; Humphrey, 2000; Oliver & Barnes, 1998). Where exclusion seemed most embedded was where these two forms of exclusionary power relations (material and symbolic) co-existed at the nexus of the social and the cultural.

My initial disability research was based on an empirical study titled: *Disability and Social Inclusion: Leisure, Sport and Culture in the Lives of Young Disabled People* conducted with Scope, the UK's largest disability organisation, and undertaken following recognition of the limited amount of data and fragmented knowledge base relating to the leisure experiences of young people with cerebral palsy (Aitchison, 2000c). The purpose of the research was to provide data, analysis and recommendations to inform future leisure provision and advocacy by Scope and other disability and leisure organisations. The research took the form of a regional study in Scope's West Country Partnership Area and aimed to map the place of leisure in the lives of young disabled people aged 11–15 and those who care for them.

The study combined the use of quantitative and qualitative methods in an attempt to generate data that would elicit details of the type, frequency and meaning of leisure. A combination of leisure diaries (for which I would like to acknowledge the input of Professor Celia Brackenridge) and focus groups held at a specially organised leisure event in an Exeter hotel was employed. The young people all had cerebral palsy and levels of disability ranged from moderate to severe: more than half of the group used walking aids or wheelchairs; the majority had moderate to severe speech difficulties; and the minority required assistance in writing their leisure diary.

Each research project brings unexpected results, not necessarily in terms of the data that are generated, but in relation to the research process, the interactions with research participants and events that happen, planned and otherwise, along the way. This project was no exception and on the Monday following the weekend focus groups and leisure activities I arrived at my office to see my answer phone flashing as if on red alert. I began to play the messages and listened to parent after parent tell me how their son or daughter had had such a wonderful time engaging in the leisure activities we had laid on and in meeting the other young people. This would be all well and good except that each message ended with the same story — that the son or daughter had not stopped talking about the event and kept asking when they would be going to the next one. It was a lesson for me in the power of the researcher and the danger in raising expectations through the research process, something that my colleagues in development studies have long been familiar with.

There were four main findings from the research. First, the young disabled people shared many of the same leisure priorities as their non-disabled counterparts. Second, the majority of leisure activities comprised informal everyday leisure with an overwhelming emphasis on electronic leisure media. Third, patterns of leisure participation differed between disabled and non-disabled young people in the amount rather than type of leisure participation and, fourth, the greatest variation between disabled and non-disabled leisure experiences was in the social circumstances surrounding participation. This was illustrated by young disabled people's tendency to participate in leisure on their own or with their parents rather than with friends or siblings. For example, during the course of the two-week diary-keeping exercise, the young disabled people averaged only one visit to or from a friend and those in mainstream schools were also more likely to spend break times on their own than with friends. In their leisure diaries the young people recorded activities such as physiotherapy and homework. Indeed the findings demonstrated that, on average, the young people made four times as many visits to physiotherapists as they did to friends during the diary-keeping period.

Disability and disabled people have been rendered largely invisible from leisure studies, which is perhaps surprising given that the central axis of UK leisure studies is an established discourse addressing the leisure lives of people deemed to be peripheral, marginal or excluded from leisure provision, participation and consumption. There are at least three explanations for this: the orthodox origins of leisure studies as a subject field; the dominance of particular and hegemonic models of disability used in leisure research; and the maintenance of conventional, and perhaps outmoded, definitions of leisure within the leisure studies literature (Aitchison, 2001a).

The origins of leisure studies can be traced to a number of disciplines and subject fields that experienced increasing status within the academy during the 1960s and 1970s. Three multi-disciplinary areas in particular played an important role in the formation of leisure studies in the UK where the sociology of work, physical education and human movement studies, and the geography of urban planning and countryside recreation were largely responsible for the development of the leisure studies canon. All three areas, however, have left an unwitting legacy from which disability and disabled people appear peripheral. The sociology of work has reified the employed body, physical education and human movement studies have valorised the able body and the orthodox aesthetic body, and urban planning and countryside recreation have emphasised the active body, the mobile body and the sighted body.

In disability studies, two explanatory models have dominated the discourse of the last twenty years: the medical model and the social model, with the medical model dominating in the field of sport science. But both critical and post-structural theories have begun to question this dualised juxtaposition of the medical and the social. Moreover, Paul Abberley (1997) cautions against the adoption of a simple materialist social model that fails to problematise the cultural and symbolic nature of oppression. In recognising the need to expand the social model to accommodate diversity of experience Tom Shakespeare and Nick Watson (1997, p. 271) suggest that

> the dominant version of the social model has favoured a materialist, if not Marxist, worldview. We argue it is possible (and indeed desirable), to retain the social model within a more nuanced worldview drawing on feminist and post-modernist discourse.

Defining leisure has preoccupied leisure scholars since the inception of the subject field. Because it is more often defined residually by what it is not than by what it actually is, leisure remains an elusive concept. Conventional definitions of leisure have focused on when people take part in leisure (leisure time), where leisure participation takes place (leisure spaces), what people do in their leisure (leisure activities), what purpose their leisure serves (leisure function) and the degree to which their leisure is freely chosen (leisure freedom).

For the young disabled people involved in the study, the findings demonstrated that leisure was not defined so much by when they took part, what they did or where their leisure took place, but by who they encountered and interacted with as part of their leisure.

Case Study Two: Sport (Gender and Sport Policy and Management in the UK and Iran)

From 1992 to 2004 I was involved in extensive research on gender and sport and leisure policy in the UK and, lately, in other countries particularly in the Middle East and specifically Iran (Aitchison, 2000a, 2005, 2006a). This work started with research that forecast and then critiqued the gendered impact of the introduction of Compulsory Competitive Tendering (contracting out or privatisation) within local authority sport and leisure services in the UK in the late 1980s (Aitchison, 1992, 1994, 1997).

This second case study seeks to outline my critical analysis of gender relations in sport and leisure management by developing a theoretical critique of gender (in)equity that integrates both social theory or earlier socialist feminist theory with cultural analyses or poststructural theory. This theoretical account was constructed inductively following the analysis of empirical data gathered in a national study of *Gender Equity in Leisure Management* conducted in 1999. Deductive analysis was then applied to similar research undertaken by others in Australia, New Zealand, Canada and the United States, demonstrating that gender–power relations in sport and leisure management are frequently produced, legitimated, reproduced and reworked at the intersection of the social and cultural, or in the social–cultural nexus of organisations (Bialeschki & Henderson, 1984, 2000; Frisby & Brown, 1991; Henderson & Bialeschki, 1993, 1995; McKay, 1996; Messner, 2002; Shinew & Arnold, 1998).

In 1998, the Institute of Leisure and Amenity Management (ILAM) commissioned a research project titled *Gender Equity in Leisure Management* and I would like to acknowledge both Professor Celia Brackenridge and Dr Fiona Jordan for their contributions to this project. The research employed a combination of quantitative and qualitative data capture methods including a questionnaire of all women members of ILAM, secondary research relating to leisure management, secondary research relating to gender equity in other service sector industries, and qualitative research in the form of individual interviews with middle and senior women leisure managers not in membership of ILAM or whose membership had lapsed.

Although there had been an increase from 568 women members in 1991 to 1151 in 1998, the respondents to the ILAM survey still testified to isolation, discrimination and harassment within the organisational culture of sport and leisure management. The characteristics of sport and leisure services include their association with informality, sociability, alcohol and different states of dress and undress. Indeed, from all areas of leisure services sport was singled out as the area where women experienced most discrimination and harassment as a result of what sport sociologists such as Jim McKay have termed 'corporate masculinity' and Mike Messner has termed the 'locker room culture' of masculinity prevalent in sport. Moreover, in spite of the increasing number of women entering junior management, there remained evidence of a 'glass ceiling' within the industry. Whilst many structural inequalities had been addressed, the glass ceiling appeared to have been maintained by cultural constraints or the interplay between the remaining structural constraints and cultural constraints which had yet to be recognised and/or addressed. These constraints were identified in organisational cultures, the implementation of equal opportunities policies and practices and the culture surrounding career appraisal and progression opportunities.

At the same time as I was undertaking this research I was also working up some theoretical writing on gender and tourism in which I was employing not only post-structural analysis but also post-colonial theory and which I will return to in the third case study. In 2002 these two paths of post-structuralism and post-colonialism converged when I was invited to undertake a lecture tour of Iran in February and March 2003. The tour was sponsored by the Iranian Ministry of Culture and Islamic Guidance, the Iranian National Tourism Organisation, the Iranian National Olympic Committee and the Iranian Women's Sport Foundation and I am grateful to those organisations and to Dr Mohammad Eshani for making the tour possible. I returned to Iran in December 2003 following my move to Bristol UWE, and both visits will, I hope, lead to further co-operation and to research partly supported by the World Leisure and Recreation Association which has long campaigned for leisure, sport and culture to be viewed as human rights. World Leisure has worked with both the UN and UNESCO to develop leisure and the UN has enshrined leisure within both the Universal Declaration of Human Rights and the Convention on the Elimination of All Forms of Discrimination Against Women:

> Everyone has the right to rest and leisure, including reasonable limitation of working hours and periodic holidays with pay (Article 24: UN Universal Declaration of Human Rights).

> Everyone has the right freely to participate in the cultural life of the community, to enjoy the arts and to share in scientific advancement and its benefits (Article 27: UN Universal Declaration of Human Rights).

> Parties shall take all appropriate measures to eliminate discrimination against women in other areas of economic and social life in order to ensure, on a basis of equality of men and women, the same rights, in particular:. . . c) The right to participate in recreational activities, sports and all aspects of cultural life (Article 13: UN Convention on the Elimination of All Forms of Discrimination Against Women).

Explanations of non-participation in sport and physical activity, developed from Western definitions of leisure, have tended to focus on material constraints. In research conducted in the West and in Iran these constraints of time, money, facilities and transport are similar in type, rank order and the way in which they are experienced. However, we have less information about the cultural constraints that influence women and girls' leisure and sport participation. What we can now begin to see from previous research conducted in the UK and North America, and from Mohammad Ehsani's extensive survey work of the leisure and sport participation patterns of 3000 young women aged 18–25 in Iran, is that there are significant cultural differences. In the West, cultural constraints are generally experienced in relation to personal socio-psychological issues related to individual self-confidence, self-esteem, body image and friendship networks. In Iran, cultural constraints are experienced in relation to intra-personal constraints related to the social institutions of family, education and religion.

Declarations of human rights, and their associated policies and practices, are frequently concerned with a flow of knowledge and values from West to East and North to South. Moreover, as Sara Ahmed (1998, pp. 36–37) has stated:

> The importance of recognising the exclusions which are authorised through rights discourse is clear if we consider the use of 'women's rights' within the context of international feminism. It is the limitations of rights discourse in practice that demonstrates the importance of a feminist critique of a universalist model of rights.

And here we might consider the ongoing disagreements within feminism concerning the wearing of the veil (Freeman, 2002; Sellers, 2002). Part of the difficulty for Iranian women's sports organisations, I have argued, has been that they have attempted to develop policy by adopting Western practices rather than adapting such practices to meet the needs of a specific local cultural context.

The social, cultural and spatial context of women's leisure and sport in Iran is different from that in the West but both activists and academics have attempted to replicate Western models of lobbying, organisation formation and specific policy development to enhance women's sport. Such differences in reasons for non-participation need to be reflected in differences in policy development and practices if sport and leisure are not to become forms of neo-colonialism.

Case Study Three: Tourism (Intersections of Gender, Sexuality and Ethnicity in Tourism Studies)

My interest in post-colonial theory and tourism, or tourism as a form of neo-colonialism, developed from the mid-1990s as I travelled extensively for both work and leisure. On a trip to Southern India in 1997 I read Arundhati Roy's *The God of Small Things*, winner of the 1997 Booker Prize for fiction:

> In Ayemena they danced to jettison their humiliation in the Heart of Darkness. Their truncated swimming pool performances. Their turning to tourism to stave off starvation.
>
> . . .In despair he turns to tourism. He enters the market. He hawks the only thing he owns. The stories that his body can tell.
>
> He becomes a Regional Flavour.
>
> In the Heart of darkness they mock him with their lolling nakedness and their imported attention spans. He checks his rage and dances for them (Roy, 1997, pp. 229–230).

Like my work in relation to leisure and sport this tourism research has sought to explore the social–cultural nexus of material and symbolic power in the construction of gender relations and gendered Others in tourism (Aitchison, 2000d, 2001b, 2005b). Unlike my earlier work that had perfected my tried and tested multi-method, multi-phase research methodology of surveys, focus groups, interviews, diaries and policy analysis, my new departure into tourism research involved content, discourse and semiotic analysis of sights, signs, symbols, tourism brochures and novels as I straddled that increasingly blurred border between the social sciences and the humanities.

Drawing on the feminist, post-colonial, critical and cultural theory of Simone De Beauvoir (1949), Edward Said (1978, 1993), Homi Bhabba (1983) and Gayatri Chakravorty Spivak (1988), I wrestled with questions of how as academics we might seek to make a difference rather than just mark difference and how we might represent Other voices without being complicit in the neo-colonial project? As bell hooks (1990) has so aptly stressed:

> I am waiting for them to stop talking about the 'Other', to stop describing how important it is to be able to speak about difference. It is not just important what we speak about, but how and why we speak. . .Often this speech about the 'Other' annihilates, erases: 'no need to hear your voice when I can talk about you better than you can speak about yourself. No need to hear your voice. Only tell me about your pain. I want to know your story. And then I will tell it back to you in a new way. Tell it back to you in such a way that it has become mine, my own. Re-writing you, I write myself anew. I am still author, authority. I am still the colonizer, the speaking subject, and you are now at the centre of my talk' (hooks, 1990, pp. 151–152).

In summary, within tourism studies 'the cultural turn' has developed alongside the 'critical turn', rather than evolving after the development of theoretical discourses that embraced critical theory as was the case in sociology, geography and leisure studies (Aitchison, 2006b). Thus, the relatively recent development of both cultural theory and critical social science within tourism studies, a subject field described only ten years ago as 'lacking in theoretical sophistication' (Apostolopolous, Leivadi, & Yiannakis, 1996), has facilitated the possibility of developing new conceptual frameworks and theoretical directions that embody the central tenets of post-structural and post-colonial theory whilst not losing sight of the structural inequalities that still exist within and outwith tourism. Here, the new sub-discipline of critical tourism studies and its key proponents, (all of whom are here this evening and collectively known as 'The Academy of Hope': Irena Ateljevic, Nigel Morgan, Annette Pritchard and John Tribe) are central to developing the discourse of identity and inclusion in tourism and thus contributing to theoretically informed policy. Such developments signal a maturing of tourism studies as evidenced by the explicit recognition of tourism studies for the first time in the UK's forthcoming Research Assessment Exercise (HEFCE, 2005).

In conclusion, my interest has been in adopting and adapting theoretical perspectives from socialist feminism, post-structural feminism and post-colonial feminism to explore the inter-relationships between the material and the symbolic or the structural and the cultural, what I have termed the social–cultural nexus. This research has demonstrated to me, and I hope to others as well, that the answers to *making a difference* appear to be located within our own ways of knowing, in translating such ways of knowing into ways of being and going beyond *marking difference* through exclusionary identities, places, policies and practices to *making a difference* through inclusive ways of knowing and ways of being.

'We need a change of soul not a change of climate' (Seneca, undated).

References

Abberley, P. (1997). The concept of oppression and the development of a social theory of disability. In: L. Barton, & M. Oliver (Eds), *Disability studies: Past, present and future*. Leeds: The Disability Press.

Ahmed, S. (1998). *Differences that matter: Feminist theory and postmodernism*. Cambridge: Cambridge University Press.

Aitchison, C. C. (1992). The need for a gender analysis of contracting out (CCT) in local government leisure services. In: C. Knox, & J. Sugden (Eds), *Rolling back the welfare state*. Eastbourne: Leisure Studies Association.

Aitchison, C. C. (1994). Women's access to leisure provision: The impact of Compulsory Competitive Tendering (CCT) in London. In: D. Leslie (Ed.), *Tourism and leisure: Perspectives on provision*. Eastbourne: Leisure Studies Association.

Aitchison, C. C. (1997). A decade of Compulsory Competitive Tendering (CCT) in UK sport and leisure services: Some feminist reflections. *Leisure Studies, 16*(2), 85–105.

Aitchison, C. C. (2000a). Women in leisure services: Managing the social–cultural nexus of gender equity. *Managing Leisure, 5*(4), 181–191.

Aitchison, C. C. (2000b). Young disabled people, leisure and everyday life: Reviewing conventional definitions for leisure studies. *Annals of Leisure Research, 3*(1), 1–20.

Aitchison, C. C. (2000c). *Disability and social inclusion: Leisure, sport and culture in the lives of young disabled people*. Cheltenham: Scope/Cheltenham and Gloucester College of Higher Education.

Aitchison, C. C. (2000d). Poststructural feminist theories of representing others: A response to the 'crisis' in leisure studies' discourse. *Leisure Studies, 19*(3), 127–144.

Aitchison, C. C. (2001a). A disabled leisure studies: Theorising dominant discourses of the employed body, the able body and the active body? In: G. McPherson, & G. Reid (Eds), *Leisure and social inclusion: New challenges for policy and provision*. Eastbourne: Leisure Studies Association (reprinted in 2006 in *Defining the field: Thirty years of the Leisure Studies Association,* edited by E. Kennedy and H. Pussard, LSA: Eastbourne).

Aitchison, C. C. (2001b). Theorising other discourses of tourism, gender and culture: Can the subaltern speak (in tourism)? *Tourist Studies, 1*(2), 133–147.

Aitchison, C. C. (2003a). *Gender and leisure: Social and cultural perspectives*. London and New York: Routledge.

Aitchison, C. C. (2003b). From leisure and disability to disability leisure: Developing data, definitions and discourses. *Disability and Society, 18*(7), 955–969.

Aitchison, C. C. (2005a). Feminist and gender research in sport and leisure management: Understanding the social–cultural nexus of gender–power relations. *Journal of Sport Management, 19*(4), 222–241.

Aitchison, C. C. (2005b). Feminist and gender perspectives in tourism studies: The social–cultural nexus of critical and cultural theories. *Tourist Studies, 7*, 207–224.

Aitchison, C. C. (Ed.). (2006a). *Sport and gender identities: Masculinities, femininities and sexualities*. London and New York: Routledge (in press).

Aitchison, C. C. (2006b). The critical and the cultural: Explaining the divergent paths of leisure studies and tourism studies. *Leisure Studies, 25*(3), 417–422.

Aitchison, C. C., Brackenridge, C., & Jordan, F. (1999). *Gender equity in leisure management*. Reading: Institute of Leisure and Amenity Management.

Apostolopolous, Y., Leivadi, S., & Yiannakis, A. (Eds). (1996). *The sociology of tourism: Theoretical and Empirical Investigations*. London: Routledge.

Ashley, C., Boyd, C., & Goodwin, H. (2000). Putting poverty at the heart of the tourism agenda. *Overseas Development Institute — Natural Resource Perspectives, 51* (March), 1–12.

Barrett, M. (1992). Words and things: Materialism and method in contemporary feminist analysis. In: M. Barrett, & A. Phillips (Eds), *Destabilising theory: Contemporary feminist debates*. Cambridge: Polity Press.

Bhabba, H. (1983). Difference, discrimination, and the discourse of colonialism. In: F. Barker, P. Hulme, M. Iversen, & D. Loxley (Eds), *The politics of theory*. University of Essex: Essex Press.

Bialeschki, D., & Henderson, K. (1984). The personal and professional spheres: Complement or conflict for women leisure service professionals. *Journal of Park and Recreation Administration, 2*(1), 45–54.

Bialeschki, D., & Henderson, K. (2000). Gender issues in recreation management. In: M. T. Allison, & E. Schneider (Eds), *Diversity and the recreation profession*. Pennsylvania: Venture Press.

Bondi, L. (1992). Gender and dichotomy. *Progress in Human Geography, 16*(2), 98–104.

Botterill, D., & Klemm, M. (2005). Special issue editorial overview: Tourism and social inclusion. *Tourism, Culture and Communication, 6*(1), 1–5.

Bourdieu, P. (1984). *Distinction: A social critique of the judgement of taste*. London: Routledge.

Coalter, F. (2004). *After the goldrush: The London olympics*. Institute for Public Policy London: Research/DEMOS.

Collins, M. (2003). *Sport and social exclusion*. London: Routledge.

Commins, P. (Ed.) (1993). Combatting exclusion in Ireland, 1990–94: A midway report. Brussels: European Commission.

Corlyon, J., & La Placa, V. (2006). *Holidays for families in need: Policies and practices in the UK. Final report to the Family Holiday Association*. London: Policy Research Bureau.

De Beauvoir, S. (1949). *The second sex*. Harmondsworth: Penguin.

de Certeau, M. (1984). *The practice of everyday life*. Berkeley, CA: University of California Press.

Davis, J. (2000). Disability studies as ethnographic research and text: Research strategies and roles for promoting social change. *Disability and Society, 15*(2), 191–206.

Department for Culture, Media and Sport. (1999). *Arts and sports: A report to the Social Exclusion Unit*. London: Department for Culture, Media and Sport.

Department for International Development. (1999). *Sustainable tourism and poverty elimination study*. London: Department for International Development.

Evans, M. (2003). *Gender and social theory*. Milton Keynes: Open University Press.

Foucault, M. (1977). *Discipline and punish: The birth of the prison*. Harmondsworth: Peregrine.

Freeman, M. (2002). *Human rights: An interdisciplinary approach*. Cambridge: Polity.

Frisby, W., & Brown, B. (1991). The balancing act: Women leisure service managers. *Journal of Applied Recreation Research, 16*(4), 297–321.

Henderson, K. A., & Bialeschki, D. (1993). Professional women and equity issues in the 1990s. *Parks and Recreation, 28*(3), 54–59.

Henderson, K. A., & Bialeschki, D. (1995). Career development and women in the leisure services profession. *Journal of Park and Recreation and Administration, 13*(1), 26–42.

Higher Education Funding Council for England. (2005). *RAE 2008: Panel criteria and working methods*. Bristol: Higher Education Funding Council for England.

hooks, b. (1990). *Yearning. Race, gender and cultural politics*. Boston, USA: South End Press.

Humphrey, J. (2000). Researching disability projects or, some problems with the social model in practice. *Disability and Society, 15*(1), 63–86.

Jackson, P. (1989). *Maps of meaning: An introduction to cultural geography*. London: Allen and Unwin.

Knight, J., & Brent, M. (1998). *Access denied: Disabled people's experiences of social exclusion*. London: Leonard Cheshire.

Messner, M. (2002). *Taking the Field: Women, Media and Sports*. Minneapolis, MN: University of Minnesota Press.

McKay, J. (1996). *Managing gender: Affirmative action and organisation power in Australian, Canadian and New Zealand Sport*. New York: State University of New York Press.

Oliver, M., & Barnes, C. (1998). *Disabled people and social policy*. Harlow: Addison Wesley Longman.

Pro-Poor Tourism Partnership. (2004). *Developing countries' share of the international tourism market*. London: Pro-Poor Tourism Partnership.

Room, G. (Ed.) (1995). *Beyond the threshold*. Bristol: Policy Press.

Roy, A. (1997). *The god of small things*. London: Flamingo.

Said, E. (1978). *Orientalism*. London: Routledge.

Said, E. (1993). *Culture and imperialism*. London: Chatto and Windus.

Seneca, L. D. (undated). *On travel as a cure for discontent*.

Sellers, K. (2002). *The rise and rise of human rights*. Stroud: Sutton Publishing.

Shakespeare, T., & Watson, N. (1997). Defending the social model. In: L. Barton, & M. Oliver (Eds), *Disability studies: Past, present and future*. Leeds: The Disability Press.

Shinew, K. J., & Arnold, M. (1998). Gender equity in the leisure services field. *Journal of Leisure Research, 30*(2), 177–194.

Social Exclusion Unit. (1998). *Bringing Britain together: A national strategy for neighbourhood renewal*. London: Social Exclusion Unit.

Spivak, G.C. (1988). Can the subaltern speak? In: C. Nelson, & L. Grossberg (Eds) *Marxism and the Interpretation of Culture*. Basingstoke: Macmillan.

Sport England and UK Sport. (1999). *Sports participation in Europe: Compass report*. London: Sport England and UK Sport.

Stanley, L. (1990). *Feminist praxis: Research, theory and epistemology in feminist sociology*. London: Routledge.

Valentine, G. (2001). Whatever happened to the social? Reflections on the 'cultural turn' in British human geography. *Norsk Geografisk Tidsskrift (Norwegian Journal of Geography), 55*(3), 166–172.

Chapter 6

Gender Analysis in Tourism: Personal and Global Dialectics

Margaret Byrne Swain and Derek Hall

Introduction

As two early contributors to gender analysis in tourism studies, we approached this joint paper through email conversations, readily acknowledging our embodiment as researchers, while intertwining tales of our personal and professional journeys as we corresponded through cyberspace. Side-stepping any gender implications for the moment, we thought about either linear evolution or spiralling dialects as the prime mover of change over time. In this representation of our conversations, we offer perspectives on our positionality and engagement with gender analysis in tourism. Coming from contrasting geographical and gender locations, we address our works' contribution to the dialectics of global scholarship in gender, tourism and development studies, as well as its shortcomings, unfulfilled aspirations and personal frustrations. We bounce our memories, observations and ideas back and forth, taking turns in this text, concluding with some suggested directions for the future, based on the 'critical turn' in tourism studies. MBS starts off because we settled on ageism rather than sexism to be the determining factor, although it was a close-run thing.

Our Stories

MBS: Can we assume that those of us who are drawn to gender issues and critical tourism studies have anything in common? What in our lives, family experiences and personalities brings us to a fascination with people in motion, the buying and selling of place, and issues of equity, all combined, and to what end? It would be good to find out more about us, collecting our stories, to understand the hows and whys of the knowledge we produce. As I have already self-disclosed (Swain, 2004), I am a red-headed, left-handed, straight, semi-dyslexic, WASP (White Anglo-Saxon Protestant) woman, born and raised in rural

The Critical Turn in Tourism Studies: Innovative Research Methodologies
Copyright © 2007 by Elsevier Ltd.
All rights of reproduction in any form reserved.
ISBN: 0-08-045098-9

New York State. How I became involved in Feminist Tourism Studies is a long tale (Swain, forthcoming) that I will mercifully abridge here.

My feminist learnings began as a child, intuitively believing that women and men are equal. For example, there were the anatomically correct snow-women I constructed in our yard as a little girl, much to my mother's bemusement. My career path was firmly set at a young age as travel and adventure called through my imagination. Armed with my rubber sword I was prepared to be the best pirate ever. That occupational choice changed a bit when I was exposed to the Disney version of Rob Roy. I wanted to be Rob Roy, heroic brigand. No gender-confusion here, it was simply a matter of seeing who had power.

In my early years destination tourism was just not in our family budget for vacations. Then my father, a high school chemistry teacher, started to take us along to summer institutes and other jobs. My father's sojourns led us to two years of living way from home in the decidedly exotic to us locations of Gainesville, Florida and New York City. In Florida I attended segregated public schools typical of the Deep South, which shocked this northern white girl as both undeserved privilege and newly experienced exclusion of others. My family also experienced a remarkable foreignness as Northern Baptists trying to understand our white Southern Baptist co-religionists. My parents wisely gave up, and in our newly found time as weekend heathens, we were tourists, visiting historic sites, beaches, and famous local attractions like the Cyprus Gardens and Manatee Hot Springs. I loved these experiences, the souvenirs, snap shots, and memories. In Florida I learned about race relations and began a serious infatuation with tourism. The following year our family lived on the outskirts of New York City where we did not quite fit in anywhere in our neighbourhood, a racially and ethnically stratified border zone between upper class and labourer communities.

Like most of my peers, as an adolescent I began to seriously contemplate gender and sex, but reading the penultimate time-travel gender bender novel *Orlando* by Virginia Woolf shaped my understanding. It changed my life, making it possible to think about time, space and people in different ways. My older sisters had gone off to college long before I did, and this represented another kind of good travel away from home. There were some life-themes developing here for me, that gender was negotiable, travel combined well with work, intellectual work in education was a good deal, and tourism nicely combined with exploring work sites.

DH: I was born in Hackney, east London, just before the UK National Health Service (NHS) came into being. We lived on the upper floor of a two-storey terraced house that my mother liked to refer to as a 'maisonette' to those who didn't know better. It had 13 stone steps down to our small piece of garden that I managed to fall down, despite a protective barrier, when I was two years old, some of the physical results of which remain with me.

My ancestry includes Irish Catholic, Protestant French Huguenot, north English Viking, some Anglo-Saxon and possibly touches of Jewish and gypsy blood. Later knowledge of this mongrel agglomeration, even though it was mostly of one colour, helped me to begin to appreciate ethnic difference and its implications. My paternal grandmother came from Cork; the Huguenot line is on my mother's side, and her prejudices, which may or may not have been derived from the persecuted history of Huguenots, included a fervent anti-Irish sentiment — which was exacerbated when my father's only experience of jury service was cut short by an IRA bomb at the Old Bailey courts in central London; and an element which only gradually diminished, of anti-German feeling as a result of her mother dying of a heart attack following an air raid in 1940.

Such a domestic context provided a sharp tension and counterpoint to the way in which my later perceptions of difference and inequality were to be framed. Indeed, to this day there are inherited genes that I feel I need to constantly suppress. It was only after my parents died that I began to be able to be a little more detached in trying to understand how my provenance shaped who I was and how that was expressed.

I attended the same Victorian primary school as film director Alfred Hitchcock, albeit sometime after he had emigrated and with somewhat less inspiration, but at a time when some families in east London were still comprised of 12 or even 15 children, and when polio was rife. Being tall and relatively strong, no doubt as the result of extended breast feeding and NHS free orange juice during the post-war period of rationing, I assumed an unreflexive 'natural' leadership role in the school football team that flattered my meagre talents. That the world was unfair was brought home in a small yet personal way at the age of 10. Along with most teammates, I was subjected to corporal punishment from the headmaster for continuing to play football in the school playground after school, after he had told us to go home. The alternative practice pitch was the next-door bombsite pitted with the rubble of war-destroyed houses overlain with shards of broken glass and stinging nettles (we wore short trousers) laced with dog and cat excrement. This was the late 1950s and reflects the fact that post-war reconstruction was slow in the less favoured parts of the UK, and bombsites were a normal and indeed integral part of my childhood landscape.

I had no siblings, and subsequently went to a single-sex secondary school. We were a stable 'upper working-class' nuclear family. My parents lived in the same 'maisonette' for almost 45 years, only during the last 20 of which were they able to buy it. My father remained in the same job all his working life, punctuated only by wartime service. Mother was a slave to the home, but had worked in a chocolate factory, as a home help, and for several years took in outside work gluing cardboard boxes, and earned a pittance. My father worked as a machinist in a canal-side timber mill in north London, and although he was intellectually capable of non-manual work he wanted to be in the fresh air and not enclosed in an office. Snapping sawmill machinery broke both his arms, removed a finger and damaged his back, while the workplace noise hastened a substantial hearing loss.

Both my parents worked long hours so that I could have the education they had never enjoyed. Yet, unlike many other working-class urban areas in Britain, we never felt isolated or introspective: London's west end was less than half an hour away on the 'Tube', and being part of the great metropolis always offered situations and places to aspire to.

Soon after I graduated and word got round the neighbourhood, a friend of my mother approached her and asked 'does that mean he's got letters after his name'? An affirmative response was greeted by a substantial intake of breath and an admiring, very obvious re-appraisal of my mother's standing locally. A quarter of a century later the same area of east London produced a somewhat more notorious male icon: the footballer David Beckham.

MBS: By my teenage years then, I had been exposed to the three basic food groups of feminism: thinking about gender, race, and class. My mom, a housewife and credentialed nurse, had recently died and, besides missing her terribly, this made me think more about women's lives, our work and value. International travel with my father, who developed a remarkable bent for adventure in his profession, took me at the age of 16 to India, blowing wide-open my worldview.

My education continued at Beloit College, where I majored in Anthropology, participated in an education abroad program in Taiwan. At the end of college, I joined my father who was working on a project in Iran. There I learned a great deal more about being an insider or an outsider, especially while working in an archaeological dig in the Zargros Mountains. In some ways I was wildly desirable, being courted by the local chieftain's son to be his third wife. Despite gallons of rose water and the OK from wives one and two, it did not work out, as it was politely suggested to the man that he needed to seek my father's permission, and that meant a day-long bus ride he could not afford. In other instances, I was offensive and reviled, as the time when a group of us foreigners and Iranians descended uninvited on a remote village to check out an interesting site. The villagers were angry and they targeted their anger towards me, the only young female wearing bandana (my head covering) and pants in the group. I was stoned, and I do not mean on drugs. Clearly my embodiment played out in both instances.

Back in the States, I went off to graduate school at the University of Washington where I was soon hooked on studying gender relations. We learned about cultural constructs of gender and how this paradigm can provide keys for us all to unlock and change sexist hierarchies of power. By then I had experienced *machismo* in the US and *purdah* as a privileged outsider, had taken in the eroticism of ancient Hindu art, stared discreetly at the bound feet of grannies living in Taipei, and learned over and over again that in terms of cultural production anywhere 'anonymous' was a 'woman'. Given my family values, circumstances and temperament, I did not interpret this into an 'us vs. them' scenario, but rather thought about variation, about how very different and very alike cultures structured women and men, and the problems of inequalities. My intellectual framework for explaining what I experienced is rooted in the perception that the personal is political. I thought about the double messages from my own society of the 1960s and 70s that women were best in the domestic sphere, yet yes, they can and should do anything. This is the Hillary Clinton syndrome of my generation.

DH: Without siblings, with a chokingly protective mother and attending a single-sex school, the omens were not good for a balanced trajectory into the social world. I became one of those gangly 'teenagers' who blushed whenever a girl passed me on the street — indeed the blush would commence as soon as she came into view. With what I considered as more than my fair share of skin blemishes, which, at that age, demanded tortuous hours of angst in front of the mirror, my body awareness, albeit skewed in its focussed naïve negativity, became a dominant determining characteristic in my 'formative' years.

Although this was approaching the height of the 'swinging' sixties, I was far from alone in wallowing in this repressed state. Indeed, at one of our first timorous forays into the world of cavernous Saturday night dance halls — in this case the *Ilford Palais* in east London — a handful of my (inevitably male) chums and I spent most of the evening dancing with chairs in the absence of having the courage to ask a girl. Interval repeat playings of the then brand new Nancy Sinatra single *These Boots are Made for Walking* at that first foray have ensured that to this day I enter (retrospective) paroxysms of despair every time I hear the opening bars of that wretched song.

These were clearly far from auspicious beginnings to encourage a later interest in gendered approaches to anything. My adolescent reading — and I do not recall actually reading a book from beginning to end until I was about 14 — was stimulated by a Christmas gift of *Animal Farm*, and from then on I avidly read much George Orwell and then Virginia Woolf, elevating her 'stream of consciousness' style to my ideal of prose perfection. Perhaps, symbolically, Orlando was her only major work I did not get round to at this time. When later my first head of department told me that he read Virginia Woolf for the sex, I could not tell if he was winding me up or whether it was a plea for help.

At the end of my first year as an undergraduate student of geography and social anthropology, in the revolutionary year of 1968, I joined a two-month overland expedition to Turkey to undertake geographical and anthropological fieldwork, ostensibly to assist tutors with their research projects. This was the result of a split moment's decision after a member of the group had dropped out at the last minute. It changed my life. This first-hand experience of a slice of central and south-eastern Europe — virtually the whole length of the then Yugoslavia and on into Bulgaria and Turkey, places and cultures of which I knew little (actually, nothing) — awakened a life-long interest in these parts of Europe and their peoples. More especially, the experience exposed me to wanting to learn more about ideologies, their philosophical underpinnings, and just what propaganda was all about, in its masking of realities, its hypocrisies and hegemonies.

Most particularly, the dialectics of Marxism–Leninism attracted me, and I thirsted for more and deeper experience of the societies it was supposedly dominating. Soon, the paradox of societies being ruled in the name of the working people, but for the benefit of a different type of élite to that experienced in my own country, stimulated me to want to know more about what this actually meant to those people in whose name it was being undertaken. This led to a gradual understanding of further paradoxes: the role of second economies, of alternative social networks, of the conditions of women, ethnic minorities and the disabled for whom formally espoused equality seemed even more hypocritical than that experienced under capitalist political economies; of working people surviving despite, rather than because of the system; and the wry humour, innovation, improvisation and imagination that triumphed over shortages and hardships — with echoes of earlier post-war Britain.

My first visit to China in 1977, and, in the following year, a funded three-month 'young scientist' research visit to India, which embraced Nepal and Sri Lanka, exposed me to further models of social and economic 'development'. My embodiment as a relatively giant, long-nosed occidental white male was to generate crowds of inquisitive people and to cause traffic jams in Changsha, and to regularly attract the wailing attention of destitute beggars and sick children as I waited for my commute bus in Delhi. Psychologically, the person I was becoming was far removed from the dance-hall shrinking violet of a decade earlier. Intellectually, I had to quickly accommodate myself in worlds that were very different from the retrospectively so safe cocoon within which I was brought up. Trying to understand and accommodate the gross inequalities and 'inhuman' suffering now continuously confronting and challenging me demanded a second watershed in my own 'development'.

MBS: True to the era, I was soon lured away from graduate school to Panama, where I married Walt Swain and became a Vietnam War era army wife, as well as the staff's pet *gringa* at the *Museo Nacional*. In the museum I learned about the San Blas Kuna Indians whose matrilocal society and ritual celebration of women's coming of age was hot stuff for a nascent feminist anthropologist. I became intrigued by the fact that Kuna women's social position, sewn 'mola' handiwork and exotic appearance were heavily used in Panamanian and international tourism promotion. My interest in a particular people and location drew me to the study of tourism for my dissertation project.

The politics of tourism in the San Blas turned out to be embedded in colonial relations and imperialist schemes. Given historical events and ongoing employment of Kuna men in US military barracks in the Canal Zone, Americans were favoured by Kuna, as reflected in the terms for humans in Kuna language: 'tule' for Kuna, 'mergi' for Americans and 'waga' for everyone else. Kuna relations with their state government were contentious, and blew up around Panamanian plans to develop tourism resorts in San Blas, leading to blood-shed and Kuna destruction of some existing resorts, including Islandia, a US run gay retreat across the bay from the community where I intended to live. Demands for sover-eignty overruled any issues about sexuality or Kuna ties to the US. The government backed down on its plans, just as I was beginning my fieldwork. In this very volatile situation, my research officially became much less about tourism and more about Kuna women.

I had also innocently assumed that tourism was a legitimate and respected academic topic and began my engagement with tourism studies by submitting an abstract for the AAA sessions being organised by Valene Smith that arguably marked a beginning in the field. Simultaneously combining this focus with an engagement in the barely emergent field of Feminist Studies became a huge challenge, demanding a map that I needed to draw myself. My chapter on the Kuna in *Host and Guests* (1977), the book Valene compiled from our AAA sessions, used the old language of 'sex roles' and was totally descriptive. I could not yet ask the theoretical questions of what it meant in terms of the big picture of gender equity, and human relations.

My embodiment caught up with my theory needs as I moved into motherhood with two girls, and midlife crisis. It was a logical response for me to learn Chinese and re-engage an academic life I had left behind ten years before, after finishing my degree. Just as I was becoming immersed, a letter from Valene Smith arrived, calling for a second edition of *Hosts and Guests*. The timing was perfect, giving me a chance to think about my research again, which I grabbed. It was news to me that I had a modest scholarly reputation based on my few publications. I was actually in the field. Besides Valene's encouragement, the fact that Dean McCannell was a colleague at UC Davis became another source of inspiration.

My new focus became Yunnan, China, a fantastically ethnically diverse part of the world where a few minority indigenous groups, including the Sani of Stone Forest, were beginning to engage in some form of tourism. It is not too surprising I guess that I have chosen to work in two indigenous societies, the Kuna and the Sani, where gender dynam-ics often balance out. In terms of my position in the field I had the semi-insider/patron sta-tus as a 'mergi' with the Kuna, based on colonial histories, while among the Sani it was the 'Martian effect' the ultimate outsider dropping in from nowhere with no history, no ties to the communist/socialist state that engulfed them. Either position however comes with the trappings of power. I learned among the Kuna about the ethics of asking too much, of inserting myself into peoples' daily routines to extract knowledge. It is important to me to find ways to give something back in an equitable way to the people I work with. One of my more creative moves led me to a collaboration with its own ethical concerns. This was the creation of a new tourism souvenir for my Sani companions to sell, little Sani cloth dolls. My rationale was to expand their commodities repertoire if they wanted to do so, while providing me with an experiment that I could measure and map out. By then I had an identity that superseded the Martian, and some of my companions said 'thanks teacher, you have helped our livelihood'.

I reclaimed my place in tourism studies in the early 1990s in two distinct ways, through ethnographic research with the Sani and engagement with feminist theory. While I was writing grant proposals for funding fieldwork in China, I was also developing a prospectus for a collection on gender in tourism as a special issue of *Annals of Tourism Research*. It soon became apparent that I was one of several tourism researchers who had simultaneously had the bright idea to stimulate new scholarship investigating gender variables in tourism. I promoted this agenda in the US (Swain, 1995), while Vivian Kinnaird and Derek Hall (1994) worked together in the U.K. Our projects met through Jafar Jafari. I still believe that the fact Derek wrote to Jafar, enquiring about his interest in their book project gave some credibility to my proposal to *Annals*.

In both cases our immediate goal was to produce a collection of articles demonstrating the utility and significance of gender analysis in tourism studies. Hearty responses to our separate calls for papers gave encouraging evidence that we were collectively on to something. In terms of *Annals*, more than 30 paper proposals were submitted for consideration in the Special Issue. Since then Derek, Vivian and I have elaborated on this synergy through correspondence about each other's projects, forming a base for ongoing collaborations over the years.

DH: My 'drift' into tourism via ideology and inequality was facilitated through an unlikely long-standing obsession with the relatively close yet unknown, demonised and almost mythical Albania (e.g. Hall, 1994). Without diplomatic relations, conventional attempts to undertake research in the country were impossible. One way to gain access in a relatively innocuous way was to act as a tour guide, a role that I took on in the 1980s and early 1990s, both in Albania, and in Montenegro, Russia, Mongolia, China and North Korea. A major ethical issue for researchers of state socialist societies was the often self-censoring fear that making (unofficial) contact with individuals would put the latter at risk. There were certainly stories — not all apocryphal — of naïve/selfish academics causing very major problems for a number of citizens of particular regimes through their blind pursuit of empirical research materials. Tom Stoppard's wonderful play *Professional Foul* manages to capture a number of the complexities and nuanced paradoxes of the naïve academic being confronted with a hypocritical regime through vulnerable intermediaries.

The tour leader role led, inevitably, to a contemplation of tourism, and reflections on its paradoxical application in inflexible societies. My eventual intersection with gender in tourism drew on the formal precepts and concepts of my formal education and training in political geography and social anthropology, and on a particular concern for inequality and hegemony experienced in a number of different contexts. This interest was complemented by the appointment of Vivian Kinnaird as a colleague at Sunderland in a de-industrializing, peripheralised northeast England.

As Vivian was working on her PhD, supervised by Janet Momsen, on gender and development in the Caribbean, I rather opportunistically suggested that we might explore the possibility of a text on gender and tourism. I had the publishing contacts to set the book up, although we soon realised that given the conditions we were labouring under at Sunderland (three full-time lecturers for geography, development and tourism programmes), we would not have sufficient time to write a full text ourselves. And it was Vivian who had the contacts to line up an excellent team of contributors, and possessed the intellect and analytical edge to drive the book through to its completion. Thus *Tourism: a Gender Analysis* was published by Wiley (Kinnaird & Hall, 1994).

Key Issues

MBS: Our efforts in the early 1990s were the first systematic attempts to combine the focuses of Tourism and Feminist Studies. In the *Annals* collection, there was no mention of sexualities, disabilities or age differences in tourism. The fact that I did not think to write about these aspects of the body in the Introduction was reinforced at the time by the lack of submissions about them for the *Special Issue*. During the following years we have begun to see more inclusive scholarship in tourism studies as evidenced by current research that takes into consideration multiple points of view and life experiences. Evolving perspectives on gender and sexuality were clearly articulated in the 'Gender/Tourism/Fun(?)' conference that I organised at UC Davis in the fall of 1997 with Janet Momsen and Dean McCannell. It was truly an international gathering of energetic scholars, about half of whom revised and published their papers in an edited collection (Swain & Momsen, 2002). Some of these authors pushed tourism studies research to engage in constructivism and embodiment theory, while others stayed clear of such post-modern talk. Their rich work evidences a growing range of approaches to the study of gender in tourism. One trend has been for researchers to write in their own voice, rather than the usual disembodied type of 'scientific' analysis. This perspective of the researcher being mindful of one's own embodiment enriches any qualitative project, in terms of results and applications of our work. This collection could be seen as a direct continuation of work in the *Annals*'s Special Issue, and more recently linked to a jointly edited collection with Derek Hall and Vivian Kinnaird for *Tourism Recreation Research* (2003).

In my own work I am currently focusing on cosmopolitanism as a gendered embodied phenomenon, exemplified by the global tourism industry in the early 21st century. This interest has grown from doing ethnography in China, and asking large-scale theoretical questions about how humans combine mobility with cultural exchange. Cosmopolitanism in this context means a consciousness of and engagement with the world outside of home community. It is based in ideals of shared power rather than linear control, and represents the cultural side of globalisation, and more. As identity and position, cosmopolitanism intersects with many other kinds of embodiment. For example, my poster-woman of cosmopolitanism, who I have known since 1987, is an illiterate indigenous farmer and tourism handicraft vendor. She is at ease talking with foreign tourists as she is calling her daughter on a cell phone or calling spirits for a séance with her shaman drum.

The embodiment and positionality of tourism researchers also needs our attention. For example, three of my students were doing field research during the summer of 2005 on embodied cosmopolitanism in distinct sites. One was in a US-Tibetan Buddhist retreat centre where gender dynamics are being challenged by both American lay practitioners and Tibetan Buddhist leaders. Another was in Beirut, Lebanon where national tourism production of a Phoenician identity has gendered dimensions. The third hung out in Starbucks,

Korea, where consumers drink their cosmopolitan identities predicted by gender. Each researcher is working from her own embodied locations as insider/outsider, based on gender, ethnicity, age, class and other factors. Their diversity reflects what I hear is going on all over the globe — young scholars engaging sophisticated gender analysis in tourism studies.

As critical theorists, our ultimate concerns have to do with how we as researchers can increase human understanding and impact lives for the greater good in the face of power politics and strife. I especially believe that we should be concerned about gender in tourism research for the very basic reason that tourism consists of interactions among women and men of diverse genders. Tourism is a human activity that mirrors ideas about gender relations and identities from all cultures. The push and pull between local and global norms provides constant material for analysis. It is significant to me that tourism practice has the potential of promoting either gender hierarchy or equity. My hope is for increased equality in this world. Like many other tourism researchers I believe that tourism can be a vehicle for the common good of humankind, but we have a long ways to go.

DH: Vivian and I soon had to acknowledge that there were critical elements largely absent from our 1994 book. These included:

- the intersection between gender and ethnicity, (and gender and disability);
- gendering the (natural) environment;
- feminist critiques;
- the interface and cross-fertilisation of gender-focused research in tourism and in leisure studies; and
- embodiment, which was emerging as an organising paradigm within the cultural turn of several subject areas.

We acknowledged some of these in joint papers we published in *Tourism Management* (Kinnaird & Hall, 1996) and *Tourism Recreation Research* (Kinnaird & Hall, 2000), and in the special edition of *TRR* with Peggy (MBS) in 2003, noted previously.

BOTH: In our *TRR* conclusion, we noted that overall, there was much promise in discourse about the interface of gender and tourism to further our understanding of tourism processes. Some areas and contexts, such as sex tourism/romance tourism, and farm tourism, seemed to have received disproportionate amounts of attention, and there would now appear to be relatively little new left to say about them. Other areas, such as exploring further embodied tourism conceptions and experiences, and the wide range of gender issues generated by tourism development processes seeking cultural authenticity in rapidly modernising societies, continued to provide a fruitful agenda. Further evolving empirical arenas offered enormous opportunities, and a specific need for, gendered critical evaluation: postcommunism, EU enlargement processes, and the globalisation of developing societies under different cultural and environmental circumstances.

We raised two major underlying and interrelated questions in the *TRR* collection:

(1) Why had there been relatively little engagement to date between feminist studies and tourism studies in the development of gender thinking in tourism? And,
(2) How was our collective research agenda in gender and tourism to be further progressed and enhanced?

In a direct answer to our prayers, as it were, in 2003, GRITS, the Gender Researchers in Tourism Studies Network, was formed by Irena Ateljevic, Annette Pritchard, Nigel Morgan and Candice Harris, to support researchers exploring the interplay between tourism, identities, genders, races, sexualities and embodiment. With the GRITS organised international conference 'Embodying Tourism Research: Advancing Critical Approaches' held in Dubrovnik, Croatia in 2005, gender in tourism research had arrived as an organised, international presence of critical theory. At the conference we were surrounded by examples of post-communism development, globalisation, and EU expansion. To quote a recent *New York Times* travel feature story on Croatia as 'a new Riviera', most Croatians . . . :

> say they are looking west in the hope of gaining admission to the European Union, which they believe would bring security to the volatile, war-torn Balkan region . . . (Dougherty, 2005, p. 11)

Since the Yugoslav wars of succession in the 1990s, government plans to make tourism a primary income generator again have moved apace. Certainly tourism business is booming, from luxury hotels, to organised tours and cruise ship stops. Foreigners are targeted at every bus, ferry, and train terminal by little old ladies and gentlemen with laminated signs in English advertising their 'private accommodations'. How does Croatia compare with other emergent economies? What is the promise of tourism development? (Ateljevic & Corak, 2006). We should ask about gender roles in home-stay businesses, the inclusion of semi-formal economy activities in tourism development and its state regulation, and the potential for tourist interactions with locals beyond the tourist bubble.

Future Directions

MBS: We contrast here our expectations for tourism to promote equity and quality of life with expectations for righteous research. Research on tourism appears to be more likely than praxis, the articulation of this research with everyday conditions to affect change. Recent research in tourism studies shows us that there is movement around the globe towards much greater engagement with theoretical debates in the social sciences and humanities, especially with feminist and other critical theories. We can no longer decry a complete lack of critical analysis, although it is fascinating to wonder why it has taken so long to catch on. In my own case, I can see how I have been part of the problem, intuitively rejecting as a patriarchal plot most theory that did not directly address gender inequality. I still have my suspicions reflected so elegantly in Veijola and Jokinen's (1994) seminal article 'The Body in Tourism' about the old boy's network of tourism studies. Then there is Judith Butler (1990) in her book *Gender Trouble* where she takes up Irigary's critique of dialectical theory as 'phallogocentric' — I just wanted to say that word. Surely a feminist reading of how agency dialectically relates to structure can acknowledge patriarchal power without perpetuating it. We know that there is critical theory that promises emancipation and transformation. It is just on whose terms and how to do it.

There is a significant trend in conferences and publications to ask questions about our philosophical underpinnings in tourism studies while also providing solid ethnography and analysis from varied disciplines. Much of this work raises issues of embodiment in terms of the feminist pantheon of gender, sexuality, race, class, ethnicity, etc. from critical and constructivist positions. Edited collections reflecting this trend include Phillimore and Goodson's (2004) *Qualitative Research in Tourism* that explores how researchers engage our ontologies, epistemologies and methodologies, how we are embodied, and what this means for the production of knowledge in tourism studies. Cartier and Lew's (2005) *Seductions of Place* instead focuses on the subjects of tourism in what they call 'touristed landscapes.' In this context to be embodied is to be emplaced, and ideas that people hold about places dialectically inform identity formation, human agency, and questions of subjectivity. Another new collection, *Travels in Paradox*, edited by Minca and Oakes (2006), combines the place/space debates of cultural geography with critical theory questions of ontology and epistemology, asking what is real about tourism and how do we know it. They address the paradoxes of tourism researchers themselves being tourists, and how mobile groups are reflexive about place. I would note a need for discussion about 'mobile people' who do not travel by leisured choice — refugees and migrants who perforce must also be reflexive about place. These people are the counter-balance, and indeed the other side of tourism.

The dialectics of critical theory could be a useful idea to further explore by researchers looking for ways to empower our research to actually make a difference. How does change occur in power dynamics of complex relations? While tourism studies dialogues with critical theory, the conversations need to be expanded. One approach would be to expand the 'adopt a French theorist' trend in critical engagement. Urry has Foucault, McCannell has Levi-Strauss and Lacan, while Baudrillard and Lefebvre are often evoked amongst others. In terms of feminist theorists in travel, Caren Kaplan can understand and utilise just about anyone in her original thinking. If I had to choose, it would be the work of Pierre Bourdeau. There is insight to be gained in tourism studies from Bourdeau's ideas about habitus or embodied conditions that dialectically engage social structure with individual agency, transforming possibilities. We need to understand how complex social and cultural systems work and our places within them in order to understand this thing we call tourism, and affect equitable change through praxis.

To achieve these goals we need to combine compatible theories with our life experiences and awareness to embody the critical mass needed to generate excellent scholarship that can make a difference. For example, I am interested in gender analysis of embodiment, habitus, and cosmopolitanism in tourism research. It is fun to think about, but what can it tell me? If I want to study 'embodied cosmopolitanism' in the back of the beyond southwest China, why bother? Is this just intellectual self-indulgence, or do I have some possibility for righteous, critical research?

My hope is for the affirmative, and yet I think that we all, no matter what our embodiment and positionality, have issues of translation. How does our desire to understand difference in this industry of differences translate to the lives of the people we are studying? Where does feminist ethics come in, the demand to promote equity among all people? How might our work relate to issues of power in capitalist global expansion, cultural renaissance, wars and terrorism? We have these possibilities of taking gender analysis in tourism into new directions, both personally and globally through our scholarship, to affect change.

DH: Embodiment, media discourses and imagery were well represented in the Dubrovnik conference papers. Having been aware of earlier (personal) research shortcomings in the intersection of tourism, power and hegemonic relations, there would still appear to be the need to reflect further on three sets of interrelated dimensions.

First, the intersection of gender with ethnicity and disability/disablement: there is only a limited literature, and there would appear to be considerable scope for more attention to be paid to the intersection of gender and ethnicity, particularly in contrasting cultural contexts and not least in societies subject to (rapid) 'transition' (e.g. Scott, 1995, 1997; Schäfer, 2001; Devedzic, 2002; see also Hall, 2004, pp. 43–46); although a number of papers have focused on the older woman traveller (e.g. Small, 2003), again there is little on the intersection of gender and disablement; this further leads to the consideration that physical and mental disabilities do of course intersect with many gender positions, so that, for example, within the masculinities literature the study of older men tourists could address interrelationships between their positionality and issues of privilege and/or 'fellow traveller' status.

Second, we have previously argued (Hall, Swain, & Kinnaird, 2003) that there has been limited engagement between gender studies and certain analytical and philosophical positions. Of course the papers that were presented at Dubrovnik do not deserve such criticism. But there is a tendency in some contemporary gender studies towards the introspective and almost indulgent rather than intellectually engaging wider realities of power inequities, hegemonies and almost literal global meltdown. As Donna Chambers (2005) argued, there may at times appear not to be a great deal of the 'critical' in 'critical studies'.

Third, to help bridge the perceived gap identified in the previous paragraph, we might suggest that there is a range of methodologies that remain to be explored from a gendered perspective (e.g. chaos theory?), and which, while inherently intellectually challenging, could also offer powerful analytical tools with which to engage those wider realities.

Finally, I am less optimistic than Peggy. I see travel and tourism both as a major symbol of global inequality and unequal access to resources and as one of the significant contributors to climate change and global degradation. I am not convinced that the industry is ready or able to face up to the enormous questions which may soon confront it (e.g. see Gössling, 2002a, 2002b). We in the developed countries have generally set poor models for the rest of the world to follow in terms of natural and human resource exploitation, social, economic and political hegemony. International tourism is still dominated by both tourists and organisations from developed countries: access to travel and recreation for those in the poorest countries is largely denied at least partly as a result of several hundred years of 'Western' domination of much of the worlds economic and political systems (e.g. see D'Sa, 1999).

Assuming for a moment that the global environment — perhaps through technological innovation — can accommodate continued growth of international tourism, and more especially if it cannot, is the developed world really going to be willing to share its resources, give up its dominant role and encourage billions of travellers from China, India, Indonesia, Brazil and other currently less developed regions to share its tourism and travel privileges? For me, therefore gender issues within tourism are both central and complementary to intersecting questions of inequity, values and power relating to ethnicity, disablement, social class relations and, not least, poverty.

But further, current inequalities in access in generating countries, a theme that tends to dominate the rapidly emerging literature in this area, emphasise poverty, disability and gender as major factors inhibiting participation. (Although, almost as an aside, the literature often fails to bring the three together or to consider the ripple of gendered impacts that the pressures of poverty and disability, separately or together, exert on kin, carers and friends: e.g. see Gladwell & Bedini, 2004.) Yet, as academics, teachers, practitioners, tourists and commentators already drawn into travel and tourism processes, do we not face a potential personal sense of hypocrisy because:

We feel it is appropriate to want to see tourism participation increased and access improved for those currently constrained from doing so — within our own societies; but by contrast, we may hesitate to contemplate the broadening of tourism participation globally, (a) because of the ethical dilemma it poses for the already threatened global environment, and (b) because it also threatens our own (already unsustainable, over-consuming) privileges in access to and participation in tourism and travel activity?

Such fundamental issues and the perceptions of them are clearly not gender-neutral.

References

Ateljevic, I., & Corak, S. (2006). New Croatia in the New Europe: Culture versus conformity. In: D. Hall, B. Marciszewska, & M. Smith (Eds), *Tourism in the New Europe: The challenges and opportunities of EU enlargement* (pp. 288–301). Wallingford, UK: CABI Publishing.

Butler, J. (1990). *Gender trouble*. New York: Routledge.

Cartier, C., & Lew, A. (2005). *Seductions of place*. London: Routledge.

Chambers, D. (2005). *Interrogating the 'critical' in critical approaches to tourism research*. Dubrovnik: Paper presented at the International Conference on Critical Tourism Studies, 30 June–3 July.

D'Sa, E. (1999). Wanted: Tourists with a social conscience. *International Journal of Contemporary Hospitality Management, 11*(2–3), 64–68.

Devedzic, M. (2002). Ethnic heterogeneity and gender in the Yugoslav seaside tourist region. In: M. B. Swain, & J. H. Momsen (Eds), *Gender/tourism/fun(?)* (pp. 143–153). Elmsford, NY: Cognizant Communication Corporation.

Dougherty, S. (2005). In Croatia, a new Riviera beckons. *The New York Times*, July 17, 5:1, 10–11.

Gladwell, N. J., & Bedini, L. A. (2004). In search of lost leisure: The impact of caregiving on leisure travel. *Tourism Management, 25*, 685–693.

Gössling, S. (2002a). Global environmental consequences of tourism. *Global Environmental Change, 12*, 283–302.

Gössling, S. (2002b). Human-environmental relations with tourism. *Annals of Tourism Research, 29*(2), 539–556.

Hall, D. (1994). *Albania and the Albanians*. London: Pinter.

Hall, D. (2004). Key themes and frameworks. In: D. Hall (Ed.), *Tourism and transition: Governance, transformation and development* (pp. 25–51). Wallingford, UK: CABI Publishing.

Hall, D., Swain, M. B., & Kinnaird, V. (2003). Tourism and gender: An evolving agenda. *Tourism Recreation Research, 28*(2), 1–11.

Kinnaird, V., & Hall, D. (1996). Understanding tourism processes: A gender-aware framework. *Tourism Management, 17*(2), 95–102.

Kinnaird, V., & Hall, D. (Eds) (1994). *Tourism: A gender analysis*. Chichester, UK: Wiley.

Kinnaird, V., & Hall, D. (2000). Theorizing gender in tourism research. *Tourism Recreation Research*, *25*(1), 71–84.

Minca, C., & Oakes, T. (2006). *Travels in paradox*. Boulder, CO: Rowman & Littlefield.

Phillimore, J., & Goodson, L. (Eds) (2004). *Qualitative research in tourism: Ontologies, epistemologies, and methodologies*. London: Routledge.

Schäfer, R. (2001). Frauen-Rechtsorganisationen in Südafrika: Ansätze und Grenzen gesellschaftlicher Transformationsprozesse. *Afrika Spectrum*, *36*(2), 203–222.

Scott, J. (1995). Sexual and national boundaries in tourism. *Annals of Tourism Research*, *22*(2), 385–403.

Scott, J. (1997). Chances and choices: Women and tourism in northern Cyprus. In: M. T. Sinclair (Ed.), *Gender, work and tourism* (pp. 60–90). London and New York: Routledge.

Small, J. (2003). The voices of older women tourists. *Tourism Recreation Research*, *28*(2), 31–39.

Swain, M. B. (1977). Cuna women and ethnic tourism: A way to persist and an avenue to change. In: V. Smith (Ed.), *Hosts and guests: The anthropology of tourism* (pp. 71–82). Philadelphia, PA: The University of Pennsylvania Press.

Swain, M. B. (Ed.) (1995). Gender in tourism special issue. *Annals of Tourism Research*, *22*(2), 247–289.

Swain, M. B. (2004). (Dis)embodied experience and power dynamics in tourism research. In: J. Phillimore, & L. Goodson (Eds), *Qualitative research in tourism: Ontologies, epistemologies, and methodologies* (pp. 102–118). London: Routledge.

Swain, M. B. (forthcoming). On the road to a feminist tourism studies. In: D. Nash (Ed.), *Toward a tourism social science: Anthropological and sociological beginnings* (not yet available, in press). Amsterdam: Elsevier.

Swain, M. B., & Momsen, J. H. (Eds) (2002). *Gender/tourism/fun(?)*. Elmsford, NY: Cognizant Communication Corporation.

Veijola, S., & Jokinen, E. (1994). The body in tourism. *Theory, Culture and Society, 11*, 125–151.

Chapter 7

Interrogating the 'Critical' in Critical Approaches to Tourism Research

Donna Chambers

Introduction

In the most recent book length exegesis of the state of qualitative enquiry in tourism studies (Phillimore & Goodson, 2004), tourism researchers were encouraged to consider the onto-logical, epistemological and methodological underpinnings of their research. Indeed, the broad aim of this work was to re-direct attention from the traditional method level focus of tourism research to those broader theoretical and philosophical issues which necessarily underpin and permeate any research undertaking. Within this context, there was an obvious move to privilege interpretative and critical approaches to research in tourism. Similarly, the *International Conference on Critical Tourism Studies* held in Dubrovnik from 30 June– 3 July, 2005, and from which this chapter has emerged, was explicit in its intention to seek further legitimacy for interpretative and critical approaches in tourism research.

However, the contention of this chapter is that despite the arguably, increasing popularity of 'critical' approaches in the tourism academy, the epistemological, ontological and method-ological underpinnings of critical research remain under-theorised and under-explored. This, it is argued, has resulted in a lack of theoretical cogency and coherency in much of what is labelled as 'critical' tourism research. The chapter commences with a brief discussion of what can be deemed a distinct 'critical' paradigm within the wider social sciences focus-ing on its philosophical assumptions rather than on its emergence or development, and then it proceeds to interrogate and reflect on, the state of tourism 'critical' research within this context. The chapter concludes with some contemplations on a possible way forward for tourism research which seeks to subscribe to the label of 'critical'.

The Critical Paradigm within the Social Sciences

It can be argued that a distinct critical research paradigm within social sciences has its ori-gins in the work of the Institute for Social Research established in 1923 in Frankfurt,

The Critical Turn in Tourism Studies: Innovative Research Methodologies
Copyright © 2007 by Elsevier Ltd.
ISBN: 0-08-045098-9

Germany (later known simply as the Frankfurt School). In the context of Frankfurt School critical theory, the term 'critical' referred specifically to the *'dialectical critique of political economy'* (Slater, 1977, p. 26). This understanding of critique while it drew on a Marxian analysis of political economy nevertheless rejected Marxism–Leninism as it was felt that this failed to provide an adequate analysis of the course of twentieth century history characterised at the time by the:

> effects of World War I, the defeat of left-wing working class movements, the rise of fascism and Nazism, and the degeneration of the Russian revolution into Stalinism. (Thompson & Held, 1982, p. 2)

So that critical theory, while it accepted the significance of political economy in the formation of late modern societies and the individuals who inhabited these societies, sought to go beyond Marxism to draw on critiques of society as a totality and perceived culture as an important component of that totality. Indeed, according to Dant (2003), critical theory is concerned with modifying Marxian analysis, sometimes utilising insights from other theoretical approaches, importantly Freudian psychoanalysis, in order to develop a critique of society which goes beyond a Marxian fixation with political economy. Critical theory, unlike orthodox Marxism:

> addresses society as a totality and treats culture not as epiphenomenal, as Marx was prone to do, but as the form in which the modern mode of production resides. (Dant, 2003, p. 4)

Evidently this critique of modern society recognised the complexities of the new social struggles that had emerged and which could not be explained solely by reference to political economy. However, that said, critical theory was not a fully articulated paradigm and was not applied in uniform fashion by all members of the Frankfurt School. Nevertheless, it is clear that they shared common assumptions and were all influenced predominantly by the dialectical philosophy of Hegel and Marx (Finlayson, 2005). Specifically, what critical theorists had in common was their rejection of 'traditional' or positivist theories as being incapable of providing adequate explanations for societal issues. Indeed, critical theorists rejected scientific knowledge on the basis that its universality led to the misrepresentation of social phenomena as immutable instead of perceiving these as historically specific and therefore alterable. For critical theorists, positivism was thus inherently repressive rendering this philosophical approach politically unacceptable (Keat, 1981).

It is possible to identify four principal characteristics of critical theory — it was interdisciplinary, reflective, dialectical and critical. By being interdisciplinary not only was critical theory challenging the traditional positivitist approach with its widespread assumption of the superiority of the natural sciences as the only valid path to truth and knowledge, but it also acknowledged the insights and richness that could be gained from working within and between several disciplines. Critical theory was reflective or:

> inherently self aware [as it] reflected on the social context that gave rise to it, on its own function within that society, and on the purposes and interests

of its practitioners, and so forth, and such reflections were built into the theory. (Finlayson, 2005, p. 3)

In other words, critical theory was a self-reflective philosophy which aimed at the creation of a more rational society in which critical theory itself comprised an integral part of societal transformation (Keat, 1981).

Importantly, critical theory was dialectical in that, unlike positivist approaches which believed that facts were fixed and irrescindable, critical theory conversely believed that there were always opposing interests in society and indeed these were necessary in order to bring about social change. In this regard, Carr (2000, p. 290) asserts that it is the existence of contradictions and tensions within society which 'give us a feeling of "unease"/estrangement and a new consciousness of what we would otherwise take for granted or accept'.

It is these inherent societal contradictions and tensions which become the catalysts for social change. This latter point brings us to the final characteristic of critical theory, that is that critical theory is critical. While this point might seem axiomatic, it is essential to clarify what this means. Critical theory was critical in the sense that not only did the theory seek to identify what was wrong with society (to criticise so to speak) but its objective was to challenge the existing state of affairs in order to help society to transform for the better. In this latter sense, Bronner and Kellner (1989) argue that critical theory was thus, potentially, politically more useful and relevant than approaches such as poststructuralism and postmodernism as it:

> Maintains a nondogmatic perspective which is sustained by an interest in emancipation from all forms of oppression, as well as by a commitment to freedom, happiness and a rational ordering of society ... against all relativistic and nihilistic excesses, critical theory seeks an emancipatory alternative to the existing order. (p. 1)

Critical theory thus posed a challenge to existing patterns of power and truth which shape modern society not in a disinterested or apolitical fashion, but with the view of initiating change. So that in opposition to traditional theory which sought merely to understand and explain phenomena by using scientific methods, critical theory aimed at critiquing existing social systems not with critique as an end in itself but using critique to bring about change. Importantly, change was sought not necessarily in a revolutionary or radical sense as in the Marxist context, but also as a *'provocation to thought — thinking differently about the social world that will lead to change in the way society is lived'* (Dant, 2003, p. 160). It is in this way that critical theoretical discourse is linked with praxis, i.e. knowledge as action.

At this point it would be pertinent to introduce the work of Habermas, as although he was a student of the Frankfurt School, there were some important differences between his thoughts and those of the original members of the School (like Adorno and Horkheimer), which adds another dimension to the philosophy of critical theory. Habermas, while he rejected the positivist claim to have universal explanations for all phenomena, nevertheless felt that there was nothing fundamentally wrong with positivism so long as it did not '*exceed the limits established by the conditions of [its] possibility*' (Thompson & Held, 1982, p. 7). In other words, Habermas believed that it was only when positivism sought to enter the realm of the social sciences, where it was not possible to technically control or manipulate objects, that it became illegitimate. So that for Habermas positivism had its place as a particular form of knowledge which he labelled empirical analytic science (or theoretical knowledge). In this respect Habermas was evidently more forgiving of positivism than his Frankfurt School mentors.

Habermas indicated that there were two further forms of knowledge — historical hermeneutic and critical social science or self-reflective knowledge. In the former, validity is arrived at through the agreement on meanings between participants, i.e. intersubjective dialogue. However, Habermas warned that this historical hermeneutic knowledge should also not lay claim to universalism as it did not take into account the consideration that language is itself a medium of social control and domination. A self-reflective critical social science is concerned with the analysis of power and ideology and is based on the 'collective interest in emancipation, in freedom from illusion, in autonomy and in the realization of the good life' (Finlayson, 2005, p. 18).

In this respect Habermas concurred with the Frankfurt School but differed from them in so far as he placed more emphasis on institutions and sought to determine what kinds of institutions are required to protect individuals against political extremism. Frankfurt School critical theorists were much more suspicious of institutions and their ability to bring about any sort of societal change. For Habermas though, the concept of intersubjective dialogue was integral to change and this meant that it was possible for institutions which could actually be forces for good, to be created as a result of this process of intersubjective communication.

From this necessarily very brief discussion of the philosophical underpinnings of critical theory it is therefore possible to summarise its main paradigmatic assumptions specifically in terms of epistemology, ontology and methodology. With regard to epistemology, critical theory is necessarily subjectivist in so far as it rejects positivist notions of objectivism which seek to create a distance between the knower and what is known. Ontologically, it is critical realist as it is based on the assumption that there is indeed a reality but one which cannot be fully apprehended (due to the existence of ideology or 'false consciousness'). And in this context it is evident that critical theory had an inherent normative dimension, as by critiquing society it was necessarily doing so from a particular vantage point or value system (hence its critical realist ontology). Methodologically, there are several dimensions to critical theory — an emancipatory cognitive interest (freeing from false consciousness); critical reflection (on the very assumptions of critical theory itself and the way that knowledge is formed); dialectical (a view of society as innately consisting of opposing interests). Importantly, it is the reflective aspect of critical theory which led its creators to recognise an inconsistency in the theory. For in critical theory contradictions are not only inherent in society (referring to its dialectical methodology) but at the same time necessary for societal change. This led to a certain pessimism in the critical theoretical project which, according to Finlayson (2005, p. 15) made it 'self-consciously aporetic; it throws a little light on a situation from which there is no way out'.

However, that said, Habermas's understandings, in contrast, are more optimistic as they hold up the ideal of free rational discussion between equals [which] though presently unfulfilled, is nonetheless worthy of pursuit. Hence Habermas's focus on what kinds of institutions should be created that could foster societal change (Finlayson, 2005).

Undoubtedly the critical theory of the Frankfurt School inspired the rise of a myriad of diverse theoretical approaches within the social sciences including cultural studies theories, feminist theories, poststructuralism, postmodernism, postcolonialism, amongst others. However, it is submitted that these subsequent theories utilised the term 'critical' in a rather loose fashion which often did not coincide with the paradigmatic assumptions that underpinned the critical theory of the Frankfurt School as discussed earlier. In a very general sense, many of these subsequent research paradigms follow a constructivist or interpretative approach which, while they bear a family resemblance to critical theory in terms of their epistemological and methodological assumptions, are nevertheless distinct in terms of their ontological underpinnings. Indeed, according to Hollinshead (2004, p. 79), methodologically, critical theory and constructivist/interpretative approaches tend towards an emancipatory, action-oriented and admittedly 'engaged' or 'political' outlook on the world. However, the difference with constructivist/interpretative paradigms lies in their ontology which is essentially relativist, in contrast to critical theory's critical realism. What this means is that those who subscribe to constructivist/interpretative approaches support the existence of multiple realities and ways of being, seeing and knowing, all of which might be equally 'truthful.' Such a relativist approach thus necessarily fails to apprehend or to acknowledge the existence of dominant ideologies which seek to suppress and subjugate. This highlights an apparent paradox in constructivist thinking — that is that it is difficult to see how a relativist ontology can co-exist with a methodology which has as a key characteristic an emancipatory cognitive interest. For seeking emancipation means making a judgement or value statement about what 'unfreedom' is, which necessarily implies a belief in a particular kind of society which is better than the one which exists. This does not 'relativise' truth as constructivists would have us to believe. So that if constructivist approaches are to lay claim to being critical, to having an emancipatory intent, then they must acknowledge that the belief in a better world necessarily implies the existence of a 'real' reality (essentially a kind of critical realism). Constructivist/interpretative approaches, in other words, should methodologically engage in critical reflection. This is important if research carried out under this umbrella is to lay claim to being critical, for critique is not just about identifying what is wrong with society and being critical about one's subjectivity within this context, but is also about identifying what is inconsistent with the entirety of one's paradigmatic assumptions.

Still, despite the apparent disparity between critical theory and more constructivist/interpretative approaches, underlying all of these philosophies is a questioning of 'Grand Narratives' not with critique as an end in itself but using critique as a means of transforming and, indeed, emancipating underserved knowledges. Admittedly the preceding discussion on critical theory and constructivist/interpretative paradigms has been grossly generalised due to the need to adhere to the word strictures of a book chapter. However, the fundamental point here is that the paradigmatic assumptions of particular research approaches that lay claim to the title of 'critical' must be discussed and made explicit. In the case of critical research in tourism, it is evident that the paradigmatic underpinnings of this kind of research have not really been explored and reflected upon and it is submitted that much of critical tourism research has still not progressed in this regard. In the next section, the state of critical tourism research will be explored.

The State of 'Critical' Tourism Research

In examining critical tourism research, focus will be on the paradigmatic assumptions (epistemology, ontology and methodology) made by authors of published work within the tourism academy. Admittedly the materials drawn upon in this context will necessarily be limited as the intention is not comprehensiveness but rather to present a primarily conceptual argument about the state of critical tourism research which, it is hoped, will direct attention to the need to ensure its theoretical cogency and coherency.

It is important to state here that there have been two interrogations of the state of qualitative tourism enquiry (under which umbrella critical research might be ostensibly located). The first by Riley and Love (2000) and the second by Phillimore and Goodson (2004) both of which sought to examine qualitative research in tourism within the context of Denzin and Lincoln's (1998) framework of the history of qualitative social research. In this framework Denzin and Lincoln (1998) categorised the historical evolution of qualitative research in the social sciences into five periods which they termed 'moments' — traditional, modernist, blurred genres, crisis in representation and fifth moment. It is not the intention of this chapter to enter into a discussion of these moments and how they reflect the state of tourism research as this has already been done competently by Riley and Love (2000) in their pre-1996 analysis of published tourism research and subsequently by Phillimore and Goodson (2004) who picked up their analysis post-1996. Rather the purpose of the current exercise is primarily to examine tourism research that lays claim to being 'critical' in order to determine whether the paradigmatic assumptions of such an approach have been explicitly conceptualised. Such a determination will be guided by this author's understanding of critical research as being underpinned by three paradigmatic assumptions — an epistemological subjectivity, a critical realist ontology and a methodology which is characterised by an emancipatory cognitive interest, a self reflective critique and a belief in the dialectical nature of the social world.

That said, the discussion is limited to published articles in the two main tourism journals — *Annals of Tourism Research (Annals)* and *Tourism Management*. These two journals were selected for two main reasons. The first is because they have dominated the tourism research landscape and have possibly the widest readership and authorships of all the mainstream tourism journals. Annals have been publishing articles for over 30 years and Xiao and Smith (2006, p. 491) indicate that it is the *'leading international scholarly journal in the field.'* A description of this journal encapsulates its *raison d' etre* as entailing a focus on the development of theory within tourism studies:

> While striving for a balance of theory and application, Annals is ultimately dedicated to developing theoretical constructs. Its strategies are to invite and encourage offerings from various disciplines ... thus to expand the frontiers of knowledge. (Elsevier, 2006a)

For its part Tourism Management is described as the *'leading international journal for all those concerned with the planning and management of travel and tourism'* (Elsevier, 2006b). Clearly both journals have different research emphases with Annals seemingly more interested in articles of a theoretical nature and Tourism Management seemingly more focused on issues of management (this is not however to imply that these two emphases are mutually exclusive!). The second reason for choosing these two journals for this discussion is that they proved to be the most easily accessible. Specifically, it was possible to search both journals electronically by keywords and indeed, according to Xiao and Smith (2006, p. 492):

> Annals is the only tourism journal that has continuously published cumulative subject indices in a consistent fashion that allows periodic examinations of the growth of tourism knowledge.

While Tourism Management does not have a searchable subject index, one can nevertheless undertake electronic keyword searches of the articles in the journal. Still, the problem that faced this author in sourcing materials from these two journals was how to determine which publications subscribed to a critical research paradigm. In the wider social science academy critical theoretical approaches are recognised as distinct types of research and so research articles that come under this umbrella would, at the very least have the term 'critical' or critique somewhere in the text. With this in mind a decision was made to undertake a keyword search of the two mentioned journals using 'critical' and 'critique' as keywords. Where an article came up that contained either of these keywords the entire articles were read in detail in order to examine their content. The investigation unearthed almost 50 articles with these key words in each journal. The articles had publication dates from 1979 to 2005 thus spanning more than a quarter of a century. Similarly, Tribe (2006) in an article in which he interrogated the 'truth about tourism' discovered in a perusal of the CABABS database over a much more limited period, that the term 'critical theory' was only evident in '*summary details of 4 out of the 12,175 articles abstracted between 1990 and 2002*' (p. 375).

However, it should be recognised that it is entirely possible that some critical research in tourism might not mention the words 'critical' or 'critique' but that this is nevertheless implicit in the assumptions underpinning the research. In this case it might be necessary to list a range of important keywords that might point to a critical theoretical approach (for example words like emancipation, dialectic, realism *inter alia*) and to proceed with a similar analysis as that conducted in this chapter. Further, it is possible that as Phillimore and Goodson (2004) suggest, the word limit strictures of journal articles preclude researchers from going into any detailed discussion of their paradigmatic assumptions. However in response to the latter contention, it is this author's feeling that this sort of engagement is not peripheral to research which subscribes to the label of critical, but is integral to it. A final point about the discussion in this chapter is that it does not include an analysis of books nor does it include any analysis of articles published in more recently established tourism journals like *Tourism Culture and Communication, Current Issues in Tourism, Tourist Studies* amongst others. Indeed, with regard to the journal Tourist Studies, a description of this journal explicitly indicates its commitment to a more critical approach to research:

> [Tourist Studies is] a multidisciplinary journal providing a platform for the development of *critical perspectives* (author's emphasis) on the nature of tourism as a social phenomenon. (Sage, 2006)

Clearly it would have been very useful for this chapter to undertake an examination of the articles in this journal. Unfortunately, it was not possible to undertake electronic keyword searches of this journal that so expressly declared its critical intent. The task of further research might therefore be to undertake such an investigation. Despite these limitations however, it is felt that the following very rudimentary analysis of articles in the two most prominent tourism journals will in some way explicate the argument being made in this chapter.

In examining the articles with keywords of critical and/or critique in *Annals of Tourism Research* it was evident that there were four general, sometimes overlapping, senses in which these terms were being applied. The first is where critical is seen as almost synonymous with critique and is taken to mean an analysis, commentary or evaluation (Mansfield, 1992; Wilson, 1994; Carr, 2002; Tribe, 1997; Jenkins, 1982; Gilbert & Hudson, 2000; Evans-Pritchard, 1989; Cohen, 1979; Arramberri, 2001). The second understanding of critical is where the term is seen to mean important or essential particularly in a managerial, operational or strategic context (Ajami, 1988; Chen & Uysal, 2002; Russell & Faulkner, 2004; Huan, Beaman, & Shelby, 2004; Douglass & Raento, 2004; Torres, 2003; Russo, 2002; Buckley, 2002; de Holan & Phillips, 1997; Tooman, 1997; Fletcher & Cooper, 1996; Moscardo, 1996; Horner, 1993; Teye, 1988; Seely, Iglarsh, & Edgell, 1980). The third use of critical is in the sense of fault-finding or criticism (Fotsch, 2004; Bendell & Font, 2004; Blundell, 1993; Siegenthaler, 2002). The fourth use of critical and the one with which this chapter is concerned is where critical is used to describe a distinct paradigmatic approach and in this case there were much fewer articles discovered. The following discussion will examine those articles which purported to undertake critical research.

Bandyopadhyay and Morais (2005) seek to examine the 'representative dissonance' (p. 1006) between the representation of India in the Western (American) media and the way in which India represents itself through the Indian government. In other words the authors seek to uncover the gap between the 'reality' of India (as portrayed by the Indian government) and the way in which India is represented by the West. The analysis is informed by postcolonial theory, and in this context the authors presume throughout that the representations depicted by the Indian government are the 'truth' about India. However, the point here is that in order to comment on dissonance in representations, there must, necessarily, be some judgement being made about what is real and what is not. It was only in the final paragraph that the authors explained that there was necessarily some confluence between the Indian government's representations and that of the American media due to India's historical experience of colonialism and imperialism and its current participation in world capitalism. Nevertheless the authors still emphasised in this conclusion that the Indian government's representations 'revealed resistance to colonialist *fantasies*' (this writer's emphasis) (p. 1017). The authors' claim that the aim of the study is to:

> probe into the ideological factors behind any observed dissonance to pave the way for more serious consideration and empowerment of Third World countries in Western touristic representations (p. 1017)

thereby declaring the works emancipatory cognitive interest. Nevertheless by sidestepping an ontological debate about the nature of reality it is difficult to accept that this article has fully engaged in research of a critical theoretical nature.

Johnston (2001) draws on feminist and the critical social theory of embodiment to deconstruct and contest tourism-based hierarchical dualisms such as mind/body, self/other, gender/sex, tourist/host, straight/gay. These hierarchical dualisms, she argues, produce hegemonic, disembodied and masculinist knowledge (p. 181). Using two gay pride parades in New Zealand and Australia, Johnston claims to illustrate the 'empirical possibilities of an embodied account of tourism' (p. 181). Johnston's work does bear some of the characteristics of critical research in so far as it is evident that it is underpinned by a subjectivist epistemology (reflected in embodiment theory) and a methodology in which an integral aspect is an emancipatory cognitive interest. The latter is reflected in Johnston's assertion that the paper is aimed at unsettling the hierarchical dualisms within tourism studies:

> thereby challenging [its] masculinism [and] focusing attention on the gendered/sexed and sexualized bodies of gay pride parades [which] can prompt new understandings of power, knowledge and social relationships between bodies and tourism processes. (p. 189)

Yet, Johnston does not engage with a reflective analysis of the ontological assumptions of embodiment theory in which there is an apparent tension between subscribing to a view of the world as being inhabited by plural and multiple realities while at the same time seeking the subversion of hierarchical dualisms so that the world can in a sense, become a better place. For the very objective of emancipation involves the creation of a subjectively hierarchical dualism between freedom/unfreedom.

Mellinger (1994) undertakes a poststructuralist (discursive) 'critical analysis of tourism representations' of African Americans in the deep South as depicted through photographic images. Mellinger's critique has a distinctly emancipatory objective as he claims that the critical analysis that he has conducted is not merely aimed at developing understanding but is also intended to:

> unambiguously condemn and disrupt the imperialist structures and colonialist fantasies that constitute much of tourism culture, and to take up a discourse of possibility that provides for the empowerment of misrepresented groups and the transformation of tourist representations. (p. 776)

Mellinger's objective is thus expressly political. Waitt (2000) also draws on poststructuralist theory, in this case to critique the historical authenticity of The Rocks in Australia. His claim is that the way in which The Rocks is historically represented by its developers, the Sydney Cove Redevelopment Authority, is merely a commodified version of the history of the area which closes off other interpretations of the area's history including that of indigenous peoples, Chinese labourers and women. These 'cultural injustices' Waitt claims, have contemporary political implications for the Australian state which has sought to embrace the philosophy of multiculturalism. Pritchard and Morgan (2000) draw on feminist and postcolonial theories to develop a critical theoretical analysis which challenges the gendered nature of tourism landscapes as being shaped by 'discourses of patriarchy and (hetero) sexuality' (p. 886). However, they express some uncertainty as to whether alternative approaches to tourism landscapes informed by a feminine and ethnic gaze (as if there were a single feminine and ethnic gaze!) 'will displace the polarizing male, heterosexist gaze to create alternative, more inclusive and insightful ways of knowing and understanding tourism' (p. 901).

Other studies which purport to conduct 'critical' research include Pretes (1995) who draws on postmodern perspectives in order to understand why tourists visit attractions such as Lapland (the fabled home of Santa Claus); and Echtner and Prasad (2003) who utilize postcolonial theory as a 'critical contextual perspective' to interpret the patterns of marketing images of Third World countries. These mentioned studies draw on postmodernist and poststructuralist perspectives which, it has been argued, are underpinned by a relativist ontology which is in conflict with an emancipatory objective. Yet in none of these studies is there a discussion of this paradigmatic contradiction.

In the journal *Tourism Management*, a similar number of articles were found with the key words critical and/or critique. However, there was a noticeable dominance in the number of articles that interpreted the term 'critical' from a managerial, operational or strategic perspective (including Ozgener & Iraz, 2006; Getz & Brown, 2006; Endo, 2005; Gursoy et al., 2005; Briedenhann & Wickens, 2004; Yuksel, 2003; Pavlovich, 2003; Mykleton, Crotts, & Mykleton, 2001; Augustyn & Knowles, 2000; Wang, Hsieh, & Huan, 2000). This predominance of managerial uses of the term is perhaps not surprising based on the title and the previously discussed intent of the journal although this should not imply that there can only be limited application of critical tourism research within a managerial or business context. The use of critical in the context of critique or analysis was less evident (including Lee & Taylor, 2005; Page, 2003; Leslie & Richardson, 2000). Importantly, there were only a handful of articles in which the term critical was used to describe a distinct philosophical approach to research and two of these will now be briefly discussed.

Hollinshead (1999) draws on poststructuralism (specifically a Foucauldian discursive approach) to critique the power of surveillance (*le regard*) in tourism. Hollinshead outlines a number of ways in which a Foucauldian perspective can be utilised within a tourism context. For example, he asserts that:

> Foucault's interpretative analytic can conceivably help decision-makers in travel and tourism self consciously measure the need in and across the industry for reins to be applied on the continuing spread of Western and other forms of a priori reasoning across the globe through the vehicle of travel and tourism. (p. 20)

Evidently, Hollinshead perceives the end of Western domination as a desirable or better state. At the same time, and somewhat paradoxically, he embraces the relativism of poststructuralism in which there are multiple realities, and ways of seeing and being, all of which are equally legitimate. Therein lies the tension in the paradigmatic assumptions of interpretative approaches like poststrucuralism which prove problematic for a coherent theory of critical research in tourism but which were scarcely discussed by Hollinshead. Pritchard and Morgan (2006) undertake a conceptual analysis of hotels as culturally contested, liminal and ideologically infused spaces drawing on insights from cultural studies and cultural geography both of which can themselves be located within a broader interpretative paradigm.

The issue with these critical tourism studies is that there is an absence of any sort of critical reflection on the paradigmatic assumptions on which the research is based. Indeed there has been a predominant use of postmodernist, poststructuralist and postcolonialist theories, all of which it is submitted, subscribe to a relativist ontology in which truth is seen as plural and perspectival. And yet in many of these tourism research undertakings there is an explicit or implicit emancipatory objective which seems to this researcher to be antithetical to a belief in the existence of multiple knowledges and truths all of which have equal 'validity.'

Conclusion

Ultimately, all tourism research and indeed all academic research should be critical where critical might be understood as critique, analysis or commentary. However, if all academic research should be inherently critical it would be tautological to speak of 'critical research.' Evidently then critical research must refer to more than just critique. It has been stated in this chapter that in the wider social sciences critical research has been understood as having distinct paradigmatic assumptions which sets it apart from other philosophical approaches. Indeed, what is now known as critical research in social sciences can trace its origins to the critical theory of the Frankfurt School which was diametrically opposed to the philosophical underpinnings of traditional positivist approaches. Critical theory was fundamentally epistemologically subjectivist, ontologically marked by a critical realism and methodologically by critical self reflection, emancipation and empowerment and a dialectical understanding of the social world. These were the philosophical assumptions that underpinned critical theory many of which were shared by constructivist and interpretative paradigms. However, while constructivist and interpretative paradigms borrowed from critical theory in terms of epistemology and methodology, they differed fundamentally in terms of ontology. It is this difference in ontology which, it has been argued, has led to a theoretical inconsistency within constructivist and interpretative approaches and which has been imported unquestioningly into tourism critical research.

Indeed, it has been the contention of this chapter that in tourism much of what is labelled 'critical research' borrows from constructivist/interpretative approaches such as poststructuralism, postmodernism, postcolonialism and feminism. However, tourism researchers have not engaged with a self-reflective analysis of the inherent tensions between the ontological assumptions of critical theory and those of constructivist/interpretative approaches. Specifically for the subscribers to the latter, reality is perspectival and plural and there is no single reality. However, such an approach necessarily denies an emancipatory objective, as if all truths are equally valid then within what context can emancipation take place? It therefore seems apparent that critical research in tourism in adopting constructivist and interpretative approaches has also adopted the tension inherent in these approaches between what is essentially a relativist ontology and a methodological approach which has as a key element an emancipatory cognitive interest.

So that in the same way that Fraser (1995) queried, "What's critical about critical theory?' this author must end the discussion with the question "What's critical about critical tourism research? There is an absence of theoretical coherency in critical tourism research which makes it difficult for it to lay claim to a distinct critical theoretical approach which includes an ontological realism. Indeed critique in tourism research should not only refer to philosophical reflections on the limits of those knowledges and truths which claim universalism (*a la* positivism) but also go beyond this to examine issues of moral autonomy *with a view to fostering social transformation/change*. And in this context a way to ensure the theoretical coherency of critical tourism research in which emancipation is a key objective is to reject ontological relativism and embrace the political underpinnings and normative values inherent in a critical realist perspective. It might be also that, in a Habermasian sense, what is required is an examination of those institutions that exist/or might be created which can foster societal change. Thus critical tourism research might become a:

> transformative endeavour unembarrassed by the label 'political' and unafraid
> to consummate a relationship with an emancipatory consciousness. [Indeed]
> whereas traditional researchers cling to the guard rail of neutrality, critical
> [tourism] researchers [should] announce their partisanship in the struggle
> for a better world. (Kincheloe & McLaren, 1994, p. 140)

So what might a critical tourism research agenda look like? First, it would involve the identification of the most important struggles within tourism today (a dialectical view of society) — these might include the tensions between the need to preserve local identities in what is a global tourism industry; the struggles of developing countries to obtain material and non-material benefits from tourism; the struggles of women to be involved as equal partners in tourism, amongst other things. Second, a critical tourism research agenda would seek to shed light on the character and bases of these struggles. Third, and importantly, a critical tourism research agenda should be self reflective in declaring and indeed in critiquing its own paradigmatic assumptions (acknowledging and addressing the tension between critical realism and relativism). But perhaps critical tourism research that aims to resist oppression in all its forms and which is expressly political might be unfashionable in a growing tourism intellectual '*milieu informed by relativism and postmodernism*' (Ray, 1993, p. ix).

References

Ajami, R. A. (1988). Strategies for tourism transnationals in Belize. *Annals of Tourism Research*, *15*(4), 517–530.

Aramberri, J. (2001). The host should get lost: Paradigms in tourism theory. *Annals of Tourism Research Annals of Tourism Research*, *28*(3), 738–761.

Augustyn, M., & Knowles, T. (2000). Performance of tourism partnerships: A focus on York. *Tourism Management*, *21*(4), 341–351.

Bandyopadhyay, R., & Morais, D. (2005). Representing dissonance: India's self and Western Image. *Annals of Tourism Research*, *32*(4), 1006–1021.

Bendell, J., & Font, X. (2004). Which tourism rules? Green standards and GATS. *Annals of Tourism Research*, *31*(1), 157–179.

Buckley, R. (2002). Tourism ecolabels. *Annals of Tourism Research*, *29*(1), 183–208.

Blundell, V. (1993). Aboriginal empowerment and souvenir trade in Canada. *Annals of Tourism Research*, *20*(1), 64–87.

Briedenhann, J., & Wickens, E. (2004). Tourism routes as a tool for the economic development of rural areas — vibrant hope or impossible dream? *Tourism Management*, *25*(1), 71–79.

Bronner, S., & Kellner, D. M. (1989). *Critical theory and society: A reader*. London: Routledge.

Carr, A. (2000). Critical theory and the psychodynamics of change. *Journal of Organizational Change*, *13*(3), 289–299.

Carr, N. (2002). The tourism–leisure behavioural continuum. *Annals of Tourism Research, 29*(4), 972–986.

Chen, J., & Uysal, M. (2002). Market positioning analysis: A hybrid approach. *Annals of Tourism Research, 29*(4), 987–1003.

Cohen, E. (1979). Rethinking the sociology of tourism. *Annals of Tourism Research, 6*(1), 18–35.

Dant, T. (2003). *Critical social theory.* London: Sage.

de Holan, P. M., & Phillips, N. (1997). Sun, sand and hard currency: Tourism in Cuba. *Annals of Tourism Research, 24*(4), 777–795.

Denzin, N., & Lincoln, Y. (1998). *The landscape of qualitative research: Theories and issues.* London: Sage.

Douglass, W., & Raento, P. (2004). The tradition of invention: Conceiving Las Vegas. *Annals of Tourism Research, 31*(1), 7–23.

Echtner, C., & Prasad, P. (2003). The context of Third World tourism marketing. *Annals of Tourism Research, 30*(3), 660–682.

Elsevier (2006a). *Annals of Tourism Research.* Available from http://www.elsevier.com/wps/find/ journaldescription.cws_home/689/description#description.

Elsevier (2006b). *Tourism Management.* Available from http://authors.elsevier.com/JournalDetail.html? PubID = 30472&Precis.

Endo, K. (2006). Foreign direct investment in tourism — flows and volumes. *Tourism Management, 27*(4), 600–614. Available from http://www.sciencedirect.com accessed 15/11/05.

Evans-Pritchard, D. (1989). How "they" see "us": Native American images of tourists. *Annals of Tourism Research, 16*(1), 89–105.

Finlayson, J. G. (2005). *Habermas: A very short introduction.* Oxford: Oxford University Press.

Fletcher, J., & Cooper, C. (1996). Tourism strategy planning: Szolnok county, Hungary. *Annals of Tourism Research, 23*(1), 181–200.

Fotsch, P. (2004). Tourism's uneven impact: History of Cannery Row. *Annals of Tourism Research, 31*(4), 779–800.

Fraser, N. (1995). What's critical about critical theory? In: J. Meehan (Ed.). *Feminists read Habermas* (pp. 21–55). London: Routledge.

Getz, D., & Brown, G. (2006). Critical success factors for wine tourism regions: A demand analysis. *Tourism Management, 27*(1), 146–158.

Gilbert, D., & Hudson, S. (2000). Tourism demand constraints: A skiing participation. *Annals of Tourism Research, 27*(4), 906–925.

Gursoy, D., Chen, M. H., & Kim, H. J. (2005). The US airlines relative positioning based on attributes of service quality. *Tourism Management, 26*(1), 57–67.

Hollinshead, K. (1999). Surveillance of the worlds of tourism: Foucault and the eye-of power. *Tourism Management, 17*(2), 133–139.

Hollinshead, K. (2004). Ontological craft in tourism studies: The creative capture of people and places through qualitative research. In: J. Phillimore, & L. Goodson (Eds). *Qualitative research in tourism: Ontologies, epistemologies and methodologies* (pp. 63–82). London: Routledge.

Horner, A. (1993). Tourist arts in Africa before tourism. *Annals of Tourism Research, 20*(1), 52–63.

Huan, C., Beaman, J., & Shelby, L. (2004). No-escape natural disaster: Mitigating impacts on tourism. *Annals of Tourism Research, 31*(2), 255–273.

Jenkins, C. L. (1982). The effects of scale in tourism projects in developing countries. *Annals of Tourism Research, 9*(2), 229–249.

Johnston, L. (2001). (Other) bodies and tourism studies. *Annals of Tourism Research, 28*(1), 180–201.

Keat, R. (1981). *The politics of social theory: Habermas, Freud and the critique of positivism.* Oxford: Basil Blackwell.

Kincheloe, J. L., & McLaren, P. L. (1994). Rethinking critical theory and qualitative research. In: N. Denzin, & Y. Lincoln (Eds). *Handbook of qualitative research* (pp. 138–157). London: Sage.

Lee, C. L., & Taylor, T. (2005). Critical reflections on the economic impact assessment of a mega-event: The case of 2002 FIFA World Cup. *Tourism Management, 26*(4), 595–603.

Leslie, D., & Richardson, A. (2000). Tourism and cooperative education in UK undergraduate courses: Are the benefits being realised? *Tourism Management, 21*(5), 489–498.

Mansfield, Y. (1992). From motivation to actual travel. *Annals of Tourism Research, 19*(3), 399–419.

Mellinger, W. M. (1994). Toward a critical analysis of tourism representations. *Annals of Tourism Research, 21*(4), 756–779.

Moscardo, G. (1996). Mindful visitors. *Annals of Tourism Research, 23*(2), 376–397.

Mykletun, R. J., Crotts, J., & Mykletun, A. (2001). Positioning an island destination in the peripheral area of the Baltics: A flexible approach to market segmentation. *Tourism Management, 22*(5), 493–500.

Ozgener, S., & Iraz, R. (2006). Customer relationship management in small-medium enterprises: The case of Turkish tourism industry. *Tourism Management, 27*(6), 1356–1363. Available from www.sciencedirect.com accessed 15/11/05.

Page, S. (2003). Evaluating research performance in tourism: The UK experience. *Tourism Management, 24*(6), 607–622.

Pavlovich, K. (2003). The evolution and transformation of a tourism destination network: The Waitomo Caves, New Zealand. *Tourism Management, 24*(2), 203–216.

Phillimore, J., & Goodson, L. (2004). Progress in qualitative research in tourism: Epistemology, ontology and methodology. In: J. Phillimore, & L. Goodson (Eds). *Qualitative research in tourism: Ontologies, epistemologies and methodologies* (pp. 3–29). London: Routledge.

Pretes, M. (1995). Postmodern tourism: The Santa Claus Industry. *Annals of Tourism Research, 22*(1), 1–15.

Pritchard, A., & Morgan, N. (2000). Privileging the male gaze: Gendered tourism landscapes. *Annals of Tourism Research, 27*(4), 884–905.

Pritchard, A., & Morgan, N. (2006). Hotel Babylon? Exploring hotels as liminal sites of transition and transgression. *Tourism Management, 27*(5), 762–772. Available from www.sciencedirect.com accessed 15/11/05.

Ray, L. (1993). *Rethinking critical theory*. London: Sage.

Riley, R., & Love, L. (2000). The state of qualitative tourism research. *Annals of Tourism Research, 27*, 164–187.

Russell, R., & Faulkner, B. (2004). Entrepreneurship, chaos and the tourism area lifecycle. *Annals of Tourism Research, 31*(3), 556–579.

Russo, A. (2002). The "vicious circle" of tourism development in heritage cities. *Annals of Tourism Research, 29*(1), 165–182.

Sage (2006). *Tourist Studies*. Available from http://www.sagepub.com/journalsProdDesc.nav?prodId=Journal201263.

Seely, R. L., Iglarsh, H. J., & Edgell, D. (1980). Goal programming: Planning process of tourism organisations. *Annals of Tourism Research, 7*(3), 353–365.

Siegenthaler, P. (2002). Hiroshima and Nagasaki in Japanese guidebooks. *Annals of Tourism Research, 29*(4), 1111–1137.

Slater, P. (1977). *Origin and significance of the Frankfurt School: A Marxist perspective*. London: Routledge and Kegan Paul.

Teye, V. (1988). Geographic factors affecting tourism in Zambia. *Annals of Tourism Research, 15*(4), 487–503.

Thompson, J., & Held, D. (Eds) (1982). *Habermas critical debates*. London: MacMillan.

Torres, R. (2003). Linkages between tourism and agriculture in Mexico. *Annals of Tourism Research, 30*(3), 546–566.

Tooman, A. (1997). Applications of the life-cycle model in tourism. *Annals of Tourism Research*, *24*(1), 214–234.

Tribe, J. (1997). The indiscipline of tourism. *Annals of Tourism Research*, *24*(3), 638–657.

Tribe, J. (2006). The truth about tourism. *Annals of Tourism Research*, *33*(2), 360–381.

Waitt, G. (2000). Consuming heritage: Perceived historical authenticity. *Annals of Tourism Research*, *27*(4), 835–862.

Wang, K. C., Hsieh, A. T., & Huan, T. C. (2000). Critical service features in group package tour: An exploratory research. *Tourism Management*, *21*(2), 177–189.

Wilson, D. (1994). Unique by a thousand miles: Seychelles tourism revisited. *Annals of Tourism Research*, *21*(1), 20–45.

Xiao, H., & Smith, S. (2006). The making of tourism research: Insights from a social sciences journal. *Annals of Tourism Research*, *33*(2), 490–507.

Yuksel, A. (2003). Writing publishable papers. *Tourism Management*, *24*(4), 437–446.

Chapter 8

A Realist Critique of the Situated Voice in Tourism Studies

David Botterill

Introduction

The chapter represents the latest contribution in my intellectual 'underlabouring' project in critical tourism studies. Underlabouring, first used by Locke, is a term borrowed from philosophy to mean a process that seeks 'to remove the idols, obstacles or ideologies that stand in the way of, or distort the understanding of, new knowledge to be produced by the sciences' (Collier, 1994, p. 19).

Thus far, expressions of this project have sought to document the UK outputs that contribute to knowledge in tourism studies at doctoral level (Botterill, Gale, & Haven, 2003) and research quality assessment (Botterill & Haven, 2003); to examine the largely unacknowledged epistemological biases in doctoral studies by showing how students' work is influenced by positivist, constructivist and critical epistemologies of the social sciences (Botterill, 2001); and through autoethnographic writing on my own research journey (Botterill, 2003) that has led me to my present Critical Realist Tourism Research (CRTR) project. Most latterly in two substantive projects I have tried to demonstrate the CRTR project through the study of tourism and social inclusion (Botterill & Klemm, 2006) and the 'internationalisation' of the tourism classroom (Botterill & Platenkamp, 2004). CRTR is also explained and demonstrated in a critique of the Tourism Area Life-Cycle Model (Gale & Botterill, 2005). The simple purpose of intellectual underlabouring and the CRTR project is to provide a more satisfactory understanding of the philosophies of social science in order to underpin research practice and the creation of knowledge in tourism studies.

This chapter represents a further public expression of a move in my underlabouring project. In offering a critique of the emergent orthodoxy of the situated voice in the social sciences and its tentative appearance in tourism studies, I want to make explicit my allegiances to realism and in particular critical realism on a philosophical level. My critique is not to argue against the adoption of the situated voice in tourism studies; indeed, I want to participate in and celebrate it. Instead I want to strengthen its contribution to 'critical' tourism

The Critical Turn in Tourism Studies: Innovative Research Methodologies
Copyright © 2007 by Elsevier Ltd.
All rights of reproduction in any form reserved.
ISBN: 0-08-045098-9

research and at the same time to assert, at a basic level, the tenets of a critical realist philosophy. The paper is also offered as an invitation to join the CRTR project because, as Sayer (2004, p. 6) reminds us, 'Critical realist philosophy offers an alternative both to the spurious scientificity of positivism and to the idealist and relativist reactions to positivism'.

I begin with a very concise introduction to Critical Realism.

Critical Realism as a complete philosophy of, and for, the social sciences, is gaining ground in a number of influencing disciplines in the study of tourism (see, e.g. Lawson, 1997 in Economics; Archer, 1995 in Sociology; and Fleetwood & Ackroyd, 2004 in Organisation and Management Studies). Originating from the writings of Bhaskar (1978, 1979) on 'transcendental realism' (his general philosophy of science) and 'critical naturalism' (his specific philosophy of the human sciences), critical realism challenges the dominant approaches of positivism and hermeneutics by defending the power of both natural *and* social science to *explain*, as well as *observe* and *interpret*. Critical Realism relies on three underlying philosophical tenets: a differentiated and stratified ontology, epistemic relativism and judgemental rationality. Of course, in the space of a chapter introduction it is only possible to briefly sketch out Critical Realism, and so I shall signpost the reader to the extensive literature in realism and the social sciences for further information.

To be realist is to hold to the view that there is a mind-independent external reality and that it can be known. Exploring and understanding the nature of that reality becomes the primary purpose of realist thinkers. Critical realists, therefore, foreground ontology over epistemology, and much of the social scientific critical realist project is founded upon an examination of 'What makes society possible?'. Consequentially, the central question of my CRTR project asks 'What makes tourism possible?'. Furthermore, critical realism proposes a differentiated ontology of social reality divided into the 'transitive domain' (our theories, concepts and discourse of research) and the 'intransitive domain' (the largely enduring structures and properties of objects that enable and constrain human agency). The realist claim to a mind-independent world does not presuppose some simplistic privileged access to social reality but, rather, a much more complex interaction in which theoretical categories inform, and are informed by, empirical materials (Gregory, 1986). This, in turn, produces fallibilist, practically adequate claims to truth based on judgemental rationality (it will become clear what I mean by this, below). We need, also, to refer here to another important position in the ontology of critical realism that not only distinguishes between the world and our experience of it, but also proposes a stratified ontology structured into: (1) the empirical, (2) the actual and (3) the real. Here, Bhaskar (1978, p. 13) was referring to the notion that knowledge of the social world is stratified into: (1) surface or experiential knowledge; (2) events that happen whether we experience them or not; and (3) a further depth strata that produces the events in the world that is comprised of what might, metaphorically, be called *mechanisms*. This deep strata — the 'real' in critical realism — should not be simply conflated with social reality as it has a distinct ontological character, and it is what distinguishes critical realism from previous manifestations of realism (see, e.g. Fleetwood, 2004). Crucially, these mechanisms:

- are hidden from the gaze of the casual observer, yet are no less real than that which can be sensed;
- are *circumstantial* rather than deterministic or, to be specific, they possess causal powers that may or may not be activated, depending on contingently related conditions (Sayer, 2001); and

- comprise a reality that is *not* a construct of a reflexive or self-referential science, despite the fact that it can only be known in terms of the discourses available to us (which is why our theories concerning that reality are, of necessity, fallible and open to falsification).

Hence, critical realism may be contrasted with 'actualism' (or 'empiricism') on one hand, and 'non-realism' (or 'idealism') on the other. The former, though not denying the reality of events and experiences, makes no provision for the existence of underlying mechanisms, since these 'are disputed and not directly observable ... and hence refractory to quantification' (Ackroyd & Fleetwood, 2000, p. 6). In contrast, the latter rules out for investigation non-discursive practices in asserting that there is nothing knowable that is independent of mind, a position that is the basis of contemporary constructivism and which has been referred to by critical realists as the 'epistemic fallacy', or the failure to separate the 'transitive' and 'intransitive' domains of social science/reality (as explained above).

'Depth' metaphors predominate in realist accounts of the natural and social worlds, thus alluding to the manner in which the multiplicity of mechanisms that conjointly provoke a given series of events and, when realised, their ensuing experiences are arranged (i.e. within open systems such as nature and society as distinct from the closed system of the laboratory). In addressing this issue, Bhaskar (1978, pp. 168–169) argues for the 'stratification of nature', that is, 'an ordered [or layered] series of mechanisms in which the lower explain without replacing the higher' (Collier, 1994, p. 48). Here, it is possible to distinguish between 'horizontal explanations', which 'move from the level of the happenings and phenomena to be explained to that of the mechanisms and structures which generate them' (Carter & New, 2004, p. 8), and 'vertical explanations', whereby one mechanism or structure is shown to be the product of another, more basic one and so on *ad infinitum*. In the natural sciences, this process of abstraction would normally be operationalised through recourse to experimental methods under laboratory conditions. However, in the social sciences, closed systems cannot be established artificially, hence experiments are irrelevant; not so the 'detective-like' skills of geologists, natural historians, meteorologists and other natural scientists who study open systems (Collier, 1998). That aside, realist social science is not grounded in a particular methodology. Quantitative and qualitative methods alike may yield the empirical data from which horizontal and vertical explanations are possible as demonstrated in Gale and Botterill (in press).

Elsewhere, I have concluded that realism, as a philosophy of *all* science, counters most of the objections attributable to positivism, constructivism and critical theory, 'yet it retains the possibility of universal and hierarchical theory, easily contains the nuance of hermeneutics and interpretation and offers the transformative power of an emancipatory science' (Botterill, 2003, p. 99). Similarly, Collier (1998) reminds us that:

> [h]uman sciences may be interpretative and non-reductive, but at the same time causally explanatory and corrective of agents' conceptions.

The Situated Voice in Tourism Research

I would argue that situated voices contribute a richness to tourism research because they:

- *celebrate the fun and fanciful experience of tourism and invite playfulness into method;*
- *embody the researcher and humanise the research process; and*

- *expose the blindness of 'orthodox' tourism research, the so-called 'God trick' of orthodox approaches where researchers claim to see everything but remain, themselves, unseen.*

In tourism research there is still only a very small amount of published literature in the field that incorporates the situated voice (see, e.g. Humberstone, 2004). To claim any sense of this movement as an emerging orthodoxy in tourism research seems, therefore, premature. However, in many social science disciplines the situated voice is much better established and is taking on the mantle of orthodoxy in many subject domains. Most of the published work in tourism is reviewed in the excellent contributions of Westwood, Morgan, and Pritchard (2006) and Ateljevic, Harris, Wilson, and Collins (2005) to two special issues of *Tourism Recreation Research* (Volume 30(2) and Volume 31(2)). Both Ateljevic et al. (2005) and Westwood et al. (2006) argue that the situated voice better captures the fractured, contradictory and context-rich social world and that the epistemology humanises the research process. The origins of the situated voice are in the rejection of positivism as a tenable philosophy in the social sciences, the crisis in Marxian-inspired material realism and critical theory, and the rise of constructivism, hermeneutics and phenomenology. And here begins the competing pulls that act upon the epistemological gain of the situated voice, when researchers are drawn to use data generated to support competing idealist, relativist or, as I want to assert, realist philosophical positions. At this point in my paper I begin my realist critique.

A Realist Critique

On first hearing, the realist claim, that there is a mind-independent external reality and that it can be known, may not be particularly startling to tourism researchers. We must all be, to some extent, minimal realists because we have to agree that the phenomenon of tourism exists independently of researchers' concepts or theories in order that it can be the object of our research. But beyond this minimal condition, things get a little more complex. For example, what do the results of our research tell us about the phenomenon of tourism? What are the truth claims that can be made? In most social science domains this has become a normal area of dispute resolved through the competing constructivist and realist philosophies. These range from strong constructivist claims that discourses are the objects of social reality to naïve empiricist claims to foundational truths. This is not yet the case in tourism research, however, where very few researchers are explicit as to what is assumed about the claims that are being made for their research results. My reading of orthodox tourism output is that the majority of authors impute a direct and uncomplicated relationship between the research findings and the object of study. In other words the results of tourism research are taken to be directly corresponding to the phenomenon of tourism, thereby many orthodox tourism researchers follow the largely discredited positivist correspondence of truth theory. Here I am in agreement with Ateljevic and Swain (2006, p. 1250) when they argue that what is partly at stake in the critical turn in tourism studies is 'the importance of exposing complexities, gaps and negotiations between the researcher and the researched'.

In orthodox tourism research the separation between the transitive and the intransitive domains is largely unrecognised and is certainly under-problematised. Consequentially, for example, the volumes of facts about tourists become 'the truth' about tourism. Such an approach implies a very simplistic relationship and one that is almost entirely rejected by the social sciences, except in some branches of economics. Critical realists accept that our knowledge of the world is always in terms of available descriptions and discourses and that we cannot step outside these to see how our claims to knowledge compare with the things to which they refer, but this does not mean that the basic differentiation between a transitive and an intransitive domain is abandoned. Tourism is an 'ism' that we use to talk about social phenomena. In doing so we ascribe tourism with certain characteristics as an orthodoxy is created through research. Now, just because under the critical turn and the situated voice in tourism research we have become reflexively engaged with the relationship between out transitive accounts of what we call tourism and the social objects that we ascribe to tourism does not mean that we can forget the intransitive phenomena. Whatever theories we hold or discourses that we engage in as part of the transitive domain, it is the intransitive domain — the world out there — that provides us with the experience of fallibility of our knowledge, of mistaking things and being taken by surprise, and it is this that provides the realist conviction that the social world is not just the product of thought, whether privately or socially constructed (Sayer, 2004). What critical realist tourism researchers would accept is that the subject–object relations become more complicated in the social sciences because of the complex, messy and contradictory characteristics of social reality and the tendency for reflexivity in social life, but that the intransitivity of tourism as an object of social research still stands. For example, the transitive domain of tourism research includes competing theories about, say tourist behaviour, or even competing social science disciplines seeking to explain tourist behaviour. But when theories about tourist behaviour are elaborated it does not follow that tourist behaviour changes too: When Boorstin's mass tourists in a protected bubble became MacCannell's recipients of staged authenticity then the tourists were largely, enduringly, the same.

So what does the move toward the situated voice mean in this critical realist metatheoretical context? As a critical realist I welcome the epistemic shift towards a more reflexive, embodied voice in the transitive domain that is easily contained by the critical realist commitment to epistemic relativism. However, from a critical realist position the judgement on the contribution of the situated voice to tourism studies lies not in the efficacy of the method but in the practical adequacy of its outcomes to explain the intransitive object of tourism or whatever sub-field of tourism is being studied; be it tourist consumption, tourism education, researching tourism or working in the tourism industry.

As I previously noted, an important position in the ontology of critical realism is that it distinguishes not only between the world and our experience of it but also proposes a stratified ontology structured into (1) the empirical, (2) the actual and (3) the real. In this schema then, we can locate the situated voices in the realm of the empirical (as we sense them) and the actual (the events that are recounted through the voice). For all the reasons given above they are potentially valuable to progressing tourism knowledge, but for the critical realist it is not until we work upon them to discover what they might tell us about the objects, their structures and their powers can we make epistemic gains in accessing the 'real' intransitive object of the social world that we label 'tourism'. Thus we are only able to begin to answer the CRTR question: 'What makes tourism possible?' if this stratified ontology is accepted. The research processes that move us into the 'real' are predicated upon the transcendent moment in critical realism and are called abduction and retroduction. A full description of these processes can be found in Danermark, Ekstrom, Jackson, and Karlsson (2002) and examples of their application in tourism research are provided in Gale and Botterill (2005).

The Epistemic Fallacy and the Slip to Relativist Ontology

The critical realist ontological position of a differentiated and stratified social world, independent of our thoughts about it, reflecting back the adequacy of our ideas, concepts and theories, provides the promised critique of the situated voice to tourism knowledge. It is quite easy to accommodate the situated voice as an epistemological move — a move towards knowing tourism in a new and different way — but the danger for a critical realist is that an epistemic move inspired by reflexivity and embodiment and one that privileges context and subjective meaning will drift into a relativist philosophical position without challenge. The danger here is to fall into what critical realists call the epistemic fallacy — the reducing of ontology to epistemology. To demonstrate this point I will use two quotations taken from examples of the situated voice in tourism. As I have previously mentioned both of these well-argued contributions are welcome expressions of the move to incorporate the situated voice, but in focussing upon them it enables me to sharpen the realist critique I am mounting here. Interestingly, both quotations are taken from the final sentences of the articles indicating, perhaps, some unresolved thoughts of the authors.

Quotation 1

Firstly from Ateljevic et al. (2005):

> Asserting the positions of the researcher and the researched are always crucial, and should be reflected on; but that such reflections cannot be abstracted from time and space they are constituted with. The researcher cannot assume that it would even be possible to abstract oneself from being in the world, that they are always and already part and co-constitutive of that world. (Ateljevic et al., 2005, p. 17)

In the thoughts expressed in the first sentence we can see the critical realist epistemic fallacy in action. Just because the epistemological conditions of the situated voice surrounding the researched and the researcher produce rich, embodied and context-specific characteristics this does not mean for the critical realist that 'roles' are indistinct. Of course, the researcher must reflect upon their 'position' 'as we are always in some position or another in relation to our objects' (Sayer, 2004, p. 53), but the crucial role of the researcher is 'to guard against forms of projection and selection which misrepresent our objects'. So it does not necessarily follow that from our epistemology we have to slip into assertions about the ontological — that the object, tourism research in the article by Ateljevic et al., is also always context specific, for example. To do so would be to slip into relativism because this produces what Harraway (as cited in Sayer, 2004, p. 52) calls the relativists 'god-trick':

> The relativist's equanimity in the face of different and often conflicting knowledges involves its own 'god-trick': it is a way of being nowhere while claiming to be everywhere equally, involving a denial of responsibility and critical enquiry.

In the second sentence we can perhaps see why the slip into relativism has been, perhaps unwittingly, made. There is recognition of the realist position that the researcher cannot step outside the transitive world but the implication of the second phrase seems to deny the possibility of knowledge of the intransitive object, in this case, the social phenomenon of tourism research. The critical realist differentiation of the domains of knowledge into the transitive and the intransitive solves this problem. Furthermore, critical realists would argue that we can move from the empirical and actual to the real through abduction and retroduction. It is the role of the researcher to come to know the real and to ask the question — what structures, objects, powers and mechanisms that lie deeply beneath the embodied voices and act upon human agents to enable and constrain their performances? It is the differentiated and stratified ontology of critical realism that offers a resolution for Ateljevic et al. should they wish to take it.

Quotation 2

In the second example taken from Westwood et al. (2006) the authors say this:

> The tourism academy needs to embrace those progressive stances which acknowledge far more variety in the way that research is conducted, interpreted and written if the field is to break new ground. In this, its scholars would do well to recognise that investigating 'the ontologies of being, meaning and identity in the contemporary age is frequently a messy matter of infinite interpretive possibilities. (Westwood et al., 2006, p. 40)

Here again we can see the slip between epistemology and ontology. In the first sentence the authors are calling for changes in the transitive domain, a new turn that I can easily contain within the epistemological relativist commitment of critical realism, but in the second sentence, in the quote from Hollinshead, the 'messy matters' become not just a creation of an epistemological turn but also a claim to ontological relativism. So in this case it is not only the epistemic fallacy but also, perhaps, the rejection of the critical realist tenet of judgemental rationality that fuels my critique. How, I am asking myself, in a social world of 'infinite interpretative possibilities' will we distinguish between 'crazy' and 'practically adequate' accounts of tourism as an object of the intransitive world?

Conclusion

Within the community of tourism researchers we should embrace the turn to an embodied, reflexive and situated epistemology, but for the critical realist this is not without its dangers.

A multiple voiced epistemology does not have to become a relativist ontology. To do so would be to commit the epistemic fallacy. The foregrounding of ontology over epistemology in critical realism provides us with a strong ontology that supports the realist pursuit of knowledge of tourism as an object in the intransitive domain. Further, we should not shy away from the responsibility to use judgemental rationality in evaluating which voices provide deeper and more practically adequate accounts of the 'real' in tourism studies.

References

Ackroyd, S., & Fleetwood, S. (2000). Realism in contemporary organisation and management studies. In: S. Ackroyd, & S. Fleetwood (Eds), *Realist perspectives on management and organisations* (pp. 3–25). London: Routledge.

Archer, M. (1995). *Realist social theory: The morphogenic approach*. Cambridge: Cambridge University Press.

Ateljevic, I., & Swain, M. B. (2006) Embodying tourism research: Gender performance among Sani and Bai women in Yunnan's ethnic tourism. In: Proceedings of *To the City and Beyond* Official Conference Proceedings (pp. 1249–1251). Council of Australian Tourism and Hospitality Educators, 2006.

Ateljevic, I., Harris, C., Wilson, E., & Collins, F. L. (2005). Getting 'entangled': Reflexivity and the 'critical turn' in tourism studies. *Tourism Recreation Research*, *30*(2), 5–18.

Bhaskar, R. (1978). *A realist theory of science*. Hemel Hempstead, England: Harvester Wheatsheaf.

Bhaskar, R. (1979). *The possibility of naturalism*. Hemel Hempstead, England: Harvester Wheatsheaf.

Botterill, T. D. (2001). The epistemology of a set of studies of tourism. *Leisure Studies*, *20*(3), 199–214.

Botterill, T. D. (2003). An autoethnographic narrative on tourism research epistemologies. *Society and Leisure*, *26*(1), 97–110.

Botterill, D., & Haven, C. (2003). *ATHE guideline 11: Tourism studies and the RAE2001*. ATHE: Guildford, Surrey.

Botterill, D., & Klemm, M. (2006). Introduction: Tourism and social inclusion. *Tourism, Culture and Communication*, *6*(1), 1–5.

Botterill, D., & Platenkamp, V. (2004). The international classroom of tourism studies: Opening Pandora's Box. Unpublished paper presented at the Association of Tourism in Higher Education annual conference, Critical Issues in Tourism Education, Buckinghamshire Chilterns University College, 1–3 December 2004.

Botterill, T. D., Gale, T., & Haven C. (2003). A survey of doctoral theses accepted by universities in the UK and Ireland for studies of tourism, 1990–1999. *Tourist Studies*, *2*(3), 283–311.

Carter, B., & New, C. (2004). Introduction: Realist social theory and empirical research. In: B. Carter, & C. New (Eds), *Making realism work: Realist social theory and empirical research* (pp. 1–20). London: Routledge.

Collier, A. (1994). *Critical realism: An introduction to Roy Bhaskar's philosophy*. Verso: London.

Collier, A. (1998). Critical realism. In: E. Craig (Ed.), *Routledge encyclopedia of philosophy*. London: Routledge. Available at: http://www.rep.routledge.com/article/R003 (accessed 1 August 2003).

Danermark, B., Ekstrom, M., Jackson, L., & Karlsson, J. Ch. (2002). *Explaining society; Critical realism in the social sciences*. Routledge: London.

Fleetwood, S. (2004). An ontology for organization and management studies. In: S. Fleetwood, & S. Ackroyd (Eds), *Critical realist applications in organisation and management studies* (pp. 27–53). London: Routledge.

Fleetwood, S., & Ackroyd, S. (Eds) (2004). *Critical realist applications in organisation and management studies*. London: Routledge.

Gale, T., & Botterill, D. (2005). A realist agenda for tourist studies, or why destination areas really rise and fall in popularity. *Tourist Studies*, *5*, 2.

Gregory, D. (1986). Realism. In: R. J. Johnston, D. Gregory, & D. M. Smith (Eds), *The dictionary of human geography* (2nd ed., pp. 387–390). Oxford: Blackwell.

Humberstone, B. (2004). Standpoint research: Multiple versions of reality in tourism theorizing and research. In: J. Phillimore, & L. Goodson (Eds), *Qualitative research in tourism ontologies, epistemologies and methodologies* (pp. 119–136). London: Routledge.

Lawson, A. (1997). *Economics and reality*. London: Routledge.

Sayer, A. (2001). Reply to Holmwood. *Sociology*, *35*(4), 967–984.

Sayer, A. (2004). *Realism and social science*. London: Sage.

Westwood, S., Morgan, N., & Pritchard, A. (2006). Situation, participation and reflexivity in tourism research: Furthering interpretive approaches to tourism enquiry. *Tourism Recreation Research*, *31*(2), 33–42.

Chapter 9

The Problem with Tourism Theory

Adrian Franklin

I am convinced that there remain some fundamental problems with how we understand tourism, how we conceive of tourism as an object/focus of investigation and how we frame the relevance of tourism in the world. In recent years, there has been good progress in the area of tourism theory and I will first try to characterise where this has occurred. In addition, there have been some further clarifications of what the problems are and I will also allude to these. Finally, as others and I have grappled with some of these problems, some new solutions seem to be emerging and these are worth including here. Notably, and no doubt annoyingly and frustratingly, I have also come to the conclusion that we need new *theory* (how do we uncover aspects of tourism that remain otherwise obscured) *less* than we need a new *ontology* of tourism (describing what tourism is/does). So, it is to this problem, rather than a review of theoretical progress and over the past few years, that I give most attention. To be perfectly clear, this paper is less about the problem with existing tourism theory than the problem of tourism *theory per se*. To put it even more bluntly: I am less inclined to look for theoretical *explanations* of tourism than to explore an account ontology of tourism. I will be suggesting that far from seeing tourism as behaviour to be explained it might be more worthwhile considering it as an *ordering*, a rather special ordering of modernity.

What has been Achieved?

A lot of good tourism works in theoretical and conceptual development have appeared in the past five years but of course there is insufficient space to pay sufficient tribute to them all here (but see Phillimore & Goodson, 2004; Tribe, 2005; Picken, 2006, for more of a review of the highlights).

Substantial progress has been made in addressing the essentially visual and symbolic registers of tourism research and part of what Tribe has called a new turn of 'new tourism research' has concentrated on exploring a more dynamic, 'entangled' tourist. There is now a healthier balance of sensual and embodied tourism work and this is advanced all the more

The Critical Turn in Tourism Studies: Innovative Research Methodologies
Copyright © 2007 by Elsevier Ltd.
All rights of reproduction in any form reserved.
ISBN: 0-08-045098-9

by the Dubrovnik conferences, beginning with *Embodying Tourism Research: Advancing Critical Approaches* in 2005, and key journals such as the *Journal of Tourism and Cultural Change* and *Tourist Studies*. Aside from the sexual, rejuvenated, excited, dancing, drinking and drugged tourist body, all of which point to important transformative performances of tourism, this research seems to have concentrated more attention on tourist subjectivities and performances and in so doing has expunged the idea of a universal tourist subject and experience. These new works have also loosened the grip of the tourism business in setting theory and research agendas.

At the same time, this new turn has begun to address broader theoretical questions about tourism and travel. Some of these have decentred the focus from sites of tourism to mobility itself, and this has produced some excellent new directions, even if it has tended to leave the theoretical question of tourism itself hanging (Sheller, 2004; Dant, 2004; Coles et al., 2005; Hall, 2005). There is now also a 'relational materialist turn' that has pursued previous observations that tourist things matter and that structuralist accounts are limiting (Lury, 1997; Kirshenblatt-Gimblett, 1998; Franklin, 2003a, 2003b, 2006a, 2006b) and combined these with new theoretical insights from Science and Technology Studies, A-NT, as well as Foucauldian studies in Tourism (Hollinshead, 2001; Picken, 2006) and critical realism (Gale & Botterill, 2005).

We are now on the cusp, it seems, of opening up tourism theory and research to a number of fronts and have left behind those days when tourism theory might be dispensed with in a couple of pages. . . . Nonetheless, the work must carry on and what follows is a very personal account of what directions this might take.

Persistent Problems

A very persistent problem in tourist studies might be called *touristcentricity*. This is the notion that the subject matter focuses properly on tourists rather than the social, cultural and political milieux and socio-technical networks that produced tourism and the desire to be a tourist in the first place and which subsequently sustain a changing context for new and changing tourisms — and tourist desires and practices. Although some work has already commenced to counter this tendency, I still see it as a problem. The idea that tourists are separable from these contexts and networks, are not part of these contexts and networks, and even by many definitions occupy a separate and singular ludic chora, is still widespread if not normative in tourist studies. Picken's (2006) recent analysis of tourism discourse shows how the binary elements used to define tourism are always centred around those of the tourist: it is the tourist's *home* and the tourist's *away* that constitute the binary — ditto with extraordinary/everyday. According to Picken (2006, p. 162), this is because:

> in order to understand 'what tourism is', the researcher became (and often still becomes) a tourist. Hence tourism as a discourse became (largely) the discourse of the tourist, and this is reflected in most disciplinary orientations and notably of economics/business/commerce where so much attention has been *demand* focussed.

Secondly, a disproportional focus on *tourist sites* that was pointed up at some length in Franklin and Crang (2001) is an artefact of this touristcentricity. We argued that this produced volumes of case study material whose legitimacy and value seemed to be measured [mainly] by its spatial–cultural uniqueness. Because knowledge of all, any, tourist site was deemed valuable in and of itself, tourist studies had become like a Victorian butterfly collection: fabulously colourful, endlessly repetitive. . . . I am no longer dazzled by variety, it's not enough.

The notion that tourists configured a unique and special type of space, which then became the social setting for studies of tourism itself, is a form of theoretical bracketing that Picken (2006) has examined in her discourse analysis of tourism. I am interested in the extent to which this tendency is an artefact of disciplinary leanings, acting independently, rather than merely accommodating a shared assumption or dominant discourse, as Picken suggests. Certainly, there seems to be connection between disciplinary orientation and the type of tourism object that was found. But further I think there was a curious convergence of disciplinary orientations that reinforced a particular and dominant tourism object.

Did geography, for example, take a particular shine to the tourism industry, in part because it could be upheld as a specifically *spatial* phenomenon? Certainly, their special interest appeared to me to have followed quickly and substantially in the wake of Rob Shields' *Places on the Margin* whose main contribution theorised tourism as a distinctively spatial phenomenon (even though it was underpinned by social structural theory) — as well as the general 'spatial turn' of the 1980s. There was something quintessentially *geographical* about tourism that was compelling to a discipline whose proper subject was often vague. Geography might have predispositions to tourism not only because tourism could be considered spatially constituted but also because geography was itself constituted *touristically*. Those intrepid explorers, folk heroes and founding fathers of the geographical societies, and the *National Geographic* writers in general, were more formative in the practice of travel and tourism than is often imagined. Certainly, they were influential in inculcating the travel and tourism impulse, as Ward and Hardy (1986) ably showed in the case of camping. The Victorian explorer/traveller/geographer remained folk heroes and their expeditions and travels were followed in specific magazines and journals by a large and popular audience spellbound by the pace and astonishment-factor of colonial expansion and consolidation in hitherto unknown cultures, places and natures. Precisely because this colonial consolidation involved at the same time the expansion of mobilities, particularly in the British Empire (where geography thrived as a discipline), it became possible for this public to convert their interest from audience to performance in a relatively short space of time. These disciplinary leanings could thus be a reason why the focus for tourism remained 'on site' rather than on the wider parameters of the tourism for it was the destination and objects of travel that was marvelled at, not travel, mobility and tourism *per se*. Often the means of travel were as incredible as the expeditions but the narratives of exploration tended to begin, in earnest, on site.

Equally, social anthropology, another core disciplinary field of tourism, tended to reify *touristic impact* as measurable in mainly *local* site terms through its disciplinary dependence on in-depth fieldwork in a specific and often closed off cultural milieux and even an endemic tendency to frame their respondent cultures as largely localised (see Clifford,

1992, for a critique). Here, tourism could be focussed on the largely negative impacts it had on a peripheral and disadvantaged indigenous people. In recent years, environmental studies embraced a similar advocacy role on behalf of natures/ecosystems and made exactly the same error, that nature was, properly those uncontaminated by the everyday and on the social/human margin (see Franklin, 2003a, 2003b, for a critique of this and Franklin, 2006a, 2006b for a more focussed critique of wilderness).

Historically, I am split between social anthropology and sociology though these days I find disciplinary boundaries more of a hindrance than anything else. Sociology has its own peculiar perspective on tourism that also, coincidentally and convergently, tended/tends to bracket tourism off as a separable, unusual and in its case also, deeply suspect social space. For most of its life, sociology had *producerist* leanings and it was the world of work, the space of employment and the social reproduction of labour power (particularly in the city) that constituted its core business. More than this, it was also populist and socially progressive (despite its overt counter-enlightenment concerns with the breakdown of family, community, tradition, etc. which surfaced particularly in one of its offspring disciplines, social anthropology) and generated very little sociology of the privileged leisure and touring classes — until tourism became a popular mass phenomenon, but even then tourism, leisure and consumerism generally have been viewed with some suspicion by the inner-core fields of sociology (Rojek, 1993).

Sociology's particular focus on a *producerist* society with its own epicentre in the metropolis meant that it too drew a boundary between core and periphery, work and leisure but particularly everyday and holiday. While in theory supporting the advance of paid public holidays (see Durant, 1938), sociology did not seem to find much of any significance to report from the pleasure beaches its workers flocked to. Indeed, there is evidence to show that at least some sociologists viewed tourism as an unfortunate, vacuous distraction, a consolation perhaps from a life of toil and routine but nothing much more. This is surely why the epic labours of the British Mass Observation Exercise yielded numerous studies of its so-called 'worktowners' in the War and post-War period, but it took until 1990 for a single volume on *Worktowners at Blackpool* to appear (Mass Observation Archive, 2006). By then, this material on the 1930s British working class pleasure beach was of *historical* interest (mainly) though it did coincide not only with an awakening of interest in leisure *per se* but also the recognition that tourism was now a major prop for its ailing industrial society. So it was really only when tourism became incorporated in work, employment and industry that sociology was prepared to embrace it as a significant sociological, albeit still spatially marginal object. Nonetheless, the notion of tourism as socially marginal and on the social margins persisted and persists.

Urry's *Tourist Gaze* emerged out of this generalised discourse on restructuring labour markets rather than a focussed interest on tourism itself, though Urry was among the first to realise the significance of tourism for sociology (see Franklin, 2001, on Urry). I find an undercurrent of incredulity and distain among many of the early sociological works on tourism, which from Boorstin onwards, seems most significant as a register of social and cultural decline. From Boorstin's finding that tourism provided an inauthentic wonder world of kitsch for culturally displaced moderns, to the scarcely veiled disappointment in Urry that former proud industrial cities were now subject to the same tourist gaze previously reserved only for those other (indigenous) peoples outside modernity's loop. All this is surely why tourism from the sociological perspective was consigned to the social and cultural periphery helping at the same time to consolidate tendencies in other formative disciplines to create it as a world apart.

Certainly, recent calls by Coles, Duval, and Hall (2005) to avoid the 'limits set by . . . discipline' are well received. Ideally, all of these disciplines could have embodied and practised the theoretical and methodological *adisciplinarity* that might describe tourism's complex nature as a mobile, networked or trans-spatial/national, globalising ordering. At the very least, they could have decentred tourism from the *tourist*. However, this is to misunderstand the nature of *interdisciplinarity* as it is so often practised. Unfortunately, interdisciplinarity preserves so well the disciplinary constitution of objects through its specific and limited theory and methodology while the prefix inter often merely indicates an object shared by others. By preserving disciplinarity, tourism studies have ironically failed to take advantage of its core feature: material, cultural, spatial, technical heterogeneity/hybridity that is both widely *distributed* and *translated*.

So, a related problem concerns the limited overview of impacts or consequences of tourism in the world. Because of the general norm of touristcentricity, tourist studies have tended to focus only on the impact (environmental, social, political, etc.) that tourists have on these specific sites. But what are the wider impacts and ramifications of tourism? And importantly, where have they impacted? How and why are they distributed and translated?

I have tried to encourage tourism scholars to become more ambitious for their field of expertise and to investigate unintended and intended consequences beyond the resort, pleasure periphery or spatial margin. I have argued that tourism is inextricably intertwined into most areas of culture and society and not just in many spatial settings (city, village, industrial zone, docklands, etc.). This is not to merely say that *the tourism market* has expanded into more and more areas of social and cultural life, even though it has (see Hannigan, 1998). Something more fundamental has happened that challenges the theoretical foundation of tourism studies. It would be a mistake to think that this is necessarily something new, that this is a recent development that requires the modification of a previously sound body of theory. If anything, the discovery of tourism everywhere ought to have signalled something that had *always been wrong with tourism theory*. In my book *Tourism* (2003), I argued that tourism had provided a new kind of stance to the world *in general*; a set of repertoires learned from touristic experience in those nations and cultures where it had taken root. This new stance and repertoire of touristic performance has been explicitly imported into everyday life as cities and suburbs (and not just the fantasy sort) progressed from the workaday routines of producerism to the leisure-rich routines and night-time economy of the consumerist or fantasy city (Hannigan, 1998; Bauman, 2000). But it has also been *invoked* as cities and social life generally become characterised by permanent flux, mobility, change and novelty and the general overloading from what Hylland Eriksen (2001) calls *fast time*, producing an endemic state of excitement and distraction and daily itineraries that allow only *fleeting* attention to passing events, places and things. In *Tourism* (2003), I also illustrated how the internet has been structured by the culture of tourism and how many other objects in common currency have a touristic genealogy? The everyday incorporation of technologies of rejuvenation and body can be traced to the regimes and repertoires of the tourist. A growing number of cities *interpellate* a touristic stance as a form of public engagement; those that do not (yet), seek ways of doing so.

I argued that from as early as the 1930s it is possible to detect the first stirrings of a process that was driven by this question: why should a life of pleasurable, dizzy distraction and constant rejuvenation be confined to those spaces defined and ordered by tourism? (Durant, 1938). Almost as soon as the holiday resort had hardened as a fixed site of modernity on the social margin, it was being imported wholesale into everyday life.

This was compounded and consolidated surely by what Wolfgang Welsch (1997) called *aestheticisation processes*. This appears not to have been noticed by those with an eye only for the tourist site. Here is Welsch pitching his claim:

> Aestheticisation is at its most obvious in the urban space, where just about everything has been subject to a facelift over the last few years. Shopping areas have been fashioned to be elegant, chic and animating. This trend has long since affected not only city centres, but also the outskirts of towns and country refuges. Hardly a paving stone, no door-handle, and no public place has been spared this aestheticisation-boom. Even ecology has largely become a further branch of enhancement. In fact, if advanced Western societies were able to do completely as they wish, they would transform the urban, industrial and natural environment *in toto* into a hyper-aesthetic scenario. (Welsch, 1997, p. 2)

What does this aestheticisation to all surfaces of culture bring to contemporary social life? According to Welsch, 'in surface aestheticisation the most superficial aesthetic value dominates: pleasure, amusement, and enjoyment without consequence'.

Further:

> This animatory trend reaches far beyond the aesthetic enshroudment of individual everyday items — beyond the styling of objects and experience-loaded ambiances. It is increasingly determining the form of our culture as a whole. Experience and entertainment have become the guidelines for culture in recent years. A society of leisure and experience is served by an expanding culture of festivals and fun. (Welsch, 1997, p. 3)

For Welsch, the object of much consumption is for the aesthetic aura rather than the object itself and this observation is similar to the distinction Bauman (1998, 2000) makes between *satisfaction* and *desire* (see Franklin's, 2003b, interview with Bauman). In an important way, Bauman's work on consumerism makes a link to a tourist sensibility that is missing in Welsch's (that seems to lack a clear sense of agency for aestheticisation or at least implies it is produced in the commercial domain rather than the cultural). Instead, Bauman argues that prior to the emergence of a consumerist society things were largely consumed for the satisfaction they gave. In many ways, this satisfaction was orientated to physical, embodied forms of satisfaction such as with use or satiating hunger. Increasingly, however, *desire* replaced satisfaction as a primary motivation. With desire, it was the anticipation of consumption and the associated intense pleasures of thinking, imagining and dreaming about acquisition and ownership that became paramount. This of course detaches the consumer from the object in a purely physical sense releasing them for the intense pleasures of *reverie*. In comparison with this, possession itself was often disappointing or a let down, hence the impulse to recreate desire again for an ever-new procession of objects and the associated state of distractedness and fleeting attention spans. Bauman's analysis of desire draws on Campbell's (1995) work on the origin of consumerism and this argues, ironically, that it was the romantic sensibility so exercised (and developed, in fact) at tourist sites — of ruins or wild nature — that generated the capacity to conjure an aesthetic sensibility of objects from mental imaginings, intellectual construction or dreamings. It seems to me that this touristic sensibility and its translation into other spheres of social life and the consequences of it as an *ordering* are poorly researched, let alone theorised. Worse, those outside tourism studies seem to be making the running. Take Richard Florida's successful pursuit of the *creative class* concept.

Even the briefest dip into Richard Florida's (2003) *The Rise of the Creative Class* suggests that this touristic sensibility is one of the most profoundly important economic foundations of successful cities and regions if not economies *per se*. It might be that cities and regions that want to thrive need to attract the creative class but it is to specifically configured cities in the likeness of tourist destinations, with what Shields (1991, p. 88) referred to as:

> aliveness' that they are drawn to live. This is clear from Florida's detailed analysis of the creative class who ideally live a life 'packed full of intense, high quality, multidimensional experiences. (*idem*, p. 166)

The description of their favoured everyday reads like an upmarket resort or destination:

> they like indigenous street level culture — a teeming blend of cafes, sidewalk musicians, and small galleries and bistros where it is hard to draw the line between participant and observer. . . . (*idem*, p. 166)

Most of all they want ethnic and cultural diversity and an atmosphere of tolerance where they can engage in social and interactive engagement. In Florida's (somewhat) cheesy language, it seems as if they seek the permanent state of touristhood inside the preferred American home-base city:

> If it is a proper street scene, there will be many people of exotic appearance: foreigners in long skirts and bright robes; young Americans with hair in colours and configurations that bend the laws of physics . . .; people dresses as cowboys, Goths, Victorians, hippies — you get the picture? And for many people, the experience of this picture is exhilarating, liberating. It is similar to the thrill of the costume party, when people literally put on new identities — including masks that obliterate or alter the social masks they normally wear — and there is a delicious sense of adventure in the air. One has an awareness of the possibilities of life. (Florida, 2003, p. 188)

The parallels with Shield's Brighton are obvious and the message is clear. These people are seeking and finding a life configured by the tourist sensibility and body. They lead active lives where sports and exercise is an everyday part of the schedule. It is a lifestyle where the body is in constant view in a number of spaces and where a toned body is keenly sought after. Rejuvenation, intense pleasure, cultural industries, creativity itself and hard work coincide and feed off each other. The opportunities for tourism research to be taken more seriously and as more mainstream need to be grasped in a world where things seem to depend on it. Needless to say, Florida's work merely illustrates the truth of this.

Repertoires and Orderings of Tourism

The experience of tourism is not merely the pleasure that begins and ends with the vacation, it is something more, something more serious and something that endures, as I argued it, as a repertoire of skills for dealing with the unfamiliar and velocity. The incorporation of tourism into everyday life should not be theorised as the extension of the tourism *industry* into the nether regions of social life, again reproducing the myth of tourism agency as being essentially *commercial*. The key point is that it has reconfigured the way we live, the manner in which an individualised and consumerised society has been reshaped — to the point where sociologists such as Bauman (1998) can talk of tourism as a metaphor for contemporary societies and individual consumers — excepting of course, those he calls *vagabonds* — the cursed minority who are, by definition, outsiders because they cannot act as/like tourists.

The liquefaction of both tradition and solid modernity, which emphasised and upheld enduring communities, local solidarities *and social bonds* themselves, was achieved in no small measure by the technologies and aesthetics of travel, mobility and freedom. For Bauman, the figure of the tourist is a metaphor of contemporary society precisely because they have no *bond* or commitment to the people or places they visit. They will stay in a given site only for as long as it continues to please them and the social relation between host and guest is unbond like, fragile and 'until further notice'. For Bauman, this state of affairs was achieved *generally* in neo-liberal times through the extension of the values of freedom and personal choice and the rapid dismantling of the nation state as an organizer of social life. However, the question remains of course as to how people so transformed could imagine a life of mobility outside stable communities and solid relationships as in any way pleasurable? I think the relationship between contemporary individualism and tourism is more than just an apt metaphor; that there may be good reason to suggest that tourism was formative in producing a culture for a more mobile, flexible and individualised world. This hinges, as I have argued elsewhere (Franklin, 2003a, 2003b, 2004), on the (dual) role that nation formation had on weakening local and immediate social ties. So, in addition to being the writer of solid modernity blue prints for a perfected and stable society — as a replacement for the inequitable solid relations of tradition — nation formation (and the tourism entangled with it) also produced the means of fragmenting such solidarities.

The extension of belonging to a wider world than the locality, family and community, region, etc., albeit one based on looser relationships, and the encouragement of performances of ritualised travel to its key historic, political, military and natural shrines at new times (predominantly *national holidays*), undermined 'national' efforts to maintain strong social bonds and enduring communities. As Gellner (1983) argued, the seductive nature of nationalism (and the travel that permitted its ritual performance by citizens) was based on the extension of 'high culture' to an entire population. This was an expansive world view based on overarching, universal themes as opposed to the more restricted themes of village and regional culture and it was by its very nature dazzling and spectacular, full of unimagined possibilities and treasures — but it also produced an acquisitive worldly culture that changed, transformed and 'improved' the initiates. National holidays produced an association of intense pleasure with the expression of freedom to move and with the less demanding form of social ties. This *communitas* among stranger citizens that was based on choice (and the ability to terminate it) rather than fate (and social boundedness or closure) foreshadowed the possibility of choice rather than responsibility as a principle. Its basis in the extension of universal, overarching interests (nature, science, history, philosophy, culture, geography, art, etc.) ensured that when the travelling impulse that was enacted in its name (as opposed to religious pilgrimage) was never restricted to national boundaries even if travel inside national boundaries was intensified (see Franklin, 2003a, 2004).

The theoretical ties between nation formation, tourism development and the touristic sensibility have been noted elsewhere (notably Löfgren, 1989, 2001), but these are barely visible as a core domain of theoretical work nor do they feature in theorisations of tourism and social change. There is a lot of work to be done: what about comparative national tourisms and the impact of international tourisms?

Post-Structural Tourisms

Definitions of tourism always seem to specify a sociological or cultural object but then fail to account for its material form or agency, or, enter into (interestingly) materially inclusive accounts of tourism in the world (its agency, content, etc.) but with no apparent sociological objectivity. So, definitions always run into the problem, sooner or later, of having to include (and account for) an expanding, boundless and materially heterogeneous assembly that includes machines, financial movements, bureaucratic systems, human bodies, technologies, places, translations, temporalities, natures, texts and a great many more, *and* providing a sociological theory that makes sense of it all. So far, definitions fail to do this and so are polarized between social and material heterogeneity on one hand and social structure on the other. By and large, business and management tourism scholars favour the former and social scientists the latter. I am more sympathetic to the wish to include everything (even though this seems tautological and absurd) than the restricted way in which social scientific accounts have been boxed into structuralist accounts, straddling unhelpful binaries.

As we have seen, the more sociological definitions seem always to insist on a separable life world of tourism situated, not very convincingly it has to be said (anymore), *at a distance* from a non-tourist life world. O'Reilly (2000, p. 43) for example, argues that many, including Graburn (1978), Smith (1978) and Voase (1995), define tourism 'more by what it is not than by what it is — it is *not* home and it is *not* work; it is a change of scenery and lifestyle, an inversion of the normal' (O'Reilly, 2000, p. 43).

These structural accounts focussing on the binaries everyday/extraordinary home/away profane/sacred, etc. still dominate much tourism work.

However, the task of avoiding these theoretical problems is not merely to look elsewhere in social and spatial terms but to question also the very ontological basis of what tourism IS. Saying it is everything to do with tourism remains true but unhelpful in answering this question. But if it does not well up from deep structures of the human condition, as expressed through different but at least theoretically linked contingencies, and if there is no theoretical linkage between commonly understood 'stages of modern tourism', then where do they all hail? I have argued (Franklin, 2004) that if we no longer have confidence in structural accounts, then each form of antecedent travel, and modern tourism itself, may need separate theorising. Equally, if modern tourism cannot be located and structurally bounded as social spaces and social practices, and has a more distributed and translated quality, then what exactly is that, theoretically? Who is doing the distribution and translation? There seems to be absence of agency and order in tourism theory.

I have tried to locate the specific origins and contingencies of modern tourism in nation formation processes, which at least provides the possibility of exploring the detailed nature of agency in a socio-political problem and movement. I have also tried to identify using the early British travel writings of John Byng (Adamson, 1996) to show the startling absence of (or indeed indifference to) a popular travelling culture or tourism during the eighteenth century, prior to the main period of nation formation movements in the nineteenth century. John Byng and Thomas Cook after him were extremely influential and *unusual* at the same time. While the conditions for the emergence of modern tourism were contingent and generally given in the currents of nation formation, it still required people of imagination to dream the dream, to envisage something entirely new. While they themselves were formed by the conditions of their lives, it seems that the nature of their dream and imagination and particularly the way they pursued them in writing/publishing and establishing a new form of travel business were important to try to understand. For what they both did was create the *idea* of tourism where none had existed before; the *objects* of tourism, which did not have this quality as things to be visited before, and the *means* of visitation which had not been widely considered before (British tourism on horseback and tourism by train, tourist maps, guides, etc.). How important were these dreams, theoretically? How do we theorise the role played by technologies (texts, horse riding, trains, maps and guides)? And what is the ontological nature of the interlinked 'thing' they unleashed on the world that became tourism? One of the problems of tourism theory is that we do not have ready answers to these questions although they are being thought about.

In my orderings paper of 2004, I thought that in ontological terms could tourism be conceived as a *becoming* or *ordering*? I argued that it certainly corresponded with what social theorists were beginning to describe as orderings.

The sociology of orderings navigates a path around the problems of *structuralist* accounts, that reduce history and cultural phenomena (such as tourism) to variations of universal operations of the human condition, and *humanist* accounts, that reduce history and cultural phenomenon to human agency alone — and particularly to intentional blueprint readings of human history (see Pickering, 1995).

As an object of analysis, tourism is both open ended, always becoming something else, and under-determined, in that there is a heterogeneous field of objects, practices and projects with none of them (and certainly not *only* the humans among them) being decisive, the only mover or the sole agent.

Nor can tourism merely be a network in the usual way this is understood, as always-already formed objects, structures and agents, existing separately and joined by (abstract) lines of association. Rather, they will be mutually constitutive, rhizomic, joined in processes of becoming or 'emergent', always shedding parts of themselves and attaching to others. Although these assemblages do not relate to a wider *order*, say a social order, they are nonetheless routinely *ordered*. And although their ordering does not reduce to the agency of humans, humans always try to manage and organize their world, a world of both humans and non-humans and in doing so their projects take on a life of their own, as the people and things so ordered respond, block, enable, modify, reconfigure, spread and inspire effects such as continuities, reproductions, refinements, failures, collapses, hybrids (Pickering, 1995).

All human projects attempt to manage and control people and things such as hydro-electric systems, banking systems, management systems, the Internet, textual technologies. Law's paper on the machinic pleasures of aircraft travel, Bennett's work on the centrality of technology for the 'Blackpool experience', demonstrate that tourism cannot be a purely social or business activity, or at least its social nature also articulates necessarily and in complex ways with non-human objects, systems, machines, bureaucratic processes, times, timetables, sites, photographs, tents, flows, desires, visitors, businesses, locals, etc. in a complex materially heterogeneous assemblage (Haldrup et al., 2006, have underlined the materiality of tourism in a recent paper).

They may have blueprint beginnings, but as orderings that persist in time and space they have a more unbounded and open-ended nature: they may not be confined to their intended object and they may not continue in the form initially conceived having range of effects intended and otherwise. It is an ontology of unintended consequences, failure, unforeseen agency and promiscuous enrolment. Orderings are pure processes. Law and Hetherington argue that 'global space' for example 'is a material semiotic effect. It has to be made'.

The Tourism Ordering?

Can tourism really be thought of as an ordering? I think it can in at least two senses. The first sense is in terms of how we investigate any one discrete tourist site, activity, place or organization but also spaces of mobility, such as airports, cars, coaches, planes, boats, highways, routes and itineraries. Here, Law's essay on machinic pleasure or the recent work on automobility (published in *Theory, Culture and Society*, 2004, p. 21) serves as a place to start. Second, world tourism itself can be thought of in these terms, historically and presently, as an ordering of global space. It is a fundamentally *connected* rhizomic entity, even if it is extremely large, and it is an *organized* entity even if it is comprised of many organizations. From the earliest of days of modern tourism, perhaps a founding part of it was the establishment of timetables and schedules of timetables that allow the tourist or agent to plot an itinerary that connects many places, carriers, travel organizations, technologies, cultures, businesses and nationalities. The Internet and computer networks have made this all the more so and simultaneous.

The tourism ordering was in part a project establishing a *smoothness* of travel connections and conditions in a world whose mobilities were hitherto ungoverned or unordered (rough to say the least), and a world network of spaces in travel — places of travel and spaces of mobility in a world hitherto consisting only of the everyday, bounded universes of the (largely) sedentary. The tourism ordering does not stand outside other orderings however, but is a positive response to some (say, nationalism) and offers resistance to others (parochialism).

In other words, tourism was an 'ordering effect' of a far more important ordering, namely the ordering of a travelling global public. How was it that suddenly, ordinary, hitherto non-travelling cultures became travelling cultures? How did they acquire an inbuilt yearning and wish to see other places? Was it because their every day was so much worse than before or was it that a widening, expanding world *interpellated* them? And if it was the latter, how did that happen? I have already located that process in nation formation which is itself of course a related though distinct ordering (Franklin, 2003a).

Organization (or management) is central to the way tourism operates and a reading of Law (1994), Crook (1999), Kendall and Wickham (2001) suggests that the notion of *ordering* is highly applicable to tourism. To the Latourian and Deleuzian emphasis on network or rhizome, or at least its post-humanist insistence on material heterogeneity, relationality, and the agency of non-humans, the Foucauldian element of governance is grafted. Ordering is like governance: 'ordering is to governance as government is to order' and while order is an impossibility, a never-to-be-attained state in the same way that government always fails, attempts at governance, and ordering attempts, are the very stuff of the world, the way the world operates as a process of becoming. Freed from the need to operate inside the restraints of abstractions such as *society, social order, social structure, etc.*, this approach suggests we concentrate on what people and things, people and things together, actually *do*. Orderings privileges attention ostensibly to human and technological interventions in the world, though in theory they are not the only actors relevant to ordering, and such interventions are never made as if that world is exclusively one of humans among themselves.

So, what can count as an ordering? According to Kendall and Wickham (2001) orderings are, in a loose sense, attempts at control or management (2001, p. 5). Orderings:

> are never simply a social matter . . . but rather a materially heterogenous set of arrangements and processes implicated in and including people to be sure, but also including and producing documents, codes, texts, architectures and physical devices.

As with governance ordering:

> involves any attempt to control or manage any known object. A "known object" is an event, a relationship, an animate object, in fact any phenomenon which human beings try to control or manage. (Hunt & Wickham, 1994, p. 24)

Ordering then can be of any magnitude and certainly every individual is engaged in ordering activities, from simple ordering of the domestic material objects around them to ordering their movement through space. All organizations, by definition make attempts to order, some larger than others. As Kendall and Wickham (2001) say, ordering is everywhere. And these various ordering attempts or programmes once released into the world have a history of their own as they interact with other orderings, especially *antiprogrammes*.

Some might enable them to change, maybe to expand their power, range or effects; others might set limitations or eliminate them altogether. And, of course, since orderings are themselves objects, they can be constituted themselves 'by being addressed by an ordering practice' (Kendall & Wickham, 2001). Some ordering projects have sought a blueprint for order itself, the idea or dream of *a* social *order*, and unleashed untold misery upon the world but most orderings are of a lower magnitude and many are associated with the more positive achievements of modernity, such as useful inventions and interventions.

Law's *Organizing Modernity* sets out a way of thinking about how orderings come into existence and how they act in the world. First, modes of ordering stem from narratives about the world:

> they tell us what used to be or what ought to happen. Here there are ordering concerns, procedures, methods or logics, dreams of ordering perhaps, nothing more. Certainly they are not 'pools of total order'. (Law, 1994, p. 9)

Second, more than mere narratives they find expression and become active only through performance:

> embodied in a concrete, non-verbal manner in the network of relations. . . I'm saying, then, that they are imputable ordering arrangements, expressions, suggestions, possibilities or resources. And third, ordering involves strategies that are not always explicitly framed or worked strategies, but, like Foucault's discourses are 'forms of strategic arranging that are intentional but do not necessarily have a subject'. (Law, 1994, p. 21)

This framework offers a very useful way of reinterpreting modern tourism as a process of 'becoming connected' but also a way of being in and of the world. It allows us to theorise the nature of Byng and Cook's dream, the technologies they devised and were replaced by, the tourists predisposition to travel and their growing demands for more, the places that were translated into tourist sites and the businesses that formed rhizomic accretions at all levels, simultaneously.

While this perspective does not dismiss all of tourism theory nor makes light of the substantial progress in the semiotics and phenomenology of tourism, it does offer an additional and less structurally *centred* theorisation of tourism, inspired by the sociology of orderings. This explicitly anti-structuralist and post-humanist hybrid of actor network and Foucauldian analysis, as expressed in works by Crook, Law, and Kendall and Wickham, encourages us to ask not what tourism means but what it does, to deploy a sociology of verbs not nouns. It also encourages us to investigate its becoming and its biography as an ordering. Tourism, I have argued, fits John Law's specification of orderings particularly in its origins as a 'dream of ordering', its pursuit as a form of management and its socio-technical ontology. From this perspective, tourism is not fragmented into a repetition of sites and an eternal presence, but a formidable socio technical rhizome, in a globalising line of flight, with a series of substantial ordering effects. In its becoming, it established one of the most important networks of connectivity that contributed to (and made possible) globalisation. In this sense, tourism has become a key cultural form of translation across the world and can hardly be confined to the social margins, resorts enclaves and times away from home. Indeed, tourism as I would have it (and I press for a new ontology rather than a replacement theory) is more or less the exact opposite of its typical theorisation.

Significantly, this is less of a new theory than a new ontology, since it does not seek to uncover something that is hidden, requiring theory to bring it to light. Rather, everything is already there available to be seen and described, on the surface. What does have to happen however is the construction of the connections, relations, translations and networks between the human and non-human elements — a relational materialism.

I am pleased to see that other theorists are working along similar lines and that a new form of tourism research is beginning to emerge. Writing from a critical realist position, Gale and Botterill (2005) also argue for a new ontological approach to tourism, reject structuralist accounts and ask the question: what makes tourism possible? Taking Butler's (1980) tourist area life cycle model as an example of an influential tourism theory, their paper demonstrates the weakness of modelling tourism theory on the resort or tourist space. Their detailed account of the decline of Rhyll and the removal of the Victorian Pier and Pavilion shows that the model cannot explain events there; that the wider tourism system needs to be investigated, particularly in relation to changing material-aesthetic sensibilities that direct decision-making. But most important of all, BETTER explanations are possible if the relational materialism of tourism is explored.

Haldrup and Larsen's (2006) recent paper is a useful summary of the intertwined and therefore theoretically central role of objects in tourism and the hybrid human–material cultures they reveal. Closer to the tourism ordering idea are those inspired by Actor-Network Theory and several papers have recently emerged to demonstrate its potential, particularly as a new way of understanding particular tourist sites (Johannesson, 2005, 2006; Baerenholdt & Haldrup, 2004). These make the case for an analysis beyond 'the social life of things' towards the more symmetrical application of agency to all objects (human and non-human) in tourism. This opens up a vast new area for investigation, particularly those poorly understood spaces of mobility and the social relations between humans and the technologies of travel and mobility.

The Tourism of Fear?

I want to end on a positive note or at least a positive note on tourism if not on tourism theory. At the beginning of this article, I referred to disciplinary influences on tourism theory but one aspect of this that remains to be considered is the persistent idea that tourism is problematic — to the perception of an authentic world, to natures, environments and places, to host cultures of the so-called pleasure periphery (and beyond), to the nature of social bonds and responsibility itself (Bauman's 'tourism syndrome', see Franklin, 2004) and even to domestic security (see Bauman's *Society Under Siege*). Every discipline in tourism studies seems to promote the fear of one or more of these impacts of tourism, and indeed it is possible to identify a dominant area of theoretical work orientated to *the tourism of fear*.

In a previous paper, which considered tourism orderings particularly through the life and work of Thomas Cook, I asked the question: what would the world be like without tourism? More to the point perhaps: what has tourism ever done for us? It seemed to me that Cook felt his zeal and energy was behind a project with certain moral worth. It was frequently alluded to by Cook (whose life took shape in times of war *and* peace) that the long history of wars between Britain and France might be halted if only the two nations knew about each other, visited each other and developed an understanding and familiarity with each other. He was proud to have produced an organization that linked all corners of the world and created a safe space for women to travel alone. The great traveller and fan of world tourism, Mark Twain (1993) wrote that 'travel is fatal to prejudice and bigotry and narrow-mindedness'. Cook and others like him were great modernising Victorians, they had a great confidence in experimentation, they looked to a better, more democratic and inclusive future and they were unswervingly on track to solve problems facing human- ity, often by major projects that were entirely new. By comparison, we seem to have lost our nerve. We seem deeply troubled by tourism, the more it becomes essential to our lives.

The idea of *a tourism of fear* is inspired by Furedi's recent *The Politics of Fear* (2005) which almost instantly made strong connections for me to tourism theory and research. Furedi's argument is that the contemporary western world is bereft of politics because we have become fearful of our own interventions in the world. A culture of fear has produced a new ethics defined by misanthropy, the precautionary principle and sustainability. All of these, he argues, lock us into a fear of the experimental, a suspicion of humanism (the search for solutions to human problems) and a morbid fear of development and science. There cannot be a politics, he argues, where important questions requiring solutions and the dream of different futures are not posed. On what basis are politicians to disagree if nothing new is on the agenda? Instead, 'the conservatism of fear thrives through the pro- motion of a diminished sense of human potential' (Furedi, 2005, p. 21). The idea that we can solve the problems that face us with the same confidence and energy of the Victorian has been lost; we *have* lost our nerve!

The disciplines that founded tourism studies *were* predisposed to look for negative impacts and there is no doubt that there have been many. But I sometimes wonder whether because of our fears and anxieties we have ever properly looked at the positive benefits of tourism. It seems to me that anthropologists and sociologists have been confused about the relative merits and demerits of tourism. Tourism may create poorly paid service industries and suck income away from third world communities, but at the same time it might bring a range of benefits such areas might otherwise not have, not least connectivity to the out- side world, the basis on which it too may dream to modernise or not. There is no doubt that there is something negative about orientalist orientations of the tourist but it is also questionable whether anthropology ought to play the role of upholding the preservation of cultures they study from currents of social change.

The epicentre of the politics of fear was not, for Furedi's, in the soulless suburbs of modernity but at recent anti-capitalist rallies:

> The anti-capitalism on the streets of Seattle and London represented not the
> old dream of human liberation, but a fear of the future and a determination
> to seek refuge in a static predictable state. (Furedi, 2005, p. 11)

The ethics of sustainability, the precautionary principle and misanthropy have all had a profound impact on the way *nature* has been managed for visitors. The fear is that tourism will overrun and destroy what few natural areas are left untouched by the hand of humanity. Surely, this fear is justified?

The problem is that it might achieve the opposite effect from the one desired. By trying to keep humanity out, by sustaining the assumption that human presence in nature is inherently problematic it may serve to reduce the personal connection to, or bonds with, these spaces and natures and thus their ultimate source of an effective political base that could preserve them against destruction. The risk of this is particularly true where people are highly managed in natural areas and kept to small areas on specific tracks and where the no-touch rule applies. This might produce, over time, a museumised nature where sensual, embodied and consumptive ties and skills are lost and where the possibility of indifference could occur. Macnaghten and Urry (1998) argue that environmental solidarity in the UK is particularly strong where people have a personal attachment to, and identify with specific natures (places, particular bird species, etc.) and it is instructive to consider how in Scandinavian countries their very close ties to the natural world through the ethic of *allemansratt* (the right to roam in nature and across land) has been extended to tourists, apparently without harm. A similar case can be made for both aboriginal ties with *country* in Australia (their term for their relations with a *nourishing* landscape) and in their own form of nature tourism businesses where tourists are taught how to forage for food (Franklin, 2006b). The point I make here is that tourist studies and tourism theory seem disproportionately focussed on the things we might fear from the tourist/tourism rather than positive things we do and might benefit from them/it.

The idea that wilderness areas should be empty of humanity and protected against them is also inaccurate historically and potentially insensitive to those indigenous people who have been removed from them in order that they can become an elitist playground for the middle class romantic for whom empty spaces have a premium. The tourism of fear in natural areas promotes the notion of doing nothing but this in itself is actually a significant intervention in ecosystems such as those in Australia that adapted and evolved to the presence of Aboriginal fire torch technology for a long while. And which ecosystems did not experience the human hand?

These simple facts demonstrate that 'doing nothing' is actually more difficult than it seems and an inequitable and racist biopolitics of nature can ensue.

Perhaps if intellectuals are to have a role here, it is to question and criticise the basis of the tourism of fear (wherever it exists) as a subset of the politics of fear and perhaps investigate a way out of its apparent stasis and misanthropic gloom and perhaps to signal where tourism, tourisms of particular kinds (allmensratt, *country*) offer a way out of the impasse. I offer a few thoughts from the area of nature tourism with which I am familiar because it is quite apparent that the tourism of fear has closed down many of the alternatives. But I hope that we may inspire new challenges to conservative practices in other areas and maintain Cook's dream of a useful and enriching tourism-orientated modernity.

In sum, the consequences of these arguments call for a more distributed and translated sense of tourism in spatial, social, historical, political and disciplinary terms. I would judge this to be achieved when those working on tourism-related themes publish key works outside the main tourism journals and in more general theory-orientated journals such as *Theory, Culture and Society*, as well as the flagship disciplinary journals, and particularly when tourism's distributed and translated qualities are researched in spaces and networks beyond the resort and tourist site.

References

Adamson, D. (Ed.). (1996). *Rides round Britain by John Byng*. London: The Folio Society.

Bauman, Z. (1998). *Globalisation*. Cambridge: Polity.

Bauman, Z. (2000). *Liquid modernity*. Cambridge: Polity.

Butler, R. W. (1980). The concept of a tourism area cycle of evolution: Implications for resources. *Canadian Geographer*, *24*(1), 5–12.

Campbell, C. (1995). *The romantic ethic and the spirit of consumerism*. Oxford: Basil Blackwell.

Clifford, J. (1992). Travelling cultures. In: L. Grossberg, C. Nelson, & P. A. Treichler (Eds), *Cultural studies*. New York: Routledge.

Coles, T., Duval, T. D., & Hall, C. M. (2005). *Tourism recreation research*, *30*(2), 31–41.

Crook, S. (1999). Ordering risks. In: D. Lupton (Ed.), *Risk and sociocultural theory: New directions and perspectives*. Cambridge: Cambridge University Press.

Dant, T. (2004). The driver-car. *Theory, Culture and Society*, *21*(4/5), 61–79.

Durant, H. (1938). *The problem of leisure*. London: George Routledge and Son.

Florida, R. (2003). *The rise of the creative class*. London: Pluto.

Franklin, A. S. (2003a). *Tourism*. London: Sage.

Franklin, A. S. (2003b). The tourism syndrome: An interview with Zygmunt Bauman. *Tourist Studies*, *3*(2), 205–218.

Franklin, A. S. (2004). Tourism as an ordering: Towards a new ontology of tourism. *Tourist Studies*, *4*(3), 277–303.

Franklin, A. S. (2006a). The humanity of the wilderness photo. *Australian Humanities Review*, *28*(April), 1–16.

Franklin, A. S. (2006b). *Animal nation: The true story of animals and Australia*. Sydney: University of New South Wales Press.

Franklin, A. S., & Crang, M. (2001). The trouble with tourism and travel theory? *Tourist Studies*, *1*(1), 5–22.

Furedi, F. (2005). *Politics of fear*. London: Pluto.

Gale, T., & Botterill, D. (2005). A realist agenda for tourist studies or why destination areas really rise and fall in popularity. *Tourist Studies*, *5*(2), 151–174.

Gellner, E. (1983). *Nations and nationalism*. London: Basil Blackwell.

Graburn, N. H. H. (1978). Tourism: The sacred journey. In: V. Smith (Ed.), *Hosts and guests*. Philadelphia, PA: University of Pennsylvania Press.

Haldrup, M., & Larsen, J. (2003). The family gaze. *Tourist Studies*, *3*(1), 23–46.

Haldrup, M., & Larsen, J. (2006). Material cultures of tourism. *Leisure Studies*, *25*(3), 275–289.

Hall, C. M. (2005). *Tourism: Rethinking the social science of mobility*. Harlow: Prentice Hall.

Hannigan, J. (1998). *Fantasy city*. London: Routledge.

Hollinshead, K. (2001). Surveillance of the world of tourism and the eye-of-power. *Tourism Management*, *20*(1), 57–74.

Hunt, A., Wickham, G. (1994). *Foucault and law: Towards a sociology of law as governance*. London: Pluto Press.

Hylland Eriksen, T. (2001). *The tyranny of the moment*. London: Pluto Press.

Johannesson, G. T. (2005). Placing tourism: The ordering of a tourism project in Westfjords — Iceland. The Inaugural Nordic Geographers Meeting *Power over time space* (pp. 1–30), Lund, Sweden, May 10–14.

Johannesson, G. T. (2006). Tourism translations: Actor-network theory and tourism research. *Tourist Studies*, *5*(2), forthcoming.

Kendall, G., & Wickham, G. (2001). *Understanding culture: Cultural studies, order, ordering*. London: Sage.

Kirshenblatt-Gimblett, B. (1998). *Destination culture: Tourism, museums, and heritage.* Berkeley, CA: University of California Press.

Law, J. (1994). *Organizing modernity.* London: Sage.

Löfgren, O. (1989). The nationalization of culture. *Ethnologia Europaea, XIX,* 2–23.

Löfgren, O. (2001). Know your country: A comparative perspective on tourism and nation building in Sweden. In: S. Baranowski, & E. Furlough (Eds), *Being elsewhere: Tourism, consumer culture, and identity in modern Europe and North America* (pp. 137–154). Ann Arbor: University of Michigan Press.

Lury, C. (1997). The objects of travel. In: C. Rojek, & J. Urry (Eds), *Touring cultures* (pp. 75–95). London: Routledge.

Macnaghten, P., & Urry, J. (1998). *Contested natures.* London: Sage.

Mass Observation Archive. (2006). Home page available at: http://www.massobs.org.uk/index.html.

O'Reilly, K. (2000). *The British on the Costa Del Sol: Transnational identities and local communities.* London: Routledge.

Phillimore, J., & Goodson, L. (2004). *Qualitative research in tourism: Ontologies, epistemologies and methodologies.* London: Routledge.

Picken, F. (2006). From tourist looking-glass to analystical carousels: Navigating tourism through relations and context. *Current Issues in Tourism, 9*(2), 158–170.

Pickering, A. (1995). *The mangle of practice.* Chicago: University of Chicago Press.

Rojek, C. (1993). *Ways of escape.* London: Routledge.

Sheller, M. (2004). Automotive emotions — feeling the car. *Theory, Culture and Society, 21*(4/5), 221–242.

Shields, R. (1991). *Places on the margin.* London: Routledge.

Smith, V. (1978). *Hosts and guests.* Philadelphia, PA: University of Pennsylvania Press.

Tribe, J. (2005). New tourism research. *Tourism Recreation Research, 30*(2), 5–8.

Twain, M. (1993). *The innocents abroad.* London: Random House.

Voase, R. (1995). *Tourism: The human perspective.* London: Hodder and Stoughton.

Ward, M., & Hardy, D. (1986). *Goodnight campers! The history of the British holiday camp.* London: Mansell.

Welsch, W. (1997). *Undoing aesthetics.* London: Sage.

Chapter 10

Tourism, Materiality and Space

René van der Duim

Introduction

In this chapter I shall theorize the relation between tourism, materiality and space by introducing a new way of looking at and researching tourism. This account is positioned within
an emerging new school of tourism studies. Tourism academics now increasingly follow
the lead of the social sciences and move into what Tribe (2005, p. 5) terms 'new' tourism
research pointing out that:

> the totality of tourism studies has now developed beyond the narrow bound-
> aries of an applied business field and has the characteristics of a fledging
> post-modern field of research

creating a wave of 'new' tourism research. This shift in thought has been labelled as a 'critical turn' in tourism studies (Ateljevic, Harris, Wilson, & Collins, 2005), and represents
a notable move towards new paradigms and new fields of research and knowledge-making
in tourism academia.

To contribute to this critical turn, I shall reconsider the way tourism is organized and
performed by fusing discourses, materiality and practices (Franklin & Crang, 2001, p.
117). More particularly, in this chapter I shall translate and perform actor-network theory
in the province of tourism studies.

Actor-network theory is an 'alternative' social theory. Although it began some 30 years
ago, it only recently became object of a systematic introduction (Latour, 2005; see also
Law, 2004), and has also entered tourism studies just recently (see Van der Duim, 2005).
Influenced by post-structuralism, actor-network theory not only tells *what* tourist scholars
study, but more importantly *how* they study tourism (Murdoch, 2006; Law, 2004). It claims
that tourism analysis (like any other form of analysis) should come down to 'following the
actor' as they stitch networks together. One should observe the trail of associations
between heterogeneous elements (Latour, 2005).

The researcher has to follow how tourism meanings and tasks are attributed to and distributed between people and things. He or she has to follow and elucidate processes of ordering, which I label 'tourismscapes' (see Van der Duim, 2005).

To study tourism in terms of tourismscapes is to refrain from explanations in terms of 'structures' or 'systems'; tourism is to be examined in terms of specific processes of association and ordering, which connect what was previously detached. In these processes, as I shall illustrate, spaces become entangled into tourismscapes by complex processes of translation. In tourismscapes spatial relations are seen as network relations. And within tourismscapes, spatial scale is reconceptualized as network length, and network length is as Murdoch (2006, p. 76) explains:

> reconceptualized as 'heterogeneous engineering' — that is, processes of network building in which entities of various kinds are assembled in ways that allow networks to undertake certain functions.

In this chapter I shall now first discuss the concept of tourismscapes. As tourismscapes consist of human and non-humans, materiality in tourism is examined. I shall then discuss the way space is contained in tourismscapes and the means whereby space is 'made' inside tourismscapes. I shall illustrate my arguments with some examples taken from Kenya (see also Van der Duim, 2006). In the conclusion, I shall summarize some of the consequences of translating actor-network theory into the provinces of tourism studies.

Tourismscapes: An Actor-Network Perspective on Tourism

Actor-network theory enables a re-conceptualization of tourism in terms of tourismscapes (Van der Duim, 2005). Analytically, these are actor-networks connecting, within and across different societies and regions, transport-systems, accommodation and facilities, tourism resources, environments, technologies, and people and organizations. Tourismscapes consist of relations between people and things dispersed in time–space specific patterns.

Tourismscapes as Actor-Networks

What does it mean when I say that tourismscapes are actor-networks? In actor-network theory, the concept of actor and network are concatenated and one cannot be defined without the other. The actor-network is reducible neither to an actor alone nor to a network. An actor-network is at the same time an actor whose activity is networking heterogeneous elements and a network that is able to redefine and change what is made of (Cordella & Shaikh, 2004, p. 4). Thus tourismscapes are 'nothing other than patterned networks of heterogeneous materials' (Law, 1992, p. 381).

As Franklin (2003, p. 279) argues, tourism is no doubt a social activity, but it cannot be reduced to the social because it is relationally linked to a wide variety of objects, machines, texts, systems, non-humans, spaces and so on, without which it would not happen and could not have become what it is: 'as an ordering it organizes a complex mesh of human and non-humans and creates ordering effects'. As soon as, for example in Kenya, the 'Big Five', the beaches of Mombassa, the plains of Maasai Mara, the 'Kilimanjaro' or the 'salty dust' lands of Amboseli, are entangled in tourismscapes they produce an effect (see Van der Duim, 2006). And tourists may be closely linked with the beaches of Mombassa, Fort Jesus or the Maasai in faraway destinations like Kenya. But take away the planes, travel books and brochures, maps, timetables, the Internet, passports, vouchers, mobile phones or internationally accepted ways of payments, and 'time–space decompresses immediately' (Verschoor, 1997, p. 42).

Material resources, objects, spaces and technologies are much more than simply the outcrops of human intention and action. They also structure, define and configure interaction. For example, the spatial concentration of tourism in Kenya in central places like Mombassa, Nairobi and only four or five national parks, is not only the result of decisions of investors based on perceptions of regions having the highest potential for immediate profit returns (Akama, 1999, p. 15), but just as well the outcome of the particular association between geological processes, historical patterns of settlement, environmental values and practices of nature conservationists, accessibility of wildlife, technology and infrastructure and, of course, choices made by people (tourists or entrepreneurs). The particular spatial configuration of Kenya's tourism is the effect of complicated processes of ordering. Seen as an ordering, this conception of tourism offers an alternative to structuralist accounts that have long influenced and inhabited tourist studies (Franklin, 2003, p. 277). It offers a new ontology of tourism (see also Van der Duim, 2005).

The methodological result of this perspective is that no *a priori* assumptions will be made about who or what will act in any particular set of circumstances. For example:

> In the flatlands of Kenya's Amboseli Game Reserve, a lioness lies resting. Every few minutes, a minivan or bus drives up and the crowd of tourists inside snap their camera shutters. The animal may remain for two hours. In that time, twenty-five vehicles might stop and stare. (Olindo, 1991, p. 23)

Who 'acts' in this example: the tourist or the lioness? Both and much more! It is the particular exchange of social (drivers, tourists) and material (lions, cameras, vans, roads) agency, the actor-network of people and things that produces the effect. Safaris as well as any other tourism activity will be the result of network construction, and networks are constructed out of all kinds of bits and pieces, some of which we might label 'social', 'economical', 'natural', 'spatial' or 'technical' and so on. In this fashion, actor-network theorists believe they are breaking down the dualisms that afflict so much sociological theorizing (see also Barnes, 2005). It is not that there are no divisions, as Law (1999a, p. 3) explains, it is rather that such divisions are to be understood as effects or outcomes. Nature/society, actor/structure, global/local — rather than being determinant of particular phenomena, these divisions emerge from heterogeneously constructed networks. Actor-networks underpin the divisions that constitute our world (Murdoch, 2001, p. 120).

Tourismscapes thus retain the main idea of what Callon and Law (1995) denote as a hybrid *collectif* of people and things (see also Verschoor, 1997). The notion of 'collectif' differs from that of a 'collective' or 'collectivity', in that a collectif is not an assembly of people who have decided to join some form of common organization; rather, 'a collectif is an emergent effect created by the interaction of the heterogeneous parts that make it up' (Callon & Law, 1995, p. 485).

In other words, 'it is the *relations* — and their heterogeneity — that are important, and not the things in themselves' (Verschoor, 1997, p. 42).

Entities in tourismscapes — whether a lion, a camera or a tourist — achieve their form as a consequence of the relations in which they are located. But they are also performed in, by and through those relations: 'if relations do not hold fast by themselves, then they have to be performed' (Law, 1992). As a consequence, everything is uncertain and reversible, at least in principle. It is never given in the order of things.

Translation

What actor-network theorists thus seek to investigate are the means by which associations come into existence and how the roles and functions of subjects and objects, actors and intermediaries, humans and non-humans are attributed and stabilized (Murdoch, 1997, p. 331). They are interested in processes of 'translation', that is, the methods by which actors bring together entities that are sometime radically different, and 'convincing' to them that they have an interest in connecting and relating (Barnes, 2005, p. 71). Through translation associations with other actors and actor-networks are established and stabilized.

Translation builds actor-networks from entities. It attaches characteristics to them and establishes more or less stable relationships between them. Translation is a definition of roles and the delineation of a scenario (Callon, 1986, pp. 25–26). It is the process in which actors attempt to characterize and pattern the networks of the social: the process in which they attempt to constitute themselves as 'collectifs' (Steins, Röling, & Edwards, 2000; Law, 1994).

As Murdoch (1998, 2006) explains, translation refers to the processes of negotiation, mobilization, representation and displacement between actors, entities and places. It involves the redefinition of these phenomena so that they are persuaded to behave in accordance with network requirements, and these redefinitions are frequently inscribed in the heterogeneous materials that act to consolidate networks. The actor-network theorists have set themselves the task to explore the tactics of translation (Steins et al., 2000, p. 7).

The 'Stuff' of Tourism

One of the most distinctive but also debated features of actor-network theory is its adherence to the principle of symmetry between people and things (see, for example, Latour, 1993, 2005; Law, 1994; Murdoch, 2001). To insist on symmetry 'is to assert that everything, more particularly, that everything you seek to explain or describe should be approached in the same way' (Law, 1994, pp. 9–10).

It thus erodes distinctions (e.g. between global and local, between those that drive and the driven, between macro and micro or people and things) that are said to reside in the nature of things, and instead ask how it is that they got to be that way as a product or effect of processes of ordering (*ibid.*, p. 12).

By doing so, the theory grants things the possibility of actor status. As Jensen (2001) explains, actor-network theory employs a semiotic definition of an actor. Actors take their form and acquire their attributes as a result of their relations with other actors. An actor is anything that acts or receives activity from others. So the scope of actors is extended far beyond individual humans. By translating lions or giraffes, baobabs and mango trees, or the Maasai Mara and Tsavo plains into tourismscapes, they become 'actants' just as small-scale entrepreneurs or Maasai acquire their attributes as a result of being part of the processes of ordering in tourism.

However, in tourism studies the objects of tourism themselves often have been left out of the picture, as if only useful as carriers of social and cultural meaning. Tourism studies ignored that 'there is such a thing as the *social life of things*, as they play critical roles (as *actants*) in the unfolding of cultural events and processes and that many things formerly considered merely 'things' are more properly hybrids of the human and non-human' (Franklin & Crang, 2001, p. 15).

The principle of symmetry between human and non-human provokes not only fierce debates (see, for example, Latour, 1999, 2005; Law, 1999a, 1999b) but also specific questions related to tourism. The most important question relates to the materiality of tourism: What is the 'stuff' of tourism?

Law and Hetherington (1999, p. 2) imagine three kinds of materials. First and foremost, it is about bodies, for bodies are material. As Wilson and Ateljevic (2006) argue, if travel destinations are viewed as embodied 'spaces', imbued with time, sensuous, feeling bodies and emotion, then no longer are destinations static places to which people travel and then return from (Crouch, 2000). Essentially, the embodiment of tourism moves us beyond the fixation with the tourist 'gaze' and the objective sightseeing of the flaneur (Urry, 2002; see also Franklin, 2003), and insists that we reflect on the 'being, doing, touching *and* seeing' of tourism (Crouch & Desforges, 2003, p. 7, emphasis in original). Travelling is not only about visual consumption and gazing at landscapes. It is not only about making mental connections and disembodied exercises. It is also about walking, travelling, relaxing and sunbathing, listening, dancing, smelling, getting ill or drunk or maybe having sex. It is not only looking at it, but also *doing things with it* (Franklin, 2003, p. 9).

Touch, a feeling of surrounding space, sight, smell, hearing and taste are worked inter-actively. All the senses are involved. However, this mode of embodied practice does not operate as a gathering device but is worked through the way the individual uses her or his body expressively — it turns, touches, feels, moves on, and dwells. Rather than set aside, the individual is engulfed by the space around him or her (Crouch, 2004, p. 87).

And similarly tourism entrepreneurs, the 'producers', are actively and bodily involved in the ordering of tourism; they bodily perform tourismscapes (see also Ateljevic & Doorne, 2005). As Haan (2005, p. 15) argues, people not only create things, they also react to them. Material appropriation, resulting in a specific physical constellation, is a meaningful act and a powerful way to structure social life.

Second, there are objects and spaces. A concern with materiality in, for example, Kenyan tourism is a concern with cars and planes; dirt roads and pot holes; cultural villages or museums, restaurants, bush camps and five-star hotels and their supplies; attractions and natural objects like seas, beaches, hills and lakes and the related flora and fauna. Indeed, tourism does seem to be more *object*- rather than simply *idea*- or *discourse*-oriented and tourists do have an intimate relationship *with* tourist sites (Franklin, 2003; his emphasis). For example, natural objects 'afford' certain possibilities. Beaches of Mombassa cannot invite sunbathing; the hills around Nairobi cannot provide viewing places; and so on. They do nothing by themselves (Haan, 2005). But they do — rather they sometimes do — because of the particular way people, technologies and environments are embedded (see also Harré, 2002). Given certain past and present relations, particular 'objects' afford a range of possibilities and opportunities; nature and other physical objects owe certain 'affordances'. Take for example the famous Amboseli region (see Van der Duim, Peters, & Wearing, 2005). The tourism space of Amboseli is a typical combination of specific natural environments (Amboseli, Kilimanjaro), tourism facilities (lodges, campsites) and 'Maasai' villages and group ranches (see Rutten, 2002); all frequented by the 'Big Five' operators. Without this specific environment there would be no tourism at all, as is the case in most other parts of Kenya. Or take the 'affordances' of the countryside:

> The unregulated and unexpected effects of climate, terrain, animals and plants are apt to impact upon the body so as to jar it from its performative normalcy. Amongst a host of potential disruptions, nettles and thistles sting, insects bite, frisky horses frighten, muddy paths may be slippery and on occasions tumbles, downpours drench and powerful smells such as silage disturb thoughts of a rural idyll. Thus the material qualities of the rural are likely to act back upon the walker whose early sauntering and visual delight is replaced by fatigue, pain and an acute awareness of gradient, surface and obstacle. What this also confirms is that the performances described above are never merely visual but involve a diverse sensual encounter with the rural, depending on the degree of temporal and physical immersion, and drawing upon tactile, auditory and olfactory senses in an engagement with space and materiality. (Edensor, 2006, p. 488)

Third, there is information and media. Texts such as travel guides, newspapers, images and photographs, CD-ROMs, maps, statistical tables and spreadsheets used by tour operators, train or airline itineraries, vouchers and credit cards, architectural designs, websites and emails: all these are information, but in material form (Law & Hetherington, 1999, p. 2). For example, 'inscribed' materials, such as passports, visas and other travel documents, play an important role in creating and sustaining actor-networks in tourism. They produce scripts of what they are making others do (Latour, 2005, p. 79). Imagine oneself at the Kenyan–Tanzanian border without a passport and visa, and suddenly one starts to realize the role of tools like travel documents (Parker, 2002; see also O'Bryne, 2001).

Of course, materials and texts have been present in what is written about tourism. But at the same time, 'they have been absent from it, perhaps because it *is* so obvious that the world is made of materials that they have been taken for granted' (Law & Hetherington, 1999, p. 2). Or alternatively — as already implied in the above — they only have been dealt with as objects of the tourism gaze. Especially Urry (2002) has argued that tourism is an essentially visual activity, and activity in which the objects of the gaze are here just to be seen. At the extreme, things themselves are potentially redundant as the signs become more significant than the signified, the things themselves. However, signs (frames, adverts, pictures etc.) are things as well (Franklin, 2003, p. 101). And these tourist things are intertwined in the practice of tourism, 'we do not merely look at them or search them out. We have become *involved* with them' (*ibid.*).

Even thinking about the pre-eminent visual and representational practice of photography, it is clear that this is not just promoting or affirming an image of places, but also about things circulating around and with tourists. Thus picture postcards that circulate among and sustain social networks, snapshots that are composed, posed, taken, developed and selected or discarded, stored or displayed all are, not just symbols but, material practices that serve to organise and support specific ways of experiencing the world (Franklin & Crang, 2001. p. 15).

In sum, tourism is held together by active sets of relations in which the human and the non-human continuously exchange properties. Through the use of certain material resources, interactions can be stabilized, summarized and extended through space and time (Murdoch, 1997, p. 327). It is the very heterogeneity of tourismscapes that allow them to become, in some sense, 'structural'. Order, power, scale and even hierarchy in tourismscapes are predominantly consolidated and preserved by material objects (*ibid*, p. 360).

In other words, there would be no social ordering if the materials, which generate these, were not heterogeneous. *Left to their own devices, human actions and words do not spread far at all* (see Law, 1994). Other materials, such as text and technologies, definitely form part of any such an ordering. So ordering has to do with both humans and non-humans. They go together. It does not make sense to ignore materials and to treat them separately, as though they were different in kind: the characterization of materials is just another relational effect (Latour, 1993). But it is an important relational effect, because certain material effects, or combinations thereof, are more durable, or more easily transported, than naked human bodies or their voices alone (Law, 1994).

Modes of Ordering

The previous section maintained that endless attempts at ordering, processes of translations and the accompanying tactics eventually produce tourismscapes. Tourism entrepreneurs, tour operators, the Tourism Boards, guides and waiters, and of course tourists, continuously try to assemble the bits and pieces, people and things, needed to build coherent actor-networks that might last for a little longer. To discover how they face and try to overcome resistance, how they try to conceal, define, hold in place, mobilize and bring into play the juxtaposed people and things we call tourism (Law, 1994), we have to render visible the analytical concept 'tourismscapes'.

How can we open up the 'collectifs' of people and things we portray as tourismscapes? The answer is simple: through empirical research. The researcher's task is to unravel the collectif under study, focusing on the linkages with material resources and less visible actors. The researcher leaves the boundaries open and closes them only when the people he follows close them, in other words, the researcher has to be as undecided as the actors he or she follows (Steins et al., 2000, p. 8; see also Latour, 2005; Law, 2004).

For example, in his *Parks beyond Parks,* Rutten (2002) followed a Group Ranch Committee and Group Ranch members, a British Tour operator, Kenyan Wildlife Society, 'liaison officers', representatives of the Ministry and many others in the negotiation and implementation process of a wildlife sanctuary in the Eselenkei Conservation Area in the vicinity of Amboseli National Park. His analysis not only revealed the way different people and organisations define tourism, but also how they perform it and the way in which they align people and things in order to make a difference.

Following Law (1994), I characterize these patterns as 'modes of ordering'. What are these modes of ordering? They are 'Foucaultian mini-discourses' (Law, 2001) that run through, shape and are being carried in the materially heterogeneous processes that make up tourismscapes and their constituent organizations. Following Ploeg's (2003, p. 111) portrayal of modes of ordering in agriculture (so-called farming styles), modes of ordering in tourism can be defined and researched at three different interconnected levels.

First of all, modes of ordering are to be seen as coherent sets of strategic notions about the way tourism should be practised. According to Ploeg (2003, p. 137), they are particular cultural repertoires. These repertoires enable calculation; they form a calculus. Every mode of ordering contains a calculus: a more or less explicit framework of interconnected concepts with which to 'read' the relevant empirical reality (in this case, tourism development and the tourismscapes in which it is embedded) and to 'translate' it into new actions. A calculus is, as it were, the backbone of a particular strategy and the related decision-making processes (*ibid.*, p. 137). It entails the way in which a tourism entrepreneur or any other actor evaluates pros and cons; it entails their 'definition of the situation'. As a result, these definitions not only organize experience but also perform tourismscapes.

Second, modes of ordering not only consist of a set of ideas, but also inculcate a certain set of practices, that is, internally and externally consistent, congruous ways of performing tourism, both informed by underlying definitions of the situation and providing the feedback that might modify these definitions.

Third, and most important for unfolding tourismscapes, modes of ordering imply particular ways of integrating with other projects and modes of ordering, as practices have to be realized through the interweaving of divergent projects (Ploeg, 2003, p. 111). Incompatible 'definitions of the situation' and resulting practices will often evoke conflicts.

More generally speaking, in performing tourismscapes modes of ordering constitute each other. The interweaving of projects of tourism enterprises (tour operators, incoming agents, hotels, transport companies and the like) and of tourism enterprises and others (banks, governments, nature conservation organizations, locals and suppliers) is fundamental for the development opportunities and directions of tourism enterprises as well as tourismscapes. Just as elsewhere in the world, tourism in Kenya is the result of complex processes of negotiation and ordering between governmental agencies, NGOs, touroperators, tourists, Groups Ranch committees and numerous fractions thereof (see, for example, Akama, 1996; Olindo, 1991; Rutten, 2002). And just as elsewhere, coherence and congruence are ordering successes (Law, 1994, p. 110).

The Spaces of Tourismscapes

As the above examples illustrate, space clearly is ubiquitous in performing tourismscapes. Space is constructed within tourismscapes, and tourismscapes are always a means of acting upon space. Spatial analysis is therefore also network analysis, as space is bound into networks and any assessment of spatial qualities is simultaneously an assessment of network relations (cf. Murdoch, 1997, 1998, 2006).

Looking at tourism in terms of tourismscapes, which is complex processes of ordering where not only people and organisations but objects, technologies and spaces are brought into play, has important implications for researching human–spatial relations.

First, generally speaking, actor-network theorists see time–space in terms of association of different actor-network topologies (Latham, 2002, p. 131). Topology is concerned with spatiality, and in particular with the attributes of the spatial which secure continuity for objects as they are displaced through a space. The central idea is that the notion of 'network' is itself another topological system:

> in a network, elements retain their spatial integrity by virtue of their position in a set of links of relations. Object integrity, then, is not a volume within a larger Euclidean volume. It is rather about holding patterns of links stable. (Law, 1999a, pp. 6–7; see also Law, 2002; Murdoch, 2006)

In this geography of topologies, time–space consists of multiple pleats of relations stitched together, such that nearness and distance as measured in absolute space are not in themselves important. The meaning of places is constructed by actors and discourses that are both local and distant (Crang, 2004). Nearness and farness are the products not of distance (though that is in all sorts of ways built into relationships), but of performing actor-networks (Latham, 2002). Therefore, actor-network theorists refrain from any shift in scale, between, say, the global and the local; rather, we should simply follow the networks wherever they may lead us to: 'the role of the analyst is to follow the actor-networks as they stretch through space and time, localizing and globalizing along the way' (Murdoch, 1997, p. 224).

This has important implications for conceptualising tourism regions and spaces. For example, modern technological networks of transport like air corridors may actually provide 'tunnel effects' that bring certain spaces and places closer together, while pushing physically adjacent areas further away. In that sense airline companies have connected the hotels in Mombassa closer to the Netherlands, Germany or the UK than Mombassa town, as well as Internet has coupled lodges, entrepreneurs or attractions with tourists and travel agents, at the same time disconnecting them from their immediate geographical and socio-economic surroundings.

Similarly, Urry (2004, p. 28) has recently distinguished five highly interdependent 'mobilities' that form and reform social life. Apart from corporeal travel by tourists, distant connections result from physical movement of objects delivered to producers, consumers and retailers; imaginative travel elsewhere through images of places and people; virtual travel often in real time on the Internet; and communicative travel through letters, telephone, fax and mobile phone. All of these perform 'at a distance' and make and maintain complex connections and patterns of presence and intermittent in tourism. So relations in tourismscapes are not fixed or located in place but are constituted through various 'circulating entities' (Latour, 1999), which bring about relationally both within and between societies at multiple and varied distances (Urry, 2004).

Obviously, there are massive inequalities in structured access to each of these mobilities (*ibid.*, p. 28). The emergence of topological networks has led to important and new questions of access and hierarchy. For example: although tourism in Kenya is extremely important in terms of income and employment, tourismscapes also generate new social inequalities of access. Some groups are well 'plugged' into tourismscapes (such as entrepreneurs with good Internet access), while others will or can be excluded. Some regions are inextricably linked to tourismscapes while others remain marginal, as the uniqueness of this or that geographical circumstance matters more than ever before (Harvey, 1989, p. 294).

Tourismscapes therefore link up, through networks of people, things and 'circulating entities', valuable functions, people and localities around the world, while switching off from their actor-networks those areas of cities, regions and parts of entire countries, constituting what Castells (1998, p. 337) calls the 'Fourth World'. So a relational effect of the performance of tourismscapes is the creation, sustaining or even deepening of the gap between the haves and the have-nots. Large parts of sub-Saharan Africa are excluded. In fact, so are large parts of Kenya; only Nairobi, certain sections on the coast (Mombassa, Malindi, Lamu) and four or five of the national parks are incorporated. And despite 40 years of tourism development around the city of Mombassa, 80% of the population still lives below the poverty line (Akama, personal communications), illustrating the lack of connectivity nearby.

Second, as Franklin (2003, p. 271) argues, through the global networked interconnectedness increasingly the difference between the everyday and spaces of tourism has become blurred if not collapsed. Tourists, objects and information enact tourismscapes in a non-linear and two-sided way. Tourists and images travel from tourism-generating regions (which are also destination regions) to tourism-destination regions (which also generate flows) and back, leading to what has been called the 'touristification of everyday life' (see Lengkeek, 2002, p. 21). Almost everyplace has become mantled with touristic properties, and our stance to the world we live in, whether at home or away, has become increasingly touristic. I have a Maasai painting in my home. Just 5 kilometres from my home I can make a walk through an 'African village' and 20 kilometres from my home I can make a safari walk, gazing at elephants, rhinoceroses, lions and giraffes. But I can also taste African food and wine, buy African herbs or plants or listen to African music whenever and wherever I wish. Indeed, tourism has ordered some of the ways in which globalisation has proceeded and been experienced (Franklin, 2003, 2004).

Third, although tourismscapes unfold in a topological way, they always ground at particular spaces and places. Tourism needs production sites and these sites are local by definition. There is no place that can be said to be 'non-local' (Latour, 2005). The complex processes of ordering I labelled tourismscapes are performed in and through local time- and space-specific manifestations and transformations (see also Saarinen, 2004; Ashworth & Dietvorst, 1995). Spaces of Mombassa, Amboseli or Maasai Mara are translated into tourismscapes to allow tourists to bathe, hike, drive, stay overnight, have sex and/or enjoy the landscape. Tangible outcome in the format of forms of land use, buildings and infrastructure reflect the way particular actor-networks stipulate the organization and production of space through legal or extra-legal means (Harvey, 1989, p. 222; see also Murdoch, 1998). It is the result of spatial practices in which people and things relationally are pooled into hotels, attractions, airports and resorts that the national parks and landscapes become attractions and landscapes become 'leisure landscapes'.

Obviously the way space is acted upon is influenced by colliding modes of ordering. Referring to the three dimensions of 'modes of ordering' as depicted in the above, these modes contain notions about the way tourism should be spatially practised. It involves the way spatial practices in tourism are represented in mental constructions, consisting of values, facts or the desires of tourism planners, tourism entrepreneurs, tourists and locals (see also Harvey, 1989; Lefebvre, 1991; Meethan, 2001). It entails the conceptualisations of what tourism 'should look like' held by tour operators, hoteliers, tourists, travel agencies and tourism offices. It is the 'imagined tourism space' (Lengkeek, 2002) like that of the 'unspoiled and wild African landscape' as portrayed on postcards or in holiday brochures, which inspired tens of thousands of 'ecotourists' to visit Kenya. It also reflects construction of our idea of Africans based on out images of African landscapes in which its people have to blend. Nairobi is not considered the 'real Africa', whereas the landscape consisting of baobabs and giraffes, the villages consisting of huts with thatched roofs and African women with water buckets on their head is considered the 'authentic Africa' (Wels, 2002, p. 55).

But modes of ordering not only entail particular 'dreams' but also spatial practices, ways of performing tourism spatially. However, these practices are seldom the result of one particular mode of ordering. In other words, the spatial developments of tourism are the result of a diversity of interacting and sometimes conflicting modes of ordering. Indeed, the particular ways space is translated into tourismscapes reflect the way different modes of ordering collide and the subsequent relations of power. In other words, modes of ordering define not only human–human but also human–spatial interactions. They are carried through by architectures, landscapes and transport infrastructures. Tourismscapes are embodied in a series of performances, a series of materials and a series of spatial arrangements.

The control by certain groups of particular resources (such as money, land, contacts or tourists) might even lead to spaces that, according to Lengkeek (2002), are 'possessed'. Here, particular power relations are consolidated and preserved by material objects and space. They might resemble what Zukin (1991) describes as 'landscapes of power', Edensor (2001) as 'enclavic' space and Murdoch (1998) as 'spaces of prescription'.

As tourismscapes unfold they can become, as Murdoch (2006, p. 98) explains, 'relatively closed — thereby establishing sharp boundaries between their own intern relations and contextual relations'.

Strongly converging networks, where particular modes of ordering dominate and subsequent translations are flawlessly accomplished, might configure 'spaces of prescription'. These are closed spaces resulting from group appropriation, imposing dominant values and exclusive access (Haan, 2005, p. 9). The preferred way of performing tourism is inscribed in architectures and spatial designs, which in turn act to consolidate the network. Gated hotel complexes in the heart of Amboseli National Park or along the Mombassa coastline leave little room for conciliation. Moreover, in highly encoded spaces, as Edensor (2001, 2006) explains, stage managers might attempt to create and control cultural as well as physical environments in order to assist and regulate performance.

Spaces shaped by networks where the links between actors are provisional and divergent, where space allows for much diversity and the unfolding of a variety of social activities and experiences, where coalitions are variable and revisable, will be more fluid, interactional and unstable; they will be 'spaces of negotiation' (Murdoch, 1998, 2006; Haan, 2005). These heterogeneous spaces are 'weakly classified', with blurred boundaries, and are multipurpose spaces in which a wide range of activities and people co-exist (Edensor, 2001, p. 64).

However, prescription and negotiation, strongly and weakly organised spaces, are two sides of the same coin: one cannot exist without the other. As we have seen, modes of ordering are never ever-lasting, complete and closed totalities: they always generate uncertainties, ambivalences, transgressions and resistances. Therefore, rather than seeing orders and resistances as being in opposition, we have to identify how these two dimensions come to depend on another within particular sets of heterogeneous relations and, secondly, how these complex relations are woven into various spatial forms (Murdoch, 1998, p. 364). Sometimes these relations are made in firmly controlled ways, while at other times they are fluid and viscous:

> as they run through spaces they weave patterns in the landscape, drawing some places together, pushing other apart. They create both proximities and distances, topographies and topologies. (Murdoch, 2006, p. 97)

This is also illustrated by the fact that spaces obviously are not only translated into (different and sometime conflicting) tourismscapes, but obviously are also subject to claims of other groups and individuals (like nature conservationists, local communities, governmental agencies) with often incompatible modes of ordering. Just as many organizations experience entrenched factional 'warfare' between constituent parts, the production, occupation and control of places are also caught up in an ongoing struggle and processes of contestation (Haan, 2005). As Edensor (2006, p. 485) explains:

> performances are increasingly acted out by competing actors on the same stage. For instance, there is a competition between adventure tourists, ramblers, hunters and farmers on the mountains of Britain, each group possessing contested ideas about what activities are appropriate to these domains.

Conclusion

In order to learn more about 'how tourism works', how it is performed and how it produces space, tourism scholars have to invest in crossing theoretical borders and to capitalize on progress made in other disciplines and fields of study. In order to enable the development of new paradigms and new fields of research and knowledge making in tourism academia, in this chapter I progressively developed a new outlook on processes of ordering in tourism by translating actor-network theory to the provinces of tourism studies (see also Van der Duim, 2005).

I introduced the term tourismscapes to denote complex processes of ordering. Tourismscapes consist of bounteous people and things interacting as cogs and wheels concurrently performing 'tourism'. Tourismscapes do not endure by themselves but need constant performance, maintenance and repair. Sometimes they create obduracy; then again they melt into air. So the main task for tourism researchers is to follow and elucidate these processes of ordering. Tourismscapes are made, done and realized, and through making, doing and realizing them, people become tourists, locals become tourism entrepreneurs, a piece of paper becomes a voucher (or passport) and spaces of Amboseli, Mombassa or Lamu become tourism spaces (see also Crang, 2004, p. 82). Everywhere in the world, tourismscapes are performed through translation. Translation builds tourismscapes from constituent entities. These entities are persuaded to behave in accordance with the requirements of the tourismscapes at stake. This involves processes of engaging, negotiating, influencing, enrolling, mobilizing and excluding. So the study of tourismscapes implies a study of processes of translation, that is, the examination of the methods and tactics employed in the ordering process to make tourismscapes last a little longer.

In performing and sustaining tourismscapes, some materials last longer than others: without the non-human, tourism would not last a second. When examining tourismscapes, one therefore should be always aware that tourism is not simply social: although it is implicated in and implicating people, it also includes and produces documents, codes, texts, architectures, buildings, environments and other physical devices. Thus, following the actors in tourismscapes means following both humans and non-humans.

Consequently, the spatial analysis of tourism is therefore always a network analysis, as space is bound into networks and any assessment of spatial qualities is simultaneously an assessment of network relations. Space is constructed within tourismscapes and tourismscapes are always a means of acting upon space. As tourismscapes come in a variety of shapes and sizes, so do the spaces of tourism. We therefore need to look in detail into how tourismscapes operate, how they 'move' from place to place, and the types of relationships that are established between tourismscapes and spatial locations (cf. Murdoch, 2006). Human–spatial relations in tourism are to be examined in terms of specific processes of association, which connect what was previously detached and link 'over there' and 'over here'. Tourismscapes unfold in a series of performances, a series of materials and a series of spatial arrangements. Together they produce the effect.

References

Akama, J. S. (1996). Western environmental values and nature based tourism in Kenya. *Tourism Management, 17*(8), 567–574.

Akama, J. S. (1999). The evolution of tourism in Kenya. *Journal of Sustainable Tourism, 7*(1), 6–25.

Ashworth, G. J., & Dietvorst, A. G. J. (1995). *Tourism and spatial transformations. Implications for policy and planning*. Oxon: CAB International.

Ateljevic, I., & Doorne, S. (2005). Dialectics of authenticitation: Performing 'exotic otherness' in a Backpacker Enclave of Dali, China. *Current Issues, 3*(1), 1–17.

Ateljevic, I., Harris, C., Wilson, E., & Collins, F. L. (2005). Getting 'entangled': Reflexivity and the critical 'turn' in tourism studies. *Tourism Recreation Research, 30*(2), 9–21.

Barnes, T. (2005). Culture: Economy. In: P. Cloke, & R. Johnston (Eds), *Spaces of geographical thought* (pp. 61–80). London: Sage.

Callon, M. (1986). The sociology of an actor-network: The case of the electric vehicle. In: M. Callon, J. Law, & A. Rip (Eds), *Mapping the dynamics of science and technology. Sociology of science in the real world* (pp. 19–36). London: The MacMillan Press.

Callon, M., & Law, J. (1995). Agency and the hybrid collectif. *South Atlantic Quarterly, 94*(2), 481–507.

Castells, M. (1998). *The information age: Economy, society and culture: Volume III. End of the millennium*. Oxford: Blackwell Publishers.

Cordella, A., & Shaikh, M. (2004). *Actor network theory and after: What's new for IS research?* European Conference of Information Systems proceedings, Naples, Italy, June, 2003. Available at: http://is.lse.ac.uk/homepages/shaikh/maha_shaikhCV.htm

Crang, M. (2004). Cultural geographies of tourism. In: A. Lew, M. Hall, & A. M. Williams (Eds), *A companion to tourism* (pp. 74–84). Oxford: Blackwell.

Crouch, D. (2000). Places around us: Embodied Lay geographies in leisure and tourism. *Leisure Studies, 19*(2000), 63–76.

Crouch, D. (2004). Tourist practices and performances. In: A. Lew, M. Hall, & A. M. Williams (Eds), *A companion to tourism* (pp. 85–95). Oxford: Blackwell.

Crouch, D., & Desforges, L. (2003). The sensuous in the tourist encounter. Introduction: The power of the body in tourist studies. *Tourists Studies, 3*(1), 5–22.

Edensor, T. (2001). Performing tourism, staging tourism. (Re)producing space and practice. *Tourist Studies, 1*(1), 59–81.

Edensor, T. (2006). Performing rurality. In: P. J. Cloke, Marsden, T & Mooney, P (Eds), *Handbook of rural studies* (pp. 484–495). London: Sage.

Franklin, A. (2003). *Tourism. An introduction.* London: Sage.

Franklin, A. (2004). Tourism as ordering. Towards a new ontology of tourism. *Tourists Studies, 4*(3), 277–301.

Franklin, A., & Crang, M. (2001). The trouble with tourism and travel theory. *Tourist Studies, 1*(1), 5–22.

Haan, H. de. (2005). *Social and material appropriation of neighbourhood space: Collective space and resistance in a Dutch urban community.* Paper for the International Conference 'Doing, thinking, feeling home: the mental geography of residential environments'. Delft, October 2005.

Harré, R. (2002). Material objects in social worlds. *Theory, Culture & Society, 19*(5/6), 23–33.

Harvey, D. (1989). *The condition of postmodernity. An Inquiry into the origins of cultural change.* Cambridge: Blackwell.

Jensen, E. T. (2001). The high impact of low tech in social work. *Outlines Critical Social Studies, 3*(1), 81–87.

Latham, A. (2002). Retheorizing the scale of globalization: Topologies, actor-networks, and cosmopolitism. In: A. Herod, & M. W. Wright (Eds), *Geographies of power: Placing scale* (pp. 115–144). Oxford: Blackwell.

Latour, B. (1993). *We have never been modern.* Hertfordshire: Harvester Wheatsheaf.

Latour B. (1999). On recalling ANT. In: J. Law, & J. Hassard (Eds), *Actor network theory and after* (pp. 15–25). Oxford: Blackwell/The Sociological Review.

Latour, B. (2005). *Reassembling the social. An introduction in actor-network-theory.* Oxford: Oxford University Press.

Law, J. (1992). *Notes on the theory of the actor network: Ordering, strategy and heterogeneity.* Lancaster, UK: Department of Sociology, Lancaster University. Available at: http://www.comp.lancs.ac.uk/sociology/soc054jl.html

Law, J. (1994). *Organizing modernity.* Oxford: Blackwell Publishers.

Law, J. (1999a). After ANT: Complexity, naming and topology. In: J. Law, & J. Hassard (Eds). *Actor network theory and after* (pp. 1–14). Oxford: Blackwell/The Sociological Review.

Law, J. (1999b). *Traduction/trahison: Notes on ANT.* On-line Paper published by the Centre for Science Studies, Lancaster University (available at: http://www.comp.lancs.ac.uk/sociology/papers/Law-Traduction-Trahison.pdf).

Law, J. (2001). *Ordering and obduracy.* On-line Paper published by the Centre for Science Studies, Lancaster University (available at: http://www.comp.lancs.ac.uk/sociology/papers/Law-Ordering-and-Obduracy.pdf).

Law, J. (2002). Objects and spaces. *Theory, Culture & Society, 19*(5/6), 91–105.

Law, J. (2004). *After method. Mess in social science research.* Oxon: Routledge.

Law, J., & Hetherington, K. (1999). *Materialities, spatialities, globalities.* Department of Sociology, Lancaster University (available at: http://www.comp.lancs.ac.uk/sociology/soc029jl.html).

Lefebvre, H. (1991). *The production of space.* London: Blackwell.

Lengkeek, J. (2002). *De wereld in lagen. Sociaal-ruimtelijke analyse nader verklaard.* Inaugural Address, Wageningen: Wageningen University.

Meethan, K. (2001). *Tourism in global society. Place, culture and consumption.* New York: Palgrave.

Murdoch, J. (1997). Towards a geography of heterogeneous association. *Progress in Human Geography, 21*(3), 321–337.

Murdoch, J. (1998). The spaces of actor-network theory. *Geoforum, 29*(4), 357–374.

Murdoch, J. (2001). Ecologising sociology: Actor-network theory, co-construction and the problem of human exemptionalism. *Sociology, 35*(1), 111–133.

Murdoch, J. (2006). *Post-structural geography*. London: Sage.

O'Bryne, D. J. (2001). On passports and border controls. *Annals of Tourism Research, 28*(2), 399–416.

Olindo, P. (1991). The old man of nature tourism: Kenya. In: T. Whelan (Ed.), *Nature Tourism. Managing for the environment* (pp. 23–38). Washington, DC: Island Press.

Parker, K. W. (2002). Making connections: Travel, technology, and global air travel networks. Paper presented to the Social Change in the 21st Century Conference, Queensland University of Technology, Brisbane.

Ploeg, J. D. (2003). *The virtual framer. Past, present and future of the Dutch peasantry*. Assen: Van Gorcum.

Rutten, M. (2002). Park beyond parks. Genuine community-based wildlife eco-tourism or just another loss of land for Masaai pastoralists in Kenya. International Institute for Environment and Development, Issue Paper 111, London.

Saarinen, J. (2004). Destinations in change. The transformation processes of tourist destinations. *Tourist Studies, 4*(2), 161–179.

Steins, N. A., Röling, N. G., & Edwards V. M. (2000). Re-'designing' the principles: An interactive perspective to CPR theory. Paper for the 8th Conference of the International Association for the Study of Common Property, Bloomington.

Tribe, J. (2005). New tourism research. *Tourism Recreation Research, 30*(2), 5–8.

Urry, J. (2002). *The tourist gaze* (2nd ed.). London: Sage.

Urry, J. (2004). Connections. *Environment and Planning D: Society and Space, 22*(2004), 27–37.

Van der Duim, V. R. (2005). *Tourismscapes*. Dissertation. Wageningen University, Wageningen.

Van der Duim, V. R., van der Peters, K. B. M., & Wearing, S. L. (2005). Planning host and guest interactions: Moving beyond the empty meeting ground in African encounters. *Current Issues in Tourism, 8*(4), 286–305.

Van der Duim, V. R. (2006). Performing African tourismscapes. Paper presented at the Atlas Africa Conference Contested landscapes in tourism: Culture, conservation and consumption. Mombassa, Kenya, February 16–18.

Verschoor, G. (1997). *Tacos, Tiendas and Mezcal. An actor-network perspective on small scale entrepreneurial projects in Western Mexico*. PhD dissertation. Wageningen: Wageningen University.

Wels, H. (2002). A critical reflection on cultural tourism in Africa: The power of European imagery. In: J. Akama, & P. Sterry (Eds). Cultural tourism in Africa: Strategies for the new millenium. Proceedings of the ATLAS Africa International Conference, December 2000, Mombasa. Arnhem: ATLAS.

Wilson, E., & Ateljevic, I. (2006). Female backpackers and independent travellers: Bringing the body into tourism research. In: K. Hennam, & I. Ateljevic (Eds). *Backpackers Tourism*. Concepts and Profiling. Clevedon: Channel View Publications.

Zukin, S. (1991). *Landscapes of power. From Detroit to Disneyworld*. Berkeley, CA: University of California Press.

Chapter 11

'Worldmaking' and the Transformation of Place and Culture: The Enlargement of Meethan's Analysis of Tourism and Global Change

Keith Hollinshead

Introduction: Meethan — The Conceptual Catalyst for 'Worldmaking'

A few years ago, Meethan (2002) produced the most valuable work which challenged much of the received thinking in Tourism Studies about the role of tourism in the production of 'society' and 'space,' and of the marketplace 'consumption' of those phenomena. Meethan's book *'Tourism in Global Society: Place, Culture, Consumption'* (hereafter *Tourism in Global Society*) is a solid and well-reasoned treatise which remonstrates against many of the conventional orthodoxies of and about tourism that Meethan found to be essentialist and reductionist (Meethan, 2002, p. 90) [*hereafter citations for Meethan 2002 are shown as 'M90', in which the last two numbers represent the page number*]. It is a fine read for those who wish to ground themselves in Pre-Fordist, Fordist, and Post-Fordist matters of cultural production (M72). It is a compact but searching treatment for those who wish to explore the role of tourism vis-à-vis key aspects of consumer aesthetics — or what some commentators call commodity aesthetics (Fjellman, 1992; Hollinshead, 1997, 1998a, 1998b, 1998c). And it is a refreshing re-rumination about the matters of authenticity, appropriation, and alienation which arise as various corporate, government, and special interest playmakers in tourism produce their contested representations of 'the primitive' and 'the modern.'

According to Meethan, too much of the conventional thinking in Tourism Studies is based upon shallow typologies, structured around stark 'binary' or 'dualistic' classifications (M163) — particularly over those matters of *authenticity* (M112) that tourism/travel are found to significantly and iniquitously rub up against. In highlighting the works of de Kadt (1979), Mathieson and Wall (1982), Pearce (1989), and Fennel (1999), Meethan laments the ways in which tourism is routinely presented as a field of activity which *itself* axiomatically commodifies things and which *itself* brings about a loss of or a corruption of forms of cultural distinctiveness (M143). In Meethan's judgement (M121) there is a powerful undercurrent of thought in Tourism Studies which is predicated upon a priori or utopian views about premodernity. Such outlooks tend to position 'tourism' as a modernistic intrusion upon received premodern worlds, and which condemns tourism for perpetually *itself* being a redefining arm of globalisation, and, to boot, always inevitably being a redefining arm of the westernisation of the world. Thus, to Meethan, commentators in Tourism Studies repeatedly overdraw the distinction between 'authentic' form of life and culture and 'inauthentic' forms, and are all too easily inclined to label things as being 'traditional' or 'non-modern' and thereby completely mutually exclusive from 'modern or 'postmodern' phenomenona (M163).

Thereafter, this chapter seeks to amplify Meethan's outlook on the cultural economy of tourism by showing how tourism is potentially — if not already — a lead vehicle in the valuation/revaluation of local places and, indeed, in the valuation/revaluation of held inheritances, cultures, and cosmologies. To that end, the paper introduces the concept of '*worldmaking*' to describe the creative and collaborative essentialising/normalising/naturalising imperatives which ordinarily and routinely run through the representational repertoire of tourism in each place. In this light, an attempt is made to show how Meethan's thinking on the social production of 'locality' 'space,' and 'culture' variously supports or advances the recent insights of Buck, Kirshenblatt-Gimblet, Fjellman, Thomas, and others, on the inventive, corrective, and highly powerful role tourism plays in such everyday *worldmaking* activities, where many of these commentators on the power and authority of tourism tend to offer their observations from research positions roosted in *other* fields and disciplines beyond what is commonly taken to be Tourism Management/Studies (hereafter termed 'Tourism Studies').

On the other hand, whilst this chapter offers general support for Meethan's judgement on the adolescence of conceptuality in Tourism Studies on matters of cultural production, it does point out that there is indeed a number of generally lone-wolf investigators positioned *within* the domain of Tourism Studies (out of which are many who have contributed to this book) who are, in their different ways, indeed scrutinising the making, de-making, and re-making of our local/global iconographies and identifications of place and culture, which has after all mobilised a recent collective movement of what is termed now 'the critical turn in tourism studies' and to which this book obviously attests. That is, the point is registered that whilst the field of Tourism Studies indeed continues to be dominated by its managerialist and non-critical prescriptivisms, it does already have its pioneering and protean individual 'critical explorers' of the ways in which the world is imagined and made through the agency and authority of tourism.

However, it is important to stress here that whilst I am acknowledging the emergence of more critical and reflexive tourism studies, it goes beyond this paper to review and engage more deeply with those individual contributions as this has been effectively provided elsewhere (see for example, Blackwell Companion to Tourism, edited by Lew, Hall, & Williams, 2004). Instead, this paper seeks to meet two key objectives. Firstly, to further distil some of the deep sensibilities that Meethan addresses in his probings into the dynamics of change and transformation across the contemporary globe by looking at the parallel analysis provided by selected lead commentators who are generally positioned 'outside tourism studies field.' Hence, my aim is to further extract what Meethan uncovers about the conduct of tourism in the political economy of cultural production by teasing out the ongoing fabricatory business of tourism as — *in vibrant association with other forces of social, cultural, and consumption production* — a maker, de-maker, and re-maker of populations and spaces. Secondly, thus, it is the purpose of this critique of *Tourism in Global Society* to run faster and further with Meethan's catalysing ideas about the mercurial role — sorry the mercurial roles — tourism has in the consolidating or emergent relationship of globalisation. It is the purpose of the paper to tease out what could fruitfully be termed as the *worldmaking* agency of tourism (Hollinshead, 2002, 2004) in the frequently subtle re-scoping of spatial and social relationships — where *worldmaking* is itself introduced and defined in Exhibit 11.1.

Hence, an effort will be made to codify the in-many-senses inventive and in-many-senses cooperative/confirmatory function of tourism in the *worldmaking* manufacture, the *world-making* de-manufacture, and the *worldmaking* re-manufacture of peoples, places, and pasts — something akin to what Callaghan (1998) attempted when he experimented with (for him) a Durkheimian outlook on the production of 'Shetlandness' in the United Kingdom. In doing so, I will begin with the prelude of the grand clichés which can be found in Meethan's observations of the contagious simplicities of and about tourism within global society which generally have resulted in perceiving tourism as a distinct and predictable phenomenon and Tourism Studies domain as a 'contained discipline.' Before considering the specific nature of insights on the social production of place, culture and consumption that Meethan gives in *Tourism in Global Society*, I will then provide a parallel analysis of the current state-of-knowledge of the subject created by other selected lead commentators who mostly come from *outside* of Tourism Studies domain. Finally, I will translate Meethan's insights on the role of tourism vis-à-vis culture and consumption to the emergent idea of *worldmaking*.

Tourism as a Distinct and Predictable Phenomenon — The Grand Cliches

Meethan's text on place, culture, and consumption is one that questions the dominant/received views of and about tourism in the literature of Tourism Studies. It questions those conventional outlooks which almost exclusively position tourism as a part of the general processes of modernity (M41), or locate tourism more precisely as part of an assumed shift from modern outlooks to postmodern outlooks. Such orthodox visions in the domain of Tourism Studies on and over the world are inclined to invest in preponderant cognitions within western thought that envision pure or traditional societies and earthly or primitive paradises as being largely fundamental and fixed phenomenon, a point which Mugerauer (2004) has addressed elsewhere. Such 'traditional societies' are held to exist within a kind of quintessential and abiding state of *otherness* — that is, within a pristine realm of The Other which is conventionally understood to be in stark opposition to The Western Self (M164) — which the Western-minded dominances of the tourism industry then upset or disturb as uncontrolled forms of travel arrive and untamed sorts of tourism appear on 'the

EXHIBIT 11.1:
WORLDMAKING DEFINED

****

WORLDMAKING, as used in this manuscript, is the creative C and often 'false' or 'faux' imaginative processes and projective promotional activities C which management agencies, other mediating bodies, and individuals strategically and ordinarily engage in to purposely (or otherwise unconsciously) privilege particular dominant/favoured representations of people/places/pasts within a given or assumed region, area, or 'world', over and above other actual or potential representations of those subjects.

****

NOTA BENE — SOME CAVEATS:

• Caveat 1:
The worldmaking imaginary tends to consist of a representational repertoire of sites, subjects, and storylines, which view the world from standpoints which are important to that 'authorising' management or mediating agency or engaged individual;

• Caveat 2:
The worldmaking imaginary tends to be platformed upon received narratives revered by the interest group/sub-population/society with which that management, mediative agency, or individual associates (or seeks to affiliate), but those foundational narratives may be given subtle or substantive (and not always recognised or admitted) re-interpretations over time;

• Caveat 3:
The worldmaking imaginary sometimes tends to purposely or unwittingly take on board interpretations of other hues (about history/nature/the cosmos) which have either originated or been consolidated elsewhere either within distant/removed/foreign invasive populations, or within collaborative industrialising corporate settings which are powerful in the prevailing regional/national/international marketplace.

• Caveat 4:
The worldmaking imaginary is always inherently (and sometimes pungently) political, inevitably advantaging some populations over others in particular ways, whilst conterminously suppressing those other peoples in large or small ways C though those who give voice to such normalising or mainstreaming acts of articulation may not always be alert to the culuro-political effects of that symbolic/significatory dominance.

Source: the above definition predominantly constitutes a condensation of the broad ideas on the *frequently fabricative* nature of the held cultural heritage and the received socio-political inheritances of populations, as given in Hollinshead (2002 and 2004). The definition does however also draw from Goodman's (1978: 6) old explanation of symbolic 'worldmaking', where the found 'ways of worldmaking' alluded to in any context, always start from worlds already on hand (i.e. C are always constructed within familiar regimes of ordering the world as already known and supported by the given worldmaker/worldmaking group).

****

Exhibit 11.1: Worldmaking defined.

traditional' scene to commodify the received world order and to alienate these Others from their 'due' lifestyles and their 'proper' cultural inheritances. In Meethan's judgement, these ascendant perspectives in the received literature of Tourism Studies are predicated upon limited theorisations about the way the world is revalued through tourism. He is disturbed by the preponderance of the view that tourism is an intrusive element within such pure or prelapsarian societies. Like Lanfant (1995) and Jacobs (2004), he is also troubled by the dominance of the view that when tourism makes its ingress into such Other-worlds it *inevitably* increases the homogenisation, the westernisation, and the general spoliation of those receiving cultures (M114).

In these fashions, Meethan follows Hall (1994) and suggests that conventional assumptions about the ways in which tourism expands across the globe tend to lack discernment about the variable interconnectives that occur between 'culture' and 'power.' In his judgement, culture tends (bewilderingly) to be accepted as an unproblematic category within the current crucibles of thought about tourism. To him, observers of global developments in tourism should particularly oxygenate their outlooks within recent thinking from sociology and from anthropology on global systems (M115). Thereby, they should take heed of schools of thought which portray 'culture' as a more versatile and mutable analytic category. Thus, Meethan insists that they should particularly note the ways in which Lefebure (1991, 1996) inspects the production of space; they should acknowledge that 'space' — here meaning, 'culture' — is profitably seen as a sometimes convergent but sometimes divergent sphere of activity in which all sorts of *unpredictable* materialisations and all sorts of *non-typical* symbol representations are inclined to be admixed.

Consonantly, in *Tourism in Global Society*, Meethan calls for a large c-r-i-t-i-c-a-l rethink about the office of tourism within processes of globalisation, something that, we could argue, is rather lacking in works like Theobald's (2005) more orthodox coverage of the internationalities of tourism — viz. Its 3rd edition remains a valuable work for the massed ranks of the professional patrimony that chiefly lead the administration and education in Tourism Management, but a work (with its hackneyed conceptualities about the political economy of culture and its largely non-critical assessments of those hallowed and reified 'impacts' of tourism) that does little to probe the more complex, contextual, and interpretive judgements as to how tourism matters and what tourism might independently or axially do to place and space. Certainly, whilst there are many fine individual prescriptivist chapters in Theobald (2005), the shallowness of the cumulative reflection about the intra-societal and the inter-societal reach and significance of tourism across the world would disturb those like Tribe (1997, 2000, 2002) who advocate that tourism is not just an everyday management matter of access to sun, sand, and sex but also inherently a day-by-day philosophical matter of acuity in stewardship of culture and nature. But I digress! Back to Meethan.

Meethan demands freshly invigorated thinking about the presumed internally consistent homogenous character of 'cultures' and the presumed bounded geography of 'cultures' (M115). To him, the role of tourism as an ambivalent and fluctuating producer of 'culture' (and of 'space' and 'consumption') at the local level must be reasserted (M114). To him tourism is important in the way it can help generate new hybrid forms of being and becoming at the local level. To Meethan, like Featherstone (1995), tourism can be a crucial originator or communicator of forms of emergent/restless/chequered culture, and its projections may be asserted for domestic consumption just as much as for visitor appeal. In his view, the received practice of continually disaggregating tourism from other trajectories of 'globalisation' and 'localisation' — he refrains from using the term 'glocalisation'! — should be suspended:

> tourism cannot be 'lifted-out' or simply isolated from other processes [of globalisation or of local renewal], nor simply squared into [its own distinct] catch-all category of culture (M162).

Though he does not use the syntax of Venn (2006), Meethan would certainly agree with him that international tourism is very much a field of complicity and co-articulation, and thereby an entangled and entangling realm of compossibility (Venn, 2006, pp. 24, 103). This significance of these co-articulative actualities and possibilities in the production of culture and place through tourism would scarcely be suspected from reading conventional managerialist studies like Ritchie and Goeldner's (1994) mammoth handbook for Tourism Studies researchers, and it is grossly understated within the narrow scripturality of Theobald's (2005) work, as parented by its large team of in-field stalwarts.

Thus, the worth of Meethan's catalytic work is that it teaches us to take care about the grand clichés which unwarily be feeding off and re-fuelling across Tourism Studies, at the expense of more carefully calibrated longitudinal theorisations about the reach and agency of tourism and travel in Tourism Studies. A list of some of the grand old conceptual chestnuts of Tourism Studies — that is, of some of the commonplace banalities about the usual intrusive indelicacies and the usual fatal prescriptions of tourism — is now given in Exhibit 11.2. Meethan is keen to remove this kind of empty talk from the discourse of the field, thereby being keen to replace the kind of totalised judgements (which stipulate universally that tourism is entirely a curse or entirely a blessing [M64]) with much more closely and critically reasoned differentiations about how tourism is articulated with particular communities and locales.

What Meethan keenly argues is that tourism is a massive field of human endeavour which is richly interlinked — sometimes robustly, sometimes in subtle fashion — with lots of other co-productive industries and institutional undertakings. He maintains that the dynamics of globalisation and localisation which stream through tourism can lead to all sorts of new or revised forms of economic, cultural, and political conditions, that is, to Venn's (2006) compossibilities. But in Meethan's judgement, whether that lived experience is a 'positive' or 'negative' matter will frequently be an intricate thing to assess and because of the scale and scope of the issue mix that tourism routinely begets, and thereby will always be perspectival in nature. This is the kind of situated and interest-group-resonant insight that the evolving conceptualisation about *worldmaking* must be primed to address. In Meethan's view — as Exhibit 11.2 implies — the existing literature of Tourism Studies tends to be tired and dull in terms of its developed capacity to trace the cultural intricacies and the competing perspectives that are ordinarily enmeshed within what the field used to call 'the impacts of tourism,' but which Lanfant (1995) has gradually taught us to recognise as *the bidirectionalities* (or rather *the multidirectionalities*) of tourism.

EXHIBIT 11.2:
THE GREAT AND GRAND CLICHES
A SELECTION OF MEETHAN'S OBSERVATIONS OF THE CONTAGIOUS
SIMPLICITIES OF AND ABOUT TOURISM WITHIN GLOBAL SOCIETY

1. SAMPLE CLICHES ON TOURISM AND AUTHENTICITY	• **1A** = *The non-modern is authentic and always decent, good, and proper: tourism is inherently/always modern, disruptive to the authenticity of things, and therefore always bad, being debilitative for those decent and proper cultural practices (M90);*
	• **1B** = *Modernity is Dystopia (which disturbs/unsettles people today): tourists therefore search for Utopia, where they can exist in bliss (however temporarily that may be) (M91);*
2. SAMPLE CLICHES ON TOURISM AND CULTURAL IDENTITY	• **2A** = *Each exhibited culture in tourism is discrete and definitely bounded: all cultural/ethnic/other important identities are therefore given (i.e. fixed, essentialised, and easily distinguishable from other such > tribal = memberships) (M141);*
	• **2B** = *The members of each significant culture have a primordial attachment to specific territories: each traditional population has a proper association with its own distinct place (M61);*
3. SAMPLE CLICHES ON TOURISM AND ITS SOCIAL IMPACTS	• **3A** = *Tourism is a distinct entity which exists in its own discontinuous state independent of culture: tourism regularly arrives uninvited as a sterile cultural force from outside to have impact upon original and distinct local societies (M138);*
	• **3B** = *All tourism activities are capitalistic and intrinsically and ideologically antagonistic to the decency of proper/ natural cultures: all tourism activity tends to commodify what is precious and esteemed in local/host/original cultures (M62-3);*
4. SAMPLE CLICHES ON TOURISM AND VIEWABLE CULTURE	• **4A** = *Each society which is regularly visited by tourists has a natural 'front' region (which tourists see) and a natural 'back' region (which they do not): things in the front region tend to be inauthentic, and things in the back region tend to be authentic C and the host population (and Tourism Studies scholars!) can readily distinguish between these two regions (M155);*

Exhibit 11.2: The great and grand cliches.

	•	**4B** = *The constant infiltration or invasion of tourists (particularly from the unknowing/uncaring 'West') tends to export > Western = preferences and to objectify/to essentialise trivial (but capturable) features — largely from the front region of the societies they briefly visit (M48);*
5. SAMPLE CLICHES ON TOURISM AND COMMODIFI-CATION	•	**5A** = *The removed communities and isolated ethnic groups which the expansionist tourism industry continually seeks out are frequently the last bastions of the 'proper'/'decent'/ 'natural' worldorder: again [in parallel to 1A above] the tourism industry is always an intrusive and commodifying force acting intrusively upon those pristine and uncontested traditions (M142);*
	•	**5B** = *The commodifying practices which are embedded within tourism (or heavily associated with it) are always an a priori negative: tourism is always inherently a force which 'encroaches' or 'interferes', and always inevitably causes forms of alienation which were never previously present in each locally distinct society it inveigles (M164);*
6. SAMPLE CLICHES ON TOURISM AND THE > SACRED = OR THE > REAL = OTHER	•	**6A** = *Tourist visitation to > other cultures = is predom-inately a quest for the sacred indulged in by travellers who are themselves disaffected by the highly secular and com-modified urban-industrial worlds in which they themselves live: the search for the authentic/the pristine/the sacred, is a vital quest for 'the real' in an increasingly non-real world (M13);*
	•	**6B** = *Tourism is naturally a human endeavour which in and of itself promotes greater understanding between peoples: when travellers from different places move closely amongst distant/faraway societies, gains of reciprocal appreciation and mutual comprehension will always result (M153–154);*
7. SAMPLE CLICHES ON TOURISM AND THE BAITED CONSUMPTION OF PLACES AND PASTS	•	**7A** = *The recent explosion of travel around the world is predominantly an outcome of the clever manipulation of tourists by all-powerful transnational corporations who are often in league with local/state/national governments: these market-controlling companies skilfully have used Fordist production techniques (and now also use more subtle post-Fordist projective techniques) to entice hordes of almost-passive tourists to consume the places and spaces which they doctor and serve up for them (M88);*

Exhibit 11.2: (Continued)

	• **7B** = *In contemporary tourism, corporate companies have been particularly acute at romanticising the past of other/ different places as lead drawcards in the promotion of international travel: > heritage tourism = has over the last century become a notably pernicious form of baited cultural production which has distorted (particularly through simulated depiction) the real culture of places for consumption by relatively unknowing/undiscerning gullible tourists (M104);*
8. SAMPLE CLICHES ON TOURISM, THE COLONISED WORLD, AND PRIVILEGED SCHOLARSHIP THEREOF	• **8A** = *Tourism is fundamentally a realm of endeavour through which the world is commodified and colonialsed, yet it is one where both the active mass of commodifiers and the receiving masses of colonised are largely docile and compliant: only lead Tourism Studies researchers really play non-passive roles, and only they are really alert to the inherent falsifications of the world which are embedded within tourism (M112);*
	• **8B** = *While tourism has expanded rapidly to destroy other cultures by turning them into mere spectacles for tourist consumption, things can gradually (and almost always) be rectified through the deployment of sound > sustainable tourism = policies: ultimately, the authenticity of cultures can be restored or substantially recaptured through the provision of proper [sic!] Tourism Studies scholarship on 'alternative'/'appropriate'/'responsible' ways of developing or doing things in tourism, and there is no area of cultural stewardship that > professional = Tourism Studies wisdoms of about sustainability cannot ever reach!! (M59–60).*

CAVEATS ON THE ABOVE CONTAGIOUS SIMPLICITIES, AS CULLED FROM MEETHAN (2002):

- The above cliches are brief interpretations of Meethan's critique of recent Tourism Studies scholarship in *Tourism in Global Society ...;*
- Most of the above assumptive bases are romanticist, privileging the supremacy of anti-modern society B.T. (Before Tourism);
- Most of the cliches speak negatively about the power/authority/influence of tourism, but some of them are roseate about the role and function of tourism;
- Many of the assumptive bases given here for the commonplace clichés in late Tourism Studies are somewhat reduced, and are admittedly offered here in concentrated fashion in order to register the said undercurrent of thought within the field succinctly;
- A number of sub-themes crop up in several of these 16 selected great and grand clichés, viz.:
  - ➢ tourism is largely an antimodern hunt for lost premodern experience,
  - ➢ host populations are tourists are both largely passive;
  - ➢ the best Tourism Studies scholars have a supreme 'God's-Eye-View' on such global processes!

Exhibit 11.2: (Continued)

Tourism Studies as a 'Contained Discipline'

Meethan frequently turns his attention to the domain-building endeavours of Tourism Studies researchers. He acknowledges Tribe's (1997) useful meditations on the expansion of tourism as 'field,' but he is perturbed by the efforts of some theorists to turn this eclectic field into a manifest 'discipline' (M2). He notes how a high proportion of Tourism Studies analysts are typically comfortable with interpretations of tourism which contextualise the subject as 'an entirely modern' or 'an entirely postmodern' entity. He worries that only a modicum of researchers in the field appear to be at ease with paradigmatic standpoints that roundly situate the subject of tourism within the broad sweep of economic, social, cultural, and political intelligences about globalisation, that is, within and under the kind of broader inspections that King (2006) advocates. Accordingly, implicit in Meethan's account is his acceptance of Tribe's judgement that the quest for a singular and contained 'discipline' is a fruitless and misconceived venture, and he joins Hall (1994, p. 187) in concluding that 'what is now tourism and what now is culture are relatively unclear' (M70).

Meethan therefore thinks that commentators in Tourism Studies have too frequently reified the subject of tourism as a *disjecta membra*. Furthermore, he considers that conventional thinking within Tourism Studies is inclined to be under-girded by a censorious moral tone which details what tourism has indeed singularly brought about in the world or peculiarly (on its own) caused for 'its' populations (M164). Consequently, tourism is generally seen as either 'a symptom of some malaise [wrecked on premodern societies] by modernity, or as a compensatory mechanism for such ills' (M164). In these respects, Meethan remarks that the commodification of things is almost always proffered as an *a priori* set of actions which alienates people from their inheritances and traditions, and which inevitably produces a litany of negative side effects. He concludes that in Tourism Studies, the commodifying appearance of tourism is repeatedly seen to bring about a deterioration in the cultural distinctiveness of places — a form of societal decomposition which can readily, under most circumstances, be calibrated on relatively non-complex 'carrying capacity scales,' 'threshold indexes,' or the like (M143). Hence the field of Tourism Studies — in Meethan's turn of the century view (M165) — is one where over-generalised classifications of and about matters of culture hold sway. It is a field replete with researchers and observers who see the process of commodification advancing in inevitable turpitude as tourism expands, thereby functioning as:

> the handmaiden of capitalism, and the result of [capitalism's] individuals spread [within and across] the shallow, inauthentic, and dystopian shadow-land of modernity (M64).

To Meethan (M5), the trajectories of consumption may be central in our need to understand what tourism affects and what it helps affect, but the literature of the field is badly under-theorised in terms of the links between the political economy and culture. Like Picard (1993), and Lanfant (1995), he judges that too many observers of the business of tourism assume that the culture of visitor-receiving destinations are static sites 'inertly subjected to exogenous factors of change' (Picard, 1993, p. 72). In disputing such depthless judgements in the received literature, Meethan is keen to challenge the field's superficially conceived orthodoxies about 'impact assessments,' about 'demonstration effects,' and about 'cultural tradition' (M161). He is particularly eager to reject analyses of tourism which have been patronisingly framed around the twin suppositions that firstly tourism is always an external (i.e., impacting) agent of change. And, secondly, he repudiates analyses of tourism which bolster the view that receiving destinations/receiving populations have always hitherto possessed 'cultures' that have been (before the onset of tourism) essentially unchanging, lacking any internal dynamism of their own (M147 and 161). Such forms of revised thinking may be standard fare in many social science fields over the last two or three decades, but — to Meethan — the penetration of such reflective, interpretive, contextualised, audienced, and reflexive views has been slow in Tourism Studies, itself.

To repeat the point, Meethan is anxious to destabilise those outlooks in the literature on the social production of place, culture, and consumption, which position tourism as a discrete, self-contained system (M5) — indeed as 'tourism' rather than 'tourisms' (M75). Overall, then, it is Meethan's purpose to reframe the questions which are asked in Tourism Studies about the relationships between tourism, globalisation, people, and place. Like Gibbins and Reimer (1999), he calls for interrogations that take more flexible but carefully connoted account of the complexities of change within the globalising world. To that end, he insists that Tourism Studies investigators generally ought to pay much more faithful attention to theorists in anthropology and sociology: they ought to particularly digest the recent insights of Hannerz (1996), Clifford (1997), and Hall (2000) on diasporic and transnational culture, together with the issue-mongering of Gregory (1994), Harvey (1993), and Tomlinson (1999) on the significance of place under the globalising condition. In Meethan's view, a more sustained spicing up of the literature of Tourism Studies with such recent cultural studies thinkers should gradually ensure that researchers in the field would develop more responsive, place-specific interpretations; such seasoning of the Tourism Studies literature should ensure that field researchers would be more readily able to cultivate salient Appadurian interrogations (after Appadurai, 1990) about the relationships between tourism and flows of people, capital, images, and ideas across the globalising/localising world (M4). Then hopefully, and by implication, we can consider that Tourism Studies commentators will be able to take a decent and decided grasp of the myriad of ways in which the field engages with connectively, advances, or helps redirect the world's symbolic economy (M169).

The State of Knowledge about the Social Production of Place, Culture and Communication — Other Selected Lead Commentators on Worldmaking

Before considering the specific nature of insights on the social production of place, culture and consumption that Meethan gives in his book, it is useful to examine the current state-of-knowledge of the subject. It is helpful to consider, in a little more depth, what other lead commentators in and around Tourism Studies have recently uncovered on the performative power of tourism in inspecting those issues of cultural commodification that are central to the relationships in tourism between globalisation and the projection of 'people' and 'place.' Thus, firstly, in Exhibit 11.3, an effort is made to reveal what Meethan concentrates upon in each of his eight chapters on the role tourism plays in the dynamics of change to places and cultures in globalised world (viz., in the left-hand column of the table). Then, secondly, the effort is taken in the right-hand column to locate a prominent researcher on the direct and indirect transformative effects of tourism on places and cultures in the globalised world to throw contemporary contextual light on the worth of Meethan's own recent contribution.

In selecting those eight thinkers and theorists on the problem of cultural commodification involved in the manufacture of populations, heritage, and destinations, the aim is to provide fresh comparative discernment or nuanced appreciation of what Meethan did and did not cover in his turn of the century writing. The insight within Exhibit 11.3 is therefore meant to be suggestive and purportive rather than exhaustive and unequivocal. Indeed, one could argue that some of the comparative commentators tabled in Exhibit 11.3 — such as Kirshenblatt-Gimblett, Rothman, and Buck — are 'panoramic' observers of the transformative effects of tourism, and do not actually restrict their own synthesis on and of the order of things to the particular 'social production of consumption' chapter in Meethan which they have here been lined up against. One could also strongly argue that a number of other lead commentators — such as Greenwood (1989), Morgan and Pritchard (1998), Urry (1990) and Poon (1993), Picard and Wood (1997), for instance — should also figure prominently in such a comparative assessment.

Nonetheless, the effort was taken to provide eight authors who had recently (in the last decade) published cutting edge analysis on the *worldmaking* role and function of tourism, though of course like Meethan, none of the eight use the term *worldmaking*, *ipso facto*, themselves. And the eight selected have — like Meethan, himself — each produced broad treatments of the performative power of tourism in its international pantheon of *worldmaking*, proffering their critiques *veluti in speculum* within multisited inspections (i.e., broadly situated assessments) rather than as scintilla observations within singe studies. Hence, Exhibit 11.3 does not bring in the *worldmaking* genius of a Bruner (in, for instance, Bruner, 1991, 1995) nor an Edensor (as evidenced in Edensor, 1998) who have written brilliant conspections on the *worldmaking* agency of tourism. These commentators have as yet only offered such perlustrations at a limited range of sites/settings, and have not yet produced a *magnus opus* on the matters of dynamic change that are conceivably imbricated in contemporary, commodifying (?), tourism. And finally, Exhibit 11.3 does not address the work of a number of Tourism Studies observers whose work is indeed used by Meethan himself in *Tourism in Global Society*: hence, the autopsies of Cohen (principally from Cohen, 1988), Harrison (principally from Harrison, 1992), and Wang (principally from Wang, 1999), amongst others, were not thereby considered for Exhibit 11.3. Meethan had already used these analysts as guide rails on his own inspections of the complexities of change *vis-à-vis* tourism.

Though some readers may quibble with the following rule-of-thumb classifications, the list in the Exhibit 11.3 contains, respectively (i) a political science, (ii) a performance studies, (iii) a historical, (iv) an anthropological, (v) a second historical, (vi) a consumer studies, (vii) a museological, and (viii) a litero-philosophical review of the miscellaneous creative and constructive agency of tourism: therefore, many leery and unadventurous 'within-discipline' Tourism Studies/Tourism Management researchers will not be acquainted with some of the

EXHIBIT 11.3:

WRITERS-IN-PARALLEL — SELECTED LEAD COMMENTATORS ON THE SOCIAL PRODUCTION OF PLACE AND CULTURE FOR (TOURISM) CONSUMPTION:

MEETHAN'S 8-CHAPTERS ANALYSIS OF TOURISM AS A GLOBAL PHENOMENON: THE RELATIONSHIPS BETWEEN TOURISM, PEOPLE AND PLACES	OTHER RECENT / EMERGENT ANALYSES OF TOURISM AS A GLOBAL PHENOMENON: THE RELATIONSHIPS BETWEEN TOURISM, PEOPLE AND PLACES
☐ *ch.1. = THEORISING TOURISM* *Tourism as a search for the authentic, the pre-modern and the primitive?; tourism as a quest for heritage?; tourism as a ritual response towards the alienations of modernity?; tourism as a 'secular' sacred-quest?*	☐ **THEORISING ABOUT POWER IN THE PRODUCTION OF THE PLACES/SPACES OF TOURISM** Tourism as a or the legitimator of populations; tourism as the definer of the character of local states; tourism as the marker of 'proper' traditionality, or the signifier of the spirit and hope of emergent populations and the representative voice of nations. • **via C.M. HALL** — principally in terms of his 1994 political science inspection of policy-making in tourism;
☐ *ch.2. = CREATING TOURIST SPACES: FROM MODERNITY TO GLOBALISATION* *Tourism space as symbolic value?; tourism as invented space?; tourism as a new signifying space of and for consumption?*	☐ **THEORISING ABOUT THE COLLABORATIVELY INVENTED MADENESS OF TOURISM SPACE** Tourism space as collaborative symbolic space C i.e., as a collaborative local hallucination of consciousness; tourism destinations as 'made' places C i.e., projected with special projections of 'hereness' as doctored by local or influential elites; tourism sites and storylines projected for 'host'/domestic' digestion as much as 'quest'/'visitor' digestion. • **via B. KIRSHENBLATT-GIMBLETT** — principally in terms of her 1998 evaluation of the performative power of tourism;

Exhibit 11.3: Writers-in-parallel — Selected lead commentators on the social production of place and culture for (tourism) consumption.

☐ *ch.3. = TOURISM DEVELOPMENT AND THE POLITICAL ECONOMY* *Tourism space as representation of the 'modern' symbolic economy?; tourism space as site of multinational corporate authority?; tourism space as 'alternative' or 'locally mediated' site?*	☐ **THEORISING ABOUT THE MEANINGS THAT ARE EMBEDDED WITHIN THE SCRIPTED EMPLOTMENTS OF THE SYMBOLIC ECONOMY OF 'INDUSTRIAL' TOURISM** Tourism space as the spirit and communicator of places; tourism as the legible and 'conventional' geography of the local/external growth coalition; tourism the powerful 'emotive' and 'affirmational' vehicle of the transformed local community. • **via H.K. ROTHMAN** — principally in terms of his (1998) breakthrough evaluation of tourism as a transformative and colonising industry;
☐ *ch.4. = TOURISM: MODERNITY AND CONSUMPTION* *Tourism sites/services as controlled and 'customised' space?; tourism sites/services as freely-chosen 'products'?; tourism sites/services as outcome of the consuming 'tourist gaze' in the West and beyond?*	☐ **THEORISING ABOUT TRANSNATIONAL CORPORATE AUTHORITY IN THE PROVISION OF/ INTERPRETATION OF TOURISM SPACE** Tourism sites/services as space regulated by powerful coalitions of like-mind corporations cross-referencing each other = s products and services; tourism sites/services as somatic offerings provided in such ways as to deny the visitor his/her own interpretive autonomy; tourism sites/services as instruments of the 'Americanisation' or the 'Disneyification' of the world. • **via S.M. FJELLMAN** — principally in terms of his 1992 scrutiny of the Walt Disney Corporation as a multi-operational, and aggrandising transnational corporation *de rigeur*;
☐ *ch.5. = AUTHENTICITY AND HERITAGE* *Tourism sites/settings as 'othered' or 'exoticised' places?; tourism sites/settings as 'authentic' or 'alienating' places?; heritage sites/settings as 'recovered' or 'invented' places?*	☐ **THEORISING ABOUT HEGEMONY IN THE SELECTION OF THEMES/NARRATIVES/SUBJECTS PRESENTATION AT 'AUTHENTIC' HERITAGE FOR SITES**

Tourism settings/sites as arenas of hegemonic 'cultural production'; tourism settings as essentialised places; tourism settings as decontextualised places; tourism settings as 'naturalised' antimodern places; heritage settings/sites as 'cleansed' places.
• **via I. MCKAY** — principally in terms of his 1994 historical assessment of the inventive and at times highly consilient role of the public and private sector in creatively manufacturing special visions of place;

□ **THEORISING ABOUT THE EXTERNAL DOMINATION AND APPROPRIATION OF CULTURE AT TOURISM DESTINATION, AND OF COUNTER-VOICES TO THAT POWER**
Tourism 'culture' as transformed space; tourism 'culture' as ideologically reproduced mythopoetic space; tourism 'culture' as intrusive music/art/craft; tourism 'culture' as conquered but appropriated 'image'; tourism 'culture' as industrialised representation.
• **via E. BUCK** — principally in terms of her 1993 transdisciplinary appraised of the appropriation of indigenous/local cultural forms in Hawai'i by the juggernaught tourism industry;

□ **THEORISING ABOUT THE QUALITY OF ENLIGHTENMENT VIS-A-VIS DEADENING TRIVIALITY EMBEDDED WITHIN THE DEVELOPMENT/PROJECTION OF 'DRAWCARD' TOURISM SITES**

□ *ch.6. = WHOSE CULTURE?*
Tourism 'culture' as homogenous/geographically-banded space?; tourism 'culture' as a symbolic mode of communication?; tourism 'culture' as commodified and political space?

□ *ch.7. = WHOSE PLACE? TOURISM, PEOPLE AND CHANGE*
Tourism presentations and the increasing flows of people and objects?; tourism presentations and old and new identities?; tourism presentations and the creation/ maintenance of 'boundaries'?

Exhibit 11.3: (Continued)

Tourism presentations as crude forms of framing and objectification; tourism presentations as unintelligent and uninspiring projections of place and identity; tourism presentations as highly selected excerpts of contained culture-hood, projected in monovocal fashions (denying counter-interpretations of history or place).

- **via D. HORNE** — principally in terms of his 1992 exposition of the sterilities and the unrefined awarenesses by and through which many government and corporate players represent peoples, places, and pasts in contemporary tourism;

□ **THEORISING ABOUT THE CHANGING NATURE OF GOVERNING REPRESENTATIONS OF PEOPLES & PLACES VIA TOURISM**

Tourism and the non-homogenous colonisation of places; tourism and historicised accounts of colonised places/ decolonised places; tourism and the complex cultural process which legitimise racial and cultural difference; tourism and the continued/emergent effects of colonial governmentality.

- **via N. THOMAS** — principally in terms of his 1994 examination of the unsuspected thoughtlines which govern the projection of tourism themes/narratives/drawcards in postmodern/postindustrial/postcolonial tourism.

□ *ch.8. = PLACE, CULTURE AND CONSUMPTION*
Tourism and the unproblematic interpretation of 'natural'/ 'steady-state' places?; tourism and the 'singular' or 'multiple'/'diverse' effects of globalisation?; tourism and the dynamic symbolic economy of particular local places?

Exhibit 11.3: (Continued)

above eight researchers. Since (out of the eight), only C.M. Hall publishes r-e-g-u-l-a-r-l-y within the Tourism Studies literature, diehard disciplinarians of and from Tourism-Studies-Unvarnished bailiwicks will probably not be cognisant of what transdisciplinarians like Kirshenblatt-Gimblett, Buck, and Thomas, and their 'progressive' multi-standpoint ilk are inclined to scrutinise. But it is important to let down the drawbridge leading to the 'discipline' (or rather 'the domain,' as some would have it) of Tourism Studies.

The fact that researchers (like the seven from Kirshenblatt-Gimblett to Thomas) tend to operate from more secure disciplinary or transdisciplinary standpoints in the broader humanities has given them certain key advantages over researchers in adolescent Tourism Studies. Historically, lead commentators in established disciplines in the social sciences have seemingly received much stronger support from national and international funding councils in the humanities (Tribe, 1997). Consonantly, a McKay, a Buck, or a Fjellman can often devote many years to the longitudinal study of such matters of authority, appropriation, and/or alienation within the *worldmaking* agency of tourism. For instance, Fjellman's (1992) inspection of the Walt Disney Corporation in Florida was the result of a 5-year ethnographic marathon; and Rothman's (1998) study of contemporary 'Wild West' identity in the USA is clearly the result of a sustained and intricate career-long review of how a veritable compendium of towns, communities, and corporations in 'America's opportunist West' have actively or passively renewed themselves. Few within-domain Tourism studies researchers are known to have the enabling funding, the home-institution ascendancy, and the exterior leverage to be able to confidently devote those sorts of long-run half-decades and certainly those long-long-run decades to any such multi-sited but dovetailed thematic research agenda. Yet, such longhaul specialists are gradually appearing, such as Graburn, who predominantly concentrate upon 'the sacred' (viz., Graburn, 1997), Hitchcock, who appears to exclusively analyse tourism developments in southeast Asia (viz., Hitchcock, 1999, 2000), and Adams, who focuses constantly upon matters of ethnic identity in Sulawesi (viz., Adams, 1997). Ergo, apart from such few longitudinal specialists, Meethan has to take his intelligences on the place of tourism in the dynamics of change from an extraordinarily-broad-in-number but generally shallow-in-individual-depth array of conventional Tourism Studies contributors. Interestingly, Meethan does cite the prolific Anglo-Australian C.M. Hall, of course, but does not address the works of any of the other seven lead thinkers on the *worldmaking* agency of tourism, as are given here in Exhibit 11.3.

Those caveats stated, Exhibit 11.3 suggests that there is much in Meethan's research agenda on globalisation, consumption, and cultural change that can be further fortified by or through an admixture with 'the eight' other selected oxygenating analysts. Meethan's valuable critical journey into the political economy of cultural commodification (and towards the global-local *jeu de théâtre*) can conceivably be further enriched with and through the following:

- by absorbing a little more of Hall's (1994) insight on the need for dialectical inspections of *worldmaking*, particularly where Tourism Studies researchers could/should 'audience' their investigative findings towards the different interests of competing communities or special-interest constituencies;
  - For a more recent account of the dialectics of audiencing, see here the third chapter by Harris, Wilson, and Ateljevic, and Hollinshead and Jamal (2006).

- by drawing a little more from Kirshenblatt-Gimblett (1998) about the contrasting *epistemological logics* (or the *ontological logics*) which various practitioners/players/publics bring to the everyday performative theatricality of tourism, almost unbeknown to each other;
  - For a more recent discussion of how the significance of such matters of epistemology — at the domain level — please refer to Tribe (2004).
- by heeding from McKay (1994) rather more pointedly how the evolving politics of identity and difference which operates nationally/internationally in tourism is very much built around singular but perduring projections of *otherness* which have evolved about the quality, richness, or merit of *other-designated* populations — that is of 'othered' groups and communities who have been under-suspectingly but ethnocentrically mis-labelled over many decades/many centuries;
  - For a more recent treatment of the praxis of othering, please read Goss (2005) and on processes of áuthentification see Ateljevic and Doorne (2004, 2005).
- by acknowledging from Buck (1993) how tourism can itself help imprison hybridising populations in difficult psychic circumstances where they contend day-in-day-out with the supremacy of *dominant mytho-poetic narratives* which the players/practitioners of tourism may have no real idea that they themselves are continuing to cosmologically maintain in very real material form through their everyday management/marketing/administrative efforts;
  - For a more recent examination of the encoded/decoded representation of the mythic naturalia and the mythic artificialia of places through tourism, please consult Lidchi (1997).
- by taking watch from Rothman (1998) as to how tourism can indeed provide — or help provide — a quite *distinctly scripted iconographic overlay*, which promises an often quite distinct psychic or affirmative 'promise' for a given population than that which can be generated by other/competing industries;
  - For a more recent set of transdisciplinary papers on the imaged projection of 'place' (in this case, of stylised visions of 'Irishness'), please inspect Cronin and O'Connor (2003).
- by ingesting from Fjellman (1992) insights about the techno-kinetic power by and through which skilled corporations are these days able to educate, entertain, and entice their visitors into swallowing their mediated or embedded messages about nuanced product-related things — but more importantly how, in the first place, those corporations become sentient to *the baseline desires* of their consumers, customer, clients before that mediated kinetic power can be decently or self-rewardingly exercised;
  - For a more recent assessment of how historic and contemporary constructions of 'people' and 'places' relate to the found or assumed motivations of tourists and other interested players, please turn to Cartier and Lew (2005);
- by appreciating from Horne the degree to which companies/corporations/councils in tourism and travel can (at each and every grand or ordinary site) learn to provide much more *empowering intellectual vitality*, on a reflexive basis with different 'reading publics' (of visitors), in order to more positively respond to the diverse psychic or cosmological imaginaries of travellers — where that said intellectual vitality is built on the capacity of those companies/corporations/councils to generate meaningfully felt awe

and respect towards the globalising/localising world rather than being some vain mongering of highbrow cultural appeals;

- ▪ For a more recent critique of what tourism practice inherently and implicitly does (and, therefore, what companies/councils/communities can strategically aim to harness), please peruse Crang (1999), in terms of his essay on spatial semiotics vis-à-vis knowledge production.
- by discerning from Thomas how there exists at each tourism site/setting *an infinity of large, small, or fragmentary starting points* within existing storylines or within possible projections about peoples/places/pasts which can be captured, kindled, or incited to tune into manifest (or, also, latent) visitor/customer/consumer historical awarenesses about the special or significant qualities of place — and how very few companies or government bodies are at all skilled in harnessing such cultural imaginaries or otherwise reaching into such cosmological imaginaries.
  - ▪ For a more recent dissection of the role of the mass media, travel providers, and host communities, et cetera, in the mediation of representations of quality experiences vis-à-vis held qualities of place, please digest the Jennings and Nickerson (2006) collation on interpreted sites and settings around the world.

Thus, there is so much in Hall, Kirshenblatt-Gimblett and others as shown in Exhibit 11.3, that can add conceptual fillip to give propulsion to Meethan's gelling ideas on the spectacle of tourist consumption (read, now, *worldmaking*). And there is so much in the later emergent critiques of Hollinshead and Jamal, and of Tribe and others as cited in the above paragraph caveats (at ▪) — which can at last help newcomers to the field (and oldstagers who have been long established in the field and unsuspectingly contained under its close managerialisms and accordant prescriptivist knowhow! [Robins, 1997, pp. 14–19]) to come towards an informed c-r-i-t-i-c-a-l understanding of who is doing what to whom, and when and where, through the agency and authority of particular constructed images under the imaginal reach of tourism.

Some observers might maintain, of course, that the above eight points of enrichment might in fact constitute no more than a gilding here and there of Meethan's conceptual lily. But the field is fast maturing in its observed criticalities: today, other field-watchdogs are much more likely to recognise that, collectively, they can be prodigiously cross-pollinative with Meethanic thought, and can thereby immediately generate all kinds of imaginative new theoretical journeys into what had been during the 1970s, 1980s, and 1990s the undeniably under-researched art and craft of *worldmaking* within tourism. Thankfully, with the recent turn of the century appearance of new journals like *Tourist Studies, Current Issues in Tourism, The Journal of Tourism and Cultural Change*, and *Tourism, Culture and Communication*, the field now has a number of regular publications which are equipped to handle researched intelligibility on such dominances, such discursivities, and such dialogues.

Meethan himself acknowledges the existence of an emergent concern in Tourism Studies for and about the inventive imaginary of tourism. To him — like Howes (1996), Wang (1999), and Whatmore (2002), that is modified by the fact that theorisation is still held back or hampered by the high proportion of researchers in the domain (and in bedfellow domains) who still predominately fuss and ferret about tired old matters of (i.e., poorly contextualised and poorly historicised approaches to) 'authenticity.' What Meethan appears to repeatedly call for is more work with the depth and width of perspective on the production and re-production of 'authentic' and 'traditional' forms of cultural life that Ateljevic and Doorne (2002) deployed in their study of the ideological reinforcements involved in the imaging and positioning of 'New Zealand' in the 1990s — or what Grunewald (2002) adopted in his investigation into the invention of tradition vis-à-vis the revival of culture in Brazil. Clearly, both Ateljevic/Doorne and Grunewald were writing at the very moment that Meethan was fine-tuning his Palgrave text! Anyhow, as AlSayyad records in his important reflection on the nexus between traditionality and transitionality, the subjects of heritage-making and culture-formation have become so poorly conceived in what he terms *the age of tourism* "that 'authenticity' has been completely cut off from its moorings" (AlSayyad, 2001).

Yet, in Meethan's view, some sub-domains of Tourism Studies were (by the turn of the century) fast taking on new leases of conceptual life. For instance, in his view, experts in 'heritage tourism' had expanded their interests way beyond the stale old concern for the provenance of objects to monger much deeper awarenesses about tangible meanings to people of presented nature (M98). Meethan does acknowledge that there is conceivably an unfolding recognition within Tourism Studies — again particularly in 'heritage settings and scenarios' — of the need for understandings that trace the political agency of tourism at different levels (i.e., at local, state, transnational, et cetera, tiers) of interest (M99–100). Hence, in his judgement, an increasing proportion of Tourism Studies scholars no longer content themselves with descriptive explorations as to what the touristic heritage of a place is, but why (a place like Skye (M100) [Meethan cites Macdonald, 1997 here]) might indeed *need* a vibrant presentation of its heritage. Thus, tourism inherently has a didactic purpose (or rather, a mix of dynamic interfeeding purposes) for both visitors to places and residents of places. Tourists have to be stimulated by awe-inspiring narratives about given places to help them to choose which to visit; coterminously, locals have to be informed about what they should really be proud of, to help them stay decently loyal to the right kind of imagined nationhood. And whilst all sorts of iconographic interpretations about places can compete — as at the Taj Mahal (M100–101) [Meethan cites Edensor, 1998 here], sometimes outsider-visitors are able to impose their own preferred vision of 'authentic place' upon locals – as has apparently transpired at Ephidvaros (M101 [Meethan cites Williams and Papamichael (1995) here]).

Future Research Agendas into 'Worldmaking'

Having provided a background of Meethan's overall coverage of the relationships between tourism, globalisation, people, and place, it is now possible to translate his main turn-of-the-century insights on the role of tourism vis-à-vis culture and consumption to the emergent idea of *worldmaking*. Exhibit 11.4 therefore comprises a table of six of the key points of critical inspection, which Meethan addresses in his Palgrave text. Again, it has to be made clear that the coding of these six reflections on the reach and authority of tourism are not precisely Meethan's, *ipso facto*, but my own (Hollinshead). The six interpreted metaphors on the projective agency and power of tourism are:

- tourism as an *under-studied* realm of representation;
- tourism as an *under-studied* agent of signification;

EXHIBIT 11.4:

A RESEARCH AGENDA ON WORLDMAKING:

THE IMPLICATIONS OF MEETHAN'S INSIGHTS ON THE SOCIAL PRODUCTION OF PLACE, CULTURE, AND CONSUMPTION FOR ENQUIRY INTO THE WORLDMAKING ROLE AND FUNCTION OF TOURISM

AREA OF CRITICAL ANALYSIS	*TOURISM AS A GLOBAL PHENOMENON: SELECTED KEY ISSUES IN MEETHAN (2002)*	*TOURISM AS A WORLDMAKING AGENT: AN EXTENSION OF THE CRITIQUE OF MEETHAN*
1. TOURISM AS A REALM OF REPRESENTATION	*Tourism is a highly potent arena of representation which acts inclusively and exclusively to define who are what a population is, and who or what a population is not. In this sense, tourism can become a realm of deep contestation where struggles over symbolic representation are as fiercely fought over as those over material resources (M27; after Harvey 1993:23).*	Tourism can play an immense role in not only the symbolic representation of peoples, places, and pasts, but in constituting (or 'making') the very world that a space/city/region becomes. It is important that tourism studies researchers investigate *the worldmaking consequences of tourism* (as it acts collaboratively with other industries and forces) to not only externally colonise distant populations, but as it acts internally to colonise the internal populations of places.
2. TOURISM AS AGENT OF SIGNIFICATION	*Tourism (as a highly potent medium of representation) is an increasingly vital vehicle by and through which privileged values of certain groups/institutions/communities are imposed on places/spaces/the environment. In this sense, tourism is not just a mere symbolic system of signification, but a means of projecting places and spaces which spawns (helps spawns) very real material processes, i.e., in capital development, transport infrastructure, building design, et cetera (M39).*	Tourism can constitute a very powerful material worldmaking order which embraces material as well as symbolic elements. It is important that, as cultures and people become ever more mobile, the transregional and transnational effects of the manufacturing power of this dynamic material worldmaking order is gauged by Tourism Studies researchers at specific places to regularly monitor the changes in symbolic and material reality being produced.

Exhibit 11.4: A reasearch agenda on worldmaking.

3. TOURISM AS ACTIVE DISCOURSE	*Tourism is fast becoming a if not the crucial medium of authority in the symbolic invention/ de-invention/re-invention of places as particularly gazes or discursive 'visions' become normalised across an area, or universalised over larger continental/global regions. In this sense, tourism does not just comprise a mix of discourse (or texts) which reflect felt differences, but constitutes a mix of authorial social practices which actually create differences through action (M162).*	Tourism can work in a myriad of complex and subtle ways to create and maintain the cultural distinctiveness of the local and global 'worlds' it makes, or rather, which it coproductively helps make. It is important that Tourism Studies researchers become proficient at identifying the worldmaking role and function of tourism as it variously reinforces (or reverses) the potentialities of other forms of external and/ or internal change. Venn (2006) would call this the 'compossibilty' of tourism.
4. TOURISM AS INTERPRETED NARRATIVE	*Tourism does not axiomatically lead to the erosion of authentic ways of life of 'other cultures' as, supposedly, it axiomatically turns them into mere spectacles for tourist consumption. In this sense, tourism should be assessed not so much as an automatic destroyer of traditional and cherished inheritances, but as a frequent creator of new emergent sorts of authenticity which can co-exist alongside received/longstanding notions of 'the authentic' (M109 and back-cover).*	Tourism is not just an external force which works in a debilitative fashion to disturb 'proper' notions of authenticity, which it imposes upon passive locals and upon passive tourists (rather it is more rewardingly seen to be a dynamic worldmaking generator of new possible compossible meanings out of which locals and/or tourists can construct new-old/ new-new authenticities and through which they can weave new identities). It is important that Tourism Studies researchers become more skilled at interpreting the personal narratives which tourists (and locals) develop as they individually/collectively negotiate the new 'worldmade' symbolic value of objects/ events/places.

5. TOURISM AS MEDIATING VISION	*Tourism very much facilitates the visual consumption of things through the accent it places/ helps place on the sightseeing of particular objects and scenes (and on the specular definition of things which that 'sightseeing' occasions). In this sense, however, Urry's (1990) emphasis on the two distinct sorts of 'romantic' and 'collective' gazes which conceivably exist within and through tourism is not entirely helpful as is: there are undoubtedly many different sorts of naturalising authorisations which run through the so-called tourist gaze, not just these two (M81–82).*	Tourism is a medium through which many essentialising and monumentalising visions course. It is important, at the turn of the millennia, for Tourism Studies researchers to become particularly practised at not only interpreting where dominant (?) (or previously dominant (?)) Eurocentric worldmaking gazes are strongly contested by surviving or emergent non-European/non-Western outlooks, but to be able to conceptualise aesthetic interpretations from various/ significant multiple standpoints.
6. TOURISM AS MAKER OF LOCALITY	*Tourism is a prominent arm in the globalisation of places, but the rationalisations of such global processes do not act in the same way at each place. In this sense, the manner in which 'new global things' are adopted and consumed at local places varies considerably: the localisation of places is no unilinear process for cultural change is not only heavily influenced by external dynamics, but it is also influenced considerably by the internal dynamics of societies (M124/5; after Watson 1997).*	Tourism is an immense agent in the worldmaking dynamics of change and transformation which are currently occurring to places and to cultures in the globalised world. It is important, however, that Tourism Studies researchers appreciate that cultures are never totalised entities, and that as tourism works in and alongside other processes to help transform places, all manner on new forms of creolisation, of hybridisation, and of indigenisation are being produced which have yet been scarcely identified within the received Tourism Studies literature.

Exhibit 11.4: (Continued)

- tourism as an *under-studied* active discourse;
- tourism as an *under-studied* interpreted narrative;
- tourism as an *under-studied* mediated vision; and,
- tourism as an *under-studied* maker of locality.

In the Exhibit 11.4, the effort is made to first synthesise Meethan's thinking on the weaknesses of vogue 1990s/early 2000s Tourism Studies conceptualisations of/about these six areas of critical analysis. Then an attempt is made to extend that particular thinking by building it into a future research agenda for the respectively targetted area of theorisation, per medium of the concept of *worldmaking* as put forward by Hollinshead (2002, 2004), and as taught under that subject title (viz., *Worldmaking: Tourism and Globalisation*) in a Masters-level module at the University of Luton — now the University of Bedfordshire — in England for the last half dozen years. In this light, Exhibit 11.4 calls for the development of more pronounced and precise lines of analysis of the dynamic and co-productive role of tourism as a global but differential change agent, and as a maker/de-maker/re-maker of the local compossible (or fantasised) worlds of populations.

Final Reflections: A More Critical and Reflexive Tourism Studies

In 2002, Meethan's analysis of tourism as a global phenomenon was a much needed exposition of the state of health of Tourism Studies. Overall, it then suggested that current Tourism Studies theorisation on the relationship between globalisation, people, and place was advancing, but only from a somewhat threadbare level. In 2002, he was able to suggest that too much of the existing thinking about tourism and the complexities of change in contemporary life was still bathetic, too frequently consisting of time-worn assessments that there is indeed an unilinear inevitability to tourism development around the world, wherever. We learn from Meethan that many sorts of dog-eared theories within Tourism Studies continually proliferate, of types that position tourism itself as a common and irreversible agent of cultural decline: in his view, compensatory thinking (which posits tourism as a conceivable executor of new and enriching cultural opportunity within existing societies) is decidedly uncommon in comparison (M122). Relatively speaking — and thankfully — many individual commentaries (as attested by this edited collection) in the last decade are certainly moving the field forward c-r-i-t-i-c-a-l-l-y to an impressive degree. But there is still merit to be had in an occasional re-read of *Tourism in Global Society*: and there is considerable value in utilising Meethan's critique of the political economy of international tourism in the refinement cum enrichment of a more flexible/transportable/accessible concept of *worldmaking* (or similar theorisation on co-production and compossibility in and through tourism).

In many ways, *Tourism in Global Society* is a critical inspection of the traditional or orthodox fashions in which tourism had been conceptualised in the late twentieth century, and it is a child of the new mixed and multi-faceted approaches that the broader emergent fold of Tourism Studies is now bringing to matters of cultural production and to issues of cultural consumption. It is Meethan's judgement that theorisation about tourism has improved considerably over the last couple of decades, and that the industry is gradually being recognised as being a cardinal player in the dynamic imaginary of places — an important catalytic 'deviser' of the ideological identifications of populations and 'designer' of the iconographic identifications of places (Bauman, 1997; Macdonald, 1997, pp. 108–111). Yet Meethan plainly believes that many old conceptualisations about tourism axiomatically being an erosive force for authentic culture linger on. Similarly, Jaworski and Pritchard (2005) claim that many researchers indeed have been slow to grasp the new thinking about tourism's dynamic didactic role in both the political economy of being and becoming and the discursive authorising of 'reality.'

Thus, after Lanfant (1995), we are competently reminded by Meethan that tourism is not just a predictable arena where the forces of globalisation act unidirectionally and uni-dimensionally to reformulate local places in like with singular and uniform conditions (read transational corporate interest?). Instead, and in terms of what Meethan could have called 'the peoplemaking'/'the placemaking'/'the pastmaking' (or aggregatively, the *worldmaking*) agency of tourism,' we are advised that tourism is a complex realm for the maintenance of cultural distinctiveness. We are informed by him what I would style the *worldmaking* agency and authority of tourism is an intricate dance of internal twists, of reverse tangoes, and of indigenised two-steps. Though the influential thinking of Bhabha (1994) on the misty locations of contemporary/postcolonial cultural formation and popu-lation projections is not cited by Meethan, we are cautioned by him that culture and con-sumable identity are not just made rootlessly by exogamous forces acting concertedly in activities like tourism upon places, but that the emergent identifications which arise in part through tourism are more wisely viewed as being fresh co-articulated entities produced along what are often difficult-to-read hybrid trajectories somewhere between old tempo-ralities and new aspirations.

Indeed, Meethan is adamant that the processes of peoplemaking/placemaking/pastmak-ing (viz., *worldmaking*) which mutate through tourism, and through other coterminous activities, do not tend to generate homogenous global spaces today, if they ever did, but will rather tend to yield places and cultures which are differentially indigenised rather than being rendered uniformly similar in character and consequence across the world. It depends, amongst other things, upon how acute and sentient the instruments of research discernment are in each single place to be able to pick up those freshly imagined local sen-sibilities, and how durable and cohesive each particular activated or created local sense of being now is. The problem is that in Tourism Studies, researchers rarely have a deep or full-toned picture about the condition of given culture *before* the involved *worldmaking* acts of external (i.e., out-group) 'cultural dominance' cum 'political coloniality' and the engaged *worldmaking* acts of internal (in-group) 'cultural effervescence' or 'political metamorphosis' ever began. The international domain and orbit of tourism has so much geography, so many abiding inheritances, and such a width of identificatory reach to cover in understanding what different competing interests deem to be important at or for a place (Cartier & Lew, 2005). The benchmark profiles of place appreciation — viz., the cultures, heritages, beings, and meanings of embraced and entangled peoples — are scarcely ever at hand and known to any penetrative degree of richness when tourism comes along to celebrate its very thereness. Oops — its therenesses!!

Hopefully, the unfolding concept of *worldmaking* can lead researchers within and beyond Tourism Studies away from the sorts of cliché-mongering that Meethan draws our attention towards improved and procreative thought on how tourism is dynamically engaged with the teeming institutions and across the old and new tribal groupings of our age in each place and space. Hopefully, the as yet inelegant and unpolished concept of *worldmaking* can be critically ventilated a little more over time to generate more robust and relevant thoughtlines to account for the role and function of tourism in the development of alternative possibilities for peoples, for places, and for pasts in our various post-colonial (?), postindustrial (?), and post-Occidental (?) contexts.

References

Adams, K. M. (1997). Ethnic tourism and the renegotiation of tradition in the Tana Toraja (Sulawsei: Indonesia). *Ethnology, 37*, 309–320.

AlSayyad, N. (Ed.). (2001). *Consuming traditions, manufacturing heritage: Global norms and Urban rorms in the age of tourism.* London: Routledge.

Appadurai, A. (Ed.). (1990). Disjunctive and difference in the global cultural economy. In: M. Featherstone (Ed.), *Global culture: Nationalism, globalisation and modernity.* London: Sage.

Ateljevic, I., & Doorne, S. (2002). Representing New Zealand: Tourism imagery and ideology. *Annals of Tourism Research, 29*(3), 648–667.

Ateljevic, I., & Doorne, S. (2004). Culture, economy and tourism commodities: Social relations of production and consumption. *Tourist Studies, 3*(2), 55–76.

Ateljevic, I., & Doorne, S. (2005). Dialectics of authentification: Performing 'exotic otherness' in a Backpacker Enclave of Dali, China. *Tourism and Cultural Change, 3*(1), 1–27.

Bauman, Z. (1997). *Postmodernity and its discontents.* London: Routledge.

Bhabha, H. (1994). *The location of culture.* London: Routledge.

Bruner, E. (1991). Transformation of self in tourism. *Annals of Tourism Research, 18*, 238–250.

Bruner, E. (1995). The ethnographer/tourist in Indonesia. In: M. F. Lonfant, J. B. Allcock, & E. M. Bruner (Eds), *International tourism: Identity and change.* London: Sage.

Buck, E. (1993). *Paradise remade: The politics of culture and history in Hawai'i.* Philadelphia, PA: Temple University Press.

Callaghan, R. (1998). Ethnic politics and tourism: A British case study. *Annals of Tourism Research, 25*(4), 818–836.

Cartier, C., & Lew, A. A. (2005). *Seductions of place: Geographical perspectives on globalisation and tourised landscapes.* London: Routledge.

Clifford, J. (1997). *Routes: Travel and translation in the late twentieth century.* Cambridge, MA: Harvard University Press.

Cohen, E. (1988). Authenticity and commoditization in tourism. *Annals of Tourism Research, 15*(3), 371–386.

Crang, M. (1999). Knowing, tourism and practices of vision. In: D. Crouch (Ed.), *Leisure tourism geographies: Practices and geographical knowledges* (pp. 238–256). London: Routledge.

Cronin, M., & O'Connor, B. (2003). *Irish tourism: Image, culture and identity.* Clevedon, England: Channel View press.

de Kadt, E. (1979). *Tourism: Passport to development.* Oxford: University Press.

Edensor, T. (1998). *Tourists at the Taj: Performance sand meaning as symbolic site.* London: Routledge.

Featherstone, M. (1995). *Undoing culture: Globalisation, postmodernity and identity.* London: Sage.

Fennel, D. A. (1999). *Ecotourism: An introduction.* London: Routledge.

Fjellman, S. M. (1992). *Vinyl leaves: Walt disney world and America.* Boulder, Colorado: Westview Press.

Gibbins, J. R., & Reimer, B. (1999). *The politics of postmodernity: An introduction to contemporary politics and culture*. London: Sage.

Goodman, N. (1978). *Ways of worldmaking*. Hassocks, Sussex: Harvester.

Goss, J. (2005). The souvenir and sacrifice in the tourist mode of consumption. In: C. Cartier, & A. A. Lew (Eds), *Seductions of place: Geographical perspectives on globalisation and touristed landscapes* (pp. 56–71). London: Routledge.

Grunewald, R. de A. (2002). Tourism and cultural revival. *Annals of Tourism Research*, *29*(4), 1004–1021.

Graburn, N. (1997). Tourism and cultural development in East Asia and Oceania. In: S. Yamashita, K. H. Din, & J. S. Eades (Eds), *Tourism and cultural development in Asia and Oceania* (pp. 194–213). Bangi: Universiti Kebangsaan Malaysia Press.

Greenwood, D. J. (1989). Culture by the pound: An anthropological perspective on tourism as cultural commoditization. In: V. L. Smith (Ed.), *Hosts and guests: The anthropology of tourism* (pp. 171–185). Philadelphia, PA: University of Pennsylvania Press.

Gregory, D. (1994). *Geographical imaginations*. Oxford: Blackwell.

Hall, C. M. (1994). *Tourism and politics: Policy, power, and place*. Chichester, England: Wiley.

Hall, S. (2000). Cultural identity and diaspora. In: N. Mirzoeff (Ed.), *Diaspora and visual culture: Representing Africans and Jews*. London: Routledge.

Hannerz, U. (1996). *Transnational connections: Culture, people, places*. London: Routledge.

Harrison, D. (Ed.). (1992). *Tourism and the less developed countries*. Chichester, England: Wiley.

Harvey, D. (1993). From place to space and back again: Reflections on the condition of postmodernity. In: J. Bird, B. Curtis, T. Putnan, G. Robertson, & L. Tickner (Eds), *Mapping the futures: Local cultures, global change*. London: Routledge.

Hitchcock, M. (1999). Tourism and ethnicity: Situational perspectives. *International Journal of Tourism Research*, *1*(1), 17–32.

Hitchcock, M. (2000). Ethnicity and tourism entrepreneurship in Java and Bali. *Current Issues in Tourism*, *3*, 204–255.

Hollinshead, K. (1997). Cross-referential marketing across walt Disney's 'world': Corporate power and imagineering of nation and culture. *Tourism Analysis*, *2*(2), 217–228.

Hollinshead, K. (1998a). Tourism, hybridity and ambiguity: The relevance of Bhabha's third space cultures. *Journal of Leisure Research*, *30*(1), 121–156.

Hollinshead, K. (1998b). Tourism and the restless peoples: A dialectical inspection of Bhabha's halfway populations. *Tourism, Culture and Communication*, *1*(1), 49–77.

Hollinshead, K. (1998c). Disney and commodity aesthetics: A critique of Fjellman's analysis of 'distory' and the 'historicide' of the past. *Current issues in Tourism*, *1*(1), 58–119.

Hollinshead, K. (2002). *Tourism and the making of the world: Tourism and the dynamics of our contemporary tribal lives*. The Year 2002 — Honors excellence lecture. The honors college. Miami: Florida International University.

Hollinshead, K. (2004). Tourism and new sense: Worldmaking and the enunciative value of tourism. In: C. M. Hall, & H. Tucker (Eds), *Tourism and postcolonialism: Contested discourse, identities and representations* (pp. 25–42). London: Routledge.

Hollinshead, K., & Jamal, T. B. (2006). Tourism and the third ear': Further prospects for qualitative research. *Tourism Research*.

Horne, D. (1992). *The intelligent tourist*. McMahon's point, NSW, Australia: Margaret Gee Holdings.

Howes, D. (Ed.). (1996). *Cross-cultural consumption: Global markets, local realities*. London: Routledge.

Jacobs, J. M. (2004). Tradition is (not) modern: Deterritorializing globalization. In: N. AlSayyad (Ed.), *The end of tradition* (pp. 29–44). London: Routledge.

Jaworski, A., & Pritchard, A. (Eds). (2005). *Discourse, communication and tourism.* Clevedon, England: Channel View Press.

Jennings, G., & Nickerson, N. P. (Eds). (2006). *Quality tourism experiences.* Burlington, MA. Butterworth-Heinemann.

King, V. T. (2006). Anthropology and tourism in South-East Asia: Comparative studies, cultural differentiation, and agency. In: M. Hitchcock, V. T. King, & M. Parnwell (Eds), *Tourism in South-East Asia revisited.* Denmark: NIAS Press.

Kirshenblatt-Gimblett, B. (1998). *Destination, culture: Tourism, museums, and heritage.* Berkeley, CA: University of California Press.

Lanfant, M.-F. (1995). Internationalization and the challenge to identity. In: M.-F. Lanfant, J. B. Allcock, & E. M. Bruner (Eds), *International tourism: Identity and change* (pp. 24–43). London: Sage.

Lefebure, H. (1991). *The production of space.* Oxford: Blackwell.

Lefebure, H. (1996). *Writing on cities.* Oxford: Blackwell.

Lew, A. A., Hall, C. M., & Williams, A. M. (2004). *A companion to tourism.* Malden, MA: Blackwell.

Lidchi, H. (1997). The poetics and politics of exhibiting other cultures. In: S. Hall (Ed.), *Representation: Cultural representations and signifying practices* (pp. 151–222). London: Sage.

MacDonald, S. (1997). *Reimagining culture: Histories, identities and the gaelic renaissance.* Oxford: Berg.

Mathieson A., & Wall, G. (1982). *Tourism: Economic, physical and social impacts.* London: Longman.

McKay, I. (1994). *Quest for the folk.* Montreal, Canada: McGill and Queens University Press.

Meethan, K. (2002). *Tourism in global society: Place, culture, consumption.* Basingstoke, England: Palgrave.

Morgan, N., & Pritchard, A. (1998). *Tourism, promotion, and power: Creating images, creating identities.* Chichester: Wiley.

Mugerauer, R. (2004). The tensed embrace of tourism and traditional environments: Exclusionary practices in Cancun, Cuba, and Southern Florida. In: N. AlSayyad (Ed.), *The rnd of yradition* (pp. 116–143). London: Routledge.

Pearce, D.G. (1989). *Tourist development.* Harlow, UK: Longman.

Picard, M. (1993). 'Cultural tourism' in Bali: National integration and regional differentiation. In: M. Hitchcock, V. T. King, & M. J. G. Parnwell (Eds), *Tourism in South East Asia.* London: Routledge.

Picard, M., & Wood, R. E. (Eds). (1997). *Tourism, ethnicity and the state in Asian and Pacific Societies.* Honolulu: University of Hawai'i Press.

Poon, A. (1989). Competitive strategies for a 'new tourism'. In: C. P. Cooper (Ed.), *Progress in tourism, recreation, and hospitality management* (pp. 91–102). London: Belhaven Press.

Ritchie, J. R. B., & Goeldner, C. R. (Eds), (1994). *Travel, tourism and hospitality research.* New York: Wiley and Sons.

Robins, K. (1997). What in the world's going on? In: P. du Gay, (Ed.), *Production of culture: Cultures of production* (pp. 11–66). London: Sage.

Rothman, H. K. (1998). *Devil's Bargains: Tourism in the twentieth-century American West.* Lawrence, Kansas: University Press of Kansas.

Theobald, W. F. (Ed.). (2005). *Global tourism* (3rd ed.). Butterworth-Heinemann: Oxford.

Thomas, N. (1994). *Colonialism's culture: Anthropology, travel and government.* Princeton: Princeton University Press.

Tomlinson, J. (1999). *Globalisation and culture.* Cambridge: Polity Press.

Tribe, J. (1997). The indiscipline of tourism. *Annals of Tourism Research, 24*(3), 638–657.

Tribe, J. (2000). Indisciplined and unsubstantiated. [Rejoinder to N. Leiper's 'An Emerging Discipline']. *Annals of Tourism Research*, 27(3), 809–813.

Tribe, J. (2002). The philosophical practitioner. *Annals of Tourism Research*, 29(2), 338–357.

Tribe, J. (2004). Knowing about tourism: Epistemological issues. In: J. Phillimore, & L. Goodson (Eds), *Qualitative research in tourism: Epistemologies, ontologies and methodologies* (pp. 46–62). London: Routledge.

Urry, J. (1990). *The tourist gaze: Leisure and travel in contemporary society.* London: Sage.

Venn, C. (2006). *The postcolonial world: Towards alternative worlds.* London: Sage.

Wang, N. (1999). Rethinking authenticity in tourism experience. *Annals of Tourism Research*, 26(2), 349–70.

Watson, J. L. (1997). Introduction: Transnationalism, localisation, and fast foods in East Asia. In: J. L. Watson (Ed.), *Golden arches East: McDonald's in East Asia.* Stanford: Stanford University Press.

Whatmore, S. (2002). *Hybrid geographies: Natures, cultures, spaces.* London: Sage.

Williams, W., & E. M. Papamichael (1995). Tourism and tradition: Local control versus outside interests in Greece. In: M.-F. Lanfant, J. B. Allcock, & E.-M. Bruner (Eds), *International tourism: Identities and change.* London: Sage.

PART 2:

METHODOLOGIES, INNOVATIVE TECHNIQUES, METHODS OF INTERPRETATION AND WRITING STRATEGIES

Chapter 12

Grounded Theory: Innovative Methodology or a Critical Turning from Hegemonic Methodological Praxis in Tourism Studies

Gayle Jennings and Olga Junek

Grounded Theory

Grounded theory is 'a methodology, a way of thinking about and studying reality' (Strauss & Corbin, 1998, p. 4). Moreover, it '*is both a strategy for research and a way of analysing data*' (Punch, 1998, p. 163). The passing of time, however, requires some updating of those definitions; more contemporary reinterpretations follow. First, the Strauss and Corbin definition: grounded theory is a '*methodolog*[ical tradition], *a way of thinking about and studying realit*[ies]'. Second, the Punch definition: '*grounded theory is a strategy for research and a way of* [interpreting empirical materials or] *analysing data*'.

Why the need for more contemporary definitions? Because, after almost 50 years of guiding research practices and processes, grounded theory has undergone interpretation and reinterpretation and presents itself as not a singular or even a dualistic approach but as a methodological tradition, which contemporaneously has multiple interpretations. The change from reality to realities in the Glaser and Strauss definition is an acknowledgment that "reality" is manifold, not singular or universal in nature and that "reality" is always under construction and reconstruction. Initially, grounded theory bifurcated into two distinctive framings: one a positivistic and the other an interpretive framing (discussed later in this chapter). Subsequently, recognizing this, Punch's definition was altered to acknowledge: (1) positivistic framings, that is, reductionist tendencies to analysing data as well as (2) interpretive framings, that is, (re)interpreting and/or (re)constructing multiple realities from social engagements that generate empirical materials and knowledges. Additionally, due to grounded theory's own inherent socially based and iterative praxis, its meanings and definitions will be constantly (re)constructed and (re)interpreted because "all scientific knowledge is always, in every respect, socially situated" (Harding, 1991, p. 10). Subsequently, the socially grounded theory/ies of tomorrow will be different to those of today and yesterday, and defining the tradition will be a continuous negotiation of meaning.

Having said this, the purpose of this chapter is to consider the background and traditional protocols/guidelines of grounded theory, provide a chronological overview of various major interpretations of grounded theory, to situate it as formerly an innovative methodology, and interpretive or analytic tool in the social sciences and more latterly as a critical turning by some tourism studies researchers from hegemonic methodological praxis in order to achieve more in-depth knowledge and understanding of the complexities of tourism phenomena. The chapter concludes with final reflections regarding grounded theory, innovation and hegemonic methodological praxis in tourism studies.

Grounded Theory: A Background

The roots of grounded theory derive from sociology (Glaser & Strauss, 1967; Glaser, 1978, 1992, 1998; Strauss & Corbin, 1990). Grounded theory was initially designed to provide an alternative to the hegemonic sociological research methodology and strategies of the 1960s. These methodologies and strategies were predicated to a *quantitative, logico*[hypothetico]-*deductive empirical studies* approach (Glaser & Strauss, 1967) informed by positivist and postpositivist (objective) paradigms. Grounded theory was, on the other hand, predicated to qualitative, holistic–inductive empirical studies informed by an interpretive/constructivist paradigm. Specifically, it generated theory grounded and induced from empirical material rather than testing of hypotheses deducted from prior knowledge. As a strategy:

> ... "grounded theory" depends on participant observation (see Schatzman & Strauss, 1973) and a method of comparative analysis aimed at constructing theories inductively. Their "constant comparative method" of analysis involves four stages: (1) comparing the data applicable to each conceptual category; (2) integrating the categories and their properties; (3) delimiting the emergent theory; and (4) writing up the theory (Glazer [sic] and Strauss, 1967, pp. 105–115). (Jorgensen, 1989, p. 113)

To iterate, the main features of grounded theory, as described by Glaser and Strauss (1967) are theoretical sampling, coding and categorising, constant comparison of categories and concepts and the emergence of substantive theory. In the development of theory, continual interaction between participants, empirical materials, researcher and interpretation takes place (Strauss & Corbin, 1994) to further "ground" theory.

Given the preceding comment about participants, an important note about participant numbers in grounded theory studies needs to be made. Predetermined participant numbers are not usually an aspect of grounded theory research design, unless of course the study is focussed on small specific cases which then might presume to use a census. In grounded theory, "sampling" of participants is dependent on "sampling" of empirical materials and interpretation. Subsequently, grounded theory uses sampling not only to drive interaction with empirical material sources but also to develop theory (Charmaz, 2003a, 2003b). The researcher moves through a continual process of interaction with empirical material sources and interpretation. Each iteration of interaction and interpretation will influence whether engagement with additional participants and sources of empirical materials may be necessary to further "ground" the conceptual categories and emerging theory. In grounded theory, this process is related to theoretical sampling, qualitative informational isomorphs, theoretical saturation and experiential interpretation.

Theoretical sampling is 'a cyclical process of data collection and analysis that continues until no new data are found only confirmation of previous [themes/] "theories" (Punch, 1998, p. 167).' (Jennings, 2001, p. 149).

Elsewhere in the literature it is also referred to as reaching a "qualitative isomorph" (Ford, 1975) or more particularly, when a "qualitative informational isomorph" is achieved, that is, there is 'redundancy with respect to information' (Lincoln & Guba, 1985, pp. 233–234). It is a state when "theoretical saturation" is reached (Strauss & Corbin, 1998, p. 143). Experiential interpretation also assists in empirical material interpretation and decision-making regarding when to discontinue empirical material collection. Experiential interpretation involves:

> the researcher, as a full participant, us[ing] her/himself as a gauge of the significance and meaning of an event, by subsequently looking inward to examine personal feelings. (Metcalf, 1986, p. 40)

These latter processes again emphasize the social nature of the research process and the embeddedness of the researchers in the processes of (re)interpretation and (re)construction.

Grounded Theory: Multiple Interpretations of the Tradition

As previously noted, since the introduction of the methodology of grounded theory (Glaser & Strauss, 1967), this methodology has developed in various directions. Of especial note is the interpretation of grounded theory by Strauss (1987) and Strauss and Corbin (1990) which led to a fundamental disagreement between the two originators of grounded theory — Glaser and Strauss. Glaser (1998), particularly, directed much criticism towards Strauss and Corbin. Glaser (1992, p. 10) contended that Strauss and Corbin presented a technique which was "full of conceptual description by a preconceived model" whereas Glaser purported that grounded theory was 'a systematic model of induction and emergence'. Glaser (1992, p. 89) further argued that Strauss used a 'verificational method which forces the deducing and testing of preconceptions in the service of full conceptual description'.

And it was to this that he referred: 'A (conditions) leads to B (phenomenon), which leads to C (context), which leads to D (action, including strategies), which leads to E consequences' (Strauss & Corbin, 1990, pp. 123, 125).

Glaser (1992, p. 58) was also critical of Strauss' mention that '*personal experience, professional knowledge, and technical literature*' assisted in analysing data. Again, Glaser (1992, pp. 56–57) reiterated that this will force the analysis rather than have it emerge through the use of constant comparison of data. The reason at the root of the differences was that Glaser viewed the *forcing of theory* as a fundamental divergence from the original Glaser and Strauss (1967) *emergence of theory*. Since the 1960s, other authors have developed directions and techniques which, whilst having grounded theory as the dominant methodology, differ in sampling, empirical material collection and analysis/interpretation techniques (Charmaz, 1997; Dey, 2004).

Linking back to the introductory statements of the chapter regarding positivistic and interpretive frames, Charmaz (2003b) distinguishes between an 'objectivist' and a 'constructivist' concept of grounded theory methodology. The objectivist view assumes there is a neutral observer, that is, the researcher and the categories will be derived from empirical material. The constructivist view 'recognises that the viewer creates the empirical material and the ensuing analysis through interaction with the viewed' (Charmaz, 2000, p. 523).

Charmaz (2003a), amongst others (Rynehart, 2004; Guba & Lincoln, 1994; Schwandt, 1994), sees constructivist grounded theory, with its multiple realities, knowledge created by the researcher and the participants and the process of interpretation of participants' views, as a more flexible, less positivist approach. Whilst acknowledging that the constructivist view of grounded theory is only one amongst many other valid views, Charmaz (2003a) sees a need to study people in social settings with a less prescriptive, rigid set of tools and techniques that have characterised the earlier works on grounded theory (Glaser & Strauss, 1967; Strauss, 1990; Strauss & Corbin, 1998). This is also a view shared by the authors of this chapter, since this approach places:

> greater emphasis on the process by which the [empirical] materials are constructed and the context in which they are constructed. . . . With [this approach] greater emphasis is placed on the processes of production of the [empirical] materials, instead of believing the [empirical] materials themselves are capable of conveying the meaning of social process. (Rynehart, 2004, pp. 63–64)

Situational Background of Grounded Theory: Innovative Methodology or Analytic/Interpretive Tool of the Social Sciences

To this point in the chapter, reference has been made in regard to objective/positivistic/postpositivistic and constructivist/interpretive approaches to research. To contextualise this further for the overall discussion of grounded theory, these are briefly reviewed here. As noted earlier in this chapter, the dominant hegemony in social sciences, and indeed tourism studies, has been positivism and postpositivism. As indicated previously, grounded theory, which is aligned with constructivist/interpretive approaches, has occupied a marginalised position in broader social sciences research. The same may be said for research designed in regard to constructivist/interpretive approaches (Jennings, 2001, 2003, 2005b). The reason for this is directly associated with the differing ways each takes to understand the world. As a consequence, these approaches or paradigms (a suite of beliefs about how the world works) have their own disparate sets of guiding principles (see Guba, 1990). These principles are broadly organised based on ontology (world view), epistemology (relationship between the knower and the known), methodology (quantitative or qualitative) (Guba & Lincoln, 1994) and axiology (values and ethics) (Lincoln & Guba, 2000). Positivism (see Jennings, 2001, 2003, 2005b) has a worldview (ontology) that assumes universal truths and laws are capable of explaining and predicting behaviours and events. It approaches know-ing (epistemology) objectively through the use of quantitative methodology. Subsequently, it purports to be value free (axiology). In the words of Comte, who coined the term "posi-tivism", the intent of positivism is:

In the final, positive state, the mind . . . applies itself to the study of . . . laws, — that is:

> their invariable relations of succession and resemblance. Reasoning and observation, duly combined, are the means of this knowledge. What is now understood when we speak of an explanation of facts is simply the estab-lishment of a connection between single phenomena and some general facts . . . (Comte, 2000, p. 28)

Over time the pragmatism of universal truths of positivism has been challenged and as a result postpositivism has emerged. Ontologically, postpositivism (see Jennings, 2001, 2003, 2005b) acknowledges 'reality' as being probabilistically and imperfectly known albeit that an objective epistemological stance is still assumed. Linked with its objectivity is the predominant use of a quantitative methodology and desire for value freedom in the research process. A form of postpositivism frequently applied in social science research is critical realism. Some critical realists assume an emancipatory axiological position. Alternately, interpretive social sciences view the world as composed by and of multiple realities. These realities are subjectively (re)interpreted/(re)constructed via qualitative methodology and a value laden axiology. The term, interpretive social sciences, is some-times used interchangeably with (social) constructionism, constructionist, (social) phe-nomenology, hermeneutics and relativism. The interpretive social sciences paradigm and related approaches reflect that:

> . . . [h]uman beings do not find or discover knowledge so much as we con-struct or make it. We invent concepts, models, and schemes to make sense of experience, and we continually test and modify these constructions in the light of new experience. Furthermore, there is an inevitable historical and sociocultural dimension to this construction. We do not construct our inter-pretations in isolation but against a backdrop of shared understandings, practices, language, and so forth. (Schwandt, 2000, p. 197)

Depending on its application, grounded theory can align with either paradigmatic per-spective. This background serves to iterate the nature of positivistic and constructivist forms of grounded theory. It also provides context for the later considerations of researchers who use grounded theory in tourism studies and the ontological and epistemological leanings they bring to the research process as socially situated and embodied beings. Additionally, it emphasizes that a move away from positivism and postpositivism, the western hege-monic research paradigms, demonstrates deviance. Deviance that we perceive as affirmative deviance (Macbeth, 1985) if not innovation in research practice. As a form of affirmative deviance, situating oneself as an interpretive social scientist, clearly accounts as a critical turn by not embracing the dominant research paradigms. The consequences of so doing have been discussed elsewhere; see for example, Scheurich (1997); Jennings (2003); Tribe

(2004); Hall (2004); Jennings (2005d). By association then, grounded theory as an under-represented methodology in interpretive research may also be (re)constructed and (re)interpreted as innovation, affirmative deviance and a critical turn.

Hegemonies, Innovation, Turns in Tourism Studies: Situating Grounded Theory

Not dissimilar to western social science research, the history of tourism studies research is based on western epistemologies founded on positivistic or postpositivistic research paradigms and linked to a preference for a quantitative research methodology (Cohen, 1988; Walle, 1997; Riley & Love, 2000; Jennings, 2001; Dann, 2005). Other approaches/paradigms or methodologies have been under-utilised and relatively limited in regard to the hegemony of literature associated with positivistic and postpositivistic paradigms. This is essentially due to the contributing disciplines and their paradigmatic biases. Works do exist, for example, see Hollinshead (1996); Jamal and Hollinshead (2001) and Table 12.1 which is specifically focussed on grounded theory examples. As a consequence, Hollinshead (1996); Riley and Love (2000); Jamal and Hollinshead (2001); Jennings (2001, 2003, 2005a); Woodside, McDonald, and Burford (2004); Phillimore and Goodson (2004), for example, see the imperative for the use of a more qualitative approach to research in tourism studies to advance knowledge in this field in order to gain a deeper and richer understanding of the tourist and travel experience beyond quantification only. In particular, Jamal and Hollinshead (2001) comment:

> we need new criteria, new dialogues, new perspectives in qualitative research to help us understand and explain the phenomenon of travel and tourism, and to help us understand in a myriad of empowering, enabling and ennobling ways the fashions by which travel and tourism may be seen to threaten or enrich the cultural, environmental and other resources of our various historical, societal, global and cosmological inheritances. (p. 22)

As more and more researchers use qualitative, interpretive research, including methodologies usually associated with other study disciplines, such as grounded theory, this will lead to a broader and more comprehensive understanding of tourism phenomena. Grounded theory is one innovation (since users reinterpret it) and a critical turn from dominant quantifying research methodologies used to understand the human in tourism phenomena. As such, grounded theory is one of a number of means to take up the earlier stated challenge of Jamal and Hollinshead (2001). Grounded theory can offer a new level of understanding to studies of tourists and their interactions within the tourist milieu. Grounded theory can generate explanations of events and relationships reflecting lived experiences of individuals, groups and processes central to the tourist experience. Hutchinson (1988) further sees grounded theory as a form of social criticism, in that it *'does make judgements about identified patterns of social interaction'* (p. 126). As already mentioned, Table 1 demonstrates examples of such usage with particular reference to grounded theory.

Table 12.1: A snapshot of grounded theory usage in tourism and hospitality studies.

Riley (1995)	*Prestige-worthy tourism behaviour* Grounded theory used to study travel prestige since it was an under researched area. Grounded theory generated dimensions of the relationship between the acknowledgers of prestige and prestige receiver(s).
Riley (1996)	*Revealing socially constructed knowledge through quasi-structured interviews and grounded theory analysis* Guidelines are provided for the conduct of engaging in grounded theory, including, for example, grounding the data by member/participant "checking".
Connell and Lowe (1997)	*Generating grounded theory from qualitative data: the application of inductive methods in tourism and hospitality management research* Grounded theory as an approach is detailed and the analytic process is outlined followed by an application of grounded theory in regard to the lived experiences of "brand expansion" in a hospitality setting. Interviews were conducted in two successive field sites — theoretical saturation was achieved in both.
Jennings (1997)	*The travel experience of cruisers* Use of grounded theory from a constructivist perspective generated a "theory" relating to the travel experience of cruisers, that is, long-term ocean cruisers living and sailing aboard their own yachts. These were then counterpointed with special interest tourists, particularly, cultural tourists in regard to their travel experiences. Grounded theory assisted further refinement of the travel experience (Killion, 1992 based on Clawson, 1963).
Jennings (1999)	*Voyages from the centre to the margin: An Ethnography of long-term ocean cruisers* Cruisers, living aboard sailing vessels, constitute a type of long-term independent traveller. Grounded theory, as both methodology and analysis, was used to generate a theory of "empowered connectivity" to explain the process of becoming a cruiser; the lived experiences of cruisers; including staying a cruiser as well as not. Modified versions of Glaser and Strauss (1967); Strauss and Corbin (1990) and Pamphilon (1999) were used.
Goulding (1999)	*Heritage, nostalgia, and the "grey" consumer* Grounded theory as per Glaser and Strauss (1968) was used to understand the leisure activity of visiting heritage sites by visitors. In the process of the research, the experiences of seniors/"grey" visitors were amplified in relation to other visitor categories. Empirical materials included observation, interviews and focus groups.

(Continued)

Table 12.1: (*Continued*)

Goulding (2000)	*The commodification of the past, postmodern pastiche, and the search for authentic experiences at contemporary attractions* Grounded theory was used to gain insight into the nature of authenticity as constructed and interpreted by visitor experiences to contemporary heritage attractions.
Hillman (2001)	*Backpackers travelling in Australia* Grounded theory was used to study the lived experiences of backpackers within Australia. Of particular interest was the notion of authenticity and how backpackers perceive authentic experiences whilst travelling. Participant observation and interviews were sources of empirical materials.
Johns and Gyimothy (2002)	*Mythologies of a theme park: an icon of modern family life* Participants in the study were selected to match the demographics of visitor profiles: nuclear families, single parents, non-family group. The study used both grounded theory and linguistic analysis to understand the experience of visitors to a theme park. Grounded theory (constant comparison) analysis was used to identify visitor perceptions of the theme park. Both analyses provided information for the site to be more appealing to adults, particularly parents as well as for children.
Hobson (2003)	*The case for more exploratory and grounded tourism research* Outlines the background of grounded theory, its modifications and employment and urges tourism researchers to consider this under-utilised research method.
Mehmetoglo and Olsen (2003)	*Talking authenticity: What kind of experiences do solitary travellers[sic] in the Norwegian Lofoten Islands regard as authentic?* Study aims to achieve an emic (insider) perspective of tourists' interpretations of authentic and inauthentic experiences. The use of grounded theory enabled the identification of three depthful insights into authentic experiences based on indepth interviews with solo travellers.
Junek (2004)	*A qualitative inquiry into leisure and travel patterns of international students: Part 1 — Background and methodology* A methodological consideration of the relevance of grounded theory to the study of the lived experiences of leisure and travel patterns of international tourism and hospitality student enrolled in tourism and hospitality programmes. Empirical materials include participant observation, focus groups and in-depth interviews.
Woodside et al. (2004)	*A grounded typology of vacation decision making* The use of grounded theory as a methodology was employed to understand how the planning for a vacation compared with the lived lived experience of the vacation. Empirical materials were generated at the end-point of the vacation experience using extended interviews.

Table 12.1: (*Continued*)

Daengbuppha, Hemmington, and Wilkes (2004)	*Using grounded theory approach: Theoretical and practical issues in modelling heritage visitor experience* Study applies the Strauss–Corbin approach (1990, 1998) to grounded theory with some modification to achieve a grounded theory of the heritage experience.
Jennings (2005c)	*Caught in the irons: One of the lived experiences of long-term ocean cruising women* Study of long-term ocean cruising women (1992–1999) and (2000–2003). Grounded theory as methodology and interpretation tool generated "theory" related to the lived experiences of women who cruise "because of" relationships. There was some complementarity with a Marxist/socialist critique within the theorized lived experiences in addition to recognition of the importance of "affect" in decision-making.
Hardy (2005)	*Using grounded theory to explore stakeholder perceptions of tourism* Due to limited theory in relation to the analysis of stakeholder facilitation of sustainable tourism, grounded theory methodology and analysis was used. The study theorized two particular sets of outcomes. One specific to the study region and the second in relation to the stakeholder facilitation of sustainable tourism.

Grounded Theory: Innovative Methodology or a Critical Turning from Hegemonic Methodological Praxis in Tourism Studies?

Table 12.1 provides a snapshot of the use of grounded theory both as a methodology and a tool for analysis or interpretation within tourism studies. Resonating throughout the examples was the use of grounded theory to (re)construct and (re)interpret experiences at a deeper level than quantification would allow. But why did each of the researchers choose grounded theory for the studies reported in Table 12.1? Answers to this question follow.

Jennings (1997, 1999) proffers that grounded theory enabled greater insight to be ascertained about the lived experiences of people in her particular studies — people engaged in cruising, as a subcultural lifestyle, as well as a form of independent travel. For her, grounded theory also generates holistic theories about such experiences, which, as a methodology and a means to interpret empirical materials, Jennings (2005c) continues to support. To iterate, for her (2005c), grounded theory as a tourism research methodology enables holistic and interdisciplinary ideals to be accommodated in the research process in order to make visible the lived experiences of travellers, in the 2005 case: women. On the other hand, Goulding (1999) indicates the benefits of grounded theory for studying social contexts of micro-environments. Additionally, she emphasizes the benefit of grounded theory for understanding behaviour. A point iterated, previously as well as later, by Goulding (1998, 2000).

As stated, Goulding (2000) specifically recommends grounded theory for studies of behaviour related to understanding the nature of consumers' experiences which are not readily quantifiable. Hillman (2001), like Jennings, sees benefits in grounded theory to represent the experience of backpackers and their experiences from a lived experience perspective.

Extending the notion of lived experiences, Connell and Lowe (1997) purport that grounded theory was able to develop theory related to social processes in action and like others have commented on its relevance for studying behaviour. Johns and Gyimothy (2002) accord with Goulding (1999) regarding the ability of grounded theory to understand behaviour beyond numerical representation. In particular, Johns and Gyimothy (2002) emphasize that grounded theory enables an understanding of 'emotional and experiential content of attraction visits' and complements more 'quantitative, questionnaire-focused approaches . . . about visitors' experiences of theme parks'. A similar perspective regarding the need to understand experiences and concepts based on self reports and reflections of participants is promulgated by Mehmetoglu and Olsen (2003), who noted that grounded theory is important for the exploration and formation of concepts. In Mehmetoglu and Olsen's case, authenticity concepts were determined through discursive practices rather than considered as steady state concepts studied using *a priori* vehicles.

In a wider consideration of tourism research in general, Hobson (2003) argues that there is a need for a refocussing of tourism research from theory testing to theory building and identifies grounded theory as a way forward to redress this. Along a similar vein, Junek (2004) argues that to understand lived experiences requires acknowledgment of social processes in action, which resonates with Mehmetoglu and Olsen and the development of theory from the participants' perspectives rather than via *a priori* theoretical lenses. Woodside et al. (2004), as did Jennings (2005c), comment on the ability of grounded theory to provide holistic understanding. Similarly, as Goulding (1999) indicated, grounded theory achieves an understanding of micro-environments as well as depthful understandings of behaviours, which in Woodside et al.'s study was decision-making.

Furthermore, drawing on Belk, Wallendorf, and Sherry (1989) as well as Geertz (1973) to substantiate the usage of grounded theory, Daengbuppha, Hemmington, and Wilkes (2004) propose that grounded theory enables a more "naturalistic inquiry" in order to achieve a "thick description" of consumer (tourists and visitors) experiences. Finally, with regard to the snapshot of researchers presented in Table 12.1, Hardy (2005), commenting with a similar perspective to Goulding, also indicates that grounded theory, as an inductive process, is germane when there is no previous theory in existence, and laments that grounded theory 'has rarely been used by tourism researchers'.

Grounded Theory: Final Reflections

The chapter will conclude by reflecting on the question: Grounded theory: innovative methodology or a critical turning from hegemonic methodological praxis in tourism studies? The chapter commenced by reframing definitions of grounded theory, this in itself was a (re)interpretation and (re)construction — an innovation and iteration that all meaning is socially situated and constantly negotiated. To that end, grounded theory was redefined as a methodological tradition, a way of thinking about and studying realities; it is a strategy for research and a way of interpreting empirical materials or analysing data (see Strauss & Corbin, 1998; Punch, 1998).

The origins of grounded theory in the 1960s are based in innovation with regard to hegemonic methodology and analytical strategies. Grounded theory was a specific and critical turning from logico–hypothetico approaches in the social sciences to holistic–inductive approaches. The first construction of grounded theory by Glaser and Strauss (1967) has been (re)interpreted and (re)constructed and innovated upon. There is evidence of a critical turning point within the tradition — a divergence from its original intent. Specifically, a divergence which generated two frames for using grounded theory: objectivist and constructivist frames. The paradigmatic roots of the objectivist and constructivist frames were presented to highlight their ontological, epistemological, methodological and axiological perspectives as well as to emphasize the nature and degree of innovation and critical turn undertaken with the innovation of a grounded theory methodology and its associated interpretive and analytic strategies. However, with the passage of time, innovations have been made in each of the objectivist and constructivist frames. Further examples of innovation were provided in Table 12.1.

Penultimately, within a tourism studies context, the history of grounded theory reflects a similar situatedness to "its" experiences in the social sciences. It is and has been positioned as a marginal methodology, connected to a marginalised theoretical paradigm — the interpretive social sciences. The western hegemonic paradigms of positivism and postpositivism prevail. Use of an interpretive social sciences paradigm albeit one that has an established place in other disciplines and fields still represents a critical turning from positivism and postpositivism for the field of tourism studies. Relatedly, this is also the case for grounded theory.

Finally, tourism is a socially constructed and determined phenomena that is constantly being reframed and reinterpreted and reconstructed. It is in a constant state of processing and flux; with continuous meaning making/sense making and reframing within and between a variety of cultural contexts. It is a complex and multiple phenomena; as Jamal and Hollinshead (2001), Jennings (2003, 2005a) and researchers presented in Table 12.1 urge, tourism needs to be considered in a more holistic way rather than in an *a priori*, segmented and controlled manner where elements of social functionality are not considered in their totality. As a consequence, we need new and different ontologies, epistemologies, axiologies, methodologies and methods (Jennings, 2005a). The innovative use of grounded theory informed by the interpretive social sciences paradigm is one way to achieve holistic, depthful, theorizing that accounts for the lived experiences of the people engaged in touristic experiences whatever their stakeholder affiliation as well as to understand the phenomena of tourism in ever changing globalscapes and connectivities.

References

Belk, R., Wallendorf, M., & Sherry, J. (1989). Development recognition of consumption symbolism. *Journal of Consumer Research, 16*(June), 1–37.

Charmaz, K. (1997). Identity dilemmas of chronically ill men. In: A. Strauss, & J. Corbin (Eds), *Grounded theory in practice* (pp. 35–63). Thousand Oaks, CA: Sage.

Charmaz, K. (2000). Grounded theory: Objectivist and constructivist methods. In: N. K. Denzin, & Y. S. Lincoln (Eds), *Handbook of qualitative research* (pp. 509–535). Thousand Oaks, CA: Sage.

Charmaz, K. (2003a). Grounded theory: Objectivist and constructivist methods. In: N. K. Denzin, & Y. S. Lincoln (Eds), *Strategies of qualitative inquiry* (pp. 249–291). Thousand Oaks, CA: Sage.

Charmaz, K. (2003b). Qualitative interviewing and grounded theory analysis. In: J. A. Holstein, & J. F. Gubrium (Eds), *Inside interviewing: New lenses, new concerns* (pp. 311–330). Thousand Oaks, CA: Sage.

Clawson, M. (1963). *Land and water for recreation: Opportunities, problems and policies*. Chicago, IL: Rand McNally.

Cohen, E. (1988). Traditions in the qualitative sociology of tourism. *Annals of Tourism Research, 15,* 29–46.

Comte, A. (2000). *The positive philosophy of Auguste Comte* (Vol. 1). [Translated by H. Martineau. Kitchener: Batoche books] [Available at: http://www.ecn.bris.ac.uk/het/comte/philos1.pdf].

Connell, J., & Lowe, A. (1997). Generating grounded theory from qualitative data: The application of inductive methods in tourism and hospitality management research. *Progress in Tourism and Hospitality Research, 3*(2), 165–173.

Daengbuppha, J., Hemmington, N., & Wilkes, K. (2004). Using grounded theory approach: Theoretical and practical issues in modelling heritage visitor experience. In: K. A. Smith, & C. Schott (Eds), *Proceedings of the New Zealand Tourism and Hospitality Research Conference 2004,* 8–10 December. Wellington (pp. 64–78).

Dann, G. M. S. (2005). The theoretical state of the art in the sociology and anthropology of tourism. *Tourism Analysis, 10,* 3–15.

Dey, I. (2004). Grounded theory. In: C. Seale, G. Gobo, J. F. Gubrium, & D. Silverman (Eds), *Qualitative research practice* (pp. 80–93). London: Sage.

Ford, J. (1975). *Paradigms and fairy tales: An introduction to the science of meanings* (Vol. 1). London: Routledge and Kegan Paul.

Geertz, C. (1973). The interpretation of cultures. In: *Deep play: Notes on the Balinese cockfight* (pp. 412–453). New York: Basic Books.

Glaser, B. G. (1978). *Theoretical sensitivity: Advances in the methodology of grounded theory*. Mill Valley, CA: Sociology Press.

Glaser, B. G. (1992). *Basics of grounded theory analysis*. Mill Valley, CA: Sociology Press.

Glaser, B. G. (1998). *Doing grounded theory: Issues and discussions*. Mill Valley, CA: Sociology Press.

Glaser, B. G., & Strauss, A. L. (1967). *The discovery of grounded theory strategies for qualitative research*. New York: Aldine Publishing Company.

Goulding, C. (1998). Grounded theory: The missing methodology on the interpretivist agenda. *Qualitative Marketing Research: An International Journal, 1*(1), 50–57.

Goulding, C. (1999). Heritage, nostalgia and the "grey?" consumer. *Journal of Marketing Practice: Applied Marketing Science, 5*(6–8), 177–199.

Goulding, C. (2000). The commodification of the past, postmodern pastiche, and the search for authentic experiences at contemporary heritage attraction. *European Journal of Marketing, 34*(7), 835–853.

Guba, E. C. (1990). The alternative paradigm dialog. In: E. C. Guba (Ed.), *The paradigm dialog* (pp. 17–27). Newbury Park, CA: Sage.

Guba, E. G., & Lincoln, Y. S. (1994). Competing paradigms in qualitative research. In: N. K. Denzin, & Y. S. E. Lincoln (Eds), *Handbook of qualitative research* (pp. 105–117). Thousand Oaks, CA: Sage.

Hall, C. M. (2004). Reflexivity and tourism research: Situating myself and/with others. In: J. Phillimore, & L. Goodson (Eds), *Qualitative research in tourism: Ontologies, epistemologies and methodologies* (pp. 137–155). London: Routledge.

Harding, S. (1991). *Whose science? Whose knowledge?* Milton Keyes: Open University Press.

Hardy, A. (2005). Using grounded theory to explore stakeholder perceptions of tourism. *Journal of Tourism and Cultural Change*, *3*(2), 108–133.

Hillman, W. (2001). *Searching for authenticity and experience: Backpackers travelling in Australia.* TASA Conference, University of Sydney.

Hobson, J. S. P. (2003). The case for more exploratory and grounded tourism research, Martin Oppermann Memorial Lecture 2001. *Pacific Tourism Review*, *6*(2), 73–81.

Hollinshead, K. (1996). The tourism researcher as bricoleur: The new wealth and diversity in qualitative inquiry. *Tourism Analysis*, *1*, 67–74.

Hutchinson, S. A. (1988). Education and grounded theory. In: R. Sherman, & R. B. Webb (Eds), *Qualitative research in education: Focus and methods* (pp. 123–140). New York: The Falmer Press.

Jamal, T., & Hollinshead, K. (2001). Tourism and the forbidden zone: The underserved power of qualitative inquiry. *Tourism Management*, *22*(February): [Online] Retrieved from http://www.sciencedirect.com.library (pp. 1–33), 20/04/05.

Jennings, G. R. (1997). The travel experience of cruisers. In: M. Oppermann (Ed.), *Pacific Rim 2000: Issues, interrelations, inhibitors* (pp. 94–105). London: CAB International.

Jennings, G. R. (1999). *Voyages from the centre to the margins: An ethnography of long term ocean cruisers.* Unpublished PhD thesis. Murdoch University, Murdoch, Australia.

Jennings, G. R. (2001). *Tourism research*. Brisbane: Wiley.

Jennings, G. R. (2003). Tourism research: Theoretical paradigms and accountability. *Targeted research: The gateway to accountability*: TTRA 34th Annual Conference Proceedings [CD Rom], June 15–18, St. Louis, MO, USA.

Jennings, G. R. (2005a). Advances in tourism research: Theoretical paradigms and accountability. *Theoretical advances in tourism economics*. Portugal: Evora. March 15–19, 2005.

Jennings, G. R. (2005b). Business research, theoretical paradigms that inform. *Encyclopedia of Social Measurement* (pp. 211–217). [Online] Retrieved from http:// www.sciencedirect.com.library (pp. 211–217), 29/04/05. San Diego, CA: Academic Press.

Jennings, G. R. (2005c). Caught in the irons: One of the lived experiences of cruising women. *Tourism Research International*, *9*(2), 177–193.

Jennings, G. R. (2005d). Interviewing — A focus on qualitative techniques. In: B. W. Ritchie, P. Burns, & C. Palmer (Eds), *Tourism research methods: Integrating theory and practice* (pp. 99–117). London: CAB International Tourism/Leisure Series.

Johns, N., & Gyimothy, S. (2002). Mythologies of a theme park: An icon of family life. *Journal of Vacation Marketing*, *8*(4), 320–331.

Jorgensen, D. (1989). Participant observation, a methodology for a human studies. In: *Applied Social Research Methods Series 15*. Newbury Park, CA: Sage.

Junek, O. (2004). A qualitative inquiry into leisure and travel patterns of international students: Part 1 — background and methodology. *The 2nd Asia-Pacific CHRIE (APacCHRIE) Conference & the 6th Biennial Conference on Tourism in Asia, 2004*, Conference Proceedings. May 27–29, Phuket, Thailand.

Killion, K. L. (1992). *Understanding tourism, study guide*. Rockhampton: Central Queensland University.

Lincoln, Y. S., & Guba, E. G. (1985). *Naturalistic inquiry*. Newbury Park, CA: Sage.

Lincoln, Y. S., & Guba, E. G. (2000). Paradigmatic controversies, contradictions, and emerging confluences. In: N. K. Denzin, & Y. S. Lincoln (Eds), *Handbook of qualitative research* (2nd ed., pp. 163–188). Thousand Oaks, CA: Sage.

Macbeth, J. (1985). *Ocean cruising, a study of affirmative deviance*. Unpublished PhD thesis, Murdoch University, Murdoch, Australia.

Mehmetoglu, M., & Olsen, K. (2003). Talking authenticity: What kind of experiences do solitary travelers in the Norwegian Lofoten Islands regard as authenticity? *Tourism, Culture and Communication*, *4*(3), 137–152.

Metcalf, W. (1986). *Dropping out and staying in: Recruitment, socialisation and commitment engendered in contemporary alternative lifestyles*. Unpublished doctoral thesis, Griffith University.

Pamphilon, B. (1999). The zoom model: A dynamic framework for the analysis of life histories. *Qualitative Inquiry*, *5*(3, special edition), 393–410.

Phillimore, J., & Goodson, L. (2004). Progress in qualitative research in tourism: Epistemology, ontology and methodology. In: J. Phillimore, & L. Goodson (Eds), *Qualitative research in tourism: Ontologies, epistemologies and methodologies* (pp. 3–29). London: Routledge.

Punch, K. (1998). *Introduction to social research — Quantitative and qualitative approaches*. London: Sage.

Riley, R. W. (1995). Prestige-worthy behaviour. *Annals of tourism research*, *22*(3), 630–649.

Riley, R. W. (1996). Revealing socially constructed knowledge through quasi structured interviews and grounded theory analysis. *Journal of Travel and Tourism Marketing*, *15*(2), 21–40.

Riley, R. W., & Love, L. L. (2000). The state of qualitative tourism research. *Annals of Tourism Research*, *27*(1), 164–187.

Rynehart, R. L. (2004). *Foruming: A theory of influencing organisational change*. Unpublished PhD. Central Queensland University, Rockhampton, Australia.

Schatzman, L., & Strauss, A. L. (1973). *Field research*. Englewood Cliffs, NJ: Prentice-Hall.

Scheurich, J. J. (1997). *Research methods in the postmodern*. London: The Falmer Press.

Schwandt, T. A. (1994). Constructivist, interpretivist approaches to human inquiry. In: N. K. Denzin, & Y. S. Lincoln (Eds), *Handbook of qualitative research* (pp. 118–137). Thousand Oaks, CA: Sage.

Schwandt, T. A. (2000). Three epistemological stances for qualitative inquiry: Interpretivism, hermeneutics, and social constructionism. In: N. K. Denzin, & Y. S. Lincoln (Eds), *Handbook of qualitative research* (2nd ed., pp. 189–213). Thousand Oaks, CA: Sage.

Strauss, A. L. (1987). *Qualitative analysis for social scientist*. Cambridge: Cambridge University Press.

Strauss, A. L., & Corbin, J. (1990). *Basics of qualitative research grounded theory procedures and techniques*. Newbury Park, CA: Sage.

Strauss, A. L., & Corbin, J. (1994). Grounded theory methodology: An overview. In: N. K. Denzin, & Y. S. Lincoln (Eds), *Handbook of qualitative research* (pp. 273–285). Thousand Oaks, CA: Sage.

Strauss, A., & Corbin, J. (1998). *Basics of qualitative research techniques and procedures for developing grounded theory*. Thousand Oaks, CA: Sage.

Tribe, J. (2004). Knowing about tourism: Epistemological issues. In: J. Phillimore, & L. Goodson (Eds), *Qualitative research in tourism: Ontologies, epistemologies and methodologies* (pp. 46–62). London: Routledge.

Walle, A. H. (1997). Quantitative versus qualitative tourism research. *Annals of Tourism*, *24*(3), 524–536.

Woodside, A., MacDonald, R., & Burford, M. (2004). Grounded theory of leisure travel. *Journal of Travel and Tourism Marketing*, *17*(1), 7–40.

Chapter 13

Immersing in Ontology and the Research Process: Constructivism the Foundation for Exploring the (In)Credible OBE?

Tomas Pernecky

When I contemplated how to begin this chapter on innovative research methodologies: an obligation imperative to new tourism research, I tried not to restrict myself unnecessarily, for limitation is not what this book sets out to achieve. On the contrary, pioneering research methodologies and innovative methods are most needed. However, this task may not be as easy as it appears, for academia can be a very critical field: new approaches can sometimes be received rather callously. For me, the innovative research methodologies of the future represent exciting, ground-breaking, fun and jubilant actions that liberate both the researcher and the researched — moving away from rigidity and impersonal processes. After all, imparting knowledge is a profound task and in the spirit of the *critical turn* let me start with a rather unusual prelude.

One evening I was reading a book by Barbara Marciniak (2004) who has been "channelling" Pleiadians: a collective of multidimensional spirit beings from the Pleiades star system. While reading, I encountered a definition of reality that I thought would suit this paper magnificently, for ontology is the main theme of this chapter. Yet this definition was provided by extraterrestrial beings called Pleiadians and I was writing an academic paper. Surely, it would be outrageous to include a piece of writing of such nature! consequently, whether one believes in extraterrestrials or not, it is for its context and exceptionality that this definition deserves to be included. The reality in our world defined by the Pleiadians goes as follows:

> Your greater world reality is founded upon a series of mass agreements, and
> your personal life is an intimate journey of self-discovery within this massive
> framework of reality, where you live out your chosen beliefs. How you grasp
> and interpret the vast array of sensations and stimuli within this multilayered

environment determines the degree of self-realization you develop. (Marciniak, 2004, p. 17)

How often do we reflect on where our reality begins and where it ends? Who defines it? Why we perceive the surroundings, situations and all the things in our lives the way we do? We define our reality on a daily basis by *choosing to believe* other people, someone's research or the news, and like a child is shaped by being told the meaning of things, we continue to select and accept certain beliefs about the surrounding world to shape our own personal reality. In hermeneutic phenomenology, Heidegger (1962) calls this *pre-understanding*, meaning that an interpretation can never be a presuppositionless apprehending of something presented to us. The question of reality is inherent as well as exciting when it comes to one's paradigm with regard to research. Therefore the importance of paradigms, ontology, epistemology and methodology in tourism studies will be explored in the pages to follow.

To follow this foreword on reality, this chapter will next define and clarify the core components of any research; the paradigms, ontology, epistemology and methods. The endeavour of this chapter is largely theoretical: demonstrating that a constructivist paradigm enables one to delve into areas of research and realities without too many methodological and academic pitfalls. It is thematically divided into two parts; the first comprises an overview and theoretical discussion of research process immersing the constructivist paradigm. The second part subsequently illustrates the primary by discussing a study on Out-of-Body travel/experience (OBE). With reference to my PhD project, these issues will be elaborated upon in the context of the specific subject of Out-of-Body travel, breaking the traditional notion of travel but also contributing to the particular branch of spirituality-related tourism: so called "New Age tourism" (Attix, 2002; Pernecky & Johnston, 2006; Sutton & House, 2003). New Age itself is a phenomenon that challenges the positivist discourse on ontological grounds: generally when it comes to the issues of spirituality, connecting with the "self" and the belief that "man is bigger than nature". As such it symbolizes a new stance on our existence as well as changing people's perceptions on reality (Pernecky, 2006).

POEM and the Research Process

Similar to a narrative poem, research also involves a series of chronologically related events that all contribute to a whole. Paradigms, Ontology, Epistemology and Methodology (POEM) are essential components of any research process and can be compared to the many elements such as diction, rhythm, line structure or imagery to make a poem work. And as the sound of a poem can be musical so can research be harmonious. These things determine the nature of our poems, for they can have a positivist, post-positivist or constructivist character seeking to answer different questions and satisfy different audiences.

Paradigms

According to Guba and Lincoln (2004) the paradigms that are currently competing or have recently competed to be accepted as paradigms in terms of guiding theory (qualitative enquiry especially) are: positivism, post-positivism, critical theory and constructivism. In their view paradigms are basic belief systems which cannot be proven or unproved and are representing the most fundamental positions we are willing to take (Guba & Lincoln, 1989). The most recent definition of a paradigm goes as follows:

> Paradigm is a set of beliefs (or metaphysics) that deals with ultimates or first principles. It represents a worldview that defines, for its holder, the nature of the world, the individual's place in it, and the range of possible relationships to that world and its parts, as, for example, cosmologies and theologies do. (Guba & Lincoln, 2004, p. 21)

Furthermore, they argue that these beliefs must be accepted on faith, for it is impossible to ascertain their ultimate truthfulness. Also a distinction exists between paradigms that define for inquirers what it is they are about, and what falls within, and what falls outside the limits of legitimate inquiry, which are so called *inquiry paradigms* (Guba & Lincoln, 2004, p. 21).

The question of one's paradigm is crucial when it comes to construction of realities as they can be appropriately judged only by criteria appropriate to the paradigm which the constructor follows and which he/she uses as a foundation of his research (Guba & Lincoln, 1989, p. 143). Therefore what paradigm we as researchers associate ourselves with is essential, for it restrains our ontological, epistemological and methodological approach to research (Guba & Lincoln, 2004). For example, assuming ontologically that there is one "reality" to be explained, restricts how we epistemologically and methodologically approach a research. It is unlikely that "reality" would be explained by choosing a non-representative sample of six people, with whom the researcher had engaged in an in-depth interview and constructed individual reconstructions, rather than providing a representative sample and generalized data.

Discussion of any paradigm involves three *major forci* (Guba & Lincoln, 2004) that need to be addressed when it comes to research. These are the questions of one's ontology, epistemology and methodology which determine the nature of one's approach to research. Increasingly, we can see scholars (mostly constructivist–interpretivist) grounding their studies in, and acknowledging the importance of, ontology, epistemology and methodology. The reason being 'we can no longer simply discuss *knowledge* but must instead discuss knowledge within the context of a particular paradigm' (Crandall, 1990, p. 221).

In other words, academics who come from different paradigms (such as positivism and constructivism) can hardly agree on issues such as those concerning "reality" as their view on that "reality" varies greatly. As a result of that, these scholars indict one another of providing "quasi statistics" or presenting research outputs on population samples of non-representative nature. Many such discussions among academics are rooted in the misunderstanding of various paradigms and at times the cause is a lack of knowledge and understanding the meaning of this terminology. Therefore the engagement in discussing one's POEM (paradigms, ontology, epistemology and methodology) is inherent when delving into realities.

Ontology

Ontology is a branch of philosophy (metaphysics) concerned with issues of existence or being (Guba & Lincoln, 1989) representing one's set of ideas or a framework of research (Denzin & Lincoln, 2003). Ontology as well as epistemology are the most essential concepts in the philosophy of science (Blaikie, 1993). The ontological question goes as follows: *What is the form and nature of reality and, therefore what is there that can be known about it?* (Guba & Lincoln, 2004, p. 21). For instance assuming there is a "real" world shapes what can be known about it; how things "really" are, or "really" work. Therefore ontological questions only relate to matters of "real" existence and "real" action. Other questions such as those concerning moral significance don't fall within the realm of legitimate scientific inquiry.

Epistemology

The epistemological question: *What is the nature of the relationship between the knower or would-be knower and what can be known?* is partially answered in how we respond to the ontological question, as not just *any* relationship can now be suggested (Guba & Lincoln, 2004, p. 21). Epistemology has seen its most fruitful phase within the last 25 years and according to Pritchard (2004), epistemology is currently enjoying a renaissance. He suggests that this renewal in epistemological theorising is thriving due to productions of new theories (such as contextualist theories), but more importantly by application of the latest novel proposals to other areas of philosophy (i.e., the relationship between content externalism and self-knowledge). The epistemological question: W*hat counts as knowledge?* should be particularly addressed by practicing researchers as they have more than anyone else to say about this issue (Smith, 1983).

Methodology

The answer to the methodological question: *How can the inquirer (would-be knower) go about finding out whatever he or she believes can be known?* is constrained by the answers given to the two previous questions (epistemology and ontology) as not just *any* methodology is suitable (Guba & Lincoln, 2004, p. 22). For instance, possible confounding factors can be mandated whether using quantitative or qualitative methods, by an "objective" inquirer who works from the ontological position of exploring the "real" reality. However it would be mistaken to diminish methodology to methods only. There is confusion over misinterpreting methodology with methods among academics. The concepts of *methodology* and *methods* are often used interchangeably and one is employed when the other is more appropriate (Blaikie, 1993). The way one "approaches" research corresponds to one's methodology, not a method. It is important to stress that by *methods* of research we mean techniques or procedures that enable us to gather and analyse data. *Methodology*, in contrast, represents the approach to how research should proceed:

> It includes discussions of how theories are generated and tested — what kind of logic is used, what criteria they have to satisfy, what theories look

like and how particular theoretical perspectives can be related to particular research problems. (Blaikie, 1993, p. 7)

Comparing Constructivism vs. Positivism

In retrospect, the history of scientific knowledge, the different methods of enquiry, as well as the perceptions of what counts as legitimate research have evolved. For the past several hundred years the conventional paradigm, also known as the positivist or scientific paradigm, has prevailed (Guba & Lincoln, 1989). The faith of scientists in the substantiality of matter and consequently the "real", has been shaken as:

> each time that science has been able to increase the power of its microscope, metaphorically speaking, that substantial reality becomes more and more insubstantial. (Guba & Lincoln, 1989, p. 91)

Today, research in tourism is slowly reaching a "mature" stage where different approaches to academic enquiry can be accepted, respected and understood. It is the beginning of a "qualitative makeover" in tourism studies which has inspired many scholars and recently been labelled as a *critical turn* (Ateljevic, Harris, Willson, & Collins, 2005) or a shift in thought, providing space for interpretative and critical modes of tourism inquiry. Correspondingly, this chapter follows Lincoln and Guba's (2003, p. 284) call for the creation of new texts that break boundaries:

> Texts . . . "that move from the centre to the margins to comment upon and decentre the centre; that forgo closed, bounded worlds for those more open-ended and less conveniently encompassed; that transgress the boundaries of conventional social science; and that seek to create a social science about human life rather than on subjects".

However, to create innovative text, innovative approaches too must be applied. In recent years, the voice of interpretive scholars has become stronger and clearer; calling for novel methodologies in contrast to the dominant positivist way of conducting research in an attempt to verify and generalize. The importance of establishing one's position by addressing the questions of ontology, epistemology and methodology has become an issue of great importance (Goodson & Phillimore, 2004; Hollinshead, 2004; Jamal & Everett, 2004). With the focus on the constructivist paradigm, researchers are now able not only to utilize new approaches in tourism studies but also to explore research topics that could not have been studied in the past for reasons such as scientific significance or validity. Constructivism therefore provides scholars with theoretical grounds and methodological foundations that grant researchers lost legitimacy.

Constructivism plays a vital role in academic inquiry, for it provides researchers not only with a variety of qualitative methods but more importantly a paradigm that enables one to situate one's research in the firm constructivist grounds of ontology, epistemology and methodology. The aim of constructivist enquiry is:

> understanding and reconstruction of the constructions that people (including the inquirer) hold, aiming toward consensus but still open to new interpretations as information and sophistication improve. (Guba & Lincoln, 2004, p. 30)

The constructivist paradigm, also known as the naturalistic, hermeneutic or interpretive paradigm has as well as positivism been in existence for several hundred years but not as widely accepted, especially in English-speaking countries (Guba & Lincoln, 1989). It was founded within the intellectual traditions of hermeneutics (generally translated as *to interpret*) and phenomenology (Blaikie, 1993). In contrast to positivism, the naturalistic or interpretive perspective assumes that 'knowledge is the outcome or consequence of human activity, rather than an entity that is out there to be discovered' (Kraus & Allen, 1996, p. 22).

Compared to positivism and largely used quantitative methods, constructivism is frequently associated with the use of qualitative methods. The constructivist ontology will be discussed in detail in the second part of this chapter.

When it comes to positivism — the fading ruler of paradigms, the core lies in a *realist* ontology: a belief that there exists a reality "out there" driven by multiple natural laws and mechanisms (Guba, 1990, p. 19). Researchers and scientists who adopt this approach aim to discover the "true" nature of reality and its principle (how it works). Within the positivistic approach to research, all phenomena happen as a result of certain laws which adhere to certain assumptions such as the *nature of reality*. Kraus and Allen (1996) define the assumption of the *nature of reality* that the world is real, and supernatural aspects such as metaphysics or magic cannot be accepted as reason for events or conditions. They suggest that the scientific method is a three-step process that uses both induction and deduction, with the end process of verification usually to test hypotheses. Also Guba and Lincoln (2004) look at conventional science as an effort to verify (positivism) or falsify (post-positivism) *a priori* hypotheses which are typically stated as mathematical propositions, or intentions that translate into mathematical formulas expressing functional relationships.

Lately, positivism has been re-invented and evolved into something called *post-positivism*. According to Guba (1990, p. 20) *post-positivism* can be best characterised as a "modified version" of positivism. Post-positivists still believe there is one reality to be explained but differ from positivists in their belief that the ultimate truth may never be uncovered. In terms of objectivity, post-positivists admit that it cannot be achieved in any absolute sense but reasonably closely by striving to be as neutral as possible and by relying on crucial tradition by subjecting inquiries to judgements of peers such as editors and referees of journals. In terms of methodology, post-positivists often employ the use of qualitative methods and research triangulation.

New Age Tourism

New Age tourism and New Age itself in particular, has transformed over the years and is still in a process of change. According to Sutcliffe (2003) the New Age between 1930 and

1960 was radically different from what it became in the 1970s and is different again in terms of what it represents today. Conceivably, that is the reason why academics find it hard to fix the boundaries of this phenomenon:

> business actors are always pushing them forward, refashioning the *lingua franca* to create new products, giving it a new spin, so that it cannot settle down into an orthodox doctrine encoded in a fixed canon. (Redden, 2005, p. 241)

As a result, more and more New Age products, services and places are being consumed, giving subsistence to the New Age tourism phenomenon. On a philosophical note, it is important to point out that New Age in the 21st century (of which New Age tourism is part of) also represents a shift in the mind of the world. The renewed interest in spirituality and related practices, the abundance of literature on spiritual awakening and enlightenment and the presence of psychic mediums on television channels are all signs of a change in people's realities — realities that allow the existence of the spiritual world to make an impact on their lives.

The study of Out-of-Body travel is underpinned by New Age tourism which corresponds to the experiences of travellers who hold a belief in the spiritual world and who visit places of spiritual importance (such as sacred and power places in Sedona or Glastonbury). A quantitative study of New Age tourists has shown that this segment can also be divided according to different levels of specialization: with regard to their experience, levels of investment and the centrality of New Age to their lifestyle (Pernecky & Johnston, 2006). According to Pernecky (2006) New Age travel is an interesting and sometimes life changing phenomenon. People travel to various sites to channel, dowse, meditate, or tune into different life energies. These are important experiences and an integral part of their lives, for New Age travellers feel the need to be connected to these energies and to the land — having a sense of communicating with a higher source.

New Age is a term that is perhaps best understood as an adjective describing New Age aspects in contemporary spirituality (Ezzy, 2003). There is a level of ideological commonality in New Age such as collective transformation and holistic conceptions of nature and the cosmos (Hess, 1993). Nevertheless, it is the personal belief of these travellers that is the key to New Age tourism:

> Being a part of the universal energy and believing that they are communicating with a universal source or exploring the biggest scheme of things is what makes their experience what it is. (Pernecky, 2006, p. 141)

Therefore what might seem to an "ordinary" tourist an ordinary rock, to a New Age traveller it represents an energy that calls for being felt by hugging and rubbing resulting in a life-time experience.

In this context, Out-of-Body travel represents one of the many aspects of this multifarious phenomenon. New Age in the present day perhaps corresponds to a paradigm that arose as a reflection of political, social and economic discourses: attending to a plethora of issues such as money, power, sexuality, nature, religion and so forth. It reflects on the post-modern way of being spiritual without necessarily belonging to only one religion and worshiping only one god. New Agers themselves believe they are in a union with the cosmic forces and many consider themselves to be gods. After all, they are "co-creating with the universe" (Pernecky, 2006). New Age and Out-of-Body travel challenge the positivist/post-positivist belief in one "real" reality: for it is a phenomenon of extraordinary nature and impossible to accept, yet to understand, whilst operating within a dualist/objectivist epistemology.

From Theory to Practice; Studying the In(Credible)

The choice of the word "in(credible)" was a purposeful attempt to show the difference between studying Out-of-Body experiences (a) under a positivist paradigm and perhaps questioning whether such study is *credible*, or (b) under a constructivist paradigm and being able to perceive such topics as perhaps *incredible*. With reference to my PhD project, it is demonstrated here that constructivism allows researchers to delve into realities that could have not been accessed in the past. Researching Out-of-Body travel (in the context of tourism and travel) is a task contributing to the particular branch of spirituality related tourism — New Age tourism, breaking the traditional notion of travel. Hence it can be considered as a unique enquiry in tourism studies: for the possibility to travel wherever one wants to and without having to move one's body is exhilarating. The Out-of-Body experience has been defined by scholars as the feeling of literally being outside the physical body (Palmer & Vassar, 1974; Podoll & Robinson, 1999) and according to Tart (1967), usually contains a combination of elements such as floating, seeing one's physical body from the outside, possessing a non-physical body as well as being absolutely convinced that the experience was not a dream.

However, studying such phenomenon can also raise many eyebrows, for it is poles apart from studying so-called legitimate tourism topics such as sustainability. Out-of-Body experiences are frequently considered as supernatural or relating to metaphysics and thus rejected by the positivist/post-positivist paradigm: for those who espouse positivism value the scientific method and empiricism. On the other hand, the foundations of a constructivist paradigm enable researchers to explore and understand many possible realities — individual reconstructions shared by participants. Therefore embracing different paradigms can result in Out-of-Body experiences being researched from a medical perspective and perhaps be regarded as a condition that requires appropriate treatment. A variety of methods can thus be utilized and consequently a number of different conclusions drawn. For instance adhering to realist ontology and rejecting the notion of metaphysics can lead to explaining the cause of Out-of-Body experiences as hallucinations.

Going Out of Body

Out-of-Body experiences are not an utterly novel phenomenon. According to Haddow (1991), Egyptians regarded man as composed of various bodies; there was "ka" the energy–body or double, directly associated with the "khat", which was the physical body.

A similar concept is held by Tibetan Buddhists; they call the astral body the "Bardo Body" which also "ensembles the second-body of the OBE and has the ability to go through matter, as a proficient Yogi is believed to be able to do in the human world" (80). Today, research estimations of OBE experiences vary from 10% of the general population (Meyerson & Gelkopf, 2004) up to 50% in special groups such as in marijuana users (Blackmore, 1991). What exactly does an Out-of-Body experience mean? The following definition provides a clear description:

> An Out-of-Body experience (OBE) may be defined as the experience in which a person seems to be awake and to see his body and the world from a location outside the physical body. (Blanke, Landis, Spinelli, & Seeck, 2004, p. 243)

OBEs provide participants with a unique feeling of separation from his/her body accompanied by sensations of floating (Meyerson & Gelkopf, 2004). According to Alvarado (2001), one of the main features of the OBE is that perceptions are organized in accordance with the idea that the person is at a distance from the body. Apart from seeing one's body and the world from a location outside the physical body (Blanke et al., 2004; Palmer & Vassar, 1974; Tart, 1967), one's awareness or the sense of self is as if separated from the physical body (Alvarado, 2001; Palmer & Vassar, 1974; Podoll & Robinson, 1999; Twemlow, Gabbard, & Jones, 1982). Once separated from one's body, OBErs commonly experience the scene as looking from ceiling heights, in particular, from corner ceiling positions (Greene, 1999) or seeing one's self from the outside (Ehrenwald, 1974). This experience can further involve a variety of phenomena such as being connected to the physical body by a cord, seeing apparitions, and having extrasensory experiences (Twemlow et al., 1982). Some OBErs claim to be able to move material objects during their experiences and various happenings were reported, such as clocks stopping inexplicably, glass unexpectedly shattering, knocking on bedroom walls etc. (Greene, 1999). Osis (1979) states that some participants report the ability to see around corners, 360-degree vision, fusion between object and OBEers, or having auras around them.

When it comes to academia, Out-of-Body experiences are rather an enigma and one has to go broader and across different disciplines to seek knowledge. The scholastic literature on OBE phenomenon has predominantly had a character of a positivist doctrine; mainly published in areas of psychical research, parapsychology, psychology, religion, and health related publications such as *Journal of Nervous and Mental Disease, Brain or Cephalalgia*. It has drawn scholars mainly from disciplines universally known as *hard science*. It has been studied in relation to symptoms of migraine (Podoll & Robinson, 1999; Wilkinson, 1999), neurology and autoscopy (Blanke et al., 2004), electric stimulation of the brain (Blanke, 2002; Frazier, 2003; Tong, 2003), as a possible seizure symptom (Brandt, Brechtelsbauer, Bien, & Reiners, 2005), aspects of body image (Murray & Fox, 2005), hypnotic states (Irwin, 1989; Meyerson & Gelkopf, 2004), physics and the Hyperspace theory (Greene, 1999, 2003). There was no literature found on OBE in tourism studies, although it seems more than appropriate to engage in understanding this phenomenon from a travel perspective. If people can leave their bodies and travel to different places what are the implications in terms of ontology of travel?

Ontology of OBE Phenomenon

When it comes to ascertaining one's epistemological and ontological position, it can be said that ontology has supremacy over epistemology. According to Guba and Lincoln (1989, p. 87), how the epistemological questions are dealt with:

> depend, in the first instance, on how the ontological question has already been 'answered' and 'taking either a *realist* or a *relativist* posture with respect to ontology places constraints on the ways in which the epistemo-logical question can be answered'.

This study is based on relativist ontology. Relativist ontology claims that there are multiple, socially constructed realities which are ungoverned by natural or causal laws and *truth* is classified as:

> the best informed (amount and quality of information) and most sophisticated (power with which the information is understood and used) construction on which there is consensus (although there may be several constructions extant that simultaneously meet that criterion). (Guba & Lincoln, 1989, p. 84)

It is individual people who try to explain their experiences with and in nature. With regard to this study, participants are being allowed by the researcher to have their Out-of-Body experiences and their view of reality was the core of the research. It is an approach opposite to the belief that there exists a single reality independent of any observer's interest, known as *realist ontology* with the aim of discovering nature as it "really is" (Guba & Lincoln, 1989). From my point of view, only in this way it can be found what really lies beyond these experiences without hypothesising.

Epistemology of OBE Phenomenon

The epistemological position on the subject of seeking knowledge and the relationship between the knower and the known is based on the constructivist philosophy. The adherents of the constructivist paradigm answer the epistemological question by asserting that separating the inquirer from the inquired-into is impossible (Guba & Lincoln, 1989). It is the interaction that creates the data emerging from the inquiry and thus, the constructivist perspective, in effect, eliminates the ontology–epistemology distinction. The epistemological approach of this study thus follows the ontological *relativist* belief that there are many realities to be explored based on individual experiences. The exciting new potential of being able to engage in a scientific investigation by employing an alternative (interpretive) paradigm — rather than following the path of overemphasising on quantitative research — has been the main driving force for this decision.

Methodology of OBE Phenomenon

When it comes to constructivist enquiry, constructivist methodology is inclined to be qualitative rather than quantitative. Although not exclusively it involves hermeneutic and dialectic methods and focuses on the social processes of construction, reconstruction as well as elaboration (Lincoln, 1990). Despite the fact that constructivism is sometimes said to originate as a contradiction to positivism, Guba and Lincoln (1989, p. 173) argue that the methodology of constructivism is more than just a response to positivism as it represents a strong position generated from its own assumptions — a "proactive posture".

According to Guba (1990, p. 27) the aim of constructivism is not to predict, control or transform the "real" world but to reconstruct the world at the only point at which it exists — "in the mind of constructors". He looks at the problem of "reality" within constructivism as existing only in the context of a mental framework (construct) for thinking about it: only possible to "see" by employing a theory (whether implicit or explicit). Therefore epistemologically speaking, if realities exist in only people's minds, then they can be accessed only by subjective interaction. Methodologically, constructivism involves a process of identifying the variety of constructions and bringing them into consensus as much as possible. This process includes *hermeneutics* and *dialectics*: in other words portraying individual constructions as accurately as possible and comparing/contrasting these individual constructions to come to terms with them.

Methodology, being closely interconnected with ontology and epistemology also includes methods, which are the appropriate tools for collecting and analyzing data. Any attempt to separate these labels is set to fail as one cannot exist without the other. Denzin and Lincoln (2003, p. 18) offer a comprehensive view on the activities defining the research process:

> the researcher approaches the world with a set of ideas, a framework (theory, ontology) that specifies a set of questions (epistemology) that he or she then examines in specific ways (methodology, analysis). That is, the researcher collects empirical materials bearing on the question and then analyzes and writes about them.

The methodology of this study was not only weighted by ontology, epistemology and methodology/methods but rather involved them too, for ontology and epistemology play an essential part in forming one's methodology. Engaging in research is an evolving course of action that includes constant interaction among all processes involved. Figure 13.1, following, describes the understanding of methodological process as applied in this study. It is shown that one's methodology or a 'composite research strategy' is not a simple process but rather a matter of reflecting and coming to understanding the research on all levels. This way it leads to a full understanding of one's position in terms of paradigms, ontology, epistemology and the choice of methods; sometimes resulting in fine-tuning and adjusting one's previous assumptions. For instance, while writing my Masters thesis, I was convinced I was operating within the constructivist paradigm, but it wasn't until I had to face my beliefs with regard to the methods I employed. I did not "get" that using a quantitative method was all right but generalizing and hypothesizing was not. It took a while to comprehend fully the difference between presenting the findings as given facts based on statistics or presenting it as the data of individuals who shared some similarities but could never have had the same experiences. Immersing in methodology was not a process of following three or four simple steps. On the contrary, it was a very confusing and frustrating time that in

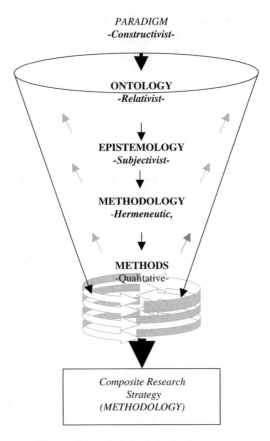

Figure 13.1: Methodological process.

later days resulted in rewarding feelings of self-achievement that my views and beliefs had become clear to me. I started to understand that:

> The major task of the constructivist investigator is to tease out the construc-
> tions that various actors in a setting hold and, so fat as possible, to bring
> them into conjunction — a joining — with one another and with whatever
> other information can be brought to bear on the issues involve. (Guba &
> Lincoln, 1989, p. 142)

Reflective Summary

This chapter and undoubtedly the whole book were written in the spirit of celebrating new paradigms, research approaches and methods, for these are inherent in innovative inquiry. It is the beginning of an era in which we can choose to delve into territories that have not been, and could not have been explored before: it is time we appreciate the influence of paradigms and open our eyes to new possibilities. For reasons such as a lack of validity and generalizations Out-of-Body experiences are hard to prove and rely mostly on qualitative research methods which have been perceived as rigid-less and unreliable sources of data. Scholars espousing positivism have tried to overcome this problem by employing tools such as EEG to monitor participants having an Out-of-Body experience with the aim of collecting rigid, reliable data. Although there is nothing wrong with basing one's research in a positivist paradigm and choosing relevant methods, it can however be limiting as to what can be found by adopting different paradigms and employing qualitative methods. When it comes to ontological assumptions the positivist/post-positivist paradigm strongly rejects any notion of metaphysics or spirituality. Therefore it automatically closes the doors before trying to understand phenomena such as Out-of-Body experiences unless there is a hypothesis or a cause of occurrence, for there must always be an explanation in relation to that "one reality" we live in. That is why constructivism is important; allowing us to legitimately approach a topic that could not have been studied before. This chapter showed how creating knowledge — our reports on reality, is different under the constructivist paradigm. The constructivist researcher lets the voice of a participant be heard with the least interference to portray his/her experiences of reality.

One of the main subjects of discussion in this book and a "buzz-word" in other recent academic sources (Ateljevic & Swain, 2006; Hall, Swain, & Kinnaird, 2003; Wilson & Ateljevic, 2007) is the body/embodiment that should not be detached from any debate concerning the tourist performance and experience among those involved in socio-cultural analyses of tourism. The physical body in New Age travel can be seen as the instrument through which people connect with energies, experience emotions and perform their rituals. Out-of-Body travel and the experience of being apart from one's body certainly highlight a different aspect of this discourse. Although this chapter and Out-of-Body travel represent the opposite quandary, de-attaching from the physical body, the role of a body (be it physical or non-physical) will continue to be one of the focal points in tourism research. This paper indeed is an indication that tourism research is at an important turning point in its development, what Tribe (2005) calls the "new tourism research".

The title of this book "Innovative research methodologies" is without doubt self-exponential, for the word innovative, in my point of view, stands for something novel, fearless and to be done with passion. This chapter has tapped into New Age travel and Out-of-Body experiences and showed the tools of legitimately researching such phenomena. It demonstrated the importance of understanding different paradigms, illustrating that Constructivism does indeed provide the grounds and legitimacy for delving into multifarious realities of humankind.

References

Alvarado, C. S. (2001). Features of out-of-body experiences in relation to perceived closeness to death. *Journal of Nervous and Mental Disease*, *189*(5), 331–332.

Ateljevic, I., Harris, C., Willson, E., & Collins, F. L. (2005). Getting 'entangled': Reflexivity and the 'critical turn' in tourism studies. *Tourism Recreation Research*, *30*(2), 5–18.

Ateljevic, I., & Swain, M. B. (2006). Embodying tourism research: Gender performance among Sani and Bai Women in Yunnan's ethnic tourism. Paper presented at the Cauthe International Tourism Conference 2006. "To the City and Beyond. . .". Victoria University, Melbourne.

Attix, S. A. (2002). New age-oriented special interest travel: An exploratory study. *Tourism Recreation Research, 27*(2), 51–58.

Blackmore, S. (1991). Near-death experiences: In or out of the body? *The Skeptical Inquirer, 16*(1), 34–45.

Blaikie, N. (1993). *Approaches to social enquiry*. Cambridge: Polity Press.

Blanke, O. (2002). Stimulating illusory own-body perceptions. *Nature, 419*, 269–270.

Blanke, O., Landis, T., Spinelli, L., & Seeck, M. (2004). Out-of-body experience and autoscopy of neurological origin. *Brain, 127*(3), 243–258.

Brandt, C., Brechtelsbauer, D., Bien, C. G., & Reiners, K. (2005). Out-of-body experience as possible seizure symptom in a patient with a right parietal lesion. *Nervenarzt, 76*(10), 1261–1262.

Crandall, D. P. (1990). Peering at paradigms through the prism of practice improvement. In: E. G. Guba (Ed.), *The paradigm dialog* (pp. 112–123). London: Sage.

Denzin, N. K., & Lincoln, Y. S. (2003). The discipline and practice of qualitative research. In: N. K. Denzin, & Y. S. Lincoln (Eds), *Handbook of qualitative research* (2nd ed., pp. 1–46). London: Sage.

Ehrenwald, J. (1974). Out-of-the-body experiences and the denial of death. *Journal of Nervous and Mental Disease, 159*(4), 227–233.

Ezzy, D. (2003). New age witchcraft? Popular spell books and the re-enchantment of everyday life. *Culture and Religion, 4*(1), 47–65.

Frazier, K. (2003). Brain site located that induces illusory out-of-body experiences. *The Skeptical Inquirer, 27*(1), 12.

Goodson, L., & Phillimore, J. (2004). The inquiry paradigm in qualitative tourism research. In: J. Phillimore, & L. Goodson (Eds), *Qualitative research in tourism* (pp. 30–45). London: Routledge.

Greene, F. G. (1999). A projective geometry for separation experiences. *Journal of Near Death Studies, 17*(3), 151–191.

Greene, F. G. (2003). At the edge of eternity's shadows: Scaling the fractal continuum from lower into higher space. *Journal of Near Death Studies, 21*(4), 223–240.

Guba, E. G. (1990). The alternative paradigm dialog. In: E. G. Guba (Ed.), *The paradigm dialog* (pp. 17–27). London: Sage.

Guba, E. G., & Lincoln, Y. S. (1989). *Fourth generation evaluation*. London: Sage.

Guba, E. G., & Lincoln, Y. S. (2004). Competing paradigms in qualitative research: Theories and issues. In: S. N. Hesse-Biber, & P. Leavy (Eds), *Approaches to qualitative research* (pp. 17–38). Oxford: Oxford University Press.

Haddow, A. (1991). Out-of-body and near-death experiences: Their impact on religious beliefs. *The Journal of Religion and Psychic Research, 14*(2), 75–85.

Hall, D., Swain, M. B., & Kinnaird, V. (2003). Tourism and gender: An evolving agenda. *Tourism Recreation Research, 28*(2), 7–11.

Heidegger, M. (1962). *Being and time* (J. Macquarie, & E. Robinson, Trans.). Oxford: Basil Blackwell.

Hess, D. (1993). *Science in the new age: The paranormal, its defenders and debunkers, and American culture*. Madison, WI: University of Wisconsin Press.

Hollinshead, K. (2004). Ontological craft in tourism studies: The productive mapping of identity and image in tourism settings. In: J. Phillimore, & L. Goodson (Eds), *Qualitative research in tourism* (pp. 83–101). London: Routledge.

Irwin, H. J. (1989). Hypnotic induction of out-of-body experience. *Australian Journal of Clinical Hypnotherapy and Hypnosis, 10*, 71–77.

Jamal, T. B., & Everett, J. (2004). Resisting rationalisation in the natural and academic life-world: Critical tourism research or Hermeneutic charity? *Current Issues in Tourism, 7*(1), 1–19.

Kraus, R., & Allen, L. R. (1996). *The scientific method: Ways of knowing* (2nd ed.). London: Allyn & Bacon.

Lincoln, Y. S. (1990). The making of a constructivist: A remembrance of transformations past. In: E. G. Guba (Ed.), *The paradigm dialog* (pp. 67–87). London: Sage.

Lincoln, Y. S., & Guba, E. G. (2003). Paradigmatic controversies, contradictions, and emerging confluences. In: N. K. Denzin, & Y. S. Lincoln (Eds), *The landscape of qualitative research: Theories and issues* (2nd ed., pp. 253–291). London: Sage.

Marciniak, B. (2004). *Path of empowerment*. Makawao, HI: Inner Ocean Publishing, Inc.

Meyerson, J., & Gelkopf, M. (2004). Therapeutic utilization of spontaneous out-of-body experiences in hypnotherapy. *American Journal of Psychotherapy, 58*(1), 90–102.

Murray, C., & Fox, J. (2005). The out-of-body experience and body image: Differences between experiments and nonexperiments. *Journal of Nervous and Mental Disease, 193*(1), 70–72.

Osis, K. (1979). Insider's view of the OBE: A questionnaire survey. In: W. G. Roll (Ed.), *Research in parapsychology* (pp. 50–52). Metuchen, NJ: Scarecrow Press.

Palmer, J., & Vassar, C. (1974). ESP and out-of-the-body experiences: An exploratory study. *Journal of the American Society for Psychical Research, 68*, 257–280.

Pernecky, T. (2006). Co-creating with the universe: A phenomenological study of New Age tourists. *Tourism, 54*(2), 127–143.

Pernecky, T., & Johnston, C. (2006). Voyage through numinous space; applying the specialization concept to New Age tourism. *Tourism Recreation Research, 31*(1), 37–46.

Podoll, K., & Robinson, D. (1999). Out-of-body experiences and related phenomena in migraine art. *Cephalalgia, 19*(10), 886–896.

Pritchard, D. (2004). Some recent work in epistemology. *The Philosophical Quarterly, 54*(217), 604–613.

Redden, G. (2005). The New Age: Towards a market model. *Journal of Contemporary Religion, 20*(2), 231–246.

Smith, J. K. (1983). Quantitative versus qualitative research: An attempt to clarify the issue. *Educational Researcher, 12*, 6–13.

Sutcliffe, S. (2003). Category formation and the history of 'New Age'. *Culture and Religion, 4*(1), 5–29.

Sutton, P., & House, J. (2003). *The New Age of tourism: Postmodern tourism for postmodern people?* Retrieved 03.03.2003, 2003, from http://www.arasite.org/pspage2.htm.

Tart, C. T. (1967). A second psychophysiological study of out of the body experiences in a gifted subject. *International Journal of Parapsychology, 9*, 251–258.

Tong, F. (2003). Out-of-body experiences: From Penfield to present. *Trends in Cognitive Sciences, 7*(3), 104–106.

Tribe, J. (2005). New Tourism Research. *Tourism Recreation Research: Theme — Tourism and Research, 30*(2), 5–8.

Twemlow, S. W., Gabbard, G. O., & Jones, F. C. (1982). The out-of-body experience: A phenomenological typology based on questionnaire responses. *American Journal of Psychiatry, 139*, 450–455.

Wilkinson, M. (1999). Out-of-body experiences in migraine art. *Cephalalgia, 19*(10), 846–855.

Wilson, E., & Ateljevic, I. (2007). Challenging the 'tourist-other' dualism: gender, backpackers and the embodiment of tourism research. Chapter 7. In: K. Hannam, & I. Ateljevic (Eds), *Backpacker Tourism: Concepts and Profiles*. Clevedon: Channel View Publications.

Chapter 14

The Beauty in the Form: Ethnomethodology and Tourism Studies

Scott McCabe

Introduction

This chapter explores the application of a little used sociologically grounded epistemological and methodological approach to tourism studies, that of ethnomethodology (EM) and its
related 'cousin' conversation analysis (CA). For whatever reasons, these approaches, which
through their interconnectedness form an important strand in qualitative sociological
research methods, have been overlooked by tourism researchers. There are perhaps many
good reasons which we might speculate: the cause of this neglect; the focus of CA on naturally occurring interactional data, something which is perhaps extremely difficult to collect
in touristic settings; the often difficult language in which EM was specified by its progenitor
Harold Garfinkel; the emphasis on past empirical research from EM/CA on medical interaction and cases; a lack of knowledge on how to use these approaches; but also perhaps, I would
argue, the particular emphasis placed from these perspectives upon what ordinary people say
and do to accomplish their activities, to make them real, meaningful and relevant to their lives,
means that clear ground rules are placed upon the depth of interpretation and abstraction made
possible through these approaches about the inner worlds of the observed (tourists) or the
speakers (touristic interaction). These restrictions have perhaps been less appealing to analysts
of touristic phenomena, a nascent field of study, wherein researchers rightly want to make
bold assertions about the phenomena under scrutiny. Indeed EM is often criticised by interpretivist sociologists as being concerned more with the 'form' than the 'being', the 'structure'
rather than the 'content', perhaps too dryly rigorous in its attention to the detail of social interaction data, perhaps too narrowly focused on questions of 'how' as opposed to 'why' of social
phenomena. And yet it is against this backdrop that I want to argue that EM, or more correctly,
EM-informed approaches to qualitative research can offer something different, unique and liberating to scholars of touristic phenomena, which can only add to our critical understanding
of tourism and to our cannon of available methodologies. It is in this sense that these
approaches can offer a critically different voice in tourism research in the context of the way

in which we treat touristic qualitative data, and in terms of how such data can be used to open up new possibilities of analytic subjects. For considerations of space and focus, this chapter focuses on EM as the root epistemological position to enable us to locate the ontological position of EM, but it refers to CA and other related approaches, notably discursive psychology (DP), where appropriate, and first outlines the basic principles of EM and its epistemological antecedents. This is followed by a description of the key concepts in EM, which will enable a comparison between EM's position and that of other interpretivist approaches. Some examples are then provided which demonstrate the richness of analysis which can be accessed using these approaches applied to tourism data and for the development of specific EM-informed tourism projects, and the chapter concludes with a discussion on the range of research topics in tourism which can be explored through an EM-informed approach.

What Is Ethnomethodology?

Ethnomethodology is a branch of sociology, a sort of paradigm for the study of accounts. Developed by Garfinkel (1967, 1994), as a way of studying the practical sociological accomplishment of everyday life, EM aimed to focus on mundane, practical activities, practical circumstances and practical sociological reasoning (Garfinkel, 1967, p. 1) as empirical topics for the first time. At its most basic level EM questions how ordinary people (members) going about their normal business come to understand each other, how members 'create and maintain a sense of order and intelligibility in social life' (ten Have, 2004, p. 14). Taking a radical stance away from Durkheimian sociology whose focus was on social facts as constitutive of sociology, EM asked how social facts are in themselves constituted through (lay) sociological reasoning. Therefore, EM was both radically social and qualitative.

In elaborating the origins of EM, Cuff, Sharrock, and Francis (1990 {1972}) identified that Garfinkel devised EM through a critical reading of Parsons and Schutz. From Parsons, Garfinkel became interested in the 'theory of action' (1990, p. 167) and the problem of social order. Radically different from Parsons was the philosophical writing of Schutz, who was interested not in social systems of action but rather from the level of action as experienced by the actor in the world of everyday life (1990, p. 168). Schutz argued that the social world is characterised by a mass of intersubjective experiences making the world exceptionally social and objectified as such by ordinary members of society who naturally orient to social understandings.

Garfinkel elaborated from Parsons the notion that 'social order' is 'produced' because social actors were able to recognise and comply with normative, social constraints. However, drawing from Schutz, Garfinkel took the idea that social actors' understandings of situations were not produced by a common culture, but locally from within the activity or setting, and so argued that social order is participant produced and endlessly being redefined within social interaction (Cuff, Sharrock, & Francis, 1990, p. 173). This is the key to EM. Garfinkel proposed that the realities of social life should be conceived as consisting in, and only in, members' understandings. Heritage (1984) interpreted that Garfinkel meant EM to be the study of commonsense knowledge and the range of procedures by which ordinary members of society make sense of, find their way about in and act on the circumstances in which they find themselves (Heritage, 1984).

Ethnomethodology is concerned therefore with the practical matters of social life — or activities — questions of how people produce and manage settings of everyday life. These activities are identical with the methods used by people in making those activities and settings accountable (Garfinkel, 1967, p. 1). According to Garfinkel, accounts (what we might call natural, everyday conversations and interactions and routines, activities and experiences) of social life have innate properties: they are reflexive and incarnate. It is these properties that make such activities and interactions the natural location of social activity and therefore the basis/site of empirical enquiry. Garfinkel explained what he meant by 'accountable':

> I mean observable-and-reportable, i.e. available to members as situated practices of looking-and-telling. I mean, too, that such practices consist of an endless, on-going, contingent accomplishment; that they are carried on under the auspices of, and are made to happen as events in, the same ordinary affairs that in organising they describe; that the practices are done by parties to those settings whose skill with, knowledge of, and entitlement to the detailed work of that accomplishment — whose competence — they obstinately depend upon, recognise, use, and take for granted; and that they take their competence for granted itself furnishes parties with a setting's distinguishing and particular features, and of course it furnishes them as well as resources, troubles, projects and the rest. (Garfinkel, 1967, pp. 1–2)

In particular, Garfinkel argued that social order could be revealed through the analysis of indexical expressions and practical actions. Indexical expressions are the opposite of objective expressions. They are the expressions in interaction (talk) that are entirely dependent upon the context of the occasion of their use. Such understandings are most often taken-for-granted in society as objective. In terms of practical actions and practical circumstances for ordinary members of society, Garfinkel noticed that in ordinary life, people do not question the meanings of actions and interactions and as such reasoning was not a topic in everyday life. In other words, the resources, aims, excuses, opportunities, tasks and grounds for arguing (1967, p. 7) employed by members of society are not of interest to them; they are taken for granted and it is this that constitutes members' reflexivity to practical accomplishments. This ongoing reflexivity in the production of indexical expressions has rational properties from which the 'social accomplishment of the organised artful practices of everyday life can be discerned' (Garfinkel, 1967, p. 62). Thus ordinary members do not continually challenge the meanings of words and situations in which they find themselves in everyday life; instead, members naturally orient their actions and interactions to the establishment and maintenance of mutual understanding. It is this taken-for-granted orientation to the production of shared meaning which can be argued to be objective and rational and therefore reportable in an 'objective' — impartial — analysis.

Garfinkel argued that this focus of EM on objective and rational properties and features within the analysis of everyday social life enabled the development of methods which focused on stable features of social interaction, and thus borrowed some of the features of 'hard' (i.e. more positivistic) social science. This has probably had the impact of making EM less attractive to more interpretivist approaches within the broader spectrum of social constructionism (SC), which embraces 'softer' and more intuitive forms of analysis to scratch beneath the surface of interaction to reveal the intersubjective meanings and hint at the elemental 'truths' of phenomena. In a relatively young field of studies like tourism, the richness of detail and the compelling nature of these interpretations have led to much deeper understandings of the nature of touristic phenomena. However, due to the paradigmatic shifts towards post-modern accounts of society and the cultural turn in research, there is currently a plethora of multitudinous and competing alternative approaches which could limit the interpretive value of some qualitative research, and which may appear too far abstracted from ordinary people's experience. I argue that EM-informed qualitative approaches to touristic phenomena and/or data analysis, which are located entirely within the perspective of ordinary people's ordinary actions or phenomena provide quite compelling and less-abstract theorising and only contribute to and complement existing social-constructionist approaches. EM techniques also open up all manner of previously unrecognised materials (data, evidence), particularly through an emphasis on 'naturally occurring' data, i.e. that which is not specifically produced as part of a research project.

Another way in which EM has the effect of liberating the researcher is in its approach to data. EM argues that if we are to understand how people accomplish their daily lives in making decisions, communicating with each other, providing reasons for their decisions using commonsense knowledge, etc., we must not treat social actors as irrational beings — as conventional sociology does — but focus our analytic attention on actors' practical experiences and thus suspend the values and norms, rules and structures from pre-existing theoretical frameworks, which are used to inform conventional sociological analyses. We must do this since the processes through which the supposed stable features of organised everyday life are not really solid but continually being recreated, renegotiated and modified (Coulon, 1995). One fundamental way in which ethnomethodological thinking has been used to re-examine tourist's experiences has been to challenge the theoretical distinction between tourism experience and everyday life (see McCabe, 2002). Using EM theory and principles has made it possible to propose that far from leaving ourselves behind at home when we go on holiday, tourist experiences allow us to continually reflect back on everyday life and therefore through tourist experiences the habits, routines and pastimes of everyday can be solidified and reified. Tourist's activities within touristic settings and their interactions in and amongst themselves and between local cultures potentially provide a unique and remarkable source of data to explore how for example 'doing being a tourist' is produced and negotiated and constituted through those activities and interactions and intercultural communications. This type of analysis can only be achieved by a focus on the practical, performed and constitutive material of ordinary, everyday activities and interactions either within touristic settings or through interview data.

Key Concepts in Ethnomethodology

In the preceding section, I mentioned how the ethnomethodologist is interested in ordinary people's ordinary talk and practical actions. At this level there is potentially little difference between EM and conventional qualitative sociologically informed approaches to tourism activity, such as that deployed so well by, for example, Edensor (2001). However, differences appear in how the ethnomethodologist approaches and analyses the materials or data. In this section, the focus is on how EM approaches are based around some key concepts. I described how EM was formulated around the principle that ordinary language is full of expressions which derive their meaning from the specific occasion of their use and whose meaning is taken for granted and reflexively oriented towards. These were called indexical expressions, and these expressions are an important concept in the analysis of interaction data within an EM approach. Coulon (1995) argues that whereas the conventional sociologist seeks ways to remedy the indexical nature of practical discourse (indexical expressions are those such as 'that', 'I', 'you', that draw their meaning from the context, that determine the contextuality of other words) to draw out the underlying meanings of the interaction, the ethnomethodologist recognises the indexical nature of interaction. What this means in practice is that although a word has a trans-situational significance, it also has a distinct significance in each situation in which it is used, and so the comprehension of the word requires indicative characteristics. As such, words only gain meaning from the context (surrounding words and sentences) in which they are used. Garfinkel argued that the entire range of natural language is indexical, and therefore for members of society, the meaning and significance of words depends on the specific occasion or in which they are used. The very intelligibility of social exchanges does not suffer from indexical expressions but rather depends on them being locally significant to the topic at the time of their use. The practical and epistemological consequence of this orientation to context is a limit on the possibility of any abstracted interpretation of meaning beyond the data. For example, it becomes difficult to show a direct causal link between the 'occasion' of use of a word/term/concept in conversation and the feelings, intentions or the 'inner world' of the speaker.

Another key concept already touched upon is that of 'reflexivity', which again is used in a different sense to its use in conventional qualitative sociology. Reflexivity refers to the taking into account of the nature of the interactional setting (e.g. interviewee–interviewer), and the roles and orientation of each participant which then informs the analysis of the data because EM argues that participants in interaction take for granted their reflexive orientation to settings and thus reflexive re-formulations are always implicit in the outcomes of any such interviews or interactions. The subject topic revealed through reflexive thinking may not be the topic of conversation or interaction. In this way topics developed through reflexive thinking represent tacit knowledge. Members use reflexive practices all the time and unconsciously. Reflexivity is oriented towards building and maintaining the meaning, order and rationality of what social actors are doing. Reflexivity refers to the equivalence between describing and producing an action, the relationship between its comprehension and the expression of this comprehension (Coulon, 1995).

Coulon goes on to describe the concept of accountability in EM whereby everyday activities are equivalent to 'methods' for making those activities visible, i.e. 'accountable' (1995, p. 23). The two defining characteristics of accountability are that it is reflexive and rational. To argue that accountability is reflexive is to accept that the accountability of an activity and its circumstances is to partly constitute those activities. In other words in narrating a story about an event or experience while on holiday — a practical and everyday conversational activity, one which as tourists returning to our normal routines, we are perhaps expected to produce — participants to the telling of that activity can be understood as practically constituting those events and/or experiences. We produce events as we recount them;

there is no formal difference. We can understand the 'what' of the events through an analysis of 'how' they are made visible through the telling, describing, explaining, etc. To argue that accountability is rational is to identify that accounts are methodically produced in a situation, in a describable, intelligible manner. These rational properties of accounts do not describe a social reality but rather they reconstruct a precarious social order to enable us to understand each other and be able to communicate in a recognised and intelligible manner, they reveal the way in which the social world is constituted, thus:

> If I describe a scene of my daily life, it is not because it describes the world that an ethnomethodologist can be interested in but because this description, by accomplishing itself, 'makes up' the world or builds it up. Making the world visible is making my action comprehensible in doing it, because I reveal its significance through the exposition of the methods by which I make an account of it. (Coulon, 1995, p. 26)

The final concept relates to that of a 'member', the concept of which does not refer to a category (a type of person) but to a person's mastery of natural language. Because people are speaking natural language they are conceived as engaged in the objective production and display of commonsense knowledge of everyday activities. People then become 'members' — or lay sociologists, since they reflexively use natural language to account for their activities and accomplish meaningful everyday life. This process allows the analyst to interpret the meaning of interaction through the documentary method of interpretation (Psathas, 1995). The documentary method is already operative by lay sociologists (members) in the processes through which people understand each other in the world. Garfinkel describes the documentary method as consisting of treating an actual appearance of a thing as the document of as 'pointing to', as 'standing on behalf of' a presupposed underlying pattern. 'Not only is the underlying pattern derived from its individual documentary evidences, but the individual documentary evidences, in their turn, are interpreted on the basis of "what is known" about the underlying pattern. Each is used to elaborate the other.' (Garfinkel, 1967, p. 78). The document has a meaning and therefore it is open to a process of interpretation. Individuals unveil social reality to each other, making it readable by building up patterns (Coulon, 1995, p. 33). The documentary method is used by members whenever they are historicizing a person's biography, or producing a biographical experience. The documentary method works to select and organise past occurrences so as to furnish the present state of affairs with the relevant past and prospects. It is this method that allows us to reconstitute the meaning of a conversation. As social actors, members are engaged in this process of interpretation continuously, selecting and giving appropriate meaning to things and interpreting what is the sense of a conversation. Therefore, through a close analysis of the form of interaction data we can obtain access to some tentative interpretations of the underlying meanings.

Perhaps this is the right moment to provide an example. The following represents a theoretical example of how members must deploy commonsense reasoning to understand and interpret an utterance in everyday conversation, or natural language. Let us consider the following statement:

> 'You had a good trip then'

This simple text which could easily be conceived in the context of ordinary interaction about tourism and travel can be interpreted in any number of different ways.

Firstly, as a straightforward inquiry into the protagonist's journey, with the addition of a question mark:

'You had a good trip then?'

Secondly, with the addition of a comma, as a fragment of a conversation that is cut short:

'You had a good trip, then. . . .'

Thirdly, as an ironic question where the questioner knows that the protagonist has had a bad trip:

'You had a good trip then?'

Each type of construction requires a choice of emphasis of intonation or stressing certain words or parts of words within the phrase. The ironic interpretation in the third interpretation requires a different method of speech, perhaps with raised intonation on certain words (such as then) and perhaps some elements of laughter, which together create a shared understanding that what is actually spoken (dictum) is not the same as what is implied by the words. This interpretation necessitates that we hear that the speaker deploys the words in an ironic sense to make light of a situation which could otherwise be interpreted as entirely negative. These interpretive resources used by the speakers to ensure that the hearer understands the meaning of the words within the situated context of their telling is the basis of EM-informed approaches such as CA. We would necessarily require some knowledge of the context in which the speaker and listener find themselves to understand more of the intelligibility of the text. For example, if we point out that the speaker is head of a panel of interviewers and has spoken this utterance as a device to make the hearer (an interviewee) feel comfortable and relaxed before proceeding with an interview, the interpretation of the text will be different than if we know that the speaker is a man picking his wife up from the airport after a period of separation. The occasion and the context of the use of speech is therefore vital in understanding what is being talked about and the choices (or resources) used by speakers in conveying meaning between each other. It is this attention to context, occasion and the close analysis of how protagonists talk which marks EM studies from other qualitative methods. An analysis of context and occasion of interaction together with the interpretive resources used to accomplish mutual understanding of an interaction sequence, necessarily impacts upon the level of analysis available into the interpretation of meaning within the topics of the interaction.

It is at this point that some differences between EM and SC can be identified. However, it must be pointed out emphatically, that the differences and similarities between types or styles of SC and an EM approach, is very complex and the subject of continuing debate within the social sciences (e.g. Hester & Francis, 1997; Hutchby & Wooffitt, 1998). And that such degrees and styles of SC and the extent that they do or do not correspond to EM are epistemological debates which focus on the different approaches to, their ontological stance on how 'reality' or 'realities' are conceived within their theorising (Francis, 1994). The boundaries of these differences and similarities are not static but are evolving with greater depth of theorising, but the following section aims to provide a gloss on the main tensions and issues.

Ethnomethodology and Social Constructionism in Dialogue

Ethnomethodology takes the standpoint that the sense of social actions is not derived from deeply embedded and culturally and historically rooted ideas about how knowledge, 'reality' is constituted, but that meaning is 'worked out' within the context, the ethnomethodologist aims to unpack the relational configurations that enable members to sense of each other or meanings to be produced *in situ* (Lynch & Peyrot, 1992), and therefore is less interested in the epistemological lacuna of the actions or interactions because these are not of concern to members themselves (Watson, 1994). One of the key criticisms of SC is that analyses are often accused of selective objectivism (Miller & Holstein, 1993), in that the meanings interpreted through the analysis often reflect the key conceptual issues in the field which subconsciously prefigure the outcomes of the analysis, and in ascribing such meanings as pointing to the 'realities' of the subjects being studied (Greene, 1990; Guba & Lincoln, 1994), SC often uses language in a misplaced way which serves to essentialise the phenomena, thus inherently, such SC studies belie a tendency to realism. Francis (1994) in a critique of Watson and Goulet's ethnography of the Dene Tha society, argues that when SC purports to show how a 'reality' is socially constituted or constructed, something is constructed in contrast or relation to or equivalent to other forms of knowledge or reality, and EM differs in that it does not assume the need to adopt a stance on 'reality' at all (Francis, 1994, p. 105). Studies in EM overcome these issues through a focus on questions of how social reality is constructed and managed, and not the topic of reality in itself. However, Czarniawska-Joerges (1992) argues that the epistemological position of EM is located on the edge between SC and existentialism on a continuum of paradigms and in her study of complex organisations, which she found to be extensively different from everyday settings, Czarniawska-Joerges argues that it was not desirable or useful to place analytic emphasis on 'how' social reality was accomplished, at the expense of 'what' was actually being accomplished in terms of topics or discourses. In the context of studies of organisations, EM was simply not practical: 'There is no soul without a body and no substance without form . . . but a solution that recommends only the study of the body and the form does not solve much.' (Czarniawska-Joerges, 1992, p. 123).

However, in practice there are many shared conventions and similarities between SC and EM. Indeed some approaches in SC are very indistinct from EM analyses. In a useful and critical discussion on the various positions adopted and applied in the context of gender and language, for example, Stokoe (2005, 2006) unpacks the theoretical issues and problems encountered by proponents of social constructionist theorising thus:

> Here, social constructionism (vs. essentialism) is conflated with social/
> cultural (vs. biological) understandings of gender: it is treated as a construction rather than as biological, or as only a construction rather than real.
> The idea that 'construction' means that gender identities are 'only' constructions rather than real is itself a re-iteration of essentialism. . . . There
> is no contrast between gender being 'constructed' and its being natural and
> prior to discourse. Its existence as natural, essential and prior to discourse
> is precisely what is constructed, in and through practices of all kinds.
> (Stokoe, 2007)

Stokoe goes on to argue that such tropes in constructionism misunderstands the constructionist project as constituted within the sociology of scientific knowledge and discourse analysis (DA). Researchers within these positions conceive both EM/CA as similar to constructionism in that they share a focus on knowledge production and both 'place reality temporarily in brackets . . . to study how people maintain a sense of a commonly shared, objectively existing world' (*ibid.*). Stokoe argues that although CA practitioners are often conceived as being extreme constructivists, it is not clear that these practitioners conceive of themselves as constructivist at all.

Both SC and EM have evolved to allow flexibility and there is more common ground between them than separates them. However, in the context of tourism studies, a strong SC has come to dominate qualitative inquiry and often tends towards essentialising 'truths' and 'realities' of subjects, and therefore I believe that EM provides a useful alternative or corrective to this type of SC hegemony in studies of tourism and tourists experience. Social constructionists and ethnomethodologists alike argue that the things we treat as 'objective facts' are discursive constructions, or locally managed accomplishments. Both perspectives aim to analyse the 'situated conduct of societal members in order to see how "objective" properties of social life are achieved' (West & Fenstermaker, 1993, p. 152). In many ways those working in either EM or SC approaches find themselves dealing with similar issues but using different means to get there. For example, Desforges (2000) argued convincingly from an SC position that when people talk about their tourist experiences they talk about their social identities. McCabe and Stokoe (2004) argued much the same from an EM-informed position using membership categorisation analysis (MCA). Each study is unique and offers fresh insights into how identity is worked up in qualitative interviews and yet they complement each other and together solidify the idea that when tourists talk about their activities and experiences, they are in effect relating to identity issues. This makes a more convincing argument that at a fundamental level, tourism is linked to social actors identity work.

Buttny (1993) argues convincingly for a conversation analytic constructionism approach, that enables an interpretation of the 'meanings' of an account (the SC concern) by drawing upon a socially constructed 'folk logic' of shared understanding, alongside an analysis of the methods used by persons to present their activities so as to render them sensible, normal, understandable (the EM concern) (1993, p. 15). However, ten Have (2004) identifies that in adopting an ethnomethodological stance, the researcher is immediately confronted with a methodological problem. Since the main purpose of EM is to study the commonplace activities and understandings of ordinary people — how the commonplace activities are constitutive of social life, and yet this is almost impossible to analyse due to what ten Have calls the 'invisibility of common sense' (2004, p. 31). As ordinary members of society are concerned with the topics and activities of social life, and not with the methods and procedures by which these topics and activities are constituted it is then problematic to shift emphasis from the topics to the properties and resources, which constitute the topics. It is perhaps because of a number of related issues that EM approaches have been less utilised in tourism studies to date: Garfinkel's over elaborated language style; the pre-eminence of SC approaches; lack of understanding of the EM position within the tourism studies academy; the difficulty in accessing naturally occurring tourist interaction data — all potentially contribute to a lack of up-take among researchers.

Ethnomethodology and Tourism

The use of an EM-informed approach is very rare in tourism studies. However, there are potentially limitless ways in which EM-informed approaches can be applied to touristic phenomena. Tourism is essentially a very organised and structured — ordered — system. Tourism, and here I refer to all forms of travel and tourism, consists of a set of activities and practices which are describable and performed by ordinary social actors who undertake the 'work' of doing being travellers or tourists largely in a taken-for-granted way. In other words, people in society do not tend to question the processes and systems, the practices and activities in which they engage while being tourists, because rightly, they are more concerned with enjoying their experiences. Similarly, the tourism industry 'orders' the production and representation of tourism spaces and destinations for touristic consumption through similarly unreflective systems and processes. Therefore, EM can be used as an approach or lens through which many or indeed any, touristic phenomena, systems and activities can be scrutinised. In fact, precisely because EM asks us to observe what's going on in a situated activity 'without presuppositions . . . by "bracketing" what you already know' (ten Have, 2004, p. 151), we can begin to challenge the more abstract myths and structures of touristic theorising to focus our perspective on the practical, mundane, observable and describable activities to build conceptualisations that are firmly driven by and located within analysis of empirical data. This challenge to the obvious, the self-evident, taken-for-granted assumptions relates very much to the current preoccupation with concerns of truth making in tourism (cf. Tribe, 2006). To risk gross over-simplification, a foundational problem in relation to truth claims for all social science relates to the epistemological question of the possibility of a correspondence between a phenomena and what is observed and reported about that phenomena. Thus if a social researcher observes a person undertaking an activity and infers the nature of that activity, how can we be absolutely sure that the inference is correct? When we observe a group of package tourists queuing up to check into their holiday apartments there is a tendency to categorise or bracket them and their activities, their motivations and personal characteristics, perhaps also their social backgrounds and livelihoods in a particular, homogenous way as package tourists. There is very little questioning of the sense or facticity of this interpretation despite the generally accepted notion that people can and do wilfully resist (stereo-)typificatory classifications. Similarly, there is very little research in tourism which questions the essentially ordering and institutionalising arrangements of the tourism industry as a set of 'instructions' through which tourism is produced and consumed. EM-informed approaches ask us to suspend conventional interpretations to ask 'just how' actual activities are produced and through which formal properties (Lynch, 2002, p. 129).

There are a series of questions we can propose to illustrate how EM-informed approaches can be used to re-specify qualitative tourism research orientations: how do ordinary people produce and order their activities as 'tourists'? This question assumes that 'doing being a tourist' requires work. The term work here denotes that there are a series of choices in accomplishing the task of being a tourist, and these choices in fact dominate the tourism process from the perspective of the industry as well as the tourist experience. Decisions about destination choice selection, the type of holiday or travel experience desired, the type of travel arrangements made, the activities undertaken whilst away from home and particularly the choices to be made within the destination, finding our way around a new environment, deciding where to go, what to eat, where to go out, what to do in an unfamiliar place, provide much evidence of the work of the tourist, and possibly the most pleasurable aspects of the exciting process that drives us to want to experience new places as tourists.

This work within the destination is perhaps more visible, observable than the choices available in the pre-trip sense, and it is here that the richness of the possibilities for EM-informed analyses can be found, although interview data can also provide similarly interesting analysis particularly in terms of the myriad ways in which tourist choices can be argued to reflect and draw upon identity work through their accounts of these choices. A large part of this focus from an EM-informed approach is through the study of language, talk and interaction, which has developed into an approach in its own through CA and its relative, MCA. Identity from the EM/CA/MCA framework is '. . . indexical, context-bound understanding of identity, in which the self (if it is anything) is an oriented-to production and accomplishment in interaction' (Benwell & Stokoe, 2006, p. 36). This approach is in stark contrast with many studies in tourism which have approached identity in tourist narratives/accounts/experiences from a performativity/social constructionist approach (e.g. Desforges, 2000; Elsrud, 2001; Noy, 2004). In their excellent recent book on identity and discourse, Benwell and Stokoe argue that despite surface similarities there are differences in understanding of the performance of identities between the EM/CA and performativity/SC approaches. They identify that in constructionist accounts, '. . . we find reference to identities, in the plural, as multiple and variable, rather than fixed, singular and rigid. What these kinds of descriptions do is produce rival ontologies of the self: the self is either multiple or fixed: constructed or essential (Edwards & Stokoe, 2004). In everyday life, people tend to think of themselves as stable, consistent kinds of persons rather than the product of fleeting, shifting identities' (2006, p. 68 their emphasis). Ethnomethodologists criticise this constructionist view because they argue that ordinary people generally treat identity as 'a real thing that they can know about themselves and other people' (as before). Benwell and Stokoe contrast this with the disinterest in the ontological status of the self for EM/CA: 'Instead, the focus is on members' orientations to identity as (un)stable, (in)consistent, (in)coherent, and so on . . . CA studies of identity do not therefore involve speculation about theory, discourses or power. Instead, they investigate how people display identity, in terms of ascribed membership of social categories, and the consequences of ascription or display for the interactional work being accomplished' (Benwell & Stokoe, 2006, pp. 68–69, their emphasis). Within the context of tourism studies more specifically, Moore argues for the benefits of discursive approaches thus:

> Discursive approaches are thus ideally suited to answer questions about how tourists 'negotiate' the tasks of being tourists, since they highlight acts and strategies that not only accomplish ends, but also help to redefine those ends spontaneously. . . . On the one hand, it can explain individual differences and dynamic and responsive flexibility, and yet also the commonalities of tourist action. On the other hand, it can do so without appeal to an individualistic and privatised account of human psychology. (Moore, 2002, pp. 52–53)

An example of this type of approach is seen in work arising out or Doctoral research by McCabe (2001), which has sought to engage different aspects of EM problems through interview data with day visitors to the Peak National Park in the UK. Interviews with couples revealed interesting insights into the ways in which gender identity categories were oriented to by couples discussing their leisure pastimes and hobbies (McCabe, 2003). This paper argued that whereas much research on gender in tourism studies — from the perspective of tourist experience focuses on the differences in participation, there was little focus on how gender is made relevant within interview contexts or on how interview respondents orient to gender identities in their elaborations of their touristic activities. The following is a short excerpt taken from McCabe (2003), which aims to show how in this case a male respondent orients to masculine identity in the context of an interview with another man:

> She says(.) 'shall we go to Castleton today?' and I say 'what do you want now?'(.) 'nothing but whilst we're there we can always have a look can't we?' (1)I'm not one of these fellas(.) I mean I hate shopping(.) I despise shopping(.) not food shopping I don't mind that because its something that I'm going for(.) but when she goes out to town(.) when she goes to Meadowhall(.) when she goes shopping(.) and I am dragged round from shop to shop to shop(.) and I really hate it(.)

L describes how his fiancé and him usually begin the process of deciding to make a visit to the Peak Park to Castleton to look around the shops which specialise in selling jewellery pieces of a locally mined semi-precious stone 'Blue John'. But immediately he orients to a masculine position 'fella' who 'hates shopping'. We can assume that men naturally dislike being 'dragged round from shop to shop', which is therefore constructed as something not hateful for 'her' when 'she goes shopping to Meadowhall' (an extremely large shopping centre or mall located in Sheffield, UK). McCabe argued that through stories of touristic accounts, people can be demonstrably seen to orient to gender roles and norms.

Following on from this work, McCabe and Stokoe (2004) sought to examine the importance of place in identity work in the same long narratives with day visitors to the Peak Park. It has been theorised that leisure practice, including tourism, are linked to constructions such as middle class identities (Munt, 1994) or a 'good' and 'moral' self (Matless, 1995). Identity is deemed to be increasingly constructed through the consumption of leisure goods, services and signs rather than through occupational categories (Urry, 1994). Additionally, people not only identify themselves and others but they also appear to ascribe identity categories to places (e.g. 'resort' or 'wilderness'). Such categorisations are not just simple, objective or factual descriptions; they construct places as 'the geographical world we know' (Schegloff, 1972; McCabe & Stokoe, 2004, p. 612). A close examination of the practices that ordinary people use in accounting for their activities within places became the focus for the analysis of previously analysed interviews with tourists. McCabe and Stokoe argued that there were few examples of empirical engagement with how people constructed identity categories in relation to places, specifically in tourists talk about the tourist destination they visited. This immediate incongruence, in that one would expect visitors to a National Park to construct themselves as 'outsiders', rather than as naturally belonging to the place, struck us as worthy of further investigation.

In the analysis, we sought how day visitors, as members of a culture, display their understandings of, and reasoning about, their identities and activities in places. We specifically looked for participants' situated descriptions of themselves and others in order to show that when people generate stories about themselves and others, as members of particular categories of 'tourist', 'visitor', or 'walker', they are engaged in aligning and realigning the social order (Goodwin, 1997) and in '. . . establishing some version of events as constituting common knowledge about what defines appropriate behaviours for such category members' (McCabe & Stokoe, 2004, p. 608). We focused our analysis on how social identity categories were negotiated in the interview narratives and how they functioned as resources that speakers used in producing accounts and descriptions. In other words, McCabe and Stokoe's analysis showed how people deployed social identity categories as tools to accomplish the business of creating a credible touristic narrative or account of their behaviour in the Peak National Park. We also considered how place formulations and identity categorisations were used in the construction of the 'social and moral order' in accounts of the activities. Descriptions of 'located activities' — i.e. within places, make inferentially available notions of what constitutes 'good' and 'bad' visitors to a place, and so therefore McCabe and Stokoe demonstrated that there is a moral order to doing being a tourist, as is evidenced by the quote:

> Hartington's always (.) always full of coach loads from Birmingham its a bit like Gulliver's Kingdom (.) it always seems to be full of coach loads from Birmingham . . . but people seem quite happy just to turn up in a bus in Hartington (.) get off the bus go and have a cream tea (.) go and buy something in the shop and get back on the bus and that's Hartington ticked off. (McCabe & Stokoe, 2004, p. 616)

This account from an interview with 'Pam' was used to allow us to elaborate how place and membership categories function to construct the moral order of place (as in tourist destination) and tourists. The choice of the member category 'coachloads' and the place category 'Birmingham' (Britain's second largest city), is heavy with implications that the recipient (the interviewer) can apply their category knowledge as members of a shared culture (Nilan, 1995). 'Coachloads', like 'swarm' in previous statements, emphasises the issue that 'bad' tourists travel in large numbers: too many people in a place ruin it and create a site of disorder (Barnes, 2000). The category 'Birmingham' also carries with it a 'relevant category environment', developing an interpretative frame within which to make sense of Pam's account, a large, urban, perceived predominance of working class population. The activities of 'bad' tourists (predominantly a culturally negative construction, cf. McCabe, 2005) are clearly articulated. They, 'turn up in a bus', 'get off the bus', 'have a cream tea', 'buy something in the shop', 'get back on the bus' and 'tick off' the place being visited. This scripted list of activities makes available the category 'tourist', and Pam's account is loaded with '. . . implicit moral evaluations about the activities that comprise the category, the incumbents of it and the place that is characterised by it' (McCabe & Stokoe, 2004, p. 617).

Outside of the interview data, McCabe (2005) has drawn analytical material from an internet discussion board (on Michael Palin's website, a famous English traveller and one-time member of the Monty Python comedy team), which asked people to contribute to a discussion on whether they considered themselves tourists or travellers. The point of the analysis here was to demonstrate how the concept of a 'tourist' is a culturally infused concept, predominantly defined in a negative and derogative sense, and to argue that it is yet treated as an objective and neutral concept by the tourism academy.

The examples above aimed to show respectively the 'just how': how interview respondents oriented to gender roles and relations in their talk about leisure experiences; how place-identity categories are deployed to create a socio-spatial moral order of tourist behaviour; and how the concept of a 'tourist' is a rhetorical and politicised cultural concept which is deployed as a resource in Internet discussion postings. These studies have specifically set out to show the relevance and use of EM-informed approaches within critical tourism studies, which provide fresh and empirically grounded alternatives to the conventional methods of qualitative inquiry into tourism systems and touristic phenomena. However, the overriding aim of these studies has been to open up debate and dialogue between social science researchers within differing and sometimes competing paradigmatic stances, on the relative benefits of alternative perspectives to the generation of research problems in tourism and to the analysis of touristic phenomena and empirical data. There are other tangential studies taking these approaches to touristic phenomena. Benwell and Stokoe (2006) refer to Dixon and Durrheim's (2003) study of informal racial segregation on Scottburgh beach in post-apartheid South Africa. They showed how identity is linked to people's use of places, through a process of zoning the beach into sections and carrying out observations to track the extent and character of segregation practices among members of the different racial groups. They supplemented this with informal *in situ* interviews with people on the beach. Of course, the object of the study here was not their leisure or touristic use of the space, but the touristic context allowed the researchers to develop revealing analysis of the social use of space and identity relationships using methods other than talk or interview data. De Chaine has similarly approached how the environment is constituted through discourse (2001), and there are numerous studies which have approached tourism from within a critical discourse studies approach which have not been included, as examples here as their approach does not directly relate back to the EM ontological position. In summary, there are many opportunities to develop research themes using EM-informed approaches not only in relation to identity but from within many different aspects of tourism studies.

Concluding Remarks

This chapter has aimed to demonstrate that very often the subjects of our research in tourism are ordinary social actors whose orientation to normative (everyday) problems of finding their way about in the world, reflexively adapting to the social situations in which they find themselves, navigating their way around the challenges brought by living in complex socialities and through processes of meaning making posed by post-modernity, shapes their actions, activities and interaction. They are not 'cultural dopes' (Garfinkel, 1994), but simply accomplishing the business of social life whereby being tourists is occasionally an important and fundamental part of that process. A rich panoply of possibilities exist as people perform and express themselves through their bodies, experiences, activities and interactions, human social life is often thought of as distilled and refracted through the lens of tourist experience, wherein the things that matter to us as individuals are given a brief spotlight (McCabe, 2002). These experiences, however, are often the result of the institutional arrangements of the tourism industry, and so the ontological and methodological choices for tourism researchers must include some way of recognition that the tourism system and tourist experience is the product of social organisation and is therefore ordered and produced. One underutilised approach to study just how touristic phenomena are produced and ordered is through ethno-methodologically informed approaches, both in terms of epistemological position and in terms of technologies of analysis through EM studies, or specifically on language and inter-action through CA and other discursive approaches. The richness of variety of touristic set-tings and systems, and hence possibilities for analysis using an EM-informed approach is like a virgin wilderness which has a beauty all of its own.

Whereas many qualitative studies drawing on ethnographic interviews of observations of touristic activity often focus on how the things tourists do and say equates to some search of meaning, authenticity or psychological state of being, EM argues that we can never be absolutely sure that our interpretations about our subjects is correct. Instead, the analyst must ground their analysis in what the speakers actually talk about and the things they orient to in their actions and interactions, or in terms of observations on what people actually and demonstrably do and in this sense, studies in EM are grounded in and driven by empirical data. Pre-existing theoretical frameworks must be suspended, or bracketed, unless we can actually demonstrate how social actors orient to them in the things they say and do.

This type of enquiry is not commonplace in studies of tourism and travel and yet there are so many instances where tourism and travel experiences challenge the very bedrock of social understandings. Where else do cultures collide against each other in such circum-stances? Where else are there so many opportunities for a breakdown in inter-social under-standing? How do members of a culture manage meaningful social interactions with members of another culture in tourism settings? How do tourists and locals interact with each other to produce all the facets which we seek from our tourist experiences: intercultural understanding, peace and cultural knowledge; a high octane adventure; a relaxing time; a bloody good laugh? How do the ubiquitous and uniform in-flight safety demonstrations work to induce a touristic feeling of anticipation? How do the other forms of institutional arrangements such as visa regulations, check-in desk security procedures, travel agency sales pitches, etc. politicise and otherwise reflect the socio-political order in a globalised world? Almost any situation, text, media story, interaction, performance, or story can be analysed using an EM approach. It has been the purpose of this chapter to elaborate how researchers might use this interesting and radically social approach to their studies of touristic phenomena and to encourage dialogue within the research community in tourism. It hopes to have offered tourism researchers an alternative to SC approaches and to develop dialogue on the potential of touristic research projects using EM-informed ontological approaches.

Acknowledgement

The author is grateful to Dr. Liz Stokoe for helpful comments and suggestions on an earlier draft of this paper.

References

Barnes, R. (2000). *Losing ground: Locational formulations in argumentation over new travellers.* Unpublished PhD thesis, University of Plymouth.

Benwell, B., & Stokoe, E. H. (2006). *Discourse and identity.* Edinburgh, UK: Edinburgh University Press.

Buttny, R. (1993). *Social accountability in communication.* London: Sage.

Coulon, A. (1995). Ethnomethodology. In: *Qualitative research methods* (Vol. 36). Thousand Oaks, CA: Sage.

Cuff, E. C., Sharrock, W. W., & Francis, D. W. (1990 {1972}). *Perspectives in sociology.* (3rd Ed.). London: Routledge.

Czarniawska-Joerges, B. (1992). Exploring complex organisations: A cultural perspective. Newbury Park, CA: Sage.

De Chaine, D. (2001). From discourse to golf course: The serious play of imagining community space. *Journal of Communication Inquiry, 25,* 132–146.

Desforges, L. (2000). Travelling the world: Identity and travel biography. *Annals of Tourism Research, 27,* 929–945.

Dixon, J. A., & Durrheim, K. (2003). Contact and the ecology of racial division: Some varieties of informal segregation. *British Journal of Social Psychology, 42,* 1–23.

Edensor, T. (2001). Performing tourism, staging tourism. *Tourist Studies, 1*(1), 59–81.

Elsrud, T. (2001). Risk creation in traveling: Backpacker adventure narration. *Annals of Tourism Research, 28*(3), 597–617.

Francis, D. (1994). The golden dreams of the social constructionist. *Journal of Anthropological Research, 50*(2), 97–108.

Garfinkel, H. (1967). *Studies in ethnomethodology.* Englewood Cliffs, NJ: Prentice Hall.

Garfinkel, H. (1994). What is ethnomethodology? In: *The polity reader in social theory.* Oxford: Blackwell and Cambridge: Polity Press.

Goodwin, M. (1997). Toward families of stories in context. *Journal of Narrative and Life History, 7,* 107–112.

Greene, J. (1990). Three views on the nature and role of knowledge in social science. In: Guba, E. (Ed.), *The paradigm dialogue.* Newbury Park, CA: Sage.

Guba, E. G., & Lincoln, Y. S. (1994). Competing paradigms in qualitative research. In: N. Denzin & Y. Lincoln (Eds), *Handbook of qualitative research.* London: Sage.

Heritage, J. (1984). *Garfinkel and ethnomethodology.* Cambridge: Polity Press.

Hester, S., & Francis, D. (1997). Reality analysis in a classroom storytelling. *British Journal of Sociology, 48*(1), 95–111.

Hutchby, R., & Wooffitt, R. (1998). *Conversation analysis.* Cambridge: Polity.

Lynch, M. (2002). The living text: Written instructions and situated actions in telephone surveys. In: D. W. Maynard, H. Houtkoop-Steenstra, N. C. Schaeffer, & J. van der Zouwen (Eds), *Standardisation and tacit knowledge. Interaction and practice in the survey interview* (pp. 125–151). New York: Wiley.

Lynch, M., & Peyrot, M. (1992). Introduction: A readers guide to ethnomethodology. *Qualitative Sociology, 15*(2), 113–123.

Matless, D. (1995). The art of right living: Landscape and citizenship, 1918–1939. In: S. Pile, & N. Thrift (Eds), *Mapping the subject: Geographies of cultural transformation* (pp. 93–122). London: Routledge.

McCabe, S. (2001). *Worlds of reason: The praxis of accounting for 'Day Visitor' behaviour in the Peak National Park. A qualitative investigation.* Unpublished PhD thesis, University of Derby.

McCabe, S. (2002). The tourist experience and everyday life. In: G. M. S. Dann (Ed.), *The tourist as a metaphor of the social world* (pp. 61–76). Wallingford: CAB International.

McCabe, S. (2003). Gender, identity and discourse in the consumption of leisure travel: An ethno-methodological approach. *Tourism Recreation Research, 28*(2), 67–75.

McCabe, S. (2005). Who is a tourist? A critical review. *Tourist studies, 5*(1), 85–104.

McCabe, S., & Stokoe, E. H. (2004). Place and identity in tourist accounts. *Annals of Tourism Research, 31*(3), 601–622.

Miller, G., & Holstein, J. A. (1993). Reconsidering social constructionism. In: J. A. Holstein, & G. Miller (Eds), *Reconsidering social constructionism*. New York: Aldine de Gruyter.

Moore, K. (2002). The discursive tourist. In: G. M. S. Dann (Ed.), *The tourist as a metaphor of the social world* (pp. 41–60). Wallingford: CAB International.

Munt, I. (1994). The other postmodern tourism: Culture, travel and the new middle classes. *Theory, Culture and Society, 11*, 101–123.

Nilan, P. (1995). Membership categorization devices under construction: Social identity boundary maintenance in everyday discourse. *Australian Review of Applied Linguistics, 18*, 69–94.

Noy, C. (2004). This trip really changed me backpackers' narratives of self-change. *Annals of Tourism Research, 31*(1), 78–102.

Psathas, G. (1995). *Conversation analysis: The study of talk in interaction*. Thousand Oaks, CA: Sage.

Schegloff, E. (1972). Notes on a conversational practice: Formulating place. In: D. Sudnow (Ed.), *Studies in social interaction* (pp. 75–119). New York: Free Press.

Stokoe, E. (2005). Analyzing gender and language. *Journal of Sociolinguistics, 9*(1), 118–133.

Stokoe, E. (2006). On ethnomethodology, feminism, and the analysis of categorical reference to gender in talk-in-interaction. *Sociological Review, 54*(3), 467–494.

Stokoe, E. (2007). Categories and sequences: Formulating gender in talk-in-interaction. In: L. Litosseliti, H. Saunston, K. Segall, & J. Sunderland (Eds), *Gender and language: Theoretical and methodological approaches*. London: Palgrave MacMillan.

ten Have, P. (2004). *Understanding qualitative research and ethnomethodology*. London: Sage.

Tribe, J. (2006). The truth about tourism. *Annals of Tourism Research, 33*(2), 360–381.

Urry, J. (1994). Cultural change and contemporary tourism. *Leisure Studies, 13*, 233–238.

Watson, G. (1994). A comparison of social constructionist and ethnomethodological descriptions of how a judge distinguished between the erotic and the obscene. *Philosophy of the Social Sciences, 24*(4), 405–425.

West, C., & Fernstermaker, S. (1993). Power, inequality, and the accomplishment of gender: An ethnomethodological view. In: P. England (Ed.), *Theory on gender/feminism on theory* (pp. 151–174). New York: Aldine de Gruyter.

Chapter 15

From Principles to Practices in Feminist Tourism Research: A Call for Greater Use of the Survey Method and the Solicited Diary

Bente Heimtun

In the chapter I address an important issue for tourism research; criteria for choosing the most appropriate research technique. Based on feminist research principles I argue for the use of the multitude of methods or techniques. The discussions revolve around two under-used techniques in feminist research whether this is related to tourism studies or the investigation of other gendered phenomenon; the survey method and the solicited diary. I show that both satisfy feminist goals. The chapter is a result of methodological considerations made while discussing appropriate methods in a feminist PhD project on Norwegian mid-life single women's holidaymaking and identity related issues. In the study the holiday was studied in three phases (Clawson & Knetsch, 1966, pp. 33–34); the anticipation and planning of the holiday, the actual holiday and the recollection of the holiday. This chapter revolves around discussion of data collection related to phase two; the actual holiday. This phase was chosen as it always proposes a challenge to the researcher to include a multitude of experiences, as the data collection often is site or time specific.

First, I examine feminist research principles such as inclusion, power relations, reflexivity and political agenda. Secondly, I briefly discuss the qualitative paradigm in feminist research which has led to a predominance of qualitative methods and point to the fact that most tourism research fall into the quantitative paradigm and the use of such techniques. This proposes a challenge for feminist tourism studies when it comes to arguing for counting and the use of surveys, and for tourism studies when legitimating in-depth knowledge. Thirdly, I examine the survey and the solicited diary as potential feminist methods in the sense that, in different ways, they each fulfil feminist goals. Fourthly, I end the chapter by briefly discussing which of the two research techniques proposes the most appropriate method in a feminist study of mid-life single women's holidaymaking and identity. The chapter is then about both research methods as the techniques of research, and research methodology as the context that emerges from epistemology and informs the choice of method. Methodology then is the theory or philosophy of how to do research (Belsky, 2004, p. 277; Harding, 1987, pp. 2–3). It determines the methods, outlines the questions and forms the analysis, and emerges from the researcher's philosophical standing.

Feminist Goals

In spite of the development of various feminist methodologies such as feminist empiricism, standpoint theory and post-structural feminism (Aitchison, 2005, pp. 27–30), and hence methods, feminist researchers are committed to common goals (see for instance Cancian, 1992, p. 640; Cook & Fonow, 1986, p. 5; DeVault, 1996, pp. 32–34; Morris, Woodward, & Peters, 1998, pp. 220–222). Cook and Fonow, and Cancian identify five principles of feminist methodologies; Morris et al. name four principles, whereas DeVault discusses three common goals. There are common characteristics in the principles identified by these researchers and I have sorted them into four categories (Figure 15.1). The first common goal is to include women in the research process. This aim is important in order to identify oppression, diversity and ideological mechanisms that affect women's lives or make the invisible visible, as Morris et al. (1998, p. 220) see it. This is a step towards challenging phallocentrism in "malestream" science. Phallocentrism refers to the texts of the white, male, Eurocentric philosophical tradition that have turned philosophy

Cook and Fonow 1986	Cancian 1992	DeVault 1996	Morris *et al.* 1998	Common traits
Include all women in research to excavate suppression	Giving a voice to everyday experience of women	Include all women in research to excavate suppression	Making the lives of women visible	An inclusive research process
Reduce harm and control over female participants in the research process	Reject rigid separation between researcher and the researched	Reduce harm and control over female participants in the research process	Treating the participants as partners and collaborators	Reduction of power relations in the research process
Change women's lives by challenging existing theories	A political agenda for improving women's lives	Change women's lives by challenging existing theories	Doing research for women	A political agenda in the research process
The researcher must anticipate every consequence the research has for the participants	A moral commitment to reduce inequality		Commitment to reflexivity and openness	A reflexive and ethical research process

Figure 15.1: Feminist research goals.

into a machine of intimidation and exclusion of women's perspectives (Braidotti, 1993, p. 2; Keller & Grontkowski, 1983, p. 220; Wearing, 1998, p. 108). For instance, the stories that are told about tourists are generally about the male, white, middle class tourist; her's and other tourist's stories are mostly forgotten.

The second common goal is to reduce power relations in the research process. This is done by developing inclusive research procedures and focusing on hierarchies of power and control in research relations (Cancian, 1992, p. 627; Morris et al., 1998, p. 221). Most feminist epistemologies question the nature of objectivity, which is fundamental in much research, instead of focusing on the equality in the relationships between the researcher and the participants (see for instance Stanley, 1990, p. 23). The third principle is an explicit political research agenda. Feminists aim to change women's lives by challenging existing theories, research practices and agendas. This is the result of epistemologies that are explicitly political. For instance, Kelly, Regan, and Burton (1994, p. 28), express such a political agenda as "our desire to do, and goal in doing, research is to create useful knowledge, knowledge which can be used by ourselves and others to make a difference".

The fourth common goal is a reflexive and ethical research process. For instance, Cook and Fonow (1986, p. 12) point to ethical concerns in the sense that the researcher must anticipate every consequence the research has for the participants. Jordan (2003, p. 12) and Morris et al. (1998, p. 222) are concerned with the importance of reflexivity, openness and intellectual honesty in feminist research. Jordan critically examines her role as a researcher by making explicit her personal and academic rationale. Related to the same principle Morris et al. (1998) introduce an important point; an awareness of possible close relationships between the researcher and the researched and the effect of such closeness:

> The closer our subject area is to our own lives and experiences, the more we can expect our own beliefs about the world to shape our work, the questions we ask, the interpretations we generate from our findings and, indeed, every aspect of the research process. (Morris et al., 1998, p. 222)

Very often the researcher and the research participants share common traits, activities, lifestyles and so on. This implies that it is important to deal with such closeness in every step of the research and to be aware of and clear about the potential influence of the researcher's voice upon the study.

To sum up this first part of the chapter, feminist methodologies are often committed to four common goals: inclusion, reduction of power relations, a political agenda and ethical and reflexive concerns. In debates on tourism methodology such principles are also asked for, especially by feminist and critical researchers. For instance, Goodson and Phillimore (2004, pp. 36, 40) point to the need for accepting the idea that the researcher and the researched are partners, and for a greater level of self-reflexivity and ethics within research agendas (see also Hall, 2004, p. 150; Ryan, 2005). Swain takes the principle of reflexivity in tourism research even further by bringing in the body:

> A focus on embodiment in qualitative research acknowledges the corporeal selves of the researchers as well as the researched "subjects" as primary factors in the research process. (Swain, 2004, p. 103)

This ongoing debate calls for attention to the importance of linking feminist principles to tourism research.

The Paradigm Discussion

The aim of this chapter is to examine one qualitative and one quantitative research technique in order to evaluate their appropriateness for feminist tourism research. I address this issue in the third section. First, I briefly examine the relationship between qualitative and quantitative methodologies and the two kinds of methods. One reason for choosing the methods of the survey and the solicited diary is to demonstrate that both, although often associated with different paradigms, are imbued with potential strengths and weaknesses for feminist research. A second reason is that both methods, and especially the method of diary-writing, are seldom used in feminist research (Elliot, 1997, p. 2) or in tourism studies (Dann, Nash, & Pearce, 1988, p. 25; Markwell & Basche, 1998, p. 229; Pearce, 1988, p. 56). A third reason is to question the notion, stemming from the 1970s and standpoint feminism, that such research is equated with qualitative techniques (Eichler, 1997, p. 11; Jayaratne & Stewart, 1991; Maynard, 1994, p. 12; Oakley, 1998, p. 724). For instance, standpoint feminists criticise quantification because it does not valorise women's ways of knowing (Mattingly & Falconer-Al-Hindi, 1995, p. 431). Feminist post-structuralists challenge the notion of a homogenous gender as an analytical category and thereby the possibility to count at all (Lawson, 1995, p. 453). According to Oakley (1998, 2000) the rejection of quantitative methods is due to feminists' lack of separation between quantitative and qualitative methodologies or paradigms and quantitative and qualitative methods:

> The uses of "qualitative" research methods have been aligned with a feminist perspective, while "quantitative" methods have been seen as implicitly or explicitly defensive of the (masculinist) status quo. (Oakley, 1998, p. 707)

I aim to show that both methods can be useful for the development of feminist tourism research and practice (Sprague & Zimmerman, 1989, p. 72; Maynard, 1994, p. 13), as feminism is not a specific method but an epistemological perspective (Reinharz, 1992, p. 241).

It is common to argue that the philosophical position combined with the nature of the research question is the foundation of choosing the "right" method (Kelly et al., 1994, p. 35; Letherby, 2004, p. 178; Oakley, 2000, p. 305). However, if the researcher does not separate methodologies from methods this ideal is not easily obtainable (Oakley, 1998, 2000). For instance, it has led feminist empiricists or first wave feminists to only use quantitative techniques in order to visualise female oppression in society (Aitchison, 2000a, 2003, p. 25; Eichler, 1988, p. 134; Harding, 1993, p. 51). Furthermore, socialist feminists or second wave feminists, who call for a feminist "standpoint" in research, have idealised women's voices heard through in-depth investigations and, hence, the use of qualitative techniques (Harding, 1993, p. 56). The close link between methodology and method is also found among post-structural feminists who reject the notion of one feminist voice and the unquestioning use of traditional methods as such (see for instance Aitchison, 2000a, p. 183; Eichler, 1997, p. 16; Stanley & Wise, 1990, p. 28). As subversion is embedded in language, deconstruction is seen as the appropriate method in this stance (Butler, 1999, p. 13; Braidotti, 1993; Foucault, 1988; Keller & Grontkowski, 1983, p. 208; Lloyd, 1984; Ramazonÿlu & Holland, 2002, p. 86). Recently, feminists have started to rethink the relationship between discourse and materiality (see for instance Aitchison, 2000a, 2005; McNay, 2000, 2004), resulting in a less rigid relationship between paradigm and method (Lawson, 1995, p. 454). This development has also provided new grounds for discussing the link between method-ology, method and research questions. It is not only feminist research that is criticised for being one-sided when it comes to the relationship between paradigm and method, the same goes for tourism studies. Most tourism research falls into the category of the "traditional period" or positivism (Botterill, 2001, p. 199; Dann & Phillips, 2001, p. 248; Phillimore & Goodson, 2004, p. 10; Walle, 1997, p. 525) and, hence, follows rigid research agendas and is about quantification. Furthermore, it does not usually question the underlying philosoph-ical perspective to the research. As quantification has been an important aim for tourism research, qualitative methods have not been given much attention or credit (Riley & Love, 2000, p. 180). This trend is finally changing as reputable journals have started to accept and ask for such research (Dann & Phillips, 2001, p. 258) and tourism scholars have called for new dialogues in tourism research (see for instance Jamal & Hollinshead, 2001, p. 79).

One way of dealing with the methodological limitation in both feminist and tourism studies is for the researcher to clearly justify the choice of method and paradigm standing (Goodson & Phillimore, 2004, p. 38) by, among others, questioning underlying ideologi-cal assumptions. Feminist tourism researchers have already started such a process, for instance, by proposing a more critical view of the research process by introducing embod-iment, reflexivity and guidance for research (Aitchison, 2005; Goodson & Phillimore, 2004, p. 32; Swain, 2004). Furthermore, feminists have added to the discussions about the research process as value loaded and as an act of collaboration. However, in spite of fem-inists' positive influence upon methodological discussions in tourism research, feminists themselves continue to have ambivalent views about specific research techniques.

In sum, in both fields more reflections upon and discussions of methodological issues have been called for. In feminist literature such discussions revolve around, among others, whether or not quantitative techniques are compatible with feminist methodologies (see for instance Kelly et al., 1994; Jayaratne & Stewart, 1991). In the field of tourism the debate is about acknowledging critical and interpretative paradigms (Goodson & Phillimore, 2004, p. 35) and the use of various qualitative methods (see Ritchie, Burns, & Palmer, 2005). The fact that feminist researchers have taken an interest in tourism studies (see for instance Aitchison, 2001, 2005; Enloe, 1989; Fullagar, 2002; Gibson, 2001; Johnston, 2001; Pritchard, 2001; Swain & Momsen, 2002) contributes positively to its development as an academic field. For instance, tourism theories are critically scrutinised (Veijola & Jokinen, 1994), tourism methodologies are questioned (Aitchison, 2000b, 2005; Swain, 2004) and new gendered research questions are raised (see for instance Jordan, 2003; Simmons, 2003; Small, 2002; Wilson, 2004). On the other side the considerable skill among tourism scholars related to quantitative techniques such as surveys may benefit feminist colleagues if they acknowledge these as a legitimate method. For instance, quantitative data is often used as a means towards political influence on a local and national level. Tourism organi-sations frequently base their decisions on statistical information. Feminist tourism research must acknowledge that, in order to influence tourism development, marketing strategies and business ventures it is sometimes necessary to conduct quantitative studies. However, the counting should, of course, not be at the expense of the relationship between the process and the product (Letherby, 2004, p. 185). Although the qualitative paradigm is the foundation of much feminist research, there is a growing awareness or positive attitude towards the use of a multitude of techniques such as surveys. Furthermore, as more feminists work with tourism issues the ideological underpinnings of "traditional" tourism research are questioned and the relationship between paradigm and method become more blurred, hopefully in both fields.

Feminist Goals — Survey and Diary

I begin this third section by briefly discussing the applicability of conducting a survey in a feminist project before I proceed to discuss the method of the solicited diary. These discussions show that it is possible to achieve the feminist goals of inclusion, power reduction, reflexivity and the adoption of political agendas by using both techniques.

A greater awareness of the non-automatic relationship between in-depth methods and liberation for women through, and as a result of, the survey technique is growing. Letherby (2004, p. 178) is one feminist researcher that openly admits that she used to celebrate the in-depth interview as the best way of knowing. But after doing research she became aware of the fact that this technique can be just as exploitative as surveys (Letherby, 2003, p. 85). Not only has a more reflective view on power relations in qualitative methods led to a more positive stance towards quantitative techniques among feminists, but, findings also demonstrate that some women would rather share personal information anonymously than in a face-to-face situation (Kelly et al., 1994, p. 35). Both Letherby and Kelly et al. then refer to the feminist principle of reducing power relations in the research process as a means for including marginalised female voices. For instance, forcing women to face their own lives through face-to-face interactions with the researcher and/or other research participants may hinder some women's participation and important voices will then not be heard. However, filling out a well-crafted questionnaire may not be such an obstacle.

There is an increasing awareness among feminist researchers that the critique of the "gendered paradigm", when it comes to research methods, has failed (Fonow & Cook, 1991, p. 8; Jayaratne, 1983, p. 158; Jayaratne & Stewart, 1991, p. 101; Kelly et al., 1994, p. 34; Letherby, 2004, p. 176; Maynard, 1994, pp. 11–12; Oakley, 2000; Sprague & Zimmerman, 1989). For instance, Sprague and Zimmerman (1989, p. 73) argue that quantitative data are not more "factual" than qualitative data, but rather provide opportunities for critique and action on a public level. Nor is it the case that all researchers conducting a survey regard themselves as "neutral researchers producing objective and value-free 'facts'" (Maynard, 1994, p. 13). Positivism is then no more intrinsic to quantitative research than feminism is to qualitative research (Lawson, 1995, p. 451). These arguments related to the survey method point to the goals of both reflexivity and the adoption of a political agenda.

Counting is then consistent with feminist goals. However, this does not mean that quantitative techniques are always the most appropriate way to produce data on women's lives (Kelly, Regan, & Burton, 1992, p. 150). I return to this point in the fourth section. When it comes to including quantification in a feminist study Rocheleau suggests asking three

questions: "Who counts? … Why and when should we count? … How can we fully integrate the gendered insights of stories and pictures with the rigour and comparative value
of quantitative method?" (Rocheleau, 1995, p. 460). This implies a discussion of power,
inclusion, reflexivity and politics. The first question refers to both the counters and the
counted. For instance, in a study of gendered interests in a social forestry program in the
Dominican Republic, women and poor people were privileged as participants (Rocheleau,
1995, p. 461). The study also wanted to avoid the detachment of the women in their community by forming a research team of both women and men:

> We sought to avoid the "women-and" orientation that can make women
> more visible, yet detaches them from both the social and ecological con-
> texts that sustain their lives. (Rocheleau, 1995, p. 461)

Such considerations demonstrate both reflexive and ethical praxis, as well as reducing
harm over the participants.

The second question is about clearly defining which technique is the most appropriate to
investigate a phenomenon. For example, Maynard (1994, p. 13) suggests that a survey is suitable for feminism when the results have potential as a political tool. She reports that studies
showing the extent and severity of violence in women's lives may influence politicians' more
than individual stories. Lawson (1995, p. 451) claims that sometimes it is the measurable elements of female experiences that are the best way to reveal how oppression operates. The
potential of counting as a means for new action towards women is also noticed by Cook and
Fonow "a well crafted quantitative study may be more useful to policy makers and cause less
harm to women than a poorly crafted qualitative one" (Cook & Fonow, 1991, p. 8).

Studies that explicitly deal with changing the lives of women may therefore benefit
from qualitative methods such as a survey. Politicians and authorities then have tools for
presenting the voices of one or more categories of women and their everyday experiences.

The third question is about mixing quantitative and qualitative research methods in a
study so that a particular phenomenon can be investigated in-breadth as well as in-depth.
In Jayaratne and Stewart's (1991, pp. 101–102) strategies for practical implementation of
a feminist perspective in social science the use of mixed methods is advocated. "*Whenever
possible, we should use research designs which combine quantitative and qualitative methods*" (Jayaratne & Stewart, 1991, p. 102, emphasis in original). The combination of methods makes the research product more powerful in the sense that it both tests theory
effectively and is more convincing. It makes it possible to include many categories of
women, as well as provide in-depth insights within each category. Executed in accordance
with feminist goals, surveys can therefore be an appropriate feminist method. However, it
is not always the right method to select in a study, as I show in the fourth section. First,
however, I examine the feminist principles in relation to the method of diary-writing.

As a qualitative technique, the solicited diary is, as such, consistent with the feminist
goals (Bell, 1998, p. 76). However, it has not been given much attention in feminist research
(Elliot, 1997; Meth, 2003, p. 195). This statement is only partly true if we include autobiographical diaries as an important source for knowledge in research (Fullagar, 2002;
Griffiths, 1995; Lesnik, 1987, p. 40; Stanley, 1992, p. 89). Such autobiographical diaries
build upon people's writings of everyday life where the writing is not related to a specific

research topic or project. The diary-writing is then not a method, but a behaviour undertaken in the course of everyday life. Such diaries are written for private and personal purposes only although, at a later point of time, might be turned into a text for academic investigations. It is the application of diaries produced specifically at the researcher's request that is less common in feminist research (Bell, 1998, p. 72). Such diaries are labelled "solicited" diaries (Meth, 2003, p. 196). The nature of a solicited diary requires an awareness of the relationship between the researcher and the participants. It is the result of negotiation between the two parties and, as such, written for a distinct purpose. It is the nature of solicited diaries and feminist goals that I examine.

The method of solicited diaries reduces the power relations between the researcher and the research participants. It is an excellent way for the researched to be heard on their own terms (Bell, 1998, p. 75) and, as such, it is an empowering method (Meth, 2003, p. 203). Although the researcher selects the topic, each participant can interpret the questions and is free to express personal experiences or not without feeling the same pressure from the researcher as might be experienced in an interview. That research participants can express such power is exemplified by Bagnoli (2004), whose one participant turned the research into a therapeutic setting for him. In many ways the researcher hands over the power of the research process to the participants by collecting data through diaries. It is an obvious risk that, in a worst case scenario, no data may be collected at all, for instance, if the diarist neglects or forgets the assignment. However, it is also a great way of showing the participants that they are considered responsible and trusted. For instance, Bagnoli (2004) engaged young people from England and Italy to write diaries in her study and reports of enthusiastic participants and a high response rate, in spite of not offering any rewards. Meth (2003, p. 197) also reports of a high response rate in her African study although she paid each diarist half a week's earnings for a completed diary. Elliot (1997) combined solicited diaries with personal interviews in her study of health experiences and found that the diaries functioned as a preparation for the interview just as much for the participants as for her. In this way the research participants' experiences were much more the basis of the interview than usually is the case in other qualitative techniques, and the power was very much in the hands of the participants. The feminist principle of empowerment is then highly accommodated through this method.

Despite eager participants Bell (1998, p. 84) questions whether the solicited diary truly represents people's stories. This concern is related to the goal of a reflexive research process. By investigating her own field diary, Bell shows how her voice was very much directed towards an audience:

> The way I was undertaking the research seems to have meant that I maintained a "public" voice (which I felt would be acceptable academically) even in my private diary. (Bell, 1998, p. 83)

This is also the case for the solicited diaries (Meth, 2003, p. 202), but it does not automatically mean that such writing is not a site for self-reflection (Jokinen, 2004, p. 341). The content in diaries is always selected, but this does not imply that the diarists are not truthful or always selective in what they choose to impart. Bagnoli (2004) reports of diaries as an instrument for self-scrutiny and change among her participants. Her close relationship with the research participants, in the sense that they were all migrants, made Bagnoli reflect upon her autobiography as well. The method of the solicited diary then proposes a site for reflexive research, both for the researcher and the participants. In these examples the researcher clearly stated this process in the publications.

The reflexive processes as a result of the diary-writing is a starting point for changes, perhaps not on a political level in the first round, but at least on a personal one (Bagnoli, 2004). Particularly in studies with multiple methods the possibility to reflect upon certain dimensions of one's life through writing and by talking to others in the same situation may bring about changes. Elliot (1997) shows that this is the case in her study of mute people. Meth (2003, p. 201) claims that the solicited diary may provide the participants with a different platform from which they can deal with their everyday lives. Very often changes occur as a result of people becoming aware of their situation. Solicited diaries are a very purposeful means towards starting such a process, and hence, fulfilling the feminist principle of political agenda.

Meth (2003, p. 203) concludes that solicited diaries are an excellent method for allowing women's voices to be heard. They can be completed by almost anybody at almost any time, and over different periods of time. Even participants that are not literate can participate, as voice diaries can provide as much insight as written ones. Diaries can be a useful technique for including several categories of tourists and types of holidaymaking. Usually research on holiday experiences is undertaken at one time because many tourists are transient (Squires, 1994, p. 10). Solicited diaries make it possible to follow the tourist in spite of changes in time and space. The method offers flexibility and variations in the stories told and it provides a temporal insight into the women's experiences (Meth, 2003, p. 198). Contrary to one-off events such as interviews or surveys, the benefit of diaries is their longitudinal character in the sense that complex topics can be voiced and followed over a longer period of time (Bagnoli, 2004, p. 1). The feminist principle of an inclusive research process is then obtainable.

A possible weakness of the diary as a feminist method is that it is decontextualised and individualistic, as the participants write their diaries in isolation from each other and the researcher. But, as Meth (2003, p. 199) concludes, the degree of decontextualisation depends upon how the participants manage the research process and how well the researcher highlights the social nature of research. In order to make the research more contextual and less individualistic she also proposes the combination of diaries and focus groups (Meth, 2003, p. 200). The two methods complement each other in the sense that the diaries give room for intimate and personal experiences whereas the focus group conversations provide interactive discussions on a range of issues.

The discussions above show that both surveys and solicited diaries fulfil feminist goals of inclusion, power relations, liberation and reflexivity. However, not every study benefits from conducting a survey or collecting data through solicited diaries. The nature of the research question often presupposes some kinds of techniques, and the techniques imply boundaries related to sample, distribution and data quality when it comes to in-depth or in-breadth input.

Surveys or Solicited Diaries in a Study of Mid-life Single Women and Holidaymaking

In this last section I discuss the most appropriate technique for investigating how the summer holiday is linked to or expresses mid-life single women's sense of self or identity from a feminist perspective. The notion of self-development as a result of leisure travel is common among tourism scholars (see for instance Desforges, 2000; Elsrud, 2001; Galani-Moutafi, 2000; McCabe, 2002; Neumann, 1992; Wearing & Neil, 2000). Following Lawson, identity matters are "uncountable" and therefore exclude the survey method (Lawson, 1995, p. 454). I partly agree with this statement although believe that it is possible to test out aspects of subjectivity and identity in a survey when profound in-depth knowledge exists. For instance, when combined with qualitative techniques that deliver knowledge about the meaning, for instance, of holidaymaking that could be tested in a survey. Although doable and in accordance with feminist research principles, a survey is not necessarily the best way to produce data on the holiday experiences and single women's sense of self as it implies predetermined questions and will not allow new insights. Furthermore, a survey only obtains descriptive patterns of the relationship between self and holiday.

I, in relation to my own research, could have distributed a questionnaire through different channels of tour operators and travel agencies, but it would not reach women that purchased their holidays elsewhere. In addition, single women who stayed at home or visited friends and relatives during their "holiday time" would not have been given the opportunity to participate as they would be too difficult to include. An understanding of the relationship between the holiday experiences and this group of women's sense of self was just as important as that of those travelling within the tourism industry. A survey was then not considered the best method in my PhD project.

An in-depth study makes it easier to capture different kinds of holidaymaking and travel. It proposes a simpler way to include different voices, in the sense that a diversity of ways to spend the holiday can be studied. By asking women to keep diaries during their holiday it is possible to collect data on home-based holidays, on visits to friends and relatives and on commercially bought holidays. A second argument in favour of solicited diaries is their longitudinal character in the sense that they give the participants the opportunity to reflect upon holidaymaking over a longer period of time. A third reason is that solicited diaries are suitable for investigating subjectivities and identity issues (Bagnoli, 2004; Fullagar, 2002). However, there is one important obstacle; the participants can refuse to keep a diary, or due to time constraints they are unable to write about experiences and activities. In a study there are ways to reduce such limitation, for instance, the researcher can build loyalty to the project through close ties to the participants, choose participants devoted to the research questions and involve the participants through more than one mode of data collections. In spite of such limitations the method of solicited diary was considered the most appropriate method in my PhD project.

In my study, the limitations were sought reduced by using two data collection methods; focus group interviews and diaries. First, the participants met in the groups; there they were instructed on the diary writing. This step was designed to ensure the participants' involvement, as they were informed that the writings would also form the basis for a second group discussion. Furthermore, the participants were explicitly asked if they were willing to keep a diary during their holiday in the recruitment process. When explained the reasons for applying this research technique most participants in this study expressed a willingness to write a diary. The worry that the participants would neglect the writing assignment was not confirmed as 28 of the 30 women kept a diary for up to 14 holidaying days.

Conclusion

In this chapter I have discussed four feminist research goals: inclusion, power relations, reflexivity and political agendas. Such principles are equally important to feminist researchers irrespective of their philosophical standings or epistemological positions, and whether they study tourism or other phenomenon. I have shown that, in spite of the rejection of quantitative methods, surveys as much as solicited diaries can fulfil feminist goals. However, not all feminist research should be concerned with quantification and counting, as research questions related to topics such as identity construction and sense of self are often better answered through qualitative techniques. When investigating the holiday experiences of mid-life single women, the solicited diary is an appropriate method in the sense that it enables the inclusion of many voices, regardless of holiday preferences. It is also a unique method for collecting data over a longer period of time as the participants carry with them the questions and a means to communicate their answers on a daily basis. For a tourism researcher this is significant in order to understand the women's tourism behaviours more thoroughly. In my PhD study the diaries even made it possible to study all kinds of holidaymaking. Traditionally tourism research is preoccupied with investigating tourists as consumers. People, who visit friends and relatives, travel to the family's holiday home or day-trippers are seldom studied. By asking a heterogeneous group of mid-life single women to keep a diary, a better insight into this category's relationship to holiday making was possible. In summary, diary-writing is then an excellent feminist research technique in the sense that it is empowering, reflexive, inclusive and potentially an instrument for change.

References

Aitchison, C. (2000a). Women in leisure services: Managing the social-cultural nexus of gender equity. *Managing Leisure*, 5, 181–191.

Aitchison, C. (2000b). Poststructural feminist theories of representing others: A response to the 'crisis' in leisure studies' discourse. *Leisure Studies*, 19, 127–144.

Aitchison, C. (2001). Theorizing other discourses of tourism, gender and culture. Can the subaltern speak (in tourism)? *Tourist Studies*, 1, 133–147.

Aitchison, C. (2003). *Gender and leisure: Social and cultural perspectives* (1st ed.). London: Routledge.

Aitchison, C. (2005). Feminist and gender perspectives in leisure and tourism research. In: B. W. Ritchie, P. Burns, & C. Palmer (Eds), *Tourism research methods: Integrating theory with practice* (pp. 21–36). Oxon: Cabi Publishing.

Bagnoli, A. (2004). Researching identities with multi-method autobiographies. *Sociological Research Online*, 9. http://www.socresonline.org.uk/9/2/bagnoli.html

Bell, L. (1998). Public and private meanings in diaries: Researching family and childcare. In: J. Ribbens, & R. Edwards (Eds). *Feminist dilemmas in qualitative research: Public knowledge and private lives* (pp. 72–86). London: Sage.

Belsky, J. (2004). Contributions of qualitative research to understanding the politics of community ecotourism. In: J. Phillimore, & L. Goodson (Eds). *Qualitative research in tourism: Ontologies, epistemologies and methodologies* (pp. 273–291). London: Routledge.

Botterill, D. (2001). The epistemology of a set of tourism studies. *Leisure Studies*, *20*, 199–214.

Braidotti, R. (1993). Embodiment, sexual difference and the nomadic subject. *Hypatia*, *8*, 1–13.

Butler, J. (1999). *Gender trouble: Feminism and the subversion of identity* (10th ed.). New York: Routledge.

Cancian, F. M. (1992). Feminist science: Methodologies that challenge inequality. *Gender & Society*, *6*, 623–642.

Clawson, M., & Knetsch, J. L. (1966). *Economics of outdoor recreation*. Baltimore: The John Hopkins Press.

Cook, J. A., & Fonow, M. M. (1986). Knowledge and women's interests: Issues of epistemology and methodology in feminist sociological research. *Sociological Inquiry*, *56*, 2–29.

Dann, G., Nash, D., & Pearce, P. (1988). Methodology in tourism research. *Annals of Tourism Research*, *15*, 1–28.

Dann, G. M. S., & Phillips, J. (2001). Qualitative tourism research in the late twentieth century and beyond. In: B. Faulkner, G. Moscardo, & E. Laws (Eds), *Tourism in the twenty-first century* (pp. 247–265). London: Continuum.

Desforges, L. (2000). Traveling the world: Identity and travel biography. *Annals of Tourism Research*, *27*, 926–945.

DeVault, M. L. (1996). Talking back to sociology: Distinctive contributions of feminist methodology. *Annual Review Sociology*, *22*, 29–50.

Eichler, M. (1988). *Nonsexist research methods: A practical guide* (1st ed.). Boston: Allen & Unvin.

Eichler, M. (1997). Feminist methodology. *Current Sociology*, *45*, 9–36.

Elliot, H. (1997). The use of diaries in sociological research on health experiences. *Sociological Research Online*, *2*, 2. http://www.socresonline.org.uk/socresonline/2/2/7.html

Elsrud, T. (2001). Risk creation in traveling: Backpacker adventure narration. *Annals of Tourism Research*, *28*, 597–617.

Enloe, C. (1989). *Bananas, beaches and bases: Making feminist sense of international politics* (1st ed.). London: Pandora.

Fonow, M. M., & Cook, J. (1991). *Beyond methodology: Feminist scholarship as lived research* (1st ed.). Bloomington: Indiana University Press.

Foucault, M. (1988). *The care of the self: Volume 3 of the history of sexuality* (1st ed.). New York: Vintage Books.

Fullagar, S. (2002). Narratives of travel: Desire and movement of feminine subjectivity. *Leisure Studies*, *21*, 57–74.

Galani-Moutafi, V. (2000). The self and the other: Traveler, ethnographer, tourist. *Annals of Tourism Research*, *27*, 203–224.

Gibson, H. (2001). Gender in tourism: Theoretical perspectives. In: Y. Apostolopoulos, S. Sönmez, & D. J. Timothy (Eds), *Women as producers and consumers of tourism in developing regions* (pp. 19–43). Westport: Praeger.

Griffiths, M. (1995). (Auto)biography and epistemology. *Educational Review*, *47*, 75–89.

Goodson, L., & Phillimore, J. (2004). The inquiry paradigm in qualitative tourism research. In: J. Phillimore, & L. Goodson (Eds), *Qualitative research in tourism: Ontologies, epistemologies and methodologies* (pp. 30–45). London: Routledge.

Hall, M. (2004). Reflexivity and tourism research: Situating myself and/with others. In: J. Phillimore, & L. Goodson (Eds), *Qualitative research in tourism: Ontologies, epistemologies and methodologies* (pp. 137–155). London: Routledge.

Harding, S. (1987). Introduction: Is there a feminist method? In: S. Harding (Ed.). *Feminism and methodology* (pp. 1–14). Bloomington: Open University Press.

Harding, S. (1993). Rethinking standpoint epistemology: "What is strong objectivity"? In: L. Alcoff, & E. Potter (Eds), *Feminist epistemologies* (pp. 49–82). New York: Routledge.

Jamal, T., & Hollinshead, K. (2001). Tourism and the forbidden zone: The underserved power of qualitative inquiry. *Tourism Management, 22,* 63–82.

Jayaratne, T. E. (1983). The value of quantitative methodology for feminist research. In: G. Bowles, & R. D. Klein (Eds), *Theories of women's studies* (pp. 140–161). London: Routledge & Kegan Paul.

Jayaratne, T. E., & Stewart, S. (1991). Quantitative and qualitative methods in social sciences: Current issues and practical strategies. In: M. M. Fonow, & J. Cook (Eds), *Beyond methodology: Feminist scholarship as lived research* (pp. 85–106). Bloomington: Indiana University Press.

Johnston, L. (2001). (Other) bodies and tourism studies. *Annals of Tourism Research, 28,* 180–201.

Jokinen, E. (2004). The makings of mother in diary narratives. *Qualitative Inquiry, 10,* 339–359.

Jordan, F. (2003). Gendered discourses of tourism: The experiences of mid-life women travelling solo. Unpublished doctoral dissertation, The University of Gloucestershire, Gloucestershire.

Keller, E. F., & Grontkowski, C. R. (1983). The mind's eye. In: S. Harding, &. M. B. Hintikka (Eds), *Discovering reality: Feminist perspectives on epistemology, metaphysics, methodology, and philosophy of science* (pp. 207–224). London: D. Reidel Publishing Company.

Kelly, L., Regan, L., & Burton, S. (1992). Defending the indefensible? Qualitative methods and feminist research. In: H. Hinds, A. Phoenix, & J. Stacey (Eds), *Working out: New directions for women's study* (pp. 149–160). London: The Falmer Press.

Kelly, L., Burton, S., & Regan, L. (1994). Researching women's lives or studying women's oppression? Reflections on what constitutes feminist research. In: M. Maynard, & J. Purvis (Eds), *Researching women's lives from a feminist perspective* (pp. 27–48). London: Taylor & Francis.

Lawson, V. (1995). The politics of difference: Examining the quantitative/qualitative dualism in post-structuralist feminist research. *Professional Geographer, 47,* 449–457.

Lensik, J. N. (1987). Expanding the boundaries of criticism: The diary as female autobiography. *Women's Studies, 14,* 39–53.

Letherby, G. (2003). *Feminist research in theory and practice* (1st ed.). Buckingham: Open University Press.

Letherby, G. (2004). Quoting and counting: An autobiographical response to Oakley. *Sociology, 38,* 175–189.

Lloyd, G. (1984). *The man of reason: "Male" and "female" in Western philosophy* (1st ed.). London: Methuen.

Markwell, K., & Basche, C. (1998). Using personal diaries to collect data. *Annals of Tourism Research, 25,* 228–230.

Mattingly, D. J., & Falconer-Al-Hindi, K. (1995). Should women count? A context for the debate. *Professional Geographer, 47,* 427–435.

Maynard, M. (1994). Methods, practice and epistemology: The debate about feminism and research. In: M. Maynard, & J. Purvis (Eds), *Researching women's lives from a feminist perspective* (pp. 10–26). London: Taylor & Francis.

McCabe, S. (2002). The tourist experience and everyday life. In: G. M. S. Dann (Ed.), *The tourist as a metaphor of the social world* (pp. 61–76). Oxon: CABI Publishing.

McNay, L. (2000). *Gender and agency: Reconfiguring the subject in feminist and social theory* (1st ed.). Cambridge: Polity Press.

McNay, L. (2004). Situated intersubjectivity. In: B. L. Marshall & A. Witz (Eds), *Engendering the social: Feminist encounters with sociological theory* (pp. 171–186). Maidenhead: Open University Press.

Meth, P. (2003). Entries and omissions: Using solicited diaries in geographical research. *Area, 35,* 195–205.

Morris, K., Woodward, D., & Peters, E. (1998). 'Whose side are you on?' Dilemmas in conducting feminist ethnographic research with young women. *International Journal of Social Research Methodology*, *1*, 217–230.

Neumann, M. (1992). The trail through experience: Finding self in the recollection of travel. In: C. Ellis, & M. G. Flaherty (Eds), *Investigating subjectivity* (pp. 176–201). Newbury Park: Sage.

Oakley, A. (1998). Gender, methodology and people's ways of knowing; some problems with feminism and the paradigm debate in social science. *Sociology*, *32*, 707–731.

Oakley, A. (2000). *Experiments in knowing: Gender and method in the social sciences* (1st ed.). Cambridge: Polity Press.

Pearce, D. G. (1988). Tourist time-budgets. *Annals of Tourism Research*, *15*, 106–121.

Phillimore, J., & Goodson, L. (2004). Progress in qualitative research in tourism: Epistemology, ontology and methodology. In: J. Phillimore, & L. Goodson (Eds), *Qualitative research in tourism: Ontologies, epistemologies and methodologies* (pp. 3–29). London: Routledge.

Pritchard, A. (2001). Tourism and representation: A scale for measuring gendered portrayals. *Leisure Studies*, *20*, 79–94.

Ramazonÿlu, C., & Holland, J. (2002). *Feminist methodology: Challenges and choices* (1st ed.). London: Sage.

Reinharz, S. (1992). *Feminist methods in social research* (1st ed.). Oxford: Oxford University Press.

Riley, R. W., & Love, L. L. (2000). The state of qualitative tourism research. *Annals of Tourism Research*, *27*, 164–187.

Ritchie, B. W., Burns, P., & Palmer, C. (Eds) (2005). *Tourism research methods: Integrating theory with practice*. Oxon: Cabi Publishing.

Rocheleau, D. (1995). Maps, numbers, text, and context: Mixing methods in feminist political ecology. *Professional Geographer*, *47*, 458–466.

Ryan, C. (2005). Ethics in tourism research: Objectivities and personal perspectives. In: B. W. Ritchie, P. Burns, & C. Palmer (Eds), *Tourism research methods: Integrating theory with practice* (pp. 9–20). Oxon: Cabi Publishing.

Simmons, B. A. (2003). Travel talk: When knowledge and practice collide. Tracking gendered discourses in popular texts; in the stories of contemporary Australian women who work in the travel industry; and women who begin international leisure travel in mid-life. Unpublished doctoral dissertation, University of Newcastle, Newcastle.

Small, J. (2002). Good and bad holiday experiences: Women's and girl's perspective. In: M. B. Swain, & J. H. Momsen (Eds), *Gender/Tourism/Fun(?)* (pp. 24–38). New York: Cognizant Communiction Corporation.

Sprague, J., & Zimmerman, M. K. (1989). Quality and quantity: Reconstructing feminist methodology. *The American Sociologist*, *20*, 71–86.

Squire, S. J. (1994). Accounting for cultural meanings: The interface between geography and tourism studies re-examined. *Progress in Human Geography*, *18*, 1–16.

Stanley, L. (1990). Feminist praxis and the academic mode of production. An editorial introduction. In: L. Stanley (Ed.), *Feminist praxis: Research, theory and epistemology in feminist sociology* (pp. 3–19). London: Routledge.

Stanley, L. (1992). *The auto/biographical I: The theory and practice of feminist auto/biography* (1st ed.). Manchester: Manchester University Press.

Stanley, L., & Wise, S. (1990). Method, methodology and epistemology in feminist research process. In: L. Stanley (Ed.), *Feminist praxis: Research, theory and epistemology in feminist sociology* (pp. 20–59). London: Routledge.

Swain, M. B. (2004). (Dis)embodied experience and power dynamics in tourism research. In: J. Phillimore, & L. Goodson (Eds), *Qualitative research in tourism: Ontologies, epistemologies and methodologies* (pp. 102–118). London: Routledge.

Swain, M. B., & Momsen, J. H. (Eds) (2002). *Gender/Tourism/Fun(?)* (1st ed.). New York: Cognizant Communiction Corporation.

Veijola, S., & Jokinen, E. (1994). The body in tourism. *Theory, Culture & Society, 11,* 125–151.

Walle, A. H. (1997). Quantitative versus qualitative tourism research. *Annals of Tourism Research, 24,* 524–536.

Wearing, B. (1998). *Leisure and feminist theory* (1st ed.). London: Sage.

Wearing, S., & Neil, J. (2000). Refiguring self and identity through volunteer tourism. *Society and Leisure, 23,* 389–419.

Wilson, E. W. (2004). A 'Journey of her own'? The impact of constraints on women's solo travel. Unpublished doctoral dissertation, Griffith University.

Chapter 16

Unresolved Power for Feminist Researchers Employing Memory-Work

Jennie Small, Kate Cadman, Lorraine Friend, Susanne Gannon, Christine Ingleton, Glenda Koutroulis, Coralie McCormack, Patricia Mitchell, Jenny Onyx, Kerry O'Regan and Sharn Rocco

Introduction

Memory-work is a feminist social constructionist method, which was developed in Germany by Frigga Haug et al. (1987 [with a second edition in 1999]). The method was developed explicitly to bridge the gap between theory and experience. It provides a way of exploring the process whereby individual woman become part of society and the ways in which women themselves participate in that process of socialisation. It is a group method, involving always the collective analysis of individual written memories. It is feminist in being explicitly liberationist in its intent.

There are three phases of the method in its basic form. In *Phase 1* the individual writes a memory focussed on a particular topic/'trigger'. *Phase 2* involves a collective examination of the memories in which the memories are theorised and new meanings result. The essence of *Phase 2* is the collective searching for common understanding, with the method allowing for the social nature of the construction of the memories to be realised. In *Phase 3* the material provided from both the individual written memories and the collective discussion of them is further theorised. This phase is essentially a recursive process in which the insights concerning the 'common sense' of each set of memories is related back to the earlier discussions and to theoretical discussions within the wider academic literature.

The use of memory-work as a method in feminist social research has become well established in Australia and New Zealand. The method has been used in a range of disciplines and fields of study including tourism and leisure studies. Feminist researchers (Crawford, Kippax, Onyx, Gault, & Benton, 1992; McCormack, 1995, 1998; Small, 2002, 2003, 2005a, 2005b) have examined women's holiday experiences through memory-work.

The Critical Turn in Tourism Studies: Innovative Research Methodologies
Copyright © 2007 by Elsevier Ltd.
All rights of reproduction in any form reserved.
ISBN: 0-08-045098-9

Crawford et al. (1992) have also employed memory-work to study men's experiences of holidays. Grant and Friend (1997) chose memory-work to analyse the relationship between the provision of leisure and the satisfaction level of the resultant leisure experience.

This chapter has been written by a memory-work collective of 11 academic women who have experience and particular interest in using memory-work as a feminist research methodology. We vary considerably in age and professional experience and have different levels of experience and expertise with memory-work methodology. We are from a wide range of academic disciplines. Four of the tourism/leisure researchers cited above (Friend, McCormack, Onyx and Small) were members of the collective.

Each of our experiences of facilitating memory-work has called upon us to investigate the dynamics of power that are played out and disrupted among researchers and participants in memory-work research projects. In undertaking the work reported here, we wanted to learn from each other's experiences of facilitating memory-work groups, specifically, the problematic positioning of ourselves as primary researchers in expressly non-hierarchical research.

Our working and writing together began when we attended a conference on memory-work as a research methodology, convened at the University of Technology, Sydney by Jennie Small and Jenny Onyx. During the course of this conference, our topic — conflicting issues around power for memory-work researchers — emerged as one that held unresolved and largely unexplored significance for us. In attempting to avoid the perpetuation of the exploitation of women (and other disenfranchised groups), feminists as researchers are particularly sensitive to the ethical issues of social research. Feminists are concerned that the traditional hierarchical relationship between researcher and participant means 'objectifying your sister' (Oakley, 1981, p. 41). Yet research contexts themselves very often make this relationship difficult to resist.

Following the formal papers presented during the first day of the conference, 11 of the delegates agreed to meet to participate in a memory-work session to explore our experiences of the method. The trigger we selected to analyse was 'Unresolved issues of power'. This trigger was designed to focus on one aspect of the methodology that we had repeatedly raised in the formal sessions the day before — the representation of voice, in particular, to what extent are participants' and/or researchers' voices silenced in both the process and the products of memory-work research. This chapter examines our perceptions of our lived experiences as researchers, the methodological dilemmas and relations of power that arose for us as we carried out the collaborative process of memory-work. Believing that we, as researchers, are active in the research process, it was important for us to understand our thoughts and feelings of our lived position in the process. The following is a candid account of 11 researchers.

Implementing the Memory-work Method

For our own project we adapted the memory-work process described in *Female sexualisation* (Haug et al., 1999), with particular reference to the interpretation of the method detailed in *Emotion and gender* (Crawford et al., 1992). Each of the memory-workers/authors came to the second day of the conference, the workshop session, with an individual written memory (*Phase 1*) relating to the negotiation of power within a memory-work group each of us had initiated. After brief discussion we agreed to form two groups, of five and six respectively, to examine and analyse our written experiences. Our collective analysis of the written memories (*Phase 2*) aimed to uncover common social understandings of events, to identify the social meanings and authority embodied and disrupted in the actions described, and to examine how these meanings were constructed. Both groups met for one and a half hours and then reported their discussions to the whole group. All sessions were taped.

Following our workshop, the taped discussions and written stories were copied and distributed to the members of the collective. As the 11 women are geographically scattered throughout Australia and New Zealand, we used communications technology to continue our collective analysis through writing (*Phase 3*). In this third phase, the material from both the written memories and the collective discussion was further theorised. Insights from 'common sense meanings' identified by the groups through their discussions were extended and related to theoretical discussions within the wider academic literature. Each member of the collective in turn wrote and rewrote the collective paper, drawing on the memory protocols, the taped discussions, and their own knowledge of the literature before forwarding it on electronically to the next writer. This process was repeated before the final editing process was carried out.

In our oral and written analyses, we discovered unexpected commonalities in our experience of unresolved power issues in the memory-work process. Few of these commonalties are addressed in the memory-work literature or emerged during our formal discussions of the methodology on Day 1 of the Memory-work Conference. Yet, many of them may be seen as a product of the methodology itself. The discussion in this chapter aims to theorise our experiences as memory-workers using the methodology by focusing on how we managed its key principles. These principles are: to use collectivity as a means of deriving common meaning; to collapse the dualism of subject and object within a specific research design; to understand the reproduction of social formation; and to reflect on memories as a means of agency and change. These issues revealed themselves as sites of struggle and anxiety for us as researchers who uncompromisingly embrace a feminist ideology within patriarchal hegemonic research structures. Our analyses moved us towards a new questioning of the core values and processes of memory-work as *method* and a re-evaluation of these fundamental principles.

Collectivity as a Means of Deriving Common Meaning

> The meanings of actions are not found in the actor's head but in the common meanings, which she/he negotiates in interaction with others. (Crawford et al., 1992, p. 53)

The common meanings are derived from the broader social, cultural context and prevailing relations of power.

As memory-work researchers, we seek to derive common meaning from our shared experiences, yet we cannot necessarily assume this commonality. The discursive construction of agency and difference within the group may foreground difference in which some may resist others' interpretations of a particular event. As Koutroulis (1993) found in her memory-work group, differences in 'reading' of events, whether through interpretation or application of a particular theory, can be regarded as inadequate or expose vehement oppositions among the group members.

Our workshop revealed a high degree of consensus rather than difference with regard to the issues highlighted by and identified within our written stories. We all continue to struggle with the powerful/powerless paradox of our positions as memory-work researchers. Issues of trust were seen to be highly significant as these are implicated in and by relations of power, and taken up 'as usual' or disrupted by researchers and/or participants. Memory-work can be painful for participants, including the researcher herself (Haug et al., 1999). However, it became apparent to us that when the researcher approaches the process with conscious intent to be participatory, to make explicit the usual relations of power and their effects and to disrupt these, trust within the research group can be quickly engendered by the process itself. The evolving, participatory dynamic of memory-work was clearly represented in our written memories of experiencing the process as researchers:

> Amazingly, great questions and discussion followed. There were also challenges by all to remember to speak in third person and not to talk over others. The group process was evolving. Three and a half hours later, after reading and analysing all the memories, they had finished. They agreed it had been a productive and fun session. 'What trigger should we use next time?' Annabel pulled out her ideas. There was discussion and other suggestions. They agreed to the trigger, 'An exhilarating clothing shopping experience' (Individual written memory).[1]

Nonetheless, for most of us, the 'collectivity' exposed a thinly disguised contradiction in our positions as researchers. These tensions were particularly strong where participants had not met as equals — where a researcher/lecturer/teacher/expert met with research participants whose co-operation she had solicited for her own research purposes and whose relative age and/or occupational status may be less powerful than hers. Our written memories and the discussion analysing these tensions highlighted the contradictions inherent in being responsible for the research, for the ultimate outcomes and for the explicit methodological feature of collectivity:

> *I felt like I was in charge; I was responsible but I didn't want to take over.*
> *I tried not to take over, but at the same time I wanted to make sure that I got*
> *out of it what I needed to get out of it…* (Collective discussion).

The contradictions and uncertainties arising from the necessary disruption of taken-for-granted relations of power inherent in more usual research methods were evidently confusing for participants and researcher alike. From a post-structural perspective these relations of power and their disruption can be seen to hinge upon particular hierarchical binaries such as speaking–silence, researcher–researched, objectivity–subjectivity, rational–emotional, male–female. The dilemmas we wrote and spoke about indicated

---

[1]Non-italicised quotations are from individual written memories (Phase 1). Italicised quotations are from the collective discussion (Phase 2).

the effects of our attempts to disrupt these binaries. In struggling to disrupt the researcher–researched and speaking–silent binaries, the researcher might be ambivalent regarding her own right to speak:

> No one commenced the discussion. Karen knew she had to start it. She wished they would take some ownership of the meeting. Through the meeting she found herself pursuing different lines. She felt she was 'facilitating' rather than being a 'co-researcher' and kept trying to stop (Individual written memory).

Collective memory-work:

> models a way of doing inquiry that promotes new forms of subjectivity via a refusal of individuality and a diffusion of the sites and practices from which dominance can be challenged. (Lather, 1991, p. 96)

However, this 'refusal of individuality' was experienced as almost impossible within the academic contexts that framed our research. We were highly sensitive to the ambiguities of our situation, and the tensions engendered were deeply felt:

> *The need to adopt as much of the responsibility as we need to, but to keep it as minimal as possible as well, then we can't police the procedures and get what we want out of it. We would be slipping into positivist and masculinist ways if we did...But in the end I was the one who was going to write the thesis, be awarded the academic award* (Collective discussion).

Regardless of the researcher's best intentions, it was difficult for both the participants and the researcher to take or give, respectively, authority in the facilitation and outcomes of the group process. One researcher (Mary) described her surprise when she still retained power as researcher after her and her co-researchers' prescribed roles in the memory-work group were disrupted:

> This was the third and final meeting of the group and arrangements had been clear. Mary [*researcher*] would do the hostess thing while they ate; over tea and coffee Liz [*other researcher*] would facilitate the session. However, now Mary had to break the news that Liz was sick and couldn't attend. Mary herself was in a complete panic...One of the participants organised the taping, another got everyone seated, and together they picked the first person to read his memory (in fact the shyest and most retiring member). Now who was facilitator? At first Mary thought her role had been changed into observer by this turn of events. During the session she realised that this wasn't so...(Individual written memory).

Although the researcher might be acutely aware of the collective processes that she hoped to engender, her reluctance to take up 'authority' could be read by participants negatively, as

a 'lack' rather than a difference in approach. One researcher recalled the following conversation in her group:

> [*researcher*] It seems to me…that there's concern that I don't give enough
> direction to the group.
> [*participant*] I don't think we said that. All I think was said was that it
> would be helpful to you, not necessarily us, if there was guidance. And didn't
> you say you had trouble concentrating on the memories and attending to the
> group as well?
> [*researcher*] Hmm, I think that's what I said. I do. I certainly do.
> [*participant*] What about if we share it [facilitation]?
> Some silence, some 'No's (Individual written memory).

As these excerpts from our stories indicate, while committed to the principles of collective memory-work, we experienced significant tensions inherent in working with a
method that requires 'going against the grain' of research-as-usual. The Memory-work
Research Conference as a whole illustrated how each woman experienced self-doubt about
her capabilities and credibility as a researcher in the eyes of the academic establishment.
We were inclined to claim the authority of the researcher over the researched and, at the
same time, to reject it. This paradoxical situation could leave us in a *terra nullius*:

> *It's a real sense of isolation — you're isolated because you're not even one
> of the group, really you don't come across as one of them and you're not
> one of them* (Collective discussion).

We felt responsible for the success of the event, but often could not or would not control
the discussion. There were contradictions and ambiguities in being, and desiring to be, at once
powerful–not powerful, controlling–open, traditional–creative, hierarchical–collaborative and
objective–subjective. These contradictions appeared at times to be mediating against the
researcher's intention to be, and to experience the method as, collaborative and participatory.

Throughout the conference there had been much debate about whether or not there might
be distinctly 'right' ways to 'do' collective memory-work. We agonised over variations in
method we had experienced or devised, and debated differences in terminology. We struggled over the question of what variations were possible for the method still to be 'memory-
work'. Particularly in the data collection phase of the memory-work processes, we had
engaged in a variety of patterns of participation ranging from virtual non-participation:

> *Feeling an outsider almost. They ignored me completely. I didn't have to
> worry about any facilitating, they were just getting on with it* (Collective
> discussion);

through subtle directing:

> *I found myself saying, 'I'm going to write a long memory' to set the stan-
> dard unobtrusively* (Collective discussion);

through reluctance:

> She felt she was being a facilitator rather than a co-researcher (Individual written memory);

to overt and acknowledged facilitation:

> *There was no doubt in my mind that that [facilitation] was my role* (Collective discussion).

The collective/control dilemma was seen to relate directly not just to the process but also to the reasons for which the group was formed, and its content:

> *I think you have to go in with something if you are the researcher. I think it's different if you come together as a collective. I think it depends on how and why the group is coming together — whether the theme emerges from the collective or whether the researcher says 'I want to know more about this'* (Collective discussion).

Thus the collective/control dichotomy reflects the difficulty posed by a key principle of the original concept of memory-work, the role of the researcher as the subject of her own research.

Collapse of Subject and Object

Haug states that collective memory-work is 'only possible if the subject and object of research are one and the same person' (Haug et al., 1999, p. 35). However, as researchers operating within defined academic structures, our roles become increasingly complex and invite further exploration. In our discussions we agreed that, for us, memory-work may be described as making the discourses within which we operate in the world more visible. Davies (1994, p. 83) describes the process of speaking and writing memories collectively as one in which researchers 'spin the web of themselves and find themselves in the act of that spinning, in the process of making sense out of the cultural threads through which lives are made'.

To achieve this requires the researcher to position herself *with* the participants. *With* the participants, we can open up the discourses and be both subject and object of our own research.

Another aspect of the research responsibility in collective memory-work, as we experienced the method, is an emotional commitment to the group. Participants should enjoy and/or gain from the experience, and we, as researchers, should use the data 'lovingly' and carefully with an eye to the potential consequences of representation. Our memories suggested that in the final analysis, this emotional commitment of a researcher to others in the group and to the integrity of the project's outcomes was a highly significant feature of the bonded collective experience generated by the memory-work method. This experience of emotional bonding was felt to be an important element, which could override tensions of subject/object positioning.

This concept of research as embodied experience is alien to many conventional notions of research, but sits comfortably with notions of feminist inquiry. We were aware that we experienced the process not just as co-researchers/facilitators but as women, as complex and embodied individuals. Being highly personal in nature, memory-work was identified as a highly emotional experience for both participants and researcher. Feminist researchers (Dupuis, 1999; Ellis, 1991; Ellis, Keisinger, & Tillmann-Healy, 1997; Friend, 2000; Stanley & Wise, 1990) have argued for the incorporation and acknowledgement of emotion in the research process, yet emotion has until recently most often been constructed as clouding reason. Barbalet (1998) and Scheff (1997) characterise emotion as comprising cognitive and dispositional elements. Emotion states include decision-making and a disposition to act, and as such, emotion contains elements of reason and action as well as of feeling. Emotion can no longer be regarded as a synonym for irrationality. Rather, our analysis suggested that emotionality is an acceptable, necessary and vital aspect of the embodiment of experience and therefore of the research process. Incorporating our feelings and emotions to understand, direct, analyse and interpret our stories in the memory-work process disrupts the rational/irrational binary that, within positivist traditions, has served to silence embodied feminist knowledges.

The Reproduction of Social Formation

A central concern of the methodology and its purpose, is to unravel 'subjectification', understood as:

> the process by which individuals work themselves into social structures
> they themselves do not consciously determine, but to which they subordi-
> nate themselves. (Haug et al., 1999, p. 59)

Unlike theories of socialisation, where the individual is a passive subject 'acted upon' by social forces, subjectification entails a degree of complicity, an active subordination of the subject within the social. As a group we recognised common ground in our struggles with issues surrounding subjectification.

A recurring concern for us was that other academics should acknowledge the methodology and us, as researchers, as legitimate and credible. The particular academic discipline, institution and academic standing of the researcher all impact on her confidence in her role within the memory-work group. One way in which this was evident in our study was as a concern about how the method should be implemented:

> *That methodology [memory-work] was so new and if I didn't do it in some*
> *sort of valid way [it would be questioned]. And there was already...debate*
> *and questions around it as a valid method. I wanted it all to go well. But I*
> *also wanted it to be seen as legitimate...[as it] was still very contentious,*
> *and probably still is. So there were all those things around the anxiety of*
> *getting started... (Collective discussion).*

Thus, despite the power conferred by academic knowledge and positioning, our stories of using memory-work highlighted the degrees of powerlessness and lack of control felt by all researchers at different stages of the method. The unresolved issues of power were not just to do with too much power but also with *lack* of power.

We wanted to be true to the feminist principles of the method but we were also aware of the conditions and sanctions produced within prevailing academic discourses that were usually applied to obtaining academic recognition and credentials. These contradictions became particularly acute where the memory-work was part of a higher degree and subject to academic supervision. Whilst some supervisors were highly supportive and encouraged their students to take up memory-work as a research methodology, others were hostile or suspicious of memory-work as a valid research paradigm. Even a benign supervisor may be conscious of the potential responses of examiners and others who will read what may be highly personal and emotive material and who will 'judge' the work in a traditional academic context.

Our acute awareness of our 'location' within the complex relations of power in academic institutions seemed in some memories even to have coloured our readings of the geographic sites we had chosen for our workshops:

> The smallish grey seminar room set in the 'power passage' between the Dean's and the school administrator's offices and across from the Graduate Studies Director's office seemed to engulf her. She opened some more windows (Individual written memory).

Adopting such an intentionally disruptive research methodology in academic disciplines which are unused to such methods can be read as dangerous, but it is also liberating, a literal 'breath of fresh air' in the suffocating halls of power.

While memory-work is widely acknowledged as a deeply felt emotional experience, it is primarily a research tool (with all that is then implied about its role in formal institutional and academic practices). We, the researchers, often found ourselves subjected to the demands of both these aspects of the process. Three powerful influences on our subjectification as situated memory-work researchers were: constructing and subjugating knowledge; the presentation of ourselves as competent researchers despite our fears; and our need to nurture.

Constructing and Subjugating Knowledge

Feminist epistemology values knowledges, which have traditionally been subjugated in academic contexts, particularly embodied knowledges that are constructed from and through lived experience. As feminist methodology, collective memory-work disrupts the conventions of positivist research with regard to 'how and where knowledge is produced and by whom, and ... what counts as knowledge' (Weedon, 1997, p. 7). In the tradition of feminist theorising, memory-work utilises experience expressed through written memory as valid data and legitimises the subjective personal voice of the researcher/researched. In so doing, memory-work creates the space for the otherwise silenced to speak of their experience. In this space all members are, or strive to be, more or less equal in terms of the knowledges constructed.

However, while such a space stimulates the sharing of personal experiences, not all of these are considered material for the public arena. There was a dilemma for us about our role in selecting which memories would be appropriate for the public arena and how the public might interpret these memories. There was concern that researchers, in suppressing certain knowledges in favour of others, which would 'count', could be acquiescing to and colluding with repressive discourses:

> *You're not wanting to disadvantage women, or whoever the group you are looking at, you don't want to disadvantage them by the outside reading so you are selecting them* (Collective discussion).

> *I think it's a major issue for me — choosing the memories — choosing how to present them, what order you present them, how much you present. Every time you make those choices it's a power decision ...* (Collective discussion).

For academic researchers, the process of selecting, molding and thus controlling the material to be exposed, was felt to be problematic.

Struggling with our positions as co-researchers in the traditional academic structure — in regard to needing to select narratives for a defined, public purpose at the same time as being collective members of the group creating those narratives — can lead us to be confused about appropriate priorities. It can make us highly vulnerable and so sensitive to the dynamics of the group and to comments made by other group members that process not only suppresses knowledge but also prevents its generation:

> One of the women started to say something, stopped, turned to her [*researcher*] and said, 'I'm not sure how you want us to do this, Sue. I don't know what you want'. Others murmured. Fear pulsed through her body, panic, she realised she did not know herself (Individual written memory).

Thus, where memory-work is used specifically for an academic goal, institutional structures can greatly influence subjectification and dominate social formation.

The Presentation of Ourselves as Competent Researchers Despite Our Fears

In academic work we usually 'decline to say' our anxieties as researchers. We are 'forbidden to name' the fleeting moments of fear about our competence and credibility. Certainty and confidence are essential qualities in presenting and defending one's research, and in pursuing academic careers. Doubts are rarely spoken aloud and even less likely to be made the focus of academic papers when the subjects themselves are successful academics.

Regardless of having successfully completed memory-work research and of our levels of credibility and experience as researchers, we all wrote about and discussed our feelings of incompetence. We recalled being anxious about 'being good researchers' both in collecting and presenting the research and about its reception by others in the wider research community. Particularly in regard to the collective process of the memory-work methodology, our anxieties were deeply felt. We felt anxious about our sense of responsibility to 'get it right'. We were responsible for the layout of the room, the furniture, the food and drink, and whether the technology worked. But more than that, we felt responsible for the participants and for the outcomes:

> She was assailed by all the last-minute doubts. Would the equipment work? Would anyone say anything other than trite banalities? Would they bring their scripts? Would anyone even turn up? Would this be the time when her veneer of competent professionalism would melt away exposing the anxieties and inadequacies beneath? (Individual written memory)

> *I think it's interesting that the first thing that came into my mind was this setting up thing and feeling responsible for the success of the group* (Collective discussion).

A strong connection between silence and the researcher's anxiety emerged through the memories. In some stories the anxiety engendered by silence became manifest in the researcher's body:

> She relaxed into her chair and listened carefully as the first woman read her memory to the group. She noted down phrases and images as she listened. The reader finished and there were low murmurs of 'Mmmm', 'very good', and sighs as if of recognition from the audience. Then there was silence. Glances criss-crossed the table, someone cleared their throat, she looked downwards at the tabletop. She had to stop herself from jumping in, not wanting to go first, to break the silence first. Her jaw grew tense, her body began to tighten (Individual written memory).

The fear provoked by the research context of memory-work was experienced as a powerfully physical force both before and after the memory-work sessions were held:

> She kept walking, imagining, remembering, anticipating, hoping. Mind racing, mouth dry, heart pumping as she pushed open the door… (Individual written memory).

> In her anxiety as to whether the session had really worked successfully, she lost power in her legs to walk…She had to get a taxi back up the hill (Individual written memory).

These feelings of anxiety about the process were unexpected. As one of us recalled, anxiety had received little mention in published memory-work texts. Rather, these texts suggested different sorts of feelings:

> I'd read Haug and I'd read the June Crawford book and I'd read some of Glenda's and everybody's work and the impression I had was a group of keen women get together, they're really enthusiastic, all this [material] comes out of it, you know, the meetings go on into the night, no one wants to leave, they can't wait for the next meeting, they want to come back (Collective discussion).

However, our own project, which focussed specifically on memory-workers doing memory-work, revealed researchers' anxieties in the same measure as their exhilaration or enthusiasm for the method.

The Need to Nurture

Nurturance, a sense of the need to nurture, emerged as a dominant theme within the stories we told. This theme goes beyond our academic training to our primary social construction as women. The stereotypical hostessing role was represented in our stories by clichés such as 'waiting for the guests to arrive', 'the frilly apron cast aside', and 'the white cloth serenely covering the table'. Within the usual conditions and habit of binary logic and the prevailing discourses of gender differences, nurturance is usually ascribed to the feminine position. It is embodied as female (Gilligan, 1982). Typically, we, as feminist researchers, felt compelled to invest time and energy into providing a nurturant atmosphere. Frequently this meant engaging in obvious, taken-for-granted practices of nurturing such as the preparation and presenting of food:

> I spent so much time and energy on the bloody food it was ridiculous (Collective discussion).

The presentation of food is not usually considered relevant to the obtaining of research data and it is certainly not specified in the prescribed practices of this method. Indeed it may seem antithetical to the expressed desire by the researcher to present as rigorous and competent. Nonetheless, in most of the memories, food takes a central part in creating an appropriate atmosphere:

> She sat around the wooden table with her writing friends. She was pleased with herself, at how well things were going, at how carefully she had prepared. There was fresh juice in a jug, good bread, cheese and fruit on the bench behind them, and wine chilling in the fridge for later (Individual written memory).

On occasions foods were even selected to 'match' the needs of particular participants. One woman, who had researched different age groups, explained:

> *I was so nervous about 'What do I offer them?' Now I think about it, the food has been a big issue for me. With the different age groups it's been different food, food that's been more suitable [for each age group]* (Collective discussion).

Nurturing the participants also went beyond the provision of food. There was a general feeling of responsibility for 'the wellbeing of the group, trying to make it nice for them', determining 'what will make people feel comfortable and not comfortable', and 'being responsible for it being all right for them!':

> *[There was the] notion of our awareness that the self-esteem of some of the participants is very fragile or vulnerable. Part of the responsibility of facilitator is to nurture them* (Collective discussion).

Also, in an extension of the nurturing role, we took great care with the intellectual preparation of the group. Many of us were concerned to share the method and the theory with the participants, not merely to use it on them. Often we would discuss this material with participants:

> All the women had brought along their blue folders from last week. They carefully discussed the extracts from Haug's and Davies's work that she'd [the researcher] photocopied for them. They'd teased out what terms like 'rationalizations' and 'explanations' might mean (Individual written memory).

Through our stories we came to realise the significance, for us, of our need to nurture, to balance the human needs and expectations of participants against the imperatives of the research process, even though none of us had articulated this before. Clearly the levels of social formation in which we were involved were multiple and highly complex.

Reflection on Memory-Work as a Means of Producing Agency and Change

The issues of unresolved power in carrying out memory-work prompted stories, which highlighted the vulnerability of the researcher. However, it was the method itself, which enabled these stories — usually silenced and secret — to emerge. Recognition that vulnerability and anxiety were experienced by most of us moved our individual emotional experiences into a different arena, one of collectively recognised and understood experience. Through the memory-work method, each one of us constructed and re-constructed our sense of self as a researcher. In so doing, we became more confident to express the specific conditions of our personal research situations and in this way agency was generated at a fundamental level.

At another level, it gradually emerged that one of the driving forces behind the pressure we put on ourselves as memory-work researchers comes from our sense of 'mission'. Memory-work itself is explicitly concerned with empowerment, with bringing about some positive change in the participants and in the world. Haug and her colleagues begin their book with the following statement:

> Our object in this book is women's capacity — or incapacity — for action and for happiness. It involves a study of the structures, the relations within which women live and the ways in which they get a grip on them. (Haug et al., 1999, p. 33)

We wanted our memory-work to lead to action, to engender some sort of personal and social change, to succeed in the larger world of creative empowerment of our participant group and others like them. Through our storying we recognised that as we evaluate the process we have initiated, we rarely lose sight of the longer term goals of creating opportunities for agency and change which the method opens up. Echoes of justification slipped into our memories:

> Alice [*researcher*] thought about her motivation for writing the memory and why others needed to know of her experiences. They need to learn from them, she thought. She [*Alice*] will tell them that this is an opportunity to participate in generating knowledge about the lives of women and children (Individual written memory).

Sometimes the impulse towards change was unfulfilled and outcomes were not understood as action. The closure of a memory-work session could be associated with a feeling of flatness — a feeling that *this didn't quite come off* and that the researcher had failed because the group had not apparently experienced any change in understanding:

> There seemed to be little more to say so Chrystal [*researcher*] wound up, asking if the group wanted to meet a third time. No, they didn't have any further issues. Chrystal said she hoped they had gained from the process. Yes, they'd found it interesting and enjoyable, but one of the women said she didn't think she had learned anything new. Others nodded. Chrystal thanked them for their participation, but felt flat (Individual written memory).

In the collective discussion, Chrystal recalled feeling flat because she felt she 'wasn't at my best in terms of enabling the group to fizz and buzz' because she was 'not tapping into stuff' and because 'one of the women said she didn't think she had learnt anything new'.

Taking responsibility for the group's increased agency, as well as for the academic validity of the results, added to our assessment of what constitutes a successful outcome. On at least one occasion participants had been inspired by the memory-work method to take their insights into the public arena themselves, thus furthering their ownership of the process and adding a dimension to the researcher's appraisal of success.

The capacity of the individual to reflect on memory is a crucial condition for intentionality, and hence agency (Shotter, 1984). During the main sessions of the Memory-work Conference we (and the other delegates) had discussed our various experiences of the method. However, it was only through 'using the method to explore the method' that we came to understand that the anxiety each member had felt in the research process was actually shared by all in the collective. We broadened our understandings of our selves as (anxious) researchers from an individual to a wider social/cultural context. It was an empowering experience.

Through this process, we began to reposition our researcher selves outside of the humanist tradition, which Haug and her colleagues describe, wherein, 'attention is focused on individuals seen in isolation from the conditions in which they live' (Haug et al., 1999, p. 222). In this tradition:

> What is demanded of the individual is an inner triumph over the surrounding conditions. Individuals are left to come to terms on their own with those conditions, and success is measured in terms of the way the individual can adjust his or her response to them. (Haug et al., 1999, pp. 222–223)

From an individualistic perspective, an anxious researcher may consider herself to be inept or unsuited to academic work. With the collective insight that memory-work brings, we began to see that what we had felt as a weakness for each of us, as individuals, could actually be a resource from which we all drew in our commitment to the success of our project for everyone involved. From this realisation we can go on to challenge the institutions and disciplines within which we work and study about procedures for gaining academic credentials and publications and about how research is conceptualised within and outside academia. Our own agency is thus multi-faceted.

Conclusion

In researching our involvement and understanding of memory-work, there was much consensus despite the many differences in topics of study. Those of us researching tourism and leisure experiences shared similar experiences of memory-work with those from different fields of study. It is hoped that, through theorising our uncertainties and anxieties, researchers employing memory-work (or other qualitative research methods) in tourism and leisure studies will come to question and understand their own position. The findings in our study contribute to the growing work on the contextualisation of the researcher. The experiences cited above echo some of the dilemmas that other feminists (as highlighted in Ribbens & Edwards, 1998) have experienced in the employment of other qualitative research methods.

In our academic work, using memory-work methodology, we have each grappled with questions of power and authority, which have sometimes been emotionally, physically and intellectually challenging. Examining and analysing our embodied experience as researchers in a memory-work collective was one way in which we could 'get a grip' on the academic and social structures and relations within which we are developing personally and professionally as feminist academics. Additionally, by unravelling our own subjectification as memory-work researchers, we have engaged in essential processes of reflexivity and critique. As feminist scholars we also aim, as Lather (1991, p. 80) describes, to develop 'the skills of self-critique, of a reflexivity which will keep us from being impositional and reify ourselves' in terms dictated by patriarchal modes of knowledge.

What had not been shared with our previous memory-work groups but emerged in our workshop collective was the reproduction of numerous acts of powerlessness through self-doubt, anxiety, 'being good', trying hard to be seen as credible, putting burdens of nurturing and perfection on ourselves, and catching ourselves being silent/silenced in the very act of making our participants' voices, including our own, heard. To a large degree, in generating our own memory-work groups, we have been active in our own 'subjectification' as anxious researchers. Our written stories provide clues into the active ways in which we have created ourselves in the social structures in which we have chosen to participate. From the many insights of our memory-work analysis, perhaps the most acute is the realisation of how hard we try to be seen as credible and competent, instead of taking that power and believing in it.

The insights and anxieties, which emerged from our analyses of practice, gave rise to on-going discussion about the nature of the methodology itself. There was some concern about the tension between the need to sustain the organic vitality of an emergent methodology and the maintenance of the integrity of memory-work *per se.* We expressed a range of views and experiences in applying, and modifying, the method as we recognised our questions regarding the status of 'principles' as against 'rules', and 'guidelines' as against 'procedures'. Finally we came to the general conclusion that, as we continue to work through the issues we have identified:

> *[We need] as memory-workers to identify a set of principles and a variety of structures, so that the structures of the memory-work process would be fluid, but that the principles would not be compromised. Because if we don't compromise the principles we've always got a methodology* (Collective discussion).

Although the written stories recorded moments of anxiety, our discussions were animated and excited, and affirmed that each of us had found that memory-work, as a research methodology, generated great joy. At short notice, we had come to the Memory-work Research Conference from interstate and international locations because of our enthusiasm, our commitment and our continuing interest in the methodology of memory-work. Within our diverse individual experiences as memory-workers and within the collective, which came into being for this project, we would concur with Haug and the original collective that:

> Despite our own experiences of bottlenecks, dead ends and running on the spot, we would nonetheless plead, in conclusion, that this form of story-writing is a solid method. Writing stories is fun. More than this, it expands our knowledge enormously, sharpens our social perception, improves our use of language, changes our attitude to others and to ourselves. It is a politically necessary form of cultural labor. It makes us live our lives more consciously. (Haug et al., 1999, p. 71)

References

Barbalet, J. (1998). *Emotion, social theory and social structure*. Cambridge: Cambridge University Press.

Crawford, J., Kippax, S., Onyx, J., Gault, U., & Benton, P. (1992). *Emotion and gender: Constructing meaning from memory*. London: Sage.

Davies, B. (1994). *Poststructuralist theory and classroom practice*. Geelong, Victoria: Deakin University Press.

Dupuis, S. L. (1999). Naked truths: Towards a reflexive methodology in leisure studies. *Leisure Sciences, 21*(1), 43–64.

Ellis, C. (1991). Sociological introspection and emotional experience. *Symbolic Interaction, 14*(Spring), 23–50.

Ellis, C., Kiesinger, C. E., & Tillmann-Healy, L. M. (1997). Interactive interviewing: Talking about emotional experience. In: R. Hertz (Ed.) *Reflexivity and voice* (pp. 119–149). Thousand Oaks, CA: Sage.

Friend, L. A. (2000). Guilty or not guilty: Experiencing and understanding Sweetie's guilt as dissatisfaction. In: J. Schroeder, & C. Otnes (Eds), *Proceedings of the Fifth Conference of Gender, Marketing and Consumer Behavior* (pp. 157–172). Urbana, IL: The University of Illinois Printing Services.

Gilligan, C. (1982). *In a different voice*. Cambridge, MA: Harvard University Press.

Grant, B., & Friend, L. (1997). Analysing leisure experiences through 'memory-work'. In: D. Rowe, & P. Brown (Eds), *Proceedings ANZALS Conference 1997* (pp. 65–70), University of Newcastle, NSW: ANZALS and Department of Leisure & Tourism Studies.

Haug, F. et al. (1987). *Female sexualization: A collective work of memory*. In: E. Carter (Trans.). London: Verso.

Haug, F. et al. (1999). *Female sexualization: A collective work of memory* (2nd ed.), In: E. Carter (Trans.). London: Verso.

Koutroulis, G. (1993). Memory-work: A critique. In: B. Turner, L. Eckermann, D. Colquhoun, & P. Crotty (Eds), *Annual Review of Health Social Science. Methodological Issues in Health Research* (pp. 76–96). Geelong, Victoria: Deakin University Press.

Lather, L. (1991). *Getting smart: Feminist research and pedagogy with/in the postmodern*. New York: Routledge.

McCormack L, C. (1995). *'My heart is singing': Women giving meaning to leisure*. MEd thesis. Canberra: University of Canberra.

McCormack, C. (1998). Memories bridge the gap between theory and practice in women's leisure research. *Annals of Leisure Research, 1*, 37–49.

Oakley, A. (1981). Interviewing women: A contradiction in terms. In: H. Roberts (Ed.), *Doing Feminist Research* (pp. 30–61). London: Routledge and Kegan Paul.

Ribbens, J., & Edwards, R. (Eds). (1998). *Feminist dilemmas in qualitative research public knowledge and private lives*. London: Sage.

Scheff, T. J. (1997). *Emotions, the social bond and human reality*. Cambridge: Cambridge University Press.

Shotter, J. (1984). *Social accountability and selfhood*. Oxford: Basil Blackwell.

Small, J. (2002). Good and bad holiday experiences: Women's and girls' perspectives. In: M. Swain, & J. Momsen (Eds). *Gender, tourism, fun(?)* (pp. 24–38). Elmsford, NY: Cognizant Communications Corp.

Small, J. (2003). The voices of older women tourists. *Tourism Recreation Research, 28*(2), 31–39.

Small, J. (2005a). *Holiday experiences of women and girls over the life-course*. Ph.D. thesis. Sydney: University of Technology.

Small, J. (2005b). Women's holidays: Disruption of the motherhood myth. *Tourism Review International, 9*(2), 139–154.

Stanley, L., & Wise, S. (1990). Method, methodology and epistemology in feminist research processes. In: L. Stanley (Ed.), *Feminist praxis: research, theory and epistemology in feminist sociology* (pp. 20–60). London: Routledge.

Weedon, C. (1997). *Feminist practice and poststructuralist theory* (2nd ed.) Oxford: Blackwell Publishers.

Chapter 17

Enhancing the Interpretive and Critical Approaches to Tourism Education Enquiry Through a Discursive Analysis

Maureen Ayikoru and John Tribe

Introduction

Tourism education is apparently one of the main sub-sectors of the multifaceted tourism world and one whose manifestation could impact on the whole of the tourism's society, directly or indirectly. Tribe defines tourism's society as including not only tourists but all those affected by tourism and the tourism world as comprising three main domains, namely: the domains of 'the tourists, the business and non-business environment' (Tribe, 1999, p. 78). The World Tourism Organisation (WTO) has singled out tourism higher education as holding a potential to achieving customer satisfaction and also improving the competitiveness of tourism businesses and regions if specific education and training are guaranteed (WTO, 1997). Tourism higher education has been researched extensively on aspects such as curriculum content and planning (see for example Leiper, 1981; Holloway, 1995; Koh, 1995; Cooper, 1997; Botterill & Tribe 2000; Tribe, 2002) and stakeholder approaches to curriculum design (see for example Cooper & Westlake, 1998; Airey & Johnson, 1999; Lewis, 2002). Other aspects have focused on teaching or knowledge transfer in tourism higher education, the interface between tourism industry and provision of tourism higher education as well as the dilemmas of future trends in tourism higher education (see for example Airey, 1995, 1998, 2003; Botterill, 1996; Cooper & Shepherd, 1997). These are but some few examples of the works done so far in tourism higher education enquiry.

Although these and other previous studies (not mentioned here) have focused on some of the salient issues in tourism higher education, none has attempted to demonstrate that the whole idea behind tourism higher education derives from and is a manifestation of a complex web of texts and discourses that operate at several levels. The outlook now is to critically interrogate these various *texts* and identify the discourses that underpin tourism higher education in the United Kingdom (UK). Likewise to come up with a possible theoretical

The Critical Turn in Tourism Studies: Innovative Research Methodologies
Copyright © 2007 by Elsevier Ltd.
All rights of reproduction in any form reserved.
ISBN: 0-08-045098-9

analytic explanation of how these discourses have come to underpin tourism higher education as well as the implications therein. The term *text* is used here to describe 'data consisting of words and/or images which have become recorded without the intervention of a researcher (through avenues such as interviews)' (Silverman, 2001, p. 119).

The underlying proposition in this study is that tourism higher education operates largely in a taken-for-granted (ideological) manner that tends to offer a partial view of the tourism phenomena to the learners.

To this end, it is considered imperative to inquire into the mechanisms that seem to not only sustain this partial view of tourism within the tourism higher education system but also attempt to critique this state of affairs with the intention to elucidate broader and for now precluded perspectives within which tourism higher education could operate. It is with this in mind that this study attempts to interrogate the texts and discourses that represent tourism higher education in the UK with the intent of revealing its discursive nature. This is done with the hope that new insights can be gained through critically interrogating what these various texts and discourses hold as well as occlude on tourism higher education. The presumption here is that 'every age sees the documents of history in a new light' (Delanty, 2001, p. 66); this 'new light' might as well be the epitome of the potential contribution of the present study to knowledge within the realm of tourism higher education enquiry.

However, it ought to be noted that what is presented here is part of a study-in-progress, and the rationale for presenting such a 'raw piece of work' in this chapter stems from an observation from Phillimore and Goodson that:

> Currently we know little about how the research process happens in tourism, because the focus is upon the outcome of research. It is important for all those working in the field to develop and share their knowledge about the kinds of struggles that arise when they are developing research problems. . . . (Phillimore & Goodson, 2004, p. 193)

Thus the discussions in the sub-sections that follow will have to be regarded as such since these encapsulate the conceptual part of a study yet to be undertaken.

Method of Enquiry

Introduction

Following the brief introduction and the rationale for this proposed study, this sub-section addresses discourse analysis as a proposed method of enquiry by briefly explaining its theoretical underpinnings and the fact that it does not fall neatly into a conventional definition of a method. Before engaging directly with these issues, it is imperative to distinguish between the terms methodology and method whereby the former term is often (mis)taken to be synonymous with the latter. Janesick (2003) describes as methodolatry, this obsession with method. Methodolatry here derives from combining the words method and idolatry to describe researchers' preoccupation with selecting and defending methods of enquiry at the expense of the substance or story being told (*ibid*). With the foregone observation in mind, a distinction is made here between these two terms; hence; methodology can be regarded as:

> A model, which entails theoretical principles as well as framework that pro-
> vides guidelines about how research is done in the context of a particular
> paradigm. (Sarantakos, 1998, p. 32)

A method on the other hand refers to 'the tools or instruments employed by researchers to gather empirical evidence or to analyse data' (*ibid.*).

This conventional definition of a method reflects closely the conception of scientific method that has close links with logical empiricist social science (Schwandt, 1998; Usher, 1996). According to Madison (1988) this scientific method can best be regarded as an abstract, formal sense of method whereby method is premised on the elimination of personal subjective judgements. And that:

> One has only to learn the method itself, in and for itself; it is an intellectual
> technique. . . . One has only to apply it to whatever subject matter one chooses;
> the only criterion in applying the method is correctness of application. . . .,
> not the subject matter to which it applies. (Madison, 1988, p. 28)

Nevertheless in principle a method cannot be selected without a regard for the underlying methodology as the latter has implications for the research questions being posed and also the choice of methods or combinations thereof that are deemed appropriate to address the questions (see Mason, 2002; Guba, 1990). In this present study, the interpretive and critical methodologies have been selected but owing to lack of space, these have not been discussed here. Detailed discussions on these methodologies can be found in Guba and Lincoln (1994, 1998, 2003, 2005) as well as Schwandt (1998, 2003), Kincheloe and McLaren (2003, 2005). Rather, attention is paid to how a discursive analysis can be deployed to enhance these methodologies in a tourism education enquiry.

Discourse Analysis (Post-structuralist Discourse Analysis)

It is noteworthy to point out here that the use of discourse analysis does not fall neatly into the preceding definition of a method; rather it is being used in this particular context for the potential it holds for furthering the research issue at hand. Existing literature shows that this approach rejects a positivistic view of reality in favour of a social constructionist and/or interpretive perspective of the world. Likewise the fact that its views of language stems from structuralist and post-structuralist perspectives whereby language is regarded not as a neutral descriptive medium but a way of constituting and shaping social reality and social practices (Gill, 1995; Usher, 1996; Chambers, 2003; Kincheloe & McLaren, 2005). What follows is a brief, generalised description of the concept of discourse and what discourse analysis entails as well as the potential it holds in furthering investigations into the proposed study. As mentioned earlier, this is a study-in-progress where much work needs to be done in scrutinising the appropriateness of the method chosen to underpin the study.

The term discourse encompasses multiple meanings and understandings (Hannam & Knox, 2005), and it has several definitions and applications (see Chambers, 2003; Phillips & Hardy, 2002) in social enquiry. The notion of discourse, regardless of its applications and many definitions, is about language (in use) not in a simplistic sense but within wider socio-cultural and political contexts (Chambers, 2003). Thus discourse studies do not describe language as a system but rather analyse language as social act and social use of language (Fiske, 1996). All these different descriptions of the concept of discourse signify that it not only encompasses the conventional linguistic concerns (with the formal structures, rules and codes of language) but also addresses issues relating to power and knowledge within language (see Chambers, 2003). Nearly all of these descriptions reflect (implicitly) Foucault's notion of discourse that to him is twosome or dyadic in nature. That is it encompasses statements and the practices that result from these statements in a way that led him to believe that discourses are 'those practices that systematically form the objects of which they speak' (Foucault, 1972, p. 49), which in turn define the limits of what can (and cannot) be said.

The application of the notion of discourse as a method of enquiry has been broadly or conveniently labelled as discourse analysis (Hannam & Knox, 2005). This broad and undifferentiated nomenclature retains the connotation that discourse analysis is a clear-cut, standardised and straightforward method. Far from being the case, Phillips and Jorgensen (2002) observe that discourse analysis entails a series of interdisciplinary approaches that can be deployed in different social domains and studies (see also Hannam & Knox, 2005; Chambers, 2003). However, they add that aside from the fact that there is no consensus on what discourses are and how to analyse them, different perspectives concomitantly appropriate the term discourse and discourse analysis for their own use.

This brief overview of the concept of discourse is by far too generalised, as it has not proffered any theoretical perspectives within which the concept operates. In other words, although the idea that the concept of discourse is not a unified one seems more apparent in these descriptions, the fact that different theories of discourse underpin the use of the concept needs to be explicated. This way the appropriation of the concept in this proposed study will be traceable to the specific perspective in question. The following sub-section will look at the Foucauldian theory of discourse and its possible use in the present study. Other common discursive approaches not discussed here are psychoanalysis and critical discourse analysis.

Foucauldian 'Theory' on Discourse

Introduction
Dreyfus and Rabinow (1982), have noted that Foucault's work covers not only a wide range of topics but is characterised by important theoretical shifts (paraphrased by Potter, 1996) all of which make it a daunting task for any one attempting to provide a brief account of Foucault. With this in mind, what is presented here is not a systematised account of Foucault's work; rather attempts have been made to elucidate those aspects that have the potential to further illuminate the present study. In other words a highly selective reading of Foucault's work is presented here in lieu of the extent to which it can serve to further investigations into the present study. Although Foucault's work is being discussed

here under post-structuralist discourse analysis, he has been variously labelled as structuralist; sociologist and historian of knowledge or better still following one of his most influential works, as an *archaeologist* of Knowledge (Potter, 1996). However, Foucault has consistently denied being placed under any of these labels that he found problematic in the first instance (see for example Foucault, 1980, 1988; White, 1979; Chambers, 2003). Instead, Potter (1996) notes that:

> To avoid becoming ensnared by epistemological questions . . . he brackets these questions. . . . To emphasise this, he uses the . . . metaphor of regimes of truth, which encourages us to see truth as related to a specific social organisation . . . that is likely to be hierarchical, potentially oppressive, and subject to radical change. . . . (Potter, 1996, p. 86)

It could be said that Foucault is mainly interested in the origins of the modern human sciences such as psychiatry, medicine, sexology; and the circumstances under which these gave rise to institutions such as the clinic, the prison, and the asylum. Likewise and most importantly he is also interested in how knowledge production is constituted by discursive regimes (Slembrouck, 2004). It is thought that by drawing attention to regimes of truth, Foucault has also discursively 'brought' an object in to the world, one that is discussible and describable (Potter, 1996). Foucault's work is generally believed to encompass three phases, namely the archaeological, the genealogical and the post-modern ethics (Phillips & Jorgensen, 2002; Slembrouck, 2004; Chambers, 2003). What follows in the next sub-sections is a brief sketch of the first two phases and the key issues that may have a bearing for this study.

Archaeology

It is within this phase that Foucault developed his concept of discourse, presented in two major works: *L'archeologie du savoir* published in 1969 and *L'ordre du discours* published in 1971. Foucault defines a discourse as:

> A group of statements in so far as they belong to the same discursive formation . . . whose appearance . . . in history might be indicated . . . made up of a limited number of statements for which a group of conditions of existence can be defined. . . . It is . . . historical . . . Posing the problem of its own limits. . . . (Foucault, 1972, p. 117)

Foucault then sets out to investigate what could be termed as the structure of a series of 'regimes of truth' or knowledge. This is based on his assertion that truth is fundamentally a discursive construction encapsulating different regimes all of which play a crucial role in delineating what is true and false (see Potter, 1996; Phillips & Jorgensen, 2002; Howarth, 2000). In essence, to him scientific truth or knowledge is inseparable from the scientific discipline that it engenders (Slembrouck, 2004) and he typically applied this reasoning to the discourse of psychiatry as well as modern medical science. The crux of the matter for Foucault is that despite the fact that there exist innumerable possibilities within which statements can be made, the statements that derive from specific domains tend to be similar and repetitive. And that as a consequence, multiplicity of statements remain unuttered; and that even if they were, the historical rules of the discourse in question would occlude these as being meaningful. This would be the result of discursive rules determining what can be uttered and thus accepted as meaningful and what ought to be precluded (see Foucault, 1972).

In terms of tourism higher education, a similar concern arises with the observation that despite the various conceptualisations and manifestations of the tourism phenomena, the prevalence of the discourses of vocationalism and managerialism tends to overshadow other possible ways in which tourism higher education could be 'spoken of'. This concern is corroborated by the findings of Airey and Johnson's (1998) survey of the aims and objectives of tourism higher education programmes in the UK in which these two discourses feature prominently. However, this point about discursive rules delimiting what statements are acceptable or capable of being uttered seems to feature as a logical contradictory in Foucault's later writings. In his work on the history of sexuality, he cautions against perceiving discourses as closed entities rather instead as entities that are nearly always conflicting upon the most acceptable way of perceiving reality. To this end Foucault (1978) asserts that:

> We must not imagine a world of discourse divided between accepted discourse and excluded discourse, or between the dominant discourse and the dominated one; but as a multiplicity of discursive elements that come into play in various strategies. (Foucault, 1978, p. 100)

The irony in this initial conceptualisation by Foucault is that on the one hand discursive rules delineate what can and cannot be uttered implying that what cannot be uttered becomes occluded at least at that particular point in time. On the other hand, discourses are not to be perceived as binary oppositions (dominant/dominated; accepted/excluded). In the end, it is not clear how one is to perceive the fact that within some specified discourses, some particular statements or groups of statements form the 'only acceptable' way of representing the discourse in question amongst the multiplicity that could have served similar functions. Therefore, if one agrees with Foucault's assertion about multiplicity of discursive elements interacting strategically then it follows that there exist several and varied discursive practices (that is, the way in which discourses operate). Foucault seems to imply just the same when he suggests that a regularity exists of rules and statements that makes communication possible, amidst the varied discursive practices (Foucault, 1991). Once the concept of discourse had been mapped out, Foucault's idea of discourse analysis entails efforts geared towards illuminating the unconscious structures that have the tendency to cloud or mask one's way of thinking. He then described his archaeological phase in the following way:

> Archaeology tries to define not the thoughts, representations, images, themes, preoccupations that are concealed or revealed in discourses; but . . . those discourses as practices obeying certain rules. . . . It is not an interpretative discipline: it does not seek another, better-hidden discourse. It refuses to be 'allegorical'. (Foucault, 1972. pp. 138–139)

This and other similar writings normally project an image of Foucault as being disinterested in the subject, what is commonly referred to as de-centring (see Howarth, 2000). Slembrouck (2004), points out that one of the key attributes of Foucault's archaeological approach and one that has relevance to discourse analysis is his reversal of the subject–statement relationship. To him, discursive rules dictate to a given subject or speaker who in turn must conform to certain conditions prior to uttering specific statements. In other words, he believes that subjects are created in discourses and he further contends, 'discourse is not the majestically unfolding manifestation of a thinking, knowing, speaking subject' (Foucault, 1972, p. 55). This disinterest in the subject or speaker becomes manifest when Foucault describes as an illusion the idea that subjects or speakers exist prior to language and that all meanings have their origins in the subject. He reiterates this reversal of the subject–statement relation by saying that:

> If there is one approach that I do reject [its that] which places its own point
> of view at the origin of all historicity. . . . It seems to me that the historical
> analysis of scientific discourse . . . be subject, not to a theory of the know-
> ing subject, but [that]. . . of discursive practice. (Foucault, 1973, p. 172)

With such an expression of overt disinterest in the knowing/observing subject, Foucault's enigmatic concept of discourse and its subsequent analysis do succumb to the critique of structural semiotics (see Howarth, 2000). However, for the purpose of the proposed study, the notion of discursive regularities and the key roles these play in ensuring the operation of discursive practices act as imperatives. In other words, the notion of discursive regularities delineating what can and cannot be uttered is perceived here as being indispensable to the emergence and thus maintenance of regimes of truth or knowledge at any one point in time. It is this aspect that will be adopted as a means of interrogating the relationships between tourism higher education and the (competing) discourses that appear to represent it. For, as intimated earlier, Foucault's archaeology that perceives discourses as practices obeying certain rules will serve to illuminate not only those discourses that seem to underpin tourism higher education but also the kind of rules they obey. Likewise, interrogated will be the mechanisms that seem to not only sustain but also perpetuate such discursive practices with respect to tourism higher education. Although there is a host of other issues covered under this archaeological phase, it is here felt that exploring all of these aspects is beyond the scope of this present chapter. However, for a detailed explication of this and other phases of Foucault's work, refer to, among others, Chambers (2003), Howarth (2000), Phillips and Jorgensen (2002), White (1979). The next sub-section looks at the genealogical phase of Foucault's work.

Genealogy

This phase took a new turn whereby it focused on issues of power/knowledge regimes as compared to the previous phase that addressed the nature of discourses (Slembrouck, 2004; Phillips & Jorgensen, 2002; Chambers, 2003). Nevertheless he did not abandon his previous work on discourses; instead one could say these two phases are complementary in that in the archaeological phase he seemed to have laid conceptual and methodical foundation of his discursive approach. Meanwhile the genealogical phase encompassed applications of how power works through discourses. Indeed Dean described this complementarity in the following words:

> Archaeology is concerned with the 'problematisation' by which human beings question what they are, do and the world around them; genealogy with the changing conditions of formation of such problematisations in particular 'practices of the self'. (Dean, 1994, p. 34)

It then follows that the concept of problematisation features prominently in this phase, whereby Foucault became concerned with the fact that 'At specific times and under particular circumstances, certain phenomenon are questioned, analysed, classified and regulated, while others are not' (Deacon, 2000, p. 127 in Chambers, 2003).

It is also in this genealogical phase that Foucault demonstrates an unprecedented effort to investigate aspects of the social world that become reified as truths simply because they seem too obvious and superficial to evoke any form of suspicion (Chambers, 2003). As intimated earlier, tourism higher education seems to be operating in a similar taken-for-granted manner that seems 'too obvious' to provoke debates on its common sense representations.

The conception of power and the way power pervades everyday life also surface as a crucial aspect of this phase, and most importantly this conception is antithetical to the traditional Marxist approach in which power is regarded as an instrument of class domination with its origins in economic interests and superstructures (see Howarth. 2000). On the contrary, Foucault contends that power is not necessarily repressive and that it does not operate in simple dualistic manner that separates the dominant from the dominated or those with power from the 'powerless' (Foucault, 1980). He vehemently opposes this perceived dichotomy between the dominant and the dominated by saying:

> I do not have in mind that solid and global kind of domination that one person exercises over others . . . but the manifold forms of domination that can be exercised within society. Not the domination of the king in his central position . . . but that of his subjects in their mutual relations. . . . (Foucault, 1980, p. 96)

What is intricate about this Foucauldian perception of power is that it implicitly reflects the earlier conceptualisation of discourses as not existing in the form of dominant and dominated but rather that there were multiple discursive elements that interact strategically (see Foucault, 1978). So that power to him did not rest so much with particular agents such as individuals or the state or groups with hidden agendas as it did across different social or discursive practices (Foucault, 1980). Through such a conceptualisation Foucault attempted to invert the negative perceptions of power — the tenets of a Marxist theory of power — to something, which can and does have positive or productive aspects, and that in fact power constitutes discourse, knowledge, bodies and subjectivities. To emphasise this productive aspect of power, he poses this question 'if power were never anything but repressive, if it never did anything but to say no, do you really think one would be brought to obey it?' (Foucault, 1980, p. 119).

He then responds to his own question by saying that:

> What makes power hold good . . . is simply the fact that it doesn't only
> weigh on us as a force that says no, but that it traverses and produces
> things . . . forms knowledge . . . discourse. It needs to be considered as
> a productive network, which runs through the whole social body. . . .
> (Foucault, 1980, p. 119)

What Foucault seems to be saying in effect is that power not only creates the atmosphere deemed necessary for the production of the social world, but it is also largely responsible for separating objects (and subjects) from one another. Likewise it is in power that objects (and subjects) become associated with certain specific attributes and also definable relationships. Foucault then applies this conceptualisation of power and knowledge to the 'objectifying' practices of prisons and the 'subjectifying' discourses of sexuality (Slembrouck, 2004). Potter illustrates this by pointing out that:

> Foucault suggests that, as institutions such as psychiatry have developed,
> they have continually produced discourses that constitutes new objects. . . .
> The notion of homosexual[ity] can be traced as a particular category that
> emerges from the development of the disciplines of medicine and psy-
> chopathology. The homosexual is produced. . . . and contrasted to the 'nor-
> mal'. (Potter, 1996, p. 86)

He thus sees power as being intricately linked to knowledge by implying that one presupposes the other (Phillips & Jorgensen, 2002; Preece, 1997). He illustrates this power/knowledge dyad by intimating that it would be difficult to imagine the modern prison system with no reference to criminology (Foucault, 1977). Thus power in the Foucauldian sense is responsible for not only creating the social world but also shaping the particular ways in which this social world can be formed and spoken about. Here then power just like discourse is viewed as determining the ways of being and talking, making it both a productive and constraining force (Phillips & Jorgensen, 2002).

What is noteworthy in this genealogical phase is that Foucault finally pays explicit attention to issues of truth and knowledge that seemed to have been less conspicuous in the archaeological phase, and also generally. More so the dyadic relationship between power and knowledge tends to reflect discourse and power in equivocal terms as both are projected as having a major role to play in producing objects and subjects and also delimiting what can or cannot be known (Phillips & Jorgensen, 2002; Preece, 1997; Kincheloe & McLaren, 2005). Within the realm of the present study, this power/knowledge dyad might form a preliminary basis for interrogating the relationship between tourism higher education and the texts/discourses that represent it. The starting point might be to adapt Foucault's idea that it is not possible to imagine the modern prison system without criminology, substituting where appropriate, tourism higher education system for prison system and the discourse of tourism for criminology. In other words, one could postulate that it is difficult to imagine a modern tourism higher education system with no reference to the discourse of tourism, how it is perceived, defined and regulated by those with authority to 'speak' about tourism as a discourse. Here then the concept of problematisation could be deployed to further examine why and how for instance tourism higher education has been and is being represented by some particular texts with connotation for particular discourses but not others.

Previous studies already show that texts with particular focus on vocationalism and managerialism seem to be the privileged locus from which the discourse of tourism and thus tourism higher education is represented (see for example Airey & Johnson, 1998; Stuart-Hoyle, 2003; Airey, 2005). Of particular interest here would then be the Foucauldian views on truth in both the archaeological and genealogical phases whereby in the former, truth was regarded as a system of procedures for production, regulation and dissemination of statements. Meanwhile in the latter phase, with his power/knowledge dyad, he contends that truth is to be found in and thus is produced by systems of power, thus linking back to his notion of regimes of truth (see for example Phillips & Jorgensen, 2002; Potter, 1996). By viewing truth in this way, he argues that 'absolute truth' is unattainable (see also Usher, 1996) and that there is no point (whatsoever) in attempting to find out if something was true or false. Rather that emphasis should be on finding out how effects of truth are produced in discourse (Phillips & Jorgensen, 2002; see also Foucault, 1988).

It is imperative to point out that this phase of Foucault's work is also imbued with some criticisms. A pertinent critique in this case focuses on the notion of truth or knowledge construction. Critics contend that in order to understand how reality is constructed it is imperative to situate power in particular groups, institutions or even individuals in a given society, something Foucault seemed to have overlooked (see Howarth, 2000). This concern was reiterated by Wetherell and Potter, who queried:

> if we are no longer to talk of groups and the power they wield, and if we
> can no longer define history as the story of who did what to whom and why,
> then what is there to say? (Wetherell & Potter, 1992, p. 92)

The implications of this for the present study are that although the discursive approach and also the power/knowledge dyad are in a better position to explicate the research issue, they focus too much on 'presences'. In principle then, it would be inadequate to explore the seemingly multiple discursive elements that encapsulate tourism higher education and the texts/discourses that represent it without explicating the role of (human) agency in shaping the discursive practices engendered. To redress this issue, it will be imperative to seek other discursive approaches that have attempted to incorporate these concerns into their theorisation. The two approaches on critical discourse analysis and discourse theory of Laclau and Mouffe are competing perspectives that might be drawn upon in this respect. These have not been discussed here due to lack of space, but the readers are encouraged to consult these two perspectives and decide which best addresses the concerns raised by critiques of Foucauldian theory on discourse and its anticipated limitation to the present study.

Sampling Strategies

The texts to be interrogated in this study include *inter alia* tourism curricula documents from various institutions of higher education in the UK. These will be drawn mainly from the university websites. Other texts such as course advertisements and promotion materials from various universities will be used. Documents from Association for Tourism in Higher Education (ATHE), Higher Education Academy (HEAC) and World Tourism Organisation (WTO) as well as the Quality Assurance Agency (QAA) proposals for tourism higher education will form a crucial part of the data for this study among others. Purposive and theoretical sampling (see Glaser & Strauss, 1976; Glaser, 1978; Mason, 2002; Morse & Richards, 2002) will be used to generate data for this study. Morse and Richards explain purposive selection of sample and study setting by saying that:

> This may involve choosing the "best" most optimal example of the phenomenon and the setting in which you are most likely to see whatever it is you are interested in. . . . Alternatively you may select a setting because it allows you to obtain examples of each of several stances or experiences (Morse & Richards, 2002, p. 67)

In this regard, the actual number of *texts* will be ascertained through a process commonly known as theoretical sampling (Glaser & Strauss, 1976; Glaser, 1978). Morse and Richards (2002) view theoretical sampling as a means of extending one's sampling strategies as one begins to understand what it is that they are studying. Thus according to them, theoretical sampling means:

> . . . . Your selection of participants is directed by the emerging analysis; and the theory being developed from data is subsequently modified by data obtained from the next participant. . . . (Morse & Richards, 2002, p. 68)

Bearing in mind the fact that the present study deals with *texts* and not participants as such, the idea of theoretical sampling in this case will entail, selecting *texts* based on the emerging analysis from the texts selected for preliminary interrogation. Once the inductive process of theory building begins, the theory derived from existing data will be modified by analysing subsequent *texts* (cf. foregone quotation). So that by using purposive sampling and also theoretical sampling the author will determine what selection of *texts* ought to be included in the study during the data collection process. Hence the sample size in this case will not be predetermined but it will emerge when redundancy with respect to information or data occurs (Guba & Lincoln, 1985). Punch (1998) describes this redundancy with regard to data as theoretical saturation; which according to him is a cyclical process of data collection and analysis that continues until no new data are found, only confirmation of previous theories. Sarantakos (1998) then summarises these sampling processes by saying that in qualitative research, it is the quality not quantity of data that determines the sample size.

Summary

This chapter presented an emerging study that attempts to investigate the discursive nature of tourism higher education in the UK. The chapter commenced with a brief introduction in which tourism higher education was recognised as one of the sub-sectors of the multifaceted tourism world with a potential contribution to the whole of the tourism's society. It was presupposed that the whole idea behind tourism higher education derives from and is a manifestation of a complex web of texts and discourses that operate at several levels, so that the need to critically interrogate this state of affairs was regarded an imperative worth undertaking. This then necessitated the adoption of a methodology, and method of enquiry deemed appropriate to further illuminate the research issue. The two methodologies selected, that is interpretive and critical methodologies, were not discussed here due to lack of space. Instead, discourse analysis was presented as a method of enquiry though with the recognition that it did not fit well with the conventional definition of a method.

The concept of discourse was defined in general terms and also a brief account of the Foucauldian theory of discourse was proffered as holding the potential to underpin enquiry into the proposed study. Here the central notions of regarding the 'truth' as existing in the form of 'discursive regimes', and discursive regularities as delineating what counts as 'truth' were considered fundamental in investigating the research issue in this study. Likewise the concepts of power/knowledge dyad in which power was shown to work through discourses and the concept of problematisation that raised an issue with why some phenomena are questioned, analysed and classified under particular circumstances while others are not seen as holding a potential for understanding the issues in this study. Some weaknesses of this Foucauldian theory of discourse were mentioned and it was suggested that readers draw on other discursive approaches, notably the discourse theory of Laclau and Mouffe or critical discourse analysis as a means to redressing some of the aporias identified. Finally, it was mentioned that data for this study will be generated through purposive and theoretical sampling whereby it will not be possible to quantify the number of texts selected for interrogation as would have been the case in a quantitative research design.

References

Airey, D. (1995). *Tourism degrees — Past, present and future.* Inaugural Professorial Lecture. The Nottingham Trent University, Nottingham, UK.

Airey, D. (1998). Exploring the links between education and industry. Paper delivered to *Tourism Education Exchange.* University of Westminster.

Airey, D. (2003). Tourism education — Dilemma of success? *Tedqual, 1*(6), 22–25.

Airey, D. (2005). Growth and development. In: D. Airey, & J. Tribe (Eds), *An international handbook of tourism education* (pp. 13–24). London: Elsevier.

Airey, D., & Johnson, S. (1998). *The profile of tourism studies degree courses in the UK: 1997/98.* London: The National Liaison Group for Higher Education in Tourism.

Airey, D., & Johnson, S. (1999). The content of degree courses in the UK. *Tourism Management, 20*(2), 229–235.

Botterill, D. (1996). *Making connections between industry and higher education in tourism.* London: The National Liaison Group for Higher Education in Tourism.

Botterill, D., & Tribe, J. (2000). *Guideline 9: Benchmarking and the higher education curriculum.* London: National Liaison Group for Higher Education in Tourism.

Chambers, D. P. (2003). *A discursive analysis of the relationship between heritage and the nation.* Unpublished Doctoral dissertation, Buckinghamshire Chilterns University College, Brunel University.

Cooper, C. (1997). A framework for curriculum planning in tourism and hospitality. In: E. Laws (Ed.), *ATTT Tourism Education Handbook* (pp. 24–27). London: Tourism Society.

Cooper, C., & Shepherd, R. (1997.) The relationship between tourism educations and the tourism industry: Implications for tourism education. *Tourism Recreation Research, 22*(1), 34–47.

Cooper, C., & Westlake, J. (1998). Stakeholders and tourism education: Curriculum planning using a quality management framework. *Industry and Higher Education, 1*(292), 93–100.

Dean, M. (1994). *Critical and effective histories: Foucault's methods and historical sociology.* London: Routledge.

Delanty, G. (2001). *Challenging knowledge. The University in the knowledge society.* Buckingham: Open University Press.

Dreyfus, L. H., & Rabinow, P. (1982). Michel Foucault. *Beyond structuralism and hermeneutics.* Hemel Hempstead: Harvester Press.

Fiske, J. (1996). *Media matters. Race and gender in US politics.* Minnesota, MN: University of Minnesota Press.

Foucault, M. (1972). *The archaeology of knowledge.* New York: Tavistock.

Foucault, M. (1973). *Madness and civilization.* NewYork: Vintage Books.

Foucault, M. (1977). In: A. Sheridan (Trans.), *Discipline and punish: The birth of the prison.* Paris: Editions Gallimard.

Foucault, M. (1978). *The history of sexuality. Volume I: An introduction.* NewYork: Random House.

Foucault, M. (1980). *Power/knowledge. Selected interviews and other writings 1972–1979.* London: Harvester Press.

Foucault, M. (1988). In: A. Sheridan (Trans.), *Politics, philosophy, culture. Interviews and other writings 1977–1984.* New York: Routledge.

Foucault, M. (1991). *The foucault effect: Studies in governmentality.* Wheatsheaf: Harvester Press.

Gill, S. (1995). *American hegemony and the trilateral commission.* New York: Cambridge University Press.

Glaser, B. G. (1978). *Theoretical sensitivity.* Mill Valley, CA: Sociology Press.

Glaser, B. G., & Straus, A. L. (1976). *The discovery of grounded theory: Strategies for qualitative research.* Chicago, IL: Aldine.

Guba. E. G. (1990). The alternative paradigm dialog. (Ed.) *The paradigm dialog.* Thousand Oaks, CA: Sage.

Guba, E. G., & Lincoln, Y. S. (1985). *Naturalistic inquiry.* Beverly Hills, CA: Sage.

Guba. E. G., & Lincoln, Y. S. (1994). Competing paradigms in qualitative Research. In: N. K. Denzin, & Y. S. Lincoln (Eds), *Handbook of qualitative research* (pp. 191–216). Thousand Oaks, CA: Sage.

Guba, E. G., & Lincoln, Y. S. (2005). Paradigmatic controversies, contradictions and emerging confluences. In: N. K. Denzin, & Y. S. Lincoln (Eds), *The Sage handbook of qualitative research* (3rd ed., pp. 191–216). Thousand Oaks, CA: Sage.

Hannam, K, & Knox, D. (2005). Discourse analysis in tourism research: A critical perspective. *Tourism Recreation Research, 30*(2), 23–30.

Holloway, J. C. (1995). *Towards a core curriculum for tourism: A discussion paper.* London: The National Liaison Group for Higher Education in Tourism.

Howarth, D. (2000). *Discourse: Concepts in the social sciences.* Buckingham: Open University Press.

Janesick, V. J. (2003). The choreography of qualitative research design: minuets, improvisations, and crystallization. In: N. K. Denzin, & Y. S. Lincoln (Eds), *Strategies of qualitative inquiry* (pp. 46–79). Thousand Oaks, CA: Sage.

Kincheloe, J. L., & McLaren, P. L. (2003). Rethinking critical theory and qualitative research. In: N. K Denzin, & Y. S. Lincoln (Eds), *The Sage handbook of qualitative research,* (3rd ed., pp. 303–342). Thousand Oaks, CA: Sage.

Kincheloe, J. L., & McLaren, P. L. (2005). Rethinking critical theory and qualitative research. In: N. K. Denzin, & Y. S. Lincoln (Eds), *The Sage handbook of qualitative research,* (3rd ed., pp. 303–342). Thousand Oaks, CA: Sage.

Koh, K. (1995). Designing the four-year tourism management curriculum: A marketing approach. *Journal of Travel Research*, 24(1), 68–72.

Leiper, N. (1981). Towards a cohesive curriculum in tourism: The case for a distinct discipline. *Annals Of Tourism Research*, 8(1), 69–83.

Lewis, A. (2002). *A case study of tourism curriculum development in the Caribbean: A stakeholder perspective*. Unpublished Doctoral dissertation. Buckinghamshire Chilterns University College, Brunel University.

Lincoln, Y. S., & Guba, E. G. (1985). *Naturalistic inquiry*. Thousand Oaks, CA: Sage.

Lincoln, Y. S., & Guba, E.G. (1998). Competing paradigms in qualitative Research. In: N. K. Denzin, & Y. S. Lincoln (Eds), *The landscape of qualitative research: Theories and issues* (pp. 1–34). Thousand Oaks, CA: Sage.

Lincoln, Y. S., & Guba, E. G. (2003). Paradigmatic controversies, contradictions and Emerging confluences. In: N. K Denzin, & Y. S Lincoln (Eds), *The landscape of qualitative research: Theories and issues* (pp. 253–291). Thousand Oaks, CA: Sage.

Madison, G. B. (1988). *The hermeneutics of postmodernity*. Bloomington: Indiana University Press.

Mason, J. (2002). *Qualitative researching*. London: Sage.

Morse, J. M., & Richards, L. (2002). *Read me first for a User's guide to Qualitative Methods*. Thousand Oaks, CA: Sage.

Phillimore, J., & Goodson, L. (Eds). (2004). *Qualitative research in tourism: Ontologies, epistemologies and methodologies*. London: Routledge.

Phillips, L., & Jorgensen, M. W. (2002). *Discourse analysis as theory and method*. London: Sage.

Phillips, N., & Hardy, C. (2002). *Discourse Analysis. Investigating Processes of Social Construction*. Thousand Oaks, CA: Sage.

Potter, J. (1996). *Representing reality: Discourse, rhetoric and social construction*. London: Sage.

Preece, J. (1997). Historicity and power-knowledge games in continuing education. *Studies in the Education of Adults*, 29(2), 121–136.

Punch, K. F. (1998). *Introduction to social research*. London: Sage.

Sarantakos, S. (1998). *Social Research* (2nd ed.). South Melbourne: Macmillan.

Schwandt, T. A. (1998). Constructivist and interpretivist approaches to human inquiry. In: N. K. Denzin, & Y. S. Lincoln (Eds), *The landscape of qualitative research: Theories and issues* (pp. 221–259). Thousand Oaks, CA: Sage.

Schwandt, T. A. (2003). Three epistemological stances for qualitative inquiry: Interpretivism, hermeneutics, and social constructionism. In: N. K. Denzin, & Y. S. Lincoln (Eds), *The landscape of qualitative research: Theories and issues* (pp. 22–331). Thousand Oaks, CA: Sage.

Silverman, D. (2001). *Interpreting qualitative data. Methods for analysing talk, text and interaction*. London: Sage.

Slembrouck, S. (2004). What is meant by "discourse analysis?" Available at: http://bank.rug.ac.be/da/da.htm; retrieved on 12/10/2004.

Stuart-Hoyle, M. (2003). The purpose of undergraduate tourism programmes in the United Kingdom. *Journal of Hospitality, Leisure, Sport and Tourism Education*, 2(1), 49–74.

Tribe, J. (1999). The concept of tourism: Framing a wide tourism world and broad tourism society. *Tourism Recreation Research*, 24(2), 75–81.

Tribe, J. (2002). The philosophic practitioner. *Annals of Tourism Research*, 2(92), 338–357.

Usher, R. (1996). Textuality and reflexivity in educational research. In: R. Usher, & D. Scott (Eds), *Understanding Educational Research* (pp. 33–51). London: Routledge.

Wetherell, M., & Potter, J. (1992). *Mapping the language of racism: Discourse and the legitimation of exploitation*. Brighton: Harvester/Wheatsheaf.

White, H. (1979). Michel Foucault. In: J.Sturrock (Ed.), *Structuralism and since* (pp. 81–115). Oxford: Oxford University Press.

World Tourism Organisation (WTO). (1997). An introduction to TEDQUAL (1st ed.). Madrid: WTO.

Chapter 18

What Lies Beneath? Using Creative, Projective and Participatory Techniques in Qualitative Tourism Inquiry

Sheena Westwood

Tourism is a people-centred experience which is ludic, sensory and pleasurable, and in which the visual is elevated above all else (Botterill & Crompton, 1987; Adler, 1989; Rojek, 1995; Ryan, 2002; Urry, 2002). For those of us who are engaged in qualitative tourism research, our aim is to make sense of human behaviours within the context of the social world. Our challenge then lies in 'finding out', and in the development of methods and techniques that will offer up the richest information and reveal experiences from the respondent's perspectives. There is some growing acceptance and use of qualitative methods within tourism (see Phillimore & Goodson, 2004; Westwood, Morgan, & Pritchard, 2006); however, there is still a need to adopt research approaches and practices that encourage respondents to open up and freely express themselves, and that reflect the characteristics which are tourism's very essence.

Qualitative studies often involve quite lengthy and time-consuming activities, which can become wearisome, and respondents may fail to fully engage or even drop out of the programme. Moreover, there are considerations of the power relationship and rapport between respondent/subject and researcher, which can affect the proceedings. In keeping with the spirit of holiday taking and tourism experiences, research methods and techniques can be developed so that they unleash the constraints of socially conformist responses, consider respondents as participants, involve them, incorporate elements of play and fun, and that are considered by the participants as being pleasurable rather than mundane and onerous. In explaining some of the projective and sensory devices that I have used, I draw attention to the value of methods and techniques that encourage participant engagement and involvement, individual, subjective expression, and that minimise prior outcome constraints and researcher interference. While my research findings are not central to this chapter, they illustrate how creative, visual and projective techniques can enable tourism researchers to penetrate the surface and mine the rich reserves of individual experience. Relatively, I call for tourism researchers to step outside the comfort zone of 'conventional', traditional approaches that involve systematic and selective data collection and reporting, to embrace diversity, recognise multiple discourses and the possibilities that this opens up for tourism knowledge (Westwood et al., 2006).

Within tourism, two of the most widely used conventional qualitative methods are semi-structured depth interviews and group discussions or focus groups. These have limitations because they tend to elicit responses that conform to societal rules and constraints, and thus fail to capture the nuances and subtlety of human behaviour. As human beings we are often reluctant to present ourselves in a light that is less than acceptable and rational, and consequently we tend to express ourselves in ways that are generally understandable and intelligible within the particular social situation. Additionally, these methods involve a high level of manipulation by the researcher who plans the interviews based on preconceived notions, has some ideas about the responses and, despite the openness and lack of structure, influences and controls the proceedings. While such methods enable the researcher to listen, follow the train of thought of the respondents, and provide opportunities for eliciting deeper information, it is the researcher who ultimately negotiates the path of the conversations according to a predetermined agenda, and as Levy (1985, p. 68) observes that 'the more specific the question, the narrower the range of information given by the respondent'. Moreover, depth interviews, particularly when the research design requires repeated interviews, can become tedious for the respondent and even for the researcher. 'We go through our days with blinders, dealing with and observing only a fraction of our surroundings' (Collier & Collier, 1986, p. 7).

Venturing beyond the rational involves delving beneath the surface to explore hidden, personal, emotional and subconscious behaviour and to encourage participants to articulate what they often do not know is there — to find the extraordinary in the ordinary. By avoiding the barriers and constraints of direct questioning, projective techniques enable participants to express themselves more openly and intuitively, thus giving insights to personal and idiosyncratic attitudes, motives and behaviours. In this chapter I begin by explaining the general concept of projective techniques, and give examples of some that I have used. However with such techniques control is still with the researcher, and I then go on to explain participatory techniques such as auto-driving and photo-elicitation, which effectively minimise researcher control. Such techniques present opportunities for self-expression and have great potential to reveal rich, hidden information from the perspective of the participant, rather than the researcher, as through their active involvement and reflexivity participants are engaged and empowered. Excerpts from the narratives of two participants illustrate how, rather than using an analytical process that fragments and fractures, such methods necessitate an approach to interpretation and presentation that enables the voices of the participants to emerge through individual, contextualised, fluent recitals.

Projective Techniques — A Brief Background

Projective techniques are described by Branthwaite and Lunn (1985, p. 101) as involving:

> The presentation of stimuli designed so that their meaning or interpretation
> is determined by the respondent who has to structure and impose meaning
> into the task.

Three of the main barriers to investigating deeper human behaviour are: repression and the unconscious; self-awareness and rationality and social influences, which often influence our responses to questions or cues (Rappaport, 1942; Askegaard, 2001). People find it difficult to articulate their real feelings, attitudes and ideas, and might not even acknowledge them to themselves. We have a tendency to say what we think we know or feel, or what we feel is socially 'acceptable' rather than what we really know or feel. In particular, personal desires, impulses, aspirations, fears and a whole range of emotions are things that we often find difficult to confront and express, particularly in an interview situation. The use of a range of ambiguous stimuli such as text, visual images, tests and tasks encourages participants to express and articulate individual subjectivities and unconscious deeper levels of thought. This can provide pathways into their mindsets and subconscious thoughts, and give insights to personality, behaviour and cultural values that otherwise would not be revealed, helping to:

> overcome self-censorship and self-consciousness; encourage expression and
> fantasy; change perspective; inhibit rationalisation and cognitive responses
> and encourage expression of personal emotion. (Branthwaite & Lunn, 1985,
> p. 109)

Originally projective techniques had a psychoanalytical application and are based on Freudian theory that reactions and responses are determined by our personalities; that subjective beliefs and anxieties are more easily dealt with if they are externalised and projected onto a third party, and that unconscious and repressed thoughts can be expressed by disassociation from reality. Therefore projective tasks, which admittedly might sometimes appear unusual and fanciful, can be instrumental in separating participants from reality, so that their responses are far less constrained and self-conscious, and thus more representative of their inner, personal emotions (Murray, 1943; Branthwaite & Lunn, 1985):

> Thus, given a standard but relatively ambiguous task — such as telling a story about a picture — what a person does reflects how he structures and interprets his life situations and reacts to them. (Levy, 1963, p. 4)

Since Murray (1943) further developed projective techniques for use in psychoanalytical diagnosis, they have been used increasingly in a wider application — particularly that of consumer research, since the 1950s (see Levy, 1980, 1981, 1985; Heisley & Levy, 1991), and more recently in marketing, where a range of projective techniques and visual and auditory stimuli are used, most usually within a focus group situation.

It is generally acknowledged that the two hemispheres of the brain respond differently to different types of stimuli, and thus activate different types of consciousness (Branthwaite & Lunn, 1985). Although we, as human beings, have dominant brain processing sides, in general both sides of the brain participate in processing the activities and experiences we engage in, with each focusing on particular aspects of the experience. The left hemisphere processes material logically and in a linear manner. It is analytical, sequential and systematic and deals in absolutes, in reality. The right hemisphere processes holistically, in a non-linear way and considers the big picture, simultaneously relating and integrating experiences. This is the side of the brain that is concerned with coherence and meaning, it is colour sensitive and is associated with creativity, intuition and the visual.

Whereas quite straightforward questions that will elicit logical, absolute verbal responses work well for gaining access to left-brained information and experiences, right-brained responses deal with subjective, complex, less reasoned information and thus are more challenging to researchers, as direct questioning is inadequate for revealing the unknown and unacknowledged subtleties of behaviour and emotions. Projective techniques can unlock the mind by overcoming some of the barriers to expression of right-brained information, as well as other barriers such as social acceptance and expectation.

There is a wide range of techniques under the heading 'projective', and it should be noted that most of these techniques will engage both hemispheres of the brain, to varying degrees. As projective techniques were originally developed for psychoanalysis, depending on the application of the techniques they will almost certainly need to be adapted and modified to fit the nature of the research in other disciplines. For example some structured, clinical psychology methods used to test personality such as the Rorschach Inkblot test and the Rosenwieg Picture-Frustration test are less appropriate for use in consumer-focused research, than for example the Thematic Apperception Test. In this 'test' participants are encouraged to extend their imaginations and make up a story around a person or people in a picture, on the assumption that they will project their attitudes and feelings on to the people in their story. As with others, this test can be adapted into an effective activity for a range of applications (Rappaport, 1942; Kassarjian & Robertson, 1991).

Although the studies referred to in this chapter have a tourism marketing and consumption behaviour focus, these techniques can be just as well adapted for use across a wide range of other tourism and leisure applications. Indeed, my key aim is to raise awareness of the power of projective and participatory techniques in tourism research, and thus to encourage their use, rather than to provide a comprehensive 'how to' guide. This is by no means an exhaustive list of projective techniques, and I have focused primarily on some that I have used in various studies, in both individual and group situations. These vary in the levels of structure and researcher control, from the more structured word and picture association, sorting and completion techniques described in the first part of the chapter, to the participant-involved auto-driving and photo-elicitation techniques described in the latter part.

From my own experience, the predominant consideration in developing the activities is that they need to be very clear and straightforward. The aim of using them is to encourage disclosure of deeper levels of emotion and feelings, and people are usually very keen to 'do it right'; therefore, it is important to guard against anything that may inhibit the responses. Keeping explanations clear and logical, avoiding tasks that necessitate long and complex explanations, not using too many different techniques and, as a moderator, being sensitive to signs of anxiety, frustration and boredom among the participants, will help to avoid misunderstanding and feelings of inadequacy and failure. Participating in the tasks however, is only a part of the process, and the real insights are to be gained through the ensuing discussions. With this type of approach the interpretation lies with the participants, and the key is to stimulate discussion and explanation of their responses. Whether it is a group situation or an individual basis, it is very important to allow sufficient time and to encourage participants to explain why they have responded as they have, and to allow them to reflect on their responses.

Word Association, Word Sorting and Sentence Completion

These techniques involve stimuli, which encourage participants to respond by association with a word, image or thought, and include word association and personification. In a study of holiday decision considerations which focused on the awareness and influence of brands (Westwood, Morgan, Pritchard, & Ineson, 1999a; Westwood, 2004) I used both these techniques to provide me with an indication of perceived attributes, image, awareness and attitudes towards a range of brands. Used early on in focus groups they proved to be valuable as 'ice breakers', relaxing participants, focusing their attention on the themes of the session, and preparing them for the activities to follow.

Word association is a method of identifying associations with certain stimulus words, and involves presenting the participant(s) with a series of words and asking them to note the first word that springs to mind when they read or hear each one. For example, in the above study the participants were verbally given a series of tourism brands and asked to note down the first word that occurred to them. Their responses were then used to generate a group discussion on salience, awareness and attitudes to tourism brands and to brands in general, and they also provided valuable material for the development of further activities.

While I did not use visual and audio texts such as pictures, photographs and sounds as associative material in this particular study, I have done so in others. For example in one study (Westwood, Pritchard, & Morgan, 1999b, 2000), I was seeking to establish reactions to gendered airline provision, and by using a range of visual and audio advertising material within focus groups I was able to observe and record the reactions of men and women to the various stimuli. Initially I did not give them long to look at the images, and only played the audio recordings once, because I wanted to observe their initial reactions. Following on from the initial exercise, I used the same material again but gave the participants much longer to look at and reflect on it, thus encouraging them to comment and expand on their first reactions and also to discuss each other's reactions and comments within the group. For example, this is the response of one woman to a print advertisement that she considered particularly inappropriate for encouraging women travellers:

> It's a shame really because I'm tall and leg room is important — but there are those pressed pin stripes and highly polished black lace ups again . . . instant switch off.

Word sorting is an exercise in identifying associations, where participants are given a selection of words, which they are then required to sort into groups according to certain attributes or other features that they consider they have in common. Or you may provide a selection of words, which they are asked to link with particular key words or brands; for example, when considering destination perceptions you might give participants words which represent different values or emotions and ask them to associate them with particular destinations. Again, in a similar sort of exercise, visual material such as pictures can be used, and this is something that can work particularly well with children.

Sentence completion is another effective activity for establishing behaviour, perceptions and attitudes, and for initiating group discussions. Participants are given a series of unfinished sentences and asked to complete them, for example *'When I'm choosing where to go for a holiday I . . .'*. In a similar way, controversial and provocative statements can be used to stimulate reactions, for example:

> *I am really surprised by all the fuss made by those environmentalists about shark diving . . . what's the problem with tourists going down in a cage — it can't do any harm . . .?*

When used in a group situation (and depending on the topic) the participants' varied responses are likely to lead to interesting, insightful and even heated discussions.

In a similar exercise, speech or thought bubbles can be used instead of sentences. Pictures or drawings of situations with empty speech/thought bubbles are presented to the participants. They are then encouraged to complete the pictures by filling in the bubbles with their ideas of what the people in the pictures might be saying or thinking.

Personalisation

Often used in marketing and consumer research, personalisation involves ascribing human personality traits to other objects or products, and is based on the understanding that just like people, objects, products and brands are perceived as having personalities with which people can identify, and which can influence attitudes and behaviour (Martineau, 1957;

Aaker, 1997, 1999; Morgan & Pritchard, 2001). Participants are encouraged to imagine an object, product or brand as a person and to describe them, for example: *if 'X' were a person what gender would they be? What would they look like? Where would they live? . . .* and so on. By bringing products and brands to life in this way, I have found personalisation exercises very effective in provoking wider, deeper feelings and thoughts, eliciting associations and attitudes, and in the avoidance of diplomatic or politically correct responses. For example, I used a brand personality exercise as a technique in a study to examine tour operator brand image and associations (Westwood et al., 1999a, 2000; Westwood, 2004). Introduced towards the end of two separate focus group sessions, when participants were relaxed and the discussions were flowing freely, each participant was asked to think of six major tour operators as personalities, and to write down a description of the type of person they were, such as their gender, their age and life-stage, the way they looked and dressed, the type of car and house, their lifestyle, leisure activities and so on. In the group discussions that followed, the perceived superiority of one tour operator emerged overall, but there was a remarkable lack of awareness of any definable image of tour operators in general, and notably the two focus groups ascribed virtually the same characteristics to several of the operators, while very low awareness of one operator was demonstrated by their failure to attribute any characteristics at all. The gendered brand and image associations were of particular interest too, with this activity indicating a strongly patriarchal seller relationship through the personification of all the tour operator brands as men, and this despite women being identified as the primary decision maker for tourism choices.

Participant Involvement and Visual Texts

The techniques I have discussed so far were used in qualitative studies, which were 'semi-structured' in nature, that is, although the participants were involved in as much as they were given a series of activities to undertake, the activities were essentially structured, led, and constrained by me, as the authoritative researcher. What distinguishes participatory research from other approaches is that it is done with, rather than on, people, and actively engages them in the programme to varying extents. For example, in a participatory study in a work environment, employees may work collaboratively with researchers within the research setting, effectively becoming co-researchers. They would receive some training and carry out various information-gathering activities, and may also be involved in the analysis (Patton, 2002). In other studies, participation is not as co-researchers in a data-gathering/analysis sense, but through their involvement in the programme by the production of stimuli materials and the activities with which they engage. Key aspects of participatory research are that openness and transparency are increased and power is devolved from the authoritative researcher to the participants. As a consequence, researcher control and interference is minimised, participant ownership, commitment and enjoyment is increased and thus they are much more likely to reveal aspects that would otherwise remain hidden — even sometimes from themselves.

Many of the techniques described so far include specific researcher prepared visual material. However, the potential of visual material for enhancing research extends way beyond these techniques, and includes photography, artwork, moving images, electronic media, illustrations and other printed material such as advertising texts and postcards (Pritchard &

Morgan, 2004). Their use within research is particularly appropriate in the context of tourism where, as Urry (2002) argues, since the mid 19th century tourism and photography have been inseparable; also Botterill and Crompton (1987, p. 152) refer to the power of using tourists' photographs as research stimuli, particularly for the way that they engender rich and prolonged verbal accounts:

> Tourists are very willing to interpret their own photographs. They often provide a rich verbal account of a situation which uses the pictorial content of a photograph as a point of departure, and extends well beyond the photographic moment. (Botterill & Crompton, 1987, p. 152)

Yet generally tourism research tends to follow the course set by the social sciences, which while acknowledging the growing interest in visual methods, still privileges words over visual texts. In other disciplines, however, their use is more developed, for example in anthropology the value of using visual texts is long accepted, and visual anthropology has emerged as a significant sub-discipline (Banks, 2001). It is my intention in the remainder of this chapter to concentrate on demonstrating the effectiveness of using participant-generated visual material as research stimuli, rather than to discuss visual methods per se. However, for informative and interesting perspectives on visual research see Collier and Collier (1986), Banks (2001), Pink (2001), van Leeuwen and Jewitt (2001), Stewart and Floyd (2004).

As Botterill and Crompton (1987) recognise, a major advantage of using visual texts is in the favourable way participants respond to them. In having something that they can see and relate to in some way, they tend to relax and find it easier to talk which results in a more prolonged and fluent flow of information:

> Beyond the cultural inventory, the photograph as a probe and stimulus to interviewing has proven to be consistently invaluable. In tests carried out for Cornell University we compared the value of interviewing with and without photographs and discovered that the picture interviewer could continue his interrogations indefinitely, as long as he continued to bring in fresh photographs. In contrast, the exclusively verbal interviews became unproductive much more quickly. (Collier, 1979, p. 281)

However, while photographs and other sensory stimuli have been used within research projects for some time they have not always been generated by the participants, and this is something that can reap huge rewards in terms of the dimension and richness of the responses. Key advantages of using participants' own materials are that they have been *selected* by them *specifically* because of some personal significance . . . as you begin to look at them, already you are entering their lives.

Collages, Photographs and Fantasy

For many consumers the true value of products, brands and objects lies in what they symbolise, and their ability to 'help construct, sustain, and reconstruct the social self' (McCracken,

1993, p. 127). Here I draw on my interpretive study, which addresses the relationships between tourism consumers and objects within the context of their holiday experiences (Westwood, 2004). I describe how the participants' own visual texts enabled me to 'unpack' their tourist experiences to get beneath the surface of their relationships with products, objects and other things. The combination of visual texts with a participatory approach encouraged them to tell their stories and weave their fantasies of tourism experiences, and I was thus able to find out about their individual embodied experiences, and how they are shaped through dialogues with consumption objects and other pleasurable, ritual, symbolic and talismanic practices.

In qualitative inquiry it is the quality and richness of information that is the priority, and some significant research has been carried out using very small samples (Botterill, 1989; Sparkes, 1994; Holliday, 2002; Patton, 2002). The strength of these studies is in the concentration on small samples, which are selected purposefully — that is, participants are selected because they have valuable, study-specific information that they can yield. The study required the participants' involvement in some quite demanding and time-consuming activities, and it was crucial that they fully engaged and were willing to participate until completion. In keeping with the spirit of holiday taking and tourism experiences, the research activities, while being acknowledged methods and techniques (Branthwaite & Lunn, 1985), were thus developed to incorporate elements of play and fun, to be considered by the participants as being pleasurable (in the spirit of holiday taking) rather than mundane and onerous. Originally nine participants were chosen purposively using the technique of 'snowballing' (on the recommendation of other participants, see Neuman, 1997), the nature of the study and their level of involvement being explained very clearly in an initial meeting. As is not unusual in quite complex studies, two dropped out, one due to re-location to another geographical area, and when the second activity was explained, another stated: '*I cannot do that, I'm not good at that sort of thing . . . I really don't want to do it*' thus reducing the final number of participants to seven.

Autodriving

The term 'autodriving' (Heisley & Levy, 1991) refers to a form of photo-elicitation, using participant-created stimuli representing their own life and behaviour. It conveys the notion of the participant being 'in the driving seat' — that is, the interview is driven by the participants whereby 'the interview is 'driven' by informants who are seeing their own behaviour' (Heisley & Levy, 1991, p. 261). By looking at a visual representation that they have made of a particular life situation, it increases their voice and authority, it affords some distance, so that they can view their everyday lives with a different perspective, and it gives them a way to explain and make it meaningful to others (Wallendorf & Arnould, 1991; Heisley & Levy, 1991). Thus, when they then talk about them they are able to explain the nuances and minutiae that make up the meaning in their lives and experiences:

> The autodriving method highlights the informants' views of ordinary realities. As they observe the moments fixed in time by the photographs, informants distinguish among elements of the typical, the unusual and the ideal.

> Autodriving thus helps in recognizing and addressing the effects that the
> researcher introduces, in contrast to the common approach that either
> assumes the researcher does not influence the informants or ignores that
> influence. (Heisley & Levy, 1991, p. 269)

I used what Heisley and Levy (1991, p. 261) term 'a multiple iteration approach to auto-driving', that is where sequential conversations were held using materials that the participants themselves had produced. The first visual texts were *ad hoc* photographs that they took of anything related to their holiday experiences that they considered significant . . . things that enhanced and enriched their holiday experiences. I supplied each participant with a disposable camera, rather than the supply of a film and processing for the participants' own cameras for several reasons. Commensurate with tourism's ludic nature (Ryan, 2002), I wanted the task to be considered fun and pleasurable, as well as being simple to undertake. Notwithstanding the logistical advantages of being neatly packaged, the disposable camera had some novelty value, which I considered would be more likely to make the task fun and distinct from other photograph taking. Following the completion of this activity, each participant brought their photographs to a meeting where they used them as stimuli for the ensuing conversations, which were guided and structured by their own visual materials and thoughts, rather than by myself.

For reasons of confidentiality and involvement, I used pseudonyms, which the participants chose themselves, and some of these too had interesting personal relevance, for example, Audrey chose hers because of her cat, which is named after Audrey Hepburn, and Jemima (who collects ducks) chose hers because of the association with the Beatrix Potter character Jemima Puddleduck. The locations of the meetings proved to be a significant factor in the comfort of the participants. It is important that participants are as comfortable and at ease in their surroundings as possible, and we mutually agreed on the locations. A great advantage of having emergent flexibility in research design is that it gives opportunities for reflection, reiteration and adaptation, so there were no pre-specified number of meetings (see Patton, 2002). Some meetings took place in the participants' work environments — this worked well and all participants in these locations were relaxed and at ease. However, when I met Elizabeth in her own home (at her invitation), she was far less comfortable than those conducted in a more neutral setting. She was initially quite nervous about the meeting and the photographs that she had taken, being concerned that she 'hadn't done it right', and being in her home location made her very conscious of her role as the 'hostess' and mine as the 'guest'. She felt she had a duty to ensure my comfort, which led to a lack of ease on her part and also on mine. Her dissatisfaction with the meeting was in fact such that we actually met again in my home to autodrive the photographs, something that proved much more satisfactory.

The vast array of invariably interesting, personal and seemingly eccentric photographs produced by the participants (plates of food, contents of suitcases, talismanic objects, choices of books and music and much more (see Figures 18.1–18.3)) and the richness of the insights bear testimony to the effectiveness of this activity. The photographs encouraged reflection and triggered memories; often the participants were transported back to time and the place of the photograph and they re-lived the moment, interpreting their own behaviour in the consideration and recounting of the thought processes that led them to take the photographs. Sometimes they expressed surprise at their own behaviour, and

Figure 18.1: Audrey's magazines to which she is 'addicted'.

Figure 18.2: Dai's 'stunning, delicious' prawns and noodles.

indeed, as Heisley and Levy (1991, p. 257) remark, the technique 'manufactures distance for the informant so they see familiar data in unfamiliar ways'.

The rich material generated by the photographs led to the development of the research and subsequent autodriving activities. Key findings from this activity were the different constraints that influenced holidays, which included choices of destination, accommodation,

Figure 18.3: Elizabeth's holiday mood music.

activities, and also enjoyment levels. While I was aware that everyone has constraints that affect and restrict behaviour, I had not considered it such a significant factor in shaping the individual experience. As the photo-elicitation activities progressed the significance of the various constraints (financial, family, time and psychological) led me to consider that their hypothetical removal might be a way to get closer to people's inner feelings, perceptions, aspirations and behaviour. 'Fantasy can offer a third way to the individual' (Gabriel, 1995, p. 479), and again in accordance with the elements of fun, fantasy and pleasure that are associated with holiday taking, I considered that if the photographs were representative of the *actual* experience within the various constraints, then it would be more revealing of the deeper feelings and meanings if the constraints were removed — in effect by representing a '*what if?*' situation, then the participants would really extend their imaginations and emotions. I thus used projective techniques to create a fantasy situation where all constraints were removed. I supplied each participant with a sheet of heavy A3 paper and some glue and explained the rationale behind the task, and that they should project their minds — to imagine that all constraints had disappeared, to let their minds run free — to daydream and, through the production of a collage, to express their imagined 'ideal' tourism experience. As Branthwaite and Lunn (1985, p. 101) acknowledge 'what these [projective] techniques have in common is that the task is highly ambiguous, novel and sometimes even bizarre'.

The participants engaged fully with this activity, drawing, pasting representations of things that depicted the places, the accommodation, the transport, the people that would accompany them and the things that they would take with them. As with the photographs, in the individual meetings that followed approximately 2 months later, the collages were used as autodriving devices, with the participants also referring back to and reflecting on their earlier conversations.

From a researcher's perspective, autodriving and the use of participants' own material have significant benefits. In a usual researcher — respondent situation, the researcher is the authoritative figure, asking questions, probing and generally controlling the proceedings, recording and writing notes, which they then take away. In participatory situations such as this, the participant is involved, and has contributed to the research in a tangible way, through the material artefacts they have brought. Already they have a vested interest and a point of reference. When the balance of authority and control is altered, the participants are no longer passive subjects, but lead and use their material to navigate conversations according to their underlying desires, influences and motives. When I have used these techniques I have been surprised and delighted that my interventions have been limited to the odd question or prompt now and again, and I have been much more relaxed and less stressed — after all, researchers too often suffer from anxiety!

Moreover, as the following comments and excerpts illustrate, participants' feel more comfortable and less self-conscious which immediately breaks down many barriers to communication and expression of deeper thoughts:

Dai:

> *It's been good fun and I found it self-revelatory too I suppose. Looking at what I put in the collage there was a mixture of OK, I'm going to look for photographs that express this, but then some of them are . . . I highly reacted to them, you weren't looking for them specifically and you come to it and you think oh, that's me or that's what I fancy doing.*

Audrey:

> *I really enjoyed it actually, it was fun and it made me think about what I do on holiday and what I think about holidays so that was interesting actually.*

Elizabeth:

> *It was a pleasure. When I got the time to actually sit down and do it. I kept having little thoughts about it, but actually doing it, I loved doing it. I could sit down and dream all day long.*

Rebecca:

> *It was good — I felt I was in control — I could find my own way around it, I wasn't always waiting for you to ask me questions, and — you know, trying to concentrate — think of answers — much less stressful and yes, I had the control, and could just talk . . . and go back to things if I'd forgotten something.*

Conventional thematic approaches to the analysis of qualitative data involve systematically grouping, comparing and contrasting the material with its consequential fragmentation, detachment and de-contextualisation. Research approaches and methods such as these produce a great wealth of individual detail and 'thick description' (Geertz, 1973, p. 6). Thus they necessitate alternative approaches to analysis, interpretation and presentation, where preservation of the individuality, ownership and fluency of the narratives is paramount. In the study, each individual's narratives were presented separately, with my interpretations incorporated as a 'discursive commentary' (Holliday, 2002, p. 98). In these next sections are excerpts drawn from the narratives of Dai and Elizabeth. They demonstrate the depth and richness of the insights and how, through the separate presentation of each individual's narratives, the involvement is preserved, the participant's voices are heard in context and the researcher influence is minimised. (For more detailed information on considerations of interpretation, voice and narrative analysis, see Riessman, 1993, 2000; Holliday, 2002; Glover, 2003.)

Dai's Experiences

'Experience' is paramount in contemporary consumption and, indeed, is the very essence of tourism. However there is a huge diversity between consumers, and between experiences — people might seek different experiences in different situations and find satisfaction and pleasure in each. There are predominantly functional experiences such as pre-travel preparations, travel arrangements, the travel itself; and there are emotional, symbolic and cognitive experiences such as excitement, relaxation, romance, education and self-actualisation. In the following excerpt, Dai (who travels frequently on business) referring to his photographs (Figures 18.4 and 18.5) reveals his airport ritual, which is a very significant part of his airport experiences:

> This is World News — somewhere else I always go to. I always go in and wander round, there's always a waiting time, so this is where I go to . . . this is a picture of Private Eye (Figure 4) — I always buy a copy of Private Eye to read . . . it's a neat package — you know when you've not got much space on the plane, you can't struggle with a newspaper — it's unmanageable, and the articles are in bite sized chunks — you know what it's like when you're travelling, sometimes it's difficult to concentrate — you get interrupted so you can pick it up and put it down when you need to. I ALWAYS buy Private Eye — nothing else will do . . . this is a real ritual. If they don't have it I'd be upset and wouldn't buy anything else . . . ahhhh the sweets (Figure 5). I always go and look at the sweets — I don't always buy them — but I always look. I like to have some sweets — I keep a packet in the car so that I can just have one when I feel like it. These are Campino — they taste DELICIOUS — really like strawberries and cream — the best things I've tasted. The trouble is, if I buy them I will eat them — they always come in large packets — if they did them in tubes then I'd buy them. Sometimes you can get them in a tube. I don't like to buy a lot in a packet . . . the whole packet is too much. Because if I eat them — which I might well do — it might take the edge off my appetite — my dinner is a very important part of the trip and I don't want anything to spoil it.

Indeed, the sensory and tactile pleasure that he gets from eating out is further demonstrated by his photographs of plates of food (Figure 18.2) and the exterior of restaurants . . . *this next photograph looks a bit peculiar — but it was absolutely stunning — it was some Thai noodles . . .*

Figure 18.4: Private eye.

Dai's collage (Figure 18.6) is visually highly active, a complete myriad of images, pre-dominantly of physical outdoor pursuits such as mountain biking and rugby, and also images of destinations and the things he would do there, such as playing cards and club-bing in Las Vegas, representations of activities normally associated with someone much younger than his 60 years. He has incorporated the words 'Carpe Diem' (Seize the Day) in the bottom corner:

> . . . I mean seize the day, in other words, sod it and just do it, you know because it doesn't, without being too morbid about these things, I'm certainly three quarters of the way into my life probably, I'm in the last quarter now, which explains that so I think I would probably take more risks now . . . doing daft things or whatever, 'oh well, I won't be coming here again so just do it', whatever it is, you don't think 'oh gosh I'm an accountant or all the rest of it', I'll never come here again, let's just sort of seize it, whatever it is . . .

Figure 18.5: Sweet choices.

Figure 18.6: Dai's collage.

He is extremely fit physically, and works hard to ensure that he stays that way. He has an extreme aversion to participating in any sport or activity that he considers to be for older people, and his conception of self and his preoccupation with ageing are strongly reflected through the type of activities he chooses (both in the actual and the imagined) and is reflected strongly in the clothes he wears and the items he takes with him on holiday. Cognitively older people consider themselves 15 years younger than their chronological age (Morgan & Pritchard, 2001; Ryall & Collier, 2001). Dai's fear of ageing and of being perceived as old — or even his actual age — is demonstrated very clearly in a tourism and leisure context throughout the study, where he reveals a lot about his own self awareness, his fear of age and the importance of communicating his self image through his leisure activities, the products he uses and the clothes he wears. Here he is referring to an image of 'Primal Wear' clothing (a brand of active sportswear) on his collage:

> I suppose it's a scream for a long lost youth I suppose, I don't know, it must be something pretty deep in there that makes me want to put a stupid t-shirt on and wear ragged cut shorts and enjoy myself with guys who are only 20 or 30 and join in on the cycling and the rest of it so . . . I suppose they are illustrative of the fact that I try not to think I'm old. Basically my interests, to be serious for a second, are of someone generally speaking a lot younger than I am, I mean the fact that I go to the gym five days a week, I go cycling, I go to pop concerts, I go to tap dance lessons, they're not the normal things that someone of my age does, they're the sort of things that people younger than me do, I don't do it because I want to be younger, I do it because that's the way I am and I suppose really these illustrate what I think I am because there are two people, I think I've told you before, I'm sorry to harp on about the age thing but you will find that you end up there's two people; there's the person you think you are and the person you feel and then there's the person you see in the mirror and in photographs where you're not posing. And they are quite different from one another and it's quite shocking sometimes. So if you notice here, there's nothing to suggest age is there? Which I didn't realise that until you pointed it out to me but there's nothing there, which would suggest age. This is what I mean, this could be enjoyed by a 20-year-old, 30-year-old, 40, 50, there's nothing there that . . . I mean, they probably think 'what a silly arse'. I mean it's not to impress them because this is what I mean . . . there are two me's if you like, there's the person I think I am and I could wear that silly shirt and think I look a cool dude and yet they would look at me and think, what's that silly old fart doing dressed like that, so it's certainly not to impress them. I would feel more part of the scene than if I was wearing something more formal amongst all these kids enjoying themselves, that's all. It's so they don't turn around and think 'well he's out of place here'. They may think I look a fool but they wouldn't think I look out of place, there's a difference isn't there, a subtle difference.

Elizabeth's Experiences

The two overriding themes in Elizabeth's narratives are time and self-actualisation. Intrinsic to Elizabeth's holiday experiences is a thirst for knowledge and self-fulfilment. She is surrounded by highly educated people and academics. Although she herself is

Figure 18.7: Elizabeth's collage.

a well-qualified professional who constantly strives to gain understanding and knowledge on a range of topics, she nonetheless has a feeling of inferiority and lack of confidence in her own level of knowledge. When she is planning a holiday she reads and digests a huge amount of information from sources as varied as tourism literature; newspaper travel articles; travel publications such as guides, novels, autobiographies and biographies; lifestyle magazines and the internet. The information is not restricted to the usual tourist attractions, but encompasses bird life, flora and fauna, food, history and music, and it is significant that her collage (Figure 18.7) is very different from those of the other participants in that it depicts many of the cognitive aspects which are so important for her, such as reviews of travel-related literature taken from broadsheet newspapers.

In the following excerpt she is describing the things that she takes away with her. Music is very important, and she chooses music which is representative of the country and culture to which she is travelling, and uses it to enhance the experience of the host destination through immersion into the culture (Figure 18.3). She is very knowledgeable about a wide range of music genres and tolerant of the varied tastes of family members. Similarly, her choice of relaxation reading and listening material reveals her level of intellect. Rather than reading magazines and light beach reading she chooses non-fiction and contemporary novels:

> Right, we're talking about what's assembled on the bed for our holiday in Sicily (Figure 3) . . . it's important to us to take CDs and portable hi-fi equipment to wherever we're staying. We usually take the kind of music that would be part of that country's music, for instance we've taken Italian

opera, arias, the tenors, all the kind of range of Italian music, baroque music as well . . . to us that is part of getting the feel of a country, whilst you're there it's very pleasurable to listen, as I say, at the end of the day sitting there with a glass of white wine and nibbly bits listening to an opera before going out for dinner in the evening. In addition we've taken . . . because my daughter's staying in the same room with us . . . her taste in music which would be hip hop, rap that sort of thing at a fairly reasonable level, plus then our other tastes in music which would range things like Billie Holiday, Django Reinhardt, whatever . . . easy listening . . . Frank Sinatra, things like that, to modern day easy listening pop like Craig David or whoever is around at the moment . . . but so it would be very important to us to pack a world band radio so we can tune in in the mornings to world service and check in on the news from home so to speak. Again of course within your hotel room most places have television these days and Sky news. We try not to put that on too much because otherwise you're never going to feel like you get away and have a change and you're bombarded with this. But as it was the World Cup football the week we were away, we did succumb and have one or two matches on or part of it. In addition we also take talking books and those sort of tapes we would listen to down in the gardens or next to the pool when you've got an hour relaxing you don't actually feel like reading a book you just want to lie there with your eyes closed listening to a story and those sort of things. We pack the batteries, the adaptors, all that kind of thing and I do find that it takes up a lot of our luggage but very often we're border line going over the weight allowance because we've packed so many CDs and books . . . there's a book on birds, Collins book on birds, we always take something like that with us, the birds of an area, and might a month or two before we go, buy books on the internet to further our knowledge, because often by buying a bird book you will find you will go to very interesting parts of the location you've arrived at that the brochures don't mention at all unless you are going for a specialist brochure like a bird watching brochure . . . then we've got, I particularly like Fay Weldon, I enjoy her style and then I've got the Tracy Chevalier book about the Vermeer paintings, talking about Vermeer the artist which I love because I like art, I like history and it's very well written, not too heavy weight and literature wise so I would say yes, books are extremely important to take on holiday.

Although she is younger than Dai (in her mid fifties) Elizabeth is also very conscious of the passing of time, but she has a very different attitude to it. In contemporary society, leisure time is an increasingly valuable commodity, and for Elizabeth, holiday taking is heavily constrained by work and family commitments (although her children are grown up she still has a very close, maternal relationship), and is linked to the academic calendar through her husband's work. In her idealised holiday, the removal of time constraints is the most significant aspect. Her travelling companion is her husband, and she imagines them both to be retired. Having time means that she can spend a leisurely 6 months planning the trip, which would span 3 years. Throughout the study she refers repeatedly to time and the luxury of not being time bound — aware of the constraints of time on her everyday life, she takes a retrospective view of travel, choosing modes of transport reminiscent of the days when travel took much longer, with the journey becoming a significant element of the experience. Her primary mode of transport is by ship and boat — which she considers is important in gaining a true perspective of distance and time.

Time/space compression is a contemporary characteristic and is partly attributed to technological advancements (Bauman, 1998). In contemporary society the increasing pace of life and time compression is leading to greater individualism and self awareness, resulting in the need for escape into experiential, introspective and reflective pursuits (Firat & Dholakia, 1998). Ryan (2002) recognises that tourism presents a time paradox — while tourism presents a time free from everyday constraints, it is in fact experienced within fixed time boundaries. In her imaginary trip, Elizabeth stretches those boundaries. Unlike Dai, whose preoccupation with age impels him to actively defy it, rushing to engage in a multiplicity of experiences before it is too late, Elizabeth is conscious of time in a totally different way. While she also discusses a range of varied experiences, it is taken at a much slower pace. For her, the imaginary holiday presents a release from the bounds of time, time to learn, to reflect and to experience time and space within the context of different countries and cultures:

> First of all I would retire from work because I am near the end of my illustrious career anyway and I would like to take six months in planning a trip. My ideal companion would be Elwyn of course and it would be very nice if we could retire and if I had Bill Gates' millions we could, so money is no object here. I was thinking to myself — mostly while I am on holiday I like to be doing something or other, learning something about where I'm at and as I didn't go to university and get a degree, you know? My education I suppose you could say . . . is lacking in a way, I'm looking upon this as a big adventure and education. So we're going to take three years over this. And I wouldn't want to be going hurtling though the sky in a metal box. My mode of travel would be ship and because I feel then you get to appreciate the time it takes to actually reach some of these far flung countries for instance when my Aunt was in the Navy and posted to Hong Kong, it took her six weeks to get there and during which time of course she stopped off at all sorts of interesting countries on the way and it gives you a real feel of you've travelled the world to get to this destination. So I just think of myself as the old days of sailing, you know, when life was so civilised, that would be my ideal form of ship travel. I think it's quite disorientating for a start with the time zones of the world and your own body clock. You can arrive in a place and you really do feel quite unhinged, a bit detached almost because you haven't been given time to prepare your body, your mind maybe because you more often that not have checked out where you're going to be arriving at so you're going to be expecting a certain amount, but it just doesn't give you such, it's almost like a shock to the system, maybe it's an age thing. Younger people, it doesn't faze them as much to arrive on the other side of the world within 24 hours and just pick up the strings and get on with it. Maybe that is it, older people like to savour the time that bit more.

Tourism incorporates daydreaming, fantasy, imagination and anticipation, and tourism consumers are ultimately seeking pleasure and (re)creation through a range of different, interconnected experiences. Both Dai and Elizabeth's experiences are characterised by a thirst for self-actualisation and knowledge. For Dai, his self-actualisation needs are satisfied through the hard, physical challenges of active leisure activities. The significance of Elizabeth's notion that she is educationally inferior to family and colleagues in influencing her life is clear, and has been the motivating factor in her drive to further her knowledge, and thus her self-image.

Summary

The strength of participant involvement, projective techniques and autodriving lies in their flexibility, unpredictability and their ability to draw out participants' stories, to find out what lies beneath and remains hidden. While some may argue that the very nature of 'story telling' is based on exaggeration and recall, and thus query its validity, others (e.g. Bochner & Ellis, 2002; Denzin & Lincoln, 2005) recognise that although the 'truths' in the stories are not necessarily objective truths, they contribute significantly to the understanding of human behaviour and reasoning. Indeed, the whole notion of 'objective truth' is inappropriate in this endeavour. Judgement of studies which adopt interpretive inquiry should be based on considerations of dependability (presenting a clearly articulated pattern of inquiry and interpretation), and authenticity (reflexive awareness of yourself as the researcher, and appreciation and understanding of the position and perspective of others — the researched, the participants and the reader). Authority, control and voice address issues of credibility but in a way that is commensurate with the nature of the research, such as through the level of rapport the researcher achieves with the participants combined with their activity and involvement in the process, rather than with those proposed by a more scientific approach (Lincoln & Guba, 1985; Sparkes, 2000, 2002; Pritchard & Morgan, 2004). Participant activity and involvement creates opportunities for self-interpretation, reflection and reiteration, and enhances the validity of the research through the levels of increased voice and authority. As Heisley and Levy (1991, p. 269) acknowledge, participants:

> . . . become projective interpreters of their own actions. The researcher then interprets further. Autodriving makes it possible for people to communicate about themselves more fully and more subtly and, perhaps, to represent themselves more fairly.

Additionally, giving participants the opportunity to read and comment on the researcher's interpretations before it is finally presented, increases their sense of control over the proceedings, whilst enabling researchers to reflect on what they had said, to reiterate and seek clarification and expansion of topics if deemed necessary.

Tourism research should be embracing innovation and progressive approaches, and exploring new ways of finding out (see Westwood et al., 2006), and there is great scope for the development of interpretive approaches, for actively involving participants in various ways and the adoption of exciting, creative and subjective methods and techniques. It has been my aim in this chapter to encourage innovation and creativity in the way that tourism knowledge is gathered. These short excerpts from Dai and Elizabeth's narratives demonstrate the power of such techniques to motivate participants to reveal their inner selves. The photographs and collages exposed things that it would not have been possible to find out using conventional interviews, where the researcher forms questions and frameworks that are limited by their own knowledge and understanding. The use of stimuli to which the participants can relate causes them to observe and consider aspects of their own, ordinary (and extraordinary) behaviour and disclose unpredicted, rich, insider information with all the implicit and contextual idiosyncrasies and nuances. This chapter describes methods and techniques that I have used in studies with a marketing and consumption behaviour focus; however, they can be developed and adapted for application across a wide range of tourism and leisure subjects. Nor should stimulus material be limited to photographs and collages. All manner of social artefacts, travel mementos and souvenirs, and personal, talismanic objects present researchers with opportunities to encourage and motivate participants to tell their stories, to explain what lies behind and beneath, and to give us valuable insights to their behaviour within the wider context of their social and cultural discourses.

References

Aaker, J. L. (1997). Dimensions of measuring brand personality. *Journal of Advertising Research,* *34*(August), 347–356.

Aaker, J. L. (1999). The malleable self: The role of self-expression in persuasion. *Journal of Advertising Research, 36*(1), 45–56.

Adler, J. (1989). Origins of sightseeing. *Annals of Tourism Research, 16,* 7–29.

Askegaard, S. (2001). Projective techniques. Unpublished lecture notes. Qualitative Research Seminar, University of Southern Denmark, Odense, November.

Banks, M. (2001). *Visual methods in social research.* London: Sage.

Bauman, Z. (1998). *Globalization, the human consequence.* Cambridge: Polity Press.

Bochner, A. P., & Ellis, C. (Eds). (2002). Ethnographically speaking, autoethnography, literature and aesthetics. Walnut Creek: Alta Mira.

Botterill, T. D., & Crompton, J. L. (1987). Personal constructions of holiday snapshots. *Annals of Tourism Research, 14,* 152–156.

Botterill, D. (1989). Humanistic tourism? personal constructions of a tourist: Sam visits Japan. *Leisure Studies, 8,* 281–293.

Branthwaite, A., & Lunn, T. (1985). Projective techniques in social and market research. In: R. Walker (Ed.), *Applied Qualitative Research* (pp. 101–121). Aldershot: Gower.

Collier, J. (1979). Visual anthropology. In: J. Wagner (Ed.), *Images of Information* (pp. 271–282). Beverley Hills: Sage.

Collier, J. Jr., & Collier, M. (1986). *Visual anthropology: Photography as a research method.* New Mexico: University of New Mexico Press.

Denzin, N. K., & Lincoln, Y. S. (2005). *The sage handbook of qualitative research* (3rd ed.). London: Sage.

Firat, A. F., & Dholakia, S. (1998). *Consuming people, from political economy to theatres of consumption.* London: Routledge.

Gabriel, Y. (1995). The unmanaged organization, stories, fantasy, subjectivity. *Organization Studies, 16*(3), 477–501.

Geertz, C. (1973). *The interpretation of cultures: Selected essays* (pp. 6–10). New York: Basic Books.

Glover, T. D. (2003). Taking the narrative turn: The value of stories in leisure research. *Society and Leisure, 26*(1), 145–166.

Heisley, D. D., & Levy, S. J. (1991). Autodriving: A photoelicitation technique. *Journal of Consumer Research, 18*, 257–272.

Holliday, A. (2002). *Doing and writing qualitative research*. London: Sage.

Kassarjian, H. H., & Robertson, T. S. (Eds). (1991). *Handbook of consumer behaviour.* Englewood Cliffs: Prentice Hall.

Levy, S. J. (1963). Thematic assessment of executives. *California Management Review, 5*(Summer), 3–8.

Levy, S. J. (1980). The symbolic analysis of companies, brands, and customers. *Albert Wesley Frey Lecture*. Graduate School of Business: University of Pittsburgh.

Levy, S. J. (1981). Symbols, selves and others. In: A. Mitchell (Ed.), Advances in consumer research, Ann Arbor, MI. *Advances in Consumer Research, 9*, 542–543.

Levy, S. (1985). Dreams, fairy tales, animals and cars. *Psychology and Marketing, 2*(Summer), 67–81.

Lincoln, Y. S., & Guba, E. G. (1985). *Naturalistic inquiry.* Beverly Hills: Sage.

Martineau, P. (1957). *Motivation in advertising: Motives that make people buy*. London: McGraw Hill.

McCracken, G. (1993). The value of the brand: An anthropological perspective In: A. Aaker & D. L. Biel (Eds), *Brand equity and advertising* (pp. 125–139). London: Lawrence Erlbaum Associates.

Morgan, N., & Pritchard, A. (2001). *Advertising in tourism and leisure.* Oxford: Butterworth Heineman.

Murray, H. A. (1943). *Manual of thematic apperception test*. Cambridge, MA: Harvard University Press.

Neuman, W. L. (1997). *Social research methods: Qualitative and quantitative approaches* (3rd ed.). Boston: Allyn and Bacon.

Patton, M. Q. (2002). *Qualitative research and evaluation methods* (3rd ed.). London: Sage.

Phillimore, J., & Goodson, L. (Eds). (2004). *Qualitative research in tourism: Ontologies, epistemologies and methodologies*. New York: Routledge.

Pink, S. (2001). *Visual ethnography*. London: Sage.

Pritchard, A., & Morgan, N. (2004). Mythic geographies of representation and identity: Contemporary postcards of Wales. *Journal of Tourism and Cultural Change, 1*(2), 111–130.

Rappaport, D. (1942). Principles underlying projective techniques. *Character and Personality, 10*(March), 213–219.

Riessman, C. K. (1993). *Narrative analysis*. London: Sage.

Riessman, C. K. (2000). Analysis of personal narratives. In: J. F. Gubraim & J. A. Holstein (Eds), *Handbook of interview research* (pp. 695–710). Thousand Oaks, CA: Sage.

Rojek, C. (1995). *Decentering leisure, rethinking leisure theory*. London: Tavistock.

Ryall, C., & Collier, P. (2001). Wrinkles and all. *Connectis, 1*(September), available at: http://specials.ft.cm/connectis/FT393C3SRRC.html, accessed 15/11/01.

Ryan, C. (Ed.). (2002). *The tourist experience*. London: Continuum.

Sparkes, A. (1994). Life histories and issues of voice: Reflections on an emerging relationship. *International Journal of Qualitative Studies in Education, 7*(2), 165–183.

Sparkes, A. (2000). Autoethnography and narratives of self. *Sociology of Sport, 17*(1), 21–43.

Sparkes, A. (2002). Auto-ethnography: Self-indulgence or something more? In: A. P. Bochner & C. Ellis (Eds), *Ethnographically speaking, autoethnography, literature and aesthetics* (pp. 209–232). Walnut Creek: Alta Mira.

Stewart, W. P., & Floyd, M. F. (2004). Visualizing leisure. *Journal of Leisure Research Special Issue, 36*(4), 445–460.

Urry, J. (2002). *The tourist gaze* (2nd ed.). London: Sage.

Van Leeuwen, T., & Jewitt, C. (Eds). (2001). *Handbook of visual analysis.* London: Sage.

Wallendorf, M., & Arnould, E. (1991). We gather together: Consumption rituals of Thanksgiving day. *Journal of Consumer Research, 18*(June), 13–23.

Westwood, S. (2004). Narratives of tourism experiences: An interpretative approach to understanding tourist–brand relationships. University of Wales PhD (unpublished).

Westwood, S., Morgan, N. J., Pritchard, A., & Ineson, E. (1999a). Branding the package holiday — the role and significance of brands for UK air tour operators. *Journal of Vacation Marketing, 5*(3), 238–252.

Westwood, S., Pritchard, A., & Morgan, N. J. (1999b). Businesswomen and airlines: A case of marketers missing the target? *Journal of Targeting, Measurement and Analysis for Marketing, 8*(2), 179–198.

Westwood, S., Pritchard, A., & Morgan, N. J. (2000). Gender blind marketing: Women's perceptions of airline services. *Tourism Management, 21*(4), 353–362.

Westwood, S., Morgan, N., Pritchard, A. (2006). Situation, participation and reflexivity in tourism research: Furthering interpretive approaches to tourism enquiry. *Journal of Travel and Tourism Research, 31*(2), 15–24 (forthcoming).

Chapter 19

Pursuing the Past: Using Oral History to Bring Transparency to the Research Process

Julia Trapp-Fallon

There are two histories of every land and people, the written history that tells what is considered politic to tell and the unwritten history that tells everything. (MacLean, 1975)
Don't you wonder sometimes
'Bout sound and vision (Bowie, 1977)

Introduction

This chapter discusses the opportunity for tourism and leisure researchers to engage with a 'holistic, integrated and all-embracing approach' advocated by Jost Krippendorf (Vanhove, 2003) and made possible by using oral history. The advantages and disadvantages of the use of this method of research in tourism and leisure have been discussed elsewhere (see Trapp-Fallon, 2003) and so this chapter will concentrate on the importance of oral commentary and its presentation in tourism and leisure research. By using recordings to hear the voice and enhance the meaning, a rich resource is created which, as Norkunas writes when speaking about tourism, '. . . offers fertile ground to look at the intersections of the politics of memory, ethnicity, public history and culture' (Norkunas, 1993, p. 1). Asking people about their past allows a reconstruction of the past and the reinterpretation of the present, and this should be added to more traditional forms of history fostering a heteroglossia, of many and varied voices. There is both art and science in this as Grayling (2002) observes and the need for this exploration of the variation in history and its interpretations helps our understanding of the way the world is now. In particular it is highlighted here that oral history can be used to find a people's history and a local history. It offers a democratic and decentralised approach, uncovering the lives of ordinary people: 'Without people willing to talk, recent community history can be a closed book'

(Iredale & Barrett, 1999, p. 193). By using technology to aid this process, research can challenge existing history, democratise research, enhance transparency and empower the researcher (Stewart & Floyd, 2004).

History from Below

The process of historiography at grassroots level is about the everyday, and means looking to local communities or neighbourhoods or group affinities as sources. The term community has 'dynamism and variability' (Black & MacRaild, 2000, p. 153) but generally it means local and will be more about an individual street than the town it's in and relates also the types of microhistories that the French have historically favoured to preserve regional distinctiveness. By examining local and regional history there is an attempt to balance mainstream historical study with a nationalist or centralist perspective (Black & MacRaild, 2000, p. 92).

Black and MacRaild believe that the way to understand community as a concept of historical enquiry lies in distinguishing between its descriptive and analytical dimensions. Community is about sentiments, values, sense of belonging; it is a series of dynamic relationships between people who share certain experiences or who seek to create links by finding or emphasising such experiences. In this type of study, insights into the community will bring understanding about identity and incorporates aspects of class, gender and ethnicity, the family and the workplace.

It is interesting to consider some of the discussions that have taken place surrounding the presentation of history. In the nineteenth century there was a move towards the primacy of facts, but upon examination this was found to be a history of events and administration, not a history of ordinary people. In fact, in 1861, Charles Kingsley Regius, professor of history at Cambridge, attacked the idea of studying the 'little man' as 'no science at all' (Black & MacRaild, 2000, p. 46). The idea that only those who achieve excellence are worthy of the study of historians continued, and Black and MacRaild see this as representative of the prevailing Victorian moral view.

During the period of the First World War, British Universities disregarded the work of Freud, Weber, Durkheim and Marx. In European Universities academics were moving dramatically away from the positivist–empiricist traditions that prevailed in Britain. Prior to that period the work of Burckhardt (1818–1897) and Michelet (1798–1874) had taken a much broader view of history, enquiring into the interaction between religion and the State, and those members of the population ignored by conventional historical narratives. It was their aim to understand everyday life in the context of history and geography (Black & MacRaild, 2000).

The idea that there are high and low forms of history led to the development of 'history from below'; a term used to describe attempts to understand the non-elite, often those not included on record. It is also called 'people's history' or 'the history of everyday life'. This is slightly different from the intention of the British Marxists of the 1960s, who were focused on working class consciousness and an understanding of the masses, but is part of the same broad movement. The British New Left fostered the development of cultural studies demonstrating much the same intention as 'the politico-cultural networks that led to the project of 'History from Below' (Macey, 2001, p. 77). The English department of Birmingham

University in the 1960s paved the way for Williams whose slogan 'culture is ordinary' (cited in Macey, 2001, p. 77) brought together many of the ideas of cultural studies and complemented the work of historians like Toynbee, who wanted to discover more about pauperism. These terms reflect the democratisation of history and the belief that different groups, like women's and gay movements have the right to pursue their histories.

The phrase 'History from below' was first used by Georges Lefebvre writing in the 1930s, but it has been suggested that it was E.P. Thompson, writing in the *Times Literary Supplement* in 1966 that raised awareness and saw its wider acceptance among historians (Black & MacRaild, 2000). Similar to the parallel work in English literature in the UK, the French Annales school were also pursuing an idea of how those previously ignored by historians should be included recognizing that statistical history could not 'unravel the past' (Thompson, 2000, p. 79). The introduction of this different way of thinking or *Mentalite* led to a shift away from a study of history through political events. Broader questions were raised about economy, society and culture (Arnold, 2000), and examined popular ideas and beliefs, which influenced everyday actions. These showed how people thought, constructed their world and their emotional values. There was an attempt 'to examine much broader sweeps of history — what they called the *longue duree* (the long-term) — and search for deep-rooted currents in the past' (Arnold, 2000, p. 98). By drawing upon anthropology, these historians were able to think about 'the unstated (and sometimes unrecognised) reasons why people do the things that they do' (Arnold, 2000, p. 100).

Carey (1987) has illustrated this development in his desire for a collection of eyewitness accounts in a collection of historical reportage. In seeking authenticity he refers to his reporter as a 'private eye working in a public area, the subject of his work should not be inward or fanciful, but pinned verifiably to the clockface of world time' (Carey, 1987, p. xxix).

He aims at bringing a sharper focus to events by bringing the 'I was there' element to the work and the belief that 'nothing is important — or unimportant — except as it is perceived'. He goes on to say:

> Of course, a lot of the pieces selected are nevertheless about big historical events, because these are the kind feel incited to record if they are around when they occur. But — to give an instance of the other kind — one of the pieces I should have defended most stubbornly if anyone had suggested leaving it out is Joe Ackerley's diary entry about going rabbiting with a small boy one afternoon. Obviously this is trivial in a sense. But because it tells how one young male began to be acclimatised to killing, it is also momentous — the loss of innocence observed through Ackerley's fastidious lens — and it is germane to all the massacres and atrocities this book logs. (Carey, 1987, p. xxx)

Tucker's (2000) more recent work in Turkey raises the issue of how information is displayed to tourists and contrasts the two forms of history by being able to compare contemporary voices in Turkish tourism. She takes two guided tours in Zelve, Capadocia and compares the voice of the establishment in an official tour by an archaeologist with one by an elderly villager. By listening to these two different guides she is able to reveal a very important distinction. There is an official history which reflects a construction of history placed in a wider context of global heritage and a more personal, strongly located voice.

There is a place for both of these within the local Zelve museum but a choice has been made to present the former as the only history and this reveals, as Tucker believes, a political agenda that seeks to avoid a number of tensions that exist in the area (Tucker, 2000, p. 86). The established professional view is clearly one that chooses to concentrate on a more traditional interpretation of history, that is, one focusing on the archaeology of the site rather than peoples' own experiences of living there.

However, a feature of 'History from below' is that it is not always written by professionals. Amateur groups of local historians have also made important contributions and, as Macey points out, (Macey, 2001, p. 186) as Macey points out, archives and the tape-recording of oral history are typical sources for this form of historiography. The nineteenth century saw some democratisation of sources (via the census for example) and this gave a new quality and quantity of information about ordinary people. Other less official observers were also investigating at this time and reporting on conditions in the homes and workplaces of families. Their findings were sometimes reported in the publications of the early statistical societies or presented impressionistically in journalism.

The Role of the Media

The recent rise of the citizen journalist and the discussion about the role of the journalist, the immediacy of information through technology and its reliability is to some extent a continuation of British discussions from eighteenth century, when the distinction between high and low history was made when Richard Rolt practised the linking of history with current political events and wrote for 'popular consumption and enjoyed significant sales' (Black & MacRaild, 2000, p. 38). The contrast here is between hack or low history written quickly and for profit compared with high history comprising a more critical and sceptical style.

The 'hack history' that was seen as inferior has a considerable role in the creation of truths in society today (Beeton, 2005). The role of the media is now even more apparent in its commentary on and documenting of social and cultural change, and the role of amateurs is one that has come to the fore. Combined with access to technology, the division between the journalist and the general public has become less clear with the rise of photographs and eyewitness accounts sent in by members of the public on the increase (Cypher, 2005). These 'citizen journalists' provided some of the most vivid firsthand accounts of Hurricane Katrina, and online forums bring news and views into people's homes with an immediacy that has never been known before. Blogging online via websites like Global voices (which has 300,000 visitors a month) is now challenging more established way in which news is presented worldwide. The blogging community sees a symbiotic relationship between the blogger and the mainstream media and this raises issues about how speech is heard. A blog that was set up in the aftermath of the Tsunami led to people around the world offering help in response to direct pleas from people in affected areas.

Dina Mehta from Mumbai is recorded as saying:

> It was one of my experiences that changed my life. . . . It wasn't the television telling you what was going on in some other part of the world; it was real voices. (Perrone, 2005)

The World Wide Web has joined radio and television to bring a feeling of personal involvement and foster responsibility. The ability of radio journalists in particular to listen to people's voices and explore the intimate details of people's everyday lives has been documented famously by radio journalists like Studs Terkel and Xinran Xue. Each were able to develop relationships of trust and sensitivity and used their years on radio and their interviews and letters over time to write books sharing the stories of people's lives that they had heard. Studs Terkel's work like *Hard Times: An Oral History of the Great Depression*, takes the form of transcripts with short biographical notes organised into chapters, often using song lyrics as a preface see Appendix for a short illustration. The beginning of the book includes a personal memoir where Terkel describes the work as a 'memory book, rather than one of hard fact and precise statistic' (Terkel, 1970, p. 5). His collections of interviews have taken years and reveal how people make sense of their past, how they connect individual experience and its social context. They see the past as part of the present, to interpret their lives and the world around them. Both Studs Terkel and Xinran Xue at opposite sides of the world in the USA and China were able over time to develop a rapport with their listeners and ask probing questions to encourage more opening up by the respondent.

Whilst journalism provides easily accessible and interesting examples of the people's voice there is now some backlash to the citizen journalist. Preston writing in *The Observer* (11/12/05) questions the validity of some of the contributions made at the time of Hurricane Katrina, emphasizing the need for a methodical approach to journalism, but Wright feels that there is the need to show sides of the conversation and that if this can take place across the world, the more the better (cited in Perrone, 2005). Reflection on this situation brings to mind Baudrillard's (2000) reservations about the immediacy of such information, believing it to be too great in volume and therefore beyond our comprehension and consequently meaningless.

There are studies in the academic literature where the methodology and objectives are clearer and personal testimony is central. The local voice has its own power and identity and it is this that has been noted by Glissant and Chamoiseau (two theorists of creolisation and the Caribbean cited by Kaup & Montgrauer, 2005 in Jamal & Kim, 2005) in the Caribbean. The traditional view of tropical paradise is one 'whose images are fixed by globalised homogenizing international tourism, and fluid local places which are always becoming minority' . . . and in this case is signified by its 'orality and variations in language' (Jamal & Kim, 2005, p. 64).

Memory and personal testimony have brought interesting insights to our understanding of women's leisure. The connection between oral history and feminist history has been described as 'symbiotic' since the late 1960s and its discoveries have challenged many traditional historical interpretations (Perks & Thomson, 1998, p. 4). An example is found in Kaufman's (1996) work based on the earlier unpublished research by Huyck, who gathered a number of 'archival and manuscript resources, photographs and 140 oral history interviews' and Kaufman added to this by interviewing a further 383 women. She called her work *National Parks and the Woman's Voice A History* and in it she details the history of women and their influence on national parks in the USA. Her aim was to document the change and development of the parks and how women had been the key to this process and previously ignored. Unlike Terkel she interleaves quotations alongside the historical information that she has collected.

Kaufman, in her recording of women's significance is part of the shift in emphasis away from what Black and MacRaild 'the nationalist or centralist perspective' (Black & MacRaild, 2000, p. 92). By recording lives that are either conceptualised individually (through oral testimony) or collectively (through community history), we develop and improve our understanding of a nation and its people. Kaufman has to some extent created a microhistory where interconnections and significance to the wider world can be made by the reader. She has written at a time where there was a wider acceptance of more theoretical research using oral and written life stories often crossing traditional disciplinary boundaries (Perks & Thomson, 1998).

Other interdisciplinary examples illustrate how our understanding of women's leisure can be advanced by using oral history and this deserves greater acknowledgement. The following examples are taken from *Oral History*, an interdisciplinary journal with a 1997 special issue on Sporting Lives. George's (1997) research about 'Women and Golf in Scotland' is revealing about the limitations and controls of life for women at the beginning of the twentieth century. The prejudices and discrimination are clearly revealed in this quotation from Ethel Jack speaking about Hazel Glennie who later represented Scotland in the Home International in 1959:

> One of the first friends I met in ladies' golf was Hazel Glennie from Falkirk and she was definitely not selected to play for Scotland because she was what we would term an 'artisan' because she worked a crane in British Aluminium in Grangemouth or Falkirk, somewhere round about there, and she was definitely not to be selected. I mean it was very obvious because she was a very good golfer. She wasn't approved of . . . she didn't speak like 'proper people'. In Scotland there were a lot of people who weren't quite accepted. But she did eventually make it in . . . but Hazel certainly had a hell of a struggle to get in, just because of the class distinction. I was all right, I went to a private school. She went to some wee school in Falkirk somewhere. (George, 1997, p. 50)

The difficulties for women engaged in sporting activity have also been highlighted by Oliver (1997) who looked at the role of Rounders in the lives of female Cotton Mill Workers in Bolton during a slightly earlier period than George's work but early in the twentieth century. Like George, Oliver has collected oral evidence and here we can see a contrast with golfing activity for women in Scotland where many:

> working class women, married and single, were actively involved in some kind of sporting activity during the period 1911–1939, and that in particular the game of Rounders was an important feature of working class women's culture. (Oliver, 1997, p. 40)

Oliver challenges the earlier work of Hargreaves (1985) about *Sporting Females*, who writes that women 'had neither the energy and time nor the money to participate or even to watch'. Hargreaves's interpretation is the established view and is evident more recently in Greer (2006), admittedly discussing women in the twenty-first century, but she too has failed to acknowledge a role for the voice that elucidates and brings women's leisure into sharp focus as the following example included in Oliver's (1997) work illustrates: Maud says:

> We used to go home from work and get washed and changed, and then back again. Our manager were very good. He were very interested in our rounders team and he used to follow us up and down. . . . We'd work really hard all day, then go back and play rounders in the evening. There'd be no transport and we would walk there and back. . . . How we had the energy to run around for another two hours playing rounders I don't know, but we really enjoyed it. It were a big thing in them days. (Oliver, 1997, p. 45)

Both the examples of the work of George and Oliver have added to an understanding of leisure in women's lives and follow the example of Henderson (1990) who believes that these oral accounts make women's lives far more visible (Henderson, 1990, p. 131). She is clearly illustrating the dual purpose of oral history technique. Her analysis of the words of women about their lives over 60–80 years as farm workers in the USA demonstrates that they were empowered by speaking for themselves which gave them a sense of control over the way that they perceived their lives (*ibid.*). She has also been able to add to the body of knowledge because using oral history allowed her to develop typologies of women's leisure. Three distinct groups of women are described, and examples of their own words bring an immediacy and understanding to her meaning that is not always found in leisure and tourism texts and far from Veblen's (1925) work introducing vicarious leisure cited by Greer (2006).

Henderson's first category is called the 'workhorses' and these were women who were always busy. She does not provide the names of these women but does give some background, for example:

> . . . a woman who [was] asked about memorable vacations she might have taken. She indicated that someone always had to stay on the farm but: a lot of people feel they need a vacation but to me my work and my pleasure were so closely related that I never felt I needed a vacation and I still feel that way. I'm enjoying what I'm doing. (Henderson, 1990, p. 126)

Her second group she calls the 'delayed gratifiers', those that thought retirement was deserved and a time to slow down. The words chosen to illustrate this were:

> I've gotten to the point that for so many years I did what I had to do, what I was expected to do and now that I am free I can do what I want to do, what I mainly want to do, and I'm really enjoying what I'm doing now. (Henderson, 1990, p. 127)

The smallest group belonged to the 'busybees'; these were women involved in activities outside work and whilst they saw volunteering or Church work as separate from leisure, they also recognised the significance of leisure in their lives:

> When one farm woman was asked if there were ever any constraints on her leisure, she replied 'No I think I belonged to everything (Laughter). Didn't make much difference, I put the kids in the car and away we'd go' (*ibid.*).

The development of work such as that cited about women's leisure during the 1980s and 1990s demonstrates how such studies take an inter-disciplinary approach. Drawing upon life story from sociology, biographical and autobiographical approaches in literary studies, anthropology, cultural studies, narrative psychology, linguistics and communication studies and related work, the relationships are explored between identity, memory and personal narrative. Thomson in Perks and Thomson (1998) claims that theoretical and methodological developments in those fields have enriched the practice of oral history, and that oral historians have contributed to the theory, method and politics of life story research through their interdisciplinary reflections on interview relationships and on ways of interpreting and using oral testimony.

Oral History Interview Technique

By illustrating the use of the oral history interview by academics it should be clear that this is more than chance reminiscence and that it can be employed to give direct and immediate testimony about life otherwise unknown. The aim is for the person to speak easily without inhibition or interruption. Familiarity with the recording equipment is therefore vital and it is important to remember that each encounter is unique and therefore 'impossible to follow a single set of techniques or rules for interviewing' (Perks & Thomson, 1998, p. 582) because it is an intuitive process.

However, there are some useful pointers:

• prepare
• establish rapport and intimacy
• listen
• ask open-ended questions
• do not interrupt
• allow pauses and silences
• avoid jargon
• probe
• minimise the presence of the tape recorder
• accept that there is no single right way of conducting an interview

Oral history researchers should also be mindful of examples from anthropology, communications studies and feminist research to remind us that the traditional perspective taken is often one that reflects a particular elite group. Therefore, the interviewer takes a balanced viewpoint about their situation and the culture they are in (Perks & Thomson, 1998) but should not be judgemental. Oakley's (1981) research into childbirth required repeated interviews and sometimes her presence at the birth itself. Consequently she advocates a more flexible, intimate and mutual approach, where there may well be some sharing of experience and the researcher:

> shows warmth and appreciation in return for what has been given to you. Accept a cup of tea if it is offered, and be prepared to chat about the family and photographs. (Thompson, 2000, p. 240)

The researcher also always has an ethical responsibility to inform those they are researching about their aim, to gain a release form so that it is agreed that the data can be used or a confidentiality statement where necessary (Maxwell & Pringle, 1983).

The previously cited work by Tucker (2000) illustrates the transparency that oral history research can achieve. By contrasting different voices in a heritage setting, revealing the questions asked help identify continuity in the researcher's thinking, for example:

> At this point, I asked if Christians and Muslims had lived here together as the archaeologist had told me. Omer replied No. No, not here. Some Christians lived in Urgup but not here. (Tucker, 2000, p. 84)

Tucker's research offers the opportunity for dialogue about the presentation of history, in this case for heritage consumers, who according to Prentice (1993 citing Sealey, 1987) have particular needs. One of these is identified as dialogue. They want 'to have a say in these processes of heritage presentation and conservation' (Prentice, 1993, p. 33) and desire nostalgia instead of aura, highlighting the extraordinary in the vernacular identified by Urry (2002) and parallels the shift that Tucker identifies from official to oral history (Tucker, 2000, p. 88). The 'proliferation of alternative or vernacular histories' as Urry identifies (Urry, 2002, p. 118) means that using the spoken word brings responsibilities for the researcher. 'Benedetto Croce (1886–1952) wrote that history is subjective because the historian himself is always present in its construction' (Grayling, 2002, p. 187) and the interviewer should see that their presence is an important part of the reflexive oral history interview process.

By making a recording, the tape should become a usable resource both for the current project and for others in the future and requires the time-consuming process of transcription and indexing. The information is now accessible and permanent and should not be tampered with and edited. Once that is done it should be referred to in this form and/or incorporated into a study with the knowledge and consent of the interviewee (Tiller, 2002) and being able to playback also brings greater flexibility in the analysis of data after the event (Dowrick & Biggs, 1983).

Augmenting the Voice

Lummis (1987) and Tiller (2002) both believe that the analysis of the spoken word can be enhanced. Tiller suggests photographs or artefacts and Lummis suggests another voice, music and visuals and believing that in this way greater validity can be gained (Lummis, 1987). To some extent the search for the local, inevitably leads to the use of different sources, for example, ballads and posters, films and videos, as each of these will have their own story and can be an illuminating insight into the past lives of a community and its cultural history.

Jamal and Kim (2005) have extensively explored the topic of heritage tourism appreciating that a:

> critically informed approach . . . recognizes that representations, enactments and displays of heritage are influenced by a network of mechanisms, industries and stakeholders

and these include the culture industries (involved in the production of film, literature, art, music, etc.) (Jamal & Kim, 2005, p. 57). They argue that a conceptual framework is needed to take the individual/local micro-level to a socio-political (macro-level) and whilst they recognise the inter-disciplinary approach needed as part of this, they too like Urry (2002) fail to acknowledge the role of the voice per se.

One of the most compelling features of oral history is its potential for use in public settings (Perks & Thomson, 1998). Presentations for a variety of media illustrate the multi-dimensional meaning of text, voice, image and performance that can engage an audience and encourage creative participation and interaction. Evidence can easily be found in the Gulbenkian Prize winning Big Pit Mining Museum in South Wales, where a strong emphasis is placed on the local voice. Miners can be heard in the background whilst viewing photographs and contributing to re-enactments of experiences working in the mine. These local voices give a very strong sense of place, and contribute to an educational role, helping to communicate important lessons about engineering and technology, for example, making them more easily digestible for the lay tourist and may also inspire new interests. The museum curator has sought different interpretive techniques to engage the visitor and by incorporating the local voice there is an acknowledgement of the importance of memory to the community and this lends distinctiveness to the museum visit. Sir Richard Sykes, Chairman of the Gulbenkian judges comments:

> . . . Big Pit offers an exceptional emotional and intellectual experience. It tells the individual stories of its community better than any museum I have visited and makes you contemplate the scale, and even the cruelty, of our industrial past which inspired a spirit of camaraderie and pride . . . museums today are not solely about displaying objects but are about the exposition of history, told with real passion alongside a commitment to a community's heritage. (http://www.artdaily.com/section/news/indexasp?int_sec=2&int_new=138 38 accessed 12 May 2006)

Urry (2002) has noted the 'pluralisation and indeed a contemporary-isation of history' (Urry, 2002, p. 118) evident particularly in museums like Big Pit, and the 'multi-mediatisation of the exhibit' (Urry, 2002, p. 119). Such harnessing of the technology transforms the experience: for example, the sound of voices in the miners' baths at Big Pit lends a special atmosphere to the space and enhances its successful interpretation. The same tool of employing the voice of experience is also used by producers of films and dramas on radio and television. In addition, the multimedia format available on CD-ROM, interactive CDs and the World Wide Web offers videotaped interviews for download, making information available to a global audience.

It is surprising therefore that the application of sound and vision to tourism and leisure research has been slow to develop, despite the acknowledgement that fieldwork with a pen and notebook has led to the loss of information (Hammersley & Atkinson, 1995). Film has been used regularly in social anthropology recognizing that non-verbal communication is not easily reconstructed.

Sipe as an historian, describes the significance of filmed oral history to add extra dimensions to the communication of a narrator's story. One example he gives is in filming

Small Happiness, a documentary about women in a Chinese village. One woman speaks of smothering her infant son because there was no food for him. Sipe views the woman's words as the bare outline seeing much more in her expression, tone of voice, breathing and body language. He believes that for these:

> 'quintessential unheard people, the visual dimension is crucial to their stories' and posits that 'moving images lessen the mediating role of the interviewer'.
> (Sipe in Perks & Thomson, 1998, p. 385)

Similarly, Hartman feels that to see and hear witnesses of the Holocaust shows the spiritual depth and resourcefulness of survivors which in itself is more heartening than seeing frightening still images and therefore the filming is seen as an extension of the oral tradition (Hartman, 2001).

The work of Belk and Kozinets is bringing filming (they call it videography) into the consumer and marketing research arena to give insights into the everyday (Belk & Kozinets, 2005). There is a recognition that the spoken and the written word can still leave space for the imagination (Stewart & Floyd, 2004) and there has been a suggestion that the introduction of the moving image is a substitution for own thoughts (Mirzoeff, 1999). There is a responsibility here about the representation that is chosen and as researchers we should be responsible as 'preservers of the historical record and the cultural memory' (Mitchell, 1994).

Interpreting the Voice

The sense of responsibility to which Mitchell refers raises an important issue for the researcher. The intention is to represent what the interviewee understands has happened and their interpretation, however it is not possible to be sure that it is correct. The whole truth of what happened in the past remains unknown, perhaps unknowable, because it is not possible for us to adopt the perspective of those in the past. The aim in pursuing the past and representing people's views is to make people stop and think and challenge accepted views (Iredale & Barrett, 1999).

The merging of subjects from the social sciences, and the interdisciplinary approach can only enrich research. Black and MacRaild (2000) note subjects like the history of crime would be without a significant method of explanation without sociological insight, and when psychoanalytical approaches are applied to the conceptual analysis of biography the result is enriched. In the study of everyday lives, there is considerable overlap between sociology and history (Black & MacRaild, 2000, p. 131) because to understand communities we need to understand relationships between all people, not just the elite or the exceptional as so often feature in history. By taking on some of the rigour of the social sciences there is more credibility to the reconstructed past that historians produce. Without it their work can be regarded as nearer to fiction than fact. A reader-friendly form called faction has been in evidence for many years and Iredale and Barrett cite the example from 1848 with Nicholas Asheton's *The Lancashire Witches* (Iredale & Barrett, 1999, p. 6). The idea of a selected re-interpretation of the past has been mentioned by a number of authors, and Norkunas cites Hobsbawm's 1983 work where he talks about history being selected, written, pictured, popularised and institutionalised by those whose function it is to do it so. A partial view can be improved by using archives where the story of the community is told directly through documentary records compiled by officials, as well as by ordinary people in diaries and private letters whose words may complement or contradict public records. Historians' theories, their analysis and speculation lead to the forming of opinions which also become part of the documentary record. The real history and what is invented is a subject for post-modernists. They believe that all history is narrative because it involves the interpretation and the imagination of the author in order to bring order and coherence to their interpretation of the past (Black & MacRaild, 2000).

Richardson and others (1990) cited in Hammersley and Atkinson (1995) see the narrative mode as essential for the organisation of everyday life taking the form of people's accounts of their experience. It is this form that dominates ethnography where information is shaped into a sociological or anthropological narrative of scholarly writing. Hammersley and Atkinson believe the narrative mode to be especially relevant for the subjects of ethnographic enquiry because it allows for the interpretation of events as they are placed on context and as part of a process.

It is through the narration of events that we can reveal how people behave and respond in certain circumstances, and can show patterns of actions and any predictable routines. In some ways the ethnographer has to recognize that they are weaving a tale of everyday life but the approach should be critical: an 'analytic power over the narrative means using reconstructions in a disciplined manner' (Hammersley & Atkinson, 1995, p. 257).

Such constructions can lead to criticism. Historians like Schama have not wished to include chapter headings believing them to privilege their explanatory force. A narrative causes criticism because it is believed to be intuitive and selective; it also ensures the information is readable and like biography follows the birth, life and death pattern. There is often an advantage in the historian knowing little, and Strachey endorsed this view believing ignorance to be the first requisite of the historian as ignorance leads to simplification and clarification, which selects and omits (Black & MacRaild, 2000).

The remembering of *their* truths is what Terkel espouses rather than *the* truth and he also acknowledges the help he receives in the transcription of the interviews. Highlighting the role of the reporter in the reporting is also a feature of Gonzo journalism. Central to the gonzo journalist's view is that there can be a greater truthfulness to their interpretation without the adherence to the strict rules of factual journalism. In literary terms gonzo has been described on the Wikipedia page by American historian Douglas Brinkley (who worked with Hunter S Thompson) as requiring virtually no re-writing, frequently employing scribbled notes, transcribed interviews, and verbatim telephone conversations. It is suggested that it brings more of the mood of the situation to their writing and greater satisfaction to the journalist (http://en.wikipedia.org/wiki/Gonzo_journalism, accessed 27 November 2005).

Conclusion

This chapter has discussed the development of the term 'history from below' which challenges the traditional methodology of history which records only the exceptional and the elite in written documentation. It has simulated the organic nature of history in that it has grown and changed by taking on aspects of the social sciences and become more interdisciplinary. The rise of the citizen journalist and the accessibility of technology for immediate communication raise much earlier historical debates about the method and style of presenting information. There is still a tendency 'to think of written language as the privileged medium of scholarly communication' (Hammersley & Atkinson, 1995, p. 189), and the chapter has addressed the value of the spoken word and identified details about the approach needed for an oral history interview. It is important for tourism and leisure researchers to remember that their research about the past or present will itself become a cultural artefact, a reflection of its time (Norkunas, 1993). The availability of the technology in small and reliable formats opens up the possibility of permanently recording (Hammersley & Atkinson, 1995) personal and popular memory about the everyday lives, and will give insights into how individuals and communities see and hear themselves, and how they tell their own story.

> ROY: They're always tellin' us that we should be glad that we got food and all that 'cause back in the Thirties they used to tell us people were starving and got no jobs and all that stuff.
> LILY: The food lines they told us about.
> ROY: Yeah! you had to stay in line and wait for food.
> LILY: And everything. You got it when it was there. If it wasn't, then you made without it. She said there was a lot of waiting.
> BUCKY: I never had a Depression, so it don't bother me really.
> ROY: From what you hear, you'd hate to live in that time.
> BUCKY: Well, I ain't livin' in that time.

References

Arnold, J. H. (2000). *History a very short introduction.* Oxford: Oxford University Press.

Baudrillard, J. (2000). *The vital illusion.* New York: Columbia University Press.

Beeton, S. (2005). Understanding film-induced tourism conference presentation on 19/7/05 at the 4th Symposium of Consumer Psychology of Tourism, Hospitality and Leisure Research.

Belk, R. W., & Kozinets, R. V. (2005). Videography in marketing and consumer research. *Qualitative Market Research, 8*(2), 128–141.

Black, J., & MacRaild, D. M. (2000). *Studying history* (2nd ed.). Basingstoke: Macmillan.

Bowie, D. (1977). *Sound and vision on the low album.* RCA Ltd, Record Division, England.

Carey, J. (1987). *The Faber book of reportage.* Great Britain: Faber and Faber.

Cypher, B. (2005). Katrina's story is told by amateur journalists. *Cardiff Post* (1/9/05), p. 15.

Dowrick, P., & Biggs, S. J. (Eds). (1983). *Using video: Psychological and social applications.* New York: Wiley.

George, J. (1997). Women and golf in Scotland. *Oral History Journal of the Oral History society Spring 1997 Sporting Lives, 25*(1), 46–50.

Grayling, A. C. (2002). The meaning of things applying philosophy to life. London: Phoenix.

Greer, G. (2006). Why women don't relax. *The Guardian,* 4/5/06, pp. 12–13.

Hammersley, M., & Atkinson, P. (1995). *Ethnography principles in practice.* (2nd ed.). London: Routledge.

Hargreaves, J. (1985). Playing like gentlemen while behaving like ladies. *British Journal of Sports History, 2*(1).

Hartman, G. (2001). Holocaust videography, oral history and education. *Tikkun, 16*(3), 51–58.

Henderson, K. A. (1990). An oral life history perspective on the containers in which American farm women experienced leisure. *Leisure Studies, 9*(2), 121–133.

Iredale, D., & Barrett, J. (1999). *Discovering local history*. Bucks: Shire Publications.

Jamal, T., & Kim, H. (2005). Bridging the interdisciplinary divide towards an integrated framework for heritage tourism research. *Tourist Studies, 5*(1), 55–83. London: Sage.

Kaufman, P. W. (1996). *National parks and the woman's voice: A history*. Albuquerque: University of New Mexico Press.

Lummis, T. (1987). *Listening to history: The authenticity of oral evidence*. London: Hutchinson.

Macey, D. (2001). *Dictionary of critical theory*. London: Penguin Books.

MacLean, C. (1975). *The highlands* (2nd ed.). Inverness: Club LeaDha.

Maxwell, G. M., & Pringle, J. K. (1983). The analysis of video records. In: P. Dowrick, & S. J. Biggs (Eds), *Using video: Psychological and social applications*. New York: Wiley.

Mitchell, W. J .T. (1994). *Picture theory*. Chicago: University of Chicago Press.

Mirzoeff, N. (1999). *An introduction to visual culture*. London: Routledge.

Norkunas, M. K. (1993). *The politics of public memory tourism, history and ethnicity in Monterey, California*. Albany: State University of New York Press.

Oakley, A. (1981). *Subject women*. Oxford: Martin Robertson.

Oliver, L. (1997). No hard-brimmed hats or hat-pins please, Bolton women cotton workers and the game of rounders, 1911–1939. *Oral History Journal of the Oral History Society Sporting Lives Spring, 25*(1), 40–45.

Perks, R., & Thomson, A. (Eds). (1998). *The oral history reader*. London: Routledge.

Perrone, J. (2005). *Found in translation*, 12/12/05, available at: http://www.guardian.co.uk/international/story/0,1665515,00.html, accessed 30/12/05.

Prentice, R. (1993). *Tourism and heritage attractions*. London: Routledge.

Preston, P. (2005). Fleet street can only see clouds in blue sky. *The Observer* 11/12/05, available at: http://www.guardian.co.uk/print/0,5352979-103390,00.html, accessed 30/12/05.

Stewart, W. P., & Floyd, M. F. (2004). Visualising leisure. *Journal of Leisure Research, 36*(4), 445–460.

Terkel, S. (1970). *Hard times: An oral history of the great depression*. Maryland: Pantheon.

Thompson, P. (2000). *The voice of the past oral history* (3rd ed.). Oxford: Oxford University Press.

Tiller, K. (2002). *English local history: An introduction* (2nd ed.). Stroud: Sutton Publishing.

Trapp-Fallon, J. (2003). Searching for rich narratives of tourism and leisure experience: How oral history could provide an answer. *Tourism and Hospitality Research. The Surrey Quarterly Review, 4*(4), 297–306.

Tucker, H. (2000). Tourism and the loss of memory in Zelve, Capadocia. *Oral History, 28*(2), 79–88.

Urry, J. (2002). *The tourist gaze* (2nd ed.). London: Sage.

Vanhove, N. (2003). Obituary of Jost Krippendorf. *Tourism and Hospitality Research. The Surrey Quarterly Review, 4*(4), 381–382.

Veblen, T. (1925). *The theory of the leisure class*. London: Unwin Books (1970 edition).

Chapter 20

The Contribution of Biographical Research in Understanding Older Women's Leisure

Diane Sedgley

Introduction

Although biographical research techniques have been widely used and recognised in sociology and history for the deep insight they can provide into individual lives, the technique has hardly been used in the field of leisure and tourism. This is a pity as biographical research methods have the potential to provide much insight into people's leisure and tourism behaviour. To demonstrate, this chapter focuses on the leisure of older women and, in particular, the leisure of Alice, an 85-year-old woman, to show how identifying the influence of both structure and agency upon her life course, allows us to understand the context and significance of her current leisure behaviour.

Older People in Context

There is a well-documented rise in the number of older people within the developed world; the United Nations (UN, 2002, p. 1) for example estimates that the number of older people in the developed world will quadruple over the next 50 years. The largest group of older people are women, who are still more likely to survive to each successive age than men (there are 18% more women than men aged over 50 and in 2002 there were 2.6 women for every man aged 85 and over (National Statistics online www.statistics.gov.uk).

Despite this, little leisure research exists on both the leisure of older people but particularly older women. The work that does exist within gerontology and leisure studies is often quantitative in nature, concerned with collecting data in order to 'measure' the characteristics of leisure and even to formulate universal models of leisure behaviour. Unfortunately, whilst such statistical accounts highlight the frequency of certain activities, they fail to uncover the variety, meanings and context of this leisure (Scraton, Bramham, & Watson, 1998, p. 108). The results also tend to shed little light on people's

The Critical Turn in Tourism Studies: Innovative Research Methodologies
Copyright © 2007 by Elsevier Ltd.
All rights of reproduction in any form reserved.
ISBN: 0-08-045098-9

attitudes, motivations and reasons for choice of leisure activities. As Long (1989, p. 69) states, merely identifying the leisure activities that people participate in is not enough. We also need 'to recognise the satisfactions and meanings that are to be derived from them (for example, creativity, relaxation and sociability)'.

Another characteristic of the quantitative research on older people is that it often highlights the negative aspects of older people's leisure, emphasising increased amounts of time engaged in solitary, sedentary, passive leisure activities such as watching television and listening to the radio. Indeed in 1991, Tokarski (1991, p. 79) observed a tendency to highlight decreases in active, competent or productive involvement in leisure amongst older people; 'only in a few cases are other tendencies mentioned'. Such conclusions are worrying because, not only do they create knowledge of older people that is inaccurate, but they also form a knowledge base which older people themselves come to believe and internalise (Wearing, 1995).

The large samples used in such quantitative research also tell us little about the diversity and variations in the leisure experiences of older people, resulting in generalised accounts (Peace, 1990, p. 4). Additionally, although many people are often interviewed for the statistical surveys, they still often result in small samples of subgroups which, as Victor (2002, p. 55) points out, 'makes analysis of specific subgroups of the older population, such as married women aged 85 or older, very problematic' Thus, the statistical nature of quantitative work in understanding older people has often meant that older people have been distanced from the analysis (Walker, 1987).

Various reasons have been forwarded to explain the predominance of quantitative research when studying older people's lives. Achenbaum (1997, p. 16), for example, suggests that the newness of the field of gerontology, compared to other sciences, has caused researchers to legitimise their area of study by emulating the hard sciences; 'gerontology's gatekeepers have been unabashedly scientistic as they tried to legitimise their area of expertise'. He even goes as far as to suggest that gerontologists are 'more wedded to positivism than physicists' as they search for a grand theory on ageing (Achembaum, 1997, p. 17). Similar observations have been made of leisure researchers who Bramham and Henry (1996) describe as traditionally 'defining themselves as 'detached scientists'.

Thus, clearly there is a need for more research on older people that addresses some of these shortcomings. For example, a need for research which rather than doing research *on* older people, involves them in the research process and allows their voices to come through. For, as Grant (2002, p. 295) quite rightly states:

> older people themselves are the authentic experts on their lives and impute meanings about what is happening in their respective worlds, we should at least attempt to get 'inside' ageing as it is experienced and let it be expressed by those living it. Such knowledge seems to be fundamental if we are to more fully realise the meaning and subtleties of ageing, leisure and a physically active older lifestyle.

Research on small groups of 'real' people can tell us much, not only about what people do with their leisure time but also why they engage in the way they do (Veal, 1997, p. 19). At the same time, such research can also lead to the negative assumptions and stereotypes surrounding older people being challenged, a re-conceptualisation of what old age means and a new way of thinking about older people (Fennel et al., 1994). Featherstone and Hepworth (1995a, p. 31), in particular, have argued for a new discourse around old age, which challenges the associations between old age and illness, disability, and disengagement, in their words, a ' radical deconstruction and displacement of negative images of ageing and the elaboration of an alternative positive imagery'. Such an approach is vital particularly because, as Betsy Wearing (1995, p. 263) points out, the study of older people's leisure can undermine the 'underuse syndrome' and has 'the potential to challenge ageism and the self-fulfilling prophesy of underuse of physical and mental abilities in old age'.

Research is also needed which, as well as allowing older people's voices to emerge in the research process, can challenge the view that the 'truth' about ageing can be measured 'objectively', recognising that it is not possible to find regularities in or predict human behaviour (Jamieson & Victor, 1997, p. 175). A shift is needed away from the dominance of positivism and empiricism, towards balanced research output which is 'as interested in the particular as in the general, in understanding as well as generalising' and which highlights aspects of older people's leisure in a way which positivist approaches cannot do (Holstein & Minkler, 2003, p. 788).

In overcoming the shortcomings of quantitative, large scale, positivist research on older people, this chapter considers the contribution biographical research can make to understanding older people's leisure, relying as it does on small samples of older people and their subjective narrative about their own lives. Consideration is also given to the contribution biographical research can make in identifying the range of personal and structural factors, over older people's life course, which determine the meanings and characteristics of their current leisure (Grant, 2002). To achieve this, the work draws from the main researcher's own ongoing PhD on older women's leisure in the 'oldest old' category, that is those aged 75 and over, a group on which little, if any, leisure research exists.

Defining Biographical Research

The term biographical interview will be used within this research, however, its exact meaning is open to interpretation, particularly as many other terms are often used to describe similar approaches to research, mainly oral history, personal narrative, biography, life history, life story. Denzin (1989, p. 27) observes for example that:

> A family of terms combines to shape the biographical method . . ., life, self, experience, epiphany, case, autobiography, ethnography, auto-ethnography, biography, ethnography story, discourse, narrative, narrator, fiction, history, personal history, oral history, case history, case study, writing presence, difference, life history, life story, self story, and personal experience story.

Bertaux (1981, p 7) argues that the range of terms, often used interchangeably to describe a whole range of biographical approaches, indicates 'terminological confusion' within the research community. Bornatt (2002, p. 118) on the other hand disputes this, observing that all these approaches have much in common, particularly the way in which they 'focus on the recording and interpretation, by some means or other, on the life experience of individuals'. Indeed, there are similarities in these approaches but there are also many distinctions. Life stories or biographies, for example, aim to focus on the past as a way of understanding people's individual lives, their identity and development, and as such are very much subject-centred. In oral history on the other hand, the emphasis is on recording detail about how the past was lived both individually and communally. In oral history, the interviews are often supplemented with historical, public and private documents or even interviews with other people to support the statements of individuals (Thompson, 2000).

History of Biographical Research

Biographical research is not new and has been used in historical and anthropological research for a long time, very often as both a way of gaining insight into non-literate societies, where there is an absence of written documentation, and also in terms of providing more in-depth and rich insights into the lives of marginal groups or individuals who would not necessarily have had a voice in the research process. As well as historians, professionals working within the field of gerontology such as social workers and health workers have also more recently recognised the benefits of biographical research in eliciting older people's attitudes (for example, in relation to residential care), understanding family relationships and learning how people coped with past difficulties and hardships (Gearing & Dant, 1990, p. 151).

In sociology, the biographical approach to research first appeared in the 1920s and 1930s when Thomas and Znaniecki (1919–1921) used it in their study of 'The Polish Peasant in Europe and America'. The approach was also later used in the 1940s in Chicago, as part of a number of studies looking at juvenile delinquency, crime and drug addiction. In both of these studies, the emphasis was on both the individual and social facts to understand individual behaviour, on objective and subjective analysis of a situation, particularly those of the 'underdog' or the 'marginal'. Plummer (1983, p. 61) observes how both of these studies indicated a rejection of a grand narrative, a whole truth about a situation. Unfortunately, issues regarding reliability, subjectivity and representativeness at that time, meant that the technique became unpopular, 'its collapse was as sudden and radical as had been its success and prestige during the 1920s' (Bertaux, 1981).

Although these early sociological studies, using the biographical technique, did not last long, they were extremely significant in that, as already stated, they represented a shift in social science away from structural determinism towards 'symbolic interactionism'. This process engaged with the individual and gave value to people's subjective experiences in order to understand how people interpret and give meaning to the world around them (Chamberlayne, Bornat, & Wengraf, 2000). Such an emphasis on the individual, rather than structural forms, to explain the nature of society and behaviour had first emerged in the work of George Herbert Mead (1863–1931) who argued that people develop and change in response to their social experiences and actively create their social environment. 'The self is something which has a development: it is not here at birth but arises in the context of social experience and activity' (Mead, 1934). Symbolic interactionism thus challenged the structural functionalist view, developed by Emile Durheim (1858–1917) and later refined by Talcott Parsons (1902–1979), which argued that social structures (work, the state and the family) determine human behaviour, assuming individuals have little control over their lives. The interactionist or subjectivist approaches aimed to shift the focus to individual meaning and choice, thus challenging functionalist accounts of social life, which were being criticised as consensual, and forming a solely societal view of the individual.

Today the use of the biographical technique continues to take from interactionism, phenomenology and ethnomethodology, its concern with subjectively defined reality and how individuals interpret the world in order to understand individual behaviour, as Roberts (2002, p. 6) states:

> The study of biographical research rests on a view of individuals as creators of meanings which form the basis of their everyday lives. Individuals act according to meanings through which they make sense of social existence.

Indeed, some observers commenting on this duality of structure and agency have observed that individual agency has become more influential than structural determinacy in determining how people lead their lives (Gilleard & Higgs, 2000, p. 3). Post-modernists in particular argue more than ever before in history, that people have the ability to make conscious decisions and choices about how they want to lead their lives. People are no longer defined purely in terms of state structures, as is the case for example with Marxism, which defined people purely on the basis of their relationship with the means of production (Gilleard & Higgs, 2000, p. 28). No longer are people regarded as purely the victims of state structures and policies such as pensions, employment and health policies (as is the case with structured dependency or political economy approaches to study older people), instead the new emphasis is on individual agency which stresses the choices people have. Indeed, the emphasis on the individual is so great that Gidden's (1991) social theory refers to the 'project of the self' in which:

> self identity becomes a reflexively organised endeavour. The reflexive project of the self, which consists in the sustaining of coherent yet continuously revised biographical narratives, takes place in the context of multiple choice . . . . (Giddens, 1991, p. 5)

Such ideas on the strength of human agency have resonance in the study of older people in that, rather than talking of them purely in terms of victims of social structures and disengagement, they allow the possibilities of old age, as a time for self-fulfilment, to come to the fore.

The Contribution and Possibilities of Biographical Research

One of the main advantages of the biographical approach is its highly personal approach, exploring people's lives *in situ*, in order to highlight the intricacies of people's everyday lives in a way which quantitative research fails to do. As Thompson (1981, p. 249) states:

> For the sociologist disillusioned with the crude mass empiricism of the quantitative survey, and the aggregating of masses of data abstracted from

their sources in timeless, impersonal slices, the life history appears to offer information which is from its very nature coherent, rooted in real social experience; and is therefore capable of generating wholly fresh sociological insights as opposed to the self-reflecting answers of predetermined questions.

The insider's or 'emic' perspective which emerges from biographical research thus places the subject at the centre of the research process, rather than the researcher, and allows the subject to highlight issues and agendas which are of significance to them (Thompson, 1981, p. 255). In doing so, biographical interviews reduce the risk of researchers applying their own values and understandings to the lives of individuals for, as Thompson (1981, p. 253) makes explicit:

> As middle class professionals working at a particular historical moment, we are too easily led to generalize from our own experience and to take for granted that it was shared in other social groups or at other periods.

Indeed, by giving voice to the older women in this research and listening to their own stories, potential difficulties of a middle class female academic doing research into the lives of women 30–40 years older, are lessened.

The focus on the individual in the biographical interviews can increase the possibility of narratives emerging, which may challenge the existing assumptions and dominant narratives around older people. Bornat (2002, p. 117), for example, observes that biographical interviews can ultimately prove to be both emancipating and empowering to older people, for example by allowing them the opportunity to challenge negatively stereotyped images of older people. Bernard, Meade, and Tinker (1993, p. 17) stress that research, which listens to the voices of older women, is particularly important, as too often, older women have been the 'objects' or 'subjects' of research that has failed to capture their resistance and spirit.

Another advantage of biographical research is that it also shifts the emphasis in research away from the formulation of 'grand narratives', which are often at the heart of quantitative research, but instead moves towards more individual, in-depth insights into people's lives and in doing so, the messiness, difficulties and struggles surrounding people's lives are often captured. In quantitative research, the detail of people's lives is often sanitised, as Goodley, Lawthom, Clough, and Moore (2004, p. 184) describe, "Lives and difficulties are disinfected and presented 'steam-cleaned', and — though creased and worn — they are offered up to the reader in a relatively painless way. These are lives served up with the appropriate dosage of painkiller to make things easier on the reader". In biographical research on the other hand, the near absence of predetermined questions, means people's histories can be explored largely in their own words, 'warts and all', often revealing the difficulties and struggles within people's lives.

As well as the ability of biographical research to provide in-depth, first hand, possibly emancipatory insights into older people's lives, the approach also reflects a belief that it is not possible to study or understand the lives of older people at a snapshot in time but that it is necessary to understand what has gone before, the social, environmental and cultural contexts through which older people have lived. Biographical interviews thus provide a perfect way of exploring the whole of people's life development rather than isolated moments, acknowledging that:

> Men and Women are not just 'old'. They are ageing people with pasts and futures. Their pasts may be personal and include all sorts of experiences that made them what they are, or stopped them living as they would have liked. (Wilson, 2000, p. 12)

The Process of Undertaking Biographical Interviews

In order to illustrate the potential of biographical research, a case study has been included in this part of the chapter, drawn from the main researcher's own draft PhD, on the leisure of women aged over 75, in order to show how biographical research may be conducted and also to show the levels of detail which the technique can provide into a person's life, in this case their leisure. Within the author's draft PhD, a series of three biographical interviews are used to supplement detail, which emerged from a number of semi-structured interviews in the same research project. Such a small sample is not unusual in biographical interviews due to their ethnographic nature, which usually involves spending long periods with participants and results in many hours of tape-recorded material (Gearing & Dant, 1990). Small research samples in biographical research are also deemed appropriate, for the aim is not to formulate rules or 'grand narratives' that can be applied to large cross sections of the population, but to explore, in some depth, the individual lives of a small group of people.

The concentration on a narrow age group in the author's own research, proved useful in that it allowed for the identification of unique structural and historical events to which the cohort had been exposed. Very often, these had been critical in determining their life chances, outlook on life, social roles, as well as opportunities for economic success and social mobility (Elder, 1981, p. 86). Indeed, the advantage of studying specific cohorts to contextualise the lives of people, first emerged in the work of Karl Mannheim (1952) who recognised that an individual's location in social and historical time resulted in distinct world-views and ways of thinking about the world.

However, the aim of biographical research is also to gain insight into the personal happenings in people's lives, as well as the shared social and historical events. To achieve this, it is important to establish a rapport with respondents during the research process. Cornwell and Gearing (1989, p. 37) advise:

> establish a style of interaction which is more that of a conversation than an interview, and a relationship in which the other person feels comfortable and relatively uninhibited about talking about themselves in the past and present.

In this research, the setting of the biographical interviews in the respondent's own homes and the minimal number of predetermined questions/prompts in the biographical interviews, ensured that the atmosphere surrounding the interviews was informal and 'more of a conversation'. As recommended by Gearing and Dant (1990, p. 150), prompts used in the biographical interviews related to the major stages of the women's lives — childhood upbringing, school, work, married life, retirement and, if appropriate, widowhood. The responses of the women were taped, with the interviews lasting between one to one-and-a-half hours, and usually ending with a shared cup of tea and biscuits. Each of the women was interviewed on three occasions.

A surprising aspect of biographical interviews, and indeed these interviews, was the extent to which the 'respondents' seemed to enjoy the meetings. Indeed, Thompson et al, (1990) in his work refers to the potential therapeutic benefits of biographical interviews, involving as they do, reminiscence, which can provide older people with an opportunity to revisit past events and memories. Cornwell and Gearing (1989, p. 37) also comment on the satisfactions which are often gained by respondents when participating in biographical interviews, observing:

> the pleasure of thinking back over the past; for others from having company
> for half a day; for others from the sense of forming a new relationship and for
> others from being able to talk — sometimes for the very first time — about
> something of significance in their past.

Indeed, the long periods of time spent with the women also meant that the researcher not only gained an insight into their lives but, in the process, also established friendships with the women. Goodley et al, (2004, p. 58) point out that this is typical of ethnographic research in which long periods of time are spent with respondents and, as such, 'digresses markedly from the classic view of the dispassionate, distanced, objective scientific observer'. Kazmierska (2004, p. 181) also observes the closeness that can emerge between the interviewer and subjects in biographical research, stating that, "The time required by a narrator to tell their life story is greater than in 'classical' interviewing, and this factor helps to strengthen the relationship between researcher and informant".

Reliability of Biographical Research

Despite the clear advantages of the biographical research method in giving voice and getting close to respondents, its subjectivity does open up questions of reliability. Fischer (1983, p. 31), for example, argues that reliance on people memories within the biographical approach is problematic for, as:

> People fail to remember, they choose (consciously or not) to lie, or they recall
> or present only partially true information. To the extent that life histories rely
> on retrospective information, it is difficult to measure the distortions.

Berger (1963, pp. 56–57) also questions the reliability of biographical interviews, maintaining that:

> as we remember the past, we reconstruct it in accordance with our present
> ideas of what is important and what is not . . . At least in our consciousness,

the past is malleable and flexible, constantly changing as our recollection reinterprets and explains what has happened.

Cornwell and Gearing (1989, p. 43) similarly observe that 'the past that is constructed orally can never be fixed; it will change to the degree that the present changes'.

However, as Veal (1997, p. 145) quite rightly argues, questionnaires and particularly quantitative data also have similar problems of reliability, as what subjects say in questionnaires is also dependent on their powers of recall, their honesty as well as the format of the questions in the questionnaire. Veal (1997, p. 145) goes on to say that information presented in numerical form, based on large numbers, does not represent 'immutable truth'. Indeed, he points out that, 'There has been very little research on the validity or accuracy of questionnaire data in leisure and tourism studies'. Plummer (1983, p. 68) similarly casts doubt on attempts in the social sciences for 'generalisability' arguing that people are not rational beings whose behaviour can be predicted. Instead, life is often ambiguous and chaotic.

> Questionnaires, experiments, attitude scales and even the perusal of existing social science literature and historical documents can often give a form and order to the world which it frequently does not have!

Hence, biographical research may be no less 'reliable' than other forms of research methods, indeed the emphasis on the subject's own voice and experiences makes it more difficult for the researcher to misrepresent respondents.

Analysis of Biographical Interviews

Fischer (1983, p. 38) maintains that methods of collecting life stories are better developed than methods of analysing them, "the application of life history to sociology is, at present, more of an 'art' than a 'science'". However, for Plummer (1983, p. 116), the lack of rigid guidelines for analysing biographical interviews is unproblematic and understandable when dealing with the ambiguity and unpredictability of people's lives. Indeed, the personal, subjective nature of biographical interviews has led some to argue that any analysis of people's life stories is unnecessary as, in the telling of a life story, the analysis and interpretation has already occurred. In fact, Booth and Booth (1994) suggest that analysing a life story can destroy the subjective realities of individuals by making the individual a subject, once again, of abstract social theory. Mitroff and Kilman (1978) similarly argue that analysis of life story can take ownership from the teller and place it in the hands of the theorist.

Whilst recognising the difficulties inherent in analysing people's life stories, the decision was taken within the main author's own research to analyse the transcripts in order to emphasise and explore the themes within the women's stories, particularly the role of both structure and agency. As Goodley et al. (2004, p. 149) state:

> analysis can serve to offer a helping hand in guiding readers to the theoretical significances of a narrative. Without analysis there is no application to any theory and the reader can interpret the story in any way they wish.

However, to ensure that the voice of respondents, in this example Alice's, was not lost in the analysis, priority has been given to using her own words where possible. In addition, to ensure that the researchers interpretation of Alice's life did not dominate, she was shown the initial version and analyses of her life story and invited to comment. In this sense the life story, which emerges, has a shared ownership ensuring that Alice was more of an equal participant in the research. In this respect, the research overcomes the criticism, levelled at much research on older people, for treating them as passive participants. The shared analysis also takes from feminist research the desire to ensure women's views of the world are privileged.

Thus, as Goodley (2000, p. 58) suggests, both the emic ('insider') view of the narrator and that of the researcher have been combined to highlight and examine the interplay between both structure and individual autonomy which have shaped Alice's life. In recognising Alice's individual, personal experiences, rather than just structure, the analysis aims to reveal Alice's subjective world. Plummer (1983, p. 57) describes such an approach as 'humanistic' sociology, in which the active, thinking individual is acknowledged, recognising that people are both the 'products and producers of their history' (Elder, 1981, p. 78).

The analysis has also been mindful of the responsibility of the researcher to challenge and dismantle dominant negative, pessimistic traditional discourses around older people, to create a more 'critical' approach to both gerontology and leisure studies. Hence, the aim is that the analysis will challenge some of negative preconceptions about older people's lives.

Pen Portrait of Alice

Alice was born in 1921 in Newcastle and was raised by her mother and grandmother after her father left the family home when Alice was a young age. To support the family, Alice's mother left Newcastle to find work as a nurse at a London hospital, leaving Alice and her brother in the care of their grandmother. At the age of eleven, after Alice's mother had saved enough money to buy a house in Shepherds Bush, Alice and her brother went down to London to join her.

At the age of fourteen Alice left school and got a job at a radio factory. After two years at the radio factory, Alice applied for a job at the Hoover factory where her mother now also worked. At Hoover, Alice was able to maintain her interest in tap and ballroom dancing, through the companies regular dance nights and annual cabaret shows. It was also whilst working at Hoover that Alice met her future husband. During courtship the two would go to Saturday morning matinees and on some Sundays, the London Palladium. Sometimes Alice's partner would hire a punt and punt to Eel Pie Island where they would have a picnic. In 1939 the couple got married and continued to live in London.

On the outbreak of war, Alice's brother joined the army and was sent to the Far East. Her husband, a key worker, training men on munitions, was sent to various sites around Wales-Machynnleth, Merthyr Tydfil, north Wales and eventually Llandaff in Cardiff. It was in Merthyr, at the age of nineteen, that Alice had her first child, a daughter, followed by a son two years later.

When the war ended, Alice's brother returned to Britain but died soon after, never having recovered from the injuries and treatment he sustained in a Japanese prisoner of war camp. Alice and her husband decided to stay in south Wales and bought a grocers shop in Cardiff. The family lived above the shop, working long hours from 9-8 in the evening except for half day closing on Wednesdays and all day on Sundays.

In any spare time they had, occasionally they would take the children to the cinema or on birthdays and anniversaries to a restaurant. Once a year the family would have a week's holiday in Ogmore, only ten miles outside Cardiff, where they would stay in one of the single-decker buses that had been converted into holiday accommodation.

After eighteen years in the shop, Alice's husband's health declined and the business was beginning to suffer from supermarket competition. The couple decided to close the shop but to continue living above it. In order to make ends meet, Alice began taking in lodgers from a local college, providing meals, cleaning and laundry services.

For Alice, the evenings were quiet times to relax watching television, however, once a week she would visit the local Conservative club for a game of bingo and a dance. During the week, Alice's husband would go out to play skittles or visit one of his three allotments where he grew vegetables.

When Alice's husband's health deteriorated further and he was told he didn't have long to live, they sold the shop premises and moved to a much smaller terraced house, round the corner from the shop; the house that Alice still lives in today. In the last months of Alice's husband's life he was bedridden and she became a full time carer. Two months after her husband's death, Alice also lost her son and, with that, contact with her sons two children, her two grandchildren.

After her husband and son's death, Alice described how she struggled and still does struggle to cope with these unhappy experiences. However despite these sad memories she has coped and worked hard to put a new life together for herself, developing new interests. Her week is full, for example Tai Chi on Monday's, keep fit on Tuesday morning and 'Tuesday Night Tarts' club in the evening (a group that Alice has formed with women she met at Slimmer's World). On Wednesdays a friend calls and Alice has her hair done at the hairdressers. Thursday afternoon is the pensioners' meeting, Thursday night is skittles. Friday is a stay at home day. On weekends she spends time shopping with her daughter.

Leisure in the Context of Constraints

A theme running throughout Alice's life relates to the constraints surrounding her leisure, most significant of which has been limited access to money. The setting for Alice's early life, for example, was the 1920s and 1930s, a time of national shortage and depression. Money and job opportunities were limited and there was no Governmental social security provision. In addition, the disappearance of Alice's father and the subsequent dependence on one income to support both Alice, her brother and grandmother made the family more vulnerable. Alice is only too conscious of this, particularly of the sacrifices and efforts her mother had to endure to ensure the family survived. She frequently refers to how her mother 'worked hard to keep us' describing also how her mother 'worked hard to buy a house' for them. She recognises however that despite her mother's efforts, life and opportunities for leisure were limited. 'We had no money, so that was a good start!' she comments on how 'I didn't have the pleasures children have today'.

Alice's move to London did open up the opportunity for her to discover dancing, a love of which has stayed with her throughout life, but again access to this did not come easily. Alice had to earn the money to pay for the tap dancing lessons; she states, 'I loved my dancing . . . Dancing was my aim' but remembers how she would have to clean the bathroom every Saturday to earn the six pence to pay for the tap dancing.

On moving to London, Alice recognises how her mother's work left her with little time to spend with her and her brother and thus constrained where and what she was allowed to do. 'Of course my mother was working and we were two young children. We were twelve, fourteen, she went to work and we were told, you stay away from this and that, so that we weren't running the streets'.

In married life, although ownership of the grocer's shop supported the family and also served as the family home, as the children were growing up in the early seventies, competition from supermarkets began to impact on the businesses viability. To make ends meet, Alice and her husband closed the shop and began to take in students from the local technical college, providing breakfast and evening meals as well as doing their laundry, it was hard work and 'Really only covered costs'. At this time, Alice's husband's health began to fail, placing the family under further financial pressures.

The legacy of these experiences since childhood, has left Alice with a careful approach to money, she talks of how 'these experiences still stick. I'm still careful with money and I think I brought my daughter up to be the same. She's the same, she'll think twice before she spends her money. You had to be'. It is these financial hardships in Alice's life that perhaps explain why her leisure in many respects has always been measured, planned carefully, budgeted for and in many ways lacked a sense of spontaneity about it. She talks of how trips to the London Palladium with her husband were on a Sunday but 'not every Sunday because we couldn't afford it', how the annual holiday to Ogmore, 10 miles from Cardiff, were carefully budgeted for throughout the year, allowing for a level of extravagance and spontaneity, impossible throughout the remainder of the year. 'We had to save up for it, we had to pay for the bus, and when we got there, we didn't think twice, if you wanted to buy ice cream you could, you could have ice cream because you were on holiday'. Trips to the cinema, meals out with the children during the rest of the year were only on special occasions, and relatively low budget affairs, she describes how meals out 'were not like meals out today. It would be a restaurant, but the restaurants then weren't like they are today. Today you could go in and spend £15–20 on a meal and think nothing of it. If you spent £5 then it was a lot of money'.

Another constraint on Alice's leisure throughout her life has not only been money but also a lack of time. Working full time, from the age of 14, left little space for leisure, indeed the attraction of working at the Hoover factory was that it allowed her to pursue her interest in dancing through their regular dance nights and annual cabaret show. Marriage at 18, followed by two children shortly afterwards, placed large demands on her time. The time commitments of the grocer's shop, working from 9 to 8, coupled with the domestic responsibilities of home and being a mother similarly left little time for leisure. When the shop closed, and Alice began to take in the lodgers, large amounts of her time were still taken up, cooking, cleaning and washing for the lodgers, as well as looking after her own children. These responsibilities not only left her with little time for leisure but also little energy "when I had the shop and the lodgers, by the time you'd finished the evening meal, washing dishes and cleaning up, you wouldn't want to go out anyway". The lack of time and energy and the realisation that home-based leisure was the most practical form of leisure open to her, eventually proved to be the incentive for buying a television. Once the shop had been sold and the lodgers had gone, there were new demands made upon her time, caring for her, by that time, bed-ridden husband, in the house that she still lives in today.

Many of the time constraints, which have faced Alice, have been very much related to being a woman and in particular the traditional expectations of women throughout much of her life. This is particularly evident in married life when Alice bore the burden of household responsibilities, in addition to working fulltime. One gets the sense in Alice's comments that the domestic tasks were a duty, which, despite lack of free time, had to be fulfilled. She describes how, on Sundays, the one-day of the week when the shop closed, 'I would not work on a Sunday. That was when my work got done, housework, washing, ironing and so forth'. The unpaid nature of this work is not recognised as work by Alice but almost as a duty that a free day allows her to fulfil.

Alice also refers, within her life story, to how her gender has excluded her from various social activities, particularly those that her husband was able to participate in freely, such as the working men's club and skittles team. 'He played skittles . . . but I didn't then, it was just the men'. Indeed the clear, traditional gender divisions around leisure are obvious in the demarcations in activities. Alice's husband would garden and grow vegetables. 'Gardening was his thing, he had three allotments. He did love his garden . . . Now and again I might go with him, but I wasn't a gardener'. On the other hand, Alice's life mainly revolved around domestic duties including freezing the vegetables that her husband grew, which as she states was 'more work again'.

The Socio-Cultural Context of Alice's Leisure

It is clear to see how historical events and cultural norms during Alice's lifetime have impacted upon her life and consequently her attitudes towards leisure. Living through the 1930s depression and wartime, for example, have affected many aspects of her life, the loss of a brother, her approach to money, her opportunities for leisure and even her move to

Wales with her husband, a key worker on munitions. Reaching the age of 14 in 1935 meant having to leave school, severely curtailing her educational opportunities and perhaps even her life chances.

The cultural expectations of women as wives and mothers throughout Alice's lifetime have also had a major impact on both her time, ability to access leisure and choice of leisure activities. Alice herself is only too aware of how both historical events and cultural norms have impacted on her life in a way that was unique to those periods in time, for example she frequently prefixes sentences with 'in those days . . .' and talks of how 'things were different then'. She observes that her marriage at the age of 18, as being young by today's standards but how it was the norm then and how having to give up full-time work on marriage and follow her husband to Wales was expected of women. 'Of course, being married in those days was different to today, you went with him . . . in those days a woman's place was in the home'.

The limited choice of leisure activities, which Alice frequently refers to while telling her life story, was also typical of those times. For example, in childhood Alice would visit Church, Sunday School and Girl Guides, not out of any religious conviction, but out of expediency, as the church was the main focus of social activity, 'I only went for my own entertainment'. She describes how marbles, hoop and a stick as being 'the only things we had to play with'. In early married life, Alice describes how they would have to entertain themselves with games of crib or games of whist with friends and neighbours. They played games of tiddlywinks and snakes and ladders with the children. 'There was nothing like there is today. Nothing whatsoever. Any entertainment you wanted, you made yourself. Your own entertainment'. Whilst Alice does refer to Working men's clubs as one impor-tant source of social activities outside the home, 'there was always the bingo and a dance' she cannot remember any other sort of club 'it was nearly all labour and conservative clubs that I can think of. I can't remember any other clubs, not that I can think of'.

The annual family holiday, only 10 miles from home was also typical of the time.

Lack of Continuity in Leisure in Later Life

Leisure in later life for Alice, particularly since her husband's death, is anything but a con-tinuum of earlier patterns of leisure. Her leisure activities seem wider than ever before as she experiences and participates in a whole range of new leisure pursuits, including Tai Chi, keep fit, 'pensioners meetings' and skittles. Both time and money are no longer constrain-ing factors and it even seems that gender constraints are no longer a barrier (she is now part of the all women skittles club, an activity open only to her husband in married life).

However, leisure in Alice's later life not only comes more easily, freed as she is from many of the earlier constraints, but also has a more important and significant role than at any other period of her life. Engagement with leisure helps to enable her to cope with the hardest things in life. Alice has had to deal with the death of her husband, followed shortly afterwards by the death of a son and subsequent loss of contact with grandchildren.

> I didn't have such a social life when he (husband) died that I've got now. I
> think the reason I am forcing myself now is because I know in the back of

> my mind that if I give in that will be it, so what I'm doing now is I'm keep-
> ing going . . . The thing is, if I didn't go to these clubs, I could sit in this
> chair and mope and get worse and I'm not going to do it.

Engagement with leisure is thus enabling her to cope with extremely difficult life experiences and, as such, is maintaining her self-esteem and determination to be positive.
However, engagement with leisure does not come easily to Alice. She has to work at it in
a way that she did not have to when younger. 'Leisure just comes when you're younger,
now I've got to think I've got to do it'. However, perhaps the great resilience Alice has
shown in managing her current leisure stems from the legacy of a lifetime spent coping
with all that life has thrown at her. It has obviously given her the ability to use and exploit
leisure opportunities in later life to the full, as well as being a source of company, an
opportunity to socialise, a buffer from sad memories and even to ensure a constructive
engagement with life.

Conclusion

This chapter has aimed to highlight the contribution biographical research can make to an
understanding of, in this instance, older women's leisure. In doing so, the work could
provide an insight into how the technique may be usefully employed in understanding
the characteristics of leisure and tourism amongst other ages and groups of individuals.
The strengths of the technique are clear: its ability to get close to people by exploring
aspects of their lives in the subjects' own words. In doing so, the technique also provides
insight into how both structure and agency affect people's life choices and lifestyles, often
highlighting the ability of people to challenge the 'knowledge' and assumptions about their
lifestyles.

In this particular case study, insight was gained into the historical and cultural backdrop
of one woman's life. In particular, key events such as the 1930s depression, the Second
World War, leaving school at the age of 14 (the norm in the 1930s), and even personal loss
have been described and have highlighted how these events affected her life, especially in
relation to economic prosperity and life chances. We have also seen the restricted opportunities for leisure, such as holiday taking, that were evident throughout Alice's life, both
the result of financial hardship and also, at times, of society's expectations and attitudes
towards women.

However, despite the minimal opportunities for economic success, social mobility, the
limited educational and leisure opportunities that are clearly evident in this biography,
there are strong elements of reflexivity running throughout Alice's life. These become evident in the way she approaches her life and leisure today. In later life, she has managed to
discover new leisure opportunities and capacities for leisure within herself, which she uses
to express her independence, to engage with peers and younger generations, to cope with
extremely difficult life circumstances, to provide a purpose in life and to engage positively
with life itself.

Thus, whilst by today's standards, Alice's leisure activities in later life might appear
unremarkable, when considered against the backdrop of her previous life, they are

remarkable in many ways. Indeed, her life would seem to support Wearing's (1995, p. 272) assertion that:

> for old people, in the contradiction between the dominant degenerative dis-
> course on ageing and the 'freedom to be' aspect of the dominant leisure dis-
> course, there is space for resisting ageism and the consequent 'underuse'
> syndrome.

Alice is a living proof of this possibility. Such a conclusion would not have been possible if a large-scale, statistical survey had been used. Biographical research on the other
hand, allowed us to get beneath the surface of Alice's life and tell the real story of the context of leisure in the face of much adversity.

References

Achenbaum, W. A. (1997). Critical gerontology. In: A. Jamieson, S. Harper, & C. Victor (Eds), *Critical approaches to ageing and later life* (pp. 16–26). Buckingham: Open University Press.

Berger, P. L. (1963). *Invitation to sociology: A humanist perspective*. London: Anchor.

Bernard, M., Meade, K., & Tinker, A. (1993). Women come of age. In: M. Bernard, & K. Meade (Eds), *Women come of age: Perspectives on the lives of older women* (pp. 1–22). London: Edward Arnold.

Bertaux, D. (1981). From the life history approach to the transformation of sociological practice. In: D. Bertaux (Ed.), *Biography and society: The life history approach in the social sciences* (pp. 29–46). London: Sage.

Booth, T., & Booth, W. (1994). *Parenting under pressure: Mothers and fathers with learning diffi-culties*. Buckingham: Open University Press.

Bornatt, J. (2002). Doing life history research. In: A. Jamieson, & C. Victor (Eds), *Researching ageing and later life* (pp. 117–134). Buckingham: Open University Press.

Chamberlayne, P., Bornat, J., & Wengraf, T. (Eds). (2000). *The turn to biographical methods in social science. Comparative issues and examples*. London: Routledge.

Cornwell, J., & Gearing, B. (1989). Biographical interviews with older people. *Oral History Journal, 17*, 36–43.

Denzin, N. K. (1989). *Interpretive biography*. London: Sage.

Elder, G. (1981). History and the life course. In: D. Bertaux (Ed.), *Biography and society: The life history approach in the social sciences* (pp. 77–115). California: Sage.

Fennell, G., Phillipson, C., & Evers, H. (1994). *The sociology of old age*. Buckingham: Open University Press.

Fischer, L. R. (1983). Sociology and life history: Methodological incongruence? *International Journal of History, 4*(1), 29–40.

Gearing, B., & Dant, T. (1990). Doing biographical research. In: S. M. Peace (Ed.), *Researching social gerontology: Concepts, methods and issues* (pp. 143–159). London: Sage.

Giddens, A. (1991). *Self and identity in modernity*. Oxford: Polity.

Gilleard, C., & Higgs, P. (2000). *Cultures of ageing*. Harlow: Prentice Hall.

Goodley, D. (2000). *Self advocacy in the lives of people with learning difficulties: The politics of resilience*. Buckingham: Open University Press.

Goodley, D., Lawthom, R., Clough, P., & Moore, M. (2004). *Researching life stories: Method, theory and analyses in a biographical age*. London: Routledge Falmer.

Grant, B. C. (2002). Physical activity: Not a popular leisure choice in later life. *Society and Leisure*, 25(2), 285–302.

Holstein, B. M., & Minkler, M. (2003). Self, society and the 'new gerontology'. *The Gerontologist*, 43(6), 787–796.

Jamieson, A., & Victor, C. (1997). Theory and concepts in social gerontology. In: A. Jamieson, S. Harper, & C. Victor (Eds), *Critical approaches to ageing and later life* (pp. 175–187). Buckingham: Open University Press.

Kazmierska, K. (2004). Ethical aspects of biographical interviewing and analysis. In: P. Chamberlayne, J. Bornat, & U. Apitzsch (Eds), *Biographical methods and professional practice: An international perspective* (pp. 181–192). Bristol: The Policy Press.

Long, J. (1989). A part to play: Men experiencing leisure through retirement. In: B. Bytheway, T. Keil, P. Allatt, & A. Bryman (Eds), *Becoming and being old: Sociological approaches to later life* (pp. 55–72). London: Sage.

Mannheim, K. (1952). *Essays in the sociology of knowledge*. London: Routledge and Kegan Paul.

Mead, G. H. (1934). In: C. Morris (Ed.), *Mind, self and society*. Chicago: University of Chicago Press.

Mitroff, I., & Killman, R. (1978). *Methodological approaches to social science: Integrating divergent concepts and theories*. San Francisco: Jossey-Bass.

Peace, S. (1990). *Researching social gerontology: Concepts, methods and issues*. London: Sage.

Plummer, K. (1983). *Documents of life*. London: George Allen and Unwin.

Roberts, B. (2002). *Biographical research*. Buckingham: Open University Press.

Scraton, S., Bramham, P., & Watson, B. (1998). 'Staying in' and 'going out'. In: S. Scraton (Ed.), *Leisure, time and space: Meanings and values in people's lives* (pp. 101–120). Brighton: Leisure Studies Association.

Thomas, W. I., & Znaniecki, F. (1958). *The Polish peasant in Europe and America*. New York: Dover (First published 1919–1921).

Thompson, P. (2000). *The voice of the past*. Oxford: Oxford University Press.

Thompson, P., Itzin, C., & Abendstern M. (1990). *I don't feel old: The experiences of later life*. Oxford: Oxford University Press.

Thompson, P. (1981). Life histories and the analysis of social change. In: D. Bertaux (Ed.), *Biography and society: The life history approach in the social sciences*. London: Sage.

Tokarski, W. (1991). Leisure lifestyle courses in old age. *Leisure Studies*, 10, 79–81.

United Nations. (2002). *Report of the second world assembly on ageing*. New York: United Nations.

Veal, A. J. (1997). *Research methods for leisure and tourism*. London: Pearson.

Victor, C. (2002). Using existing research and statistical data: Secondary data analysis. In: A. Jamieson, & C. R. Victor (Eds), *Researching ageing and later life* (pp. 51–66). Buckingham: Open University Press.

Walker, A. (1987). Ageing and the social sciences: The North American way. *Ageing and Society*, 7(2), 235–242.

Wearing, B. (1995). Leisure and resistance in an ageing society. *Leisure Studies*, 14, 263–279.

Wilson, G. (2000). *Understanding old age: Critical and global perspectives*. London: Sage.

Chapter 21

The Language(s) of the Tourist Experience: An Autoethnography of the Poetic Tourist

Chaim Noy

Introduction: The Tourist State of Mind[1]

> And she said why, why don't we drive through the night
> We'll wake up down in Mexico?. . .
> Tell me why, why won't you love me for who I am where I am?
> (Paul Simon, *Hearts and Bones*)

It has been ten years since I began researching tourists and their experiences, and yet, during this time what the "tourist experience" is has become increasingly less clear to me. During this time, rather than developing a more analytical and defined perception of the array of concepts, theorems and methods that comprise the (inter-/sub-)discipline of tourism research, I have found that defining or delineating what tourism means to people living in modern times has become an increasingly more evasive task.

In the beginning of the classes on tourism that I teach, I routinely suggest — in a somewhat provocative manner — that tourism "is a state of mind". That is, that to partake in tourist activities means to partake in a symbolic dimension, wherein an altered state of mind is in fact witnessed. Quoting the philosopher–phenomenologist, Alfred Schutz (1945, 1970), who wrote that "the world is composed of multiple realities", I tell my students that the culture(s) of tourism may be fruitfully approached from a *symbolic perspective*, i.e. from the unique experiences of tourists, or from the "the tourist state of mind".

At a later point during the course, when the class discusses the semiotics of souvenirs, I tell the students a well-known and rather kitsch tale. The tale tells of a person who fell asleep, and dreamed of flowers or butterflies, only to wake up to find that there was a flower or a butterfly (respectively), on her/his chest. The tale, I suggest, relays what is so

---

[1] I am indebted to Nehama Uni for the many constructive suggestions made to earlier versions of this chapter, as well as to Paul Lynch for coining the term "poetic tourist".

emotionally unique and powerful about souvenirs as metonyms of tourism: their ability to "travel back" from other "worlds", "realms", "spheres" or Schutzian "finite provinces of meaning". The point I would like to make, I continue, is that when people recall and recount their tourist-related experiences, they take on the expression of re-calling a dream, a daydream or a (religious) vision. They seem to be focusing on a point that lies elsewhere, beyond or past the here-and-now's of everyday spaces and routine practices. As Berger and Luckmann famously observed (in line with Schutz):

> [a]s I move from one reality to another, I experience the transition as a kind
> of shock. This shock is to be understood as caused by the shift in attentive-
> ness that the transition entails. Waking up from a dream illustrates this shift
> most simply. (Berger & Luckmann cited in Young, 1987, p. 7)

What is true of retrospective recollections is, of course, true of prospective fantasies as well. When people expect and imagine a vacation they will take, the views they envision transcend those of the "everyday": different landscapes, different bodies, different move-ments and different selves. Persons fantasizing or reminiscing in these ways, bearing these experiential expressions, might be regarded as being in or under the "tourist state of mind". This "state of mind" is pervasive in affluent societies. In the current era, people in these societies enjoy almost constant access to various cultures of tourism, and are, in one way or another, "much of the time 'tourists'" (Urry, 1990, p. 82). "Tourists' dreams colonize all those other fifty weeks, when we are not on vacation", as Lofgren (1999, p. 7) so elo-quently puts it. Indeed, this supports MacCannell's (1999) early claim, that the tourist is no less than the symbol of modernity, indeed "one of the best models available for modern-man-in-general" (p. 1).

But how do we go about researching this unique "state of mind"? How do we not lose, by excessively theorizing and through overly analytical categorization and reductionist conceptualization, the delicate language of tourists' experience? Lastly, what is the language — the syntax and the grammar — of the *inquiry* into tourists' experience, through which subtleties and ephemerality can be studied?

The contributions that this chapter offers address these questions. First and foremost, the chapter offers a methodological proposition in the form of an autoethnographic study of tourists' language of experience, as well as of the experience of tourists' language. The chap-ter also includes a discussion of theoretical concerns, and empirically illustrates the method of autoethnography and its consequences. It shows how autoethnography enables one to communicate experience and reconstruct it in vivid, lively and sometimes even painful ways, in ways that are not "purely" academic or that result in an over-intellectualization of the *sense* of having an experience. By pursuing the research of experience in an evocative fashion, the resulting presentation is often more insightful, and can evoke a deeper appreciation of the subject matter of the tourist experience. In this regard, the present research should be viewed as a branch of the more recent advancements in tourism research methodologies (Aitchison, 2000; Ateljevic, Harris, Wilson, & Collins, 2005; Botterill, 2003).

Second, the chapter explores and sheds light on the relations and correspondence between tourism, on the one hand, and everyday life, on the other. Truly, tourism research literature has yet to conceptualize the oxymoron of the "everydayness of tourism". For the present exposition, tourism and everyday life are viewed as co-related and complementary symbolic orders or structures. Indeed, it is commonly argued that the possibility of mass-tourism, and its accelerated growth over the last half century, was both a prerequisite and an outcome of the inherently modern notion of "everyday life" (as identified and described by Foucault, 1979; Goffman, 1959, 1974).

In this capacity, this chapter joins and contributes to the established tradition within sociological research into tourism — that of the "tourist experience" (Cohen, 1973, 1979). The notion of the "tourist experience" entails a dazzling array of human experiences that emerge when people engage in the sphere of tourism, via its many institutional extensions, representations and guises. These emotions emerge as a result of the construction of tourist activities — whatever they come to include in different cultures — as transcending the order of the everyday.

Performing Travel Writing: A Tourist Autoethnography

According to Ellis and Bochner (2000), whose views of autoethnography I find both provocative and productive, an autoethnography is "an autobiographical genre of writing and research that displays multiple layers of consciousness, connecting the personal to the cultural" (p. 739).

Autoethnography is a critical and reflexive method of inquiry that developed over the last decade or so within the North American Qualitative movement in the social sciences. Appreciating the strengths and weaknesses of this mode of inquiry, as well as of the implications it bears, and its impact on various fields of research, necessitates acknowledging its inherent relation to the diverse family of qualitative research methodologies (Denzin & Lincoln, 2000). While much can be said of the elements common to qualitative research methods and autoethnography, for the present exploration it suffices to note that the qualitative method involves:

> an interpretative, naturalistic approach to the world. This means that qualitative researchers study things in their natural settings, attempting to make sense of, or to interpret, phenomenon in terms of the meanings people bring to them . . . to describe routine and problematic moments and meanings in individuals' lives. (Denzin & Lincoln, 2000, p. 3)

This broad definition indicates that at the heart of qualitative research lies the desire to understand and make sense of "meanings in individuals' lives". Within the family of qualitative research methodologies, however, autoethnography represents an extreme form, a radically subversive and oftentimes provocative relative. Indeed, autoethnography is a mode of inquiry that is wholeheartedly — morally, emotionally and ideologically — committed to the *subject* of the research, namely to people and to their complex, intricate lives and experiences. In this respect, autoethnographical research can be compared with performance studies, symbolic interaction, various feminist research and similar schools of thought, both recent and traditional, within the social sciences.[2]

The term autoethnography literally defines the inquiry procedure: The researcher addresses herself or himself ("auto"), as a subject of a larger social or cultural group ("ethno"), by ways of revealing research and writing ("graphy", Ellis, 1997, see also Bochner & Ellis, 2002; Ellis, 2003). The autoethnographic work aspires to describe those constitutive dimensions that in ordinary, conventional sociological research are erased, or play a backstage role. In addition to personal, lived experience, autoethnographic research explores voice, emotions, processes (rather than results or products) etc., as a part of "the guerilla warfare against the repressive structures of everyday lives" (Denzin, 1999, p. 572). Frequently, autoethnographic research is an investigation into the relationship between researchers, their fields of inquiry and their informants, thereby supplying innovative perspectives on the underlying assumptions of various academic disciplines, as well as on the process of disciplinary socialization in academia. As a method that is centered on the scholar herself or himself, autoethnography is inescapably an emotionally painstaking exercise, a type of ethnography that "breaks your heart" (Behar, 1996).

Exploring tourist-related experiences by means of autoethnography suggests an exciting, even volatile nexus. It forces the tourists — ourselves — to inquire into and to challenge our own experiences, which would otherwise be dismissed as "recreational", "superficial", "fun" etc., in a reflexive and informed manner. Autoethnographizing one's tourist experiences reveals a broader, more complex and challenging aspect to the sphere of tourist experience than the conception of tourist experience as, almost without exception, leisurely or positive. Rather, this type of critical and reflexive research forces us to admit the extent to which much of one's tourism-related experience resonates with feelings of alienation, sadness, aloneness and other bleak and disconcerting experiences.

Furthermore, tourists are performers; they are constantly under the gaze of other people — tourists, locals, tourist operators etc., and their behavior is constantly regulated and monitored so as to avoid "improper" expressions (Aitchison, 2000; Fullagar, 2002). This particularly occurs in enclavic tourist spaces (Edensor, 2000, p. 49), where the exhibition of only certain behaviors is acceptable and gratifying, while other behaviors are discouraged. Indeed, on the stage upon which international tourists find themselves, the show must go on, and "deviant" behaviors, emotions and experiences are effectively, albeit subtly, sanctioned.

Exploring tourists' experiences autoethnographically bears an additional merit. It illuminates the fuzzy and liminal space that lies between tourism experiences and everyday experiences. While tourism-related practices clearly generate unique experiences, these experiences interestingly interrelate with a sense of everyday life. This interrelation will be explored hereafter.

---

[2]It is relevant to point out here that various phenomenological and reflexive methods of inquiry are not recent developments, but have in fact been applied for over a century. Similar to the Qualitative paradigm in general, the recent emergence of autoethnographic inquiries can and should be seen as part of a "pendulum" movement in the history of research methods in the humanities and social sciences (for a review see Ellis & Bochner, 2000). In addition, it would not be inaccurate to suggest that autoethnography, like ethnography or interview studies, is not a single research method, but rather a cluster of methods that share an underlining approach.

Lastly, because autoethnographic research accesses a different type of lived experience than do other qualitative methods, and because it is ideally suited to explore the relationship between researchers and their fields of inquiry, it is potentially a (self-)empowering endeavor. The autoethnographic method has the capacity of revealing and rearranging traditional academic institutional relationships by illuminating the normative, taken-for-granted axioms of various fields. This form of auto-inquiry stimulates critical reflections about one's scholarly involvement, attitudes, constraints and ideological and epistemological commitments (Jones, 1998; Noy, 2003).

Put differently, although the materials tourism scholars research often have a seemingly trivial appearance, they are in fact ridden with ideologies (as grand as "capitalism") and power dynamics and relations. Within these tricky circumstances reflexive monitoring promotes the understanding of the positions of the different actors within the field of tourism, and consequentially, the comprehension of the nature of the field as a whole as well. Reflexivity carries the potential of shedding light on the ideologies tourist scholars themselves hold, partly in the capacity they too are tourists "much of the time" (Urry, 1990, p. 82), and thus are as susceptible as anyone else to commercial-ideological suggestion.

Ellis and Bochner (2000, p. 739) note that autoethnographic texts appear in a variety of forms, including poetry, fiction, novels, personal essays, fragmented and layered writing and more. These forms are tailored to the social and cultural reality that is being studied. The present exploration includes the interpretation of a poem, "In-between sanctity and profane", as well as a discussion of some five additional poetic texts, all of which were composed between 1996–2006.

All the poems presented hereafter concern vacation trips to Sinai. Beside the last contribution, they were all written by a naive author, as yet unfamiliar with research into tourism. As I am not an accomplished poet, the pieces are best conceived as stylized journal entries, as part of a travelogue or a scripted souvenir densely depicting memories and feelings I had whilst in (or on the way to or back from) Sinai. As poems, they can be viewed, at least partly, as tourist performances of the type of "reminiscing" (Edensor, 1998, pp. 135–148), revealing the emotions and experiences — alienated, exhilarated and reflexive — in tourism.

Sinaiscapes: Topography of (Extra) National-collective Experience

The texts to be discussed were written by a single tourist — myself, about a single tourist destination — the beaches of the Sinai Peninsula by the Red Sea. The advantages, and shortcomings, of this particular combination of tourists and destination can be examined against other possible combinations, such as an autoethnographic travel biography that addresses different sites visited by a single person (or a single social unit, such as a family); or research on a larger scale, that explores different people (or social groups) in relation to a single destination or to a number of destinations. Since the present inquiry, however, is concerned with a single destination, I will briefly introduce some background information on Sinai, which will clarify the setting in which and in regard to which the pieces have been composed.

The Sinai Peninsula is located between the Suez Canal and the Red Sea, and is a mountainous desert of the Saharan belt. During the twentieth century the Sinai Peninsula changed hands time and again (see review in Lavie, 1990, pp. 45–84). In the second half of that century it was conquered by Israel from Egypt in 1967 and later evacuated in 1982. In the late 1970s, when the area was still under Israeli occupation, it played a unique role as a truly liminal tourist space (Azaryahu, 2006; Cohen, 1987; Lavie, 1990). This was partly due to its spectacular beaches, which had been popular destinations, providing an ideal place of escape for many. In more ancient time and in mythical history, the Sinai Peninsula played an important role in the Exodus and emancipation of the Jewish People from Ancient, Pharaohnite Egypt. For this reason, too, the sharp peaks of the granite Sinai Mountains, and the dramatic contradictions that they evince with the deep-blue Red Sea, suggested — and still suggest — a mysteriously attractive scenery of mythical richness.

Indeed, throughout the centuries the pregnant scenery of the Granite Sinai desert and the gulf of the Red Sea, have attracted a wide and varied range of travelers and wanderers, poets and novelists, pilgrims, ascetics and hermits. "The equation", Michael Tobias (1995) explains, "was obvious: one look at the Sinai, with its tortured colors and windless furnace, its incessant midges and stinging nights, suggested all the ingredients of penance" (p. 21).

In the function of a more mundane resort space intended for the consumption of modern mass tourism, Sinai can be viewed as the pleasure "periphery belt" of Israel.[3] It is an interesting — liminal and peripheral — destination precisely because it is *not* located at a great geographical distance from the Israeli homeland. It is easily accessible via land transportation, and can be traversed in only a few hours of travel. The traveler to Sinai does not need to pass through airports or to check-in luggage. The geographical continuity of the land and the relatively easy accessibility of the destination offer a perplexing equation of differences and distances in the visiting tourist imagination; it is located away, but not far away. This condition has also fostered different types of spatial constructions and tourist performances in Sinai (Coleman & Crang, 2002), as well as longings to Sinai, which are referred to in the poem presented shortly, in the form of what Smadar Lavie has termed "colonialist nostalgia" (Lavie, 1990).

The poem below, "In-between sanctity and profane",[4] is dated March 31, 1996, and was penned during a vacation to Dahab, Sinai, that I took with my (future)-wife.

---

[3]The 1977 Peace Agreement with Egypt affords relatively easy entry into the Sinai Peninsula for Israeli citizens, who are not required to obtain visas in order to do so. This factor contributes to the popularity of Sinai among Israeli tourists, many of whom choose to spend their holidays and vacations on Sinai's beaches. However, this state of affairs has dramatically changed as a result of the recurring terrorist bombing attacks, mostly aimed at tourists.

[4]The title of the poem is an Hebrew expression (which appears in the Old Testament and in the Jewish Prayer Book). The Hebrew word in the title that is translated to "profane"or "mundane"is h,ol (*Bein kodesh uvein h,ol*), which also means "sand". The poem plays on this double meaning, contrasting sand as something earthly with spirituality or the divine. For the purpose of its inclusion in this chapter the poem has been translated from the original (Hebrew), and five verses have been omitted. Hebrew words are italicized and words originally in English are underlined.

In-Between Sanctity and Profane

Back at Sinai for
the third time, more or less
with a book in Hebrew and a book
in English (*Inta Omri* and LILA)[5]
Passover, *Hatashnav,*[6] is approaching.

The muse in me has been silenced.
The sand of gold has poured from the mountains
the reefs
the Red Sea breeze.

This entire peninsula —
one giant reef
fossilized corals
of stones of Tablets of the Covenant
between a starfish and a coral
between a sea-sponge and a sea-anemone.

The last time here
I was seven.
From inside a Renault 4
emerged a tent
and six people: uncles, parents, children,
cousins.
And one dawn
half-asleep I wondered to the
nearby palm trees and saw:
a man at rest reading a book,
his huge penis hanging-limply,
and two Scandinavian women as
bare and as tanned as the sand
quiet as the sand
warm and soft as is the sand —
perhaps.

Then too a Red Sea Front was approaching
and at night the wind struck the tent with fury.

And in the time before that
the desert was as arid as it is today

---

[5]The Hebrew title *Inta Omri* is a transliteration from Arabic, meaning "you are my love".
[6]*Hatashnav* is the transliteration of the Jewish year count (5756), corresponding to the year 1996.

and some of us were passionate, and some compassionate
and some the earth had swallowed
and some just wanted to make it
through
and Jehovah supplied us with food and
seemed
annoyed,
and promised to watch over us.

But this of course is an impersonal
recollection
another contemplation in the History of the
Jewish People
the fourth visit
the fifth visit, the
s-c-r-i-p-t-u-r-e
the revealed Torah
the Elders, Judges, Kings, Kingdoms, Prophets, Diasporas,
the Messianics, Healers, Ministers, Fascists
the sand
sand
sand.

Muzeina
An elderly Bedouin woman as
wrinkled as a desert shrub
black as the night
recounted how her uncle's wife's husband-in-law
pushed her wounded back
and cried,
and later laughed,
and told my lover she is
'from the Bedouins'
because the shade of her skin is dark
and her hair so black.
And to me, with a colorful tourist hat on my head,
she said:
'and you,
you are from the hat'.

This sand, blinding, purifying,
hot, boiling,

Sand
blinding purifying

retaining heat
traces of a snake
of a partridge
hunting a lizard
of a beetle
of horse of camel
of wind of a Bedouin jeep.
And this sand
I will bring to my Jerusalem apartment
like bottled multicolored sand
in your shoes
in my shoes
in your tan (your face there was completely dark, and your eyes shining)
in our armpits
and
in-between our toes and
inside our ears
and our hair
and in the poem
. . .

Jerusalem —
the eve of Passover, *Hatashnav*

scrubbing my whole body:
my feet that were cut in the sand and became swollen
and have dried and hardened
the little blood-red caps left by
bedbugs on our feet
and behind our ears,
like *Hames*.[7]

The Language of the Tourist Body

The language of the tourist experience as it is represented in "In-between" is essentially embodied. It is not only a set of lexical, grammatical and syntactical choices and correlations, but is, first and foremost, a language of embodied practices, or performances. Hence, before addressing the various bodies, and bodily postures, senses and transformations described in "In-between", I first wish to suggest the notion that the poem itself conveys an embodied state. Written by an author at leisure on the pristine sands of Sinai, the poem's length, the repetitions it evinces, and the narrative it unfolds in a gradual manner — all convey a notion

---

[7]*Hames* means leavened dough, the consumption of which is strictly prohibited during the Passover holiday according to the Jewish dietary rules (*kashrut*).

of extension or expansion. Very much like the relaxed tourist body vacationing on the Red Sea beach, the poem too has a "relaxed" quality, and evokes sense of contemplation that is typical of the type of reflexivity often indulged in by tourists on vacation. That is to say the frame of mind in which one feels one "gets away from it all", and also have the time and opportunity to look back and take stock from a wider perspective. Hence, in this capacity, the poetic form amounts to a souvenir of sorts, one crafted by the tourist himself. The poem has the power to relay bodily sensation in that in reading the poem, it is possible to rekindle the type of bodily senses that were experienced by the tourist-author *at the destination.*

A good deal of "In-between", however, is dedicated to the description of the different bodies that share the spaces of tourism. Bodies first emerge in the poem in an indirect manner, during a recollection that the trip to Sinai has triggered (verse #4). "The last time here" opens a tourist scene within a tourist scene, one that took place when I was seven (in 1975, twenty-one years before the poem was written). Literally, "last time here" juxtaposes spatial sameness (i.e. "here" or vacationscapes), and temporal or chronological difference (travel biography), having the effect of creating the "emotional phenomenology of return", but not to the place that is perceived as "home". It touches on one of the tourists' mottos: "To be back again", as Lofgren (1999, pp. 149–150) reminds us.

In the author's recollection, different bodies are engaged in different practices. First, in a way that is almost transformatory, the six of us "emerged" from a tiny Renault 4, the group comprising, in fact, three different families and members of families: my aunt, uncle and their two children, another aunt (who is single), and myself. In that constellation I was the oldest of the children. No physical details are provided with regard to our bodies beside the fact that we all move from one enclosed space, that of the moving automobile, to another, that of the stationary tent.

There is another "emergence" which occurs at dawn. The second instance of recollected bodies portrays three Scandinavian nudists whom we happened to lodge in close proximity to (in hindsight, it begs the question as to whether the location of our tent in a nudist colony was in fact accidental?). As dawn approaches, probably still half asleep, what I witnessed when I left the safe and predictable familial confines (in the shape of the tent), was registered as nothing less than a vision. Down South, beyond and "under" the borders of national sovereignty, the "tourist body" was powerfully present (Crouch & Desforges, 2003). It primarily takes the form of a naked Scandinavian male body, with what then seemed to me to be a huge flaccid penis, next to two nude female companions (I realize in hindsight, that it was the first uncircumcised penis I ever saw, as well as the first vulva). The physical proximity to a foreign and adult male body left me shocked, and aroused pre-pubertal anxiety (I remember how concerted I was with the thoughts, "when will my aunts wake up? Something must be done about this"). Note the perspective (the "gaze"): a young male tourist looking at the body of a mature male tourist. The blurring of social borders in this heterogeneous space — between the normative and the transgressive, the clothed and the unclothed, and later in the poem, the blurring of social borders between the Bedouins (native), the Israelis (tourist), and the Europeans (tourist), was of a liminal quality, and left a powerful imprint in my memory.

The third instance of recollected bodies includes collective bodies inhabiting national-mythical space. These are largely anguished bodies, passionate and compassionate, passing through the Sinai desert on the way to the Promised Land. While some of the members of the mythical Tribe of Israel met a horrible fate during their travels/travails (such as that of followers of Karachi whom God punished by having the ground swallow them whole, [see Numbers, Chaps 17–18]), others are described in more mundane language: they "just wanted to make it through". In any case, the caterer of foods, beverages and accommodation during the period of forty years that the Tribe of Israel spent crossing the Sinai desert, as well as the implementer of discipline (punishments and rewards), is not the capitalist industries of tourism, but God himself.

Through the threading of ancient and contemporary visits to Sinai, the poem "In-between" indicates that the accumulative nature of these visits and re-visits transcends the notion of an individual travel biography on various levels. Akin to other symbolic sites (Edensor, 1998), whether natural or man-made, visiting Sinai ties the tourist individual or the tourist group to a larger historical (or mythical) chain of visitings. Interestingly, under these conditions, the distinction between individuals, groups and collectives is blurred.

I indicated earlier that Sinai is a liminal and somewhat paradoxical destination (at least this is so for Israelis), precisely because it is *not* located at a very great distance from "home". For instance, among the many Israelis who backpack throughout Asia and South America, Sinai is referred to as "a stop on the way back home". That is to say that Sinai is symbolically perceived as existing betwixt-and-between the homeland and more distant destinations and fantasies. For many Israelis Sinai is foreign, but at the same time not entirely foreign. This point is made in "In-between", via the recapitulation of different "visits" to Sinai, both historical (real) and mythical (imaginative), occurring both in the past and in the future. Thus, the present trip can be seen as located in-between various dimensions or temporal and spatial spheres.

The next body presented in the poem is of a different nature altogether — Muzeina's (verse #8).[8] Muzeina's body is the body of the native, and it suggests various contrasts to the bodies of the European tourists: it is vulnerable (old and wounded), but it also possesses a voice (Noy, 2006c). And unlike the nudists, it is completely veiled behind a black *Higab* (one of the verses I omitted from the present version includes the line, "Muzeina/clothed in the blackness of Bedouin wool/from head to toe"). Although she is veiled, the skin-color of the actors in this tourist scene is referred to, for the second time. The first reference describes the nudists' practice of tanning, and the second reference is by Muzeina, who addressed my partner's shade of skin, which is considerably darker than mine. Muzeina addresses not only genetic dimensions (concerning the colour of skin), but also acquired ones, i.e. practices: while my wife enjoys the sun and does not wear a hat, I favour wearing a (synthetic colourful) hat in order to protect my lighter skin. Through reporting the sad and then humorous "hat" exchange with Muzeina, we are positioned in the poem as particular types of tourists. Somewhere between Western nudists and local Islamic traditions, Israelis seek to locate themselves in the Levant, in this case through the practices of tourism. In this and other cases, heterogeneous and multinational tourist spaces supply pubic arenas wherein collective-national is negotiated (Edensor, 1998; Noy, 2006a, 2006b, 2006c).

---

[8]In Arabic, Muzeina (or colloquially Mzeina) means pretty or decorated. It is also the name of a Bedouin tribe located near Dahab (see Lavie, 1990).

In the verse, Muzeina is captured through the poetic tourist's pen, in a way that resembles to some degree the tourists' cameras, which capture and portray the "native" (the image of which is indeed most commonly feminine). However, unlike the silent image of the "native", Muzeina has a voice with which she speaks. Following Lavie's (1990) ethnographic work with the Mzeina Bedouins, the actual woman we met, and the stories she shares with us, can be interpreted as more general allusions. Her vulnerable body, on the one hand, and her interaction with and perception of tourists on the Dahab beaches (which are Mzeina territory, or rather were Mzeina territory before the Bedouins were dispossessed), on the other, are also allegorical: Egyptian sovereignty, the Israeli occupation (in the years 1967–1982), and then, presently, the "tourist occupation", engender a set of power relation and dynamics, where the Sinai Bedouins are repeatedly the oppressed (Lavie, 1990). Note that this notion supplies part of the *local* motivation for Bedouin collaboration with and participation in anti-tourist and anti-Egyptian terror attacks in the Peninsula.

The last two evocations of bodies refer to our bodies, the tourists' bodies, from within the trip (verse #11, the second-to-last verse), and outside of the experience — after the trip has been concluded (the last verse). These are the only instances in which a process (a transformation) is described. While vacationing in Sinaiscapes, our bodies are soaked and immersed in sand. Shoes, tans, armpits, eyes, hair and the poem too, are bodily organs that are mentioned apropos the sea/sand bath we bath in. They are described, or better, prescribed as yet-to-be souvenirs ("I shall bring to the Jerusalem apartment/like bottled multicolored sand"). The tourist knows that the inevitable countdown to the end of the trip, and to the end of the poem, has begun. Preparations, in the form of the accumulation of souvenirs, have therefore commenced. The poem, and the organs, and the clothes that are mentioned, are indeed ideal souvenirs: ears, shoes, armpits and hair are places where sand can be kept and can be transferred from one location to another. Akin to bottled, multicolored sand, sold by Bedouins on occasion, the tourists' bodies capture and retain sand — in its symbolic capacity — authentically indicating that they truly were at that desired liminal location, where the earth meets the water, i.e. "the beach" (Cohen, 1982, 2005).

However, having returned home, the tourists in "In-between" comply with the prescriptions of the approaching Jewish Holiday, known for its strict and detailed dietary prohibitions. They scrub and wash their bodies of the Sinai sand, viewing the sand — again, in symbolic and semi-religious terms, as unacceptable (or un-kosher) *Hames*. The cleansing of the body indeed recalls orthodox purification rights pursued at Passover, whereby the house is examined inch by inch, in search of impurities. Thus there is here a third "emergence", the emergence out and away from tourist spaces and states of mind and body. The proximity to the Passover Holiday contextualizes the tourist actions in a *ritual framework*: in this case scrubbing the body extensively is part of the tourists' ritualistic practices of returning to everyday life. In other words, the Passover Holiday only emphasizes the necessary and accepted condition whereby it is expected that no tourist would return to the workplace after a vacation with sand behind her or his ears or inside the armpits.

Lastly, while attending to the tourist's "whole body", now back under everyday hygienic discipline, scars are observed. Albeit temporal, bedbug bites cannot be scrubbed away like sand; they are not simply "dirt" but are inside the tourist body ("blood-red"). As Haldrup and Larsen (2003) observe of tourists, "[m]emory moves and lives in the body" (p. 40).

The Language of the Tourist Experience: Circumstances and Performances

An autoethnographic exploration of the "poetic tourist" suggests that at the focus of our attention is not the language *of* the tourist experience as much as the *tourist experience itself as a language*; as a polyphonic nexus of "languages", and of modes of consuming and producing inscriptions.

Earlier, I mentioned that the poem "In-between" is an embodied discursive medium. It both embodies the tourist "body-on-the-beach" and describes various bodies, bodily postures and organs. I would like to return now to the former type of embodiment, that of tourist "body-on-the-beach", which is the body of the author. In the capacity the poem serves as a souvenir, it is inscribed — produced — by the tourist while vacationing. After all, the core ideas, which later developed into the present form of the poem, had to have been written, or (more realistically) scribbled, down "In between" — that is, while on vacation. This operation is best conceptualized in performative terms: "In-between" is not only or simply a souvenir of a vacation in Sinai, with its experiences and stimulated fantasies, it is also a souvenir of an embodied tourist state, that of writing. Just like walking, photographing, gazing, remembering (Edensor, 1998) and storytelling (Noy, 2004), are embodied performances pursued by tourists, so is reading (to which I shall return shortly) and writing. This is why part of the domain considered under the title the language of tourists, must include *the embodied circumstances and possibilities of inscriptions available to tourists, and these inscriptions' performances*.

The poem "In-between" stops short of reflecting on the very act of the poem's inscription within a tourist setting. I can attest to my habit of taking a yellow office pad with me, and can recall scribbling an initial draft of the poem on the pad. While I generally like to write (with preference to poetry), taking a paper pad with me on trips offers me the opportunity to document travel events, experiences and reflections in particular, in a way similar to recording by camera and camcorder. It is a tourist tactic adopted to overcome and to compensate for distances and divides. Furthermore, "performing" writing while on a tour, positions me differently in relation to most other tourists (who are the tourist's primary reference group). Why they, I tell myself, are "passive consumers", because they read books and tourist brochures; I am active and agentic, because I read *and write*. I produce something.

I mentioned the performance of reading. This embodied performance is alluded to in "In-between" several times. The first occasion is in the first verse: (*Inta Omri* and LILA). At this strategic point, mentioning the books helps to mark the practices described later in the poem as "touristic": they denote the duration of the tourist's time spent on vacation as "free time", and infuse it with different languages (English and Arabic), and additional narratives and imagined meanings relating to the books' content. In other occasions, the nudist tourist is reading a book, as are the relaxed Israeli tourists, who are reading books under palm trees (a frequent sight, which is described in a verse I omitted).

Lastly, these occasions of reading allude indirectly to two further acts of reading: the reading of the tales of the *Haggadah* (which is the central part of the Passover night, see Zemel, 1998), and the reading of the poem "In-between" itself. While the former is alluded to by the references made to the scriptures and to the *Torah*, the latter allusion arises from the very function of the souvenir. "We need or desire souvenirs of events that are reportable", Susan Stewart (1993) writes, "events whose materiality has escaped us . . . events that thereby exist only through the invention of narrative" (p. 135).

In discursive souvenirs the portable and the reportable are enmeshed: the very object that is portable is the repot.

Other poems I wrote about excursions to Sinai also express a linguistic polyphony, and describe the spaces of tourism as discursive nexuses. For instance, a short piece dated March, 1999, concerns translation in a fairly literal manner. The main part of the poem (untitled) is simply a very short Hebrew-Arabic lexicon. The transliteration of eight Arabic words is supplied, followed by their translation into Hebrew. The outcome corresponds with a known genre of tourist publication, namely the "tourist phrase booklet". However, while commercial (institutional) phrasebooks construct — enable and limit — the discursive possibilities of the host-guest interaction, this poem emerges *in and from* the interaction: it describes more than it prescribes. The short list reflects the very minimal contact between guests (Israeli tourists) and hosts (Bedouins) in the heterogeneous tourist spaces of the Sinai beaches (Edensor, 2000), and addresses the notion of translation — so inherent to the many divides (linguistic and other), that exist within tourism. Poetically, the list of eight word-pairs also amounts to a cursive "picture" of a Sinai beach, its sounds and meanings, at a given point in time. *N'ballesh* ("let's begin"), *hawali* ("approximately"), *awal imbareh*, ("the day before yesterday"), and other Arabic-cum-Hebrew words, portray the beach's soundscape, and are, at the same time, also a souvenir.

Another short poem, titled "On the way to Sinai" (dated January, 2002), expresses the polyphonic discursive dimension of tourist endeavors in a different way. The poem refers to an earlier trip made around 1989—1990,[9] together with three close friends.

On the Way to Sinai

> The four of us packed in a Fiat 127,
> 4 a.m. by the Dead Sea Scrolls, we roll around laughing as
> the SW radio commands:
> *ras dva tre chetiri!*
> *ras dva tre chetiri!*

"On the way to Sinai" captures or "freezes" a moment in motion: the four of us in Guy's mother's old Fiat, leave Jerusalem before dawn, and hear, near the Dead Sea, a program broadcasted from one of the former Soviet Republics. The early morning program, which is the only transmission the car's radio receives, is a morning exercise drill (of the type which the Israeli Broadcasting Authority used to broadcast in the 1970s). The radio program consisting of an authoritative and severe male voice, accompanied by a piano, counts loudly to the rhythm of stretching movements for the exercising listener: *ras dva tre chetiri!*

Hence, similar to the previous texts, "On the way to Sinai" evokes foreign words, sounds and rhythms that permeate our social space (this time through long-distance, short-wave transmission). The poem captures a unique moment because the Russian words

---

[9]I am thankful to my friend Dedi Laniado for clarifying these dates.

capture in a discursive form the "foreignness" of the experience of leaving familiar spheres. In addition, the moment depicted in the poem is also a moment of jubilation: the tourists in the Fiat take a particular pleasure at the contrast between the authoritative disciplining instructions, thundering in a bass voice, and the ludic and joyful tourist state. We are out of the reach of the symbolic Father, to employ an Oedipal-Freudian language.

However, unlike the two poems discussed earlier, "On the way to Sinai" captures a moment that occurs during *the liminal phase of traveling*. In other words, even before we actually arrive at Sinai, the polyphonic nature of tourism, and its discursive or linguistic manifestations, is manifest. The liminal dimension of traveling is interestingly alluded to through the descriptions of the proximity to the Dead Sea ("the lowest place on earth", as the commercials describe it) — a place, that for me, always had a special aura, through the twilight quality of dawn, and through a sense of isolation (the Judean Desert and lack of radio reception). Similar to the notion conveyed in Paul Simon's words in this chapter's motto, after "we drive through the night", or through other liminal zones, wake up elsewhere transformed — "wake up down in Mexico". The Renault 4 and the Fiat 127 — akin to a Boeing 707-200, are modern vehicles not only of (material) transportation, but also of (symbolic) transformation.

The evocation of the famous Dead Sea Scrolls, described by some as the "most outstanding archeological findings found in Israel", adds a mythical flavor to the spaces through which the old Fiat is traveling. The Dead Sea Scrolls also introduce into the poem yet another form of discursivity: while the rhythmic count in Russian arrives from a great *geographical* distance, the Scrolls represent texts that have transcended great *chronological* spans. (Indeed, the evocation of the Dead Sea Scrolls, albeit documented historical facts, in "On the way to Sinai", corresponds with the mythical Exodus mentioned in "In-between", in creating a "tourist prehistory"). The point is that the "tourist state of mind" embodies a unique composition — that of polyphonic discourses and multilayered meanings, regardless of whether it is at the destination, or while traveling there or back, or even before the trip has commenced or after it has concluded.

Note that there is one autoethnographic piece of information that is missing from the description above, which is the trigger that has led to the composition of the poem "On the way to Sinai", some twelve years after the trip it describes has occurred. I regrettably did not record and cannot recall the "tourist moment of reminiscence", which occurred sometime in January, 2002, and which re-evoked the earlier experience of elated laughing on the way to Sinai. It might well be that it was yet another excursion to Sinai that has brought the earlier one into remembrance.

Back in/to Everyday: Writing the Return(s) from Sinai

The poem "In-between" includes several indications concerning tourists' more general travel biographies, in the form of evocations of earlier and future trips to Sinai (both real and fantasized). In this respect, the poem's last verse, describing the trip's aftermath, amounts to a short chapter in a history of homecomings. That is, within an accumulated documented history of reflections, recollections and reminiscences of *returns from Sinai*. Of shaking the golden Sinai sand off our sheets, towels and shoes, and packing our belongings into the colourful wool packs that we brought back from Nepal; of driving along the scenic road leading to the Taba Border Checkpoint and crossing over from the Egyptian side to the Israeli side; of driving the hot, dry and mind-numbing road that leads from Eilat through the Arava Desert for over three hours; of unlocking the door of our cool Jerusalem apartment, of putting our daughters to bed, our clothes to the laundry, and ourselves back (in)to routine. As if it all didn't happen. Or that it happened, but in a dream — in a shared altered state of consciousness of the type that memories are made of.

Indeed, subtle tourist transformations occur before the trip commences, as well as after its conclusion. These transformations suggest that a more nuanced model should account for the overall tourist experience (if a model is to be suggested at all). The model should not be triadic: pre-trip, trip and post-trip, as is typically the case in tourism literature. This can be illustrated by my own recent experience. Two weeks prior to our family's most recent vacation in Sinai, when attempting to comfort my daughter Noa (who was seven years old at the time) during a moment of frustration, I found myself referring to the upcoming vacation:

> Noa, think of Sinai and cheer up. We're gonna take your floating mattress
> for the sea and your buoys for the pool. Wow. Just think about it — it's
> going to be *really* great.

However, as can be expected, it wasn't long before I had to stop myself from referring to the very same (expected) vacation in a contrary, and threatening context; during a moment of anger, I just barely prevented myself from uttering something like: "Noa, if you keep up this nasty attitude of yours we're simply not going to go to Sinai!" These illustrations, which are likely familiar scenarios to most caregivers, capture a phenomenology of tourist preparations. The event of the trip, or the trip's eventfulness, permeates our daily lives, and adds layers of language and meaning to existing dialogues.

Toward the conclusion of this discussion, I wish to turn to the tourist's phenomenology of "the return", such as the one described in the last verse of "In-between". The issue I would like to address here, then, is not related to the experiences that occur during the journey to or back from the destination, or during the vacation itself (see "On the way to Sinai"). Instead, I inquire into reflections and hindsight, aftermaths and aftereffects; into a state that is the mirror image of the planning, expecting and preparing state that precedes the trip.

The last occasion of return from Sinai took place fairly recently, at the end of our last Passover vacation (April, 2006). We traveled to Sinai contra to the recommendations of worried relatives and friends, who insistently reminded us of the many pending and specific travel warnings against visiting Sinai (issued by the Israel Foreign Ministry), and that the place is prone to terror attacks (a position that was reinforced when a terror bomb attack in Dahab claimed the lives of twenty-three people a week after we had returned. However, while on vacation, another suicide bomb attack took the lives of nine people in a kiosk in Tel-Aviv).

Keeping in mind this chapter, I tried to observe, as closely as I could, the fluctuations in my experiences during the return. Diligently applying an (auto)ethnographical method, I made sure not to be caught without my pen and yellow writing pad upon which I recorded any experiential vicissitudes (see Figure 21.1). But nothing outstanding was revealed.

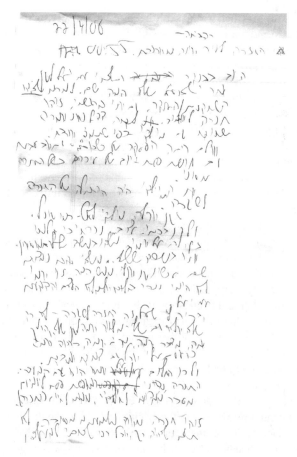

Figure 21.1: Writing a souvenir: a tourist's yellow writing pad.

Instead, everything on our way back went quite smoothly: no particularly emotional moments, unique rituals of passage, homecoming or interactions. With the exception of a vivid daydream that I had during the trip back, about visiting a popular Jerusalem pub on the evening of our return (which, I realized I would probably be too exhausted to do), my mental sonar did not detect any unique emotional movement. Perhaps I had tried too hard, I thought. Perhaps I had looked too eagerly, or with an overly academic focus, and had missed something; or worse, I suspected that my self-conscious analysis had prevented an experiential association from occurring, thus preventing such an association from enriching the overall experience of the trip and its aftermath. In this regard, I admit to feeling a sense of some disappointment and of a triviality with regard to my return.

The last entry in my yellow notepad is dated April 22, 2006, 00:55 (the day after we returned):

In the morning I am walking Yael, my three year old, to her nursery school. It's located two blocks away from our apartment, and we usually walk along this path together. Yael hasn't been at the nursery, with her teachers and toddler friends, for over two weeks, because, prior to the holiday, and to our vacation, she had smallpox and missed the last few days. So we are really excited. As we leave home in the morning, I notice that at first, she wants to take a small seashell she brought from Sinai with her (she always likes to take small things with her). Then, right near the door, she changes her mind. She leaves the shell at home and instead takes a chocolate yogurt from the refrigerator, of the type she usually takes with her everyday to the nursery ("Milky"). I can't tell what is going on inside her mind (is she worried that her friends will not appreciate the shell as much as she wants, etc.), but I make a mental note to myself that she is returning to her routine; that she is regaining her everyday practices, minute by minute: "Milky" > a shell from Sinai.

At the nursery it emotionally dawns on me.

We get there quite early, sit on tiny chairs near tiny tables, and peel the aluminum foil off the "Milky" yogurt. Yael is consuming it slowly. Tablespoon by tablespoon. Her tiny hand is shaking slightly, and I'm deeply moved. Now I'm suddenly teary, and I'm not sure why. I'm trying to hide my reddened eyes from her and from Na'ama, her nursery teacher. I'm supposed to be happy. Right at this moment I recall a moving dream that I dreamt the night before. I dreamt of my mother who died in 1997. I guess I had simply forgotten the dream. I didn't dream of her in a long while, and I was now shocked to recall that I had dreamed of her office. It was empty, and yet there were other people there who I didn't know: I think there a woman there who replaced her as the Curator of the Prehistory Department at the Israel Museum. I cannot recall exactly the emotions that I felt in the dream, but the feeling was clearly despairing. Her office was always full of Neolithic stone tools, flint arrowheads and even human bones, and was a great place to spend adventurous childhood mornings. In the dream there was only alienation and distance: the space of the office wasn't mine any more in any way. It was her place but she wasn't there. In this case sadness has triggered a dream, and not the other way around. I say good-bye to Yael and leave the nursery quickly, and now I can express my sadness openly and cry.

Yael is returning to her everyday routine, and so am I: walking her to the nursery, chatting with her, absorbing her childish blows (she practices hitting me with her small fists, with marked pleasure) and making her laugh. My return to our routine is reflexive because I observe myself observing Yael. When I do, I slip (back) into the role of the parent, *her* parent, observing her and Noa on a daily basis. In line with Haldrup and Larsen (2003), tourism might indeed be said to produce symbolic spaces of recreation, mainly re-creating social relations — familial relations in the present case (p. 24). Families are indeed effected by tourism, both during the trip, but also before and after it has actually occurred.

The return from Sinai has triggered dreaming, which partly serve to mediate and negotiate the transformations that occur between different states of mind and being, or between "everyday-life and tourism-life" (Haldrup & Larsen, 2003, p. 25). These transformations are fairly common, and indeed various returns from Sinai, as well as from other destinations, were followed, in my experience, by particularly vivid, life-like dreams. These dreams, which are real, i.e. they actually occurred (unlike the excursions to Sinai, which are not "real" dreams), converse with altered states of consciousness. The evocation of the death of my mother in this context suggests additional terrains of reminiscences and nostalgia. While I wish to avoid simplistic symbolic interpretations of the dream, it is fairly clear to me that returning to "everyday life" means realizing — time and again — the enduring absence of my mother (illustrated in the dream through a similar language to that employed in tourism: spaces — inhabited and vacated). And death, too, is transformative, although under modern worldviews, death is not viewed as a state from which one returns or from which homecomings are possible. It remains, however, unclear to me why it is my mother's workplace that I visit in the dream, rather than, say, my parents' warm living room or the cozy kitchen that she had liked so much. My guess is that this recollection concerns my return to my (academic) workplace, and particularly to the act of writing — a sphere about which I feel very close to my mother's experiences (see Noy, 2003). In any case, the fact is that it has been years since I last thought of, or imagined, that somewhat peculiar office, which embodies an interesting (and neglected or forgotten) aspect of my childhood spaces and experiences.

Conclusion of the Poetics of Sinai Journeys

> By following the tourists, we may be able to arrive at a better understanding of ourselves. (MacCannell, 1999, p. 9)

At the onset of this chapter I proposed the notion that an autoethnographic inquiry can offer a singular contribution to the exploration of tourists' "languages of experience". The poetic texts described in the chapter suggest that tourism amounts to a nexus of both language and discourse — a nexus of different languages (such as Hebrew, Arabic and Russian), as well as the different syntaxes of various experiences. These (symbolic) languages are both the result and the means of translations of experiences across different Schutzian (1945, 1970) "provinces of meaning", primarily between the spheres of tourism and of everyday life. In the chapter I endeavored to illustrate this idea through examining a heterogonous — as well as heteroglossic (Bakhtin, 1981) — corpus of trips, experiences, recollections, languages and texts (written in the last decade, 1996–2006), of which there are only two homogeneous aspects: there is only one tourist — myself, and only one destination — the serene beaches of Sinai by the Red Sea.

As a methodology, autoethnography should be viewed in the present context as yet another "language", which relates to the field of research. Indeed, the experience of writing autoethnographies embodies a strong sense of "language": the author departs from traditional social science discourse in favor of attending to, and re-evoking specific discursive spheres. The autoethnographic exploration introduces additional languages into the already polyphonic semiotics of the tourists' experience. It is, then, not a neutral and impartial "method". Rather, by definition, it evokes the experiences of, and the prevailing ideologies in the field in which it is applied as a method of inquiry in an attempt to highlight them and discuss them critically.

Because the texts presented in this chapter were initially penned while the author was on vacation, they are viewed as souvenirs, those metonymically materialized products of the abstract notion of "tourist semiotics". What Haldrup and Larsen (2003) write with regards to the social role photographing plays in tourism, can well be said about productions of tourists' texts-as-souvenirs. In both cases, the tourist "is both the subject and the object of the photographic event – [she or he] is both in front of and behind the camera" (p. 42).

This leads to the observation that the poetic tourist's texts have an embodied quality, which can be discerned at both ends — in the texts' production and in its consumption. This embodied quality is related to the fact that the texts are created, or "entextualized" (to borrow from Silverstein & Urban, 1996) within a lively social setting, as a product of tourist performances. Much like the production of other tourists' texts — from eighteenth century postcards to contemporary electronic blogs and mail — tourists' poems require particular conditions for their production. Likewise, the reading of such texts in this chapter was also viewed as a tourist performance — akin to the consumption of a variety of discursive objects within sphere of tourism (commercials, guidebooks etc.).

At the outset I also proposed that, with time, the notion of tourists' experiences is increasingly less clear and more elusive to me. The autoethnography presented above attempts to address this condition, but not in linear ways. It does not suggest, test and accept or reject further hypotheses or analyses. Rather, it conveys a "thick" (Geertzian) and emotionally loaded description, which touches upon and evokes the intricacies and subtleties of which the sphere of tourism is so rich with, and arrests or freezes fleeting moments, which, too, are so inherent to the same.

The nature of an autoethnographic inquiry is holistic or "Gestaltian". It is therefore presently employed as an inquiry into *the whole of the tourist experience*. This is why the chapter organically "follows the tourists" (MacCannell, 1999, above) — from the journey to the destinations, through the sounds and rhythms of the vacationscapes of the beaches of Sinai, to the phenomenology of the return(s). Indeed, the chapter's final section is devoted to experiential vicissitudes and transformations, which transpire in the course of negotiating "everyday-life and tourism-life" (Haldrup & Larsen, 2003, p. 25). The observation that people are tourists most of the time (Urry, 1990), does not lead, to my mind, to the view that everyday and the touristic spheres are homologous, but rather that transformations and translations are more frequent and are negotiated more subtly than before. They amount to moments of "awakenings" which the chapter tried to highlight.

References

Aitchison, C. (2000). Poststructural feminist theories of representing others: A response to the 'crisis' in leisure studies discourse. *Leisure Studies, 19*(3), 127–144.

Ateljevic, I., Harris, C., Wilson, E., & Collins, F. L. (2005). Getting 'entangled': Reflexivity and the 'critical turn' in tourism studies. *Tourism Recreation Research, 30*(2), 9–21.

Azaryahu, M. (2006). The beach at the end of the world: Eilat in Israeli popular culture. *Social & Cultural Geography, 6*(1), 117–133.

Bakhtin, M. M. (1981). Discourse in the novel. In: M. Holquist (Ed.), *The dialogic imagination: Four essays* (pp. 259–422). Austin: University of Texas Press.

Behar, R. (1996). *The vulnerable observer: Anthropology that breaks your heart*. Boston: Beacon Press.

Bochner, A. P., & Ellis, C. (Eds). (2002). *Ethnographically speaking: Autoethnography, literature, and aesthetics*. Walnut Creek, CA: AltaMira Press.

Botterill, D. (2003). An autoethnographic narrative on tourism research epistemologies. *Loisir et Societe/Society and Leisure, 26*(1), 97–110.

Cohen, E. (1973). Nomads from affluence: Notes on the phenomenon of drifter tourism. *International Journal of Comparative Sociology, 14*, 89–103.

Cohen, E. (1979). A phenomenology of tourist experiences. *Sociology, 13*(2), 179–201.

Cohen, E. (1982). Marginal paradises: Bungalow tourism on the islands of southern Thailand. *Annals of Tourism Research, 9*(2), 189–228.

Cohen, E. (Ed.). (1987). *The price of peace: The removal of the Israeli settlements in Sinai — an ambiguous resolution of an existential conflict* (Vol. 23 (special issue of the *Journal of Applied Behavioral Sciences*)).

Cohen, E. (2005). The beach of 'the beach': The politics of environmental damage in Thailand. *Tourism Recreation Research, 30*(1), 1–17.

Coleman, S., & Crang, M. (Eds). (2002). *Tourism: Between place and performance*. New York: Berghahn Books.

Crouch, D., & Desforges, L. (2003). The sensuous in the tourist encounter. *Tourist Studies, 3*(1), 5–22.

Denzin, N. K. (1999). Two-stepping in the 90's. *Qualitative Inquiry, 5*(4), 568–572.

Denzin, N. K., & Lincoln, Y. S. (Eds). (2000). *Handbook of qualitative research* (2nd ed.). Thousand Oaks, CA: Sage.

Edensor, T. (1998). *Tourists at the Taj: Performance and meaning at a symbolic site*. London: Routledge.

Edensor, T. (2000). Staging tourism: Tourists as performers. *Annals of Tourism Research, 27*(2), 322–344.

Ellis, C. (1997). Evocative autoethnography: Writing emotionally about our lives. In: W. G. Tierney, & Y. S. Lincoln (Eds), *Representation and the text: Re-Framing the narrative voice* (pp. 115–142). Albany: State University of New York Press.

Ellis, C. (2003). *The ethnographic I: A methodological novel about autoethnography*. Walnut Creek, CA: AltaMira Press.

Ellis, C., & Bochner, A. P. (2000). Autoethnography, personal narrative, reflexivity: Researcher as subject. In: N. K. Denzin, & Y. S. Lincoln (Eds), *Handbook of qualitative research* (2nd ed., pp. 733–768). Thousand Oaks, CA: Sage.

Foucault, M. (1979). *Discipline and punish: The birth of the prison* (A. Sheridan, Trans.). New York: Vintage Books.

Fullagar, S. (2002). Narratives of travel: Desire and the movement of feminine subjectivity. *Leisure Studies, 21*(1), 57–74.

Goffman, E. (1959). *The presentation of self in everyday life*. Garden City, NY: Doubleday.

Goffman, E. (1974). *Frame analysis: An essay on the organization of experience*. Boston: Northeastern University Press.

Haldrup, M., & Larsen, J. (2003). The family gaze. *Tourist Studies, 3*(1), 23–45.

Jones, S. H. (1998). *Kaleidoscope notes: Writing women's music and organizational culture*. Walnut Creek, CA: AltaMira Press.

Lavie, S. (1990). *The poetics of military occupation: Mzeina allegories of bedouin identity under Israeli and Egyptian rule*. Berkeley: University of California Press.

Lofgren, O. (1999). *On holiday: A history of vacationing*. Berkeley: University of California Press.

MacCannell, D. (1999). *The tourist: A new theory of the leisure class*. Berkeley: University of California Press.

Noy, C. (2003). The write of passage: Reflections on writing a dissertation in narrative/qualitative methodology. *Forum of Qualitative Social Research [On-line Journal]*, *4*(2).

Noy, C. (2004). "The trip really changed me": Backpackers' narratives of self-change. *Annals of Tourism Research*, *31*(1), 78–102.

Noy, C. (2006a). Israeli backpacking since the 1960s: Institutionalization and its effects. *Tourism Recreation Research*, *31*(3), 39–54.

Noy, C. (2006b). The poetics of tourist experience: An autoethnography of a family trip to Eilat (submitted to publication).

Noy, C. (2006c). *Narrative community: Voices of Israeli backpackers.* Detroit: Wayne State University Press.

Schutz, A. (1945). On multiple realities. In: M. Natanson (Ed.), *Collected papers I: The problem of social reality* (pp. 207–259). The Hague: Matinus Nijhoff.

Schutz, A. (1970). *On phenomenology and social relations.* Chicago: University of Chicago Press.

Silverstein, M., & Urban, G. (1996). The natural histories of discourse. In: M. Silverstein, & G. Urban (Eds), *Natural histories of discourse* (pp. 1–17). Chicago: University of Chicago Press.

Stewart, S. (1993). *On longing: narratives of the miniature, the gigantic, the souvenir, the collection.* Durham: Duke University Press.

Tobias, M. (1995). *A vision of nature: Traces of the original world.* Kent, Ohio: Kent State University Press.

Urry, J. (1990). *The tourist gaze: Leisure and travel in contemporary societies.* London: Sage.

Young, K. G. (1987). *Taleworlds and storyrealms: The phenomenology of narrative.* Dordrecht, The Netherlands: Martinus Nijhoff.

Zemel, A. (1998). The Passover *Haggadah* as argument, or why is this text different from other texts? *Argumentation*, *12*(1), 57–77.

Chapter 22

Re-Peopling Tourism: A 'Hot Approach' to Studying Thanatourist Experiences

Ria Ann Dunkley

Uzzell and Ballantyne (1998, p. 152) contend that 'to deny the emotional side of our understanding and appreciation of the world and our relationships is to deny the very humanity that makes us part of the human race'. Yet within tourism research little recognition has been given to the emotional aspects of tourism experiences. Additionally, the traditional tourism researcher has been encouraged to remain impersonally aloof from her research (Westwood, Morgan, & Pritchard, 2006). The 'rules of the academic game' as Hall (2004, p. 143) puts it, deterring tourism researchers away from 'playful and reflexive' approaches in favour of seemingly objective methods and writing styles approved by gate-keepers within tourism studies. Furthermore, amongst the social science community of which tourism academics are a subcommunity (Hall, 2004), the author's voice is repressed; this is seen as a method of purporting rigour within qualitative research (Holliday, 2002). Consequently, relatively little tourism research has been conducted taking into account the positionality of the researcher and the author's influence is commonly excluded from text. As a result, studies are generally written in distant third person prose where the author is made to appear invisible. In contrast to this tradition, this chapter focuses on taking a passionate and situated approach to research. My interest in which came about whilst exploring the thanatouristic experience,[1] during which time it became clear to me that taking a cool and distanced approach to the field was not going to be simple or even desirable given that it is such an emotive subject. Rather, I opted against the traditional convention of creating 'cold, depersonalized, unsigned, voiceless' (Clandinin & Connelly, 2000, p. 149) documents, in a move away from post-positivist methodologies favoured within the social sciences and tourism studies (Wilson, 2004), towards the adoption of a 'softer' approach which embraced the emotional aspects of the experience.

Although within our society a 'detached, cool and objective approach' (Uzzell & Ballantyne, 1998, p. 152) to an abundance of lived experience is generally favoured, Janis

---

[1]Thanatourism (also known as dark tourism), involves the visitation of sites of, or associated with death and depravity (Seaton, 1996; Foley & Lennon, 1996).

The Critical Turn in Tourism Studies: Innovative Research Methodologies
Copyright © 2007 by Elsevier Ltd.
All rights of reproduction in any form reserved.
ISBN: 0-08-045098-9

and Mann (1977, p. 45) view the 'desirability of cool detachment' as a highly questionable ideal. Human nature deters us away from emotional detachment, thus we must recognise the undeniable presence of the researcher within the research setting and allow the voice of the 'vulnerable observer' (Behar, 1996), the researcher, to emerge from the field texts which she constructs. Taking a passionate and situated approach has the capacity to inform and inspire researchers and writers. Consequently, this chapter exposes my emotionally turbulent relationship with thanatourism. I hope that it will be as inspiring and insightful for you, as papers which reveal personal experience (Botterill, 2003; Hall, 2004) have been for me. For instance, I have been particularly encouraged by authors such as Tillmann–Healey (1996, p. 80) who bravely uses her own experience as a bulimic as primary data in order to understand bulimia and help others 'see and sense it more fully'. In a comparable manner, here I provide a discussion of my own development as a researcher, focusing on three sequential autoethnographic episodes of thanatourism experience between 2002 and 2006. These episodes are counterpoised with an exploration of the issues associated with situating the self within tourism research. As I move through my accounts I address areas which at different stages of my development became particularly salient, beginning with my disenchantment and subsequent struggle with conventions. I then move on to consider fear experienced within the field and trepidation related to writing the emotional self. Finally I provide a review of the many selves that we bring to the field as researchers, which disallow us to remain detached from the fields we study.

To begin from the beginning, I had unknowingly encountered thanatourism on a number of occasions as a child and teenager, visiting such places as, the Arnhem–Oosterbeek War Cemetery and the Overloon War and Resistance Museum as a sea-cadet. However, I became formally aware of the subject during my undergraduate degree when it was mentioned, in passing, in my first year of study. It stayed in my mind and I knew that it would be something I would like to study, perhaps for my undergraduate dissertation. I have always had an interest in warfare; my father would tell me stories about wars through history, we would watch old war films such as 'A Bridge too Far' together and we had a bookshelf full of material on war. At school I had taken history throughout and learnt about the First and Second World Wars and the Vietnam War, and had always found these aspects of history fascinating. Whilst writing the proposal for my dissertation, I decided to visit the Imperial War Museum (IWM) in London on Friday 18th October, 2002. This visit deeply affected me, and I feel it was a turning point in my fascination with thanatourism. This is the story of my experience that day.

An Afternoon with Death and Depravity

I came out of the holocaust exhibition at the Imperial War Museum and sat in the contemplation area, a space which allows the visitor to make sense of what they have seen. I sat in front of the screen which plays a continuous loop of interviews with holocaust survivors and I began to cry, so upset about what I had just seen in the holocaust exhibition that I felt disillusioned with humanity, everything I knew to matter did not, along side this. To view the video footage and photographs of piles of dead bodies lying on top of each other in mass graves, and then to see an actual table from Mauthausen concentration camp where fatal medical experiments were carried out was too much to bear. I tried to hold back my tears, no one else was crying, all looked sombre, expressionless, indifferent but they did not show any signs of sadness. I felt like a silly little girl getting upset, so I held back my tears and composed myself. The recorded interviews came to an end and then rewind to the beginning, and it is at this point that I decide I must go.

I went to the museum shop, as I forgot my note pad and wanted to write some research notes while the event was fresh in my mind. I spotted the book *Poems of the Great War*. I had the intention of buying a book specifically from the museum, containing the poem 'In Flanders field' by John McCrae. This poem meant a great deal to me, I first heard it during an English class on the Great War poets at school. I went home from school that day, typed the words up on my mother's typewriter and affixed it to the first page of my poetry book. At this time I was suffering the personal upheaval of my parents' separation and poetry, both my own and that of others was of great solace to me. 'In Flanders Field' represented perfection and so it occupied an honorary position there. I flicked through the book and to my delight I found the poem, and so I bought it.

I also wanted to get something that would remind me of the visit so I chose the notebook because of the Flanders's poppy field on the front of it, I remember spending quite sometime standing in front of the shelf deciding whether it was a good idea to spend the six pounds ninety-nine on the notebook, when I could buy a simple note book for sixty pence. This would have been a much better idea, taking into account that I had about fifty pounds left to live on until the end of term. I used the note pad throughout the dissertation as a reminder and inspiration for the journey I had chosen to embark on.

While sitting in the museum café, thinking about the proposal for my dissertation and the ominous task ahead of me, I tried to make some objective observations which would help in the understanding of the subject, something that would prove to my tutors that this would make a good dissertation. I could not think of anything objective, I could not make distanced reflections; that afternoon I sat in the café and did what I always did when I tried to make sense of difficult issues that I came across. I wrote my thoughts and feelings down and tried to make sense of them. This was, however, the only time during my undergraduate studies that I wrote such an account, and over the next two years I would produce generalised findings in relation to thanatourism experiences in line with social sciences positivist tradition (Tonkin, 2005). When I sat down in that café I knew that I would not abandon this subject and felt that in some small way by studying it, I would better myself and perhaps carry an important message of humanity forward. The following extract is from the diary that I wrote in the café that day:

> The museum has had a huge impact on me, studying the atrocities of Nazi Germany and war, for example, nothing can prepare you for the harshness of seeing actual things, people, photos of things that were there at the time of the events. A completely gut-wrenching experience. These people in the photographs are on death row, the girl who wore that coat is now dead and for what? This is why I think it is crucial to deliver the message of caution to the world, to make sure this never happens again and as harsh and disgusting as the events are, the whole world and we as sophisticated human beings have an obligation to deliver the warning to future generations. There should be museums like this

in every city and town of the world. Prevention is far better than cure and people need to be educated, they need to learn from the past, especially now with the threat of war posed once more. It begs the question, along with many other questions, 'would this be happening if nations were better educated?' if they knew about these things and are prepared and cautious. Because if Hitler can attack Jews, Bin Laden can attack America and maybe one day someone will have it in for Britain. The lesson we need to learn, is that we have to be less selfish in our ways of life, too often do people think 'oh, well it's not effecting me or my family, so why should I bother getting involved'.
It is this kind of attitude that allows six million people to be murdered and then something is done.

So, now I feel like I have identified what effect visiting the museum should have, I need to find out what impact on people they do have. I can say that if everyone in the world felt the same as I do right now, there would be, no more wars. It is also important to note that these people should not have died in vain. Yes, it is painful to see these atrocities but it also reminds us of how lucky we are not to have been caught in these atrocities. People are so fickle as Nazi Germany showed. They need to see the negative impacts of dictators, such as Hitler and also remember what is important in life, not money, or power, or success but love, comradeship, and human compassion. . . As time goes on memories fade and that's why these sites should remain, so they are a reminder, so that memories never fade.

Hiding the Humane: Struggling with Convention

In contrast to supposition that our own personal subjectivities do not come into our research decisions (Hall, 2004), it is clear that 'we study the things that trouble or intrigue us, beginning from our own subjective standpoints' (Hertz, 1997, p. xvi). It was my own subjective experience at the IWM in 2002 that led me to believe that 'evocative forms of writing are not merely desirable, they are essential' (Charmaz & Mitchell, 1997, p. 195). My above diary entry with all its grammatical errors, innocence and rawness shows how I felt about thanatourism as a tourist not as an academic. It shows how I struggled with convention in my desire to reflect on my experience, revealing a great deal about my inner state of being at the time of writing and although through a dedication to scholarship my ideas have been refined, my key values remain the same. It also illuminates the deep psychological and sociological forces that interplay within a tourism experience, which is important in terms of how I have subsequently chosen to research thanatourism. For example, I felt that I should remain 'composed', while really wanting to cry after seeing evidence of the holocaust, influenced by the actions of others around me. Items purchased are also significant, providing an echo back to a painful time of my life. Additionally, how I chose to record this emotional experience, using the same technique as I had always done, that is, writing my thoughts down, is of significance.

The 'reflexive turn' of the 1980s meant that the consideration of the fieldworker within the research setting began to be addressed (Svasek, 2005, p. 15). The recognition of the involvement of the subjective researcher within the research process is increasingly perceived as a positive aspiration (Coffey, 1999; Ellis & Bochner, 2000; Westwood, 2004). However, Charmaz and Mitchell (1997, p. 193) were correct when they stated that scholarly writers have long been cautioned to work like Victorian children, that is, to 'be seen (in the credits) but not heard (in the text)'. Furthermore, because of the tourism academy's encouragement of objective approaches to study (Westwood, et al., 2006), such 'hot approaches' to research as the one discussed here, written in the first person, passionately and intimately, are actively discouraged in accordance with traditional research culture.

When I began my research career I was certain that I would follow the post-positivist path, having been schooled in traditional research methods and enticed by the security which large-scale surveys offered. However, whilst carrying out a pilot survey of one hundred questionnaires at the IWM in 2004, I realised that I was not getting the in-depth information which I desired about these people's experiences (Westwood, 2004, p. 102). I certainly was not reaching the depths of emotions which I myself had experienced at the museum two years previously. I realised therefore, that in order to reach deep wells of tourist emotions and subsequently achieve what I had promised the university I would within my research degree proposal, I needed to take an alternative approach. In a broader context, the view that social settings are settings that can be quantified and categorised is being challenged increasingly by social scientists (Lincoln, 1990; Ellis & Bochner, 2000; Holliday, 2002) not least tourism researchers (Phillimore & Goodson, 2004; Westwood, 2004; Wilson, 2004). What is now suggested is that such an objective approach to the study of peopled fields is undesirable in terms of gaining an accurate view of that field and many recognise the value of alternative methodologies (Jamal & Hollinshead, 2001; Westwood, 2004; Wilson, 2004; Westwood et al., 2006).

Ignorance and suppression of the fact that fieldwork is peopled by both the researcher and the researched may lead to the possibility of disregarding information which provides valuable insight into the lives of participants. Therefore we must recognise that 'fieldwork is itself a "social setting" inhabited by embodied, emotional, physical selves' (Coffey, 1999, p. 6). As Botterill and Crompton (1987, p. 154) argue, there is a need to pursue 'a more emic, or actor-centred approach towards understanding tourist behaviour' and there is a necessity to position the researcher within the research texts which she constructs. However, within tourism academia very little previous research has been carried out which takes into account the personal narratives (Westwood, 2004) of the author, exposing the writer's voice as my above account does. My struggle with these conventions when trying to research an emotional form of tourism led me to approach my research differently. Rather than excluding accounts, such as the one above, I began to see that there was a place for and value to integrating this and similar accounts within my actual writing because as Bochner and Ellis (1996, p. 20) state 'we cannot help but read something into what is there, because we are there with it'.

The anthropologist Rosaldo (2004, p. 167) explains how it was only following the death of his wife Michelle Rosaldo whilst they were in the field researching the Ilongots, that he was able to understand 'headhunters rage', the Ilongot man's way of dealing with bereavement. What Rosaldo (2004) brings to light, is that in order to understand the experiences and emotions of those we study it is crucial that we are able to empathise with their position. Through giving up 'ones academic cloak of objectivity' (Behar, 1996) and taking an evocative, subjective and emotionally powerful approach, as Rosaldo (2004) does in 'Grief and headhunters rage', it is possible to achieve deep insights into the phenomena which we seek awareness of. As researchers we will never observe what would have occurred had we not 'been there' (Behar, 1996) and there is merit in recognising our own presence within the research setting. Indeed, Behar (1996, p. 177) stresses the need to recognise the emotional aspects of lived experience within research in response to criticism of emotionally powerful work such as Rosaldo's (2004) by stating that anthropology 'that doesn't break your heart just isn't worth doing'. We must therefore give recognition to the personal nature of research both in terms of the implications of the researcher's involvement on their research as well as to the identification of the researcher as a credible research participant. Coffey (1999) notes that 'while there is increasing address of the personal nature of fieldwork, the self in the field is not something to which method text gives substantial attention' (Coffey, 1999, p. 1). Yet the information gained from observing, interacting and conversing with participants, supported by autoethnographic accounts, can help to provide the 'thick descriptions' of situations which Geertz (1973) refers to.

Autoethnography and the construction of personal accounts is still relatively controversial (Coffey, 1999) for it is one of the major challenges to the conventions of 'silent authorship' (Holt, 2003, p. 2).Writing conventions are derived from social science as well as the academic community (Holliday, 2002), and despite gradual acceptance, gatekeepers to tourism research are still hesitating to acknowledge the value of alternative approaches (Westwood et al., 2006). Indeed, Hall (2004) states that it would be highly unlikely that any of the tourism academic journals would publish a paper written entirely in the first person without, at least, major modifications, should it get published at all. However, writing in the first person allows the author to embrace subjectivity not only through the exposure of her own voice within autoethnographic narratives, but as narrator in the presentation of the findings, dispelling the myth of silent authorship (Charmaz & Mitchell, 1997). The reader is therefore put in a position to understand the truth which is interpreted out of both — the author's own experiences and the experiences of the research participants. In this chapter I invite you, the reader, to see inside my experiences and to construct your own interpretations of them (Mykhalovskiy, 1997).

A Close Encounter with Dennis Nilsen

It is 31st October 2005, and I am at the Princess Louise Public house, the site where Dennis Nilsen picked up the second of his young male victims Kenneth Ockendon and the final stop on our 'Horror London' walking tour. David the tour guide tells us of the events which proceeded Nilsen's encounter with the young Canadian and dares us now to go in and have a drink. It's all dealt with in a very humorous and light-hearted manner, but this only happened in 1979, the story is real, a twisted tale, people died and David is making on this tour alone, at least one hundred and eighty pounds by telling people about it. I feel so uncomfortable in my own skin, after having listened to a marathon of stories about the horrific aspects of London's past, Jack the Ripper's murdered prostitutes, Mrs Lovetts human pies, and I desperately want to get back to reality and stop looking at all this stuff that makes me feel so uncomfortable. David makes an announcement that I am a researcher and that I would like to speak to some of the tour members about their experiences and I wait anxiously for someone to agree, secretly hoping that the seemingly eccentric American man and his wife, with the oversized camera will volunteer. To my joy they do and we go in for a drink.

Sally, Jim's wife offers to buy me a drink, refusing my original offer, because I am in her words the 'starving student' and Jim and I perch ourselves on some barstools in the corner. I am glad that I can come back down to earth in the purposeful form of research, but I'm not best pleased about being in this pub. We have an enlightening discussion about what the tour meant for all of us, agreeing to keep in touch and swapping email addresses before we leave. Jim and Sally pose for photographs outside the pub as they wave me off into the distance. It is night time now and my mind switches track, back to the land of the living, I hurry down this busy London street to meet my partner Andrew at the next tube stop. My anxiety surprises me I am checking behind me all the time to make sure no one is following me. The buildings now personify fear, towering above me and surrounding me as though slowly closing in. I don't understand, surely I cannot be this scared, I've walked through the streets of London alone at night many times before but this time is different. These buildings now have power in what has happened in them, every one seems to tell a story and evoke fear in my mind.

After a seemingly long train journey back to Holborn, I meet Andrew who has agreed to go on the Halloween's evening tour with me. I tell him how scary the tour is going to be, but he does not seem fazed. After dinner we make our way back to Holborn tube station to meet David and forty or so tourists who are all geared up for a spooky Halloween. The tour runs to schedule with the same frights and chills as earlier in the day, and even though it is my second time round, I am quite pleased Andrew is here for me to hang on to, and I wonder if he is at all scared, it is rather dark, which does undoubtedly add to the atmosphere. The streets are so quiet that it does feel like you could be in another time, but it is much the same.

After the tour, Andrew suggests that we go into the Princess Louise for a drink; I agree, it is after all a lovely looking pub and it wasn't so bad earlier. We follow the rest of the tourists in and sit down on stools near the bar. A balding, wiry man sitting in the corner in a lumberjack shirt, smoking rolled-up cigarettes appears to be staring intensely at me, my anguish leads me to stare back and unfortunately I catch his eye. . .I need the toilet. . .but I am too scared to go. . .I think to myself, 'I've got to be brave, just go'. I run down the stairs to them, faster than I did in the pizza express earlier, when I was scared because there seemed to be some form of vault on the door and I thought it would be something sinister.

My imagination is in overdrive,
I lock the door,
I hear footsteps, my heart is pounding
I've got to get out quickly. . .
Before the lady next door does. . .
'What if he's come down behind me and he is going to murder me?'
Thoughts are rushing through my head, I try to calm down but I just can't,
I can't seem to bring myself back to a rational state of mind.

I run out of the toilets and sprint up the stairs, when I get to the top; I try to act casual, as there is a group from the tour sitting to my left. I return to my table, the man has left his seat, horror bolts through my mind. . .he's at the bar getting another drink.

'Have we got time for another?' Andrew asks.

'No come on lets get out of here, we better get across to Paddington for the train' I say, glad that the day is over, and in the realisation of how difficult researching such an uncomfortable subject, which I've never been comfortable viewing, is going to be and it is at this point I realise that to do it well I've really got to get in deep with this stuff.

On Writing Fear and Fear of Writing

Within the above narrative I expose different aspects of my 'self' and a very different set of emotions is evoked as opposed to the first account, emphasising the diversity of thanatourism experiences (Dunkley, 2005). The account reflects the strength of a thanatourism experience to affect feelings and actions. It also reveals the different selves which we bring to the field (Reinharz, 1997), for example, in this case the self as a researcher, a frightened girl and a girlfriend, and also the selves which are imposed on us by others within the field (Clandinin & Connelly, 2000), for instance, Sally's understanding of me as 'the starving student'. This narrative was also the most difficult to share. I must be completely honest within my research; however, the seemingly irrational emotions which I experienced during this episodic narrative, where an innocent pub reveller became momentarily Dennis Nilsen, make me embarrassed of my always overactive imagination.

As I write this, therefore, I am in fear as I was during my horror tour experience. I am fearful of exposing these seemingly irrational anxieties and fearful of appearing over-zealous or self important in my decision to share my stories with you. These fears relate to my personal self and thus the very intimate aspects of my self are vulnerable. I am also anxious as an academic for I know that as emergent fields, narrative inquiry (Clandinin & Connelly, 2000) and autoethnography (Reed–Danahay, 1997) in particular have come under scrutiny. There are those who argue that the manner in which ethnography and autobiography are combined in explicit and self-conscious ways (Coffey, 1999, p. 122) is a cause for concern, questioning autoethnographies validity as a research technique, stating that such personal accounts have a more justifiable place within acknowledgments and forewords of texts. Such approaches have also been discussed as having more credence within therapeutic and literary disciplines. My reputation and how I am perceived as a novice academic is therefore exposed. For these reasons personal narrative inquiry is a research methodology which involves an element of risk and subsequently fear for the researcher within tourism studies where such approaches are rarely articulated.

To a certain extent, I am able to dispel some of these fears, by defending narrative enquiry and autoethnography against these arguments espousing their usefulness, authenticity (Reed–Danahay, 1997) and their potential to take us to that 'somewhere we couldn't otherwise get to' which Behar (1996, p. 14) discusses. However, within research we must also be aware of the reasonable criticisms and ethical implications of our work. Emotionally powerful writing must not be seen as being beyond criticism and thus undiscussable (Behar, 1996, p. 175), rather alternative forms of criticism 'which are rigorous yet not disinterested' must be applied to such writing. As Clandinin and Connelly (2000, p. 170) express, ethical matters are never far from 'the heart of our inquiries no matter where we are in the process' and it is most important that we do not ignore the voices of our critics. Instead, we must listen to them closely and exhibit the ongoing reflection which they term 'wakefulness', that is, an awareness of the risks of 'narcissism and solipsism' within narrative inquiry. Clandinin and Connelly (2000) argue that through exhibiting wakefulness narrative researchers are able to develop criteria for judging the value of narrative inquiry. Thus although traditional scientific criteria may not be helpful for such studies, we must however be aware of the pitfalls and shortcomings of our research and take into account concerns about 'confidentiality, validity, replication and generalisation' (Hertz, 1997, p. xvii).

A Grave Encounter

It is the 28th January 2006 and I am at Tyne Cot Cemetery in Belgium. I managed to spot a Dunkley on the memorial wall to the missing; I was amazed because I had been walking along staring at each wall and nothing, so I began to tire of looking. I didn't even know my family on my Dad's side, I know nothing about the name, so what exactly I was looking for I didn't know. But then suddenly as I walked passed this column I had a strong urge to look up and see if there was a Dunkley, and there it was, Dunkley, W. H. A strange rush of feeling came over me, I felt excitement, like I had just won a prize, like I had made a connection, like I had a right to be here, like there might be a great mystery behind my name. I really wanted to know if this person was related to me. Either way I wanted to know if any of my relatives were involved in this war because this is my heritage, I want to be proud of where I am from. Instead, I don't even know. I don't even know who my Dad's family are and I felt that if I could at least find out about a relative who maybe did this most honourable thing of fighting for ones country, then I would be proud of my heritage, I would be proud to be a Dunkley and I would not disinherit myself as my father has done himself.

Whilst staring at the wall I realise, hang-on this person is serving under an Irish regiment, as far as I know my family are not from Ireland, chances are it's nothing to do with me. So my search is not over, I think to myself 'now that I've found one, there's got to be more' and I make it my personal mission for the next few days to try and find my family name. As I see Bob, one of the battlefield tourists from our group, bounding across the field to find his family name, I can understand why, 'Go on Bob' I think and I am pleased that he too would have experienced the joy of finding his own surname on a headstone, in realising that his own family would have played a part in this event which was so nationally important.

Seeing Tyne Cot Cemetery was an intensely moving experience, very overwhelming, there are simply too many graves, too many dead people, too many young lives lost, too many grieving families and we have thirty minutes to look and we then must get back on the bus. If I was here alone then I would like to sit here a while and contemplate what happened to these people. I would like to sit down on the lawn by myself and think about all the lives lost; think about the Dunkley's and most of all I would like to cry. I would like to sit here and cry to know that my visit has served its purpose that I have empathised, that

I have understood so well the sacrifice that it has moved me to tears. I want to be alone here, I want to feel the pain, in order to justify me being here, in order to know myself that I have grieved and so I can move on. Instead we must get back on the bus and I have no time to think about it, I do not cry, there are others here. But I imagine myself sitting in the middle of the cemetery on a summers day crossed-legged and playing with the freshly clean cut grass and thinking about the people that are here but gone and hoping that they know that one day a girl from Wales travelled to see them and I cry now, for this lost beautiful moment and for the lost beautiful soldiers for it is so unfair that they died and so unfair that people don't get to cry and I feel guilty for not sitting and staying a while and most of all I feel guilty for not crying. It is, however, freezing cold and so I am glad to get back on the bus.

Later, we arrive at Pozieres British Cemetery as a request stop, I sit and debate whether to get off or not, I decide that I will and I get off the bus alone and walk towards the register. I get it out of its metal encasement to look for my name as I have done at every cemetery we have been to and suddenly, there it is in front of me:

> 'Sergeant F Dunkley, 1211, "A" Bty. 59th Bde., Royal Field Artillery, Aged
> 23, son of John and Ellen Dunkley'.

A rush of excitement comes over me and I hurry to find James the tour guide, who is talking to a guide who is conducting a personal tour:

'James, I found my name, I want to see it, how can I find it?' I exclaim.

'Ok well you look up the numbers and that tells you where it is, look there we are, plot three, tier twelve, third row, three from the back on the end'.

I am so excited and determined to see it that I am almost running through the cemetery, and I find it, the last grave in the row next to the path, and I feel happy that even if this person is not related to me, they will mean something to me because I came to see their grave and they are a Dunkley too. A tear stings my eye and a content smile broadens across my face. I find myself alone, the cold having discouraged many of the tourists from disembarking the tour bus, and with the same feeling that you get when a film has a happy ending or in the case of a great relief. I feel sorrow for this person who was only the same age as me and died on Christmas Eve, how terribly sad I feel. Back on the bus I write in my journal:

> I found a Dunkley, after my eternal quest for the Dunkley name; it was
> Sergeant F. Dunkley who died on the 24th December 1916. It was very
> strange to see your own name on a gravestone. I literally ran across the ceme-
> tery to find the grave, I take four photographs. I feel the letters and I say good-
> bye, I feel emotional but I need to walk on by as I need to get back on the bus.
> It is a lovely cemetery with big white pillars and a cross at the top. I can't
> believe I found a Dunkley, son of John and Ellen Dunkley. Amazing, even if
> he is not related to me, now I know how Bob felt at Tyne Cot.

I walk away thinking that maybe I would have liked to come back on a summers day and sit with Fred for a while and remember him, for him to know that someone is thinking of him. I walk quickly back to the bus feeling content and with an excitement about telling Dad that I found our surname. It was an incredible experience that I doubt many will understand and I feel it would be difficult to get anyone to listen for long enough to do so. I tell everyone around me that I found my name on a stone; as mutual battlefield tourists they are all excited for me.

The Return to the Self: Reaching Deep Wells of Emotion

During my tour of the First World War Cemeteries, I was constantly searching for my surname and implicitly a link to the past and my identity. I included this episode to precede this reflection on the return to the self, which characterises my research, because I feel that a number of conflicting selves emerged from this narrative as opposed to the researcher self. This led to an intensely emotional experience, allowing me to empathise with the other battlefield tourists from an insiders perspective. There is much to be learned from accounts which expose intense thoughts and feelings. For example, the quest for my lost identify in the above account led to me becoming more than a researcher or even a tourist at Tyne Cot and Pozieres Cemeteries, for during parts of the experience, I felt more like a pilgrim, a mourner, however, perhaps most prominently underpinning all of this, a Dunkley.

All three of the narratives within this chapter emphasise that we can be drawn into experiences in intensely engaging ways and on occasion it is impossible to stand by as a passive observer. As a researcher it is possible to become captivated in the 'total immersion' of the experience. However, this total immersion as Coffey (1999, p 36) states is not a weakness but the researcher's involvement is one of the strengths of research. Within all three accounts I expose the humaneness of my research given that as a person I am programmed with 'emotions and unconscious motives as well as cognitive abilities' (Janis & Mann, 1977, p. 45) and in recognising this I am able to use it to my advantage within my research and attempt to reach deep wells of emotion by beginning with the subject I know best, myself (Hall, 2004).

The self has been described as 'a key research tool' (Reinharz, 1997, p. 3), however, the subject of the multiple selves within which we embody the field as in the above account have seldom been discussed within tourism research. When carrying out research, we bring many aspects of ourselves to the field, of which being a researcher is just one (Reinharz, 1997). For example, just as Reinharz (1997), I am able to identify, here, a number of different selves within the three narrative accounts presented including being a researcher, a girlfriend, a frightened girl, a tourist, a starving student, a pilgrim, a Welsh/British citizen, a Dunkley and a mourner. Each of these selves impacted on my research at different stages, for example, my identity as a Dunkley was particularly salient when I visited the First World War battlefields; however, during the horror tour my self as a frightened girl was most prominent. The point here is that although being a researcher is the most important self within the field (Reinharz, 1997), we cannot help to bring a number of other selves with us. These different selves bring different insights and empathies to the field and we need to recognise this in order to maximise the benefits of our own involvement.

A reflexive approach is seen as a way of being self aware and recognising the human element of research (Westwood et al., 2006). Jamal and Hollinshead (2001) note that the interpretive paradigm involves the acknowledgement of people's affect on the knowledge creation process in that they are actively involved in this process. They also note that the researcher's voice becomes just one of the many within interpretive research. Taking into account my own background, biases and the multiple selves within which I occupy the field as, allows me to carefully considering the consequences of my presence. Thus the activity of situating myself within the research provides unique insights into my own thanatourism experiences and firmly establishes my own voice. Reflexivity allows me to adopt an approach which is personal and takes into account the importance of my emotional experiences at thanasites adding greater depth to my work (Westwood et al., 2006). In being true to myself, I am able to expose the deep wells of emotion, which thanatourism reaches, and then to use my own experience to encourage others to share their stories with me. These accounts are, however, far from narcissistic because they add to the bigger research picture in terms of understanding thanatourism experiences or as Charmaz and Mitchell (1997, p. 208) put it 'voice is one more source of insight from which readers can construct images of the goings-on'. Wikan (1992, p. 471 in Svasek, 2005) describes this process as 'resonance' which is the ability to use our own experiences in order to understand the meanings of the experiences of others. As Bochner (2001, p. 131) responds, to critics of narrative who regard personal narratives as 'privileged, romantic and/or hyperauthentic' there is a strong case for the acceptance of narrative research as a valid method which should exist alongside traditional methods.

Therefore, writing self narratives not only provides you, the reader, with an insight into my experiences but provides an insight into the thanatourism subculture which I am part of (Botterill, 2003). A reflexive approach therefore enables me to better understand the meaning of my own experiences in order to empathetically interpret 'meaning in the experience of others' (Ellis, 1991, p. 27). Ellis (1991, p. 25) suggests that such introspection as that which is considered here offers the opportunity to explore the deeper aspects of emotional experiences, highlighting that it is important to consider both private and social aspects of emotion, and thus makes a case for carrying out research which involves the self. The process of introspection is made all the more interesting in consideration of the following points which Ellis (1991, p. 29) identifies concerning how we make sense of our experiences and the social forces which interplay within these experiences. She highlights that introspection is:

> a social process as well as a psychological one. It is active thinking about one's own thoughts and feelings; it emerges from social interaction; it occurs in response to bodily sensations, mental processes, and external stimuli as well as affecting these same processes. It is not just listening to one voice arising alone in one's head; usually it consists of interacting voices, which are products of social forces and roles.

The consideration of our own experience, therefore, fits into the wider context of lived social experiences as a whole, the ultimate aim being to strive towards something akin to Dylan Thomas's play 'Under Milk Wood'. Within this play of voices, Dylan Thomas is the powerful first voice and the characters emerge out of the darkness to reveal themselves. In parallel, by taking a personal approach to research, the reader is drawn into the writing through emotional evocation; and just as in Dylan's play, the reader gets to know thanatourism intimately. In a similar way as the listener of Under Milk Wood comes to know Llareggub 'through sights and speech, description and dialogue, evocation and parody, you come to know the town as an inhabitant of it' (Dylan Thomas, 1951 in Ferris, 1985).

Conclusion

Within this chapter I aimed to carefully consider and exhibit what my involvement within the research and the multiplicity of selves which I take to the field means for my research. In reflection of my central role within the research and writing process, I wrote in the first person and as a result I was able to present my thanatouristic accounts in a passionate manner. This was appropriate to the nature of the research itself given that the subject of death, fundamental to the human condition, arouses such intense emotion (Hertz, 2004, p. 197). In this sense, I am present both as a narrator and as a central character within my autoethnographic writing (Mykhalovskiy, 1997, p. 241). I wanted not only to provide a discussion of the contention surrounding alternative approaches, such as narrative inquiry and autoethnography in tourism research, I also wanted to provide you, the reader, with an insight into emotionally situated research such as that of thanatourism exploration, so that you are able to comprehend the value of this approach within this and other contexts.

Autoethnography is still a relatively new and contentious research methodology which has received criticism from the traditional sphere of the social sciences where 'the conventions mitigate against personal and passionate writing' in favour of 'dull, distant, abstract, propositional essays' (Ellis & Bochner, 2000, p. 734). However:

> ethnographers have realised for quite some time that researchers are not
> invisible, neutral entities; rather, they are part of the interactions they seek
> to study and influence those interactions. (Fontana & Frey, 2000, p. 663)

It is clear that personal narratives have always formed an important part of the research process, in the form of private journals used to record 'feelings, emotions and personal identity work that comes with prolonged engagement' (Coffey, 1999, p. 115). Indeed, as the diary entry in the introduction to this chapter shows, I too have long been accustomed to the process of recording and reflecting on my experiences, though not by means of incorporating these within my academic writing. Within this chapter I wanted to exhibit the process which I have undertaken from the beginning of my research career, when I was forced to exclude such accounts in line with convention. To the stage now where in recognition of changing perceptions and with the support of supervisors who encourage me to make my voice heard, I have been empowered to include myself and my experiences in my writing.

In this chapter the subjectivity of my voice as researcher and thanatourist was not discounted but openly acknowledged as an undeniable presence which will inevitably affects the research outcomes. However, rather than viewing this as negative, subjectivity was embraced and utilised to add to the quality of the writing, by considering my influences and the effect that this will have on the research process and by examining my own experiences of thanatourism in an intensely passionate manner. As Coffey (1999, p. 118) expresses, research should aim to provide a chorus of voices made up of the researchers own and those of other research participants, and autoethnography can be perceived as a movement towards this provision. Research no longer has to be 'dull or distant' (Ellis & Bochner, 2000) now that we are aware of approaches which can breath life and meaning into our research.

References

Behar, R. (1997). *The vulnerable observer: Anthropology that breaks your heart.* Boston: Beacon Press.

Bochner, A. P., & Ellis, C. (1996). Talking over ethnography. In: A. P. Ellis, & C. Bochner (Eds), *Composing ethnography: Alternative forms of qualitative writing* (pp. 13–45). London: Sage.

Bochner, A. P. (2001). Narrative's virtues. *Qualitative Enquiry, 7,* 131–157.

Botterill, T. D., & Crompton, J. L. (1987). Personal constructions of holiday snapshots. *Annals of Tourism Research, 14,* 152–156.

Botterill, T. D. (2003). An autoethnographic narrative on tourism research epistemologies. *Society and Leisure, 26,* 97–110.

Charmaz, K., & Mitchell, R. G., Jr. (1997). The myth of silent authorship: Self, substance, and style in ethnographic writing. In: R. Hertz (Ed.) *Reflexivity and voice* (pp. 193–215). London: Sage.

Clandinin, D. J., & Connelly, F. M. (2000). *Narrative inquiry: Experience and story in qualitative research.* San-Francisco: Jossey–Bass.

Coffey, A. (1999). *The ethnographic self: Fieldwork and the representation of identity.* London: Sage.

Dunkley, R. A. (2005). The thanatourist: A fascination with death and depravity? In: *Dark tourism: Cashing in on tragedy?* Unpublished conference paper. London: The Tourism Society.

Ellis, C. (1991). Sociological introspection and emotional experience. *Symbolic interaction, 14,* 23–50.

Ellis, C., & Bochner, A. (2000). Autoethnography, personal narrative, reflexivity. In: Y. Lincoln, & N. Denzin (Eds), *Handbook of qualitative research* (pp. 733–768). London: Sage.

Ferris, P. (1985). *Dylan Thomas: The collected letters.* London: J.M. Dent & Sons.

Foley, M., & Lennon, J. J. (1996). Special issue: Dark tourism. *International Journal of Heritage Studies, 2,* 194–244.

Fontana, A., & Frey, J. (2000). The interview: From structured questions to negotiated text. In: Y. Lincoln, & N. Denzin (Eds), *Handbook of qualitative research* (pp. 645–672). London: Sage.

Geertz, C. (1973). *The interpretation of cultures.* New York: Basic Books.

Hall, M. (2004). Reflexivity and tourism research: Situating myself and/with others. In: L. Goodson, & J. Phillimore (Eds), *Qualitative research in tourism: Ontologies, epistemologies and methodologies* (pp. 137–155). London: Routledge.

Hertz, R. (Ed.). (1997). Introduction: Reflexivity and voice. *Reflexivity and voice* (pp. vii–xviii). London: Sage.

Hertz, Robert. (2004). A contribution to the study of the collective representation of death. In: A. C. G. M. Robben (Ed.), *Death, mourning and burial: A cross-cultural reader* (pp. 197–212). Oxford: Blackwell.

Holliday, A. (2002). *Doing and writing qualitative research.* London: Sage.

Holt, N. L. (2003). Representation, legitimation, and autoethnography: An autoethnographic writing story. *International Journal of Qualitative Methods, 2,* 1–22.

Jamal, T., & Hollinshead, K. (2001). Tourism and the forbidden zone: The underserved power of qualitative inquiry. *Tourism Management 22,* 63–82.

Janis, I. L., & Mann, L. (1977). *Decision making: A psychological analysis of conflict, choice and commitment.* London: Macmillan.

Lincoln, Y. (1990). The making of a constructivist: A remembrance of transformations past. In: E. Guba (Ed.), *The Paradigm Dialog* (pp. 67–87). London: Sage.

Mykhalovskiy, E. (1997). Reconsidering 'Table Talk': Critical thoughts on the relationship between sociology, autobiography and self indulgence. In: R. Hertz (Ed.), *Reflexivity and voice* (pp. 229–251). London: Sage.

Phillimore, J., & Goodson, L. (2004). Progress in qualitative research in tourism: Episomology, ontology and methodology. In: L. Goodson, & J. Phillimore (Eds), *Qualitative research in tourism: Ontologies, epistemologies and Methodologies* (pp. 3–29). London: Routledge.

Reed-Danahay, D. E. (1997). *Auto/ethnography: Rewriting the self and the social.* Oxford: Berg.

Reinharz, S. (1997). Who am I? The need for a variety of selves in the field. In: R. Hertz (Ed.) *Reflexivity and voice* (pp. 3–20). London: Sage.

Rosaldo, R. (2004). Grief and a headhunter's Rage. In: A. C. G. M. Robben (Ed.) *Death, mourning and burial: A cross-cultural reader* (pp. 167–178). Oxford: Blackwell.

Seaton, A. V. (1996). Guided by the dark: From thanatopsis to thanatourism. *International Journal of Heritage Studies,* 2, 234–244.

Svasek, M. (2005). Introduction: Emotions in anthropology. In: K. Milton, & M. Svasek (Eds), *Mixed emotion: Anthropological studies of feeling* (pp. 1–24). Oxford: Berg.

Tillmann-Healy, L. M. (1996). A secret life in a culture of thinness: Reflections on body, food and bulimia. In: C. A. Ellis, & A. P. Bochner (Eds), *Composing ethnography: Alternative forms of qualitative writing* (pp. 76–108). Walnut Creek, CA: Alta Mira.

Tonkin, E. (2005). Being there: Emotion and the imagination. In: M. Svasek, & K. Milton (Eds), Anthropologists' Encounters, in mixed emotions: Anthropological studies of feeling (pp. 55–69). Berg: Oxford.

Uzzell, D., & Ballantyne, R. (1998). Heritage that hurts: Interpretation in a postmodern world. In: D. Uzzell & R. Ballantyne (Eds), *Contemporary issues in heritage & environmental interpretation.* London: The Stationery Office.

Westwood, S. (2004). *Narratives of tourism experiences: An interpretative approach to understanding tourist–brand relationships,* Ph.D. thesis. Welsh School of Hospitality Tourism and Leisure Management, University of Wales Institute Cardiff, Cardiff.

Westwood, S., Morgan, N., & Pritchard, A. (2006). Situation, participation and reflexivity in tourism research: Furthering interpretive approaches to tourism enquiry. *Journal of Travel and Tourism Research, 31,* 33–42.

Wilson, E. C. (2004). *A 'Journey of Her Own?': The impact of constraints on women's solo travel.* Ph.D. thesis. Department of Tourism, Leisure, Hotel and Sports Management, Griffith Business School Griffith University, Australia.

Chapter 23

Processes of Becoming: Academic Journeys, Moments and Reflections

Stephen Doorne, Stephanie Hom Cary, Graham Brown, Jo-Anne Lester, Kath Browne, Tomas Pernecky, Susanna Curtin, Martine Abramovici and Nigel Morgan

Stephen Doorne

If there is a starting point on my academic journey, it was probably that first taste of real research during my Masters thesis. It was especially meaningful for the naivete that surrounded it. I was working in a new area and my understanding could make a difference. The sustainability of tourism growth was where I first encountered the politics of tourism and later the politics of academia. The end of my masters was quickly followed by a scholarship to do a PhD (from big business — see I was a funding slut even then) and the birth of my first child (more on this later). These were heady days exploring the inversions of Foucault, Baudrillard, Le Fevre and the rabid cynicism of David Harvey. I was studying the politics of tourism development and the landscapes of power, and what was then the vogue of political resistance, place. I was working as a cable car driver in downtown Wellington. At the top of my run I remember seeing the city below as a political landscape with no singular truth, only argument and perspective. This landscape became my research, a billion dollar redevelopment scheme with all the ingredients of public/private/community/place and culture.

A trapdoor was opening beneath my feet and with it an exhilarating, terrifying sense of freefall. There was no neutral place to stand, no truth, no end, and nowhere to stop. A PhD, however, demands shape, perspective, coherence, and argument. In writing the thesis I realised that academia, for all its promise of unbounded exploration, is an act of joining the dots, playing the game, and getting your ontological highs when and where you can. I began working for the academy. The submission of my PhD encountered egos, bureaucracy and, I have to say, largely male power games. Research and writing would never be the same again.

Fortunately, I was not alone, my first day at work was also the first day for Irena, also a tourism geographer I had met at a conference. We shared a religious fervour for the new ways of interpreting the world and a healthy cynicism of structures and processes that surrounded us. Here we were, two geographers in a business school teaching tourism management. We learnt and played this new fangled game, designing courses, lecturing, writing papers, running up against the politics of publishing, and concocting research projects in weird and wonderful places.

But I digress. Academia does that, it sucks you in. Actually, the most remarkable and life changing experience of that time was the birth of my son and becoming a father.

Over the next six years, my wife and I had another two children, the last quite unplanned. I took a year off work (I think, I was already eager to step back) to look after three little people and be a part of their lives. It was the most challenging, most direct, hands on, and rewarding thing I had ever done in my life. I began to see academic life in terms of sitting in an office and staring at a computer, interrupted by periods of stress performing in front of a sea of faces.

I am not a natural teacher and in the end it has been the teaching that has caused me to move away. I am a shy person and relatively introvert. It was always the research I loved. The act of lecturing did not come naturally, but I learned the skills and became respected by my students (I still cannot believe that simply having a PhD gives you licence to teach). I returned to work only to burn out quickly. Staff shortages doubled my teaching load together with new courses, restructuring, administration, and little time for research, let alone my family.

I became a cynic. I could not reconcile teaching in a business school to students who saw a degree as a stepping stone to a job in the world's most glamorous industry. There were no jobs, at least not the sort of jobs they expected. Yet still, we devised new courses to cater for rapidly growing demand.

It was time to move on. I took a job at the University of the South Pacific in Fiji, and in doing so I stepped back a few years to my undergraduate and early postgraduate studies and the geography of developing countries. This was where my tourism interest first emerged, and the work of Steve Britton and Mowforth and Munt revived my interest in the power structures and contradictions of third world tourism. My postmodern leanings were satisfied by the more methodologically driven perspectives of Robert Chambers, and the big questions posed by Gilbert Rist and Cowan and Shenton. They reignited a fire that had been slowly smothered.

I began grass root research projects, more backpackers, and hit the big time spending Japanese aid money on a project which was, in reality, driven by my CV. Life was good for a while. Irena and I managed some creative writing and research with much to-ing and fro-ing (she was now in Auckland). My cynicism surely returned and much of it centred around the drag of teaching. This time it was the culture of rote learning, which stifled critical thinking in the classroom together with a suffocating and on occasions corrupt bureaucracy which accounted for my withdrawal from academic life. Not to mention parasitic tourism corporates injecting the overarching capitalist system into communities least able to resist them.

These were not healthy attitudes with which to continue an academic career, so I am now taking a break. I am still contracted to USP, supervising postgraduate theses so still have an oar in the water and am enjoying the enthusiasm of my students. For the most part, however, I am being an active parent to my still-young children, renovating the house, playing and teaching music, and applying myself mentally and physically to the art of taekwondo. I am also supporting my wonderful wife, whose energy and motivation for her career and study I greatly admire.

So far, my retreat from academia has lasted about a year. I am on the consulting register of New Zealand Agency for International Development, but am not pushing the boat out for work. I feel that academia is something I will drift in and out of. The fascination with theoretical nuance is never far away. If I could do the bits I like and ditch the rest, it would be perfect.

Stephanie Hom Cary

My journey into tourism studies begins neither as an academic nor as a tourist, but rather from my experience as "the toured." Growing up in the heart of Honolulu, many of my earliest memories involve being the object of a tourist's gaze: from hula performances, to getting my picture taken as one of the exotic locales, to being asked questions like, 'Do you surf to school?' and 'Where are all the grass shacks?'

As such, tourism profoundly shaped my everyday life. I did not realize the extent to which it influenced my behavior, language, worldview, and sense of humor until I left the islands to pursue my own ideas of exotic Otherness (e.g., Europe, and Italy in particular). After university and a three-year stint as a journalist on both sides of the Atlantic, I arrived as a new graduate student in Italian Studies at the University of California, Berkeley. Little did I know then, but I was about to stray from the *diritta via* of Italian into the world of tourism studies where I was to find a remarkable mentor in Professor Nelson Graburn.

I took Nelson's course on the anthropology of tourism in my second semester of graduate school. As I read the tourism studies "canon," all of the hypotheses and case studies — from MacCannell's staged authenticity to Cohen's phenomenology — intuitively made sense to me given my upbringing. I marveled at Nelson's deep knowledge of the field and the institutional memory that he brought as one of its pioneers, as well as his endless enthusiasm for junior scholars like myself. In one class, I even remember him waxing prophetic about his Shelby Cobra, and I ignorantly thought to myself, 'Wow. He's an herpetologist, too?'

As both a mentor and a friend, Nelson was unquestionably the determining factor in my burgeoning career as a tourism studies scholar. He indefatigably pushed me to publish my first article in the *Annals of Tourism Research*. Our long conversations helped me to envision my role as an academic who bridges the humanities and social sciences. He personally introduced me to key scholars in the field, and most importantly, put me in touch with other graduate students studying tourism. Together, we would all go on to create our own academic community in the form of the UC Berkeley Tourism Studies Working Group (TSWG).

The working group was born in the spring of 2003 in a local café. Nelson, myself, and two other graduate students, Charles Carroll and Naomi Leite, were pondering the state of tourism studies at the university. After a long lunch of chicken quesadillas and vegetarian pad thai, we had a collective epiphany; *we* constituted a core community of tourism scholars, not only in the Bay Area, but also in the United States. With that, we set out on a mission to create an interdisciplinary forum, wherein the exchange of ideas would truly enrich the academic discourse on tourism and travel. In other words, we hoped that the TSWG would become a "home" of sorts to all of us studying tourism.

For me, it has indeed become an academic home. I have enjoyed many discussions and many a dinner with my working group colleagues who have, in turn, also become close friends. We have traveled to conferences together, in such exotic locales as Harrogate and Wageningen. We have critiqued each other's field statements, edited job letters, and helped one another practice for qualifying exams. And in the spring of 2004, we began to think about how to enlarge our Berkeley community by reaching out to other tourism scholars around the world.

A year later in October 2005, we hosted an international conference entitled, "On Voyage: New Directions in Tourism Theory." With more than 150 scholars in attendance, the conference embodied, for me, a moment of sublation. Collectively, it made real our working group's mission to unite scholars across disciplines and generations. Personally, I was no longer the academic misfit on the margins of the humanities and social sciences, but rather an integral part of a larger tourism studies community. To be a part of such an inspiring scholarly community — which only seems to gain momentum with every passing moment — I look to the future with a profound sense of hope.

Graham Brown

I used to live in Geography, but I have spent quite a bit of time visiting Sociology, Marketing and Environmental Psychology. The objects collected and the lessons learned en route have all been brought to Tourism. Tourism studies demand a nomadic lifestyle and the academic must scour the landscape for widely dispersed sources of knowledge. We must welcome the challenge of constantly taking new routes and we seem, of necessity, to be much more mobile than colleagues in other fields of enquiry. They seem to more clearly identify with their immediate surroundings and there is a danger of becoming envious of the security of their foundations. Their structures have existed for much longer than those built by our recent ancestors and contemporaries.

My Tourism journey has been all consuming and has benefited from good timing. Opportunities to pursue areas of interest and to develop an academic career coincided with the expansion of tourism studies in higher education. I was involved in helping establish some of the first tourism degrees to be offered in England and Australia. On reflection, much of the curriculum development was completed at a frantic pace and was very time-consuming, but the early degrees were in great demand from highly motivated applicants with very good qualifications. It was pleasure to teach these students who were also able to benefit from the "sandwich" industry experience that was an integral part of the degrees. They were developed, mainly, by the Polytechnics and Institutes of Higher Education that existed in England, at that time. Unfortunately, the desire to provide students with relevant knowledge and skills seems to have been replaced by a willingness to accede to the dictates of industry representatives in curriculum design to the detriment of educational outcomes. However, the establishment of industry panels is only a small part of the administrative workload associated with new programme development, and people who accept these responsibilities can find it hard to allocate sufficient time to other outcomes that are more highly regarded by promotion panels.

The expansion of tourism education has been international. It has taken different forms in different places, but working with international colleagues is one of the most enjoyable aspects of academic life. Renewing contacts at international conferences serves to recharge motivational batteries and reading emails in the morning in Australia from colleagues in Europe and Canada who have been working on papers while you have been sleeping tends to take precedence over exchanging local news with the person in the next office.

Being a tourism academic is a life's work. You never finish and you can never do enough. There is always another chapter to write, another article to review, a better way to present your ideas in class or on-line. Achieving these outcomes requires excellent time-management skills, discipline, and a self-centred attitude that works against achieving the type of work-life balance that many of us read and write about. In addition, no matter where we go, we are always working, but this is a preoccupation that I really enjoy. As tourism academics, we are offered opportunities to meet fascinating people at home and abroad, to study behaviour in interesting settings, to examine events of international importance, and we can share all these experiences with students from a wide range of cultural backgrounds. After twenty years, it is the moments of meaningful connection with students that continues to give the greatest rewards.

Jo-Anne Lester

In developing my research ideas for my PhD I gave little thought to the fact that my area of enquiry and methodological approaches may be considered, by some, somewhat unconventional. Certainly, in the early stages of developing the proposal and refining my ideas, I was fairly comfortable in answering the question 'What is your research about?', but less prepared for rigorous enquiry and questions along the lines of 'What is the purpose of your research?'; 'Will your findings help managers in the industry?'; 'How does your research underpin tourism management studies?'. These questions were often followed with suggestions that my research is conceptual, non-empirical, and highly subjective and thus problematic.

What I learnt very quickly was that my enthusiasm for the topic area was not enough to justify its legitimacy. Given the fact that researchers in tourism studies have made some excellent progress in adopting more interpretive approaches in their research, I made the rather naïve assumption that this, given my methodological approaches, would be readily accepted. For researchers like me, challenging the traditional positivist paradigms long associated with tourism research may be symptomatic of some of the cross-disciplinary approaches being adopted in much tourism research. In my case, I am investigating cruise tourism discourses, primarily focusing on a popular film and therefore my study draws on literature and associated methodologies from various disciplines including that of media and film studies.

The challenge I faced convincing some fellow academics about the seriousness of my research may be one of perception. Hours of lounging around on a comfortable sofa, feet up, cup of tea watching popular movies such as Carry on Cruising and Titanic cannot be serious research, can it? Perhaps not, however, hours of grappling with technology to organise the film data frame by frame, to engage in the analysis of the narratives constructed through aural and visual text, and the application of critical discourse analysis constitutes in my opinion, a challenging and credible research approach.

There is no doubt that I have had to think very carefully about the purpose of my research. In many ways asking about links with the industry is a valid and legitimate question; however, some research will not explicitly draw links with industry and this should not mean that it is any less valid. In my case it very swiftly dawned on me that the potential results of my research are not intended to provide the industry with a set of findings and recommendations that they could draw upon to inform elements of their business and management. So, for example, ground-breaking knowledge that can inform marketing strategy or product development is not the targeted outcome of my research, rather it seeks to investigate the ways in which cruise tourism is represented in a popular film. This is only one small area of enquiry within the 'cultural circle of representation' (see Hall, 1997; Jenkins, 2003).

For me, the PhD journey is a very personal one, and it was not long ago that I made the bold statement that I was never going to do a PhD. Perhaps this was an issue of confidence — what to research; how to approach and carry out the research; people's perceptions of my research; self-questioning about ability, and achievement are all issues to contend with. So initially when confronted with such challenges from those that appeared not to understand and/or have sympathies with my particular perspective or world view, it was easier to retreat and sit in the shadows hoping that no one would notice what I was doing. What I found particularly challenging was responding to expectations that I should have all the answers to the questions posed, particularly about methodology, before I had really embarked on the journey.

Some of these issues have made me reflect on my school days and fond memories of the art studio on a Wednesday afternoon. Without reason I had made an odd choice of foregoing the tradition of spending such afternoons enjoying sport to stay inside and play in the art studios instead. I say 'odd choice' because I actually liked sport and 'play' because I had no experience of art and design. So to some extent my actions defied logic, however what actually happened was extraordinary in many ways.

The most significant memory I have is the fact that the tutor would not tell me how to paint. I remember so vividly being pointed in the direction of the paper, paint, and brushes and told to 'just paint'. Perplexed, confused, frustrated, annoyed? Yes, I felt all of these, however it was my choice to be in the art studio rather than outside on the sports field, so in some senses I just got on with it.

Admittedly I spent the first few weeks just playing around, literally. It was great, loads of space, big displays of water stretched paper, a classroom table as my paint pallet, mixing lurid colours, and generally making a mess — great fun! After about 3 weeks later and 15 pieces of paper with paint on them, at the request of the tutor, I embarrassingly pinned them up in a sequence around the wall of the art studio. The art tutor and myself sat and just looked, contemplated and started to discuss what was in front of us. Of course what became quickly apparent was that there were many things to learn and techniques to explore, but the tutor wanted my approach to painting, the implementation of techniques and style to be unique to me. So two years later, as with all his students, I confidently painted 'my way' and walked away with an 'A' level qualification in modern art.

The point I am making here is that for me the PhD is very much a journey of discovery, highly personal, creative, and imbued with emotions. For me I enjoy the freedom and space to be creative and to nurture my research ideas and could not imagine being locked in the positivist paradigm, just because this approach has long traditions in the field of tourism research. However, I am conscious of the legitimacy of my research and will also find the journey difficult to endure unless I believe in its purpose, rigor, and credibility. Therefore, as I venture out of the shadows to face the questions, to a large extent I can thank those who have, and continue to challenge me, to share their interest in my research because importantly such discussion, debate, and argument has helped me to better understand and articulate my approaches.

In many ways I feel very privileged to be so well supported and encouraged in the pursuit of my research ideas. However, reflecting back some 20 years ago to that art studio, I am also mindful that there is much to learn and discover and that I need to look out for the signposts along the way to ensure that I do not stray too far from the path. When heading in the wrong direction, I hope that I pay good attention when the gentlest of hands from my expert guides redirect me. When I question myself about whether I should be taking such a philosophical position and am at a risk of loosing confidence, I will ask what the world of art would have missed had the likes of Pablo Picasso not defied convention?

References

Hall, S. (Ed.) (1997). *Representation: Cultural Representations and Signifying Practices*. London: Sage.

Jenkins, O. H. (2003). Photography and travel brochures: The circle of representation. *Tourism Geographies*, 5(3), pp. 305–328.

Kath Browne

I remember my very first 'feminist conference'. It was a scary place to be for a nervous postgrad who was not sure where she stood on labelling her feminism, her lesbianism, herself. I struggled to identify with those who were supposed to be 'the same'. Since then I have learned that critic is performed in a very specific way — often through polite conference questioning followed by fierce submitted journal article reviews and have at times felt that 'turf wars' have prevailed in the reviews I receive. In Dubrovnik I learned two very important lessons that I think could change the way academia is done — and short of that will hopefully inform the development of critical tourisms. Perhaps these are states that reflect periods other sub disciplines have 'passed through' but which have now moved into the memory on the way to 'mature' critic. This movement and assumptions of 'maturity' potentially does not allow for other possibilities of knowing. After the bitter wars fought elsewhere, perhaps, there are other ways of doing difference, which will always be important and need to be validated. Dubrovnik's 'project of love' celebrated and validated something else that moved beyond the performance of critic.

My first Dubrovnik lesson was how to suspend critic, to do critical thinking differently — not solely looking for 'the' fault, 'the' flaw, 'the' problem to tear down the study, the argument, and the theory. What was different in Dubrovnik was the absence (in my experience) of those who critique when you/the speakers are not present. These 'after presentation' discussions create spaces to where it is necessary to demonstrate 'prowess' by tearing apart arguments, research and findings, thus 'making your mark'. There was no space or approval for unsupportive critic of others' work — rather interested parties challenged key points in a constructively critical way, often outside the public performance of critic. There was an appreciation in Dubrovnik that had something to do with the organisation and everything to do with how people engaged with each other and with academia. I imagine the early embattled spaces of feminist academia to be like this — where the masculinism forced a common aim, a common goal, but more than that a sense of relief at just being supported.

Of course, there were keynotes in Dubrovnik, discussions of work, studies, and other 'academic' related conversations. However, the 'critical' aspect was focused elsewhere — not at the work of others, but at those who were not at the conference, who prevented this work, critiqued it as 'not real', challenged the validity of 'critical tourisms' in the already embattled subject field of tourism. As the area inevitably changes, I hope in its establishment it will not lose this element of support that from my place on the 'outside' seems integral to its beginnings. Those who create it will hopefully recognise the accessibility of this conference where things could truly be 'tried out' in a supportive environment. More than this, I hope this will continue to move beyond the spaces of conferences, in the reviewing, comments, and publication processes. My worry is that the emergence of hegemonies and powerful elites in critical tourism studies will allow some to use their power as reviewers and editors to determine 'the' new critical agenda, one that celebrates certain theoretical perspectives and postitionalities. This is not simply a call for plurality, it is a bid not to lose the 'project of love' but allow this to become a different way of knowing and doing knowledges. Although we can find niches of support, networks and friends, could a sub-discipline that not only builds on (comes from?) such supportive networks but comes from them, such that they are integral to its progression, offer some alternative ontologies and epistemologies?

I am of course romanticising the Dubrovnik experience — yet in this (over emphasised) memory is the hope for another way of doing academia. Could the 'project of love' offer supportive critic? How can critical tourism keep hold of some aspects of this atmosphere, while still growing, diversifying, and potentially offering diverse and opposing critics? I do not have the answer (as if there is only one!) but even in the questioning perhaps it can be put on the agenda. For me one key aspect of developing these questionings is how we can respect, acknowledge, understand, and experience difference and hierarchisations without losing supportive contexts and spaces. This has to acknowledge, not only power relations that disempower, but also explore how power is employed and deployed. It, for me, means acknowledging that whilst I 'work hard', there are other external reasons as to how and why I can attend such amazing conferences, speak, and have my voice heard and listened to (or at least to have some of my research and thoughts in print) (Butz and Berg 2002). In other words, I want to participate in discussions where our power is not only acknowledged but actively questioned and challenged when this is needed. This could simultaneously recognise that power relations can empower and use this to ensure people's work is valued, validated as well as constructively questioned.

The second thing I learned was that 'networking' is not just about making contacts, it can very much be about making friends. That, however, is the excess of this paper and something that for the moment needs to be felt rather than theorised! Just to say it maybe in these friendships that the 'project of love' has begun/can begin, it is not about 'them' doing something different to create these other ways of knowing — it is about us!

Reference

Butz, D., & Berg, L. (2002). Paradoxical space: Geography, men, and duppy feminism. In: P. Moss (Ed.) *Feminist geography in practice* (pp. 87–102). Oxford: Blackwell.

Tomas Pernecky

There was a small village. It was old and charming, sheltered by tall mountains on one side and open to a beautiful sea on the other. The village was not large but it was not small either. Every morning the streets would fill with the delicious smell of freshly baked bread to which the village would lovingly awake.

The delightful smell came from a little bakery. It was rented by a man who would get up every morning at four o'clock and start making the dough for the many buns, breads, and pies he would sell. The baker was very sought-after and sometimes people from neighbouring villages would go out of their way to buy his bread. He led an ordinary life; of course he had many dreams and visions, but somehow ended up being a baker. But he did not complain. Occasionally, the baker would get sick, there were times he struggled with love, he would worry about his children, he had to deal with his workers. He was happy but sometimes he would also be sad.

One day he woke up and thought . . . *What is the point of getting up at 4 o' clock every morning just to bake bread? There must be other jobs that are better and more meaningful.* But he got up anyway and continued his day as always. That morning, however, three familiar faces walked into the shop. They were three women who grew up in the village and used to buy bread from the baker. They met after many years of not seeing each other and decided to pay a visit to a person who meant a lot to them. The first one looked into his eyes and said, Thank you for being so hard on me when I was a girl. It was difficult growing up without a father, but every morning you would stress how important school was and later reward me with sweets for good marks. If it were not for you, I would not be a doctor today. Then the second woman said, every time I saw you there was a smile on your face. You always found the right words and were kind to me saying how pretty I was, although other children would make fun of my looks, and for that I thank you. The third woman said, I am sorry for the many struggles you had with the landlord. He is my father and not many people know how hard his life has been, but he does not know how to deal with it and takes it out on other people. Then each of the women bought a piece of bread and left the shop . . ..

Is the baker still there or has he found a more meaningful and interesting job? Perhaps he has, and perhaps he has not. This is for you to ponder. The moral of the story is that, no matter who we are, no matter what we do, and no matter where we are, we have an impact on people's lives. The classroom is our stage and on that stage we can do amazing things although we think we cannot. And this is when LOVE comes into play. There is love for your self, love for others, and love for what you do. I know some think it is not appropriate to mix love and academia, but I believe that will change in the years to come. We academics are in contact with young souls and thus in a privileged position to influence them more than others through teaching and writing, and also simply by being. After all, is there anything more inspiring than being loving, supportive, funny and enjoying ourselves, and sharing it with others?

We, like everyone else, have our struggles. The baker did not have to mark assignments until midnight but he had to get up at four in the morning to start his work. He did not have to deal with difficult academic committees, journal reviewers or employers, but he had his own issues with his landlord. But somehow he managed to find love and kindness and make a change in people's lives. The point is that at the end of the day we are all the same (be it the baker or the landlord): sometimes confident and assertive but at other times weak and vulnerable. Although some could call me a "baby academic" as I am in the process of completing my PhD, nevertheless, for the past years I have seen, I have experienced, I have struggled, I have felt, and I asked many questions. Hence the story of the baker and the importance of LOVE for yourself, LOVE for others and LOVE for what you do.

Susanna Curtin

It seems to me that academic life is rather like surfing; sometimes you are on top of a wave feeling exhilarated and alive, and at other times you are beneath the water struggling to come up for air. The bad times can leave you feeling totally baffled, exhausted, and unsure of yourself but the good times are wonderful: the sense of achievement, the sense of 'being someone' and, above all, the sense that you have journeyed a long way.

And this has indeed been a long and interesting journey for me: intellectually, personally, spiritually and professionally. At secondary school I was labelled as a 'no-hoper' and so happily dropped out mid-A levels to go off back-packing around Europe. I travelled with a tremendous sense of adventure and absolutely no care for the future. It was not until I was married and had two children trying to live the good life on a pitiful income that I realised what the education that I had so wilfully given up could have given me. I was 28 when I went back to school to do my A levels, 30 when I first went to university and 35 when I achieved my Masters. From there, I drifted into research and academic life swept by a warm current which I interpreted as serendipity. Once embroiled, I very soon realised that a Masters degree wasn't enough and in order to progress or even just succeed, you needed a doctorate. Four years on from this realisation and I am still studying; still proving myself, and making up for lost time. Just like those ocean waves, my part-time PhD and journal articles are moving at a steady pace but so often during the ride I have to jump off with the weight of teaching and marking, not to mention the need to maintain a healthy mind, body, and home life.

On top of this, as a qualitative researcher working in tourism studies, and a female one at that, there is still the notion that your science is automatically 'soft'. Several reviewers have deemed my tendency to use 'emotional language' as 'not appropriate for a scientific journal'. This stops me in my tracks: imagine a life without emotion. Tourism is a life experience and an emotionally laden one at that; why is it so difficult to embrace this in our studies? Why should creativity, novelty, or even personal opinion be stifled and 'corrected' into the traditional, established academic mould, and why cannot we write convincingly in the first person?

I see being research active as an essential part of academic life if you are to receive promotion or at least negotiate a reasonable teaching load. However, I do question who reads these journal articles and what, other than for promotion, is the point in publishing in this forum especially when the hoops are so difficult to jump through and given that you have to write them in your spare time? Would it be more financially rewarding and exciting, I wonder, to write for the trade press or travel industry. Perhaps this is what I might aspire to when I have that golden qualification.

Hopes and aspirations like these are wonderful things for they are our internal drivers. So in spite of the difficulties and hurdles, I gladly join the 'academy of hope'. With the help of some wonderful people, I have achieved a great deal and will continue to do so. The Dubrovnik event allowed me to be myself and this was a 'eureka' moment. I felt very privileged to be in such a beautiful place and with such open and like-minded people. Instead of focussing on the struggle, I began to smile and to be comfortable with who I am, what I have achieved, and where I hope to be in the future and from that point on, it has been onward and upward.

Martine Abramovici

My holistic approach to academia, bringing together my interests, my intellectual capacities, my values, and my philosophy of life, is finally taking shape as the critical turn enables this reality to be lived and expressed at its fullest. It is through a complete spiritual and intellectual requestioning of the self that I detached myself from the 'expected path' I was to follow and instead followed my heart into the academy of hope.

Being a good student at school, and in a French school, I was automatically guided into undertaking a scientific Baccalaureat, this being considered the superior option within this schooling system. I then naturally continued at university and graduated with a Masters degree in Information technology. It is of interest to point out that I had always been creative, artistic, passionate about languages, interested in society, and a good communicator, however this had no influence over a clear-cut path to success within French society. At the age of 22, I started a male-dominated career as a research engineer in the field of computer science in Paris. I was proving the female gender to be as intelligent as the male gender was perceived to be. Being naturally positive in my approach to life and work, I made my job an enjoyable one and even managed to bring creativity and communication into the world of logic and computers. This was my internal drive in a world where rationality was the pulling force. Although intellectually stimulating, my job felt contriving, however I did not question the system, feeling privileged to be employed in the scientific world where few women succeeded.

At the age of 30, pregnant with my first child, I took the opportunity to have a break from work and travelled the world with my husband and new baby, ending up a year later in New Zealand. Long-term travelling implying by nature being out of 'the system' thus away from any pressure of 'expected behaviour', it is the ideal moment for re-evaluating what one wants from life, and of particular interest to this chapter, what I wanted from work. My overwhelming desire to express my creativity and use my much held-in imagination flourished in the form of modelling clay. For 2 years, I was a part of the potters association in Wellington, New Zealand, where a constant flow of love could be felt. I attributed this wonderful community spirit to the world of arts and thrived in it. However, after a few years and another baby, I started to miss the stimulation of intellectual work. I thought about what I missed from my old job, what I liked from my present pottery world, my passion for travels, my natural ability for understanding people, and perceived my resulting intellectual goal to be carrying out research on people and this through their travel experiences. The field of tourism represented a way of pulling together my personal interests and intellectual desires.

A few years down the track, carrying out my masters thesis as part of my Tourism Masters degree at Victoria University of Wellington I am confronted with similar male gatekeepers to those I had left behind in the computer world, however, maturity, a deeper spiritual understanding of myself and the world, a drive to listen to my inner voice, and the opportunity to change supervisors half-way through my Masters research project, all contributed to my being able to carry out the interpretative research I wanted to, and resist the strong pressure the tourism group was applying for me to modify my research to suit the head of department. The latter was heavily positivist in his approach to academia and had a tendency to make any non-positivist piece of work as a joke. The joy of working with my new supervisor, who not only understood my research aims, took me seriously and supported me, but also stimulated me through her own academic work, as well as her enthusiastic attitude to work. . . a living example that if work is carried out in a positive light through love, both the process and the outputs will benefit. Following this experience. I started my exciting and on-going journey along the path of PhD, chosing my supervisor rather than a university of convenience, even though it meant carrying out my research as a distant student. It became apparent to me that not only was it important to bring together personal interests and intellectual interests, but that values and life choices also needed to be integrated into my work, this creating a general well-being and inner richness. A stimulating, holistic, emotional, open approach to research is what I strive for today, leaving the patriarchal, positivist, unemotional, and detached approach far behind.

The community spirit, as lived during the Dubrovnik conference, was strangely close to the community spirit of love I had associated with the world of arts. This is then the academy of hope, enabling entanglement of love, life values, respect, and openness with the intellectual world of research. Communication among like-minded people, guided by love and their desire to make the world a better place, is what took place during the Dubrovnik conference. The academic world benefits from this community for it helps the positive flow within the network of researchers and academia, hence strengthening research and pushing it well beyond its present boundaries.

Nigel Morgan

When writing this reflective piece I began to ask how was it that I moved from reading feminist history to thinking 'can I "do" feminist tourism enquiry?' After all, gender has been central to my engagement with critical tourism work. What makes critical research?

What is it about research in tourism that makes it critical? What sorts of things do you need to know about before you can do critical research? I don't have any definitive answers. What I do know is that I have been passionate about social inequalities for ages now, ever since (and probably before) my days as a history student reading Stephen Humphries' Steal to Survive: The Social Crime of Working Class Children for my final year essays. I used to spend ages in the library ploughing through the pages of *History Workshop* (a Marxist/Feminist journal) for my essays and seminar presentations and I despaired at not getting a scholarship to take this further in a PhD. The only funded bursary available was for a doctoral candidate to study maritime history — and so I wrote a proposal to study working class tourists' use of leisure space at the seaside. Then, in the first few months of my immersion (or drowning) in the literature I 'discovered' leisure sociology and became inspired by the work of Chris Rojek, John Clarke and Chas Critcher. And so, much to the amusement of (and against the advice of) my supervisors who were both 'traditional' historians, I began my thesis with a chapter entitled 'Perceptions of Leisure', which I opened with this quote from John Wilson (1988: 2): 'Leisure is . . . part of the struggle for the control of space and time in which social groups are continually engaged'. And so began my engagement with the study of tourism, leisure, and social inequality.

After a break of five or six years whilst I worked in sports and tourism policy (including two years at the Sports Council for Wales working on largely unsuccessful initiatives intended to use sport to break down social exclusion), I returned to academia. A chance look through the jobs pages brought me to UWIC (then Cardiff Institute of Higher Education) where I was appointed as a senior lecturer in marketing (my last job had marketing in its title and so I was quickly assimilated into this discipline group). And yet, interesting though marketing became and still is (I enjoy writing marketing texts), marketing was not really where I wanted to be. Fortunately, the day I was appointed, so was my wife Annette, who was deeply interested in gender issues and who had just completed her Masters dissertation on gendered representations in men's magazines. So now both of us were working in a school of tourism and leisure in a vocationally-oriented higher education institution and we knew that what we wanted to write was 'critical' research — although we didn't call it that back then.

As two people new to the murky (and now we know, power-laden) world of academic publishing, it was fortunate for us that our first few attempts were accepted by the reviewers. Buoyed by our early success and too naïve to know any better, we then decided to write a book proposal about marketing, power, and representation (what became *Tourism Promotion and Power*) because to us that was what academics did — write books. One of the proposal's reviewers commented that it read as though a marketing man had been hijacked by a feminist sociologist. Funny how people make assumptions about our research interests and our passions based on our genders. To us, we both shared the same agenda and now, after over a decade of writing together, it is hard to know where Annette's ideas stop and mine start — they just seem to flow together. Maybe writing *with* a woman gave me the confidence to write *about* women but I have always been very conscious of my own positionality (long before I knew what this meant). What gives me the right as a white, able-bodied, middle-class heterosexual man to write about anyone else's marginality? Nothing I guess is the real answer. And yet, there have been times when if I did not speak, who was there to put the case for what otherwise might be rejected because it did not 'fit' some people's ideas of academic norms? Like the time when I used to sit on the University's

Research Degree Committee and proclaimed myself a feminist during a discussion over the 'validity' of a research proposal advocating situated scholarship. That a man could say he was a feminist provoked mild amusement in a gathering dominated by (mostly male) natural scientists. Since I have read and reflected further though, I have realised that I cannot really be a feminist. I cannot be a feminist as a man, but what I think I can do is to be pro-woman in my writing and to embrace the principles of feminist scholarship in my research practice. I can recognise the implications of my location and my points of privilege and at least try to work through the impacts of the masculine, western dominance in the politics of knowledge production. Life (and promotion to a personal chair) has been easier for me than for most. I cannot be a feminist just as though I cannot be an aboriginal person or a person of colour, but it is important for me that I at least try to embrace the values (such as anti-oppression, social justice and advocacy of self-determination) which underpin their scholarship. Otherwise what is the point of it all?

Subject Index